AF715538

ASIAN DEVELOPMENT OUTLOOK 2018

HOW TECHNOLOGY AFFECTS JOBS

APRIL 2018

AN DEVELOPMENT BANK

ADB

Creative Commons Attribution 3.0 IGO license (CC BY 3.0 IGO)

© 2018 Asian Development Bank
6 ADB Avenue, Mandaluyong City, 1550 Metro Manila, Philippines
Tel +63 2 632 4444; Fax +63 2 636 2444
www.adb.org

Some rights reserved. Published in 2018.

ISBN 978-92-9261-120-0 (print), 978-92-9261-121-7 (electronic)
ISSN 0117-0481 (print), 1996-725X (electronic)
Publication Stock No. FLS189310-3
http://dx.doi.org/10.22617/FLS189310-3

The views expressed in this publication are those of the authors and do not necessarily reflect the views and policies of the Asian Development Bank (ADB) or its Board of Governors or the governments they represent.

ADB does not guarantee the accuracy of the data included in this publication and accepts no responsibility for any consequence of their use. The mention of specific companies or products of manufacturers does not imply that they are endorsed or recommended by ADB in preference to others of a similar nature that are not mentioned.

By making any designation of or reference to a particular territory or geographic area, or by using the term "country" in this document, ADB does not intend to make any judgments as to the legal or other status of any territory or area.

This work is available under the Creative Commons Attribution 3.0 IGO license (CC BY 3.0 IGO) https://creativecommons.org/licenses/by/3.0/igo/. By using the content of this publication, you agree to be bound by the terms of this license. For attribution, translations, adaptations, and permissions, please read the provisions and terms of use at https://www.adb.org/terms-use#openaccess.

This CC license does not apply to non-ADB copyright materials in this publication. If the material is attributed to another source, please contact the copyright owner or publisher of that source for permission to reproduce it. ADB cannot be held liable for any claims that arise as a result of your use of the material.

Please contact pubsmarketing@adb.org if you have questions or comments with respect to content, or if you wish to obtain copyright permission for your intended use that does not fall within these terms, or for permission to use the ADB logo.

Notes:
In this publication, "$" refers to US dollars.
ADB recognizes "China" as the People's Republic of China and "Vietnam" as Viet Nam.
Corrigenda to ADB publications may be found at http://www.adb.org/publications/corrigenda.

Cover artwork by Ana Verayo/2018.

Contents

Foreword

The economic growth outlook for developing Asia remains vibrant. *Asian Development Outlook 2018* foresees continued momentum after growth accelerated to 6.1% in 2017. The region is expected to expand by 6.0% in 2018 and 5.9% in 2019. Excluding Asia's high-income newly industrialized economies, the prospects for growth are even higher, at 6.5% in 2018 and 6.4% in 2019. Traction for economic expansion will come from strong external demand, which is supported by a further pickup in growth this year in the major industrial economies, and robust domestic demand. Growth in the People's Republic of China is seen to continue its gradual moderation, to 6.6% this year and 6.4% next, as the authorities take actions to address financial risks, while India recovers from a temporary growth setback in 2017, rebounding to 7.3% in 2018 and 7.6% in 2019.

Certain risks to this outlook require monitoring. The upswing in trade could be threatened by rising trade tensions. Although the measures implemented by the United States as of the end of March this year are unlikely to have a significant impact, the move away from trade openness is worrying. Further measures and countermeasures could dent business and consumer confidence. Meanwhile, capital flows to the region could diminish if the US Federal Reserve raises interest rates faster than expected to keep fiscal stimulus there from igniting inflation. Within the region, the buildup of private debt in some economies in the past few years needs close monitoring. Fortunately, most Asian economies are well positioned to meet these challenges.

This year's publication draws attention to opportunities and concerns presented by new technologies in the workplace. The application of new technologies will boost productivity, but at the same time it will displace certain types of jobs. Evidence shows, however, that rising demand and higher output will create jobs, outweighing job displacement, especially with the addition of new occupations and industries that will arise to meet the new needs of producers and consumers. This transition will require a skilled workforce and could put the less-skilled at a disadvantage. The challenge for governments is to ensure that workers are equipped with foundational skills to enable lifelong learning and have the specialized skills required for working with new technologies. Governments must act to enhance and adapt skills development, labor regulation, social protection, and income redistribution. Finally, they must ensure that new technologies develop in ways that benefit people and protect their rights.

TAKEHIKO NAKAO
President
Asian Development Bank

Acknowledgments

Asian Development Outlook 2018 was prepared by staff of the Asian Development Bank (ADB) in the Central and West Asia Department, East Asia Department, Pacific Department, South Asia Department, Southeast Asia Department, and Economic Research and Regional Cooperation Department, as well as in ADB resident missions. Representatives of these departments constituted the Regional Economic Outlook Task Force, which met regularly to coordinate and develop consistent forecasts for the region.

The authors who contributed the sections are bylined in each chapter. The subregional coordinators were Kenji Takamiya and Fatima Catacutan for Central Asia, Akiko Terada-Hagiwara for East Asia, Masato Nakane for South Asia, Kwang Jo Jeong and Dulce Zara for Southeast Asia, and Rommel Rabanal and Cara Tinio for the Pacific.

A team of economists in the Economic Research and Regional Cooperation Department, led by Joseph E. Zveglich, Jr., director of the Macroeconomics Research Division, coordinated the production of the publication, assisted by Edith Laviña. Technical and research support was provided by Shiela Camingue-Romance, Cindy Castillejos-Petalcorin, Marthe Hinojales, Nedelyn Magtibay-Ramos, Pilipinas Quising, Aleli Rosario, Dennis Sorino, Lea Sumulong, Priscille Villanueva, and Mai Lin Villaruel. Additional research support was provided by Emmanuel Alano, Raymond Gaspar, and Michael Timbang. The economic editorial advisors Robert Boumphrey, Joshua Greene, Srinivasa Madhur, Richard Niebuhr, and Reza Vaez-Zadeh made substantive contributions to the country chapters and regional outlook.

A team of economists preparing the theme chapter was led by Rana Hasan, director of the Development Economics and Indicators Division in the Economic Research and Regional Cooperation Department. In addition to the contributors named in the byline and the authors of the background papers, the theme chapter benefited from inputs by Roehlano Briones, Dene Chen, Peter Drury, Yang Du, Peng Jia, Md. Golam Mortaza, Albert Francis Park, Stefanie Sy, Laura Villadiego, and Pankaj Vashisht. Detailed discussions with Abdul Abiad, Duncan Campbell, Jesus Felipe, and Fahad Khan helped clarify critical issues. James Bessen, Nattapong Puttanapong, Arun Ramamurthy, Priya Ranjan, and Yudo Wicaksono provided feedback on selected material. The valuable support and guidance of Yasuyuki Sawada, Juzhong Zhuang, and Joseph E. Zveglich, Jr., throughout the production process is gratefully acknowledged. Guy Sacerdoti and Josef Yap provided editorial advice on the theme chapter. Illustrations were created by Rhommell Rico.

Peter Fredenburg advised on ADB style and English usage. Alvin Tubio handled typesetting and graphics generation, in which he was assisted by Heili Ann Bravo, Elenita Pura, and Azaleah Tiongson. Art direction for the cover design was by Anthony Victoria, with artwork from Ana Verayo. Critical support for the printing and publishing of the report was provided by the Printing Services Unit of the ADB Office of Administrative Services and by the publications and web teams of the ADB Department of Communications. Fermirelyn Cruz and Rhia Bautista-Piamonte provided administrative and secretarial support. The Department of Communications, led by Vicky Tan, Omana Nair, and Erik Churchill, planned and coordinated the dissemination of *Asian Development Outlook 2018*.

Definitions

The economies discussed in *Asian Development Outlook 2018* are classified by major analytic or geographic group. For the purposes of this publication, the following apply:

- **Association of Southeast Asian Nations** comprises Brunei Darussalam, Cambodia, Indonesia, the Lao People's Democratic Republic, Malaysia, Myanmar, the Philippines, Singapore, Thailand, and Viet Nam.
- **Developing Asia** comprises the 45 members of the Asian Development Bank listed below.
- **Newly industrialized economies** comprises Hong Kong, China; the Republic of Korea; Singapore; and Taipei,China.
- **Central Asia** comprises Armenia, Azerbaijan, Georgia, Kazakhstan, the Kyrgyz Republic, Tajikistan, Turkmenistan, and Uzbekistan.
- **East Asia** comprises Hong Kong, China; Mongolia; the People's Republic of China; the Republic of Korea; and Taipei,China.
- **South Asia** comprises Afghanistan, Bangladesh, Bhutan, India, Maldives, Nepal, Pakistan, and Sri Lanka.
- **Southeast Asia** comprises Brunei Darussalam, Cambodia, Indonesia, the Lao People's Democratic Republic, Malaysia, Myanmar, the Philippines, Singapore, Thailand, and Viet Nam.
- **The Pacific** comprises the Cook Islands, the Federated States of Micronesia, Fiji, Kiribati, the Marshall Islands, Nauru, Palau, Papua New Guinea, Samoa, Solomon Islands, Timor-Leste, Tonga, Tuvalu, and Vanuatu.

Unless otherwise specified, the symbol "$" and the word "dollar" refer to US dollars. *Asian Development Outlook 2018* is generally based on data available up to **9 March 2018**.

Abbreviations

ADB	Asian Development Bank
ADO	Asian Development Outlook
AI	artificial intelligence
ASEAN	Association of Southeast Asian Nations
BPO	business process outsourcing
DLT	distributed ledger technology
EEC	Eastern Economic Corridor (Thailand)
EEU	Eurasian Economic Union
EU	European Union
FDI	foreign direct investment
FSM	Federated States of Micronesia
FY	fiscal year
GDP	gross domestic product
GFC	global financial crisis
GST	goods and services tax
GVC	global value chain
ICT	information and communication technology
IMF	International Monetary Fund
IT	information technology
LAN	local area network
Lao PDR	Lao People's Democratic Republic
Libor	London interbank offered rate
M1	money that includes cash and checking accounts
M2	broad money that adds highly liquid accounts to M1
M3	broad money that adds time accounts to M2
mbd	million barrels per day
MSMEs	micro, small, and medium-sized enterprises
NIE	newly industrialized economy
NPL	nonperforming loan
OECD	Organisation for Economic Co-operation and Development
OPEC	Organization of the Petroleum Exporting Countries
PNG	Papua New Guinea
PPP	public–private partnership
PRC	People's Republic of China
Q	quarter
R&D	research and development
RMI	Republic of the Marshall Islands
ROK	Republic of Korea
RPC	Regional Processing Centre (Nauru)
saar	seasonally adjusted annualized rate
SDA	structural decomposition analysis
SMEs	small and medium-sized enterprises
SOE	state-owned enterprise
TVET	technical and vocational education and training
US	United States of America
VAT	value-added tax

ADO 2018—Highlights

Developing Asia enjoys buoyant prospects as external demand remains strong. The region is forecast to expand by 6.0% in 2018, just 0.1 percentage points off the 2017 rate, and by 5.9% in 2019. Excluding Asia's high-income newly industrialized economies, growth should reach 6.5% in 2018 and 6.4% in 2019.

With oil prices edging up and robust consumer demand continuing, inflation is poised to pick up after dipping slightly last year. Consumer prices are projected to rise by 2.9% in both 2018 and 2019, or 0.6 percentage points more than in 2017.

Though prospects are firm, risks are clearly to the downside. Protectionist measures and retaliation against them could undermine the recent pickup in trade growth. In response to fiscal stimulus, the United States Federal Reserve may need to raise interest rates faster than currently expected, which could diminish capital flows to developing Asia.

New technologies drive higher productivity, the foundation for better-paid jobs and economic growth. While new technologies displace jobs, they also unleash countervailing forces that generate more jobs. As some workers may be left behind, governments in developing Asia should respond to this challenge by ensuring that workers are protected from the downside of new technologies and prepared to harness the new opportunities they provide. This will require coordinated action on skills development, labor regulation, social protection, and income redistribution.

Yasuyuki Sawada
Chief Economist
Asian Development Bank

Turning strength into opportunity

Strong tailwinds but tricky crosscurrents

- **Asia and the Pacific continue to enjoy steady growth.** The region picked up steam throughout last year to average 6.1% growth in gross domestic product (GDP), a 0.2 percentage point uptick from 2016. Excluding the high-income newly industrialized economies, growth was 6.6%. The strong showing reflected both solid export demand and rapidly expanding domestic demand, including in the People's Republic of China (PRC). Momentum is likely to moderate only slightly to 6.0% in 2018 and 5.9% in 2019, or 6.5% and 6.4% excluding the newly industrialized economies.

  - **Growth accelerated across the major industrial economies.** Aggregate growth in the United States, the euro area, and Japan rose to 2.3% from 1.5% in 2016, while unemployment rates reached their lowest since the global financial crisis of 2008–2009. The pace of growth will continue at 2.3% in 2018, with US fiscal expansion sustaining growth for the group as a whole, before slowing to 2.0% in 2019. Gradual monetary tightening in the US is expected to keep inflation in check. Rising business confidence in the euro area and Japan will be supported by accommodative monetary and fiscal policies.

  - **PRC growth accelerated on strong demand from home and abroad.** The service sector grew by 8% on buoyant domestic demand, and net exports expanded as trade in intermediate manufactures rebounded. Assuming mildly tighter monetary and fiscal policies in the PRC, growth is expected to moderate from 6.9% in 2017 to 6.6% in 2018 and 6.4% in 2019. Further progress on reforms such as strengthening financial sector regulation and supervision, and addressing debt issues would lay a foundation for solid macroeconomic stability.

  - **India is set to rebound from a dip in growth following reform.** Growth in fiscal 2017 was estimated at 6.6%, 0.5 percentage points below the previous year. The demonetization of large banknotes in late 2016 had lingering effects on small business and private credit, and reform that introduced a national goods and services tax temporarily slowed business activity early in fiscal 2017. While industry and agriculture slackened, services grew by a solid 8.3%. Improved business regulation and buoyant tax revenue will bolster growth to the forecast horizon, as it accelerates to 7.3% in 2018 and 7.6% in 2019.

  - **Growth in Southeast Asia is forecast steady this year and next.** Although an expansion of technology exports in 2017 will moderate somewhat, recovery in global commodity prices should continue to support exporters of primary goods. Growth in Indonesia, the Philippines, and Thailand will accelerate thanks to strong investment and domestic consumption, while Viet Nam will benefit from continued expansion of its industrial base. Southeast Asia is expected to maintain its 2017 growth rate of 5.2% in 2018 and 2019.

» **Events temper resource revivals in the Pacific and Central Asia.** Growth in the Pacific will linger at the 2017 rate of 2.2% in 2018, following earthquake damage that has temporarily disrupted gas production in Papua New Guinea, before accelerating to 3.0% in 2019. Higher crude prices boosted growth in Central Asian oil producers in 2017, lifting subregional growth to 4.3%. However, as a rebound in industry in Kazakhstan moderates, growth in Central Asia is forecast to slow to 4.0% in 2018, picking up somewhat to 4.2% in 2019.

- **Strong consumer demand and rising commodity prices will lift inflation.** The region experienced broadly stable inflation at 2.3% in 2017, but higher incomes today and oil prices tomorrow will bring increases. With average Brent crude oil prices rising above $60/barrel in 2018 and 2019 from $54 in 2017, inflation is projected to accelerate to 2.9% in 2018 and 2019. Despite the pickup, moderated inflation expectations will hold price rises below the 10-year average of 3.7%. Both years will see accelerating price rises in all subregions except Central Asia, where price-stabilizing policy will seek to tame inflation that reached double digits in 2016.

- **Developing Asia's trade rebound will taper modestly.** Exports grew in 2017 by 4.9% in real terms in the region's 10 largest economies, and imports by 7.7%. In US dollar terms, exports rose by 9.6%, with growth in the second half hitting 7.9% in the PRC and 16.5% in the five largest economies in Southeast Asia. Commodities and manufactures alike saw export growth, which was particularly strong for trade within Asia of intermediate manufactures for assembly into electrical and electronic goods, machinery, and equipment. Trade growth is expected to slow somewhat in 2018 and 2019. Despite the rebound in exports, the current account surplus of the PRC fell by 0.4 percentage points to equal 1.4% of GDP in 2017. This helped narrow Asia's current account surplus with the rest of the world to 0.5% of global GDP.

- **Favorable as the growth outlook is, the risks to it are on the downside.** Risks to trade are high on the list. Protectionist trade measures implemented by the US so far in 2018 have not discernibly dented buoyant trade flows to and from developing Asia. However, further actions and retaliation against them could undermine the business and consumer optimism that underlies the regional outlook. Another risk is diminishing capital inflows if the US Federal Reserve needs to raise interest rates faster than markets expect to keep fiscal expansion from overheating the economy. The trade revival last year has, however, reinforced strong trade links within Asia and built up financial buffers in many Asian economies, in particular in recovering commodity exporters. Asia should therefore be in a strong position to withstand most shocks.

Private debt and economic growth

- **Developing Asia continues to accumulate private debt.** Since the global financial crisis of 2008–2009, the ratio of private debt to GDP has declined in the US and other advanced economies as companies and households strove to deleverage. In contrast, ratios of household and nonfinancial corporate debt to GDP have continued to rise in emerging markets, including those in Asia. In the PRC, for example, the corporate debt ratio rose from 96% of GDP at the end of 2008 to 163% at the end of the third quarter of 2017. In the same period, the household debt ratio rose from 50% to 67% in Malaysia, 74% to 94% in the Republic of Korea, and 45% to 68% in Thailand.

- **Does the private debt buildup pose a risk to regional growth?** Private debt accumulation spurs growth only in the short run. Evidence shows that the positive effect of household debt growth in emerging economies typically dissipates after 2 years, turning negative in the medium term. The pattern is broadly parallel in advanced economies. Similarly, corporate debt growth does not seem to have any persistent positive effect on output growth. Further, as the amount of private debt rises, the impact of additional debt on output growth becomes smaller.

- **The results argue for closely monitoring the buildup of private debt.** The region would benefit as well from macroprudential measures that help prevent excessive credit buildup. The accumulation of both household and corporate debt may pose a medium-term threat to the currently benign economic outlook for the region. However, the lack of a persistent positive effect on output suggests that not all of the added private debt is channeled into productive investments and activities. Strengthening regional financial systems would improve the quality of private debt.

Outlook by subregion

- **Most of developing Asia will pause after a pickup in 2017.** As only 14 of 45 individual economies are forecast to see growth accelerate in 2018, aggregate growth rates in most subregions are projected to be unchanged or lower this year. South Asia is the exception, as a rebound in India will lift growth above 7%, making it the fastest-growing subregion in developing Asia. Across the region, domestic demand will remain as the key sustainer of growth. Central Asia and the Pacific will bounce back in 2019.

- **East Asia slows on moderating PRC growth and external trade.** Economic growth in East Asia picked up by 0.3 percentage points to 6.3% in 2017 as strong external and internal demand lifted every economy in the subregion. Growth accelerated to 6.9% in the PRC on robust exports and private consumption, and surging coal exports and mining investment lifted Mongolia's growth rate fourfold to 5.1%. Expansion in the PRC should moderate to 6.6% in 2018 and 6.4% in 2019 as economic policy leans further toward financial stability and a more sustainable growth trajectory. Other economies in the subregion will see lower growth as well, mainly on account of moderating export growth. These developments will tamp down East Asian economic expansion to 6.0% in 2018 and 5.8% in 2019. Inflation dipped in East Asia last year, reflecting moderation in the PRC, where food prices fell. It will trend higher from 1.6% in 2017 to 2.3% in 2018 and 2.2% in 2019 as food prices rise, the PRC deregulates prices, and wages improve in most economies.

- **South Asia anticipates revived growth after a 2-year slowdown.** Aggregate growth slipped 0.3 percentage points to 6.4% in 2017. This reflected slackening in India, where growth fell to 6.6% with the lingering effects of demonetization in 2016, businesses adjusting in 2017 to a new goods and services tax, and agriculture subdued. The South Asian giant is expected to bounce back to 7.3% in fiscal 2018 and firm to 7.6% in 2019 as the new tax regime improves productivity and as banking reform and corporate deleveraging take hold to reverse a downtrend in investment. Elsewhere in South Asia, growth will stay robust but generally not improve. The need to carry out revenue-enhancing fiscal reform and to strengthen economic policy will temporarily brake expansion in Bangladesh, Pakistan, and Sri Lanka. Growth in South Asia as a whole is forecast to rise to 7.0% in 2018 and 7.2% in 2019. Very modest food price rises in India following bumper harvests there pushed average inflation in South Asia down to 4.0% in 2017. Inflation is forecast to revive to 4.7% in 2018 and to 5.1% in 2019, mainly on higher oil prices.

- **Southeast Asia is poised to sustain a higher growth path.** Growth accelerated to 5.2% last year, 0.5 percentage points higher than in 2016. A turnaround in exports and robust domestic demand underpinned solid economic performances across the subregion. As export growth moderates from last year's rebound, stronger domestic demand—fueled by ambitious public infrastructure spending, solid foreign direct investment, and robust household consumption—should see the subregion sustain average annual growth at 5.2% this year and next. Growth this year in 8 of the 10 economies is projected to be equal or exceed the 2017 rate, but Malaysia and Singapore are likely to unwind from last year's rapid expansion toward their long-term potential growth rates. Inflation, having edged up 0.7 percentage points to 2.8% in 2017, is seen stabilizing at about 3.0% this year and next, buoyed by strong domestic demand, higher minimum wages, hikes in administered prices, and rising international oil prices. Only Malaysia will see inflation cool in both 2018 and 2019 after changes to the price-setting mechanism for fuel and lubricants spiked transport costs in 2017.

- **Central Asia moderates after a notable recovery in 2017.** Average growth in the subregion rose to 4.3% from 2.7% a year earlier as recession ended in Azerbaijan and expansion accelerated in six other economies, particularly in predominant Kazakhstan. Growth slowed only in Uzbekistan, where sharp currency devaluation to unify the exchange rate and other economic reform forfeited some expansion last year for future growth. Following a strong pickup in growth last year, Kazakhstan is projected to slow to 3.2% in 2018 but bounce back to 3.5% in 2019 as investment quickens. With expansion moderating in most of its economies, Central Asia is projected to slow to 4.0% in 2018 and reaccelerate to 4.2% in 2019 with faster growth in all eight countries. A more stable exchange rate almost halved inflation in Kazakhstan, trimming average inflation in the subregion to 9.2% in 2017 from 10.6% in 2016, even though inflation accelerated in the other seven economies, particularly in Uzbekistan. As recent currency devaluations slip further into the past, inflation is projected to settle at 8.5% in 2018 and 7.9% in 2019.

- **The Pacific will grow more slowly than the other subregions.** Growth at 2.2% in 2017 was determined largely by events in Papua New Guinea, the largest Pacific economy, where growth at a similar rate reflected a slowdown in agriculture and contraction in oil and gas. Elsewhere, performance was mixed, with Palau and Timor-Leste contracting. While these two economies will bounce back in 2018, all others will either maintain the pace or slow. Following an earthquake in February, growth in Papua New Guinea is expected to falter to 1.8%, but recovery in Timor-Leste is expected to keep growth in the subregion as a whole unchanged at 2.2% in 2018. An expected recovery in Papua New Guinea and continuing strength in Timor-Leste should contribute to aggregate growth of 3.0% in 2019. Although inflation in the Pacific fell 1.0 percentage point to 3.8% in 2017, prices rose faster in eight economies, half of them escaping deflation in the previous year. As higher global commodity prices will boost inflation in most economies in 2018, subregional inflation is forecast to reach 4.1% in 2018 before tapering to 3.9% in 2019.

How technology affects jobs

Summary

- New technologies drive higher productivity, the foundation for better-paid jobs and economic growth.
- Despite growing concern that new technologies could cause widespread job loss, optimism about developing Asia's job prospects springs from several observations:
    - New technologies often automate only some tasks of a job, not the whole job. ATMs, for example, have not replaced bank tellers but broadened their role in customer relationship management.
    - Job automation goes ahead only where it is both technically and economically feasible. Both requirements tend to be met in capital-intensive manufacturing, where employment shares were already low in 2015.
    - Rising demand offsets job displacement driven by automation. In 2005–2015, jobs created by rising domestic demand more than compensated for job losses to technological advances.
    - Technological change and economic growth create new occupations and industries. Many new job titles have arisen in ICT, and new types of jobs will arise in health care and education and in finance, insurance, real estate, and other business services.
- Nevertheless, new technologies alter the skills required of the workforce and may cause unemployment as some firms downsize or close. They make the less-skilled more likely to experience lower wage growth, exacerbating income inequality.
- Governments should respond to these challenges by ensuring that workers are protected from the downside of new technologies and able to harness the new opportunities they provide. This will require coordinated action on skills development, labor regulation, social protection, and income redistribution.
- Governments should use new technologies to improve education and skills development, as well as to deliver such public services as social protection programs. Government support for new technologies must benefit people and protect their rights and privacy.

Rising concern over technology displacing jobs

- **Developing Asia has done remarkably well in creating jobs for its workers.** Over the past 25 years, the region has created 30 million jobs annually in industry and services. Job creation has come with improved productivity, rising earnings for workers, and large reductions in poverty. Contributing to this process are shifts in employment from sectors with low productivity and pay, typically subsistence agriculture, to sectors with higher productivity and pay, typically in modern industry and services. But a larger part of productivity gains come from technological advances within sectors, such as high-yielding crop varieties in agriculture, modern machine tools in manufacturing, and information and communication technology (ICT) in services. The creation and adoption of new technologies is driven not only by investments in education, infrastructure, and research and development, but also by international trade and foreign direct investment. At the same time, macroeconomic stability and an investment climate conducive to business have provided a foundation for technological advance, sustained growth, and job creation.

- **Technological advances fuel productivity but also threaten jobs.** Emerging technologies such as robotics, three-dimensional printing, artificial intelligence, and the internet of things will help drive future prosperity. Yet they also pose challenges for workers. The apparel and footwear industries, for example, are experimenting with completely automated production. Similarly, it is becoming technically feasible to automate more complex service tasks such as customer support. These developments have raised concern that automation could cause widespread job loss, slow wage growth, and worsen income inequality in developed and developing economies alike. Some studies indicate that over half of the jobs in some economies in developing Asia are at risk.

Reasons for optimism on job prospects

- **New technologies often automate only some tasks of a job, not the whole job.** Any job consists of a number of tasks, and the tasks can be classified as either routine or not, and either manual or cognitive. Automation targets mainly routine tasks, such as soldering components onto a circuit board repeatedly on an assembly line, which is both routine and manual, or counting and dispensing cash in a bank, which is routine and cognitive. While task automation may displace some types of jobs, in other cases it restructures the job such that machines handle only the routine tasks, freeing up workers to focus on more complex tasks. The introduction of ATMs, for example, changes the job for bank tellers to one of customer relationship management.

- **Job automation goes ahead only where both technically and economically feasible.** Data on industrial robots in Asia show the two largest users to be electrical and electronics industries and automobile manufacturers, each accounting in 2015 for 39% of the total robot use but, together, only 13.4% of total manufacturing employment. By contrast, producers of textiles, apparel, and leather goods and of food and beverages together accounted in the same year for only 1.4% of robot usage but 31.4% of manufacturing employment. This pattern reflects both technological and economic feasibility. More technological sophistication is required to give a robot the dexterity to stitch cloth, for example, than to handle large metal parts. At the same time, low pay in apparel and footwear is a disincentive to automation. In 12 economies in developing Asia that account for 90% of employment in the region, an estimated 40% of manufacturing and service jobs entail mostly routine tasks, either manual or cognitive. However, many of these jobs are unlikely to be lost. Some will be restructured instead, and automating others will not be technically or economically feasible.

- **Rising demand offsets job displacement driven by automation.** New technologies allow a given output to be produced by fewer workers. While some workers are displaced, improved productivity and lower prices often spur higher demand. Increased demand may even expand the number of jobs in factories that automate part of their production process. Moreover, the productivity benefits of new technology in one industry lower production costs in downstream industries through input–output channels, contributing to increased demand and employment across industries. An increase in demand and production in one industry heightens demand for upstream industries as well.

» **Data show rising demand more than compensating for jobs displaced by technology.** Using productivity as a broad measure of technological advance, input–output analysis of 12 economies in developing Asia was conducted for 2005–2015, when modern machine tools and ICT equipment spread into factories and offices in a big way. If output had remained the same, higher productivity would have brought a 66% decrease in employment, equal to 101 million jobs per annum. However, concurrently higher demand for goods and services more than offsets this with an associated 88% increase in employment, equal to 134 million jobs per annum.

» **Production returning to advanced economies may not threaten employment in Asia.** Even if automation in advanced economies attracts some factories back to the home market, this is unlikely to happen on a large scale for lack of economic feasibility. In addition, in the 12 Asian economies studied, employment in 2015 that depended directly and indirectly on final demand in advanced economies was only 10%. Developing Asia is growing fast and relying less on exports and more on consumption-driven growth as a rising middle class generates higher demand for goods and services, including those that are traditionally export-oriented. This suggests that so-called "reshoring" may not be a major threat to employment in the region.

- **Technological change and economic growth create new occupations and industries.** New technologies give rise to new occupations and industries. Auto repair workers and car salesman emerged alongside the car industry in the 1900s, and more recently software engineers and app developers accompanied the development of ICT. In addition, the greater complexity of modern production and growing demand for new personal services in health care, education, finance, and others areas are countervailing forces against job loss to technology as they create new occupations.

» **New types of jobs have emerged to handle new technologies.** A detailed analysis of occupation titles in India, Malaysia, and the Philippines found that 43%–57% of new job titles that emerged in the past 10 years are in ICT. A large share of new job titles emerged in one of India's fastest growing occupation categories: craft and related workers. This was driven mainly by the different types of specialized technicians needed to work with computer-controlled machines. Such trends will continue.

» **Comparing occupations across regions shows scope for job growth in many sectors.** Health care and education provide 15% of employment in the US, for example, while finance, insurance, real estate, and other business services provide 19%. In lower- and middle-income economies in developing Asia analyzed, health care and education provide only 3.5%–6.0% of jobs, and business services 1.5%–6.0%, suggesting considerable scope for job growth in these services.

Some worker concerns remain

- **Even as new technology creates jobs, automation will hurt workers in routine and manuals jobs.** New jobs will appear, but they may require skills that such workers do not possess. Further, as firms and industries adjust to new ways of producing and distributing goods and services, the resulting disruptions along existing supply chains may cause unemployment. In addition to more job losses, routine and manual workers will likely experience lower wage growth, worsening income inequality.

    - **Demand will grow most for nonroutine cognitive, social, and ICT tasks.** Jobs requiring routine and manual tasks will be less in demand. This is suggested by analysis of five economies in developing Asia showing that, over the past decade, annual expansion of employment in jobs intensive in nonroutine cognitive tasks, social interactions, and the use of ICT was 2.6 percentage points faster than total employment. Average real wages for these nonroutine jobs increased faster than for routine and manual jobs.

    - **Workers with weaker foundational skills could find themselves left behind.** Foundational skills—those that are best learned as a schoolchild, encompassing not only basic reading, writing, numeracy but also digital literacy and teamwork ability—support transition into jobs that require higher intensity of nonroutine and cognitive tasks. Without adequate skills development or retraining, workers with weaker foundational skills face hurdles in seizing the opportunities that new technologies provide.

- **Even some cognitively oriented but routine jobs may be displaced.** The business process outsourcing (BPO) industry is a case in point. Industry experts estimate that, in 2016, 47% of BPO workers in the Philippines worked at process-driven tasks requiring little abstract thinking. With the advent of new technologies, such jobs are likely to decline as a share of all BPO jobs. There will be new opportunities driven by greater demand for more complex BPO services, which can expand along with technologies. But they will require more specialized training. Workers employed as medical transcriptionists, for example, may lose their jobs to increasingly sophisticated software able to recognize voice, text, and image signals. Transitioning these workers into nonroutine cognitive jobs in the BPO industry will require retraining and skills development.

The role of government in harnessing technology for workers

- **Governments must pursue education reform and promote lifelong learning.** Schools need incentives to strengthen foundational skills that enable individuals to learn—and to relearn. For imparting the specialized skills needed to work with new technologies, universities and institutions specializing in technical and vocational education and training (TVET) are key, and they will have to cater not only to the rising number of graduates from secondary education but also to adults seeking to upgrade their skills or retrain. These institutions must be better integrated, as through credit transfer systems that enable TVET graduates to pursue higher education and university students to acquire specific technical skills.

- **Labor market flexibility needs to be accompanied by programs that support the unemployed.** Labor markets will need to be flexible to accommodate the reallocation of labor across firms and industries necessary to realize the benefits of new technologies. Some governments need to eliminate excessive regulatory barriers to hiring and firing. All governments must pursue active labor market programs that provide job placement services to match unemployed workers with emerging employment opportunities, as well as training and retraining programs that equip workers with skills in high demand.

- **Social protection systems must be strengthened.** Workers need protection from income losses on account of unemployment. Social protection systems are essential as well for workers who may still be employed but in low-paid informal jobs. Systems need to be strengthened in terms of unemployment benefits, expanded health insurance, public works programs, and income transfers. Minimum wage laws should complement the role of social protection in supporting workers' welfare and tackling widening inequality.

- **Tax policies must fund social protection and counter widening income inequality.** The actions needed, as noted above, on education and skills development, active labor market programs, and social protection will help address worsening inequality. Funding these initiatives will require governments to raise more revenue. Broadening the tax base and improving tax administration are important, especially because government revenue is a low share of gross domestic product in many Asian countries. Additionally, scope exists to make income taxes more progressive and to expand receipts from taxes on capital gains, inheritance, and property, which will raise more revenue and narrow inequality.

- **New technologies can facilitate skills development, job-matching, and social protection.** Machine learning and big data analytics are increasingly able to personalize services. Adaptive learning technology, for example, changes the content taught and its sequence in response to student performance. This technique has enhanced learning outcomes in schools. New technologies can improve job-matching by assessing and monitoring the evolution of occupations and providing users with instant feedback on what skills employers seek and how to acquire them, or what job is best for career growth. Finally, technological advances in biometric identification can improve how social protection programs function by reducing costs, overcoming implementation challenges in sophisticated unemployment benefit systems, and enabling the tracking of job-placement services.

- **Governments must ensure that new technologies develop in ways that benefit people and protect their rights.** Given the central role the internet plays in new technologies, developing a nationwide broadband backbone and other ICT infrastructure is essential, as is basic infrastructure for electricity supply and transport. Public investments are needed to extend internet access to remote and lagging regions. Appropriate regulation of mobile and internet providers is needed to ensure affordable services. Governments need to come to grips with the protection of personal data and privacy. Competition policy has to evolve to ensure that large technology firms abide by the norms of fair competition. Appropriate public policy interventions are critical to ensure that new technologies serve economic and social development.

GDP growth rate and inflation, % per year

	Growth rate of GDP					Inflation				
	2015	2016	2017	2018	2019	2015	2016	2017	2018	2019
Central Asia	3.1	2.7	4.3	4.0	4.2	6.3	10.6	9.2	8.5	7.9
Armenia	3.2	0.2	7.5	4.0	4.2	3.7	–1.4	1.0	2.7	2.2
Azerbaijan	1.1	–3.1	0.1	1.7	2.0	4.0	12.4	12.9	7.0	8.0
Georgia	2.9	2.8	5.0	4.5	4.7	4.0	2.1	6.0	3.5	3.0
Kazakhstan	1.2	1.1	4.0	3.2	3.5	6.6	14.6	7.4	6.8	6.2
Kyrgyz Republic	3.9	4.3	4.6	3.5	4.0	6.5	0.4	3.2	4.0	4.5
Tajikistan	6.0	6.9	7.1	6.0	6.5	5.1	6.1	6.7	7.5	7.0
Turkmenistan	6.5	6.2	6.5	6.5	6.7	6.4	6.0	8.0	8.0	8.0
Uzbekistan	7.9	7.8	5.3	5.5	5.6	8.5	8.0	14.4	16.0	14.0
East Asia	6.1	6.0	6.3	6.0	5.8	1.3	1.9	1.6	2.3	2.2
Hong Kong, China	2.4	2.1	3.8	3.2	3.0	3.0	2.4	1.5	2.2	2.1
Mongolia	2.4	1.2	5.1	3.8	4.3	6.6	1.1	4.3	8.0	7.0
People's Republic of China	6.9	6.7	6.9	6.6	6.4	1.4	2.0	1.6	2.4	2.3
Republic of Korea	2.8	2.8	3.1	3.0	2.9	0.7	1.0	1.9	1.9	2.0
Taipei,China	0.8	1.4	2.9	2.9	2.8	–0.3	1.4	0.6	1.1	1.1
South Asia	7.4	6.7	6.4	7.0	7.2	4.9	4.5	4.0	4.7	5.1
Afghanistan	1.3	2.4	2.5	2.5	2.5	0.7	4.4	5.0	5.0	5.0
Bangladesh	6.6	7.1	7.3	7.0	7.2	6.4	5.9	5.4	6.1	6.3
Bhutan	6.2	7.3	7.5	7.1	7.4	6.6	3.3	4.3	4.6	5.4
India	8.2	7.1	6.6	7.3	7.6	4.9	4.5	3.7	4.6	5.0
Maldives	2.2	6.2	6.5	6.7	6.8	1.0	0.5	2.8	3.1	3.0
Nepal	3.0	0.0	6.9	4.9	5.5	7.2	9.9	4.5	5.5	6.0
Pakistan	4.1	4.5	5.3	5.6	5.1	4.5	2.9	4.2	4.5	4.8
Sri Lanka	5.0	4.5	3.1	4.2	4.8	3.8	4.0	7.7	5.2	5.0
Southeast Asia	4.6	4.7	5.2	5.2	5.2	2.8	2.1	2.8	3.0	3.0
Brunei Darussalam	–0.4	–2.5	0.8	1.5	2.0	–0.4	–0.7	–0.2	0.1	0.1
Cambodia	7.0	7.0	7.0	7.0	7.0	1.2	3.0	2.9	3.2	3.5
Indonesia	4.9	5.0	5.1	5.3	5.3	6.4	3.5	3.8	3.8	4.0
Lao People's Dem. Rep.	7.3	7.0	6.8	6.8	7.0	1.3	1.6	0.8	2.0	2.5
Malaysia	5.0	4.2	5.9	5.3	5.0	2.1	2.1	3.8	2.6	1.8
Myanmar	7.0	5.9	6.8	6.8	7.2	10.0	6.8	5.3	6.2	6.0
Philippines	6.1	6.9	6.7	6.8	6.9	1.4	1.8	3.2	4.0	3.9
Singapore	2.2	2.4	3.6	3.1	2.9	–0.5	–0.5	0.6	0.9	1.4
Thailand	3.0	3.3	3.9	4.0	4.1	–0.9	0.2	0.7	1.2	1.3
Viet Nam	6.7	6.2	6.8	7.1	6.8	0.6	2.7	3.5	3.7	4.0
The Pacific	8.1	2.4	2.2	2.2	3.0	4.3	4.8	3.8	4.1	3.9
Cook Islands	3.2	8.8	3.5	3.5	3.0	3.0	–0.1	–0.1	0.5	1.0
Federated States of Micronesia	4.9	–0.1	2.0	2.0	2.0	0.0	–1.0	0.5	1.0	1.0
Fiji	3.8	0.4	3.9	3.6	3.3	1.4	3.9	3.3	3.0	3.0
Kiribati	3.5	1.8	2.5	2.3	2.3	0.6	0.7	2.2	2.5	2.5
Marshall Islands	–0.4	1.9	4.0	2.5	2.5	–2.3	–1.5	0.5	1.0	1.0
Nauru	2.8	10.4	4.0	–4.0	0.5	11.4	8.2	5.0	2.0	2.0
Palau	11.4	0.5	–0.5	3.0	3.0	2.2	–1.3	1.0	1.5	1.5
Papua New Guinea	10.5	2.0	2.2	1.8	2.7	6.0	6.7	4.7	5.0	4.5
Samoa	1.6	7.1	2.5	0.5	2.0	1.9	0.1	1.4	2.0	3.0
Solomon Islands	2.6	3.4	3.2	3.0	3.0	–0.5	1.1	0.1	2.5	3.0
Timor-Leste	4.0	5.3	–2.0	3.0	5.5	0.6	–1.3	0.6	2.0	3.0
Tonga	3.7	3.1	2.8	–0.3	1.9	–1.0	2.6	7.4	3.8	0.5
Tuvalu	2.6	3.0	3.2	3.0	3.0	3.2	3.5	2.9	2.5	2.8
Vanuatu	0.2	3.5	3.5	3.2	3.0	2.5	0.9	3.2	4.8	2.5
Developing Asia	6.0	5.9	6.1	6.0	5.9	2.2	2.4	2.3	2.9	2.9
Developing Asia excluding the NIEs	6.6	6.4	6.6	6.5	6.4	2.4	2.7	2.4	3.0	3.0

Note: The newly industrialized economies (NIEs) are Hong Kong, China; the Republic of Korea; Singapore; and Taipei,China.

1

TURNING STRENGTH INTO OPPORTUNITY

Turning strength into opportunity

Asia and the Pacific had a remarkable year, with growth accelerating throughout 2017 and into 2018. The strong showing reflected solid export demand, both from the advanced economies and from within the region, with trade growth continually surprising on the upside. Trade links that had laid dormant from 2014 to late 2016 revived, with positive spillover across the region. Domestic demand, particularly household consumption, showed robust gains in economies both large and small. Developing Asia thus accounted for more than 60% of global growth in 2017 and a quarter of global income in 2016 (Figure 1.0.1). Moreover, inflation remained moderate despite a 23% increase in oil prices during the year.

Going forward, countries should be able to build on these economic gains, even as growth tapers somewhat (Figure 1.0.2). Domestic demand is expected to be the key driver as confidence builds during 2018 and 2019.

The outlook has downside risks. First, while the direct impact of protectionist trade measures implemented by the US in March 2018 is unlikely to affect the outlook for developing Asia, further measures and retaliation would have larger ramifications. Second, expansion in the US that is faster than expected, fueled by recent tax cuts and spending increases, may prompt the US Federal Reserve to raise interest rates more rapidly than markets currently anticipate. The trade revival last year has, however, reinforced strong trade links within Asia and built up financial buffers in many Asian economies, in particular in recovering commodity exporters. Finally, caution is necessary when private debt grows very quickly, as this is found to correlate with larger subsequent declines in gross domestic product (GDP).

1.0.1 Global share of income, 2016

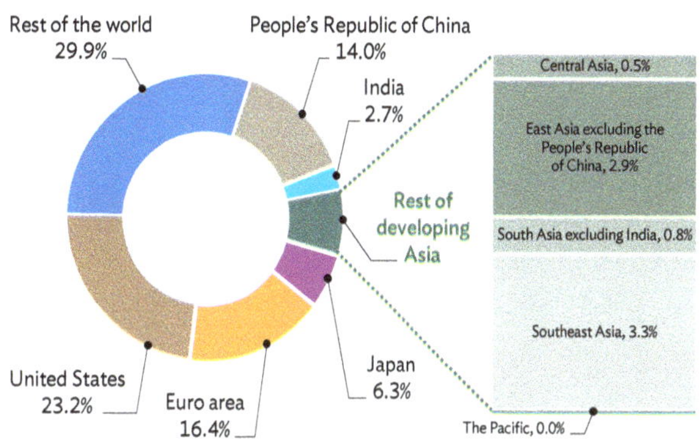

Note: Weights are based on gross national income in current US dollars, Atlas method.

Source: ADB estimates using data from World Development Indicators online database (accessed 30 March 2018).

1.0.2 GDP growth outlook for developing Asia and the industrial economies

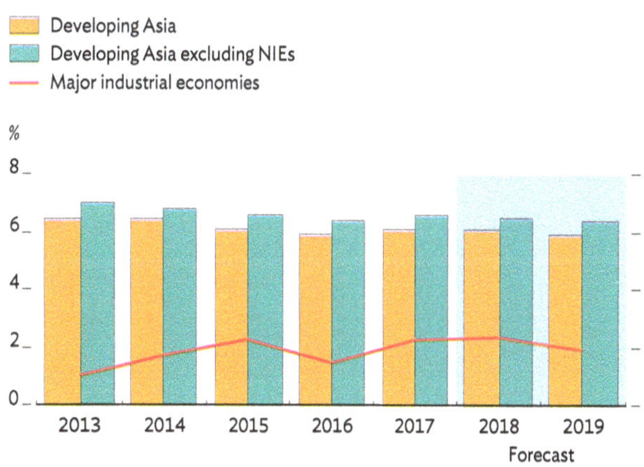

Notes: The major industrial economies are the euro area, Japan, and the United States. The newly industrialized economies (NIEs) are Hong Kong, China; the Republic of Korea; Singapore; and Taipei,China.

Sources: US Department of Commerce, Bureau of Economic Analysis, http://www.bea.gov; Eurostat, http://epp.eurostat.ec.europa.eu; Economic and Social Research Institute of Japan, http://www.esri.cao.go.jp; Consensus Forecasts; *Asian Development Outlook* database; ADB estimates.

This chapter was written by Valerie Mercer-Blackman, Benno Ferrarini, Donghyun Park, Shu Tian, Arief Ramayandi, Madhavi Pundit, Shiela Camingue-Romance, Cindy Castillejos-Petalcorin, Marthe Hinojales, Nedelyn Magtibay-Ramos, Pilipinas Quising, Dennis Sorino, and Priscille Villanueva of the Economic Research and Regional Cooperation Department, ADB, Manila.

Strong tailwinds but tricky crosscurrents

The aggregate GDP growth rate in developing Asia reached a 3-year high of 6.1% in 2017 with subdued inflation, but the pace of growth should slow gradually over the next 2 years. Regional economies are projected to expand by 6.0% on average in 2018 and 5.9% in 2019 (Figure 1.1.1). Exports, which boosted growth last year, will still be a key driver of growth, albeit at a slightly moderated pace. Exports have been supported by growth in the advanced economies, which is expected to continue to the forecast horizon (Box 1.1.1).

With exports set to weaken, domestic demand in the region will likely take up the slack, even as some economies return to trend after exceptional growth in 2017. Much of the decline reflects moderating expansion in the People's Republic of China (PRC), however, that will more than offset faster growth elsewhere, notably in India and the larger economies of Southeast Asia. Inflation in developing Asia is forecast to rise from 2.3% in 2017 to 2.9% in 2018 and 2019, mainly on strong consumer demand and rising global commodity prices (Figure 1.1.2), but remain well below its 10-year average of 3.7%. The region's current account surplus will narrow from 1.8% in 2017 to 1.4% in 2018 and further to 1.3% in 2019 as the surge in global exports fades somewhat.

1.1.1 Subregional contributions to GDP growth in developing Asia

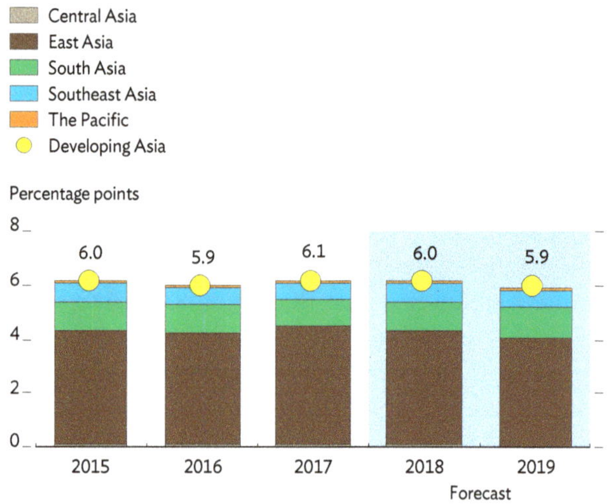

Note: Contributions from Central Asia and the Pacific are less than 0.1 percentage points.

Source: *Asian Development Outlook* database.

1.1.2 Inflation in developing Asia

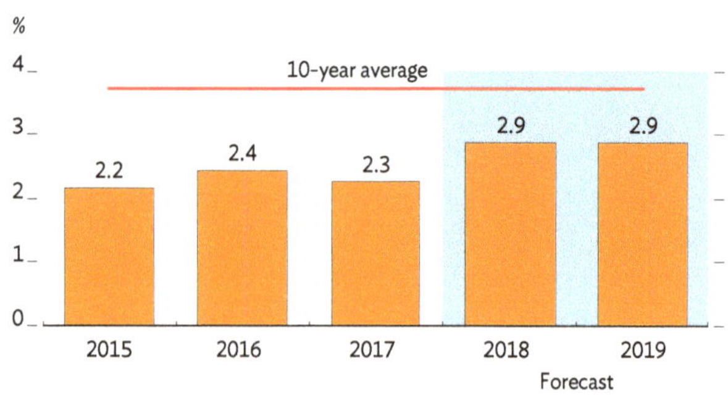

Source: *Asian Development Outlook* database.

Stellar growth in 2017

Developing Asia enjoyed a stellar performance in 2017, as most of the region's large economies comfortably exceeded growth expectations. Regional growth expanded by 6.1%, the highest in 3 years, mirroring a surprise pickup in the PRC and economic dynamism elsewhere in the region. Growth accelerated in more than 70% of the region's economies thanks to solid export demand from the industrial economies and from within the region, as well as strong domestic consumption. Central, East, and Southeast Asia performed well, but South Asia and the Pacific grew more slowly than in 2016.

1.1.1 Strong global demand lifts outlook

The major industrial economies of the United States, the euro area, and Japan enjoyed solid recovery in 2017, with growth accelerating in all three and aggregate growth rising from 1.5% in 2016 to 2.3% (box table). Growth momentum is expected to remain strong to the forecast horizon, with US fiscal expansion lifting growth for the group as a whole.

GDP growth in the major industrial economies (%)

	2016	2017	2018	2019
Area	Actual		ADO projection	
Major industrial economies	1.5	2.3	2.3	2.0
United States	1.5	2.3	2.7	2.3
Euro area	1.8	2.5	2.2	1.9
Japan	0.9	1.7	1.4	1.0

ADO = Asian Development Outlook.

Notes: Average growth rates are weighted by gross national income, Atlas method. More details in Table A1.1 on page 35.

Sources: US Department of Commerce, Bureau of Economic Analysis, http://www.bea.gov; Eurostat, http://ec.europa.eu/eurostat; Economic and Social Research Institute of Japan, http://www.esri.cao.go.jp; ADB estimates.

In the US, GDP grew by 2.3% in 2017 after slower expansion early in the year. Private consumption led the way, accelerating throughout 2017 to a seasonally adjusted annualized rate of 4.0% in the fourth quarter (Q4). Acceleration was reflected as well in higher import demand, which grew significantly faster than exports in Q4, such that net exports subtracted from growth. The domestic rally came as a strong labor market supported faster wage growth. The contribution of investment remained small until Q4 2017, when nonresidential investment rose, mainly on double-digit growth in equipment. In sum, trends underlying private consumption suggest that it will remain strong, as confirmed by preliminary data for Q1 2018.

Upbeat industrial production and purchasing managers' indexes in early 2018 may argue for further expansion in domestic investment, as do tax incentives under the Tax and Jobs Act, 2017—provided that they are not undercut by recent protectionist moves. The unemployment rate remained in early 2018 at a 17-year low of 4.1%. With these developments, the US economy is expected to grow by 2.7% in 2018 and moderate somewhat to 2.3% in 2019, though protectionist moves could slow expansion.

US headline inflation has hovered around 2.0%, while core inflation has remained softer at 1.8%. Along with the steady decline in the unemployment rate, the upward trend in inflation from greater fiscal stimulus and additional purchasing power will likely prompt the Federal Reserve to advance its gradual normalization of monetary policy. The assumption in this analysis is that the Fed will gradually raise its benchmark rate as many as 5 times in the next 16 months to reach 2.9% by late 2019.

The euro area recorded growth in 2017 at 2.5%, its best rate since before the global financial crisis of 2008–2009. Domestic demand expanded robustly, buoyed by high market confidence and supportive monetary and fiscal policies. Spurred by strong job creation and optimistic businesses, the unemployment rate fell to 8.7% in December.

The euro area shows early indications that it entered 2018 on a high note, with political uncertainty appearing to recede. Growth is forecast to remain strong in 2018 but moderate slightly to 1.9% in 2019. Last year's tailwinds are likely to continue into 2018 and offset weakening fiscal incentives in several economies as external demand continues to grow. By 2019, however, external factors that have supported growth in the recent past will fade somewhat. Investment spending will benefit substantially from faster disbursement of funds under the European Union's 2014–2020 programming period. However, developments surrounding the scheduled exit in March 2019 of the United Kingdom may delay large investment decisions. Negotiations on Brexit bore fruit in late March 2018 and will now move to discussing future ties.

Full-year inflation in the euro area was 1.5% in 2017, below the 2.0% target set by the European Central Bank. Since January, the central bank has been moderating its monthly asset purchases under its quantitative easing program. With wage pressures contained and some slack in the labor market, inflation will still likely remain below the central bank target in 2018 and 2019.

Japan continued to recover to the end of 2017, supported by strong global demand and accommodative monetary policy. GDP grew by 1.7% in 2017, up from 0.9% in 2016, and marked 8 consecutive quarters of growth. Stronger economic activity has reduced unemployment and created more jobs, which should spur consumer spending, but wage growth remains sluggish.

Early indications for Q1 2018 suggest a soft start for the year, but business sentiment remains very positive and consumer confidence elevated. Moreover, prospects for higher demand look good as the unemployment rate fell in January to 2.4%, its lowest in 25 years. The forecast is for growth at 1.4% in 2018 and 1.0% in 2019. The government is slated to increase sales taxes in October 2019, which may dampen household spending. Risks to the forecast are a possible slowdown in the People's Republic of China and uncertainty in global trade policies.

Consumer price inflation approached a 3-year high of 1.5% year on year in February. The Bank of Japan has kept its inflation target at 2% and maintained its accommodative monetary policy, with the short-term policy rate at −0.1% and the yield on 10-year Japanese government bonds capped at about zero.

Key growth drivers

On the demand side, much of the impetus for growth in developing Asia came from an unexpectedly large rise in external demand. Exports accelerated across the region as global demand picked up. However, import demand rose even faster, to support the renewal of domestic demand that ensued, such that the contribution to GDP growth from real net exports declined in 2017 from 2016. In 8 of the 11 large regional economies with 2017 data, net exports subtracted from GDP growth (Figure 1.1.3). Private consumption remained the dominant source of growth in over half of the 11 large economies.

Consumer confidence recovered last year in eight of the nine large economies examined, after declining during most of 2016 (Figure 1.1.4). Confidence improved the most in Hong Kong, China; the PRC; and the Philippines but fell in India, where demonetization and the implementation of a goods and services tax temporarily battered consumer confidence. In the PRC, the consumer sentiment index reached its highest in more than 2 decades as optimism picked up over job prospects and personal finances, particularly in lower-tier cities, with help from supportive government policy, infrastructure investment, and more affordable housing. In Hong Kong, China, optimism rose on the economic outlook, job prospects, and spending plans as a rebound in tourist arrivals buoyed consumer confidence. Optimism rose in the Philippines on the same issues, along with improved expectations for peace and security. In Indonesia, consumers remained upbeat about government reform programs and expectations of job growth

1.1.3 Demand-side contributions to growth, selected economies

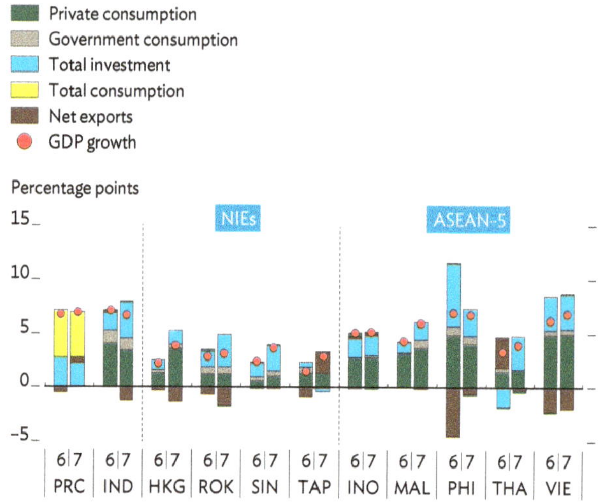

6 = 2016, 7 = 2017, ASEAN = Association of Southeast Asian Nations, HKG = Hong Kong, China, IND = India, INO = Indonesia, MAL = Malaysia, NIE = newly industrialized economy, PHI = Philippines, PRC = People's Republic of China, ROK = Republic of Korea, SIN = Singapore, TAP = Taipei,China, THA = Thailand, VIE = Viet Nam.

Note: Data for India are fiscal years ending on 31 March of the next year.

Sources: Haver Analytics; CEIC Data Company (both accessed 20 March 2018).

1.1.4 Consumer confidence and expectations, selected economies

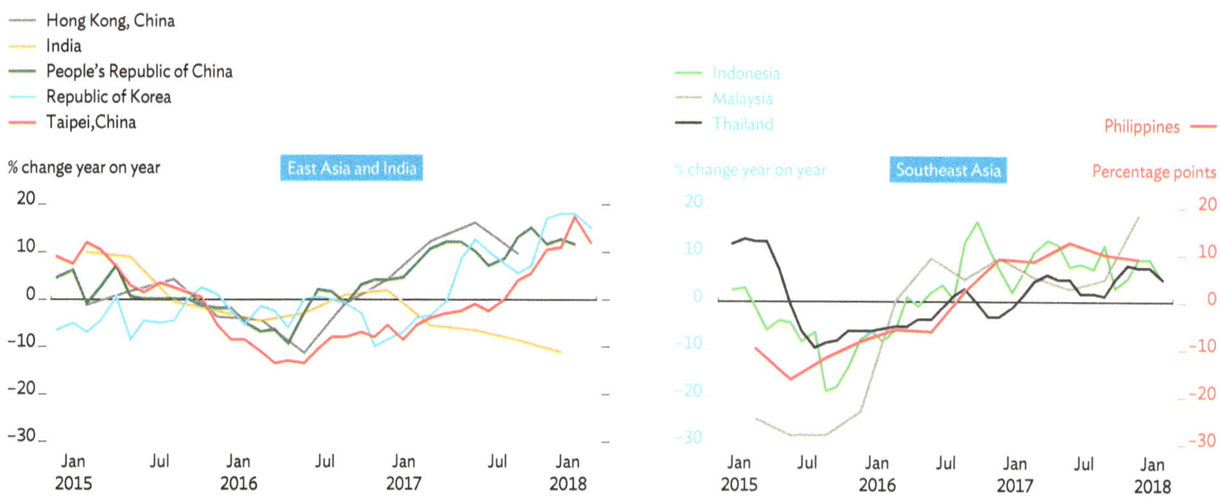

Notes: Data for the Philippines give the percentage of households that were optimistic less the percentage that were pessimistic. Above zero indicates a favorable view, negative unfavorable. Data for Hong Kong, China; India; Malaysia; and the Philippines are quarterly.

Sources: Haver Analytics; CEIC Data Company (accessed 20 March 2018).

1.1.5 Growth of retail sales, selected economies

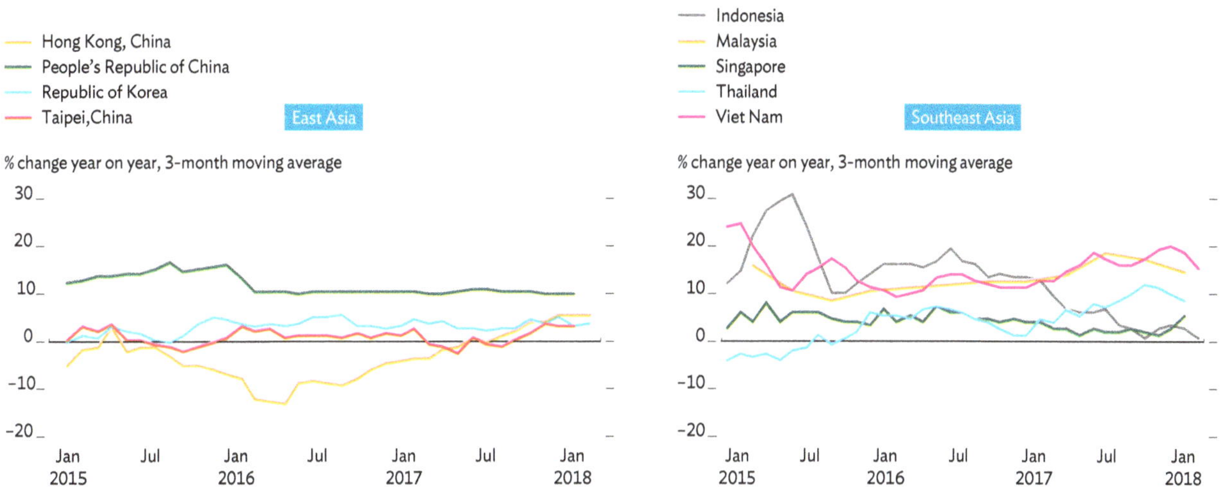

Note: Data for Malaysia are quarterly percentage change year on year.
Source: Haver Analytics (accessed 20 March 2018).

and higher incomes. Consumer confidence rose to a near 7-year high in the Republic of Korea (ROK) as improvements to the economic outlook, higher global demand for electronics, and an easing of geopolitical tensions brought optimism about incomes and equity prices. Higher equity prices and the government's decision to raise public sector wages by 3% in January 2017 and relax work hours boosted optimism in Taipei,China.

Retailers in the region saw growth improve in 2017 as rising incomes and wealth factored into highly optimistic domestic markets (Figure 1.1.5). Retail sales in Hong Kong, China experienced their best growth since February 2015, reflecting strong consumer demand and higher spending by tourists, particularly from the PRC. Retail sales remained strong in the PRC too as higher incomes helped boost spending on clothing and durables. Taipei,China ended the year on a strong note despite reduced department store clothing sales early in 2017 because of a warm winter. In Southeast Asia, Malaysia and Viet Nam registered the largest gains in retail spending, thanks to rising incomes and higher employment. Continued expansion in online shopping supported retail sales growth, particularly in Malaysia and Thailand. Growth in retail spending was slower in Singapore, as sales of recreational goods, clothing, furniture, and other consumer goods moderated, and in Indonesia, as the return to normal consumption patterns after the end of Ramadan and Eid al-Fitr celebrations weakened sales in mid-2017.

Trends in industrial production supported robust economic expansion in export-oriented economies (Figure 1.1.6). In East Asia, growth in industrial output surged by 3.0% in Taipei,China and by 6.5% in the PRC as a wide array of manufacturing industries including electronics and electrical

1.1.6 Industrial production indexes, selected economies

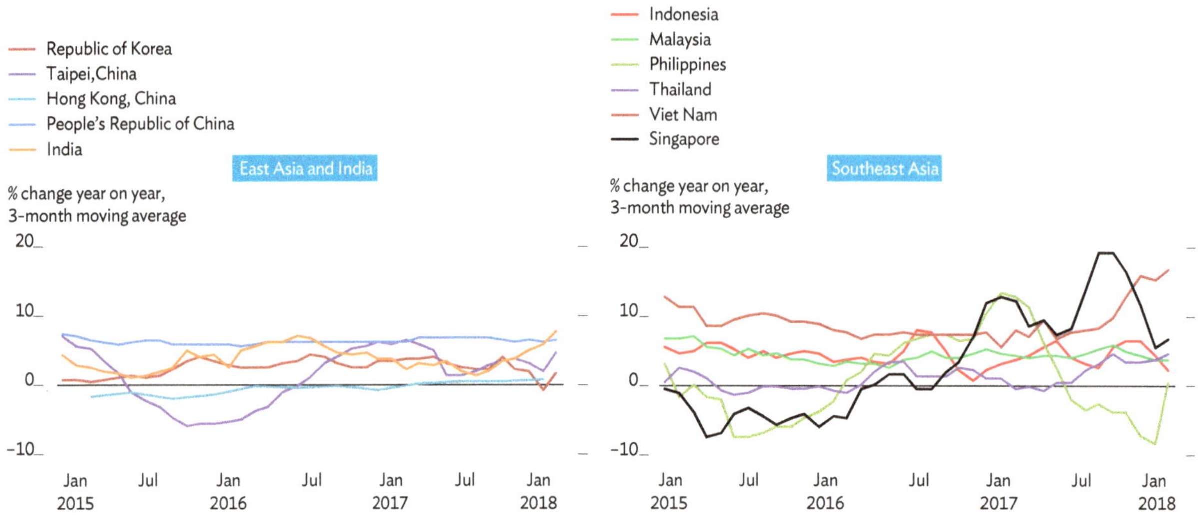

Note: Data for Hong Kong, China are quarterly percentage change year on year.
Sources: Haver Analytics; CEIC Data Company (both accessed 30 March 2018).

machinery benefitted from a global upswing in high-tech trade. Industrial production fluctuated in the ROK, rising in the first half of 2017 and slowing toward the second half as weak demand for automobiles and auto parts in the PRC hurt manufacturing. In Southeast Asia, industrial production also accelerated except in the Philippines, where it fell by 0.8% following unusually rapid expansion in 2016. Singapore recorded the fastest pickup, at 10.4%, aided by strong demand for semiconductor exports. Viet Nam followed closely with 10.0% growth as rapid expansion in mining added to strong gains in manufacturing, particularly in the latter part of the year. Malaysia continued to post solid gains thanks to strong performance in key manufacturing sectors, and petrochemicals and metals led growth in Indonesia.

Last year saw business conditions improve as well on solid expansion of production and new orders, following an anemic performance in 2016. In seven of the nine economies in developing Asia surveyed by Markit, purchasing managers' indexes had slowly returned to above 50 by the end of the third quarter of 2017 and stayed close to this level to the end of the year, showing that growth momentum held up well (Table 1.1.1). Much of the growth in manufacturing came from the tech upcycle that prevailed through 2017, which enabled the open economies of Southeast Asia to benefit handsomely from the trend. As firms expanded and built up inventories further, capital spending rose, boosting private investment.

Solid expansion in the private sector and higher public investment spending helped boost investment in most of the larger economies (Figure 1.1.7). Gross investment rose in 8 of

1.1.1 Markit purchasing managers' index

	2016												2017												2018	
Economy	Q1			Q2			Q3			Q4			Q1			Q2			Q3			Q4			Q1	
Developing Asia																										
India	51.1	51.1	52.4	50.5	50.7	51.7	51.8	52.6	52.1	54.4	52.3	49.6	50.4	50.7	52.5	52.5	51.6	50.9	47.9	51.2	51.2	50.3	52.6	54.7	52.4	52.1
Indonesia	48.9	48.7	50.6	50.9	50.6	51.9	48.4	50.4	50.9	48.7	49.7	49.0	50.4	49.3	50.5	51.2	50.6	49.5	48.6	50.7	50.4	50.1	50.4	49.3	49.9	51.4
Malaysia	48.6	47.8	48.4	47.1	47.2	47.1	48.1	47.4	48.6	47.2	47.1	47.1	48.6	49.4	49.5	50.7	48.7	46.9	48.3	50.4	49.9	48.6	52.0	49.9	50.5	49.9
PRC	48.4	48.0	49.7	49.4	49.2	48.6	50.6	50.0	50.1	51.2	50.9	51.9	51.0	51.7	51.2	50.3	49.6	50.4	51.1	51.6	51.0	51.0	50.8	51.5	51.5	51.6
Philippines	53.0	54.1	54.4	56.5	55.8	55.5	56.3	55.3	57.5	56.5	56.3	55.7	52.7	53.6	53.8	53.3	54.3	53.9	52.8	50.6	50.8	53.7	54.8	54.2	51.7	50.8
Rep. of Korea	49.5	48.7	49.5	50.0	50.1	50.5	50.1	48.6	47.6	48.0	48.0	49.4	49.0	49.2	48.4	49.4	49.2	50.1	49.1	49.9	50.6	50.2	51.2	49.9	50.7	50.3
Taipei,China	50.6	49.4	51.1	49.7	48.5	50.5	51.0	51.8	52.2	52.7	54.7	56.2	55.6	54.5	56.2	54.4	53.1	53.3	53.6	54.3	54.2	53.6	56.3	56.6	56.9	56.0
Thailand	49.4	50.0	49.4	50.2	49.7	49.4	49.3	49.8	48.8	48.8	48.2	50.6	50.6	50.6	50.2	49.8	49.7	50.4	49.6	49.5	50.3	49.8	50.0	50.4	50.6	50.9
Viet Nam	51.5	50.3	50.7	52.3	52.7	52.6	51.9	52.2	52.9	51.7	54.0	52.4	51.9	54.2	54.6	54.1	51.6	52.5	51.7	51.8	53.3	51.6	51.4	52.5	53.4	53.5

PRC = People's Republic of China, Q = quarter.

Note: Pink to red indicates contraction (<50). White to green indicates expansion (>50).

Source: Bloomberg (accessed 22 March 2018).

the 11 economies surveyed. Higher outlays for industrial machinery and equipment, construction, and inventories to meet rising orders for tech exports and to execute planned investment projects benefitted investment expansion in Hong Kong, China; India; Indonesia; Malaysia; Singapore; and Viet Nam. A decline in investment in the PRC reflected mainly lower real estate investment following restrictions on purchases introduced in a number of cities, along with weak investment by heavy industries with excess capacity and high debt.

1.1.7 Investment growth, selected developing Asia

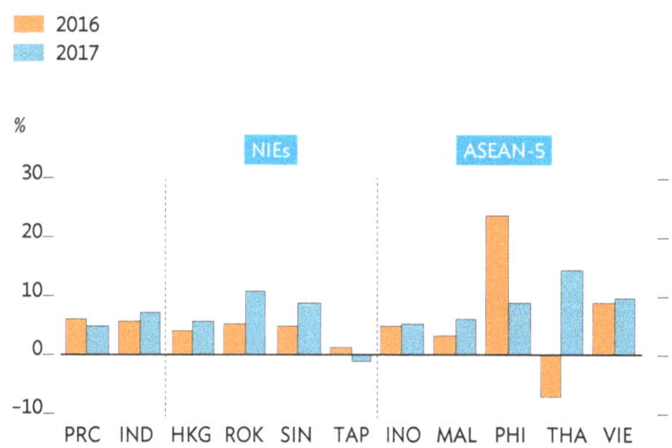

ASEAN = Association of Southeast Asian Nations, HKG = Hong Kong, China, IND = India, INO = Indonesia, MAL = Malaysia, NIE = newly industrialized economy, PHI = Philippines, PRC = People's Republic of China, ROK = Republic of Korea, SIN = Singapore, TAP = Taipei,China, THA = Thailand, VIE = Viet Nam.

Sources: Haver Analytics; CEIC Data Company (accessed 20 March 2018).

Growth by subregion

Growth in East Asia reaccelerated to 6.3% in 2017, after slowing to a 15-year low of 6.0% in 2016, as healthy domestic demand in the PRC spilled over to the rest of the subregion. The PRC grew by 6.9% on robust domestic consumption and surprisingly strong external demand, which facilitated further economic rebalancing toward consumption and services. Growth quadrupled to 5.1% in Mongolia, while it doubled in Taipei,China, as buoyant investment added to demand, propelled by higher construction and strong consumption fueled by higher incomes and upbeat economic sentiment. Growth accelerated as well in the ROK, expanding by 3.1% in 2017 from 2.9% in 2016 as the election of a new government in May 2017 helped boost domestic demand, and as external demand flourished on the global pickup in semiconductor exports and warming relations with the PRC, a top trade partner.

Growth in South Asia eased to 6.4% in 2017 from 6.7% in 2016 even as six of the eight economies posted higher growth. The deceleration came largely from India, where growth slowed to 6.6% in 2017 from 7.1% in 2016 with the lingering impact of demonetization of high-denomination banknotes in November 2016 and teething problems attending the implementation of a new goods and services tax. Growth also fell in Sri Lanka as agriculture and government spending shrank. Meanwhile, growth accelerated markedly in Nepal to 6.9% as trade flows and electricity supply normalized after devastating earthquakes in 2015 caused stagnation in 2016, and as a favorable monsoon enabled better harvests. The return of normal monsoon rains supported steady and broad growth in other South Asian economies as well.

Growth in Southeast Asia improved to 5.2% in 2017 from 4.7% in 2016 as the subregion benefitted from higher demand for tech products, recovery in global fuel prices, and procyclical fiscal policies. Brunei Darussalam enjoyed the highest growth acceleration, largely from oil prices, followed by Malaysia, Singapore, and Thailand, partly because of their extensive participation in electronics supply chains. Malaysia rebounded strongly, with growth rising 1.7 percentage points to 5.9% in 2017. Gains in electronics and precision engineering also helped raise Singapore's growth rate to 3.6% in 2017 from 2.4% in 2016, with tech exports offsetting a decline in fixed investment. In Thailand, growth improved to 3.9%, its highest rate in 5 years, as stronger consumption aided by higher rural incomes and increased tourist arrivals added to a robust pickup in exports of commodities and manufactures. Growth in Viet Nam was broad-based, continuing to benefit from an expanding industrial base and policies to boost domestic demand. Huge drawdowns in inventory limited Indonesia's growth improvement to only 0.1 percentage points. Meanwhile, growth in the Philippines slowed to 6.7% from 6.9% in 2016, the unusually large expansion that year attributed to election spending.

In Central Asia, growth strengthened to 4.3% in 2017 from 2.7% in 2016 as seven economies—all but Uzbekistan—posted higher growth. Contributors to the growth rebound were higher global oil prices, stronger demand both at home and abroad, and a return of growth in the Russian Federation, a key trade partner and source of remittances for the subregion. A recession ended in Azerbaijan thanks to higher oil prices and gains in services and agriculture, which helped offset a decline in industry caused by currency devaluation that started in 2016. Growth improved the most in Armenia, by sevenfold over 2016, as higher lending and remittances propelled growth in consumption and investment. Expansion in petroleum and natural gas-dependent Kazakhstan and Turkmenistan also accelerated, reflecting increased investment and household spending as well as higher hydrocarbon exports. In Tajikistan, growth improved marginally, up 0.2 percentage points on higher remittance flows and continued public investment. Growth slowed in Uzbekistan as a huge devaluation of the local currency in September slowed expansion in industry and private consumption.

In the Pacific, aggregate expansion eased slightly in 2017 to 2.2% from 2.4% in 2016, though growth recovered in the larger island economies. Improved metal and gas prices helped boost mining in Papua New Guinea, the subregion's largest economy, but overall growth remained below the 10-year average of 5.4% as poor access to foreign currency weakened consumption. Growth picked up in Fiji with a recovery in agriculture and increasing tourist arrivals, but GDP contracted in Timor-Leste on lower public spending and depressed private investment.

India and the PRC trading places

1.1.8 Demand-side contributions to growth: PRC and India

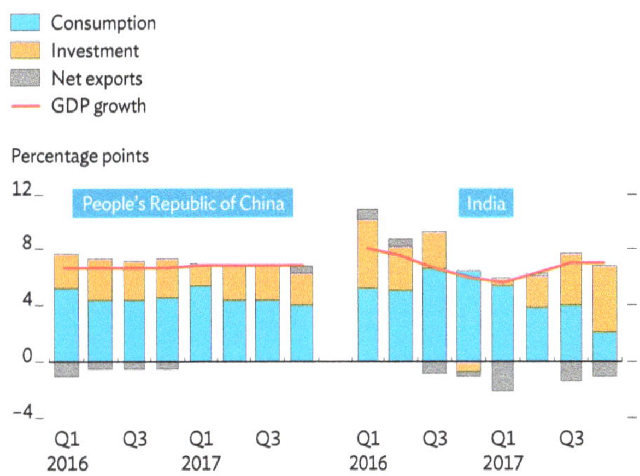

Q = quarter.
Source: *Asian Development Outlook* database.

India and the PRC provide a story of contrasts despite significant efforts by both governments to deepen reform (Figures 1.1.8). Together they contributed 50% of global growth in 2017. As the economic giants of developing Asia, providing about 70% of aggregate GDP, their impact on the region is monumental. In *Asian Development Outlook 2017*, India was projected to be the fastest growing economy in Asia, at 7.4%, while the PRC was expected to grow by 6.5% or less, in line with a planned long-term moderation in growth. Instead, expectedly high oil prices drove down India's real net exports, and bumps from financial and fiscal measures cooled business activity and slowed growth, probably to 6.6% in 2017. In contrast, unexpectedly strong external demand from the industrial economies propelled the PRC.

Both economies have seen services become important contributors to growth. In the PRC, the service sector remained the main driver of growth in 2017 from the supply side, accelerating to 8.0% from 7.7% in 2016 and contributing 4.0 percentage points to growth. Nonetheless, services comprise just over 51% of GDP in the PRC, which is low by international standards. In India, services also grew by a healthy 8.3%, notably passenger and cargo transport services. Services, particularly business service exports, remain a mainstay of the Indian economy.

Recent developments in the two economies have differed in three ways. First are different trends in rural–urban income disparities. The PRC has had some success in recent years in closing the rural–urban income gap as rural households saw real income increase faster than did urban residents in 2017, for a ninth straight year—though urban households still earned 2.7 times more than their rural counterparts.

In India, rural wage growth slowed in 2017 as procurement prices in agriculture rose only sluggishly and as the effects of demonetization lingered, especially affecting cash-dependent remote areas. With slowing rural wage growth, private consumption growth in India slowed to 6.1% in 2017, the lowest rate in 5 years.

The second difference is how the trade balance affected growth. While both economies experienced significant trade growth, only the PRC saw net exports increase—and more than expected. With price increases of nearly 23% for oil and 21% for metals in 2017, incomes rose in neighboring commodity-producing countries, raising their demand for PRC exports by more than expected, particularly in the second half of 2017. By contrast, net exports subtracted from growth in India, particularly in the second half of the year. Oil imports rose by 24% as international prices increased, but real demand was also higher, particularly from firms. In addition, demand for imports of gold and precious stones grew by 51.3%.

The third difference is the ratio of investment to GDP, which is higher than desired in the PRC and considered too low in India. In the PRC, investment still provides almost 40% of GDP, which is very high by international standards. Various reforms have been applied to reduce that share in recent years because the government realizes that overinvestment in some sectors is inefficient use of resources. In 2017, fixed investment contributed 2.4 percentage points to GDP growth. In India, while the share of investment in GDP was a healthy 31% in 2017, it could be higher. On a positive note, robust growth in manufacturing exports including iron and steel will improve investment prospects in India, which should boost the share of investment in GDP. This follows a lull in production amid confusion related to goods and services tax reform in mid-2017 (Figure 1.1.9).

Neither India nor the PRC has shied away from structural reform despite its possible impact on short-term growth. Indeed, both countries choose to forego additional growth now, as needed to allow reform to take effect, for the sake of financial stability later. New challenges concern the tax structure and tax base, which India has recently begun to tackle with some success. Strong direct tax collection in 2017 helped bolster GDP, but lower corporate tax rates will dampen growth in corporate tax revenue in 2018. By contrast, the PRC ratio of tax revenue to GDP has stagnated at 17.5%, with heavy dependence on indirect taxes in the PRC atypical at its stage of development. The authorities there should broaden the tax base while ensuring that the revenue system is progressive.

1.1.9 Merchandise exports and purchasing manager's index: the PRC and India

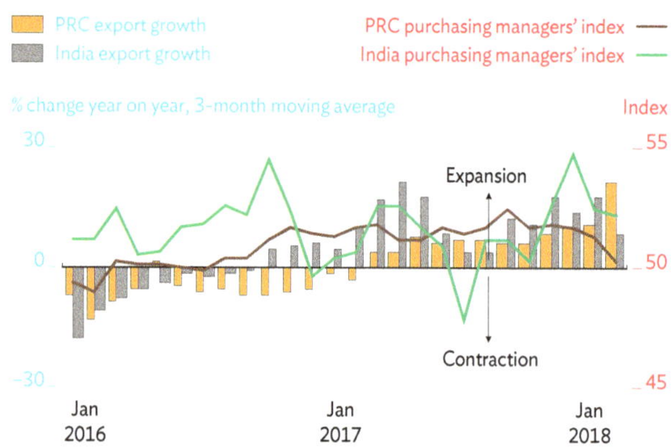

Sources: CEIC Data Company; Bloomberg (both accessed 20 March 2018).

Subdued inflation despite rising oil prices

Inflation slowed in Asia and the Pacific in 2017, though more than 60% of regional economies experienced higher prices. The regional decline stemmed mostly from price changes in the PRC, the region's largest economy. Consumer price inflation there slowed to 1.6% from 2.0% in 2016 as food prices fell thanks to favorable weather and improved supply, as well as reflecting a high base effect. Inflation was highest in Central Asia, and particularly in Uzbekistan, as prices for gasoline, most of it imported, rose by 39.7% in the 12 months to November 2017, while utility tariffs rose by 7.1%. Inflation accelerated notably in Georgia on higher excise taxes and import prices, faster growth, and the lagged effect of currency depreciation in 2016. Sri Lanka experienced higher inflation as its crucial agriculture sector experienced its worst drought in 4 decades and then severe flooding in May, causing double-digit increases in food prices, particularly for staples such as rice. Elsewhere, especially in Southeast Asia, rising incomes, faster growth, and higher fuel prices added to inflationary pressures. In East Asia, inflation was generally benign except in Mongolia, where prices quadrupled as huge depreciation of the local currency forced up import prices and a summer drought disrupted domestic food supply. Inflation slowed in the Pacific, largely reflecting moderation in food prices in Papua New Guinea.

Producer price indexes rose across the region, in some economies much faster than consumer prices (Figure 1.1.10). Monthly data showed producer price inflation in 2017 spilling over from 2016 in some economies, having lagged consumer price inflation at that time, while falling below consumer price inflation in some other economies. Inflation is expected to accelerate to 2.9% in 2018 and 2019 in line with forecast higher oil prices. All subregions will see higher prices except Central Asia, where inflation will moderate under government efforts to stabilize prices (Figure 1.1.11).

1.1.10 Consumer and producer prices, 2017

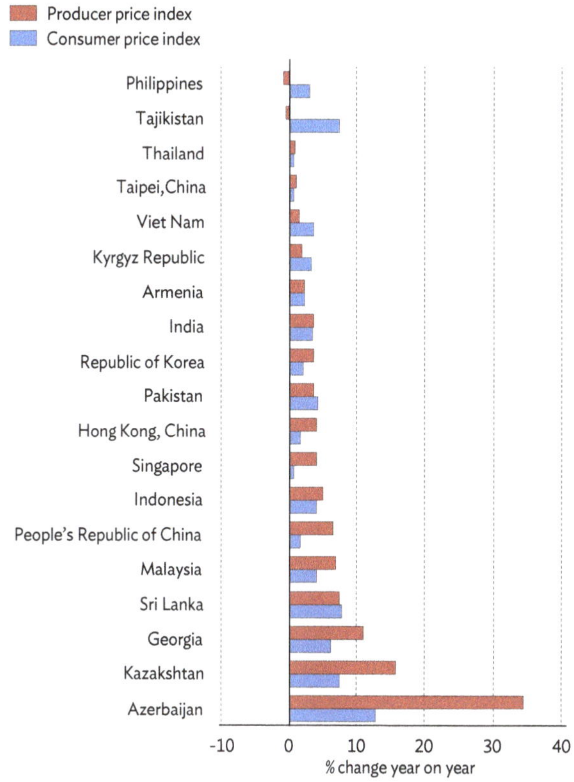

Source: CEIC Data Company; Haver Analytics (both accessed 20 March 2018).

1.1.11 Subregional inflation

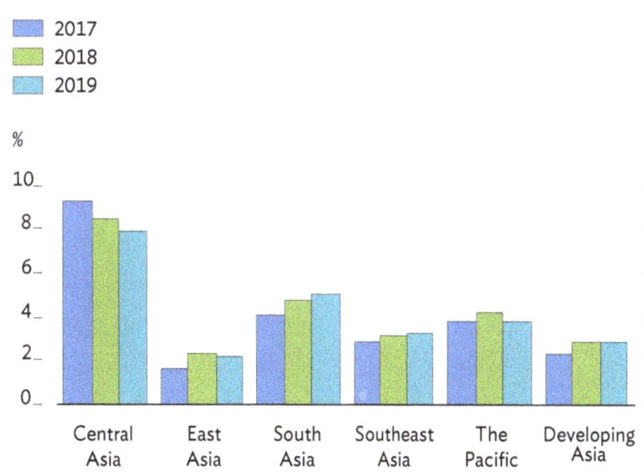

Source: *Asian Development Outlook* database.

Trade lifts the tide

Trade in developing Asia staged a strong turnaround in 2017, with exports driven in large part by external demand from the industrial economies and a revival of manufacturing supply chains, many financed by foreign investors. Import growth was even higher with recovering commodity prices and robust domestic demand, slightly narrowing the regional current account surplus with the rest of the world—a welcome development.

Robust trade despite rising tensions

Trade growth in developing Asia rebounded sharply in 2017 in response to robust external demand. Expansion was especially strong in the second half of the year, particularly in the PRC and the five largest economies in Southeast Asia. Trade within Asia grew by 13.1%, slightly outpacing 12.7% growth in total trade but not enough to significantly alter the share of intra-Asia trade in total trade, estimated at over 45% in 2017. The rise in external demand came not only from the industrial countries but increasingly from within the region, spurring synchronized export growth (Figure 1.1.12)

1.1.12 Export growth, selected economies

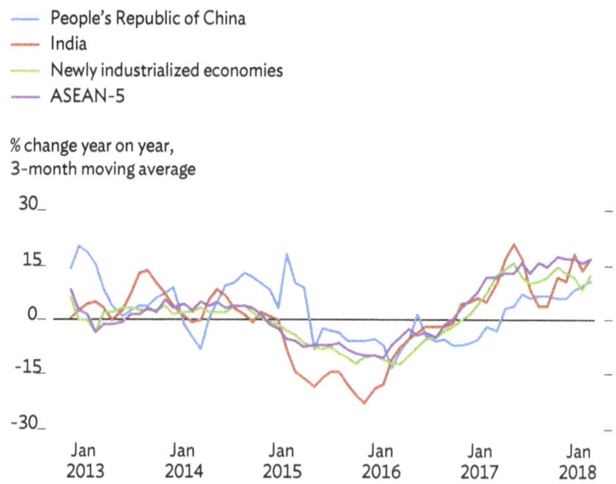

Note: The ASEAN-5 are the five largest economies in the Association of Southeast Asian Nations: Indonesia, Malaysia, the Philippines, Thailand, and Viet Nam. Newly industrialized economies are Hong Kong, China; the Republic of Korea; Singapore; and Taipei,China.

Source: CEIC Data Company (accessed 19 March 2018).

Export demand across the region exceeded expectations (Figure 1.1.13), lifting regional exports by 10.9% after declining by 5.4% in 2016. Commodity exports grew the most in both nominal and real terms. While prices for energy commodities rose by 23.7% in 2017, the volume of commodity exports from the region's 10 largest economies (comprising about 90% of total exports) rose by 8.6% after falling slightly in 2016. Real manufacturing exports in these economies rose by 4.5% after a slight decline in 2016. Manufacturing exports grew the most quickly, especially intermediate goods for machinery, transport, and electrical and electronic equipment. Higher commodity prices spurred export growth not only in oil and gas exporters in the region—particularly Azerbaijan, Kazakhstan, and Papua New Guinea—but also in metal exporters such as Indonesia, the Kyrgyz Republic, Mongolia, and Papua New Guinea. Rubber and palm oil prices increased, boosting raw material exports in Indonesia and Malaysia, among others.

Like exports, imports increased faster than expected, by 16.5% in US dollar terms. Imports of commodities and primary products, which comprise about 70% of all imports, grew by 29% after falling by 10.5% in 2016. Imports of commodities, especially oil and industrial metals, were high, particularly in the PRC. Likewise, India's oil imports grew by 26%, reflecting increases in both price and volume, while gold imports surged by 42.3% on robust local demand and a bump in the first half from a change in gold taxation.

Both exports and imports of manufactured goods grew substantially in 2017 in real terms, by 4.5% and 4.0% respectively, with the direction of trade in intermediate goods revealing links through global value chains. The pickup in

1.1.13 Change in nominal exports and imports, selected economies

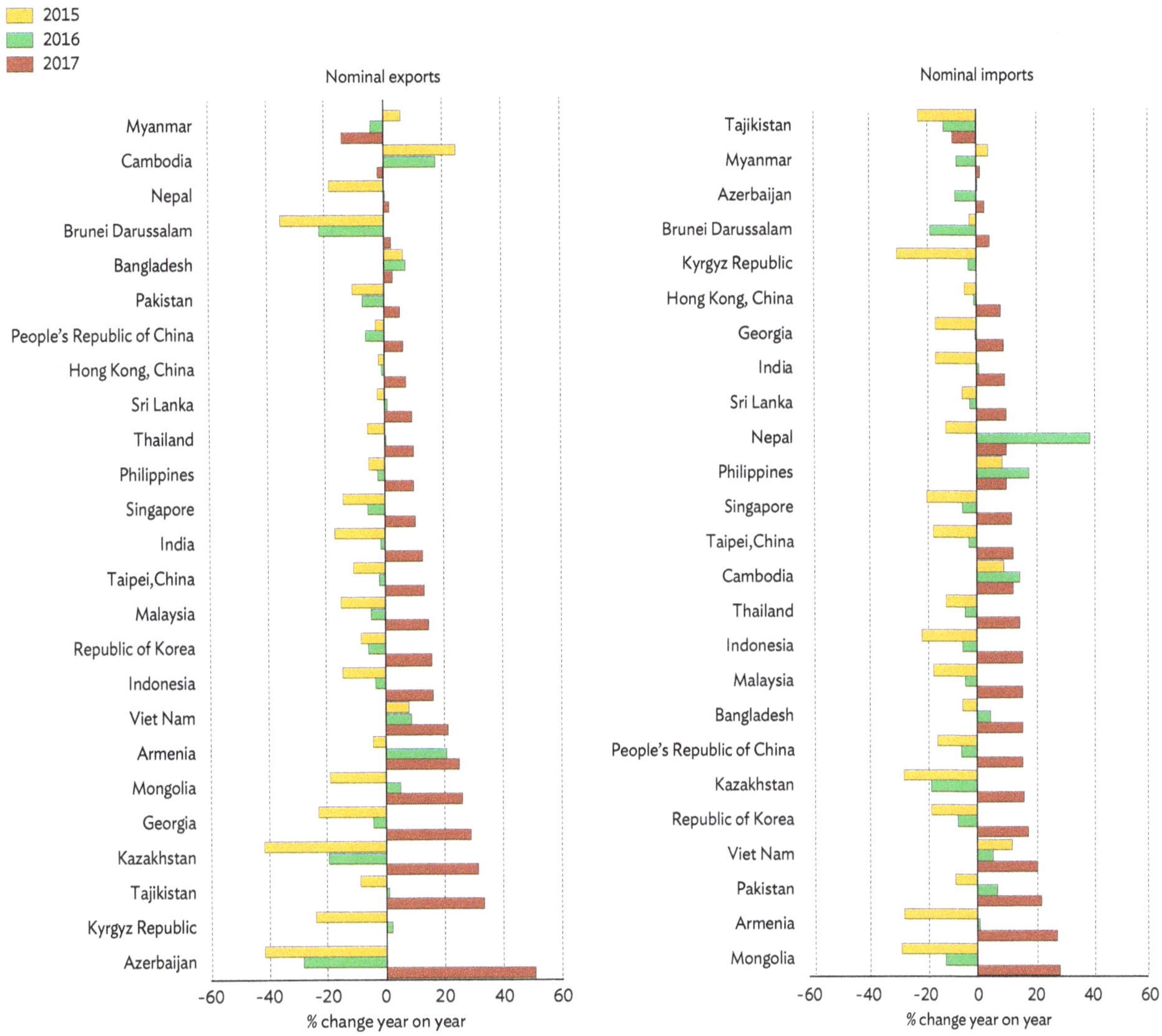

Note: 2017 data for Brunei Darussalam, Cambodia, and Myanmar are as of November and for the Kyrgyz Republic, as of April.
Sources: CEIC Data Company and Haver Analytics (accessed 3 March 2018).

export demand from the industrial economies was amplified by this trade in intermediates as global value chains transmitted shocks across participating economies. Open sectors, those with exports and imports prominent as shares of GDP, are more linked to global production processes, particularly in high-tech manufacturing (Figure 1.1.14).

Trade is expected to grow in 2018 and 2019, albeit more slowly. Data available to February 2018 suggest that growth in trade continues (February itself being seasonally slow because of the Lunar New Year). However, growth is expected to slow to half of the 2017 rate as effects from the strong pickup in 2017 wane. Domestic demand in developing Asia will take the driver's seat as private consumption and investment expand, triggering continued high growth in imports.

1.1.2 Estimated direct impact of pending US tariffs on exports from developing Asia

Item protected and proposed tariff rate	Exports of selected products to the US as a share of total exports to the US (%)					Estimated incremental tariff payments as a share of export value
	Solar panels 30%	Washing machines 30%	Iron and steel 25%	Aluminum 10%	All Items	
Developing Asia	1.0	0.0	0.9	0.2	2.2	0.08
India	0.0	0.0	1.3	0.2	1.5	0.06
Malaysia	7.5	0.0	0.2	0.1	7.7	0.39
People's Republic of China	0.5	0.0	0.4	0.3	1.2	0.06
Republic of Korea	1.9	0.1	3.8	0.1	5.9	0.19
Singapore	2.2	0.0	0.0	0.0	2.2	0.03
Taipei,China	0.9	0.0	2.8	0.1	3.7	0.12
Thailand	1.9	0.0	0.4	0.1	2.5	0.09
Viet Nam	1.2	0.0	1.3	0.1	2.6	0.15
Other developing Asia	0.4	0.0	0.4	0.3	1.1	0.01
Rest of world	0.8	0.1	7.7	4.1	12.7	
Share of developing Asia's item exports to total US imports, %	78.3	24.1	25.1	14.6	79.0	

Note: Iron and steel includes flat-rolled products, tubes, and bars. The Republic of Korea is partly exempted under a free trade agreement with the US. Export data are for 2016, the latest year available with this detail.

Source: ADB calculations using data from UN Comtrade database. https://comtrade.un.org (accessed 2 April 2018).

Tariffs imposed by the US as of 31 March 2018 are unlikely to weaken developing Asia's prospects. Early in January 2018, the US imposed tariffs of 30% over a 4-year period on solar panels and washing machines. In March, it imposed a 25% tariff on steel and 10% on aluminum. While many economies were temporarily exempted from the tariffs—notably Australia, Canada, the European Union, and Mexico—the Republic of Korea was the only economy in developing Asia to receive this special treatment. Based on the share of these exports from Asia to the US, the direct cost was estimated at $4.62 billion annually, equal to 0.08% of developing Asia exports in 2017—a negligible amount (Table 1.1.2).

Moreover, prices for aluminum and iron ore (iron being the bulk of stainless steel) rose by 23% in 2017. This raised profits in the producers' home economies more than enough to offset the impact of tariffs, had they been imposed a year earlier. Profits in heavy industry, including large steel producers in the PRC, rose by 21% in 2017 thanks to higher prices and government-imposed production quotas, allowing these industries to service their debt and reduce borrowing while trying to shed excess capacity. Thus, these producers should be able to manage lower demand expected from the US, given the small share of exports to the US directly affected.

1.1.14 Developing Asia's GVC participation and trade share, by sector

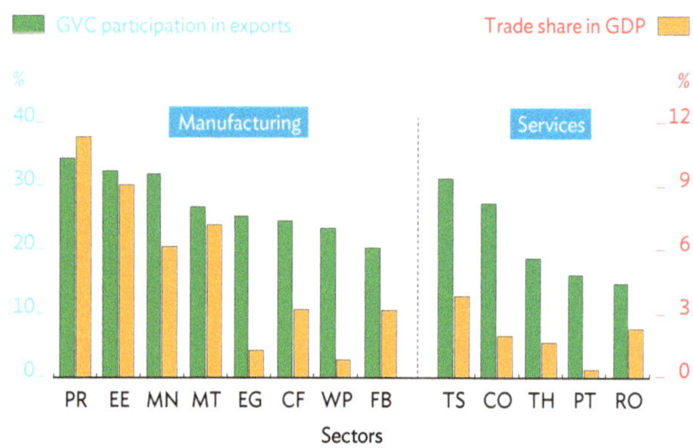

CF = clothing and footwear, CO = construction, EE = electrical and optical equipment, EG = electricity, gas, and water supply, FB = food, beverages, and tobacco, GVC = global value chain, MN = metals and nonmetallic minerals, MT = machinery and transport equipment, vehicles, and manufacturing, PR = petrochemicals, refining, rubber, and plastics, PT = post and telecommunications, RO = business services and machinery rental, TH = tourism, hotels, and restaurants, TS = transport services, WP = wood and paper products.

Notes: "GVC participation in exports" is domestic value added as a percentage of the export value of the product or service category. "Trade share in GDP" is the value of international trade in the product or service category—to, from, and within developing Asia—as a percentage of developing Asia GDP. Year is 2016. See Wang, Wei, and Zhu (2013) for details. Based on data from 2016, the latest year available. Selected economies in developing Asia are Bangladesh, Bhutan, Brunei Darussalam, Cambodia, Fiji, India, Indonesia, Kazakhstan, the Kyrgyz Republic, the Lao People's Democratic Republic, Malaysia, Maldives, Mongolia, Nepal, Pakistan, the Philippines, the Republic of Korea, Sri Lanka, Taipei,China, Thailand, and Viet Nam.

Source: ADB calculations using ADB's Multi-Regional Input-Output Database.

Steady foreign investment inflows

A concern regarding trade tensions is their potential effect on investors, considering that foreign direct investment (FDI) into Asian manufacturing generally finances exports. FDI inflows for new "greenfield" projects in developing Asia reached the equivalent of an estimated 1.7% of GDP in 2016, bouncing back from a low of 1.2% in 2012 in the wake of the global financial crisis of 2008–2009 (Figure 1.1.15). Preliminary data for 2017 suggests that greenfield FDI declined, largely on concerns over new policies in developed countries at the beginning of the year. However, the number of greenfield projects has been fairly steady since 2012. Including mergers and acquisitions, which are about a third the size of greenfield investment in developing Asia, the trend has changed little over time. FDI into developing Asia is most prominent in natural resources and financial services. That said, more than a quarter of FDI is tied to manufacturing value chains.

The US is an important investment partner in developing Asia, providing about 16% of total FDI into the region in 2017. The US directs 30% of its outbound FDI to developing Asia for a diverse set of sectors: a third going to extractive sectors such as oil and gas, and most of the rest to high-tech services and manufactures (Figure 1.1.16). Some policy makers worry that the recent US tax cuts may curtail future FDI flows into developing Asia. However, evidence suggests that other drivers are more important than tax cuts when it comes to new greenfield investment (Box 1.1.2).

Current accounts move toward balance

Current account balances moderated in 2017, despite strong exports, because of even stronger growth in imports, a trend that will continue in 2018 and 2019 (Figure 1.1.17). Developing Asia's current account surplus will narrow from the equivalent of 1.8% of aggregate GDP in 2017 to 1.4% in 2018 and 1.3% in 2019. The regional outcome reflects the narrowing of current account surpluses in East and Southeast Asia and the Pacific, as well as a widening current account deficit in South Asia. East Asia's current account surplus shrank from 2.8% of regional GDP in 2016 to 2.4% in 2017 and is expected to moderate to an average of 2.0% of regional GDP in the forecast period. Southeast Asia will continue to have a healthy surplus, though it will narrow

1.1.15 Total greenfield investments to developing Asia

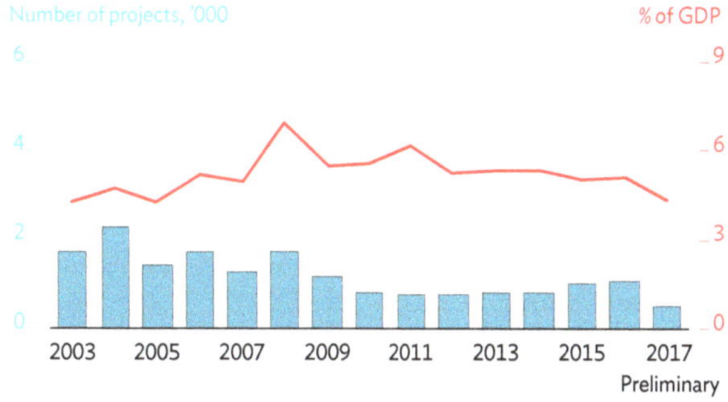

Note: Developing Asia covers all but the following member countries: Mongolia, the Cook Islands, Kiribati, Nauru, Palau, Timor-Leste, and Tuvalu.

Sources: ADB calculations using data from fDi Markets (https://www.fdimarkets.com), Zephyr (https://www.bvdinfo.com), and Haver Analytics.

1.1.16 Total greenfield investments in developing Asia by sector

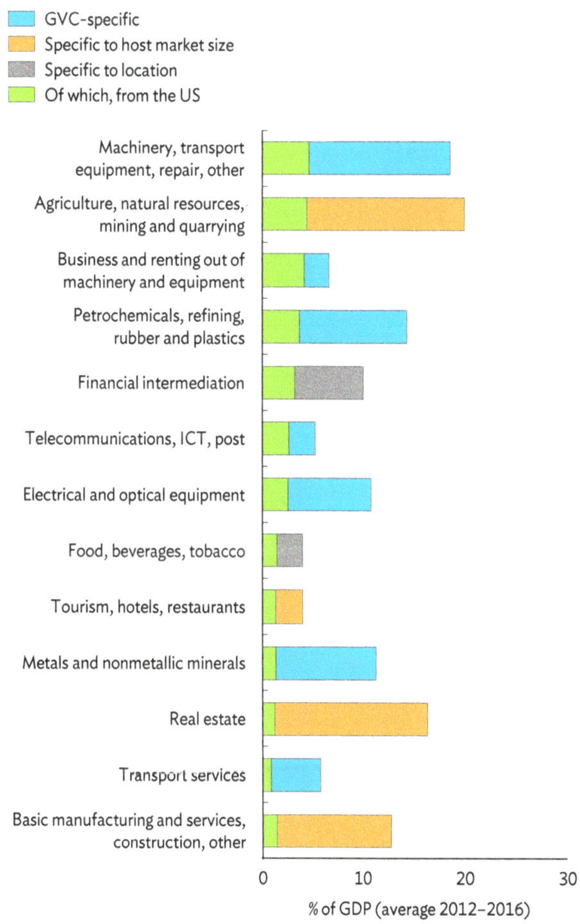

GVC = global value chain, ICT = information and communication technology.

Note: Developing Asia covers all but the following member countries: Mongolia, the Cook Islands, Kiribati, Nauru, Palau, Timor-Leste, and Tuvalu.

Sources: ADB estimates using data from fDi Markets (https://www.fdimarkets.com), Zephyr (https://www.bvdinfo.com), and Haver Analytics.

1.1.2 Effect of US tax policy on foreign direct investment in Asia

The question is whether recent changes in US tax policy may inhibit inflows. The recently enacted Tax and Jobs Act, 2017 reduced the corporate tax rate in the US from 35%, the highest in the Organization for Economic Cooperation and Development (OECD), to 21%, below the average Asian rate (box table). The 21% tax rate applies to profits earned abroad, as well as to domestic earnings. The law includes various other incentives for new investment into the US such as lower tax rates for cash repatriated and an immediate 100% tax deduction for spending on capital equipment. The fiscal impetus from this law on developing Asia's GDP is positive but negligible.

The impact of the tax rate is not immediately obvious. There are three channels through which US tax reform could affect prospective FDI, particularly to developing Asia.

The first channel is the repatriation of past profits to US, which would reduce the supply of funds available to FDI. Companies could repatriate as much as $2.5 trillion in profits held overseas, equal to about a third of almost $6.4 trillion in US outward stock, or 13% of 2017 GDP (US Treasury 2018). This foreign cash was held abroad before the tax law to take advantage of an earlier rule deferring tax on foreign profits if they were not brought into the US. Indeed, following the signing of the law, prominent US software giants announced their intention to repatriate profits. However, this is likely to be gradual. Reflows will occur as new project opportunities arise, which may take some time.

The second effect is the possibility that US firms heavily invested in developing Asia will immediately uproot physical assets. This is highly unlikely because the cost of doing so would be prohibitive. The difference between the corporate tax at home and abroad constitutes only a small part of the total costs of production, while the fixed costs of destocking capital for long-term investments such as oil and gas, for example, would be many times larger than the savings from slightly higher after-tax profit.

A third consideration is the decision where to locate new greenfield investment. Investors still have flexibility in this regard, and thus bargaining power, so they will carefully consider many structural factors before deciding. Still, the economic literature suggests that tax rates are generally not a priority consideration for investors when deciding about location, and this is likely to be even more true in developing Asia. Studies on emerging markets show that once other factors are considered—such as the size of the market, availability of natural resources,

continued next page

Corporate tax rates and FDI restrictiveness, selected economies

Country	Corporate tax rates	FDI index
Brunei Darussalam	18.5%; 55% for oil and gas companies	0.327
Cambodia	20%; 30% for oil and gas companies	0.052
Hong Kong, China	16.5%; two-tiered profit tax regime on or after 1 April 2018	...
India	30% for Indian companies, 40% for foreign companies	0.212
Indonesia	25%; 20% for nonresident companies in the form of permanent establishment	0.315
Lao People's Democratic Republic	24% with a 5% reduction for companies listed in the Lao stock exchange	0.187
Malaysia	24% but 18% for Malaysian resident small and medium-sized companies	0.211
Myanmar (average)	25% for companies established under the Myanmar Foreign Investment Law, otherwise 5%–40%	0.356
People's Republic of China	25%; 15% for high and new technology enterprises	0.327
Philippines	30% on net income for resident companies, or 2% based on gross income; 30% on gross income for nonresident companies	0.398
Singapore (strict)	17%	...
Thailand	20% on net worldwide income; 30% on foreign companies for earnings in Thailand; 3% of gross receipts for transport companies	...
Viet Nam	20%; 32%–50% for oil and gas enterprises	0.115
United States	35% excluding deductions but 21% starting in 2018, plus state taxes of 3%–5%	0.089
OECD average	22.34% for corporate income tax; 22.2% excluding deductions for subnational taxes; 24.8% for combined corporate income tax	0.067

... = not available, FDI = foreign direct investment.

Note: FDI Index is based on OECD FDI Regulatory Restrictiveness Index, where 0 = close, 1 = open.

Sources: Organisation for Economic Co-operation and Development. http://www.oecd.org; Worldwide Tax Summaries. https://www.pwc.com/gx/en/services/tax/worldwide-tax-summaries.html#online-tool; Asia Briefing. http://www.asiabriefing.com/news/2014/12/analysis-asias-tax-rates-part-one-corporate-income-tax; and KPMG. https://home.kpmg.com.

1.1.2 Continued

business environment, and host country potential for demand growth—tax differentials between the guest and the host country tend to be unimportant (Echandi, Krajcovicova, and Qiang 2015, James 2009). If the investor is already enmeshed in a tightly knit global value chain, shifting out of the network may entail substantial fixed costs required to link to a new supply chain in a new location (Swenson 2008). For investors with a long-term horizon targeting natural resources, the literature suggests that certainty about the fiscal regime and governance are more important than the tax rate itself (Hassett and Metcalf 1999, Hvozdyk and Mercer-Blackman 2009).

A breakdown by sector is instructive toward understanding investors' motivation when deciding about location (Figure 1.1.16). Stöwhase (2005) and Obeng (2014) found that the impact of taxation can vary substantially across sectors. For example, FDI in food processing has alternative locations, so it may be more sensitive to changes in the tax differential. FDI in export-oriented activities—which are very important in Asia—may occur in an enclave such as a free trade zone, so domestic tax rates are less relevant than relative labor costs. More generally, higher tax rates in host countries may indicate higher tax revenue used to improve the infrastructure and human capital that is crucial for attracting high-tech investors. This is why high tax revenue in a host country positively correlates with higher FDI (Bénassy-Quéré, Gobalraja, and Trannoy, 2007). Indeed, most US investment goes to other OECD countries, where average effective tax rates are much higher than in developing Asia (PwC 2016). Policy makers in developing Asia should thus worry about improving the business environment instead of considering a race to the bottom on corporate tax rates.

from 3.5% in 2017 to 2.7% in 2018 and 2.5% in 2019. Strong import demand in South Asia caused the current account deficit to widen to 2.1% of GDP in 2017, and it will widen further to 2.5% in 2018 and 2.6% in 2019. Bucking regionwide current account trends, Central Asia's current account deficit narrowed sharply from the equivalent of 6.5% of GDP in 2016 to 1.7% in 2017, largely because oil and gold price rose but also with increased trade volumes. These gains are expected to be sustained as the subregional deficit holds at 2.1% of GDP to the forecast horizon.

As a share of world GDP, developing Asia's current account surplus is forecast to narrow from 0.5% in 2017 to less than 0.4% in both 2018 and 2019, even as exports expand in many Asian economies. This suggests rising demand and domestic activity in the region, as many economies move closer to their growth potential, and continued rebalancing in the PRC economy, which caused its surplus to shrink further to less than 0.2% of world GDP (Figure 1.1.18).

1.1.17 Current account balances by subregion

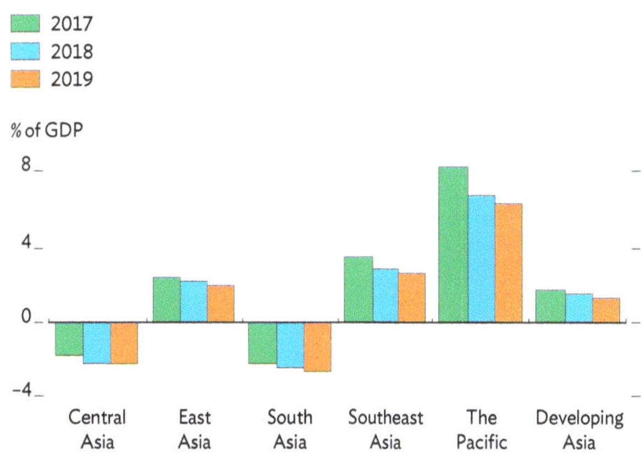

Source: *Asian Development Outlook* database.

Growth outlook remains stable

Growth in domestic demand is expected to become the main driver of GDP expansion as growth in trade decelerates moderately. Heightened confidence should continue to the forecast horizon. Aggregate GDP in developing Asia will grow by 6.0% in 2018 and 5.9% in 2019, slowing marginally from

6.1% in 2016. Excluding the newly industrialized economies, growth will slow from 6.6% in 2017 to 6.5% this year and 6.4% in 2019. Expansion will be sluggish in more than two-thirds of the economies in the region as growth returns to trend. India will lift regional output, but its contribution will be offset by controlled deceleration in PRC, which accounts for 58% of regional GDP (Figure 1.1.19). The region will nevertheless remain the fastest growing in the world and the largest contributor to global growth, accounting for more than 60% (Figure 1.1.20).

East Asian growth is expected to slow to 6.0% in 2018 and further to 5.8% in 2019, tracking growth moderation in the PRC. The PRC itself is likely to grow by 6.6% in 2018 and 6.4% in 2019, slowing under the effect of further reduction in excess capacity, the gradual unwinding of financial sector vulnerability, and a shift of growth drivers from capital accumulation to total factor productivity. The effect of slower PRC growth will extend to trade and manufacturing in the rest of the subregion, even with acceleration from domestic drivers such as private consumption and government and private investment. Growth is therefore forecast to moderate in Hong Kong, China; the Republic of Korea; and Mongolia but remain broadly unchanged in Taipei,China as the government there spends heavily on infrastructure.

South Asian expansion is forecast to accelerate to 7.0% in 2018 as India regains its footing and further to 7.2% in 2019 as expansion accelerates in the rest of the region as well. In India, continued government reform and deleveraging by private corporations will support recovery in investment, and strong growth prospects in the industrial economies will boost exports this year and next. Growth in India is expected to accelerate slightly to 7.6% in 2019, boosting the subregional average and offsetting a projected slowdown in Pakistan.

In Southeast Asia, growth is forecast to remain at its current rate of 5.2% in 2018 and 2019 as the cyclical upswing from 2017 continues, though with individual growth patterns varying. Energy exporters should benefit from the pickup in global commodity prices, but larger contributions are expected from private consumption and public spending on infrastructure. Growth in the Philippines and Thailand will benefit from higher consumption and a continued rise in public investment, in addition to slower but still solid expansion in tech exports.

1.1.18 World current account balance

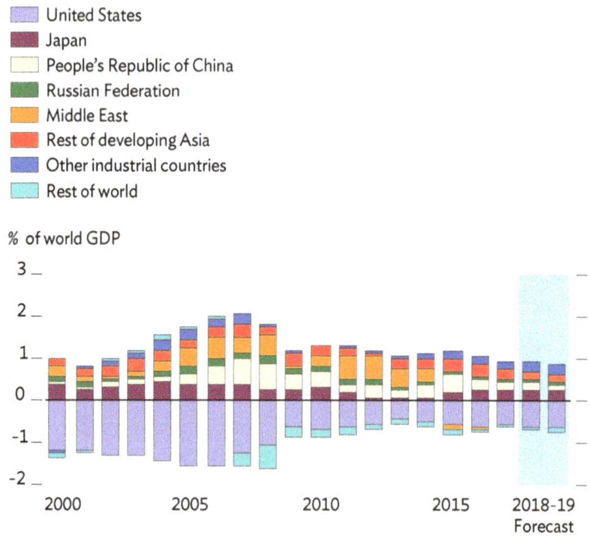

Source: Haver Analytics (accessed 19 March 2018).

1.1.19 GDP growth, by subregion

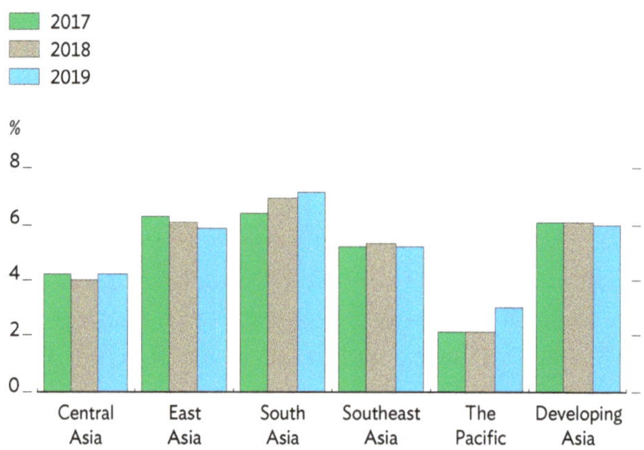

Source: *Asian Development Outlook* database.

Central Asia will reverse last year's growth acceleration as growth moderates in Kazakhstan. Higher oil prices should benefit oil-exporting economies, but as consumption and manufacturing growth slows in heavily-weighted Kazakhstan, growth in the subregion as a whole will moderate to 4.0% in 2018 and 4.2% in 2019.

The Pacific is seen to keep its aggregate growth rate at 2.2% in 2018 and rise further to 3.0% in 2019, determined largely by events in Papua New Guinea, the subregion's largest economy. In Timor-Leste, improvement will hinge mostly on the political outlook, particularly with a parliamentary election in May, and in Palau on a gradual recovery in tourist arrivals. Expansion will slow in Fiji and Vanuatu as most cyclone reconstruction ends.

Regional inflation is projected to accelerate from 2.2% in 2017 to 2.9% this year and next because of rising global commodity prices and higher consumer demand. Inflation will rise in all subregions except Central Asia, where it will be constrained by price stabilization efforts in Kazakhstan. Uzbekistan will continue to experience double-digit inflation fueled by higher tariffs and the effects of earlier currency depreciation as they pass through from imports to consumer prices. In the PRC, the key drivers of inflation remain strong consumer demand for commodities other than food and for services, higher wages, and continued price deregulation for health care in particular. Higher producer prices will further boost inflation in the PRC, which will accelerate to 2.4% this year before easing marginally to 2.3% in 2019.

South Asia will see consumer prices rise by 0.7 percentage points to 4.7% in 2018 and further to 5.1% in 2019. Inflation is expected to accelerate in every country except Sri Lanka. Inflation in India will increase to 4.6% in 2018 largely on rising global oil prices, likely higher procurement prices for food, and strengthening rural wages. Price rises in the Pacific will reflect higher inflation in Papua New Guinea from the pass-through of higher global fuel prices and excise tax hikes on domestic fuel, and in Timor-Leste from higher food and fuel prices and a weaker US dollar, which serves as the national currency.

1.1.20 GDP growth, developing economies

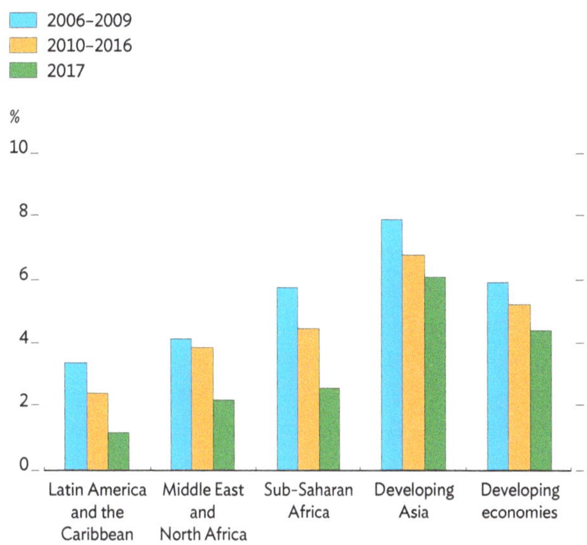

Note: Latin America and the Caribbean, Middle East and North Africa, and Sub-Saharan Africa are classifications in the International Monetary Fund's World Economic Outlook database. "Developing economies" combine these regions with developing Asia.

Sources: Haver Analytics (accessed 14 March 2018); *Asian Development Outlook* database; ADB estimates.

Risks to the outlook

Prospects may be positive following robust growth recovery in 2017, but the risks are mostly on the downside. The big risk, of course, would be worsening trade friction. Another would be rapid capital outflows that could materialize if the US Federal Reserve needed to raise interest rates faster than markets expect. Finally, the continued build up of private debt in some regional economies since the global financial crisis could undercut growth. Developing Asia is well positioned to respond to these shocks.

Trade risks

Risks to trade are high on the list. As noted above, new trade tariffs implemented by the US to the end of March 2018 have not discernibly dented buoyant trade flows to and from developing Asia. However, further action and retaliation against it could undermine the business and consumer optimism that underlies the regional outlook.

Some countries have managed to negotiate exemptions from US steel and aluminum tariffs—notably the ROK—but this has done little to ease heightened trade worries globally. Tensions between the US and the PRC in particular have ratcheted up. The US announced in 3 April 2018 possible tariffs of 25% on more than 1,300 specific goods, affecting an estimated $50 billion a year of imports from the PRC, equal to 2% of PRC exports in 2017 or 0.4% of GDP. The tariffs overwhelmingly affect PRC exports of intermediate inputs, especially for renewable energy, electricity generation, and electrical and optical equipment. In response, the PRC announced reciprocal 25% tariffs on imports from the US that affect 128 categories of mainly agricultural goods, also worth $50 billion. Most of these tariffs will take effect in the coming months unless forestalled by a conciliatory agreement between Beijing and Washington.

While the direct tariff costs of the announced measures may be small compared with growth in trade forecast for 2018, their disruption to supply chains could sabotage business expansion plans in related industries, and uncertainty over the global environment could dampen currently strong consumption growth. Moreover, US firms have strong links with Asian value chains in manufacturing. Any shift of US investors out of Asia would risk possibly interrupting, diverting, or severing global production chains now operating in the region.

Stronger intraregional links may help mitigate any effects of rising global trade tensions. Consider the Trans-Pacific Partnership. US withdrawal in January 2017 did not, as some feared, spell the end of negotiations. Instead, 11 Pacific Rim economies moved ahead, albeit with modifications. The resulting Comprehensive and Progressive Agreement for Trans-Pacific Partnership was signed in March 2018 by four governments in developing Asia—Brunei Darussalam, Malaysia, Singapore, and Viet Nam—and other countries may be allowed to join as new members. Although signatories still need to ratify the agreement, their intent to maintain movement toward trade openness is clear. Also, the Regional Comprehensive Economic Partnership, led by the Association of Southeast Asian Nations and encompassing 30% of global GDP and more than 3.5 billion people, is progressing well. By opening up new markets, both initiatives could dispel the clouds gathering over an otherwise bright horizon.

Capital flow risks

A less headline-grabbing but nevertheless real risk is diminishing capital inflows if the Federal Reserve decides to raise interest rates faster than markets expect to keep fiscal expansion from overheating the US economy. The baseline assumption is that the Fed will gradually raise its benchmark rate 2 or 3 more times in 2018 to bring the midpoint of the federal funds rate to about 2.1% by the end of 2018 and then raise it perhaps 2 more times in 2019 to reach 2.9% by the end of the year. This roughly aligns with market expectations. The Fed raised its policy rate by a quarter point to 1.50%–1.75% on 22 March 2018, as most market watchers expected, having predicted inflation accelerating in the coming months. If US core inflation threatens to exceed 2%, the Fed may need to enhance both the pace and the size of its policy rate adjustments, which could cause rapid capital outflows from developing Asia.

Such outflows could create US dollar scarcity, possibly appreciating the dollar and ramping up the local currency cost of servicing foreign currency debt. While the financial effects of such repatriation would be unlikely to upend any economy's balance of payments, it could very well mire developing Asia's trade-driven growth. No sign has yet emerged of the US dollar appreciating significantly in the short run, however, so there is little incentive at this point to move additional capital from the region. In any case, with banks that are well regulated and capitalized, and with ample foreign reserves, developing Asia is in a strong position to weather any capital outflow likely to materialize.

1.1.21 Bitcoin price

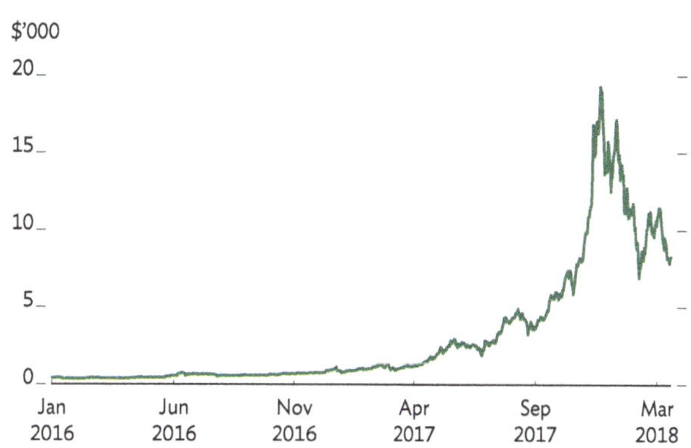

Source: CoinMarketCap.

Finance sector risks

There is concern that the region's financial sector may be facing unknown risks from emerging financial technologies. Virtual currencies like Bitcoin have proliferated in recent years. A speculative frenzy caused the price of Bitcoin to triple to nearly $20,000 in the 3 months to December 2017, before a major selloff (Figure 1.1.21). Virtual currency assets remain too small to pose a threat to national or global financial systems, their total market capitalization in mid-March 2018 equaling a mere 0.19% of global equity and bond capitalization. Wary policy makers have nevertheless been restricting their use and circulation and are gearing up to ringfence financial systems. International coordination is essential to address these challenges and ensure adherence to national rules and regulations.

However, an emphasis on "crypto mania" misses the promise in the underlying technology. Blockchain or distributed ledger technology opens up opportunities in development finance and related efforts (Box 1.1.3). Policy makers and development lenders can facilitate development-friendly distributed ledger technology through targeted infrastructure investments and regulation that either uses a test-and-learn sandbox approach to fine-tune new technologies before implementing them on a wider scale or adopts the results of experience in other countries.

In addition to new risks, the region's financial sector faces more familiar challenges. The ongoing rise in US interest rates and the consequent tightening of global liquidity pose challenges to financial stability. The buildup of private debt in the region since the global financial crisis of 2008–2009 has amplified this risk. More specifically, there are concerns that the post-crisis debt buildup may adversely affect financial stability and economic growth, especially in Asian countries that have experienced rapid expansion of household or corporate debt. In light of such possible effects, the next section analyzes the relationship between growth in private debt and economic growth. The analysis finds no positive relationship between private debt growth and economic growth beyond the short term. This raises concerns about the quality of the added debt and strengthens the case for closely monitoring debt trends and building more efficient financial systems.

Conclusion

The downside risks to a generally benign economic outlook are far from negligible. However, the trade revival last year reinforced strong trade links within Asia and built up financial buffers in many Asian economies, especially commodity exporters. The stronger fiscal and financial position of many countries in 2017 should allow them to manage risks. The best recourse for Asia is to take advantage of the current good times to deepen structural reform that is otherwise difficult to impose. Such reform would put Asia in an even stronger position to withstand future shocks.

1.1.3 Distributed ledger technology and its promise for development finance

The blockchain technology underlying Bitcoin is viable and ripe for broader application. Indeed, distributed ledger technology (DLT), to use the broader but usually interchangeable term, opens opportunities for applications that can revolutionize the financial sector. DLT-based clearing and settlement is beginning to replace inefficient back-office infrastructure, for example, and operations such as exchanging cash for securities will increasingly be accomplished in a matter of seconds, rather than days as is currently the case. DLT has far-reaching implications for the developing world in multiple areas. Remittances, microcredit, and trade finance are just a few of the many possible applications.

Remittances. Remittances are a stabilizing source of foreign exchange for many economies in Asia and the Pacific, accounting in 2016 for 30.5% of GDP in the Kyrgyz Republic, the highest percentage in the region, and for 9.8% even in the relatively large Philippine economy. However, sending money to relatives from abroad is slow and costly. Transfers may take several days, and banks and money transfer companies typically charge 7% of the amount transacted and sometimes much more (World Bank 2015). To avoid these costs, remitters often transfer funds through informal channels, such as a visiting friend or relative carrying cash.

Several companies now offer DLT-based remittance services in several Asian economies. Compared with traditional channels, which require a centralized entity to perform the actual remittance, DLT services save time and transaction costs by making the role of corresponding banks less central to the settlement process. The widespread use of internet-enabled mobile phones among the poor enables DLT-based remittances to reach the unbanked far beyond the reach of the traditional financial channels (Dong et al. 2016).

Microcredit. Catering to the financially excluded, microcredit continues to expand, especially in developing Asia and Latin America. It typically operates at the village level, leveraging the capacity of poor communities and economically disenfranchised groups, in particular women, to assume joint liability and monitor peer compliance. Lenders seek to lower the high transaction costs of small-scale lending but often incur substantial costs in dispatching loan officers to periodic community meetings. As a peer-to-peer communications system that distributes trust among members of a shared network by ensuring decision by consensus, DLT is particularly well suited to microcredit and to microfinance more broadly. It functions as an open accounting system, placing borrowers' transaction histories on a shared ledger, which eliminates the need for outside audits or documentation of loan applicants' credit and income histories.

DLT enables unbanked individuals to build a personal credit history and thus a bankable reputation gradually and organically. It lets lenders monitor and assess the capital loaned, the areas of operation, and any development opportunities. Pilot applications suggest that, compared with traditional centralized microfinance operations, the DLT-powered mode incurs significantly lower overhead and achieves faster transaction times. In 2016, for example, Japanese companies successfully operated DLT microcredit transactions in Myanmar. The evidence gathered during these trials suggests that the DLT platform will, assuming full-fledged commercial implementation by 2019, reduce costs to a tenth of those incurred by traditional microcredit operations in Myanmar (Redaktion 2016, Del Castillo 2016).

Trade finance. The global trade finance gap was estimated at $1.5 trillion in 2016 (ADB 2017b). Shortfalls were particularly severe in Asia, which accounted for the largest share of proposals—firms' requests to banks for trade finance support—and rejections. Access to trade finance is particularly difficult for small and medium-sized enterprises (SMEs) because they often lack collateral, a documented history of past commercial and financial transactions, or sufficient knowledge of the finance industry and instruments on offer. National and regional initiatives to bridge this gap, including some led by multilateral development banks, increasingly look forward to technology that can make a difference.

Some innovation is coming from leading companies in global e-commerce. They have established their own lending arms, catering mostly to SMEs, or provide training and advice tailored especially for smaller companies. However, except in the PRC, these services have yet to penetrate developing Asia, where the supply gap for SME financing remains particularly acute (The Banker 2017). In these economies, DLT could be a real game changer by lowering costs and doing away with the paperwork and bureaucratic hurdles that preclude access for SMEs.

Source: Ferrarini, Maupin, and Hinojales 2017.

Private debt and economic growth

Some economies in developing Asia have since the global financial crisis of 2008–2009 (GFC) experienced rapid growth in private debt, both corporate and household. Concern is rising that the buildup of private debt may threaten financial stability, especially as interest rates rise with monetary policy normalization in the advanced economies. Further, some studies find that private debt buildup, in particular by households, predicts lower GDP growth and higher unemployment in the medium term (Mian, Sufi, and Vernier 2017). These counterintuitive results, if confirmed, have major implications for economic policy and development. An empirical study presented in this section sheds light on the nature of the relationship between private debt accumulation and economic growth, particularly in Asia.

Private debt mounting in Asia as the advanced economies deleverage

Low global interest rates since the GFC, reflecting unprecedented monetary expansion in the advanced countries, encouraged Asian households and companies to borrow heavily, driving up the ratio of private debt to GDP in many Asian economies (Figure 1.2.1). Concerted deleveraging efforts in the US, the United Kingdom, and other advanced economies in the aftermath of GFC lowered their ratios of private debt to GDP, but such efforts were absent in developing Asia.

1.2.1 Ratio of debt to GDP in selected economies in developing Asia

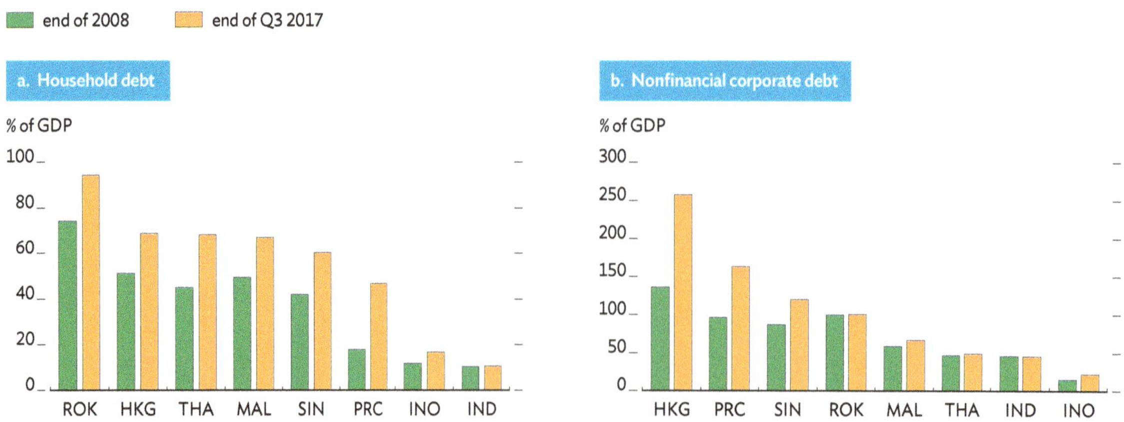

GDP = gross domestic product, HKG = Hong Kong, China, IND = India, INO = Indonesia, MAL = Malaysia, PRC = People's Republic of China, Q = quarter, ROK = Republic of Korea, SIN = Singapore, THA = Thailand.

Source: Institute of International Finance.

1.2.2 The dynamics of private debt, household debt, and corporate debt

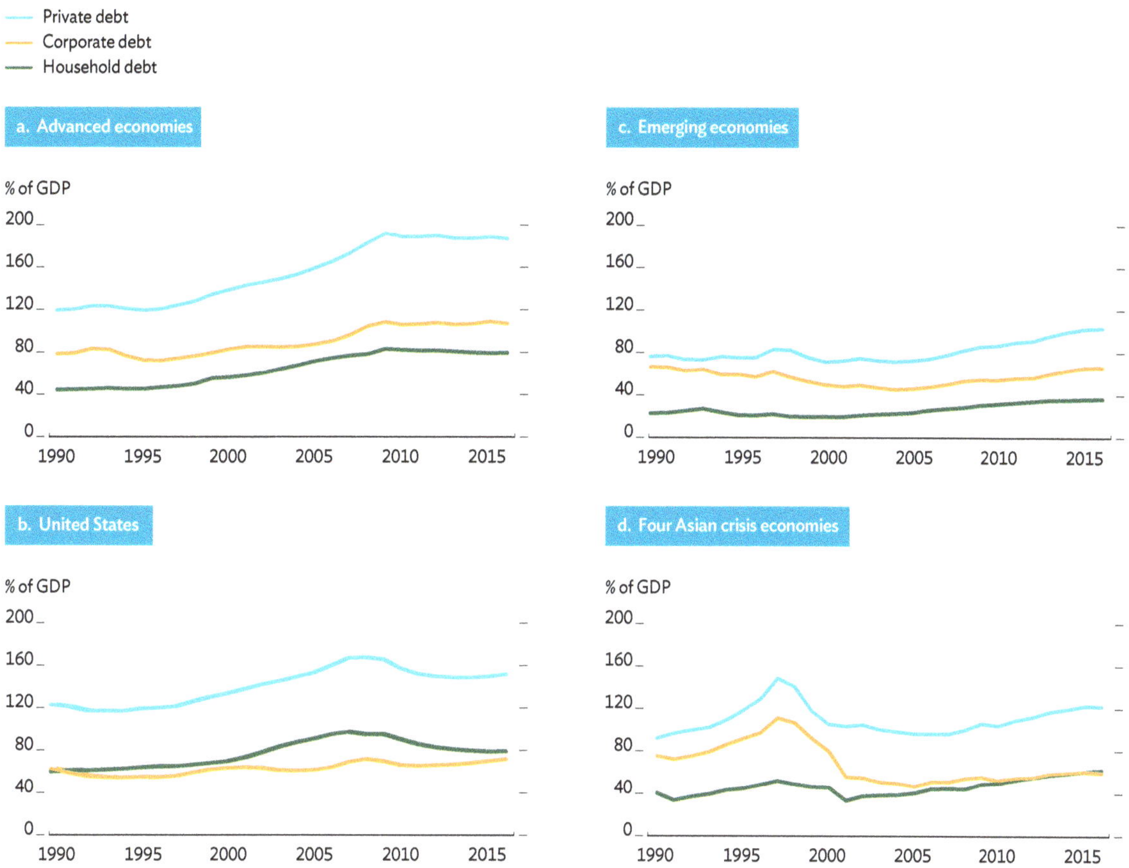

GDP = gross domestic product.

Notes: Debt is measured as a share of GDP. The advanced economies are Australia, Austria, Belgium, Canada, Denmark, Finland, France, Germany, Greece, Ireland, Italy, Japan, the Netherlands, New Zealand, Norway, Portugal, Spain, Sweden, Switzerland, the United Kingdom, and the United States. The emerging economies are Argentina; Brazil; Colombia; the Czech Republic; Hong Kong, China; Hungary; Indonesia; Israel; Malaysia; Mexico; Poland; the Republic of Korea; the Russian Federation; Saudi Arabia; Singapore; Thailand; and Turkey. The four economies hit hardest by the Asian financial crisis of 1997–1998 are Indonesia, Malaysia, the Republic of Korea, and Thailand.

Sources: ADB calculations based on the BIS Debt Securities database.

In the advanced economies, corporate and especially household debt increased sharply before the GFC (Figure 1.2.2a). In the post-crisis period, corporate debt stabilized while household debt decreased. Narrowing the focus to the US, the dynamics of private debt were more dramatic, rising rapidly before the GFC and falling after, mostly led by household debt (Figure 1.2.2b). This is consistent with the widely held view that the main cause of the GFC was a rapid increase in household debt under lax credit appraisal and approval.

Unlike the advanced economies, emerging economies continued to accumulate private debt even after the GFC (Figure 1.2.2c). In Indonesia, Malaysia, the Republic of Korea, and Thailand, the four Asian economies hardest hit by the Asian financial crisis of 1997–1998, the pronounced increase in private debt before the earlier crisis was driven largely by corporate debt (Figure 1.2.2d). This is consistent with the popular view that the crisis was precipitated by Asian companies borrowing heavily in foreign currency to finance investment projects such as property that generated revenue only in local currency, and that the surge of borrowing drove down the quality of investment.

It bears noting that private debt expansion is not necessarily a cause for concern in itself, especially in emerging economies with immature financial systems. It may reflect simply the development of the national financial system from a low base. Further, ease in borrowing can smooth investment and consumption to the benefit of all. That said, rapid debt accumulation can affect growth adversely through several channels. First, households and corporations may not be able to service their debt, undermining bank health, especially if loans are not backed by adequate collateral. Second, the need to allocate resources to pay debt service can syphon funds from consumption and investment. Rising interest rates accentuate both of these risks.

Third, excessively leveraged firms and households can inflate asset prices. When the bubble bursts, banks and other financial institutions suffer a surge of bad loans and have to cut back on their lending, which hurts investment and consumption. Because it generally takes some time for banks to repair their balance sheets, credit to firms and households will be disrupted for some time. Further, firms and households have to cut back on investment and consumption to repair their own damaged balance sheets. This is why recessions stemming from financial stress tend to be deeper and more persistent than recessions from other causes, exacerbating volatility in the business cycle.

The experience of the developed countries sheds light on how harmful private debt buildup can be to economic growth. The immediate cause of the GFC and the bad recession that followed was the rapid buildup of US private debt, which taxed procedures to appraise loans for creditworthiness. The world economy has yet to recover fully from the loss of growth momentum caused by that recession.

In light of these considerations, the ongoing escalation of global interest rates is putting the spotlight on the buildup of private debt in Asia, in particular in Malaysia, the Republic of Korea, and Thailand, where household debt is large and growing, and in the People's Republic of China, where corporate debt is fast expanding (ADB 2017a). Although developing Asia currently enjoys a positive economic outlook, rising corporate and household debt poses risks to growth over time.

Intuitively, is private debt buildup bad for growth?

The discussion above indicates that private debt buildup can either boost economic growth or hinder it. A positive credit demand shock can result from an expectation that productivity or long-term income will increase, bringing subsequent output growth. The current Fourth Industrial Revolution, for example, is encouraging firms to borrow and invest in potentially game-changing new technologies, and it is encouraging individuals to borrow to invest in firms that stand to benefit from the revolution. On the other hand, if credit supply shocks are driven by lenders' irrationally exuberant expectations and disregard for downside risks, debt accumulation in high-risk sectors eventually brings about a reversal in investor sentiment and subsequently harms growth. A recent example is the US subprime mortgage crisis that morphed into the GFC.

In sum, theoretical ambiguity renders the relationship between private debt growth and economic growth an empirical issue. Unfortunately, the literature on empirical experience is thin (Box 1.2.1).

1.2.1 Empirical studies on private debt and growth

The link between public debt and economic growth is well established in the literature, examined in, for example, Baum, Checherita, and Rother (2013), Checherita and Rother (2012), Égert (2015), Kumar and Woo (2010), and Reinhart and Rogoff (2010). However, only a few studies have empirically examined the impact of private debt on economic growth, and they have been largely confined to the advanced economies. Mian, Sufi, and Verner (2017) found a significant negative relationship between economic growth in the advanced economies and private debt, especially household debt, accumulated through credit shocks positive for either demand or supply. By decomposing private debt into household debt and nonfinancial corporate debt, the study showed household debt more than corporate debt closely related to the boom-and-bust cycle.

Sutherland and Hoeller (2012) examined the impact of debt in different sectors—government, private financial, private nonfinancial, and household—on economic stability in member economies of the Organisation for Economic Co-operation and Development (OECD). It found private sector debt not consistently related to GDP volatility but household debt positively associated with consumption volatility, and short-term private sector debt with investment volatility. Cecchetti, Mohanty, and Zampolli (2011) examined the separate impact of public, corporate, and household debt on economic growth in OECD economies. It showed both corporate and household debt having significant negative correlation with growth in GDP per capita, but only corporate debt significantly positively related to volatility in growth of GDP per capita. Further, it found that excess private debt not only constrained the capacity of financing to smooth economic cycles but also caused large swings in asset prices, which tended to trigger recessions when an economy slows down.

While these studies looked mostly at the amount of private debt, it is worthwhile to examine how the speed of private debt accumulation affects economic growth and the occurrence of recessions. Jordà, Schularick, and Taylor (2013) showed that recessions caused by financial crises were costlier than others, and that economic expansions with rapid credit buildup were followed by deeper recessions. These results were confirmed by Claessens, Kose, and Terrones (2012). Bernardini and Forni (2017) found the effect of private debt buildup to have even more pronounced effects on the duration and intensity of recessions in emerging economies.

Empirical evidence on private debt buildup and economic growth

Park, Shin, and Tian (forthcoming) empirically analyzed the effect of private debt growth on output growth. The study followed the basic empirical framework of Mian, Sufi, and Vernier (2017) but extended it to emerging economies. In addition to looking at the effect of the speed of debt buildup, it explored how the initial debt amount influenced the effect of the speed of debt buildup on output growth. In addition to the effect of private debt growth on output growth, the study investigated its effect on consumption and investment growth. Box 1.2.2 describes the data and methodology.

1.2.2 Econometric analysis of the relationship between private debt buildup and economic growth: data and empirical methodology

Park, Shin, and Tian (forthcoming) followed and extended Mian, Sufi, and Vernier (2017) to estimate the fixed effects regression on the dynamic relationship between private debt growth and economic growth, shown in the equation below. The procedure was to identify business-cycle frequency correlations. The rationale for the procedure, justification of the variables and parameters used, and estimation methodology are described in Mian, Sufi, and Vernier (2017) and not repeated here.

$$\begin{aligned}\Delta_3 y_{it+k} = \beta_0 + \beta_H \Delta_3 d_{it-1}^{HH} + \beta_C \Delta_3 d_{it-1}^{Corp} + \beta_{H1} d_{it-1}^{HH} \\ + \beta_{C1} d_{it-1}^{Corp} + \beta_{H2} \Delta_3 d_{it-1}^{HH} * d_{it-1}^{HH} \\ + \beta_{C2} \Delta_3 d_{it-1}^{Corp} * d_{it-1}^{Corp} + u_{it+k}\end{aligned} \quad (1)$$

where

$\Delta_3 y_{it+k}$ = change in log per capita GDP of country i from year t + k to t + k − 3,

d_{it-1}^{HH} = household debt as a share of GDP of country i at time t − 1,

d_{it-1}^{Corp} = corporate debt as a share of GDP of country i at time t − 1,

$\Delta_3 d_{it-1}^{HH}$ = change in household debt as shares of GDP from t + k to t + k − 3, and

$\Delta_3 d_{it-1}^{Corp}$ = change in corporate debt as shares of GDP from t + k to t + k − 3.

To estimate the relationship between private debt growth and consumption growth, Park, Shin, and Tian (forthcoming) simply replaced log per capita GDP with log per capita consumption, and did the same to estimate the relationship between private debt growth and investment growth.

The BIS Debt Securities database was the source of data on private nonfinancial sector debt as a share of GDP in 21 advanced economies and 17 emerging economies selected on the basis of data availability (Table 1.2.1 note). This aggregate was divided into household debt and nonfinancial corporate debt. Real GDP, real consumption, and real investment data were collected from the Penn World Table 9.0. Park, Shin, and Tian (forthcoming) provides the full definition of data sources of these variables and other control variables, the methodology for calculation of per capita values, and the summary statistics of all variables used in the empirical analysis.

The mean values of household debt and corporate debt as shares of GDP are higher in the advanced economies, at 55.5 and 83.7, respectively, than in emerging economies, at 26.0 and 55.3. In both groups, household debt is smaller than corporate debt but grows slightly faster. However, the standard deviation of annual increases in corporate debt is much higher than that of household debt, at 2.8 versus 5.4 in the advanced economies and 2.1 versus 5.3 in emerging economies. Serial correlation is higher for household debt, and this feature is more pronounced in the advanced economies.

1.2.1 Expansion in household and corporate debt versus subsequent growth rates

Growth in real GDP per capita	Advanced economies							Emerging economies						
	Year 0	Year 1	Year 2	Year 3	Year 4	Year 5	Year 6	Year 0	Year 1	Year 2	Year 3	Year 4	Year 5	Year 6
Increase in household debt ratio	+	+	+	–	–	–	–	+	+	+	+	–	–	–
Increase in corporate debt ratio	+	–	–	–	–	–	+	–	–	–	–	–	+	+
Household debt ratio	–	–	–	–	–	–	–	+	–	–	–	–	–	–
Corporate debt ratio	–	–	–	–	+	+	+	–	–	–	–	–	+	+
Interaction of household debt ratio and increase in household debt ratio	–	–	–	+	+	+	+	–	–	–	–	+	+	+
Interaction of corporate debt ratio and increase in corporate debt ratio	–	–	+	+	+	+	–	+	+	+	+	+	–	–
Observations	671	650	629	608	587	566	545	330	313	296	279	262	244	228
R^2	0.314	0.355	0.354	0.346	0.370	0.360	0.328	0.276	0.268	0.249	0.188	0.163	0.159	0.184

Notes: Blue shading denotes significance at 1%, orange 5%, and green 10%. The household debt ratio is the ratio of household debt to GDP. The corporate debt ratio is the ratio of corporate debt to GDP. Fixed effects are controlled in estimation. The advanced economies are Australia, Austria, Belgium, Canada, Denmark, Finland, France, Germany, Greece, Ireland, Italy, Japan, the Netherlands, New Zealand, Norway, Portugal, Spain, Sweden, Switzerland, the United Kingdom, and the United States. The emerging economies are Argentina; Brazil; Colombia; the Czech Republic; Hong Kong, China; Hungary; Indonesia; Israel; Malaysia; Mexico; Poland; the Republic of Korea; the Russian Federation; Saudi Arabia; Singapore; Thailand; and Turkey.

Source: Park, Shin, and Tian (forthcoming, which has full results and coefficient estimates).

The results for real GDP growth per capita confirmed results in Mian, Sufi, and Vernier (2017) for the advanced economies (Table 1.2.1). While the coefficients of household debt growth on output growth in the same and the following year are positive and statistically significant, those for the third year and later are negative and statistically significant. These results suggest that, while a buildup of household debt boosts output growth in the very short run, it predicts lower output growth for 3 years starting with the fourth year. In contrast, no buildup of corporate debt ever increased output growth, even in the short run, but rather predicted lower output growth in 1–3 years, implying that corporate debt buildup was likely a positive supply shock, prompted by eager banks. While the estimated coefficients of corporate debt were smaller, their negative impact was comparable to that of household debt.

The results also indicated that, as the debt amount rose, the negative impact of debt growth on output growth declined. Yet, in the advanced economies where the existing debt amount was relatively high, further additions to debt harmed output growth in the medium term. This implied the possible existence of a threshold amount beyond which debt growth threatened to harm economic growth.

In emerging economies, which were generally less financially developed and indebted, growth in household debt had a significantly positive impact on output growth in the short term, but the effect turned negative in the fifth year and persist in the sixth year. By contrast, corporate debt growth had a significantly negative impact on output growth in the first 4 years.

Again, the opposite sign of the coefficients on interaction terms between debt amount and debt growth suggests that financial sector development helps to stabilize the effect of debt growth on output growth. Further, in emerging markets, the household debt amount had a negative impact on output growth after 5 years but did not have any significant impact in the short term. On the other hand, the amount of corporate debt generally had no significant impact on output growth in the long run.

The empirical analysis further indicated that, in advanced and emerging economies alike, household debt was lower than corporate debt but increasing slightly faster, while the annual growth rate of corporate debt was more variable.

Concluding observations and policy implications

Evidence revealed in Park, Shin, and Tian (forthcoming) suggests that the positive effect of private debt growth on output growth is short-lived in emerging economies, and the effect is limited to household debt growth. In fact, the evidence indicates that the relationship between both household debt growth and corporate debt growth on the one hand, and economic growth on the other, is negative in the medium term. This strengthens the case for policy makers in developing Asia to closely monitor the buildup of private debt, especially in light of the potential risk that debt buildup poses for financial stability as global liquidity tightens. In addition to monitoring credit developments, it could be useful to pursue macroprudential measures that stemmed excessive credit buildup. Also useful would be early warning systems that could trigger action from supervisory authorities if signs emerged of excessive borrowing, falling lending standards, or inability to service debt. The analysis further points to the need for financial sector development as a means to alleviate the impact of private debt growth on boom–bust cycles.

These results may be controversial, but they are first steps toward empirically examining the relationship between private debt growth and output growth, an important policy issue that merits further research. Park, Shin, and Tian (forthcoming) focused on the quantity of debt, but the quality of debt matters at least as much to financial stability and economic growth. If debt is used to finance unproductive activities, its effect is more likely to be negative. If private debt growth largely reflects credit supply shocks driven by irrationally exuberant lenders who ignore downside risks, debt will build up in high-risk sectors, as it did in the US housing market before the US subprime mortgage crisis and in many Asian corporations before the Asian financial crisis.

Debt buildup eventually erodes investors' confidence and causes subsequent growth decline. The evidence thus reinforces the case for stronger prudential financial supervision and regulation—a case that has gained force since the GFC and its recession upended the global financial system and the world economy.

Background paper

Park, D., K. Shin, and S. Tian. Forthcoming. *Household Debt, Corporate Debt, and the Real Economy: Some Empirical Evidence*. Asian Development Bank.

References

ADB. 2017a. *Asian Economic Integration Report*. Asian Development Bank.

——. 2017b. Meeting Asia's Infrastructure Needs. Asian Development Bank. http://dx.doi.org/10.22617/FLS168388-2.

Baum, A., C. Checherita, and P. Rother. 2013. Debt and Growth: New Evidence for the Euro Area. *Journal of International Money and Finance* 32.

Bénassy-Quéré, A., N. Gobalraja, and A. Trannoy. 2007. Tax and public input competition. *Economic Policy* 19.

Bernardini, M. and L. Forni. 2017. Private and Public Debt: Are Emerging Markets at Risk? *IMF Working Paper* No. WP/17/61. International Monetary Fund.

Cecchetti, S., M. Mohanty, and F. Zampolli. 2011. The Real Effects of Debt. *BIS Working Papers* No. 352. Bank for International Settlements.

Checherita, C. and P. Rother. 2012. The Impact of High and Growing Government Debt on Economic Growth: An Empirical Investigation for the Euro Area. *European Economic Review* 56(7).

Claessens, S., M. A. Kose, and M. E. Terrones. 2012. How Do Business and Financial Cycles Interact? *Journal of International Economics* 87.

Del Castillo, M. 2016. Myanmar Microfinance Firm Trials Blockchain. *Coindesk*. 7 July. https://www.coindesk.com/myanmars-largest-microfinace-company-conducts-blockchain-experimetn/.

Dong, H., K. Habermeier, R. Leckow, V. Haksar, Y. Almeida, M. Kashima, N. Kyriakos-Saad, H. Oura, T. Saadi Sedik, N. Stetsenko, and C. Verdugo-Yepes. 2016. Virtual Currencies and Beyond: Initial Considerations. *IMF Staff Discussion Note* SDN/16/03. https://www.imf.org/external/pubs/ft/sdn/2016/sdn1603.pdf.

Echandi, R., J. Krajcovicova, and C. Z. Qiang. 2015. The Impact of Investment Policy in a Changing Global Economy: A Review of the Literature. *World Bank Policy Research Working Paper* 7437. Washington, DC, October.

Égert, B. 2015. Public Debt, Economic Growth, and Nonlinear Effects: Myth or Reality? *Journal of Macroeconomics* 43.

Ferrarini, B., J. Maupin, and M. Hinojales. 2017. Distributed Ledger Technologies for Developing Asia. *ADB Economics Working Paper Series* No. 533. Asian Development Bank.

Hassett, K. and G. Metcalf. 1999. Investment with Uncertain Tax Policy: Does Random Tax Policy Discourage Investment? *Economic Journal* 109.
Hvozdyk, L. and V. Mercer-Blackman. 2009. What Determines Investment in the Oil Sector? *IDB Working Paper Series* No. 209. Inter-American Development Bank.
James, S. 2009. Tax and Non-tax Incentives and Investments: Evidence and Policy Implications. Facility for Investment Climate Advisory Services. World Bank.
Jordà, Ò., M. Schularick, and A. M. Taylor. 2013. When Credit Bites Back. *Journal of Money, Credit, and Banking*, 45 Supplement (2).
Kumar, M. and J. Woo. 2010. Public Debt and Growth. *IMF Working Paper* No. 10/174. International Monetary Fund.
Mian, A., A. Sufi, and E. Verner. 2017. Household Debt and Business Cycles Worldwide. *Quarterly Journal of Economics* 132.
Obeng, C. K. 2014. Effect of Corporate Tax on Sector Specific Foreign Direct Investment in Ghana. *Munich Personal RePEc Archive (MPRA) Paper* No. 58454 (10 September). http://mpra.ub.uni-muenchen.de/58454/.
PwC. 2016. International Comparison of Effective Corporate Tax Rates. Prepared for Alliance for Competitive Taxation. September. http://www.actontaxreform.com/wp-content/uploads/2016/09/International-Comparison-of-Effective-Corporate-Tax-Rates_FINAL_20160926.pdf. PricewaterhouseCoopers.
Redaktion. 2016. *The First Blockchain Microfinance Service is Implemented by Japanese Tech Firms.* https://www.bitcoinnews.ch/4237/microfinance/.
Reinhart, C. and K. Rogoff. 2010. Growth in a Time of Debt. *American Economic Review* 100(2).
Stöwhase, S. 2005. Tax-rate-differentials and Sector-specific Foreign Direct Investment: Empirical Evidence from the EU. *FinanzArchiv* 61.
Sutherland, D. and P. Hoeller. 2012. Debt and Macroeconomic Stability: An Overview of the Literature and Some Empirics. *OECD Economics Department Working Paper* No. 1006. Organisation for Economic Co-operation and Development.
Swenson, D. L. 2008. Multinationals and the Creation of Chinese Trade Linkages. *Canadian Journal of Economics* 41(2).
The Banker. 2017. Small Firms Go Global. October. 168(1101).
United States Treasury International Capital System. 2018. https://www.treasury.gov/resource-center/data-chart-center/tic/Pages/index.aspx (accessed January 2018).
Wang, Z., S. Wei, and K. Zhu. 2013. Quantifying International Production Sharing at the Bilateral and Sector Levels. *National Bureau of Economic Research Working Paper* No. 19677. http://www.nber.org/papers/w19677.pdf.
World Bank. 2015. *Remittance Prices Worldwide.* https://remittanceprices.worldbank.org/en.

Annex: Sustaining growth momentum

The major industrial economies of the United States, the euro area, and Japan recovered in 2017, with growth accelerating in all three and aggregate growth rising from 1.5% to 2.3% (Table A1.1). Growth is expected to continue to the forecast horizon, with the US sustaining growth for the group at 2.3% in 2018 and a bit lower at 2.0% in 2019 as tax cuts boost private spending. Meanwhile, growth in the euro area and Japan will moderate in both years. Fading fiscal incentives in several euro economies offset the area's favorable employment conditions, positive market sentiment, and accommodative monetary stance. In Japan, domestic manufacturing and corporate investment are still expected to contribute to growth. However, expansion may be limited by tepid consumption spending and exports constrained by an appreciating yen.

A1.1 Baseline assumptions on the international economy

	2016	2017	2018	2019
	Actual		*ADO 2018 Projection*	
GDP growth (%)				
Major industrial economies[a]	1.5	2.3	2.3	2.0
United States	1.5	2.3	2.7	2.3
Euro area	1.8	2.5	2.2	1.9
Japan	0.9	1.7	1.4	1.0
Prices and inflation				
Brent crude spot prices (average, $ per barrel)	44.0	54.3	65.0	62.0
Food index (2010 = 100, % change)	1.5	0.7	1.2	1.2
Consumer price index inflation (major industrial economy average, %)	0.7	1.7	1.8	1.7
Interest rates				
United States federal funds rate (average, %)	0.4	1.0	1.8	2.7
European Central Bank refinancing rate (average, %)	0.0	0.0	0.0	0.0
Bank of Japan overnight call rate (average, %)	0.0	0.0	0.0	0.0
$ Libor[b] (%)	0.5	1.1	1.8	2.7

ADO = *Asian Development Outlook*, GDP = gross domestic product.

[a] Average growth rates are weighted by gross national income, Atlas method.

[b] Average London interbank offered rate quotations on 1-month loans.

Sources: US Department of Commerce, Bureau of Economic Analysis, http://www.bea.gov; Eurostat, http://ec.europa.eu/eurostat; Economic and Social Research Institute of Japan, http://www.esri.cao.go.jp; Consensus Forecasts; Bloomberg; CEIC Data Company; Haver Analytics; and the World Bank, Global Commodity Markets, http://www.worldbank.org; ADB estimates.

Recent developments in the major industrial economies

United States

After a disappointing first quarter (Q1) in 2017, the US economy grew by 2.3% in the full year. The economy slowed to a still strong 2.9% seasonally adjusted annualized rate (saar) in Q4 2017, less than the 3.0%-plus saar in the previous 2 quarters. Q4 decelerated mainly because private investment slowed and net exports subtracted heavily from growth (Figure A1.1). However, neither factor raises much concern about the strength of the economy. The contribution of private investment fell to 0.8 percentage points in Q4, mainly from a drop in nonfarm inventories, while fixed investment continued to soar. Net exports trimmed 1.3 percentage points from GDP as imports grew twice as fast as exports, which surged by 7.0% in the quarter despite the strong US dollar. Private consumption remained the main pillar for growth, contributing 2.8 percentage points to Q4 2017 growth, while a rebound in government spending added 0.5 percentage points.

Private consumption accelerated throughout 2017, hitting 4.0% saar in Q4 2017. Retail sales improved steadily in 2017 and stayed strong in the first 2 months of 2018. This is consistent with the continuing employment and wage strength in the labor market. The index of consumer confidence remained upbeat throughout 2017, reaching a 17-year high of 124.4 in November 2017 (2007 = 100) and a new peak of 126.6 in February 2018 (Figure A1.2). This result suggests that recent stock market volatility has had little impact on consumer sentiment. Recently passed tax cuts may have cheered consumer sentiment by boosting disposable income, thereby lifting aggregate demand. In sum, the trends underlying private consumption suggest that it will remain strong, with private consumption in Q1 2018 potentially much stronger than in the past 2 years.

Though contributing little to GDP growth, private investment grew at a healthy 4.7% in Q4 2017. Fixed investment expanded even more, with 6.8% growth in nonresidential investment outpacing 4.7% growth in Q3 2017, mainly reflecting double-digit growth in equipment. Residential investment rebounded in Q4, expanding by 12.8% after 2 quarters of contraction. These improvements in

A1.1 Demand-side contributions to growth, United States

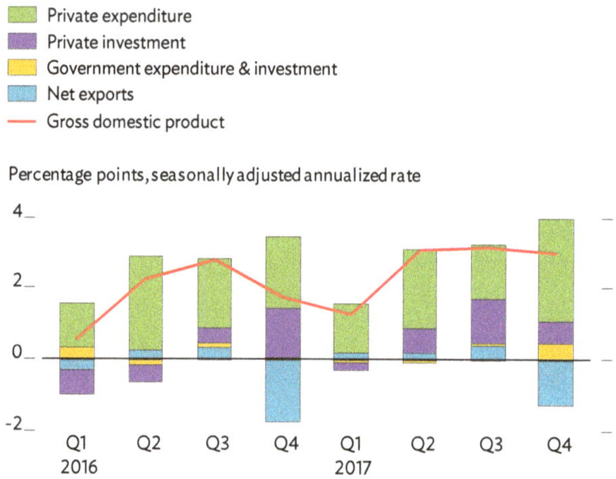

Q = quarter.

Sources: US Department of Commerce. Bureau of Economic Analysis. http://www.bea.gov; Haver Analytics (both accessed 26 March 2018).

A1.2 Business activity and consumer confidence indicators, United States

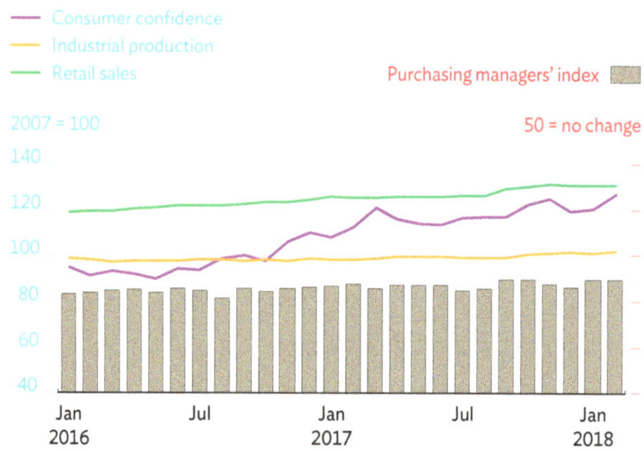

Note: For the purchasing managers' index, a reading below 50 signals deterioration of activity, above 50 improvement. The index is compiled by the Institute for Supply Management.

Source: Haver Analytics (accessed 26 March 2018).

aggregate fixed investment, which contributed 1.3 percentage points to GDP growth, were only partly offset by declining inventories. Nevertheless, even after contracting in Q1 2017, total investment contributed 0.6 percentage points to annual GDP growth.

Further investment growth is possible, as the outlook is still robust. The purchasing managers' index approached 60 in both January and February, its highest since August 2005 and up from 56.4 in December 2017. In addition, the industrial production index continues to hover above 100, indicating that production has been somewhat better than in the base year, 2007. Together, the two upbeat indexes suggest continued expansion in US production. This momentum may, along with the tax cuts, spur further expansion in domestic investment to complement continued growth in private consumption.

Linked to the upbeat trend in aggregate demand, the positive trends in the labor market in 2017 continued into 2018. A further 313,000 nonfarm jobs were added in February 2018 after a strong 239,000 increase in January. Moreover, the unemployment rate has remained at a 17-year low of 4.1% since October 2017, with the possibility of further decline (Figure A1.3). The average duration of unemployment shortened, to 22.9 weeks in February 2018 from 25.1 weeks a year earlier. Average weekly earnings rose by 2.9% in February 2018, up from 2.8% in January.

The continuing strong growth in US economic activity should eventually stir domestic inflation. Headline inflation recently inched above 2.0%, but core inflation has remained soft at 1.8% (Figure A1.4). Along with the steady decline in unemployment, the upward trend in inflation from greater fiscal stimulus and additional purchasing power will motivate the Federal Reserve to advance its gradual normalization of monetary policy. How fast normalization progresses will depend on growth and inflation during the year. Current thinking is that the Fed may gradually raise its benchmark rate in each quarter of 2018, bringing the federal funds rate to about 2.1% by year-end. At least two more increases in the first half of 2019 are planned, raising the rate to about 2.9%.

With these developments, the US economy is expected to grow by 2.7% in 2018, reflecting the short-term impact of tax cuts and higher spending, before moderating somewhat to 2.3% in 2019 with the lagged effect of tighter monetary policy. Inflation is projected to accelerate to 2.3% in 2018 but ease to 2.1% in 2019 in response to monetary tightening. A drift toward

A1.3 Unemployment rate and average duration, United States

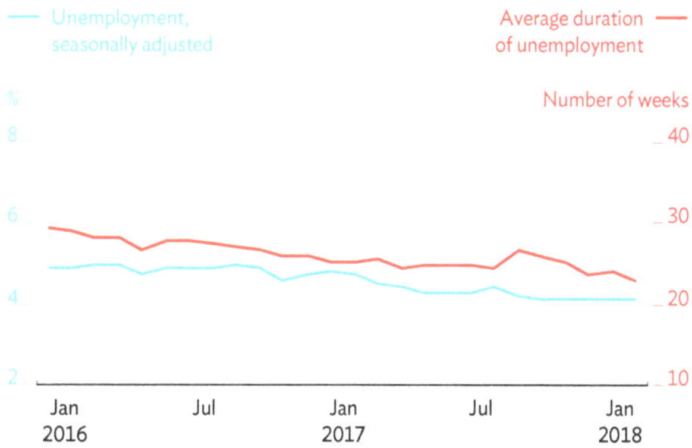

Source: Haver Analytics (accessed 26 March 2018).

A1.4 Inflation, United States

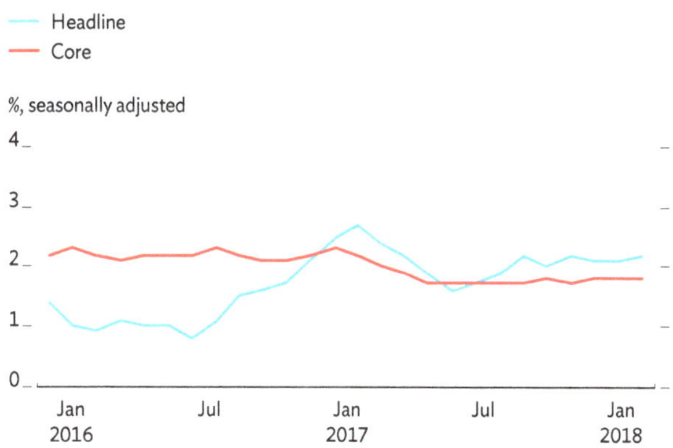

Source: Haver Analytics (accessed 26 March 2018).

trade protectionism, however, poses a downside risk to the forecast. Recently imposed tariffs on steel and aluminum may slow growth by increasing domestic production costs. Possible retaliation from trade partners could trigger a global trade war, creating serious downside risks to the global economy.

Euro area

With GDP rising by 2.4% saar in Q4 2017, the euro area recorded its best growth since the global financial crisis of 2008–2009. The region expanded by 2.5% in 2017, up from 1.8% in 2016 (Figure A1.5). Domestic demand continued to contribute growth, buoyed by high market confidence, supportive monetary and fiscal policies, and labor market recovery. Investment recovered notably in Q4 2017 to contribute 0.7 percentage points to growth, equal to the combined contributions of government and private consumption. However, net exports contributed the most to growth in Q4, at 1.8 percentage points. Strengthening global demand supported a healthy rise in exports and helped offset the strengthening euro, which reached its highest value in 3 years. Growth appears robust across economies. Germany grew by a strong 2.5%, though less than in Q3 2017. Italy and Spain showed similar trends. Among the gainers, the Netherlands expanded the fastest, at 3.2%, while Belgium more than doubled its growth rate from Q3. France, Greece, and Portugal also improved from Q3, though at a slightly less buoyant pace.

A1.5 Demand-side contributions to growth, euro area

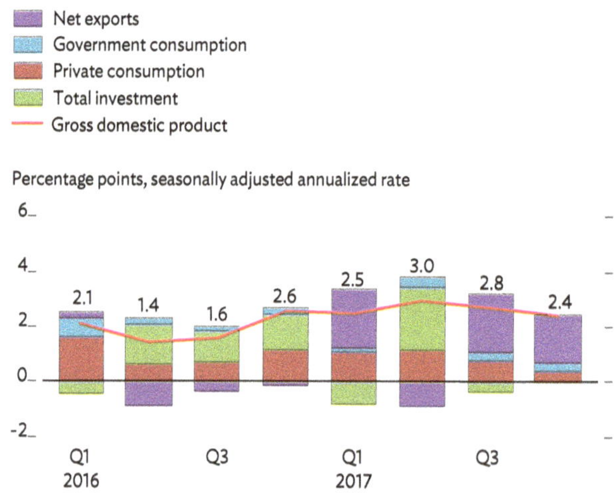

Q = quarter.
Source: Haver Analytics (accessed 8 March 2018).

Economic sentiment in the euro area held strong during much of 2017, spurred by strong job creation, higher savings expectations, and optimistic businesses. Unemployment fell to 8.7% in December, its lowest rate since January 2009 and a boost to consumer confidence and retail spending across euro economies (Figure A1.6). In December, the consumer confidence index moved into positive territory for the first time in 16 years. Business sentiment held strong on higher orders and improved profit margins. The composite purchasing managers' index remained well above the 50 threshold, with broad growth in output and hiring. Industrial production expanded twofold over 2016, driven by robust production of capital goods.

A1.6 Selected economic indicators, euro area

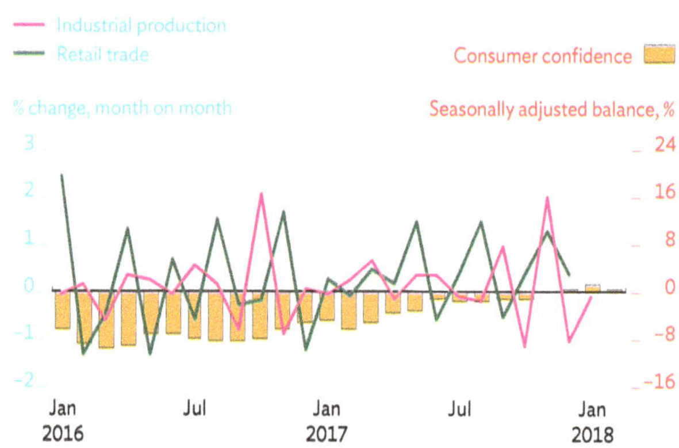

Source: Haver Analytics (accessed 9 March 2018).

Early indicators suggest that the euro area entered 2018 on a high note. The purchasing managers' index rose in January to its highest since 2006 in anticipation of business expansion in the coming months, then softened somewhat in February.

Consumer confidence rose further in January, and economic sentiment in the euro area remained strong (Figure A1.7). However, economic sentiment weakened in February, with export orders and hiring plans expected to slow somewhat from historic highs across sectors.

Inflation downshifted to 1.4% in December 2017, 1.3% in January 2018, and 1.2% in February, mainly because energy prices stabilized after their peak in Q1 2017 and food prices were lower. Euro area full-year inflation stood at 1.5% in 2017, significantly above 0.2% in 2016 but short of the European Central Bank target of 2.0%. However, recent strengthening of the euro against the US dollar has dampened inflationary pressure. The European Central Bank kept its interest rates unchanged at its March 2018 meeting: zero for refinancing and –0.4% for the deposit facility. Starting in January, monthly asset purchases in the quantitative easing program halved to €30 billion from the previous €60 billion, a rate of purchase set to continue until September.

A1.7 Economic sentiment and purchasing managers' indexes, euro area

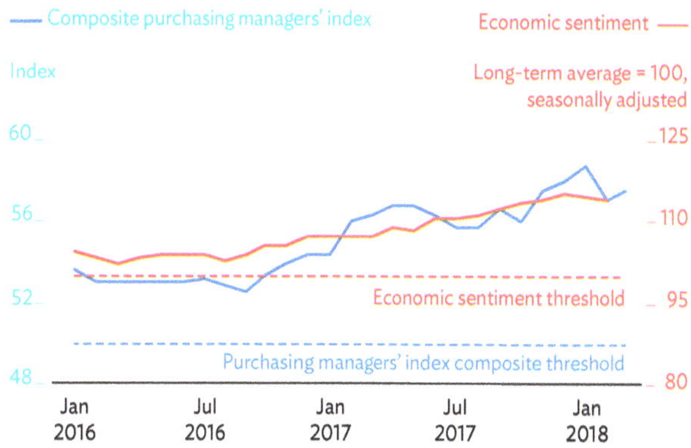

Sources: Bloomberg; Haver Analytics (both accessed 9 March 2018).

Growth is forecast to remain strong in 2018, moderating slightly to 2.2%. Last year's tailwinds in the form of favorable employment conditions, strong market sentiment, and accommodative monetary stance are likely to continue this year, offsetting weakening fiscal incentives in several euro economies. Rising real wages and continued job creation will keep household spending healthy, while stronger demand will support high capacity utilization and investment growth. A strengthening global economy is likely to keep export growth robust. However, its contribution to GDP growth may moderate this year if growth in global trade slows or the euro continues to appreciate. With wage pressures contained and some slack in the labor market, inflation will still likely remain below the European Central Bank target.

Political uncertainty has receded notably from last year, but challenges remain. The outcome of the elections in Italy—putting a Eurosceptic majority in Parliament—poses some risk to the euro area political landscape. Germany's two major parties eventually agreed to form a coalition government, which will have to provide the impetus necessary for critically needed reform to the European Union. Negotiations on the United Kingdom's exit from the union progressed in late March. The parties agreed on the legal text for the transition period following withdrawal in March 2019. Negotiations will now move to discussing future ties, including the terms of a trade agreement and other contentious issues.

By 2019, temporary factors that have supported growth in the recent past will have faded, and GDP growth is expected to slow further to 1.9%. Inflation is expected to accelerate, however, because of higher energy taxes and the fading impact of earlier low energy prices. Improved labor markets and favorable financing conditions will continue to support higher domestic demand. However, employment growth is likely to moderate, especially as public sector employment will start falling in some economies, and skills shortages may begin to emerge. Investment spending will receive substantial support from faster disbursement of funds under the European Union's 2014–2020 budget programming period. However, developments leading to the United Kingdom's scheduled exit in March 2019 may constrain large investment decisions.

Japan

Recovery continued to the end of 2017, when the economy expanded for an eighth consecutive quarter. Supported by strong global demand and accommodative monetary policy, GDP grew by 1.7% in 2017, up from 0.9% in 2016. On the positive side, stronger economic activity has created more jobs and reduced unemployment, which should spur consumer spending. Wages and prices are rising only sluggishly, however, posing risks to sustained economic growth.

In Q4 2017, economic growth slowed to 1.6% saar from 2.4% in the previous quarter (Figure A1.8). The economy benefitted from a rebound in private consumption, which contributed 1.1 percentage points to GDP growth. Private investment added 0.7 percentage points, suggesting a strengthening of domestic demand, though government consumption and investment contributed little to growth. The external sector, which played a key role in economic recovery earlier, subtracted from growth as a surge in imports offset strong export growth. While growth lost some momentum toward the end of 2017, data showing strong imports could be a positive sign that domestic demand is picking up.

A1.8 Demand-side contributions to growth, Japan

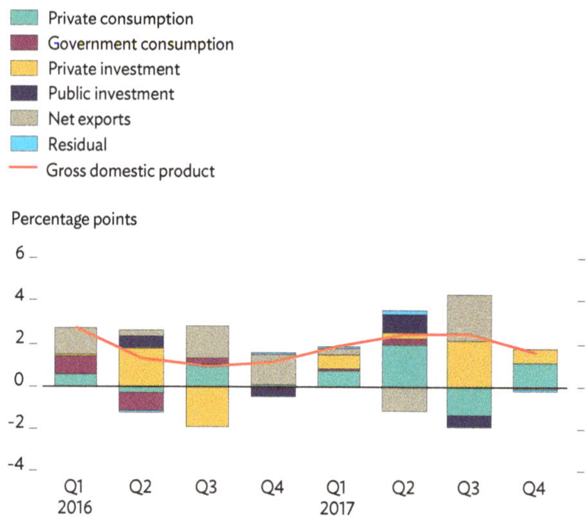

Q = quarter.
Source: Haver Analytics (accessed 8 March 2018).

Early Q1 2018 results suggest, however, that the year had a soft start. Industrial production, which had recorded 7 relatively strong quarters fueled by buoyant external demand, slowed sharply in January from the previous month (Figure A1.9). The Nikkei Japan manufacturing purchasing managers' index slid to 54.1 in February from 54.8 in January. However, the index is still hovering near a 4-year high, and its value above the threshold of 50 indicates that manufacturing activity is improving. Core machinery orders—a leading indicator for business investment, particularly capital expenditure—had plummeted in December but rebounded strongly in January.

Reinforcing this is highly upbeat sentiment about business conditions expressed by Japanese firms. The index of the Tankan survey of large manufacturing enterprises rose for 5 straight quarters to Q4 2017, reaching its highest value since 2006.

Consumption trends inspire confidence despite a decline in retail sales in January 2018 by a seasonally adjusted 1.8% from the previous month. This followed increases in November and December. Consumer confidence also slipped, from 44.3 in January to 43.7 in February, which analysts suggest reflects the impact of stock market volatility on consumer finances. Confidence nevertheless remains elevated in recent terms, and prospects for higher demand are good thanks to favorable labor market conditions. In January, unemployment fell to 2.4%, its lowest rate in 25 years, down from 2.8% in December. Job gains are expected to raise incomes, boosting spending and inflation.

Despite a tight labor market, wage growth has been sluggish, and inflation pressures are building only slowly. Consumer price inflation rose in February to 1.5% year on year from 1.3% in January, the highest in nearly 3 years (Figure A1.10). It remains, however, below the Bank of Japan medium-term target of 2.0%. Core inflation, which excludes more volatile fresh food and energy components, edged up to 0.4% in February. The Bank of Japan has kept its accommodative monetary policy unchanged, with the short-term policy rate at −0.1% and 10-year Japanese government bond yields capped at about zero.

The all-important export sector, which had propelled recovery since 2016, continued to grow strongly in 2017, driven by demand for machinery and transport equipment, in particular motor vehicles and semiconductors. Much of the growth in demand for these items came from the People's Republic of China. Imports grew faster than exports in Q4 2017, however, generating a trade deficit. In January, exports rose by a strong 16.3% over the previous year, while imports increased by 11.8%.

External demand may continue to feed into domestic manufacturing and private investment bolstered by accommodative financial conditions. However, a plunge in industrial production at the start of the year and tepid consumption spending cloud the outlook for domestic demand. And yen appreciation against the US dollar since the start of 2018 may undermine future export demand. These factors inform an outlook for moderate growth at 1.4% in 2018,

A1.9 Consumption and business indicators, Japan

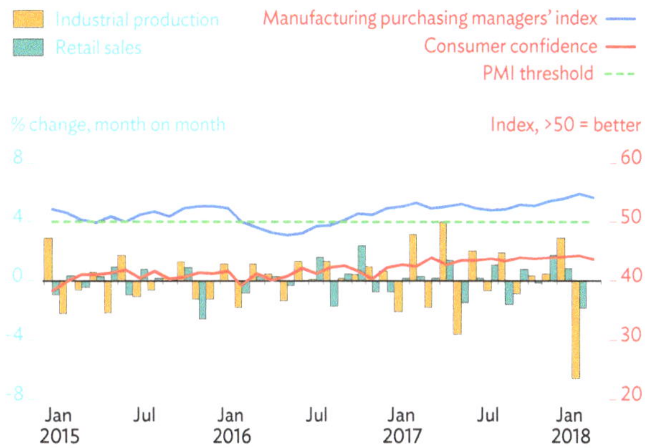

PMI = purchasing managers' index.

Sources: Haver Analytics; Bloomberg (both accessed 1 March 2018).

A1.10 Inflation, Japan

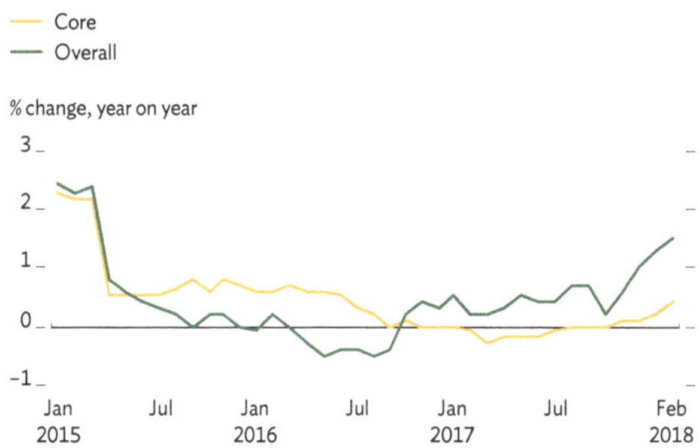

Source: Haver Analytics (accessed 23 March 2018).

decelerating to 1.0% in 2019. On the domestic front, the government plans to increase sales taxes in October 2019, which may dampen household spending. A possible slowdown in the People's Republic of China and uncertainty over global trade policies pose potential risks to growth in exports.

Australia and New Zealand

The Australian economy expanded by 1.5% saar in Q4 2017, well down from 2.8% growth in Q3 (Figure A1.11). Consumption was almost the only growth driver, contributing 3.6 percentage points, with change in inventories adding 0.1 points. Meanwhile, net exports deducted 1.9 points and fixed capital formation 1.2 points. Seasonally adjusted retail sales rose by 0.1% in January 2018 after falling by 0.5% in the previous month. The index of consumer sentiment rose to 103.0 in March from 102.7 in February, further above the 100 demarcation of optimism from pessimism. The business confidence index, which subtracts the percentage of pessimists from that of optimists, subsided to 9 points in February from 11 points in the previous month, still way above the zero threshold. The seasonally adjusted unemployment rate rose marginally to 5.6% in February from 5.5% in January. The Australian Industry Group's manufacturing performance index declined to 57.5 points in February from 58.7 in January, still well above the threshold of 50 indicating expansion in manufacturing. Inflation ticked up to 1.9% in Q4 2017 from 1.8% in Q3, still less than the Reserve Bank of Australia target of 2.0%–3.0%. The Reserve Bank of Australia retained its all-time low policy rate of 1.5%. With positive growth in retail sales and consumer sentiment remaining optimistic, private consumption is expected to continue to drive economic growth. Also boding well for higher growth are continued expansion in manufacturing, measures of business confidence indicating huge optimism regarding future economic conditions, and a robust labor market. FocusEconomics panelists forecast GDP expanding by 2.7% in 2018 and 2019, with economic growth supported by accommodative monetary policy and stronger exports of liquefied natural gas, even as activity rebalances away from mining.

New Zealand grew by 1.5% in Q4 2017, slowing from 4.1% growth in Q3 (Figure A1.12). Change in inventories was the biggest contributor to growth, adding 5.4 percentage points. Consumption added 3.0 points to growth, and fixed capital 2.1 points,

A1.11 Demand-side contributions to growth, Australia

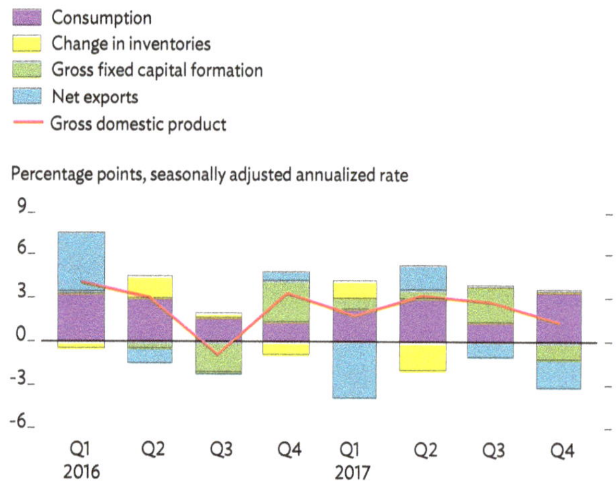

Q = quarter.
Source: CEIC Data Company (accessed 12 March 2018).

A1.12 Demand-side contributions to growth, New Zealand

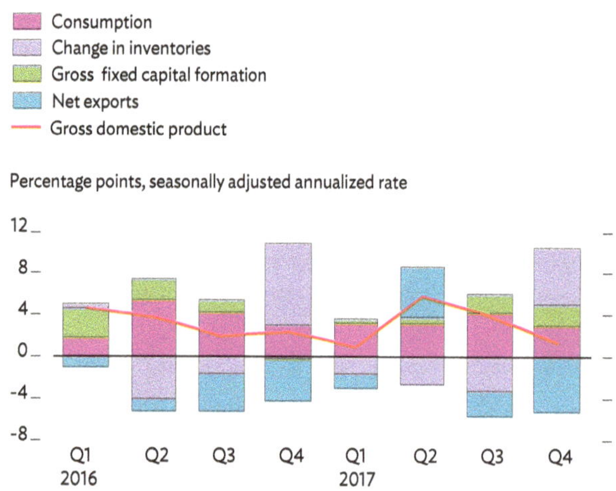

Q = quarter.
Source: CEIC Data Company (accessed 15 March 2018).

while net exports subtracted 5.1 points. Retail sales expanded by 6.3% in Q4 2017, up from 6.0% in the previous quarter. The seasonally adjusted performance of manufacturing index decreased from 54.4 in January to 53.4 in February, staying above the threshold of 50 indicating expansion. The business confidence index improved to −19.0 in February from −37.8 in December but remained deep in negative territory. However, consumer confidence remained positive, rising to 127.7 in February from 126.9 in January, with values above 100 indicating optimism. Inflation slowed to 1.6% in Q4 2017 from 1.9% in the previous quarter, comfortably within the Reserve Bank of New Zealand target of 1.0%–3.0%. The seasonally adjusted unemployment rate dropped marginally to 4.5% in Q4 2017, the lowest since 2008, from 4.6% in Q3. Pessimistic business sentiment persists, but signs of recovery in the housing market and higher consumer confidence could further increase private consumption, as signaled by higher retail sales. Expansion in manufacturing and lower unemployment at the start of this year support the expectation of a stable growth. FocusEconomics panelists forecast economic growth at 2.9% in 2018 and 2.7% in 2019 on expected expansion in government spending, continued record-low interest rates, and looser fiscal policy to maintain support for growth.

Commodity prices

Average commodity prices rose in 2017, with oil prices buoyed by robust global demand and by restraints on production agreed by members of the Organization of the Petroleum Exporting Countries (OPEC) and other producers. Oil prices are forecast to remain below $70/barrel, however, as upward pressure from higher global demand and reduced OPEC output is tempered by increases in oil production outside the cartel, doubts that the OPEC production cut will last, and appreciation of the US dollar, in which prices are denominated. Food prices are forecast to post a small gain, edging up by just over 1% in the next 2 years in response to strong demand and higher oil prices. Adequate supply will, however, limit the rise in food prices.

Oil price movements and prospects

Brent crude finished 2017 at $67/barrel, or $11 higher than at the end of 2016 and the highest end-of-year price since 2013. Brent crude oil prices averaged $54/barrel in 2017, up by $10 or 23% from the 2016 average (Figure A1.13). Lower production engineered by OPEC and robust global demand supported crude oil price increases in 2017. The 30 November 2017 agreement by OPEC

A1.13 Price of Brent crude

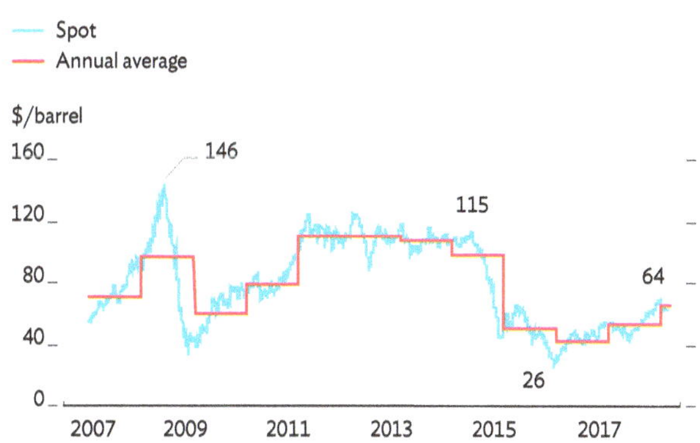

Sources: Bloomberg; World Bank. Commodity Price Data (Pink Sheet). http://www.worldbank.org (both accessed 16 March 2018).

members and other producers to extend negotiated oil output cuts until the end of 2018 exerted further upward pressure on crude oil prices toward the end of 2017.

Global oil supply continued to pick up in 2017, rising by 0.4 million barrels per day (mbd), a somewhat smaller increment than the 2016 increase. Oil supply from outside OPEC rose by 0.7 mbd in 2017, partly offsetting a 0.8 mbd decline in 2016. The US produced most of the increase as its crude oil production grew by 5.3%, from 8.9 mbd to 9.3 mbd, even surpassing 10.0 mbd in November for the first time since 1970. Conversely, supply from OPEC fell by 0.4 mbd, the first annual decline since 2013. Saudi Arabia posted the biggest strategic decline, reducing its supply by 0.6 mbd, or 21% more than its agreed cut. Venezuela had the biggest unplanned decline, at 153 thousand barrels per day, as its oil industry reeled from insufficient investment, delayed payment to suppliers, and US sanctions. World oil demand increased by 1.6 mbd in 2017, or 21% above the 1.3 mbd increase in 2016. With oil demand increasing faster than supply, global oil inventory declined by 0.5 mbd in 2017 after 3 consecutive years of inventory increases.

Oil prices have been volatile in recent months. Price support has come from the OPEC decision in November 2017 to extend to the end of 2018 the agreement to cut production, as well as from unplanned supply disruption. Meanwhile, constraint on prices has come from rising US production; seasonal refinery maintenance around the world, which temporarily suppresses demand for crude oil; and a strengthening US dollar, which makes the dollar-denominated commodity more expensive for countries paying in other currencies. After piercing $70/barrel in mid-January for the first time since December 2014, Brent crude oil prices retreated and were trading below $65 at the start of March 2018.

The International Energy Agency report *Oil 2018* said that oil markets seemed adequately supplied up to 2020. Growth in global oil demand is forecast to be 1.4 mbd in 2018, slightly down from the 1.6 mbd estimated for 2017. The main swing factor for world oil supply will be US production. According to the US Energy Information Agency, US crude oil production is forecast to average 10.3 mbd in 2018, which would be the highest in US history. The agency forecasts production to increase to an average of 10.8 mbd in 2019 and to surpass 11.0 mbd by the end of the year. OPEC, meanwhile, is doing its part to alleviate the global oil glut and keep a lid on oil flows. Group oil output fell in February to a 9-month low as most members reduced production by more than what their agreement required.

Despite signs that the global oil glut is shrinking, the increase in Brent crude oil prices is tempered by rising output from US shale oil producers, continued concern about whether participants in the OPEC deal can stick to their production quotas, and the strengthening US dollar. Futures markets show Brent crude trading above $60/barrel in the forecast horizon (Figure A1.14). Barring a major supply disruption, the price of Brent crude is forecast to average $65/barrel in 2018 and $62/barrel in 2019.

A1.14 Brent crude futures and spot prices

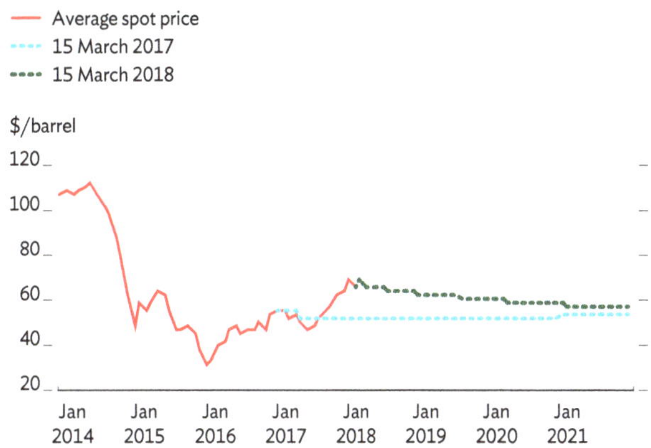

Source: Bloomberg (accessed 16 March 2018).

Food price movements and prospects

Food prices, as measured by the World Bank food price index, edged up by 0.7% in 2017, but this was solely from a rise in the "other food" component (Figure A1.15). The retreat on the edible oil index came primarily from soybean. Prices for soybean fell by 1.2% and for soybean meal by 5.6% with good harvests in the US and forecasts of ample global availability in the 2017/18 crop year. Palm oil prices were little changed from a year earlier as growing conditions in Malaysia and elsewhere in Southeast Asia were favorable. Turning to grains, declines in prices for maize and barley offset slight increases for wheat and rice that reflected tight supply and buoyant demand. Maize prices continued to decline for a fifth consecutive year, mostly because of ample supply and a comfortable supply outlook for the short term.

The food price index averaged 93.47 points in February 2018, or 2.2% higher than in January but just 0.4% above February 2017. The grain price index averaged 86.9 points in February, up by 11.2% from a year earlier. The February increase marked the eighth consecutive month of index increases year on year. Grain prices rose as well month on month, bolstered by rising demand and concern over unfavorable weather hitting US winter wheat and Argentine maize. International rice prices also strengthened owing to firm import demand. Prices for most vegetable oils weakened amid prospects of a growing global glut in the 2017/18 crop year. Palm oil price quotations dropped the most, undermined by disappointing exports and rising inventories in Indonesia and Malaysia. International sugar prices remained under downward pressure as production by major producers such as India and Thailand continued to expand. Sugar markets remained depressed on the expectation of a sharp rise in European Union production in 2017/18, boosted by higher beet yields and the removal last year of output quotas.

A1.15 Food commodity price indexes

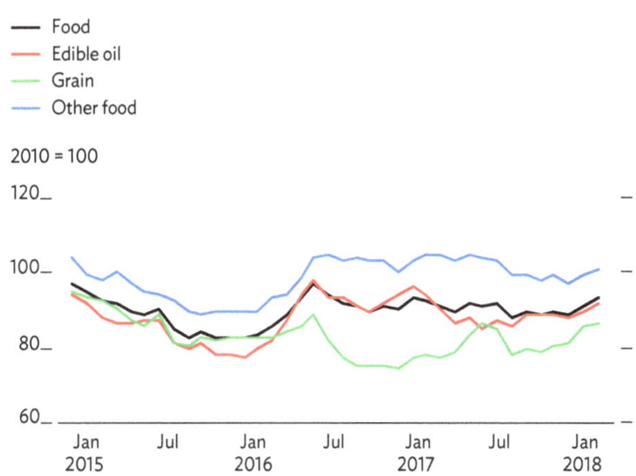

Source: World Bank. Commodity Price Data (Pink Sheet). http://www.worldbank.org (accessed 16 March 2018).

Early indications for the 2017/18 crop year point to high crop yields. The US Department of Agriculture raised its global grain production projection from 2,556 million tons in

December to 2,567 million tons in March, slightly below the previous year's estimate but still above the 5-year average. For two of the three primary grains, wheat and rice, ratios of stock to use are projected to reach multiyear highs (Figure A1.16). Demand is still forecast to dip but not as much as supply, thus lowering the ratio. The outlook for oilseed, edible oil, and meal remains favorable, with the US Department of Agriculture forecasting higher production, exports, and ending stocks in 2017/18. Global production for these commodities is forecast at 1,107.6 million tons, up by 20.9 million from last year.

The Food and Agriculture Organization of the United Nations reported in March 2018 little risk of La Niña weather disturbances or associated disruption to agriculture for the rest of 2018. Higher crude oil prices are expected to exert upward pressure on food prices, along with increased demand and, inevitably, unfavorable weather in some areas. But with well-supplied markets for most grain, oilseed, and edible oil, the food commodity price index is forecast to rise only by 1.2% in the next 2 years.

A1.16 Ratio of stock to use

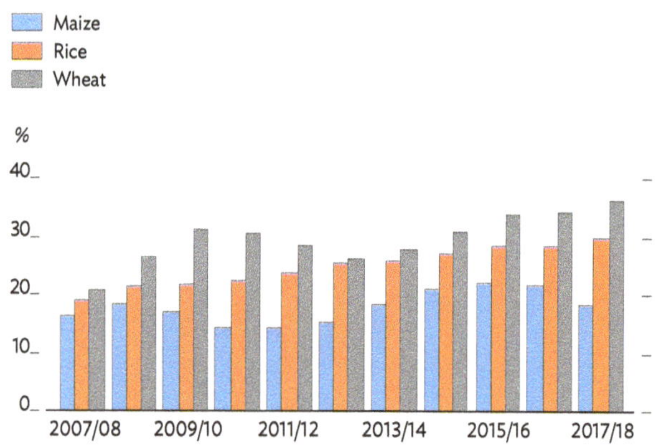

Note: Years refer to crop years.

Source: US Department of Agriculture. Production, Supply, and Distribution Online. http://www.fas.usda.gov/psdonline/psdQuery.aspx (accessed 16 March 2018).

External environment in sum

As the solid recovery in the major industrial economies gains ground, developing Asia should experience stronger external demand. The boost in US private spending led by fiscal stimulus and higher import demand should pay a dividend to commodity exporters in the region. While oil prices are expected to remain subdued, higher global demand is applying upward pressure on commodity prices. Monetary policy continues to be accommodative in the euro area and Japan, but a rising trend in inflation and purchasing power in the US is driving a gradual tightening there. Monetary authorities in most Asian economies will nevertheless keep policy rates low. In sum, developing Asia enjoys a broadly supportive external environment and looks ahead to further economic expansion.

2

HOW TECHNOLOGY AFFECTS JOBS

How technology affects jobs

Developing Asia has created 30 million jobs annually in industry and services over the past 25 years. Job creation has been accompanied by improved productivity, rising earnings for workers, and large reductions in poverty. Contributing to this process are shifts in employment from sectors with low productivity and pay, such as agriculture, to sectors with higher productivity and pay. However, a larger part of the aggregate productivity gains come from sector-specific improvements in productivity, mainly thanks to technological advances such as high-yielding crop varieties in farming, modern machine tools in manufacturing, and information and communication technology in services.[1]

The jobs challenge is far from over. From 2015 to 2030, the labor force in developing Asia is projected to increase by about 11 million per year. So Asia needs more jobs but also better jobs. The broad contours of action and policy needed to meet the jobs challenge are well known: timely and appropriate investments in education, infrastructure, and research and development, as well as a policy framework emphasizing macroeconomic stability, openness to trade and foreign direct investment, and an investment climate conducive to business (ADB 2015a, 2017a). However, concern is growing that some elements of this framework will no longer improve labor market outcomes for many workers. Paradoxically, the concern stems from the fundamental driver of human progress throughout history: technological change.

This chapter was written by Elisabetta Gentile, Rana Hasan, and Sameer Khatiwada, all in the Economic Research and Regional Cooperation Department, with technical support from Donald Jay Bertulfo, Erik Jan Eleazar, John Paul Flaminiano, Pia Marie Medrano, Rhea Molato, Orlee Velarde, and Mia Kim Veloso. It draws on the background papers listed at the end of the chapter. Contributions from Valerie Mercer-Blackman, Kathleen Farrin, Mahinthan Joseph Mariasingham, and Arturo Martinez, Jr., of the Economic Research and Regional Cooperation Department, and Tania Rajadel of the Sustainable Development and Climate Change Department, are gratefully acknowledged. Other contributions are listed in the Acknowledgments section.

While future prosperity is sure to derive from advances in robotics, three-dimensional printing, artificial intelligence (AI), and the internet of things—technologies that enable the often-cited Fourth Industrial Revolution—some of them also pose new challenges for workers. In particular, the growing sophistication of robotics and AI raise the possibility of unprecedented automation and displacement of labor. In apparel and footwear manufacturing, for example, "workerless factories" are being tested using completely automated production. In services, it is becoming technically feasible to automate more complex tasks in occupations such as customer support. How will new technologies affect developing Asia's ability to generate more and better jobs?

This is the central question of this chapter. Considering the many uncertainties that arise in any analysis of a nascent and rapidly evolving phenomenon, the question is addressed through several exercises that together shed light on how the relationship between technology and jobs will likely play out in the region. The exercises are embedded within an analytical framework that clarifies the different channels through which technology affects jobs. Moreover, they focus on different aspects of technology and capture their effects in various ways, some more direct than others. Thus, while some exercises look at the effects of automation through, for example, the adoption of industrial robots in manufacturing, others take a broader view of technology and capture its effects through more efficient production or distribution of goods and services along the global supply chain.

The analysis concludes that several forces will likely work against the pervasive job displacement that some predict. In the first place, the economic feasibility of automating in many parts of Asia today lags technological feasibility, leaving the adoption of the latest laborsaving technologies some ways off. Perhaps most importantly, higher productivity will generate more demand for novel goods and services, providing a powerful countervailing force to automation-driven displacement of labor. Moreover, technological advances and economic growth will generate new occupations and industries, further contributing to job growth.

Clearly, though, new technologies and automation will impose hardships on some workers. Several types of jobs will be lost. While new ones will appear, they will require skills that workers do not yet possess, and they may arise in locations removed from the homes of displaced workers. Low wage growth and higher unemployment among the less-skilled could become, alongside other causes of income inequality, a feature of labor markets if governments fail to take action. Accordingly, this chapter looks at the implications for public policy, especially on education and skills development, and on labor regulations and social protection systems, while touching on other topics.

Rising concern over technology displacing jobs

An overview of labor markets in Asia and the Pacific reveals how important higher productivity is to reducing poverty and improving the quality of jobs to make them more remunerative and formal. Technological progress plays a vital role in raising productivity but inevitably raises nagging concerns about job security. Today, robotics and AI promise ever greater improvements to productivity, but will these benefits come with ever worsening job prospects for working people? Assessing this possibility is important but not straightforward. Technology affects job prospects through several channels, calling for an analytical framework that clarifies the various channels and the conditions under which they operate. The first step in constructing such a framework is to consider the shape of the labor market and workplace in developing Asia today.

Asia at work

Developing Asia has the largest regional labor force in the world, with nearly 2 billion workers. India and the People's Republic of China (PRC), the region's two giants, account for almost 70% of the total (Figure 2.1.1a). The regional labor force is projected to grow by 0.5% annually from 1.9 billion in 2015 to 2.1 billion in 2030 and 2.2 billion in 2050. India is projected to account for 30% of the regional total labor force by 2030, with the PRC share declining to 37%. One cause of this shift is that the labor force is aging. The decline in the share of the 15–24 age group and an increase in the share of the three oldest age groups are quite evident for the region as a whole (Figure 2.1.1b). Considerable variation in age distribution exists by country, with different implications for growth in the national labor force (Figures 2.1.2 and 2.1.3). Economies with relatively young current populations, such as Nepal and Pakistan, will experience larger increases in their labor force and need policies to ensure an adequate number of

2.1.1 Labor force in developing Asia

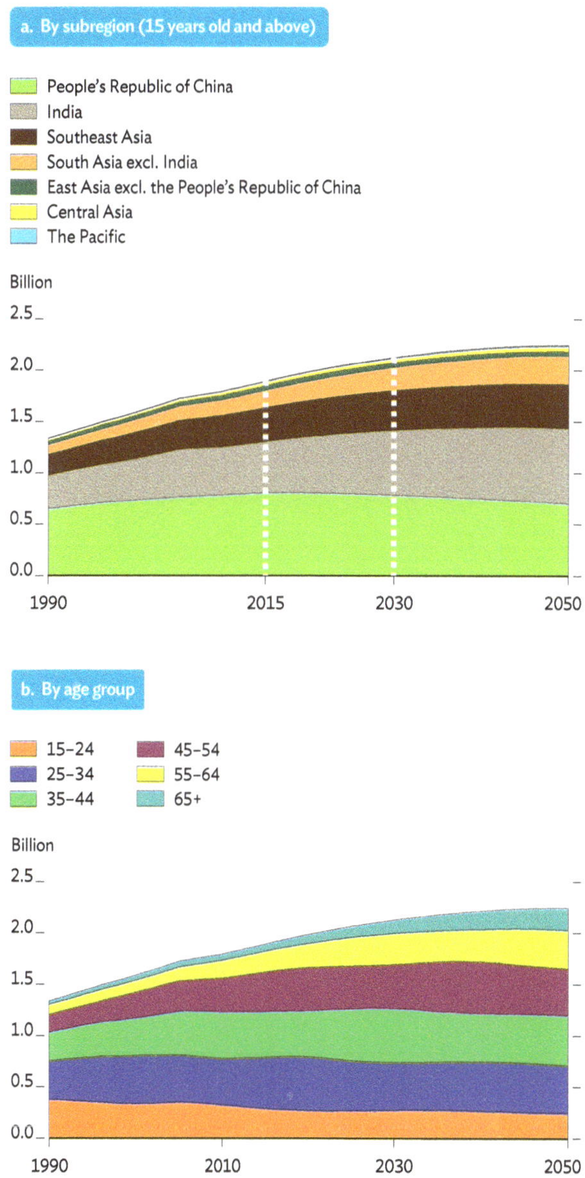

Note: Southeast Asia includes Brunei Darussalam, Cambodia, Indonesia, the Lao People's Democratic Republic, Malaysia, Myanmar, the Philippines, Singapore, Thailand, and Viet Nam. South Asia excluding India includes Afghanistan, Bangladesh, Bhutan, Maldives, Nepal, Pakistan, and Sri Lanka. East Asia excluding the People's Republic of China includes Hong Kong, China; Mongolia; the Republic of Korea; and Taipei,China. Central Asia includes Armenia, Azerbaijan, Georgia, Kazakhstan, the Kyrgyz Republic, Tajikistan, Turkmenistan, and Uzbekistan. The Pacific includes Fiji, Papua New Guinea, Samoa, Solomon Islands, Timor-Leste, Tonga, and Vanuatu.

Source: International Labour Organization. ILOSTAT. http://www.ilo.org/ilostat (accessed 10 August 2016).

2.1.2 Percent change in labor force size, 2015 to 2030 (%)

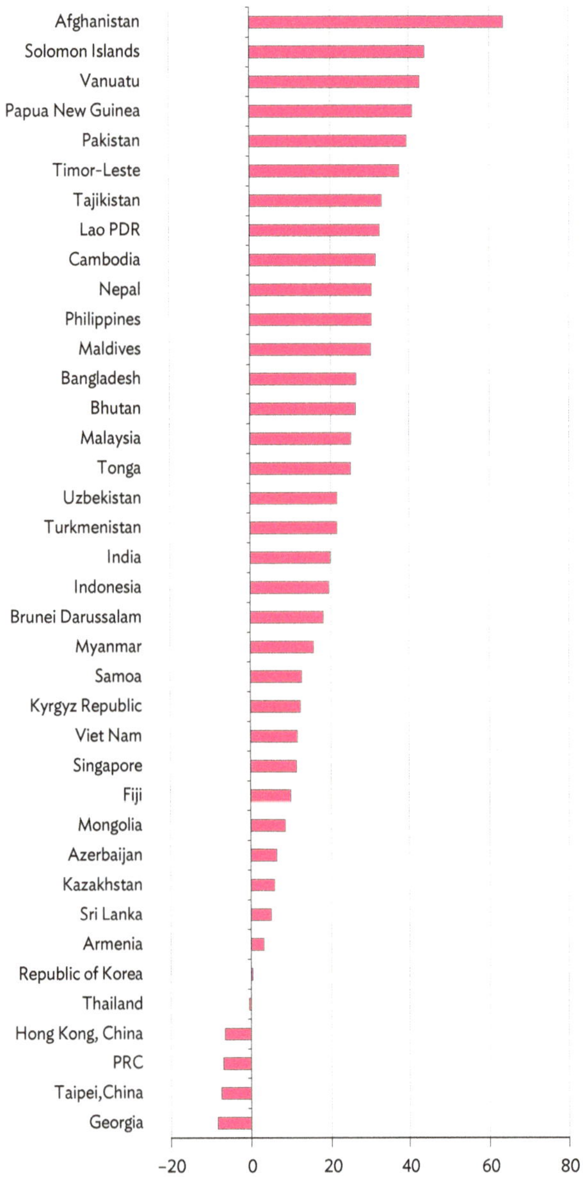

Lao PDR = Lao People's Democratic Republic, PRC = People's Republic of China.
Source: International Labour Organization. ILOSTAT. http://www.ilo.org/ilostat (accessed 22 February 2018).

2.1.3 Distribution of labor force by age group, 2015 (%)

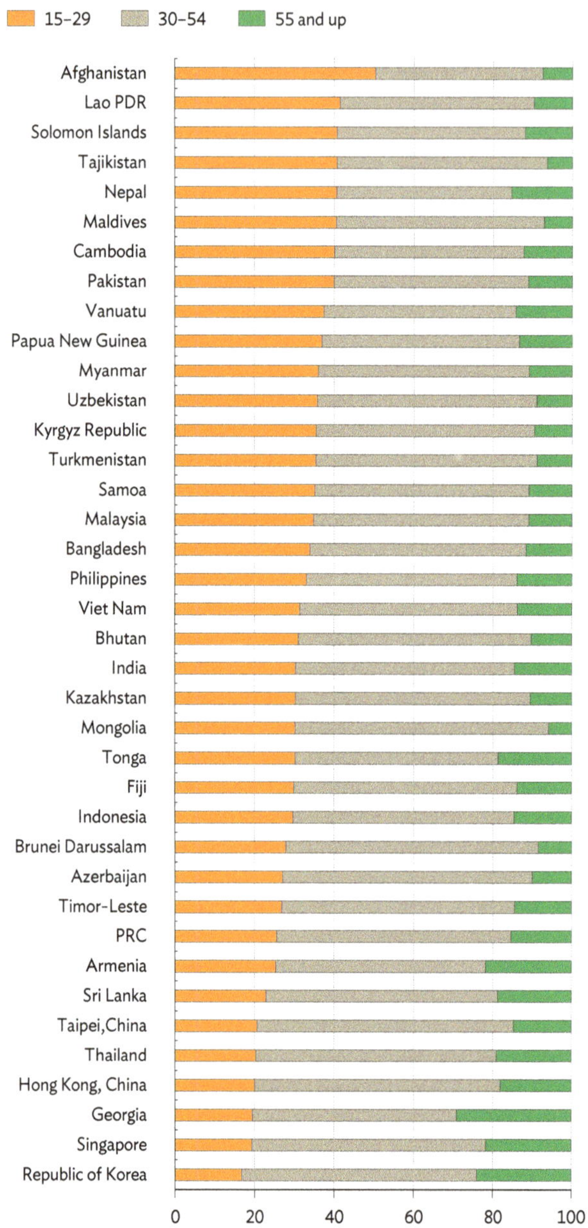

Lao PDR = Lao People's Democratic Republic, PRC = People's Republic of China.
Source: International Labour Organization. ILOSTAT. http://www.ilo.org/ilostat (accessed 22 February 2018).

productive jobs. Meanwhile, economies with aging populations, such as the PRC and the Republic of Korea, must ensure that workers are well looked after when they retire and that productive opportunities exist for those older workers who wish to continue working.

On average, agriculture employs one-third of the workforce in developing Asia, excluding high-income economies, where it employs less than 5% (Figure 2.1.4). In general, the share

2.1.4 Employment by sector, selected developing Asia, 2016

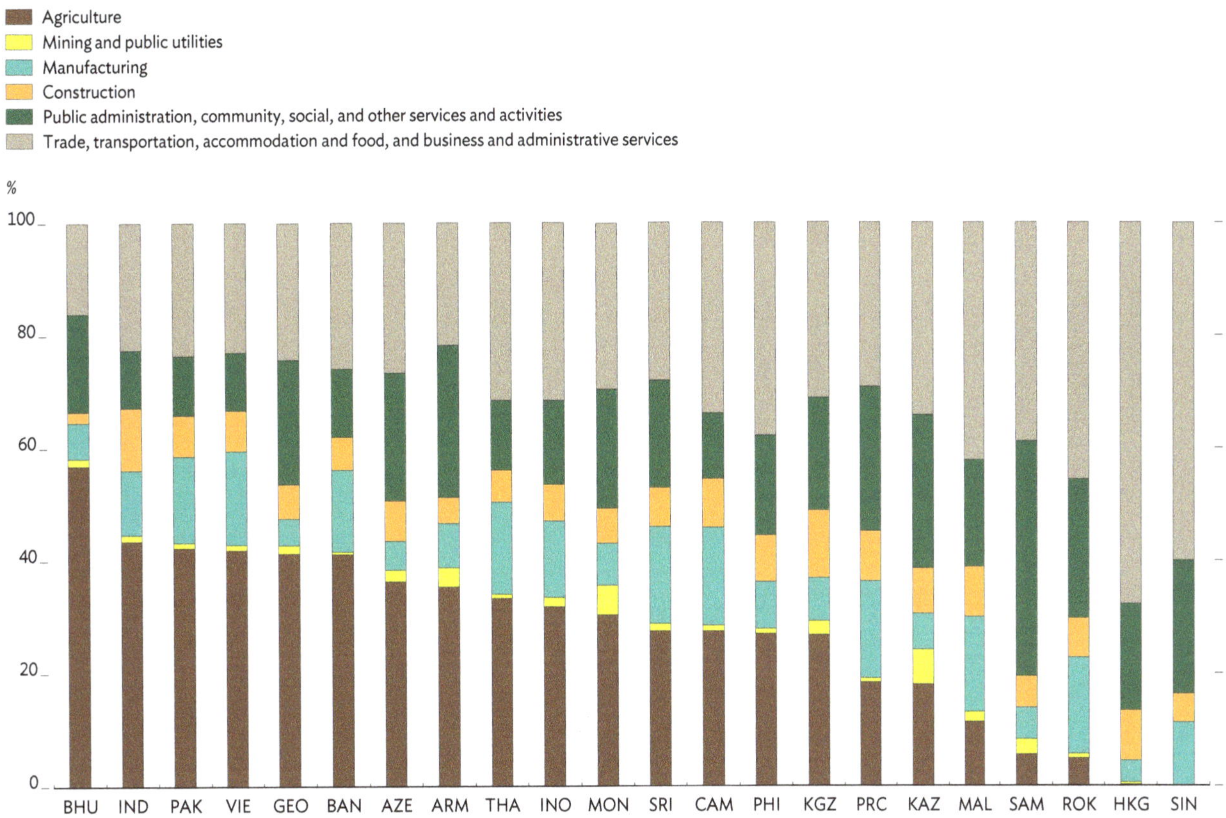

ARM = Armenia, AZE = Azerbaijan, BAN = Bangladesh, BHU = Bhutan, CAM = Cambodia, GEO = Georgia, HKG = Hong Kong, China, IND = India, INO = Indonesia, KAZ = Kazakhstan, KGZ = Kyrgyz Republic, MAL = Malaysia, MON = Mongolia, PAK = Pakistan, PHI = Philippines, PRC = People's Republic of China, ROK = Republic of Korea, SAM = Samoa, SIN = Singapore, SRI = Sri Lanka, THA = Thailand, VIE = Viet Nam.

Source: International Labour Organization. ILOSTAT. http://www.ilo.org/ilostat (accessed 15 March 2018).

of employment in agriculture (which often entails paid work off the farm) declines as gross domestic product per capita rises. Conversely, as economies grow richer, the share of employment in manufacturing and especially services increases. The structural shift, however, occurs at different speeds across countries.

Another way of characterizing employment is in terms of the types of tasks done. This, too, varies by stage of development. Workers in lower-income economies generally carry out tasks that are often termed lower-skilled (Figure 2.1.5a). Also, low-income economies generally have a larger portion of workers with low educational attainment (Figure 2.1.5b).

How well are Asia's workers doing?

Whether individuals in the labor force are able to find jobs is usually the first metric used to judge labor market performance. On this count, developing Asia does well for adults. The median unemployment rate is relatively low at 3.0%, and the mean

2.1.5 Employment share by skill and education

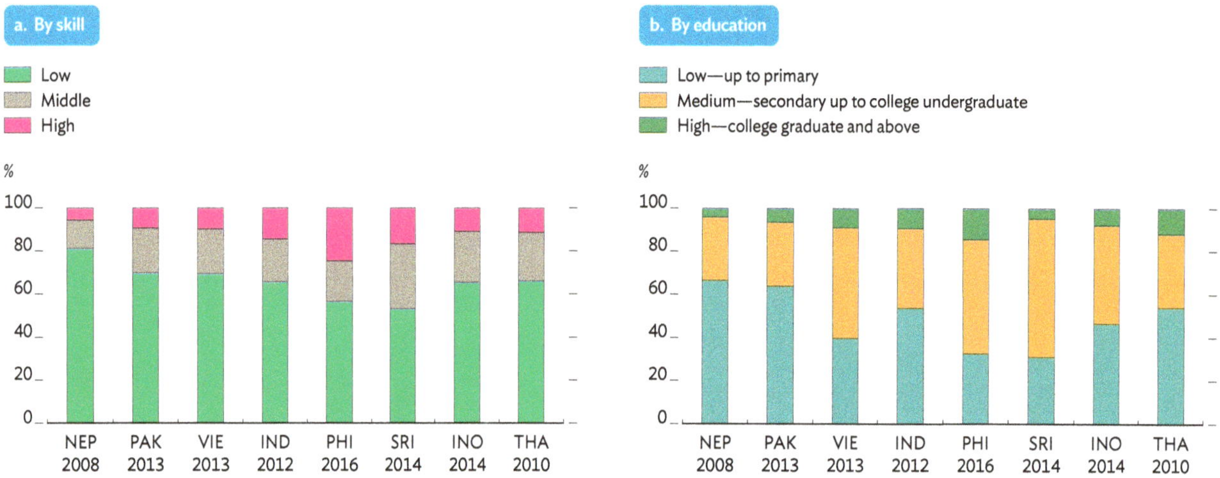

IND = India, INO = Indonesia, NEP = Nepal, PAK = Pakistan, PHI = Philippines, SRI = Sri Lanka, THA = Thailand, VIE = Viet Nam.
Note: Skills classification is based on World Bank (2016).
Source: ADB estimates using labor force surveys, various countries.

at 3.8% (Table 2.1.1). While unemployment rates are higher for young participants—the median at 10.7% and the mean at 12.6%—the bigger developmental challenge for the region is underemployment. This can mean workers employed for fewer hours than they would like, or involuntary underemployment, but is most apparent as workers employed in low-paying, less-productive jobs—both common features of the informal sector and fundamental determinants of whether a job is good or not.

This raises the question of what determines workers' earnings. Empirically, a key determinant is where a person is employed. Table 2.1.2 shows that, among the three sectors with relatively large shares of total employment, typically 10% or above, average wages are lowest by far in agriculture. In fact, average wages in manufacturing and in the services wholesale and retail trade, hotels, and restaurants—that is, services that typically do not require tertiary education—are often 50% higher in nominal terms. This wage gap is wider than typical urban–rural cost differentials.

A variety of factors determine a worker's earnings: worker supply and demand, regulatory and institutional issues like minimum wage and collective bargaining laws, and even social norms on "fairness" and gender relationships. However, a key determinant of wages is labor productivity, or how much output a worker produces. Table 2.1.2 shows average labor productivity in agriculture considerably lower than in manufacturing and services.

2.1.1 Employment, unemployment, and informal employment in Asia and the Pacific, 2015 or latest

Region	Economy	Working-age population ('000)	Ratio of employment to population	Youth unemployment rate	Adult unemployment rate	Informal employment share of nonfarm employment
East Asia	People's Republic of China	1,132,960	68.4	10.1	3.6	...
	Republic of Korea	43,017	60.3	10.5	3.1	...
	Taipei,China	19,842	56.4	12.0	3.1	...
	Hong Kong, China	6,384	59.2	10.5	2.7	...
	Mongolia	2,023	56.9	13.1	3.9	24.5
South Asia	India	763,132	51.5	10.1	1.2	84.7
	Pakistan	111,515	50.2	6.6	2.5	78.4
	Bangladesh	106,265	54.7	9.9	2.9	...
	Sri Lanka	16,671	51.3	20.7	2.6	62.1
	Nepal	14,878	64.7	2.2	1.0	...
	Bhutan	559	61.6	10.7	1.3	...
Southeast Asia	Indonesia	186,101	61.7	22.6	2.9	72.5
	Viet Nam	69,736	76.1	7.0	1.3	68.2
	Philippines	64,936	59.7	15.0	4.0	70.1
	Thailand	55,238	68.8	1.0	0.3	37.7
	Myanmar	33,935	64.2	1.6	0.5	...
	Malaysia	21,388	65.8	10.7	1.5	...
	Singapore	3,300	65.7	10.3	2.0	...
Central Asia	Kazakhstan	12,831	67.6	3.9	5.4	...
	Azerbaijan	6,678	61.9	13.4	3.8	...
	Kyrgyz Republic	4,079	57.7	15.0	5.9	...
	Georgia	3,010	59.7	30.8	10.2	...
	Armenia	2,107	50.9	32.0	16.4	17.6
The Pacific	Fiji	588	52.0	19.2	5.5	...
	Vanuatu	143	66.0	10.6	3.7	...
	Samoa	117	29.4	19.1	6.4	...

... = data not available.

Note: Data are for 2015 except working age population in India 2012, Nepal 2008, Bangladesh 2013, Fiji 2010, Vanuatu 2009, and Samoa, 2014; youth unemployment and adult unemployment rate in Fiji, Kazakhstan, the People's Republic of China, and Singapore 2013; informal employment share of nonfarm employment in Thailand 2016, Mongolia 2014, India 2012, Pakistan 2010, Sri Lanka 2009, Indonesia 2009, Viet Nam 2009, and the Philippines 2008.

Source: International Labour Organization. ILOSTAT. http://www.ilo.org/ilostat (accessed 1 September 2017).

The imperative of improving labor productivity

Given the pattern of relative labor productivity and wages across sectors described above, some combination of raising agricultural productivity and shifting agricultural workers into more productive sectors should improve labor market performance considerably. In fact, evidence indicates that economies that are more successful at moving workers from low- to high-productivity sectors—that is, at effecting structural change—have done better on several dimensions of labor market performance, including larger reductions in poverty (Figure 2.1.6a) and self-employment (Figure 2.1.6b).

2.1.2 Wages and relative productivity by sector

Country	Year	Sector	Share in total employment (%)	Share in total wage employment (%)	Share of workers with less than college (%)	Ratio to agriculture sector	
						Wage	Productivity
India	2012	Agriculture	47	36	97.29	1.00	1.00
		Manufacturing	12	14	90.92	1.79	3.01
		Trade, hotels, & restaurants	12	7	87.31	1.79	2.54
Philippines	2016	Agriculture	29	14	97.75	1.00	1.00
		Manufacturing	8	11	88.72	1.75	9.48
		Trade, hotels, & restaurants	24	18	86.71	1.50	2.57
Indonesia	2014	Agriculture	35	14	99.42	1.00	1.00
		Manufacturing	13	20	96.98	2.00	4.28
		Trade, hotels, & restaurants	23	14	95.84	1.75	1.93
Nepal	2008	Agriculture	65	17	98.91	1.00	1.00
		Manufacturing	8	19	95.86	2.21	1.59
		Trade, hotels, & restaurants	11	8	94.47	2.21	2.30
Viet Nam	2013	Agriculture	47	11	98.97	1.00	1.00
		Manufacturing	14	29	93.60	1.15	2.86
		Trade, hotels, & restaurants	17	10	93.45	1.15	2.07
Pakistan	2013	Agriculture	43	15	99.03	1.00	1.00
		Manufacturing	14	22	94.19	1.50	1.86
		Trade, hotels, & restaurants	16	10	94.33	1.33	2.24
Sri Lanka	2014	Agriculture	28	14	99.64	1.00	1.00
		Manufacturing	18	21	98.86	1.36	3.16
		Trade, hotels, & restaurants	16	11	98.96	1.45	2.90

Notes: Trade, hotels, & restaurants includes both wholesale and retail trade. Relative wages are based on median monthly wages of wage workers.
Sources: ADB. The Statistical Database System. https://sdbs.adb.org (accessed 8 January 2018); Labor force surveys, various countries.

Another significant part of making jobs more productive is raising productivity within sectors. In fact, a larger portion of economy-wide or aggregate labor productivity growth in Asia derives more from rapid increases in labor productivity within sectors than from movements of labor from low- to high-productivity sectors (Figure 2.1.7).[2]

Technology is a key driver of improvement in within-sector productivity growth

While within-sector productivity growth can be achieved by reallocating workers from low- to high-productivity firms and farms, it also occurs by improving the productivity of individual firms and farms. A key driver of this process is the use of new technologies. The adoption of new, high-yielding varieties of grain, fruit, vegetables, and even livestock—used in combination with improved fertilizers, irrigation, and machinery—has boosted agricultural productivity on

2.1.6 Structural change, poverty reduction, and self employment

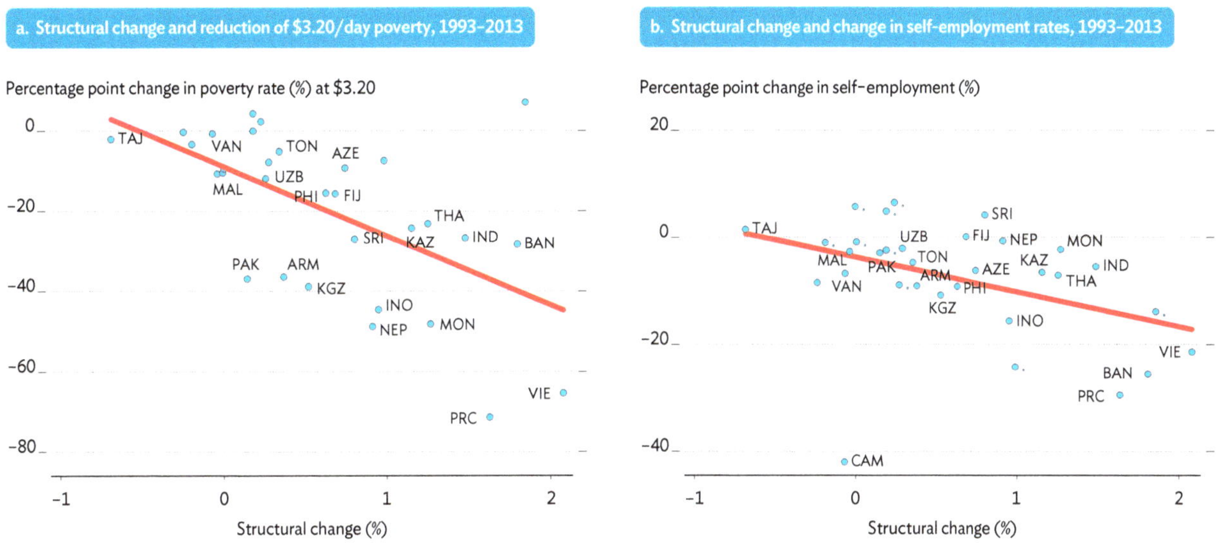

ARM = Armenia, AZE = Azerbaijan, BAN = Bangladesh, CAM = Cambodia, FIJ = Fiji, IND = India, INO = Indonesia, KAZ = Kazakhstan, KGZ = Kyrgyz Republic, MAL = Malaysia, MON = Mongolia, NEP = Nepal, PAK = Pakistan, PRC = People's Republic of China, PHI = Philippines, SRI = Sri Lanka, TAJ = Tajikistan, THA = Thailand, TON = Tonga, UZB = Uzbekistan, VAN = Vanuatu, VIE = Viet Nam.

Notes: Panel A contains 31 countries and panel B 32 countries classified as low- and middle-income countries by the World Bank in 1993. Following Mcmillan, Rodrik, and Verduzco-Gallo (2014), changes in economy-wide labor productivity can be broken down into two components: improvements in sector-specific labor productivity and structural change. These computations are based on three sectors: agriculture, industry, and services.

Sources: International Labour Organization. ILOSTAT. http://www.ilo.org/ilostat (accessed 15 March 2018); World Bank. PovcalNet. http://iresearch.worldbank.org/PovcalNet/ (accessed 8 March 2018); World Bank. World Development Indicators. http://databank.worldbank.org/data/home.aspx (accessed 1 March 2018).

2.1.7 Components of labor productivity growth, 1993–2013

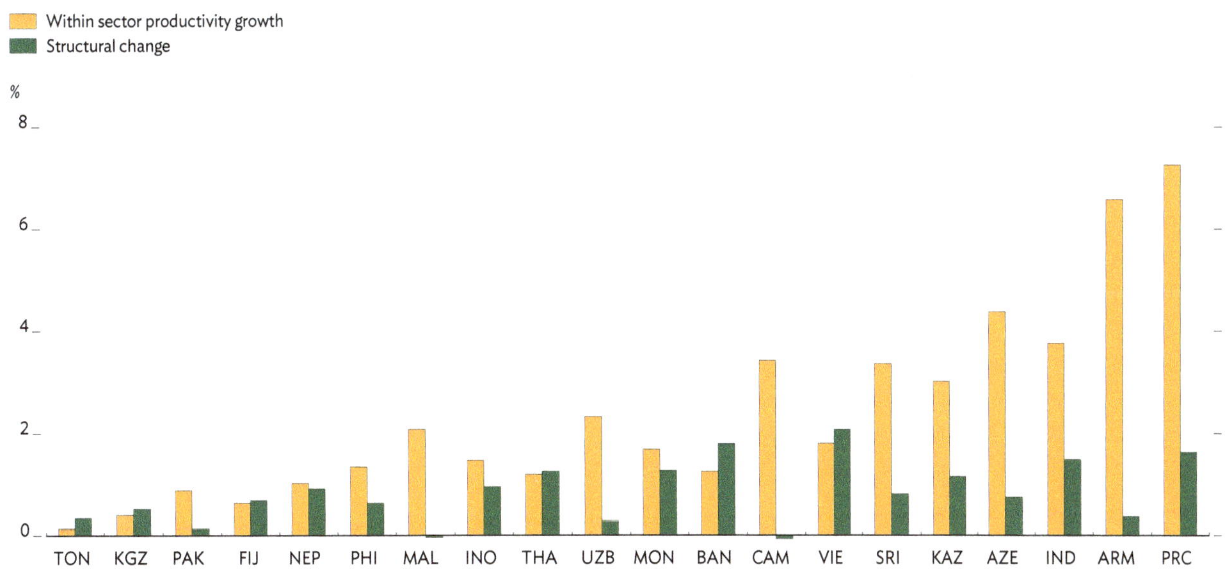

ARM = Armenia, AZE = Azerbaijan, BAN = Bangladesh, CAM = Cambodia, FIJ = Fiji, IND = India, INO = Indonesia, KAZ = Kazakhstan, KGZ = Kyrgyz Republic, MAL = Malaysia, MON = Mongolia, NEP = Nepal, PAK = Pakistan, PRC = People's Republic of China, PHI = Philippines, SRI = Sri Lanka, THA = Thailand, TON = Tonga, UZB = Uzbekistan, VIE = Viet Nam.

Note: Three sectors—agriculture, industry, and services—were used to calculate these components of labor productivity growth.

Sources: International Labour Organization. ILOSTAT. http://www.ilo.org/ilostat (accessed 15 March 2018); World Bank. World Development Indicators. http://databank.worldbank.org/data/home.aspx (accessed 1 March 2018).

Asian farms and raised rural standards of living. It has enabled workers to move out of subsistence farming while allowing those who remain to produce more food (Estudillo, Sawada, and Otsuka 2006). Similarly, the use of modern machine tools such as numerically controlled lathes in manufacturing, and of information and communication technology in services, has been crucial in raising factory and office productivity, allowing better wages for workers.

However, concern is growing that the very latest technologies could prove to be disruptive for workers, displacing jobs without creating nearly enough new ones. This could be particularly problematic for countries with a lot of young workers. For example, recent research suggests that manufacturing—a sector instrumental to economic success in developing Asia—may have lost its power as an engine of job creation (Felipe, Mehta, and Rhee 2018). One reason behind the lower peak for industrial employment share could be technology. Ever-increasing opportunities for automation can enable more manufactured goods to be produced without a correspondingly large increase in employment. Even in many services, new technologies are raising the specter of labor-displacing automation.

Understanding the relationship between technology and jobs

From knitting machines and power looms to electricity and computers, automating production has been at the heart of economic development. Since the first industrial revolution starting with the steam engine, being able to automate tasks in a production chain has been instrumental to raising labor productivity (Figure 2.1.8). Across history, automation has always displaced workers, generating anxiety about technological change. However, displacement has been accompanied by the emergence of new occupations, and job opportunities have not diminished. Moreover, not all technology displaces human labor. Magnetic resonance imaging and X-ray machines, for example, perform functions humans cannot, thereby complementing, not displacing, human labor in medical care. However, the advent of the Fourth Industrial Revolution has heightened automation anxiety. Underpinned by more sophisticated robots and computing power, automation is taking over more and more tasks once thought to be uniquely human (Box 2.1.1). The key issue is whether the Fourth Industrial Revolution is different from previous ones. Is widespread “technological unemployment”—as warned by notable thinkers such as David Ricardo, Karl Marx, and John Maynard Keynes—more likely this time around?

2.1.8 Industrial revolutions: four episodes of technological breakthrough

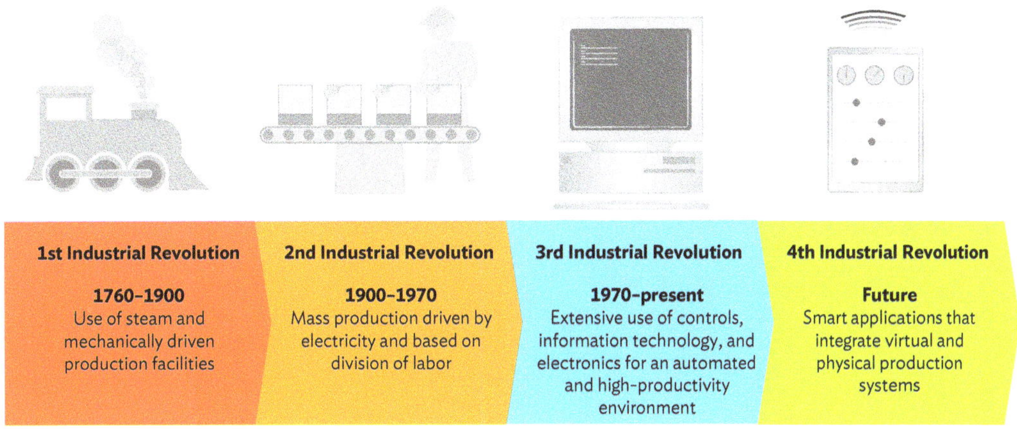

Source: ADB based on Schwab (2017).

This section presents an analytical framework that explains the different channels through which technology affects jobs.

A useful framework for analyzing the impact of new technologies on jobs is provided in Autor, Levy, and Murnane (2003), Acemoglu and Autor (2011), Autor (2015), and Acemoglu and Restrepo (2018). This framework recognizes that any given job consists of a bundle of tasks. They can be classified along two dimensions: either manual or cognitive, and routine or not. The technical feasibility of automating tasks

2.1.1 Technological advancements that define the Fourth Industrial Revolution

- **Artificial intelligence** (AI) is the science and engineering of rational, intelligent machines that act, work, and solve problems the way humans do. Machine learning—or "deep learning," a subset of AI—is the science of teaching computers to learn and apply data without being explicitly programmed.
- **Quantum computers** are powerful machines that run new types of algorithms to process information more holistically. They may one day enable revolutionary breakthroughs in the discovery of new materials and drugs, the optimization of complex synthetic systems, and AI.
- **Biotechnology** covers a broad range of technologies that employ living organisms to make products such as drugs and therapeutics, nutritional compounds, biofuels, and materials with novel functions.
- **Blockchain technology** is an incorruptible digital ledger of economic transactions that can be programmed to record not just financial transactions but virtually anything of value. This type of technology powers cryptocurrencies such as Bitcoin and Ethereum.
- **Three-dimensional printing**, a manufacturing process that additively builds three-dimensional objects using computer-aided design, allows the construction of complex objects with less material than traditional manufacturing.
- **New generation robotics** such as sewbots, Baxter, and the *leichtbauroboter* (lightweight robot) intelligent industrial work assistant, better known as LBR iiwa, open new possibilities for automating tasks on factory floors, particularly in light manufacturing such as textiles and apparel.

Sources: Blockchain Research Institute 2018; IBM Q Network webpage; Lee 2016; McCarthy 2007; Winston 2010.

using some combination of machines and computing power tends to be higher for routine and manual tasks, such as repetitive physical operations. Further, a particular task may be automatable but the associated job safe from being displaced because automation may only restructure the job, such that workers are freed up to focus on other tasks. By implication, only jobs consisting mainly of routine and manual tasks, such as machine operator and assembler, will likely be displaced. Jobs that entail some routine and manual tasks, such as clerk and IT assistant, are less likely to be displaced.

To illustrate, Figure 2.1.9 shows that occupations with a larger share of routine tasks are more likely to be automated, while those with a lower share are less likely. Workers in occupations in quadrant 4 (researchers and managers) are safe because the majority of their tasks are difficult to automate and new technology augments the value of their labor. In contrast, workers in quadrants 1 and 2 hold jobs with mostly routine tasks, including cognitive routine jobs (accountants and bank tellers) and manual routine jobs (sewing machine operators and assembly line workers). These jobs are at risk of displacement by laborsaving technology. Manual and nonroutine jobs in quadrant 3 (cook and hairdresser) are not yet heavily affected by laborsaving technology.

Concern that automation could cause widespread job loss is cited in many recent studies (Table 2.1.3). However, the concern appears to stem from considering only the displacement effect of automation, many of these studies ignore other effects (Figure 2.1.10). Channels through which automation has an impact on jobs can be divided into within-firm or -industry effects and between-industry effects.

Within-firm or -industry effects. There are three main channels through which new technology affects labor demand within a firm or industry:

(i) **Displacement effect.** Because robots and computers are good at routine tasks, demand will fall for jobs comprising mainly routine tasks. A manual worker in an industrial warehouse whose job is to fetch products from shelves, for example, is likely to be displaced, perhaps by Kiva system robots, which can traverse large floor spaces to find products much faster than humans. Interestingly, though, displacement is bounded by tasks that humans accomplish effortlessly but computer programmers struggle to code into routines. Polanyi's Paradox recognizes that we know more than we can tell (Autor 2015, Polanyi 1966).

(ii) **Productivity effect.** Sometimes called a scale effect, it is when automation improves productivity and lowers production costs. Under normal conditions, this lowers the price of goods and services, which raises demand for them. As industrial robots become

2.1.9 Impact of automation on jobs

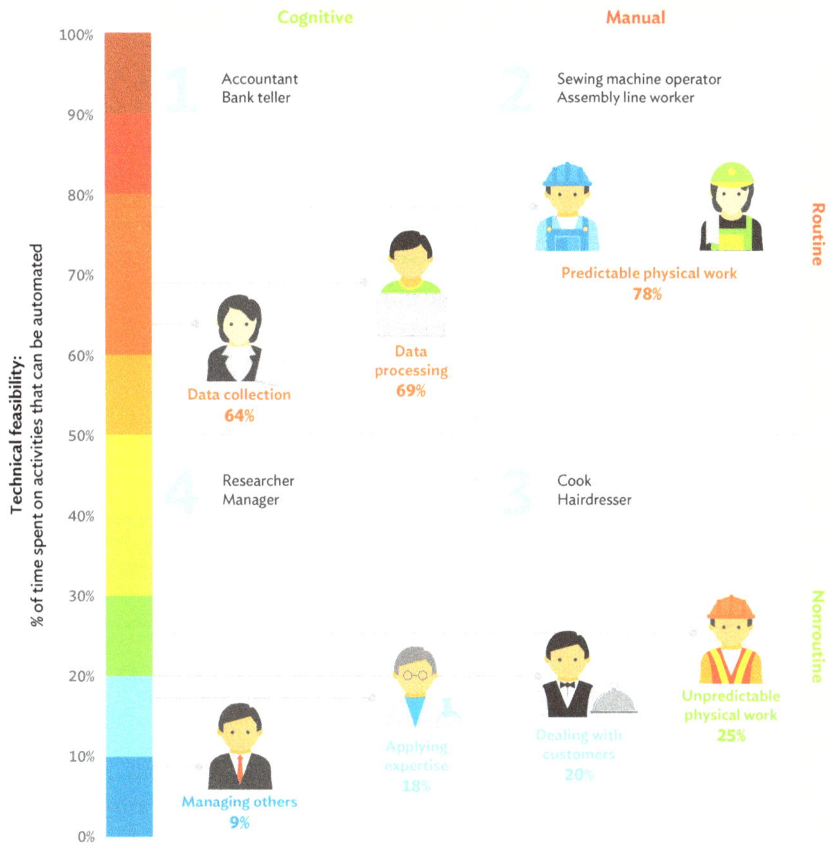

Note: Percentages are from Frey and Osborne (2017) estimates on probability of automation. Framework is based on Acemoglu and Autor (2011).

2.1.10 Analytical framework of countrywide effects

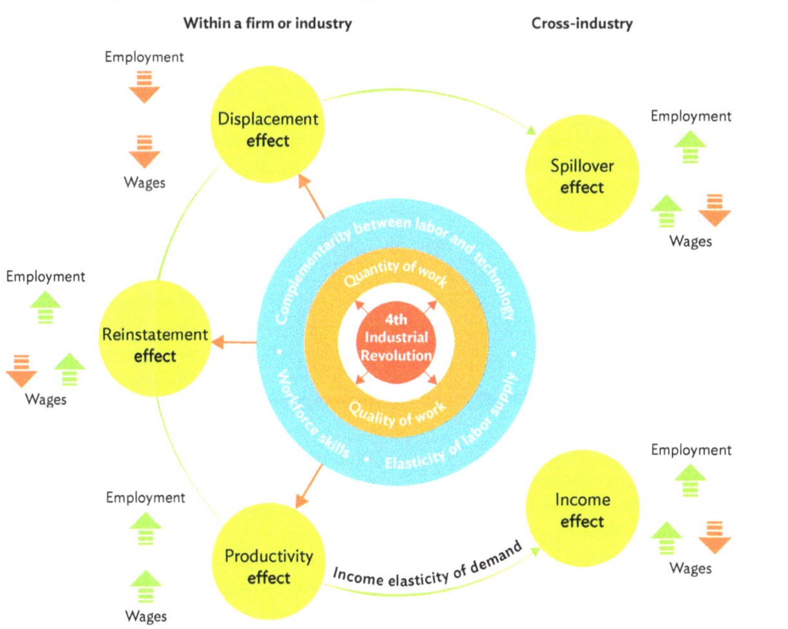

Notes: Arrows indicating a rise or fall in employment or wages reflect empirical findings from existing studies, but they do not necessarily mean the result is obtained each time the effects are studied (Table 2.1.3).

Source: ADB based on Autor (2015) and Acemoglu and Restrepo (2018).

2.1.3 Recent studies on the impact of automation on jobs

Study	Key findings	Impact of technology	Country coverage
Acemoglu and Restrepo 2017a	☐ During 1990–2007, adding industrial robots correlated negatively with employment and wages. ☐ Each robot cut six jobs and reduced wages by 0.5% per 1,000 workers. ☐ In manufacturing, routine manual and blue-collar jobs were most affected.	E↓ W↓	US
Autor and Salomons 2017	☐ During 1970–2007, combined productivity growth was associated with increased employment countrywide. ☐ Each 1.0% rise in total factor productivity predicted a 0.3% rise in employment. ☐ Productivity growth in one industry had positive job spillover elsewhere in the economy.	E↑	19 OECD members
Bessen 2017	☐ During 1984–2007, computer use was associated with 3% average annual job loss in manufacturing and 1% annual job gain elsewhere. ☐ Demand in manufacturing or mature industries was weak, while productivity gains created new demand elsewhere or in newer industries.	E↑ nonmanufacturing E↓ manufacturing	US
Chang, Rynhart, and Huynh 2016	☐ Technology will increase productivity, rendering some occupations obsolete and creating new ones. ☐ ASEAN members relying heavily on labor-intensive jobs are most vulnerable to automation. ☐ Up to 70% of salaried workers—in automotive, electronics, and textile manufacturing and in retail service sectors—face automation.	E↓ W↓	ASEAN members
Frey and Osborne 2017	☐ By 2033, 47% of US jobs could become automated. ☐ Transportation and logistics, office and administrative support, and production labor will be most affected. ☐ Wages and educational attainment relate negatively with an occupation's probability of automation.	E↓ W↓	US
Frey and Rahbari 2016	☐ Automation will likely replace jobs faster in developing countries. ☐ The PRC risks losing 77% of jobs to automation, India 69%, and Ethiopia 85%, against an OECD average 57%. ☐ Technology-using sectors like professional services have expanded rapidly as many jobs became tradable.	E↓	OECD members plus Ethiopia, India, and the PRC
Graetz and Michaels, forthcoming	☐ During 1993–2007, industrial robot use increased labor productivity, total factor productivity, and wages. ☐ Robotics accounted for 10% of GDP growth and 16% of labor productivity and wage growth in industries with high robot density. ☐ Robots replaced low-skilled and some middle-skilled jobs but had little effect on high-skilled jobs.	E↑ W↑	17 developed countries—14 in Europe, plus Australia, the Republic of Korea, and the US
Mann and Püttmann 2017	☐ During 1976–2014, automation was associated with positive effects on total employment. ☐ Every new automation patent per worker brought a 0.2 percentage point increase in the ratio of employment to population. ☐ Automation is associated with jobs lost in manufacturing and in routine work, but with growth in jobs elsewhere.	E↑	US
McKinsey Global Institute 2017a	☐ Automation could raise productivity growth globally by as much as 1.4% annually. ☐ At least 30% of the work done in some 60% of occupations could be automated. ☐ Manufacturing, retail trade, accommodation and food service, and some middle-skill jobs are most susceptible to automation.	E↓ W↓	46 countries, both developing and advanced

continued next page

2.1.3 Recent studies on the impact of automation on jobs

Study	Key findings	Impact of technology	Country coverage
McKinsey Global Institute 2017b	☐ Automation could displace up to 15% of work globally by 2030. ☐ Up to 375 million workers globally, or 14% of the global workforce, will likely need new jobs and new skills if automation is rapid. ☐ Income inequality could grow in the US and other advanced economies as demand rises for high-wage jobs and falls for middle-wage jobs. The PRC and other emerging economies will likely see the highest net middle-wage job growth—in services and construction, among other areas—boosting the middle class.	E↓ W↓	46 countries, both developing and advanced
PricewaterhouseCoopers 2017	☐ By the early 2030s, automation could replace 38% of jobs in the US, 35% in Germany, 30% in the UK, and 21% in Japan. The risk in the UK is 56% in transportation and storage, 46% in manufacturing, 44% in wholesale and retail, and 17% in health care and social work. ☐ New automation technologies will create new jobs and, through productivity gains, generate new income and spending, creating new jobs that are more difficult to automate, primarily in services. ☐ In the UK, the average income should rise with productivity gains, but income inequality could worsen.	E, net long-term impact unclear in the UK W↑ UK	Germany, Japan, the UK, and the US
UNCTAD 2017	☐ During 2005–2014, more robot use is associated with a slight drop in manufacturing employment share and real wage growth across the sample, except in Mexico, Portugal, and Singapore. ☐ Robots displace routine tasks usually done by workers in the middle of the pay scale.	E↓ W↓ manufacturing	64 countries

ASEAN = Association of Southeast Asian Nations, E = employment, EU = European Union, FDI = foreign direct investment, GDP = gross domestic product, OECD = Organisation for Economic Co-operation and Development, PRC = People's Republic of China, UK = United Kingdom, UNCTAD = United Nations Conference on Trade and Development, US = United States, W = wages.

Note: Studies listed above were released between 2015 and 2018. This is not an exhaustive list of recent studies.

more sophisticated and widely used in production lines in Asia and the Pacific, for example, the cost of producing cars could go down, pushing down prices and spurring increased demand for cars. To the extent that increased demand requires hiring more workers, it could offset the displacement effect from automation.

(iii) **Reinstatement effect.** Automation can spawn new labor-intensive tasks and jobs, raising demand for labor. New job categories could emerge as AI is introduced into production, for example, or when a more sophisticated industrial robot is introduced on a factory floor and needs programming or tending.

Cross-industry effects. Adopting new technology in one industry has an impact on productivity and jobs in other industries. There are two main channels through which cross-industry effects change labor demand.

(i) **Spillover effect.** As one industry adopts new technology, positive spillover affects other industries in at least three ways. First, firms in downstream industries benefit from cheaper and/or better-quality inputs, while firms in upstream industries benefit if the output of the automating industry expands. Second, other industries learn the benefits of adopting the new technology. Third, workers with new skills and knowledge move between industries, spreading technological know-how.

(ii) **Income effect.** When technology complements labor, workers' higher incomes create positive spillover on other industries through increased demand for goods and services. A software developer whose income has increased thanks to complementarity between automation and human labor, for example, may want to buy a bigger car, a faster computer, better health care, more vacations, or other leisure services.

Aggregate impact on employment. Still other factors influence how technology affects jobs.

(i) **Complementarity between labor and technology.** If workers carry out tasks that are complemented by automation, demand for such workers will likely increase, as will their wages. If workers perform tasks that can be done solely by machines, they are likely to be displaced. That said, the technical feasibility of automating a set of tasks does not necessarily make automation economically viable. The price of new technology relative to labor cost is a crucial determinant of whether automation takes place.

(ii) **Elasticity of labor supply.** An example would be a within-industry effect with technology complementing human labor. Even if demand for tasks supplied by a software developer rises, there can be no significant change in employment unless there is an adequate supply of appropriately skilled workers. Assuming labor supply is not very elastic, wages earned by software developers and researchers tend to rise, which incentivizes more workers to enter those jobs. However, high labor supply elasticity—an abundance of workers with the requisite training as a software developer—could mitigate wage gains.

(iii) **Demand response to income elasticity.** Rising incomes in one industry create demand for goods and services in other parts of the economy, but this depends on how responsive demand is to increased income. Consider again the example of software developers whose labor is complemented by automation. How much of the increase in wages are they willing to spend on goods and services supplied by other sectors? The answer will help determine employment and wages in the other sectors.

(iv) **Workforce skills.** To take advantage of automation and new types of tasks created in the economy, workforce skills need to match technological requirements. New tasks require new skills, and education and training are key. A mismatch between skills and technologies slows the adjustment of employment and wages, hindering productivity growth.

Indeed, careful investigation of time series data spanning many decades shows these forces at play, countering the job displacement effects that arise when new technologies allow a given output to be produced by fewer workers (Box 2.1.2).

2.1.2 Productivity and employment: different forces at play

Bessen (2017), an analysis of employment data spanning decades, powerfully illustrates the idea that laborsaving technologies can raise employment in adopting industries. With the introduction in 1814 of textile power looms in the US, productivity soared, reducing prices, raising incomes, and increasing demand for textile products. Similarly, the assembly line Henry Ford introduced in 1913 increased productivity in the automobile industry, reducing prices and increasing demand for cars. Long-term employment trends in the US show that strong employment growth took place in the decades when technological advances improved labor productivity (box figure). Bessen (2017) called this the "inverted U" pattern of employment, wherein employment expands for an extended period before it starts declining. Employment in the US textile industry, for example, grew for about a century before it peaked and began declining.

Similarly, Autor and Salomons (2017) studied 19 high-income countries and shed further light on whether laborsaving technological progress erodes employment. As in Bessen (2017), the relationship between productivity growth and employment growth was positive in aggregate. However, at the industry level, rising labor productivity forces down employment within the industry, and this phenomenon prevails across all industries. The study reconciles these seemingly opposite results by showing that, when one industry improves labor productivity, spillover affects employment in other industries. Spillover stems from the income effect pushing up final demand and interindustry demand linkages.

To fully understand the impact of technology on employment, it is important to examine the impact of productivity gains using input-output analysis, as this sheds light on interindustry linkages and final demand effects (Autor and Salomons 2017). Later in this chapter, this method is used with multiregional input-output tables produced by the Asian Development Bank to show that, indeed, countervailing forces are at play thanks to rising demand.

Long-term trends in employment in manufacturing

a. Textile, thread, and fabric jobs in the United States

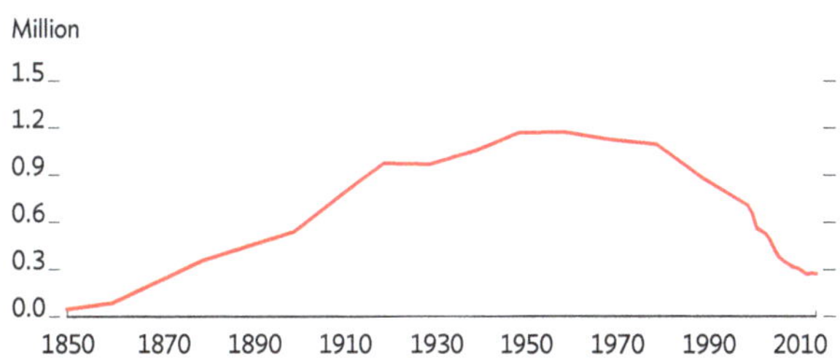

b. Auto and auto equipment jobs in the United States

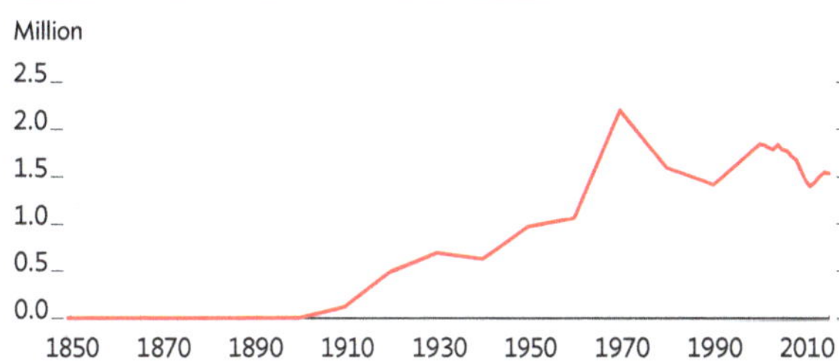

Source: Minnesota Population Center. Integrated Public Use Microdata Series, International: Version 6.5. http://doi.org/10.18128/D020.V6.5 (accessed 23 February 2018). Cited in Bessen (2017).

Reasons for optimism on job prospects

Empirical evidence presented in this section shows that the anxiety over automation is overblown, and that predictions are unfounded that a majority of jobs in the developing world may be lost to automation. Three empirical exercises are conducted to back this statement.

First, this section examines trends in Asia's robot usage and shows that robots tend to be concentrated in capital-intensive and high-wage industries. A key point is that, even if it is technically feasible to replace a job with machines, it may not be economically feasible.

Second, analysis of the relationship between technology and employment in global value chains provides further insight into how various forces have affected jobs and will shape their future. Decomposition of employment changes from 2005 to 2015 using a demand-based input–output approach is instructive about how different forces affect job numbers, types, and locations in global value chains. While the technologies needed for extreme automation are only just starting to appear, advances such as computer numerically controlled machines and modern ICT tools were already coming online in factories and firms in Asia over the period covered. Two results stand out: Rising demand, spurred by improved efficiency or labor productivity, more than compensates for technology-induced displacement of jobs. Further, any "reshoring" of production to advanced economies may not be a major threat to employment in developing Asia.

Third, this section examines changes in occupation titles, which show that advances in technology have created new jobs. This is a prominent countervailing force against the displacement effect of technology (Lin 2011). A detailed analysis of occupation titles shows that new types of jobs have emerged in highly skilled occupations. Moreover, a comparison of occupations in the region with those in advanced economies show great scope for job growth.

Industrial robots and employment outcomes

Industrial robots are the epitome of new technology and automated systems in production processes. Robots take many forms and shapes and can do many human tasks. The International Federation of Robotics (2016) defines a machine as an industrial robot if it can be programmed to perform physical, production-related tasks without the need of a human controller. The federation database provides information on industrial robot deliveries and robot stock from 1993 to 2015, covering 55 economies including 23 in Asia.

Asia's use of industrial robots is accelerating, its operational stock having risen from 2010 to 2015 by 70% to 887,400 units. The PRC is the world's largest market for industrial robots, annually taking 43% of all sales in Asia and the Pacific, followed by the Republic of Korea with 24% and Japan with 22%. International Federation of Robotics estimates suggest, moreover, that by 2019 almost 40% of the world's industrial robots will be in the PRC. The federation predicts that robot installation will continue to grow in all major Asian robot markets. Robot sales by industry show the largest share of robots in Asian manufacturing going into electrical and electronic goods and the automotive industries. Metal processing comes next, closely followed by plastic and chemical products (Figure 2.2.1a). The robot skillset lends itself to the standardization and fixed nature of automotive and electronics assembly using hard materials, as opposed to soft material such as the fabric used in apparel (United States Government 2016).

The capital-intensive industries that use increasing numbers of industrial robots do not employ many workers (Figure 2.2.1b). The two largest users of industrial robots in Asia, electrical and electronics industries and automotive manufacturers, each accounted in 2015 for 39% of Asia's robot stock but only 9.2% and 4.2%, respectively, of manufacturing employment. In contrast, food and beverages accounted for 1.3% of Asia's industrial robots but 12.3% of Asian manufacturing workers, and textiles, apparel, and leather for 0.1% of robots and 19.2% of workers. The data imply that any adverse employment effects from the use of new technology, particularly robots, will not be widespread. The more labor-intensive manufacturing industries have low rates of robot deployment, largely because automation is not economically viable. The one exception to this trend is the PRC, which employs large numbers of workers in capital-intensive sectors where the potential for robot deployment is high (Box 2.2.1). This means that the PRC is more exposed to automation than other economies in developing Asia.

2.2.1 Annual supply of robots and sectoral employment

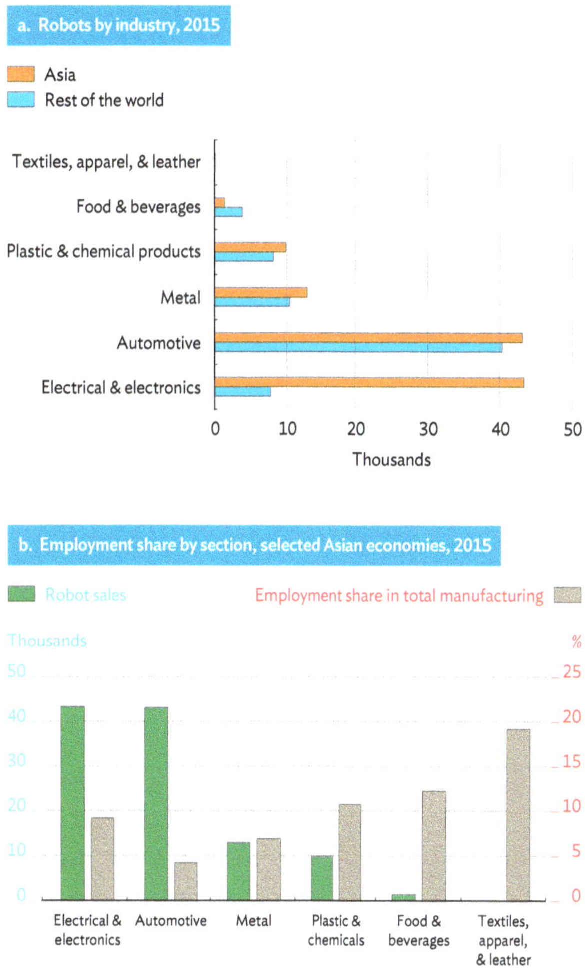

Note: Asia includes India; Indonesia; Malaysia; the People's Republic of China; the Republic of Korea; Singapore; Thailand; Taipei,China; and Viet Nam.

Sources: International Federation of Robotics. World Robotics Statistics Database (accessed 23 March 2018); World Input-Output Database–Socioeconomic Accounts (Timmer et al. 2015).

Technical versus economic feasibility

Many recent studies that looked at the impact of automation on jobs focused on the technical feasibility of automating a set of tasks. But technical feasibility is one thing, economic feasibility another. For new technology to significantly

2.2.1 Robots, automation, and jobs in the People's Republic of China

Rapidly rising wages in the PRC have induced firms to embrace automation and robots in a trend that will shift the nature of work and demand for new skills. From 2013 to 2016, annual robot purchases by the PRC increased by 106%, compared with 65% globally. In 2016, the PRC became the world's largest robot market, receiving 30% of global sales. By industry, robots are concentrated in automobiles at 39%; computers, communication, and consumer electronics at 24%; and metal processing at 10%. Because the PRC has a very large workforce, the ratio of robots to workers remains much lower than in advanced countries, but the government announced an ambitious plan to triple the ratio from 49 robots per 10,000 workers in 2015 to 150 by 2020.

According to the China Employer-Employee Survey, which covered over 1,100 manufacturing firms in Hubei and Guangdong provinces in 2016, 49% of workers are in firms with computerized numerically controlled machines, including 9% in firms with robots. The survey found 13% of firms received subsidies for robots purchased in 2013, 20% in 2014, and 18% in 2015. The average subsidy was 20% of the cost.

What kinds of firms automate?

Firms that automate tend to be larger, older, more capital intensive, high-tech, and located in special economic zones—and firms using robots even more so (box table 1). Compared with both unautomated firms and those using numerically controlled equipment, firms using robots are more globalized in that they export a larger share of their production and are more likely foreign owned.

Characteristics of automated firms, by number and type of worker and by wage level

Automated firms generally have twice as many employees as those that are not, and those with robots have 6 times as many. Employees at firms with robots have higher educational attainment and are paid better across all occupations (box table 2). They also have a lower proportion of managers to production and technical workers. The wage premium for technical workers over production workers is 30% in firms with no automated equipment (90% for managers) and 50% in firms with robots (180% for managers). Regression analysis finds the relationship between relative wages and automation persists even after controlling for other company characteristics. Although not necessarily causal, the results are consistent with automation being more complementary to skilled than to unskilled work, suggesting the trend toward automation will likely increase demand for skilled workers in the PRC.

1 Firm characteristics by degree of automation

Feature	No automation	Numerically controlled machines but no robots	Robots
Share of firms (%)	51	40	9
Employees (number)	445	811	2,721
Firm age (years)	11	13	16
Ratio of capital to labor (CNY'000 per employee)	251	296	321
Located in economic zone (%)	56	68	77
Ownership (%)			
State	12	11	15
Domestic private	68	67	43
Foreign	20	22	41
Export share of sales (%)	22	20	29

Source: Jia, Park, and Du 2018.

2 Firm employment and wages by degree of automation

Feature	No automation	Numerically controlled machines but no robots	Robots
Education of employees (%)			
Junior high school and below	50	46	35
Senior high school	33	36	40
College and above	17	18	25
Occupation of employees (%)			
Production workers	73	74	77
Technical workers (Ratio of technical to production workers)	8 (0.11)	10 (0.14)	12 (0.16)
Managers (Ratio of managers to production workers)	13 (0.18)	11 (0.15)	6 (0.08)
Monthly wage by occupation (CNY)			
Production workers	3,887	4,294	4,779
Technical workers (Wage ratio of technical to production workers)	5,062 (1.30)	6,200 (1.44)	7,242 (1.52)
Managers (Wage ratio of managers to production workers)	7,424 (1.91)	9,071 (2.11)	13,372 (2.80)

Source: Jia, Park, and Du 2018.

displace human labor, it needs to become economically viable (Figure 2.2.2a). For example, sewing robots—assuming they are sophisticated enough to work with fabric—would have to be sufficiently cheap to displace a Bangladeshi garment worker who earns $68 per month (Box 2.2.2). Hence, even in certain industries where automation is technically feasible, robot deployment is low.

Figure 2.2.2b links the use of robots in manufacturing in selected Asian economies with proxies for the technical and economic feasibility of automation. Bubble size represents robot stock in 2015. The vertical axis of technical feasibility is based on an index of routine task intensity provided by Marcolin, Miroudot, and Squicciarini (2016).

2.2.2 Technical versus economic feasibility of automation

a. Economic feasibility of new technology

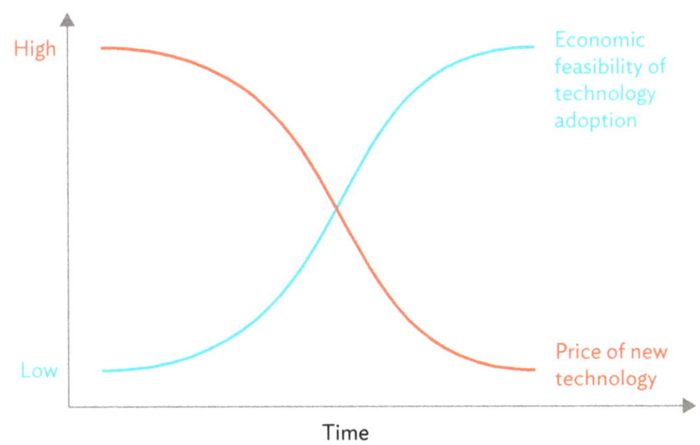

b. Evidence from manufacturing, selected Asian economies

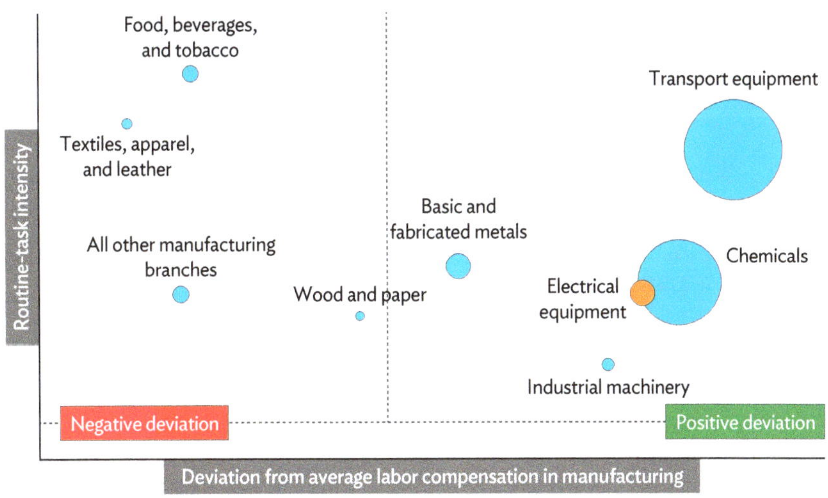

Notes: Bubble size represents robot stock in 2015. Wage and robot stock data cover India, Indonesia, Pakistan, the Philippines, Thailand, and Viet Nam.

Sources: Inspired by Mayer (2017) and UNCTAD (2017). Panel A, ADB. Panel B, wage data from labor force surveys in India, Indonesia, Pakistan, the Philippines, Thailand, and Viet Nam; routine intensity index by sector from Marcolin, Miroudot, and Squicciarini (2016); robot stock data from the International Federation of Robotics.

2.2.2 Automation in garment manufacturing in Asia

Garment manufacturing has long been a path out of poverty for low-income economies in developing Asia because it provides steady employment for a workforce with few skills. After agriculture and construction, garments are the third largest employer in the three economies examined here: Bangladesh, Cambodia, and India.

Automation in all three has moved quickly over the past decade, but the main driver differs in each case. Three formerly manual-intensive processes—cutting, spreading, and ironing—are now done more accurately, twice as quickly, and with one-tenth of the workers. A Jacquard weaving machine increases daily output per worker sixfold. Automation reduced labor costs per garment but, more importantly, reduced delivery time for greater flexibility, encouraging factory expansion for exploiting economies of scale. In the three economies, labor equals only 10%–20% of basic garment variable cost. As a result, costs are only marginally affected by wage increases on the one hand and reductions in unit labor cost on the other. Instead, savings from automation derive more from reduced waste and higher volume—and therefore better return on fixed costs. Still, profit margins in recent years have been squeezed by intense competition as suppliers chase sluggish demand growth in consumer markets.

It is difficult to predict how long before full automation occurs. Sewing is a very labor-intensive process. Technological advances in sewing machines have improved accuracy but have not yet replaced jobs. Most executives of large garment exporters say replacing operators with sewing robots is unlikely in the next decade because it is barely feasible, either technically or economically, and the industry would need to adapt. One current estimate says the unit labor cost of producing a cotton shirt in the US is about $7. The approximate cost of producing the same shirt in India is $0.50, in Bangladesh $0.22, and in Cambodia $0.33. Sewing robots should narrow the gap, with some observers saying robotics will reduce basic apparel production costs in the US and Europe to about $0.40. Developing countries would lose their competitive edge, which would encourage reshoring, or reversing the outsourcing of production. However, as discussed below, rising demand from within Asia could be an important offset to job displacement on account of either automation or reshoring.

It shows routine task intensity within manufacturing highest in food, beverages, and tobacco; textiles, apparel, and leather; and transport equipment. The horizontal axis is labor compensation, or wages calculated using labor force surveys. It shows job displacement by robots to be economically more feasible in capital- and skills-intensive manufacturing such as transport equipment, chemicals, and electrical equipment. Bigger bubbles on the right show robot usage more common in sectors where wages are higher.

Robot density and employment

Several new studies examine the impact of industrial robots on employment. The empirical evidence is inconclusive. Acemoglu and Restrepo (2017b) found industrial robot adoption negatively correlated with employment and wages, and this holds across industries. Developments in the US from 1990 to 2017 showed that each additional robot displaced six workers, and raising robot density by one new robot per thousand reduced wages by 0.5%. In manufacturing, the most affected occupations are routine manual—typically blue-collar workers without college degrees. By contrast, Graetz and Michaels (forthcoming) found in 17 developed countries that, from 1993 to 2017, robotics accounted for 10% of GDP growth and, in industries with higher robot density, 16% of labor productivity and wage growth. This study found no evidence of robotics driving down aggregate employment. However, results vary by skills group, with robotics reducing hours worked and wages for low- and middle-skilled workers, but having had no significant effect on high-skilled workers.

So, simple correlation between robot density and employment growth yields a somewhat ambiguous picture. When jobs are divided into routine and not, however, routine employment negatively correlates with robot density, while nonroutine employment positively correlates (Figure 2.2.3). Empirical analysis corroborates these descriptive trends.

Indeed, there is no significant relationship between adopting robots and overall employment (Table 2.2.1a). But when robot adoption is disaggregated by type of employment, the relationship is different: Routine employment decreases with the increased usage of robots, while nonroutine employment increases (Table 2.2.1b). In addition, robot adoption significantly correlates with a decrease in routine manual occupations such as production workers and an increase in nonroutine cognitive occupations such as managers and professionals (Table 2.2.1c). Most important is the difference between developing and developed countries, as the impact of robots on labor demand is larger in developed countries than in developing countries (Table 2.2.1d).

2.2.3 Robot density and employment, routine versus nonroutine

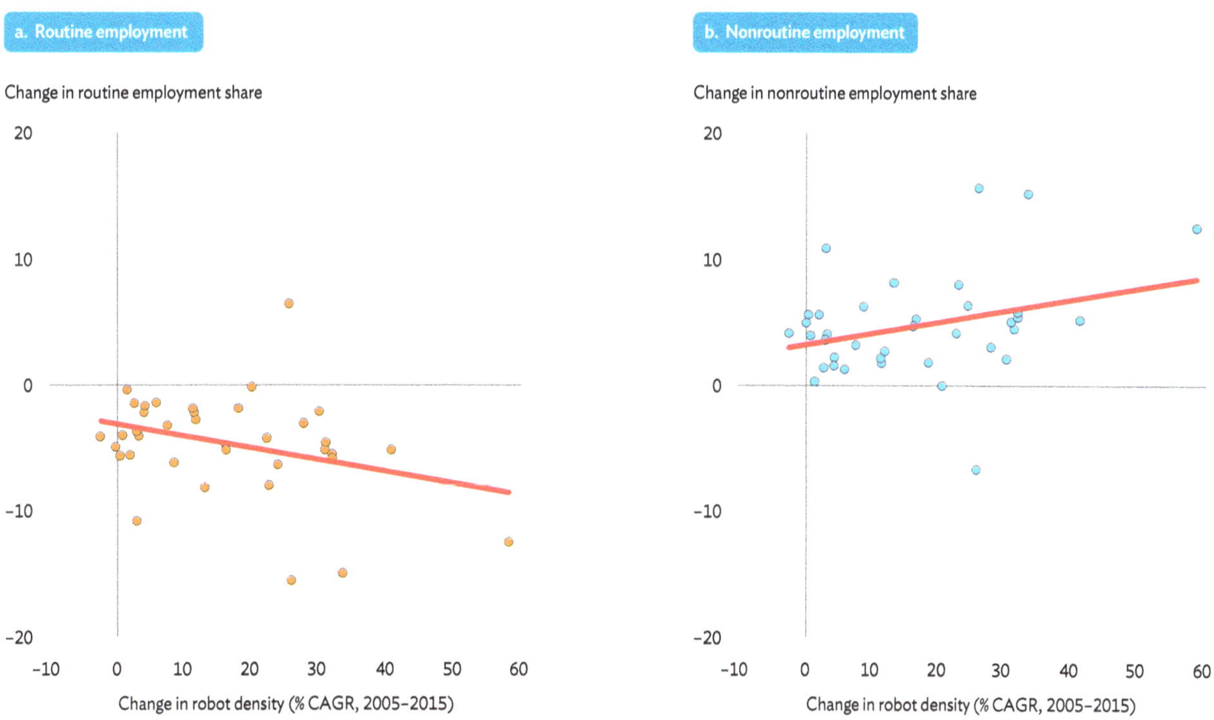

CAGR = compounded annual growth rate.

Notes: Robot density is the number of robots per 10,000 workers. Routine and nonroutine classification is based on Autor and Dorn (2013).

Sources: International Federation of Robotics. World Robotics Statistics Database (accessed 23 March 2018); International Labour Organization. ILOSTAT. http://www.ilo.org/ilostat (accessed 23 March 2018); results of structural decomposition analysis of jobs using ADB Multiregional Input-Output Tables.

2.2.1 Change in robot inputs and impact on employment, 2005–2015 (ordinary least square estimates)

a. Overall employment

	Change in employment		
	(1)	(2)	(3)
Robot adoption	-0.212 (0.37)	-0.212 (0.73)	-0.663 (0.61)
Country trends	Yes	Yes	Yes
Controls			Yes
Clustered standard errors		Yes	Yes
Observations	758	758	757

b. Routine employment

	Change in routine employment share		
	(1)	(2)	(3)
Robot adoption	-0.048*** (0.01)	-0.048*** (0.01)	-0.048*** (0.01)
Country trends	Yes	Yes	Yes
Controls			Yes
Clustered standard errors		Yes	Yes
Observations	777	777	776

c. Occupational employment shares

	Change in employment share of			
	(1)	(2)	(3)	(4)
	Routine manual	Routine cognitive	Nonroutine manual	Nonroutine cognitive
Robot adoption	-0.055*** (0.02)	-0.002 (0.00)	-0.004 (0.01)	0.061*** (0.01)
Country trends	Yes	Yes	Yes	Yes
Controls	Yes	Yes	Yes	Yes
Clustered standard errors	Yes	Yes	Yes	Yes
Observations	776	776	776	776

d. Developed versus developing countries

	Change in routine employment share		
	(1)	(2)	(3)
Robot adoption	-0.056*** (0.01)	-0.056*** (0.02)	-0.056*** (0.02)
Developing country x robot adoption (Interaction term)	0.038 (0.03)	0.038** (0.02)	0.036** (0.02)
Country trends	Yes	Yes	Yes
Controls			Yes
Clustered standard errors		Yes	Yes
Observations	777	777	776

* = p<0.1, ** = p<0.05, *** = p<0.01.

Note: Robot adoption is the percentile in the weighted distribution of changes in robot density. Controls include real changes in gross fixed capital formation share in value added and changes in value added. Robust standard errors in parenthesis. Regressions are weighted by 2005 within-country employment shares.

Source: Bertulfo, Gentile, and de Vries, forthcoming.

Technology and employment in global value chains

Driven by revolutionary advances in information technology, production processes have been unbundled across national borders to form global value chains (GVCs).[3] A GVC includes all the interrelated production units that contribute one task or more to the creation and delivery of a final good or service to end consumers. Production units can be nearby or located anywhere on the globe, and labor contributes to virtually every task along the chain. Two additional factors have made this unbundling possible: trade liberalization and lower transport costs through improved logistics, infrastructure, and transport technology. This process redistributed global economic activity, with Asian economies emerging as key players. In 2016, Asia's GVC participation, measured as the share of gross exports of value added used for further processing through cross-border production networks, was 61.1% (ADB 2017b). This was second only to the European Union.

GVCs significantly affect employment in participating economies. Changes in the structure of GVCs, in particular those caused by new technology, have corresponding effects on employment. Developing economies that boost production for the export market often see a significant increase in manufacturing jobs. In Bangladesh, for example, the emergence of GVC-oriented garment exports has created more than 3 million new jobs over the past 2 decades (Farole and Cho 2017). In most low-cost, routine, labor-intensive GVCs such as garments, footwear, and electronics, the largest employment share is occupied by young women, many of them newcomers to the workforce.

GVCs have made it easier for developing economies to adopt new technologies. For example, technologies developed in high-income economies, such as numerically controlled machines and modern ICT tools, are used by factories and firms all along GVCs. Arguably, business use of ICT has been a boon for women in the labor market (Box 2.2.3).

While new technologies improve productivity, they raise two main concerns for developing economies. First, extreme automation can have significant implications for jobs. As Fourth Industrial Revolution technologies such as digital manufacturing become more sophisticated and cost-effective, firms in developing economies could lose many jobs if reshoring production back to advanced economies becomes feasible. In fact, however, if the cost of new technologies lowers significantly, it is conceivable that firms in developing economies may use them too.

Second, to the extent that upgrading technology is skill-biased, it shifts demand from workers with lower skills to those with higher skills, widening inequality. This poses a problem for developing economies competitive in low- to medium-skill activities, as using advanced technology could create a shortage of high-skilled workers and surplus of medium- and low-skilled workers.

Combining multiregional input–output tables developed by the Asian Development Bank with employment data from labor force surveys[4] allows research that examines the relationship between technology and jobs along supply chains in 12 economies in developing Asia, covering 35 sectors from 2005 to 2015.[5] The 12 economies accounted for 90% of employment in developing Asia in 2015.[6] In the tables, a GVC is defined by final products produced by a particular industry in a particular economy. For example, "textiles and textile products finalized in the PRC" is considered a GVC that encompasses a wide range of final products, from garments to awnings and canopies (Timmer et al. 2014).

The analytical framework developed in Reijnders and de Vries (2017) is used to analyze changes in demand for jobs by modeling the input–output structure of the world economy. The focus is on the relative importance of changes in various determinants of demand for jobs in economies and the sectors within them. This analysis is among the first to frame the quantification of these effects in a setting of internationally fragmented GVCs in Asia.

2.2.3 How information technology skills help women find better jobs in Viet Nam

Information and communication technology (ICT) would seem to be gender-neutral, but in fact businesses' increased use of ICT has positive effects for women in the labor market. Chun and Tang (2018) examined this by exploring the interplay between firms' ICT use, demand for tasks, and employment by gender and skill group. Using data from Viet Nam, which has one of the world's most inexpensive broadband networks, recent research found that greater ICT use increases the female share of employment, benefiting in particular college-educated women (though gender disparities in education and training limit the benefit).

Chun and Tang (2018) used data on firms' use of ICT from the Annual Enterprise Census of Viet Nam, 2005–2009. The study measured an industry's task complexity, evaluated by occupation.[a] Complex industries are the most innovative in the economy, heavily relying on highly technical engineering skills, while less complex industries provide basic products and services. The study used the gradual liberalization of broadband internet across provinces from 2006 to 2009 to construct an instrument to measure firms' ICT use, controlled for region, industry, and year fixed effects. The three main findings are as follows.

- **Adopting ICT has a positive effect on a firm's female labor share.** A 10% increase in the number of internet-connected computers per worker increases a firm's female labor share by 3 percentage points. The share increase is 3.5 percentage points when computers are also connected to a local area network (LAN). Compared with firms not using ICT, a firm using a LAN has a higher female labor share by 14 percentage points, one using the internet by 15 percentage points, and one hosting a website by 30 percentage points. These numbers support the observation that ICT use increases relative demand for nonroutine interactive tasks, raising the relative share of women employed.
- **The positive effect is larger for the female share of skilled employment.** ICT raises both the share of skilled college-educated workers and the share of women employed by a firm. A 10% increase in the number of computers connected to the internet per worker increases the female share in college-educated employment in firms by 8 percentage points, and connection to a LAN by 9 percentage points. A firm's use of a LAN correlates with a higher female labor share among the college-educated by 31 percentage points, use of the internet by 46 percentage points, and hosting a website by 69 percentage points.
- **But the effect is weaker in more complex industries.** The interaction terms between ICT variables and the sectoral measure of complexity have negative coefficients, such that women benefit less from ICT in more complex sectors. In these sectors, men may have comparative advantage over women because a higher proportion of men train in highly technical skills. ICT may thus worsen gender inequality in industries more dependent on complex tasks.

These results illustrate the potential that ICT has to generate growth in high-quality employment for women, compared with programs narrowly focused on providing to women capital and training. The results underscore the importance of addressing gender differences in education and training, toward improving gender equality in the workplace. The study highlights ICT as a force for female empowerment in labor markets and the importance of acquiring the ICT skills necessary for the complex computerized and digital tasks essential to innovative industries.

[a] The study constructed an index on occupation complexity, a measure of the need for complex problem-solving skills in each occupation, based on the US Department of Labor's Occupational Information Network.

Source: Chun and Tang 2018.

Decomposition by occupation shows technology, considered alone, reducing labor demand

Three main forces affect employment in economies and industries participating in GVCs. First is the location of a production task and its associated jobs. Second is the use of technology along the GVC, which may affect the number of workers required to meet given demand, the direction of impact on employment depending on whether new technologies replace jobs or complement them. Third, GVC employment is influenced by conditions in the economy and globally, such as total demand for goods and services and changes in consumer preferences.

Structural decomposition analysis (SDA) of the multiregional input–output tables achieves two objectives. First, it quantifies changes in labor demand associated with technological change and task relocation. Second, it examines the relative magnitude of these GVC-specific channels with respect to conditions globally and within an economy.

The decomposition of change in an economy's number of jobs from 2005 to 2015 occurs on two levels (Figure 2.2.4). At the first level, the change in employment is decomposed into change *within* the GVC, or changes in employment within the production structure or GVC of a specific final product, and change *between* GVCs, or changes in employment resulting from shifts in consumer demand for different products. If, for example, consumers suddenly spend more on electronics than garments, there will be greater demand for employment in the electronics production chain and less in the garments chain. Finally, income refers to changes in employment caused by changes in global demand for goods and services. In practice, higher income in real terms will increase demand for goods and services, which in turn will increase employment.

The SDA further decomposes the within-GVC channel into (i) technology within the GVC, or changes in employment associated with changes in efficiency within a specific GVC; (ii) task relocation, or changes in employment as the location changes for one production task or more; and (iii) country-level efficiency, or changes in employment from efficiency changes in the economy.[7]

The GVC for garments in the PRC is used to illustrate how to operationalize technology within the GVC and task relocation. If machines replace workers at one or more of the production tasks in the GVC, this will lower the number of jobs in the GVC needed to meet given demand. This channel is labeled "technology within GVCs." If PRC garment manufacturers decide to relocate one or more of the production tasks to Thailand, the jobs for those tasks will be lost in the PRC and gained in Thailand.

2.2.4 Decomposing changes in labor demand

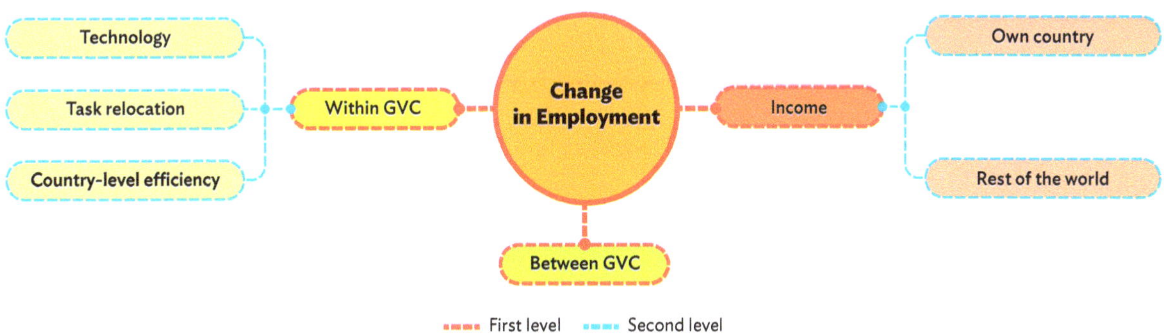

GVC = global value chain.
Source: Based on Reijnders and de Vries (2017).

Assuming other factors are constant—for example, workers in the PRC and Thailand are equally productive—the total number of jobs in the GVC is unchanged, but fewer workers are employed in the PRC and more in Thailand. This is task relocation.

The use of the within-GVC technology channel to capture the effects of industry-specific technological change on jobs operates along the lines of recent research that uses measures of labor productivity growth that vary across industries as an all-encompassing proxy for the effects of technological progress (Autor and Salomons 2017). It bypasses the formidable difficulty of examining the employment implications of specific technological innovations. As noted in Autor and Salomons (2017), the diversity of specific innovations defies both consistent classification and comprehensive measurement. In the model presented here, countrywide economic conditions, which would include the effects of improved economic institutions or rising educational attainment, are captured by country-level efficiency, while technology within the GVC transcends national boundaries and captures technological advances along a specific production chain.

Finally, the second stage of the SDA further decomposes the income channel into "own country," or demand for goods and services originating within a specific country, and "rest of the world," or demand from abroad for goods and services. The purpose is to see what fraction of employment depends on domestic demand and what fraction foreign demand.

This analysis has two outliers. During 2005–2015, the global commodities bust hit hard in Mongolia, an economy heavily reliant on mining, causing a major decline in employment in services. The second outlier is Sri Lanka, where a 30-year civil war ended in 2009, followed by a period of record-breaking economic growth. Particularly affected were the employment numbers for manufacturing. Therefore, they are not always presented in figures (though these may be found in Bertulfo, Gentile, and de Vries, forthcoming[b]).

Figure 2.2.5 presents the results of the SDA for employment in agriculture, manufacturing, and services. The results show that, all other things being equal, technology improvements within GVCs accompany lower employment across all sectors. In the PRC, for example, the decrease in employment associated with technology is 77% in agriculture, 68% in manufacturing, and 44% in services. Notable exceptions are employment in services in the Philippines and Viet Nam, where technological change within GVCs increases demand for certain service occupations: information technology and business process outsourcing in the Philippines, and information technology services in Viet Nam.

2.2.5 Structural decomposition analysis of changes in employment by sector, 2005–2015

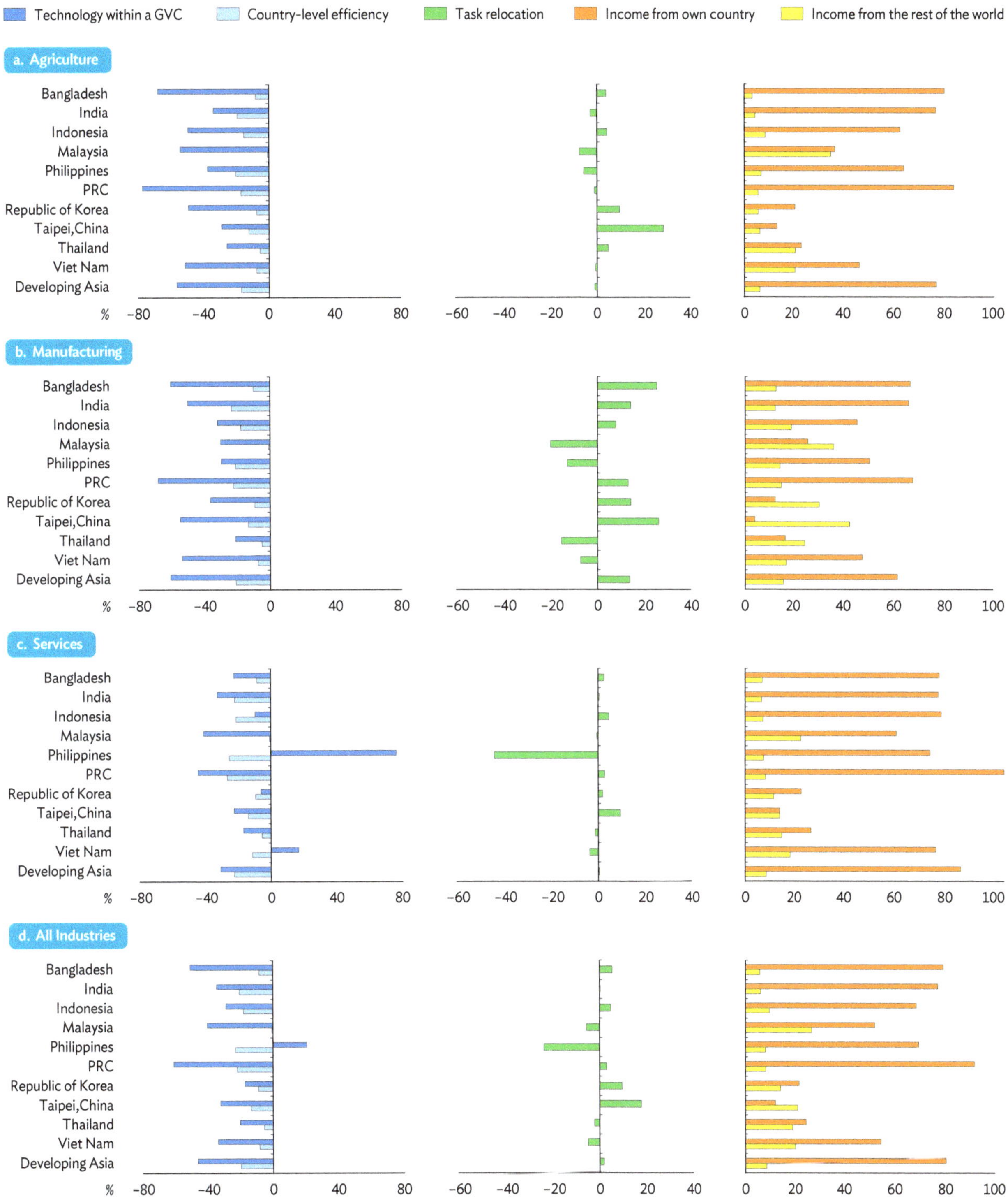

GVC = global value chain, PRC = People's Republic of China.

Note: Because manufacturing excludes the industry subsectors electricity, gas, and water supply and construction, "all sectors" is larger than the sum of agriculture, manufacturing, and services. Developing Asia in the decomposition analysis includes Bangladesh, India, Indonesia, Malaysia, Mongolia, the People's Republic of China, the Philippines, the Republic of Korea, Sri Lanka, Taipei,China, Thailand, and Viet Nam.

Source: ADB estimates using the ADB Multiregional Input-Output Database (accessed 20 November 2017); Labor force surveys, various countries; World Input-Output Database—Socioeconomic Accounts (Timmer et al. 2015).

Task relocation is associated with changes in employment that are much smaller and mixed. Bangladesh, India, Indonesia, and the PRC, which are well integrated into GVCs, experience net increases in employment, while others experience net decreases. This suggests that task relocation was not the main driver of changes in employment during 2005–2015.

Rising incomes more than compensate for employment demand suppressed by new technology

The last column of Figure 2.2.5 compares the magnitude of changes in domestic employment associated with changes in income from within the domestic economy and from the rest of the world. It is noteworthy that domestic income effects are generally much larger than those from the rest of the world. In the PRC, for example, the increase in employment associated with own-country income is 83% in agriculture, 68% in manufacturing, and a staggering 105% in services, as opposed to 6%, 15%, and 8% associated with income from the rest of the world. This is an encouraging sign of newly rising consumers in developing Asia, now able to generate domestic demand for products and services. Moreover, the figure shows that increases in employment associated with both sources of income are large enough to offset the combined decrease in employment from changes to technology in the GVC and efficiency in the economy (Box 2.2.4). In fact, in developing Asia, the combined impact of efficiency gains at the country level and technological advances within the GVC, holding all other components constant, is a 66% decrease in labor demand, equal to 101 million jobs per annum. However, concurrently higher demand for goods and services more than offsets this with an 88% increase in labor demand, equal to 134 million jobs per annum.

2.2.4 Rising income offsetting employment losses from technology

The world has witnessed three major technological revolutions, each reducing the labor required to produce a given output. It has not, however, witnessed any increase in structural unemployment. This implies the existence of channels that counterbalance the negative impact technology has on employment. Researchers have in fact identified various such channels, most of which expand aggregate demand, as described by Bessen (2017), for example, in the previous section. Technological innovation generally reduces the prices of goods and raises income per capita. Both effects push up demand, which can outweigh the direct negative impact of technology on employment.

Consider India, which has a large population with income per capita growing at a healthy rate. In 2015, income per capita was about $1,600 annually, and the Indian apparel market was estimated at $59 billion. If the economy grows at 7% annually over the next 16 years, annual income per capita will rise to $2,800 in 2021 and $4,900 in 2031. The apparel market can be expected to expand in response. Using 0.8 for income elasticity, it is expected to reach $93 billion in 2022 and $149 billion in 2032. This increase of output by 2.5 times over the next 16 years can be expected to counter job displacement from future automation in the garment industry.

Routine occupations are more at risk than others

Of major interest is which occupations are more vulnerable to displacement by technology. The taxonomy developed in Autor, Levy, and Murnane (2003), which classifies occupations as routine manual, routine cognitive, nonroutine manual, and nonroutine cognitive, allows for an SDA of changes in employment by occupation type. Unfortunately, this exercise is not possible for agricultural employment because it is difficult to distinguish routine and nonroutine occupations in the sector.

The results of the SDA by occupation type are presented in Figure 2.2.6 for manufacturing and services. The trends are the same as in Figure 2.2.5, but changes in employment are distributed across occupation types. It can be observed on the left that technology change within a GVC correlates with lower employment across countries and occupation types in both manufacturing and services. However, the decrease in nonroutine employment, especially nonroutine cognitive employment, is less pronounced than for routine employment. Bangladesh, the Philippines, and Viet Nam even show an increase in nonroutine employment in services. The findings suggest that technological advances along the supply chain may have been skill-biased in 2005–2015. This should not be surprising, as modern machine tools and ICT have been used in production for some time.

It can be observed on the right that task relocation in manufacturing appears to have a positive effect on nonroutine employment as well. In India, Indonesia, and the PRC, task relocation is associated with increases in nonroutine occupations, both cognitive and manual (Box 2.2.5). Bangladesh and Thailand show increases in nonroutine manual occupations, and Malaysia shows an increase in nonroutine cognitive occupations. In services (excluding outliers in the Philippines and Viet Nam), changes in employment are generally very small and mixed.

New technology pushing up the share of nonroutine jobs

The analysis above quantifies the prevalence of routine and nonroutine employment. In Figure 2.2.7, the focus shifts to employment shares. In general, the magnitude of the change in employment share for manufacturing is smaller and more uniform than for services, which have more diverse dynamics. An increased employment share of nonroutine cognitive occupations accompanies technological advances within the GVC (Figure 2.2.7a). For nonroutine manual occupations, roughly half the economies show increased employment share, the rest decreased. Finally, the change in employment share for both routine cognitive and routine manual occupations associated with new technology is decidedly negative for manufacturing and mainly negative for services. These results follow from Figure 2.2.6, which shows that, although the impact of technological advances is generally a reduction in both routine and nonroutine jobs (conditional on their satisfying the same demand), it is larger for routine jobs. The impact of task relocation is relatively small and mixed.

2.2.6 Structural decomposition analysis of changes in employment by sector and occupation type, 2005–2015

BAN = Bangladesh, DA = developing Asia, GVC = global value chain, IND = India, INO = Indonesia, MAL = Malaysia, PRC = People's Republic of China, PHI = Philippines, ROK = Republic of Korea, TAP = Taipei,China, THA = Thailand, VIE = Viet Nam.

Note: Developing Asia in the decomposition analysis includes Bangladesh, India, Indonesia, Malaysia, Mongolia, the People's Republic of China, the Philippines, the Republic of Korea, Sri Lanka, Taipei,China, Thailand, and Viet Nam.

Source: ADB estimates using the ADB Multiregional Input-Output Database (accessed 20 November 2017); Labor force surveys, various countries; World Input-Output Database—Socioeconomic Accounts (Timmer et al. 2015).

Final demand from advanced economies likely to become less important for employment in developing Asia

The evidence thus far indicates that technological change within a GVC generally accompanies decreased employment across all occupation types, though routine occupations are more affected. As noted above in this section, production technologies such as industrial robots have been used for decades but are now becoming more flexible and affordable.

2.2.5 Routine and nonroutine jobs in GVCs: examples from textiles and electronics in the PRC

Box figures 1 and 2 illustrate the GVC concept using final production in the PRC of electronics and textiles. The examples show that producing manufactured products generates substantial indirect labor demand, that labor demand shifts over time toward occupations intensive in nonroutine tasks, and that substantial variation exists across industries in the indirect demand for labor they generate, as well as in relative demand for routine versus nonroutine jobs. Occupation data in each industry and economy are used to characterize occupations by their index of routine task intensity (Autor, Levy, and Murnane 2003). Occupations with scores above average on routine task intensity are considered routine. Other occupations are not considered routine task intensive.

The left panel of box figure 1 shows routine and nonroutine jobs in the PRC involved in the production of electronic products finalized in the PRC. The findings suggest that increased demand for final PRC electronic products increased PRC jobs numbers from 15 million in 2000 to 38 million in 2015. Demand for routine jobs doubled, but demand for nonroutine jobs increased almost threefold. Estimated demand for jobs includes jobs both directly and indirectly involved in the production of electronics finalized in the PRC. As intermediate inputs needed to produce electronics require their own intermediate inputs (for example, hard disks requiring electric circuits), indirect labor effects can be substantial. The right panel explicitly indicates indirect employment effects.

Box figure 2 shows jobs involved in the production of textiles finalized in the PRC, with several notable similarities to box figure 1 and several differences. First, the number of jobs involved in the production of textiles finalized in the PRC was comparable to electronics in 2015. However, the increase in job numbers was much faster in electronics than in textiles. Second, the share of routine workers involved in the production of textiles is higher than for electronics—in 2015 about 75% in textiles compared with 49% in electronics. Third, indirect employment effects from textiles are substantially smaller than from electronics, the ratio of indirect to direct demand for jobs being about 2 for textiles but almost 3 for electronics in 2015. These differences suggest that industry specialization affects demand for routine versus nonroutine jobs. In addition, the strength and importance of intermediate input linkages differs substantially across products.

Foreign workers
PRC, nonroutine workers
PRC, routine workers

Foreign workers
PRC, indirect effect on job demand
PRC, direct effect on job demand

a. GVC jobs in the production of electronics finalized in the PRC

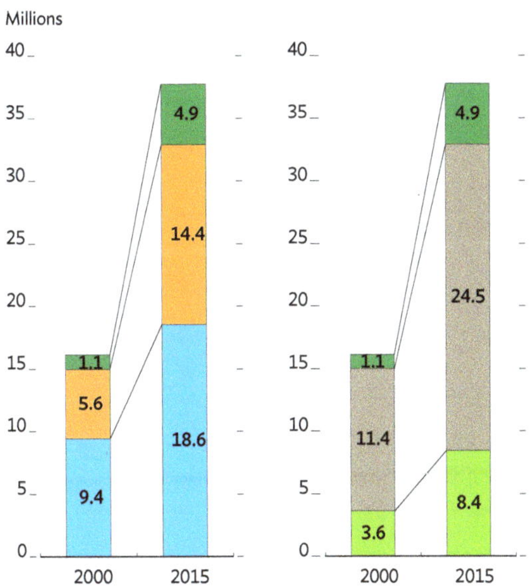

GVC = global value chain, PRC = People's Republic of China.

Notes: The right panel shows the number of workers directly and indirectly involved in producing electronic products finalized in the PRC. The left panel decomposes this demand for workers by foreign and domestic and by routine and nonroutine task intensity.

Sources: ADB estimates using data from the ADB Multiregional Input-Output Database (accessed 20 November 2017); Labor force surveys, various countries; World Input-Output Database—Socioeconomic Accounts (Timmer et al. 2015).

b. GVC jobs in textile products finalized in the PRC

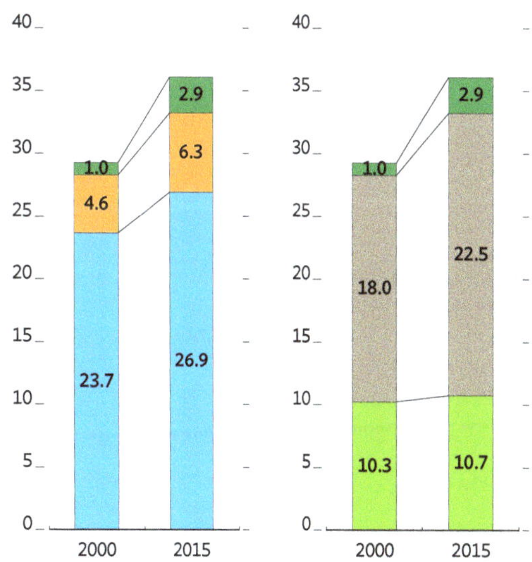

Notes: The right panel shows the number of workers directly and indirectly involved in producing textiles finalized in the PRC. The left panel decomposes this demand for workers by foreign and domestic and by routine and nonroutine task intensity.

Source: ADB estimates using data from the ADB Multiregional Input-Output Database (accessed 20 November 2017); Labor force surveys, various countries; World Input-Output Database—Socioeconomic Accounts (Timmer et al. 2015).

2.2.7 Changes in employment share with technological change and task relocation by occupation type, 2005–2015

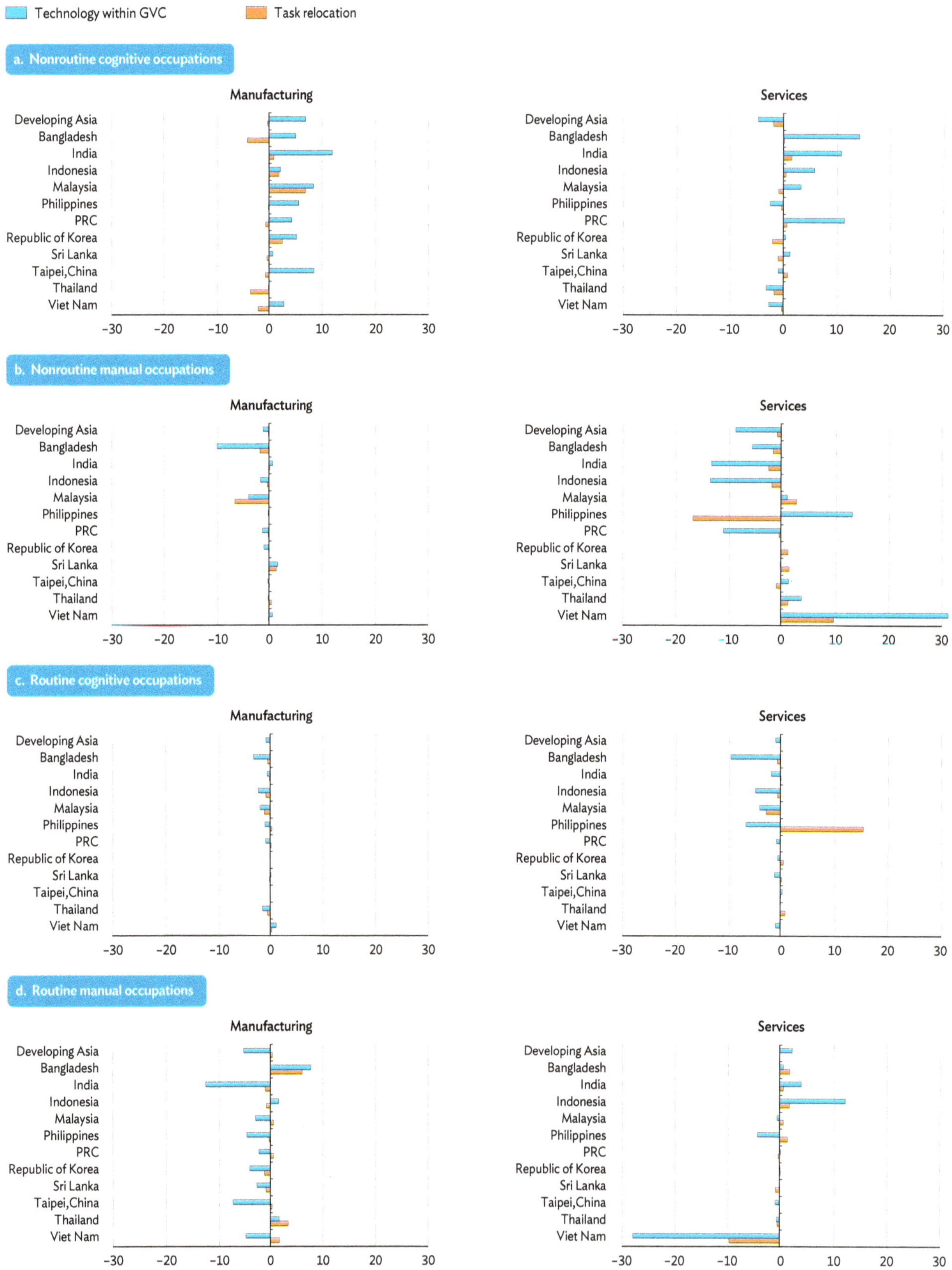

GVC = global value chain, PRC = People's Republic of China.

Note: Developing Asia in the decomposition analysis includes Bangladesh, India, Indonesia, Malaysia, Mongolia, the People's Republic of China, the Philippines, the Republic of Korea, Sri Lanka, Taipei,China, Thailand, and Viet Nam.

Sources: ADB estimates using the ADB Multiregional Input–Output Database (accessed 20 November 2017); Labor force surveys, various countries; World Input–Output Database—Socioeconomic Accounts (Timmer et al. 2015).

Developing economies that have benefited from production tasks offshored from advanced economies are now concerned about reshoring. They fear, in other words, that it could become economically feasible to move those production tasks back to the home market. In an SDA, reshoring would appear as a sizeable decrease in labor demand from task relocation. Indeed, that reshoring did not happen in 2005–2015 does not mean it will not happen in the near future.

To determine how dependent employment in developing Asia is on final demand from advanced economies, the approach adopted in Los, Timmer, and de Vries (2015) is used. Figure 2.2.8 shows the share as well as the total number of jobs servicing final demand in 2015 decomposed into domestic final demand, final demand from advanced economies, and final demand from the rest of the world.

Figure 2.2.8 shows that 82% of employment in the 12 Asian economies depends on domestic final demand, which demonstrates rebalancing away from a growth model led by manufacturing for export to growth led by services and domestic consumption. However, variation across countries has domestic demand in Taipei,China a low 53% and in Viet Nam at 55%, and much higher in Bangladesh at 88% and India at 87%.

About 10% of jobs in the 12 Asian economies service final demand from advanced economies. Taipei,China and Viet Nam are relatively vulnerable to reshoring because they have the highest share of jobs dependent on final demand from advanced economies, at 25% for Taipei,China and 26% for Vietnam. However, bearing in mind that reshoring aims to move production closer to customers and thereby shorten the time required to get a product to market, lower production costs, and improve efficiency, it is noteworthy that consumer markets in advanced economies are increasingly saturated, even as demand from Asia's expanding middle class increases. Figure 2.2.8 shows that, while the share of jobs servicing final demand from the rest of the world is only 7% in the 12 economies as a whole, it is well over 20% in Malaysia; Taipei,China; and Thailand. Markets in the rest of the world have a high potential for growth as well, such that the importance of final demand from advanced countries to employment in developing countries will likely decline over time.

Emergence of new occupations and new industries

One of the less-appreciated channels through which technology affects the labor market is its creation of new occupations and entirely new industries with new jobs. Indeed, from 1980 to 2007, new tasks and job titles and their expansion explained about half of US employment growth (Acemoglu and Restrepo 2017b). Carefully examining growth in occupation titles is one way, however imperfect, to predict which new occupations and industries will emerge in the future.

2.2.8 Job shares servicing foreign and domestic demand, 2015

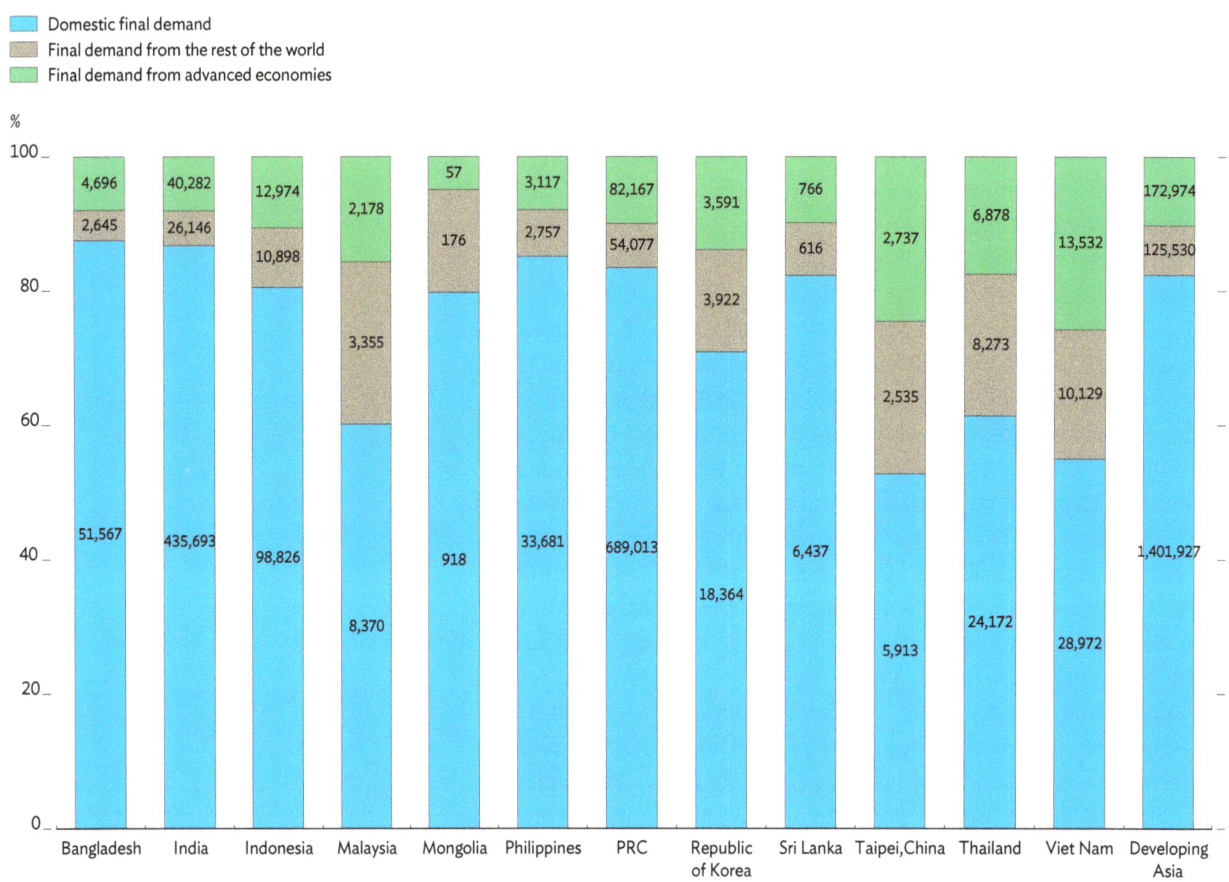

PRC = People's Republic of China.

Note: The advanced economies are Australia, Austria, Belgium, Canada, Denmark, Finland, France, Germany, Greece, Ireland, Italy, Japan, Luxembourg, the Netherlands, Portugal, Spain, Sweden, the United Kingdom, and the United States. For each of the 12 Asian economies in the figure, the rest of the world includes the other 11 as well as other economies at various stages of development. Developing Asia in the decomposition analysis includes Bangladesh, India, Indonesia, Malaysia, Mongolia, the People's Republic of China, the Philippines, the Republic of Korea, Sri Lanka, Taipei,China, Thailand, and Viet Nam.

Numbers indicate jobs (in thousand) servicing foreign and domestic demand in 2015.

Sources: ADB estimates using the ADB Multiregional Input-Output Database (accessed 20 November 2017); Labor force surveys, various countries; World Input-Output Database—Socioeconomic Accounts (Timmer et al. 2015).

Where new jobs have been created is evident in changes in employment share by broad occupation category. In nearly all economies considered, occupations categorized as professional or in services and sales increased (Figure 2.2.9). These two types of occupations are both nonroutine. But professional work is classified as cognitive while services and sales are classified as manual. Across developing Asia, then, nonroutine jobs have increased both in manual and cognitive tasks. On the other hand, the importance of skilled workers in agriculture and related sectors has declined.

A more systematic analysis can track the emergence of new occupations by comparing various waves of a country's national classifications of occupations (NCO). Because classifications are periodically updated and revised, changes in the types of jobs and specializations available in different fields indicate

2.2.9 Annual change in employment share by occupation, selected Asian economies

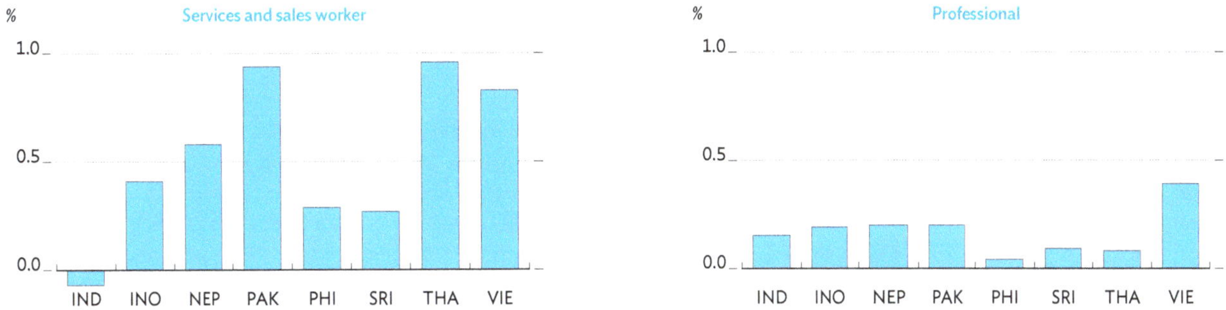

IND = India, INO = Indonesia, NEP = Nepal, PAK = Pakistan, PHI = Philippines, SRI = Sri Lanka, THA = Thailand, VIE = Viet Nam.

Note: India 2000–2012, Indonesia 2000–2014, Nepal 1998–2008, Pakistan 2002–2013, the Philippines 2001–2013, Sri Lanka 2004–2014, Thailand 2000–2010, and Viet Nam 2002–2013.

Source: Labor force surveys, various countries.

structural changes and the emergence of new technologies in the labor market—as when, for example, the proliferation of cable television in India in the 1990s fueled increased demand for cable television installers. Lin (2011), for instance, used "new work," or jobs requiring new combinations of activities (the phrase borrowed from Jacobs [1969]), to observe how US workers and firms adapt to technological change. Successive versions of the US Index of Occupations were compared to identify new job titles and match them with microdata to estimate worker selection into new occupations. Following this approach, the emergence of new occupations can be investigated for several economies in developing Asia that have the necessary data (Box 2.2.6).

Analysis of NCO lists finds the emergence of 60 new job titles out of 2,945 (2.0%) in India in 1968–2004, 120 out of 3,600 (3.3%) in India in 2004–2015, 28 out of 2,338 (1.2%) in Malaysia in 1998–2008, and 42 out of 3,698 (1.14%) in the Philippines in 1990–2012. As in Lin (2011), most new job titles, 43%–57%, are related to ICT. Moreover, as seen from Figure 2.2.10, occupations with the highest proportions of new job titles are mainly nonroutine cognitive. Nearly 40% of job titles under ICT operations and user-support technicians in India were created from 2004 to 2015, and more than 20% in Malaysia from 1998 to 2008.

New job titles are mostly in nonroutine cognitive occupations

In all countries studied, new job titles appear primarily in professional categories (Figure 2.2.11). India presents a particularly interesting case. The 1968–2004 figure shows 93% of all new jobs as professionals, with 36 new job titles, and associate professionals, with 20. A closer look into these two groups reveals that several of the new job titles are mainly engineering and data analyst positions and directly related to the use of personal computers, reflecting

2.2.6 Estimating the emergence of new occupations

As a first step in tracing the emergence of new jobs, an economy's national classification of occupations (NCO) is compared with its preceding version at the most disaggregated level available using an official concordance between the two classifications. Job titles are then identified in the newer NCO that did not exist in the previous one, while controlling for any form of relabeling or reclassification. It is also important to check which International Standard Classification of Occupations the NCO editions are patterned after for two reasons: First, one can identify which technological advances were made during the time studied. Second, one gains insight on what types of new job titles may emerge.

As a second filter and robustness check, the remaining job titles are further compared with the US Index of Occupations. The US Index of Occupations provides occupational titles down to the smallest unit, which means a large number of occupational titles are included. To illustrate, the number of titles listed ranged in 1950–2000 from 25,000 to 31,000 (Lin 2011). The 1950 index lists over 80 titles that contain "engineer" and includes over 10 types of economists with different specializations and functions. The index version used should account for a lag in the emergence of job titles given different stages of development between the country studied and the US. This exercise therefore assumes that job titles in the country at time t is equivalent to the job titles in the US at time $t-n$. For example, the comparison of India's new job titles in NCO 2004 with its previous version in 1968 is cross-checked against the new job titles with the 1950 US Index of Occupations (US at time $t-n$) in the second filtration process. The assumption here is that job titles in India in 1968 are equivalent to job titles in the US in 1950. If the job title in NCO 2004 did not exist in the 1950 US Index of Occupations, it is considered new.

Other indicators of new jobs are used. In some cases, job titles specifying a type of technology not widely used in the previous NCO year are categorized as new. This involves investigating when the technology penetrated the market.[a] For example, managerial positions are generally categorized as old job titles unless the specification entails a new type of technology. Job titles listed as "others," or "not elsewhere classified" but are newly added to the later list are not considered new.

Among the limitations to the technique are measurement error from checking occupation titles manually, the subjective judgment whether a technology was widely used in the previous NCO year, and the use of the US Index of Occupations as proxy for an economy's list of occupations in the previous version. The exercise nevertheless provides insight into the link between the emergence of new types of jobs and new technology in developing Asia. A potential extension of this analysis is to use microdata to check how many individuals in the labor force were actually employed under these new job titles (Lin 2011).

[a] A job title using a technology introduced in 1967 may still be categorized as new if the technology was still not widely used in 1968.

Source: Flaminiano et al., forthcoming.

2.2.10 Occupations with the highest proportion of new job titles, selected Asian economies

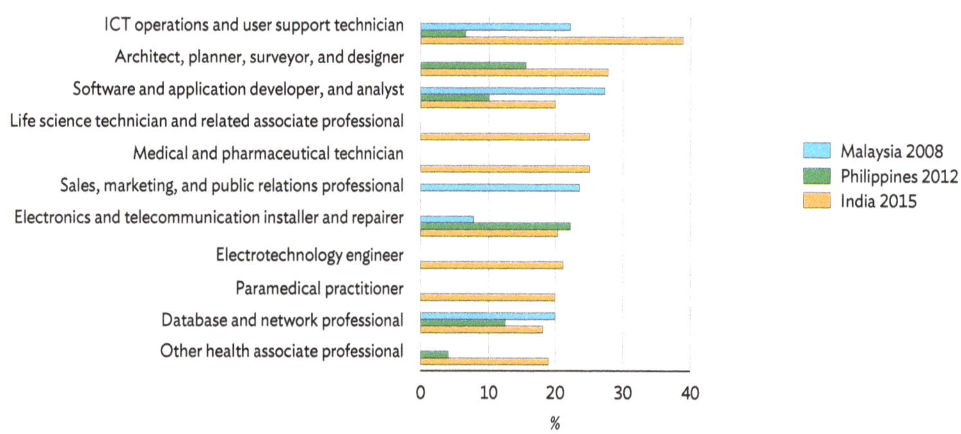

ICT = information and communication technology.

Note: These are occupation groups with the highest proportion of new job titles. Calculations are based on comparisons made between national classification of occupations (NCO) 2004 (based on International Standard Classification of Occupations 1988 [ISCO-88]) and NCO 2015 (ISCO-08) for India, PSOC 1990 (ISCO-88) and PSOC 2012 (ISCO-08) for the Philippines, and MASCO-1998 (ISCO-88) and MASCO-2008 (ISCO-08) for Malaysia. As a robustness check, the 1970 US Index of Occupations was used as proxy for a comprehensive list of occupations in the base year of the economies studied.

Source: Flaminiano et al., forthcoming.

2.2.11 Share of new job titles per broad occupation group

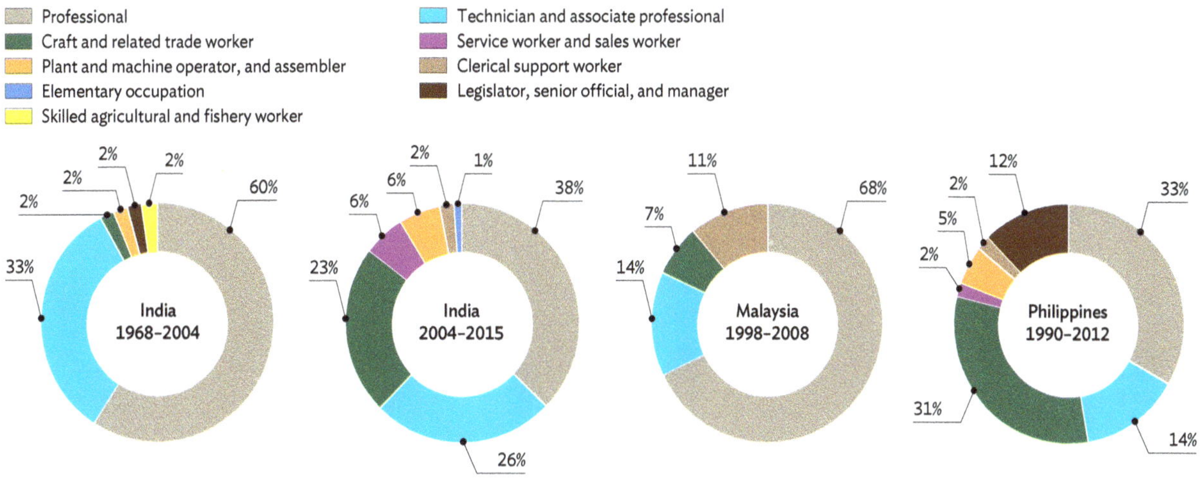

Source: Flaminiano et al., forthcoming.

rapid advances in digital technology in the 1980s: software engineer, system programmer, database design analyst, computer system hardware analyst, computer quality assurance analyst, and computer security specialist, among others. Once again, this resembles findings in Lin (2011) in the US in 1977. By contrast, none of the occupation groups clerks, service and sales workers, and elementary occupations show new job titles, despite employment growing in these occupations. In fact, all three economies show growth in routine cognitive and nonroutine manual employment. For example, in 2004–2015 in India, a third broad occupation group—craft and related trade workers, specifically electrical trade workers, categorized as routine cognitive jobs—hold a significant share of new job titles. Interestingly, the majority of the new job titles in this occupation group are computer numerical control technicians, who are machinists whose jobs entail operating computer-driven machine tools. Examples of job titles are computerized numerical control (CNC) operator machining technician, CNC setter-cum-operator–vertical machining center, CNC programmer, CNC operator–turning. Other new job titles in this occupation group include smartphone repair technician, solar panel installation technician, and optical fiber technician.

Technological progress and economic growth also creating jobs

The growing complexity of life and the modern workplace—the result of technological change and economic growth—will contribute new occupations. A comparison of occupations in the region with those in advanced economies shows great scope for job growth in many sectors. For example, health care and education provide 15% of employment in the US, while finance, insurance, real estate, and other business services provide 19%. In lower- and middle-income economies in developing Asia, health care and education provide only 3.5%–6.0% of jobs, and business services 1.5%–6.0%, suggesting considerable scope for job growth in these services. Similarly, urban parts of developing Asia show much greater variety of occupations than rural parts. As the region urbanizes, many jobs will emerge.

Further, technology will transform some existing occupations. A case in point is informal retail, perhaps the most ubiquitous occupation. In many parts of developing Asia, informal retailers are increasingly using social media platforms to reach many more customers than before (Box 2.2.7).

2.2.7 Informal retail transforming into social commerce

Despite rapid growth in internet use, e-commerce in Southeast Asia remains in its infancy for lack of well-developed digital finance or logistics (Chadha 2016). In Southeast and South Asia, less than a third of companies have their own websites, and only about half use e-mail to communicate with clients and suppliers (ADB 2017b). However, despite small e-commerce markets, developing economies lead the world in social commerce, or unofficial e-commerce using social media.

Social commerce is characterized by online sales and offline payments. It begins on a social media platform, followed by direct communication between buyer and seller, usually using instant messaging apps, and closes using offline payment (Malabuppha 2017). Cash on delivery is widely used (International Trade Center 2017). The popularity of social media turns these venues into cheaper e-commerce platforms than traditional e-commerce. Whereas websites charge commissions, selling on social media is free.

The world's most avid social media shoppers are in Thailand, where 51% of online shoppers report buying on social media, and India at 32% (box figure). Facebook is the preferred platform for selling online in Viet Nam (Asia Pacific Foundation of Canada 2017) and Indonesia (JakPat 2015), and it is widely used in the Philippines (Llamas 2017). Social media sales account for 30% of e-commerce transactions in Southeast Asia (Chadha 2016).

India and Southeast Asia are the largest Facebook and Instagram users globally.[a] Social mobile use is also large and growing. In Southeast Asia, 47% of people are active on social media, with 42% accessing platforms from mobile devices (Klemp 2017).

Social commerce in the region is largely domestic. However, small businesses worldwide are becoming "micro-multinationals" by using digital platforms—including social media—to connect with international customers and suppliers (McKinsey Global Institute 2016). This has created new opportunities for informal retailers. Studies find that small and medium-sized enterprises using e-commerce increase revenues, lower costs, boost profits, add jobs, and are more likely to export and innovate. As digital payment infrastructure and logistics improve, the informal sector will be better able to tap global markets. In an age of digital expansion, the rise of social commerce is making e-commerce a reality for many sellers with few resources or formal skills.

Where online shoppers said they purchased directly through a social media channel

PRC = People's Republic of China.
Source: PricewaterhouseCoopers 2016.

[a] India has the most Facebook users globally at 250 million. Indonesia is fourth with 130 million, the Philippines sixth with 67 million, Viet Nam seventh with 55 million, and Thailand eighth with 51 million. Indonesia ranks third in the world for Instagram users at 53 million, and India fourth with 52 million (Statista 2018).

Some worker concerns remain

So far this chapter has categorized occupations mainly as requiring tasks that are either routine or not, and manual or cognitive. This section considers a more disaggregated classification of tasks. In addition, the degree to which an occupation is intensive in these various tasks is explicitly quantified to further refine the analysis of the impact of new technology on employment and wages. Analysis of India, Indonesia, the Philippines, Thailand, and Viet Nam shows the employment structure in the region shifting toward jobs intensive in nonroutine cognitive, social interaction, and ICT tasks. These tasks generally complement technological progress and may not be readily automated. They tend to require more education and/or relatively advanced training. At the same time, the labor market is moving away from jobs intensive in manual tasks, which tend to require skills that workers with basic education can acquire. Such jobs are more likely to be replaced by machines. The magnitude of these changes in the past decade or so is sizable, and the trend will likely persist. The major challenge for Asian economies is to cope with this structural transformation in the nature of jobs. If Asia's workers are not given the skills in demand—particularly to fill jobs intensive in nonroutine and cognitive tasks—they may be left behind. Incomes for the few with the required skills will rise, exacerbating inequality.

Trends in employment and wages by task intensity in the region

Five indicators here describe the intensity with which workers are required to perform various types of tasks. Four of them pertain to nonroutine cognitive, social interactive, routine cognitive, and manual tasks.[8] A fifth indicator, for ICT tasks, describes computer use at work to capture jobs intensive in tasks that may directly complement new technologies. The methodology used to construct these indicators is presented in Box 2.3.1. Task intensity can be measured, making it possible to examine the task-biased technical change hypothesis: Technological progress and information technology (IT) will likely displace jobs consisting of mainly routine and manual tasks while increasing demand for jobs that involve a lot of abstract and complex cognitive tasks. Occupations and industries in which workers are frequently required to provide advice, teach, or negotiate, among other tasks, score high in social interaction, while high scores in the complex or nonroutine cognitive indicator indicate high intensity in tasks such as writing, using advanced mathematics, or solving complex problems.

2.3.1 Constructing task intensity indicators

Constructing a set of indicators that account for task intensity by occupation and industry requires an appropriate methodology. The indicators are constructed using publicly available country surveys conducted in the 27 OECD member and partner countries (OECD 2013a, 2016a).

Besides background information on education, industry, occupation, sex, and age, the surveys gather information from workers on the requirements of their jobs. Requirements include cognitive skills that encompass reading, writing, mathematics, and the use of information and communication technology (ICT). Questions extend to interaction and social skills, covering collaboration and cooperation, planning, time use for oneself and others, communication, and negotiation. Subjects are asked about physical motor skills, both gross and fine. In addition, they are asked about the frequency and intensity of various tasks their jobs require. There are more than 50 questions on job requirements in the survey. Most questions are coded on a scale from 1 to 5, with greater values indicating greater frequency and/or intensity of the task required at work. Following previous studies on the polarization of employment and given the information provided in Program for the International Assessment of Adult Competencies (PIAAC) surveys, the tasks are grouped into five categories (box table).

Step 1. Assigning survey questions to categories
First, questions in the PIAAC survey providing information pertaining to the five task categories were identified. Principal component analysis determined the extent to which questions from the survey conveyed similar information and was used to compute a summary indicator for each category.

Step 2. Constructing indicators by occupation and industry cell
To account for diverging stages of development in countries in the PIAAC survey, and to ensure robust indicators of country-specific characteristics, the final indicators were obtained from regressions that controlled for country fixed effects. For each of the five task categories, workers' summary indicator of intensity (cat) was regressed on a set of dummy variables accounting for the worker occupation and industry (occ_ind) and a set of country dummies (c) as follows:

$$cat_i = \alpha + \sum_i \gamma_j occ\_ind_{ij} + \sum_k \delta_k c_{ik} + \varepsilon_i, \quad (1)$$

where i denotes workers, j the occupation-industry combinations, and k countries. The coefficients on the occupation-industry dummies (γ) can be thought of as a rank that measures the task intensity of an occupation-industry combination after controlling for country-specific characteristics. The industries and occupations covered are based on 1-digit ISIC Rev. 4 classification and 2-digit ISCO-08 classification, respectively. To reduce distortion from changes in national classifications in the region over time, as well as those arising from the harmonization with international classification standards, steps 1 and 2 were also conducted using the 2-digit ISCO-88 classification for occupations.

Categories of tasks within occupations and industries

Category	Interpretation	Examples of specific tasks
1. Social interaction and influencing	Frequency of nonroutine interactive tasks	Influencing and advising other people, teaching, giving speeches or presentations, negotiating with people inside and outside of firm, planning the activities of others
2. Cognitive nonroutine	Frequency of nonroutine cognitive tasks	Writing letters, emails, or articles in newspapers, magazines, or newsletters; preparing charts, graphs, or tables; using advanced math or statistics such as complex algebra, trigonometry, or regression analysis; solving complex problems
3. Cognitive routine	Frequency of routine cognitive tasks	Calculating prices, costs, or budgets; using or calculating fractions, decimals, or percentages; using a calculator or spreadsheet software
4. Manual	Frequency of manual tasks	Relying on hand or finger dexterity (methodology and data do not allow manual tasks to be disaggregated into routine and nonroutine)
5. ICT	Use of ICT at work	Ranging from no ICT use to performing complex tasks such as programming

ICT = information and communication technology.

continued next page

2.3.1 *Continued*

Step 3. Merging task intensity indicators with Asian labor force surveys

Information was gathered on employment and wages in India, Indonesia, the Philippines, Thailand, and Viet Nam using country labor force surveys at two points in time. The time frames vary across countries, with Viet Nam the shortest (2007–2015), followed by Thailand (2000–2010), India (2000–2012), the Philippines (2001–2013), and Indonesia (2000–2014). The indicators obtained in step 2 were merged with country data based on worker occupation and industry.

Step 4. Constructing employment and wage trends for high- and low-intensive tasks

For each country and task category, the employment-weighted mean of the intensity indicator at the beginning of the sample was calculated separately for wage employees and all workers (i.e., wage employees and the self-employed). Occupations and industries whose task intensity fell below the weighted mean were classified as low and those above the mean as high. Changes in employment and wages in high-intensive occupations and industries were compared with low-intensive ones.

Step 5. Comparing the distribution of employment by intensity of tasks across countries

In the previous step, the country's weighted mean was used as a threshold to classify occupations and industries into low- and high-intensive. For illustrating trends over time within countries, this is the preferred threshold because it best describes employment and wage trends representative of the mean worker in each country. However, this country-specific threshold cannot be used when comparing employment distribution by task intensity across countries. As such, for comparison with OECD countries and across Asian economies, the simple average for each type of task was used as a threshold. For example, occupations and industries whose ICT intensity is above the simple mean of the ICT indicator are classified as high and those below as low.

Source: Khatiwada, Lennon, and Zilian, forthcoming.

These two indicators are used to characterize jobs intensive in nonroutine tasks. To describe jobs intensive in routine cognitive tasks, information is obtained on the frequency with which workers are required to use simple arithmetic, for example, in calculating prices and costs. Jobs that require a lot of use of hands or fingers are considered intensive in manual tasks. Finally, information on ICT use provides the basis for determining the intensity of ICT tasks of jobs. With these indicators, jobs in the economies considered can be classified in terms of whether they are high-intensive or low-intensive with respective to the five task categories. These classifications are used to reveal employment and wage trends over time.

For both wage employees and all workers, jobs that are intensive in cognitive, social interaction, and ICT tasks have expanded faster than jobs that are less intensive (Figure 2.3.1a). In fact, in some countries—Indonesia, Thailand, and Viet Nam, for example—jobs less intensive in these categories have contracted. The only exception is the Philippines, where jobs intensive in nonroutine cognitive tasks expanded at a slower pace than their counterparts. This coincided with growth in employment in other categories, including jobs intensive in routine cognitive tasks, a category that includes many types of jobs in IT-business process outsourcing—the call center jobs that provided much of the growth of employment in the sector, which expanded from less than 100,000 jobs in 2004 to almost 1 million in 2013. However, this may change as this large industry shifts toward more nonroutine cognitive tasks (Box 2.3.2).

The opposite occurred for jobs intensive in manual tasks. Low-intensive manual jobs expanded faster than high-intensive ones. Moreover, employment in high-intensive manual jobs has contracted in Indonesia, Thailand, and, to a lesser extent, India.

2.3.1 Annual employment growth by task intensity

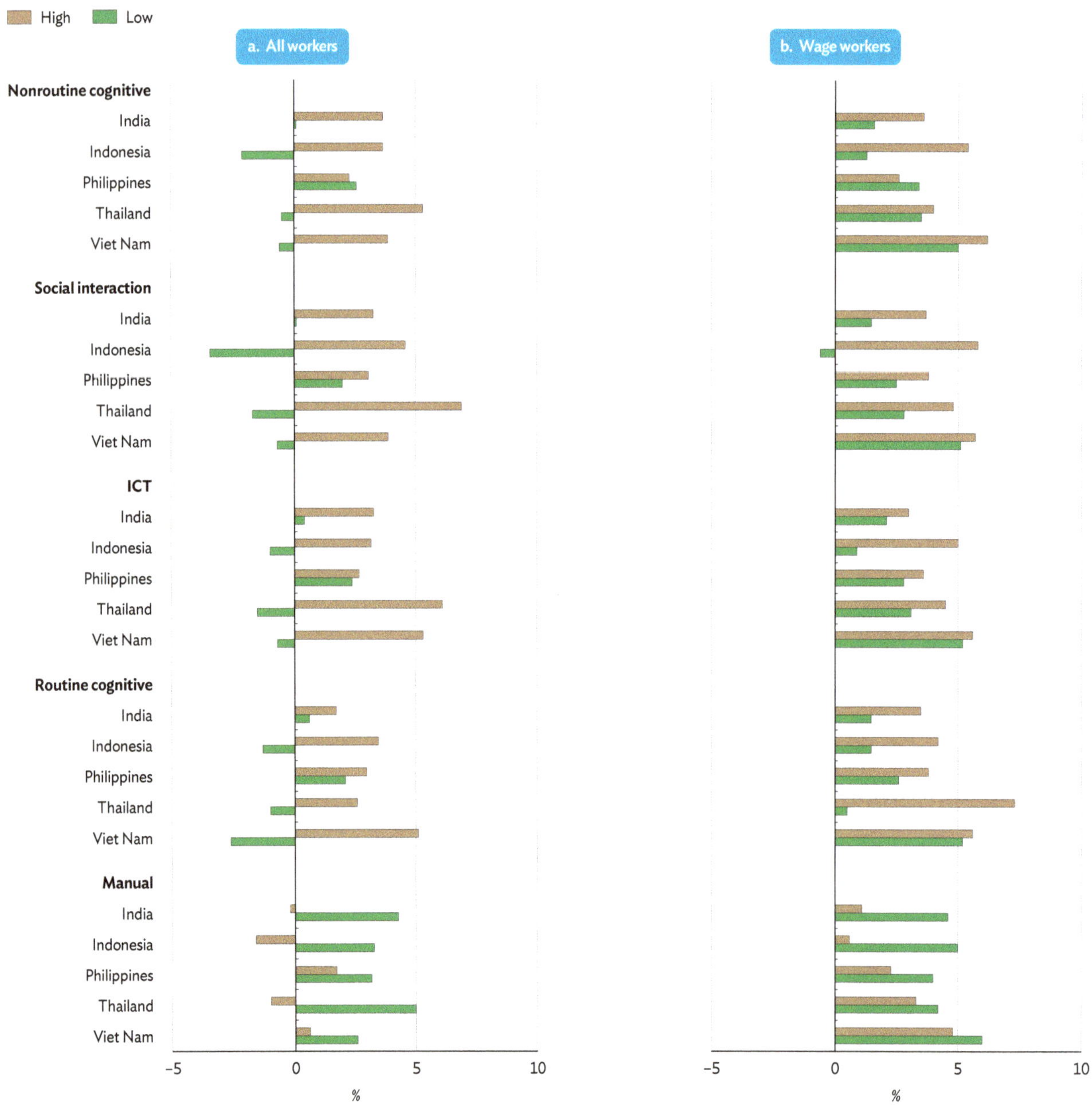

ICT = information and communication technology.

Note: Jobs are classified in terms of whether they are high-intensive or low-intensive with respective to the five task categories. These figures use employment estimates for workers aged 15 and above.

Source: Khatiwada, Lennon, and Zilian, forthcoming.

2.3.2 Business process outsourcing in the Philippines

Business process outsourcing (BPO) grew out of increased connectivity as information technology (IT) and other advances created business opportunities for those able to deliver customer service at reduced cost. Estimates give the Philippines 13% of global BPO market share.

In 2013, BPO provided 20% of Philippine exports, 6% of GDP, and 4.2% of wage employment.[a] More recent industry estimates from 2016 put IT-BPO revenue at $22.9 billion, equal to 7.5% of GDP. With formal job creation low in the Philippines, BPO is an attractive option for young graduates. Clerical support dominates BPO jobs, and education and skills requirements vary across the industry. A 2016 labor force survey shows 62% of IT-BPO jobs in clerical support. Nearly 85% of call center workers are either college students or high school graduates, while only 13% have earned college degrees. By contrast, animation BPOs, which require more technical or advanced skills, fill 72% of their entry positions with college graduates. Similarly, college graduates fill 68% of entry positions in medical transcription and 55% in computer-related activities such as software development.

Service delivery automation, in particular robotic process automation, will transform BPO, affecting job creation. Technologies such as artificial intelligence, big data analytics, and cloud computing will alter the type of workers employed, the wages they earn, and the services they deliver to overseas clients. However, even the most pessimistic projections of employment growth show steady increases in IT-BPO job creation in the Philippines. As industry leaders reported at the IT-Business Process Management Summit in Manila in November 2017, demand from North America, Europe, and Australia will continue to fuel employment growth in the industry, as will demand from within Asia and the Pacific as these economies get richer.

The Information Technology and Business Process Association of the Philippines says the share of low-skilled BPO workers will decline from 47% in 2016 to 27% in 2022. Medium-skill occupations will increase from 38% to 46% in 2016, and high-skill occupations from 15% to 46% (box figure).

One of the proposals presented by IT-BPO leaders is a skills-development fund to train IT-BPO workers in new technology and familiarize them with automated service-delivery models. Industry leaders believe the government should contribute to the fund to provide incentives for firms to upskill and reskill. Further, as most BPO workers are university students or graduates, industry leaders believe that educational streams must better align with industry needs. Given growth in computer-related BPO, it is imperative that university education in computer and IT-related majors align with industry needs.

[a] This is from official statistics provided by Bangko Sentral ng Pilipinas and the Philippine Statistics Authority. Reference years for data vary depending on information source. From these two sources, the most recent year is 2013. When data are from labor force surveys, or official sources on labor market data, the latest is 2016. The Information Technology and Business Process Association of the Philippines provides 2016 data based on industry estimates.

Skills composition of the workforce as IT-BPO adjusts to automation

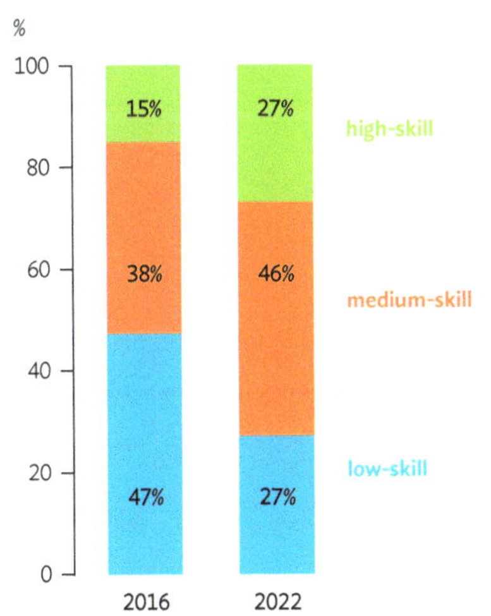

	Tasks	Jobs
high-skill	Complicated tasks that require specialized expertise, abstract thinking, and autonomy	Computer programmer, computer engineer, health professional (nurse), financial expert, design professional
medium-skill	Complicated tasks that require experience, abstract thinking, and situational response	Accounting and bookkeeping clerk, computer assistant (animation, data analysis, digital production), health assistant
low-skill	Simple entry-level, process-driven tasks that require little abstract thinking and autonomy	Customer support clerk, data entry assistant, medical transcriptionist

IT-BPO = information technology-business process outsourcing.

Source: ADB using estimates from the Information Technology and Business Process Association of the Philippines.

Considering only wage employees, the data show a similar but less pronounced pattern (Figure 2.3.1b). The growth difference between jobs with high and low task intensity means that employment is shifting toward occupations and industries requiring high cognitive, social, and ICT task intensity. This is consistent with relatively slow growth in demand for manual work and for work not intensive in the use of congnitive, social, and ICT skills.

In some countries, the shift in employment across job types has been substantial. From 2000 to 2014, more than 25% of Indonesian workers shifted into jobs intensive in social interaction, 20% migrated to high-intensive jobs in nonroutine cognitive tasks, and 17% moved away from high-intensive manual jobs. Similarly in Thailand, 18% of those employed shifted into high-intensive ICT jobs within just 10 years.

To properly compare the speed of these changes across economies, the growth rate of the share of jobs with high intensity across task types is annualized, which is much like comparing employment growth in these jobs with growth in total employment (Figure 2.3.2). The speed of change varies by the type of task and worker. The categories nonroutine cognitive, social interaction, and ICT show that changes are occurring faster in higher-income Asian economies considered here. Thailand stands out when both wage and self-employed workers are considered, for example, and Indonesia for wage workers alone. In particular, Thai growth in employment in high-intensive jobs in these three categories has outpaced that of total employment by 4.7 percentage points on average. Less dramatic shifts have occurred in the Philippines and Viet Nam. However, the mean speed of change is considerable. Each year, growth in Asian employment in jobs intensive in ICT, social interaction, and nonroutine cognitive tasks is on average 2.6 percentage points faster than overall employment.

How have wages evolved across job types? This information is presented in Figure 2.3.3 using average wages in constant local currency. In most countries, wage gains were larger for jobs intensive in cognitive, social interaction, and ICT tasks than for those less intensive. By contrast, jobs intensive in manual tasks experienced lower increases in wages. This pattern is particularly pronounced in economies with relatively large shifts in employment from low- to high-intensive cognitive, social interaction, and ICT jobs and from high- to low-intensive manual jobs, like Indonesia and Thailand. The Philippines is an outlier, as the trends in average wages are reversed there, except for nonroutine cognitive tasks.

2.3.2 Deviation of high-intensive job growth from all employment growth

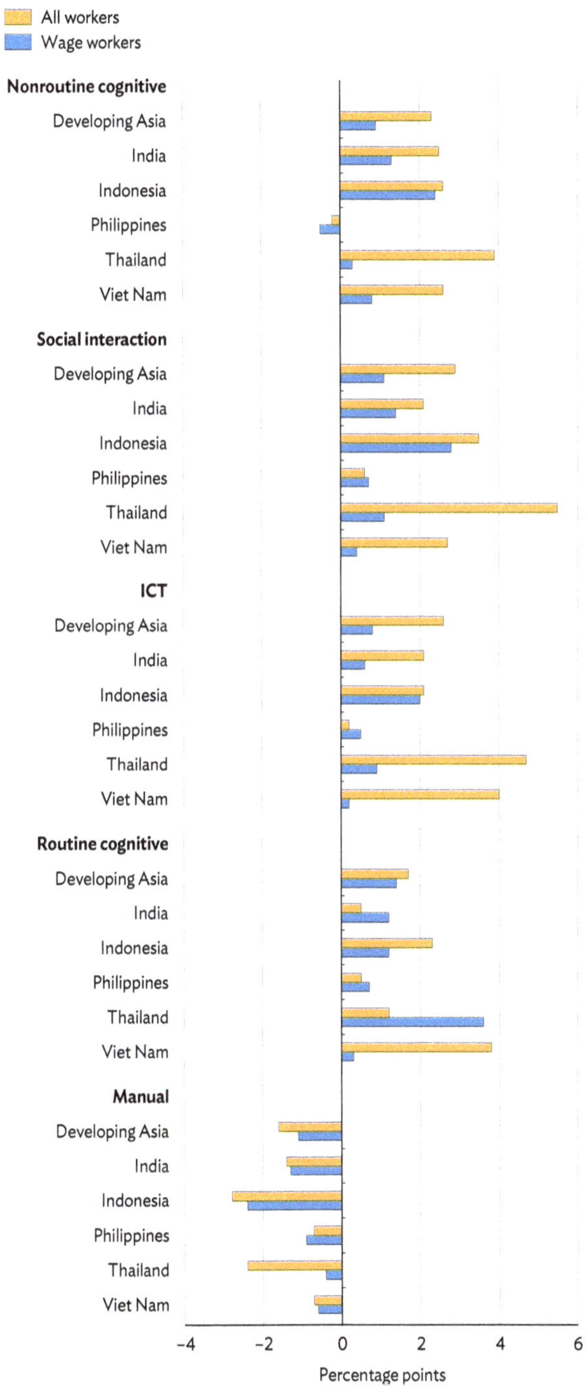

ICT = information and communication technology.

Note: Developing Asia here comprises five economies: India, Indonesia, the Philippines, Thailand, and Viet Nam. Employment estimates are for workers aged 15 and above.

Source: Khatiwada, Lennon, and Zilian, forthcoming.

2.3.3 Change in average wages by task intensity

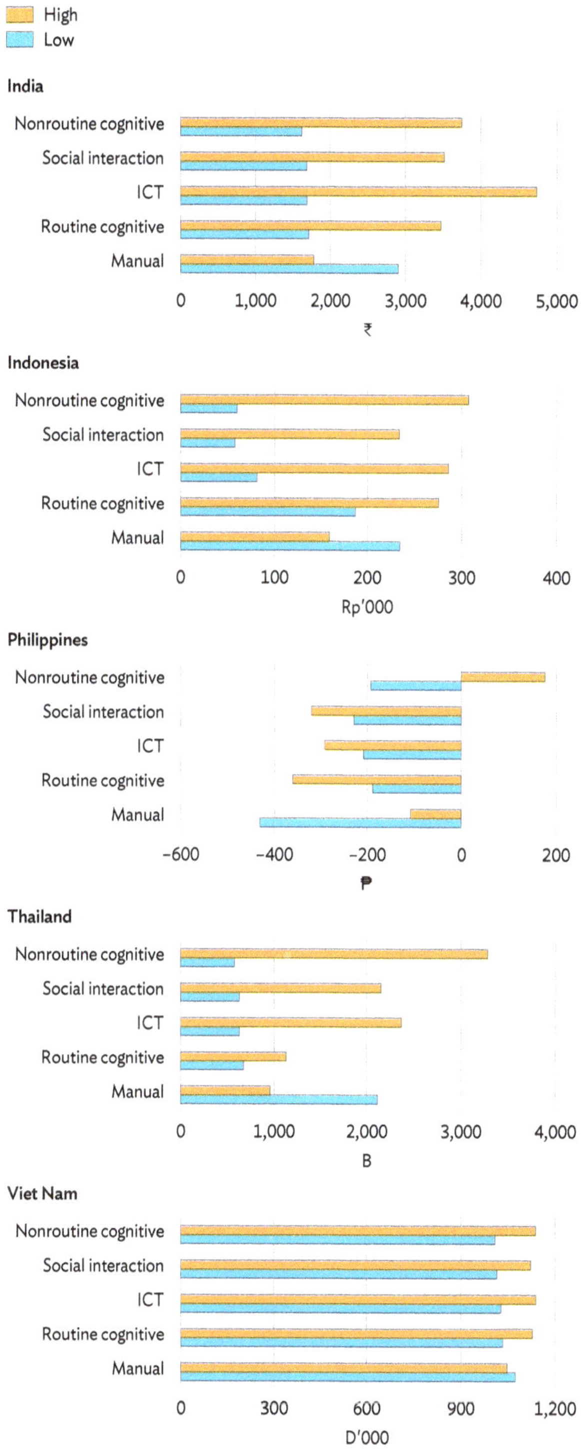

Note: Wage estimates by task intensity for wage workers aged 15 and above. Data on monthly wages in local currency are drawn from each country's labor force survey, deflated using national GDP deflators from World Development Indicators. Changes in average wages are over the entire period of analysis: India 2000–2012, Indonesia 2000–2014, Philippines 2001–2013, Thailand 2000–2010, and Viet Nam 2007–2015.

Source: Khatiwada, Lennon, and Zilian, forthcoming.

Analysis thus far has shown substantial differences in employment and wage trends by task intensity indicator.

Employment in the region is shifting toward jobs intensive in nonroutine tasks and toward jobs that complement new technologies. Further, jobs intensive in nonroutine and ICT tasks see faster growth in wages than do jobs intensive in manual tasks. Interesting differences surface between wages in newly created occupations and existing ones (Box 2.3.3). Employment and wage trends strongly suggest that demand is rising for jobs intensive in nonroutine cognitive, social interaction, and ICT tasks relative to demand for manual intensive jobs.

Findings for routine cognitive jobs are perhaps the most surprising in view of the task-biased technical change hypothesis. Rather than contracting as predicted by the hypothesis, demand for routine cognitive jobs is still expanding in the region. One of the reasons behind this continuing expansion may be that these jobs occupy a smaller share of employment in developing Asia than in the developed world. Further, new technology has opened opportunities for workers that are outside of formal employment. Indeed, even among the low-paid and low-skill workers in the informal economy, there are examples where digital technology in particular has allowed productivity and wages to rise in Asia (Box 2.3.4).

2.3.3 Wage differentials between new and old occupations

Studies have shown that new occupations, particularly in new technology industries, tend to pay better than existing ones. Matching identified new job titles with microdata to estimate worker selection into new occupations in the US, Lin (2011) found that better-educated workers are likely to be found in newly created jobs and that these workers earn higher wages than similar workers in older jobs. Wage data by occupation title in Asia was used to study the difference in wages between new and old work.

A survey of business process outsourcing conducted in the Philippines in 2013 found a wage differential in favor of software developers (Bangko Sentral ng Pilipinas 2013). Software developers were the highest-paid employees, with an average annual wage of $18,453, or 6.2% above their average wage in the previous year. Computer programmers were the fifth-highest paid occupation in the Philippines, according to a survey in 2016 (Philippine Statistics Authority 2017). The survey also found that middle- and low-skilled workers in ICT and professional, scientific, and technical activities (PSTA) received wages above average. The average monthly wage of low-skilled workers was highest in these two industries, at ₱13,010 for ICT and ₱12,923 for PSTA, which compared with a low-skilled average monthly wage of ₱10,162 across all industries.

Meanwhile, software developers and programmers in Sri Lanka and Viet Nam earn higher average wages than other ICT professionals. In Sri Lanka, software developers and application programmers earn an average monthly wage of SLRs56,536, more than twice the average monthly wage of SLRs23,333 for database and network professionals or SLRs25,000 for web and multimedia developers. Likewise in Viet Nam, software developers are the highest-paid professionals in ICT, earning average monthly wages of D8,520,000, compared with, for example, D6,297,000 for web and multimedia developers.

2.3.4 Informal jobs, the promise of new technology, and Indonesia's Go-Jek

Informal work remains a prominent fixture across developing Asia, ranging from 33% of nonfarm employment in the PRC to 87% in Bangladesh. The median is over 70% in the 10 economies in developing Asia with data. Informal workers earn less than formal workers, their income only 20% of what formal workers make in Bangladesh and 64% in Pakistan (box figure 1). In eight countries with available data, the median informal worker wage is half that of formal workers.

Informal work is often a fallback when formal job opportunities are lacking. Registered firms tend to be larger and more productive, pay higher wages, and serve larger and wealthier markets. Either the formal economy needs to expand to absorb informal workers, or informal productivity needs to rise. The rise of the digital economy seems to be contributing on both fronts and is beginning to affect GDP. In Southeast Asia, for example, the internet economy provided 2% of regional GDP and is growing rapidly (Anandan et al. 2017). Since 2015, ride-hailing has had a compounded annual growth rate of 43%, e-commerce 41%, and online media 36%. Ride-hailing in Indonesia is fiercely contested between international companies like Uber, regionals like Grab, and locals like Go-Jek, Indonesia's informal motorbike service. Go-Jek revolutionized Jakarta's informal transport sector after its January 2015 launch.

Go-Jek is a play on English "go" and Indonesian "*ojek*," or motorcycle taxi, a popular option in notoriously gridlocked Jakarta. With *ojek* drivers spending much of their time waiting for customers, they were not very productive (Ford and Honan 2017). Enter Go-Jek, which supplied *ojek* drivers with a ride-hailing app instantly connecting them to customers. Go-Jek uses global positioning to instantly match passengers to the nearest driver. This allows drivers to serve more customers and waste less time. Passengers are far more satisfied, and drivers get better daily pay, even though Go-Jek drivers' fares can be less than a third of what others charge.

Go-Jek drivers have expanded services to package and food delivery, further boosting earnings (box figure 2). Go-Jek links its drivers increasingly to middle-class customers, whose preference for ride-hailing apps gives them a distinct advantage. But greater connectivity and, hence, productivity require some capital investment. Go-Jek drivers receive credit to purchase smartphones and training in how to use them. The investment pays off for many

1 Informal–formal wage ratio, various years

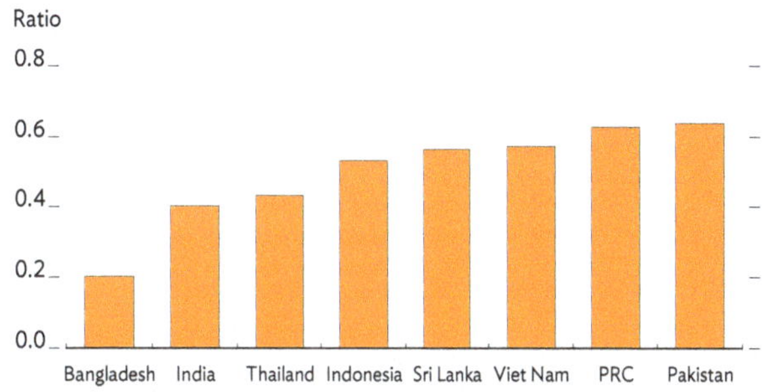

Notes: Indonesian figures use wages in Yogyakarta and Banten.

Sources: ADB and BPS 2011; Chen and Hamori 2011; Dasgupta, Bhula-or, and Fakthong 2015; Gunatilaka 2008; Irfan 2008; Maligalig, Cuevas, and Rosario 2009; Nguyen 2013; Unni 2005.

2 Ride hailing in Southeast Asia

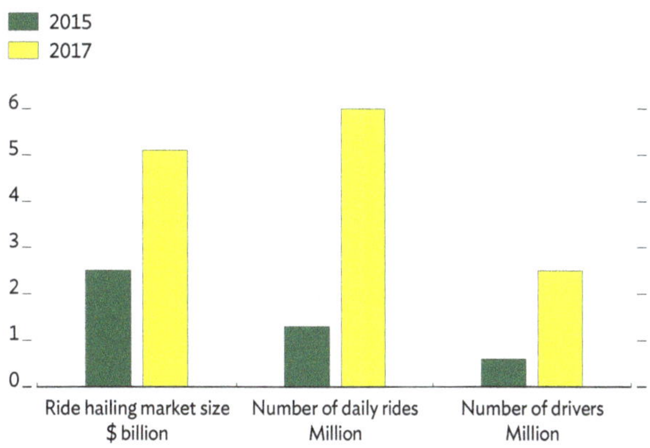

Source: Anandan et al. 2017.

Go-Jek drivers, who can earn 3 times or more than conventional *ojek* drivers and several times above their old income, either as offline *ojek* drivers or in other informal jobs, or even in some formal employment (Fanggidae, Sagala, and Ningrum 2016).[a] Go-Jek (2017) said its drivers' monthly income increased by 15% since August 2016.

[a] Go-Jek drivers make at least Rp150,000 per day, while regular drivers earn Rp50,000–Rp100,000 per day (Ford and Honan 2017). A certain female Go-Jek driver earns 12 times her pay in a previous job as department store sales promoter. A GrabBike driver earns 10 times more than in his former construction job (Yap 2016).

Comparing employment distribution in the region with developed economies

The distribution of employment by task intensity in the region can be compared with the distribution in developed countries. The latter is generated using data from the Program for the International Assessment of Adult Competencies Surveys (OECD 2013a, 2016a) that cover mainly of OECD economies (Figure 2.3.4). As may be expected, economies in Asia and the Pacific have far greater employment shares in manual-intensive jobs and much lower shares in ICT-intensive jobs. If Asia and the Pacific were to have an employment distribution similar to that in OECD countries in nonroutine cognitive, ICT, and manual jobs, some 160 million jobs would have to be transformed in terms of their task structure. To make Indonesian employment structure, for example, look like that of a developed economy, as many as 25% of Indonesian workers would need to migrate to high-intensive jobs in ICT and nonroutine cognitive tasks, and about 20% of workers would need to migrate away from manual-intensive jobs.

While the evolution of Asia's employment structure is unlikely to mirror exactly that of the advanced economies, the broad trends will surely increase employment requiring proficiency in nonroutine cognitive and ICT tasks and remove opportunities in intensive manual work. Indeed, in Indonesia, Thailand, and Viet Nam, jobs less intensive in ICT and nonroutine cognitive tasks, and jobs intensive in manual tasks, are already disappearing.

This has important implications for policy. Not surprisingly, workers in jobs intensive in nonroutine and ICT tasks in particular have high educational attainment. For instance, the average wage worker in high-intensity nonroutine cognitive jobs has completed either secondary school or a short tertiary program, while the average wage worker in a job with low intensity for these tasks will likely have completed only primary education. In addition, wages for jobs intensive in cognitive, social interaction, and ICT tasks are more than twice as high as wages for corresponding low-intensity jobs. Further, wages for jobs with low intensity for manual tasks are 1.8 times higher than those with high intensity for manual tasks.

2.3.4 Difference from OECD in employment distribution by task intensity

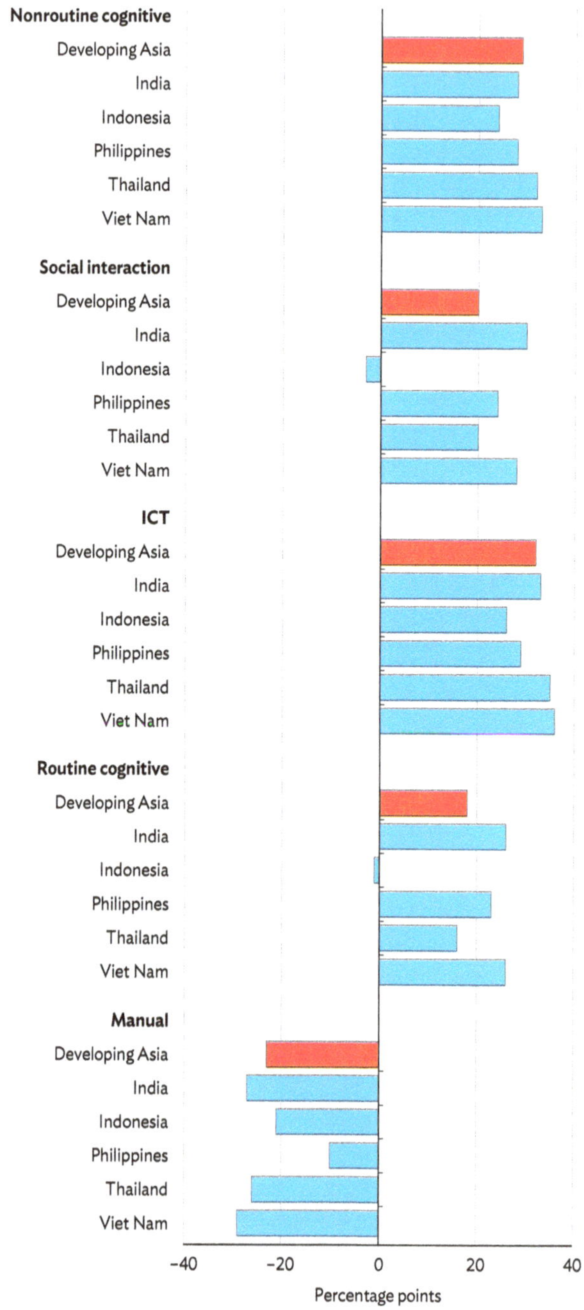

ICT = information and communication technology, OECD = Organisation for Economic Co-operation and Development.

Note: Differences in employment distribution are calculated by task category as the share of high-intensive jobs in the OECD minus the share of high-intensive jobs in developing Asia, here comprising five economies: India, Indonesia, the Philippines, Thailand, and Viet Nam. This figure describes how distant the region's employment distribution by task intensity is with respect to the OECD average. Employment shares for Asian economies are from the last year available: 2010 for Thailand, 2012 for India, 2013 for the Philippines, 2014 for Indonesia, and 2015 for Viet Nam. Employment shares for the OECD are from 2011/2012.

Source: Khatiwada, Lennon, and Zilian, forthcoming.

Thus, even as new technology creates jobs, workers engaged in manual work without the skills to carry out nonroutine cognitive tasks or work with emerging technologies are unlikely to be able to seize opportunities as they arise. In other words, new jobs will appear, but they will require skills that many workers do not possess. Workers who carry out mainly routine and manual tasks will likely experience lower wage growth and worsening income inequality. Further, as firms and industries adjust to new ways of producing and distributing goods and services, the resulting disruptions along supply chains may cause unemployment. As discussed in the next section, tackling this downside of new technology will require coordinated action on skills development, labor regulation, social protection, and income redistribution.

The role of government in harnessing technology for workers

While new technology remains central to creating productive jobs, there are some concerns from a worker's perspective. The previous section showed that job prospects for occupations intensive in cognitive, social interaction, and ICT tasks will likely expand, while those intensive in manual tasks will likely shrink. Given the smaller supply of workers proficient in cognitive, social interaction, and ICT tasks, it is not surprising that wage increases have been higher in these occupations. If the trend persists, inequality in the region will continue to deepen (ADB 2012). The worst case would see the wages of less-skilled workers hardly increase at all, which is what happened in the developed economies of today during the first industrial revolution. Then, the average wage of workers barely increased over several decades despite a dramatic increase in labor productivity in manufacturing (Bessen 2015).[9]

The other major issue is labor displacement. Disruption affecting particular types of occupations, industries, and firms will render some of their workers unemployed, unless and until they acquire the skills needed for emerging occupations and industries. The process is neither easy nor cheap.

This section presents various options on how policy makers can deal with these issues. First, education and skills development systems will need to equip Asian workers with the skills required to fill the jobs generated by new technologies. Second, labor regulations and social protection systems must be designed to protect worker incomes, even as firms retain flexibility to adjust workplace practices and job numbers as economic conditions change. Finally, policy on taxes and expenditure will need to ensure sufficient resources for education and skills development and for social protection, and they should bring about more equitable income distribution.

Education and skills development

Despite tremendous progress in expanding access to education, skills gaps remain a concern across developing Asia. More than 100 million children of primary and secondary school age are not in school, and many more leave school without basic literacy and numeracy. This has ripple effects on their employment prospects and widens skills gaps in the labor market. In 2016, 46% of employers in Asia and the Pacific reported difficulty in filling vacancies for skilled positions (ManpowerGroup 2016).

Asymmetric information aggravates skills gaps and mismatches. Educational curricula often misalign with labor market needs, while education and training programs are typically slow to adapt to changes in skills demand. Although workers may want to acquire new skills, they often do not know what skills employers want or their own employment or earnings prospects. Employers, for their part, consider training a risky investment because newly trained employees may leave the company, perhaps leveraging their newly acquired skills. This creates a vicious cycle of employers looking to hire those already with the needed skills while jobseekers do not know the skills they need and have no opportunity to learn them on the job.

Even when individuals have the right skillsets for certain types of jobs, they may struggle to connect with the right employer. Progress is being made in matching jobseekers with potential employers thanks to the diffusion of recruitment portals. No longer relying solely on personal networks, jobseekers can now learn about hundreds of vacancies and their skills requirements. So far, these portals benefit mainly urban mid- to high-skilled workers, but they are expanding rapidly. In Indonesia, for example, the networking platform LinkedIn doubled its users from 4 million to 8 million between 2015 and 2017, with 70% of new users in the 25–44 age group.

The big challenge facing Asia and the Pacific today is to improve learning outcomes and to prepare for a structural transformation of the economy and the workplace. The good news is that technology, having contributed to the problem, can offer solutions.

Foundational skills in a technology-driven economy

A technology-driven economy makes it more important than ever to learn how to relearn. Solid foundational skills continue to be a crucial prerequisite to further learning. Traditionally, foundational skills included basic reading, writing, and numeracy, but they have grown to encompass two more categories: social and emotional skills, and digital literacy (Figure 2.4.1). These skills build on each other to promote further learning (Acosta et al. 2017, Durlak et al. 2011, OECD 2013b). High social and emotional skills are associated with better reading, writing, and numeracy skills, for example, and solid reading, writing, and numeracy skills are prerequisite for digital literacy.

Digital literacy is fast becoming indispensable for such everyday functions as digital finance and e-government, as well as further education and lifelong learning. It includes not only the ability to use digital devices and platforms, but also knowing how to use them appropriately. The importance of using digital tools intelligently is often overlooked, as many

2.4.1 Skills in a technology-driven economy

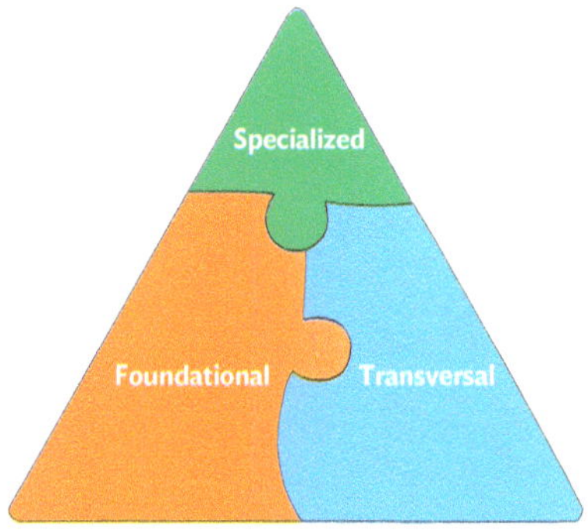

Specialized

- Acquired through TVET, higher education, and lifelong learning
- Relate to a specific job, task, academic discipline, or knowledge area
- Can depreciate with technological change and/or lack of practice, so need regular upgrading

Transversal

- Acquired through education and life experience
- Include a range of skills, from critical thinking to creativity and interpersonal skills such as communication skills
- Are transferable across occupations and sectors

Foundational

- Acquired through basic education
- Include reading, writing, numeracy, socio-emotional skills, and digital literacy
- Are a stepping stone to further education and full participation in society

TVET = technical and vocational education and training.
Source: Adapted from UNESCO (2014).

training courses focus exclusively on the mechanics of using a device or specific software. However, learning how to do research—to make sense of and analyze digital content—is now as essential as basic reading and writing skills (OECD 2016b).

Beyond hardware, two elements are fundamental to successful digital literacy programs (World Bank 2016). First, such programs are more effective when embedded in mainstream learning. Standalone programs are less effective because they do not contextualize the use of technology. This requires adapting curricula and learning materials for traditional subjects to integrate digital technologies. Second, teachers must train to adapt pedagogical practices and understand how to use digital technologies to support learning. Many programs have failed because they focused on hardware use, with inadequate attention to teacher training.

Social and emotional skills affect a range of individual outcomes, including learning, employment trajectories, health, and overall life satisfaction. Definitions and terminology vary, but social and emotional skills are generally understood as skills "involved in achieving goals, working with others, and managing emotions" (OECD 2015). They include behavioral traits such as perseverance, self-control, and resilience, as well as such social skills as interacting effectively with others. These skills are malleable, particularly from early childhood to adolescence, and therefore can best be taught and strengthened through childhood education.

Recognizing that different types of foundational skills build on one another, pedagogical approaches are now evolving to develop these skills in tandem. For example, many schools are now encouraging students to adopt a "growth mindset." The concept is based on the idea that one's skills are not inherent but can be developed through effort, commitment, good learning strategies, and support from others (Dweck 2007). Failure and errors provide opportunities to grow and thus become part of the learning process. A similar principle is often used in educational software, especially through the gamification of learning, which relies on trial and error and on learning by doing.

Leveraging new technologies to build foundational skills

Educational technology and e-learning are rapidly growing globally, not least in Asia. With some 600 million young students increasingly connected and eager to use game- and social-based learning, new services and products are flooding the region. Interest in mobile learning is growing as smartphone usage increases.

These initiatives, driven by global and Asian information technology startups, are changing the education landscape. Some are developing initiatives removed from traditional educational arenas, while others are developing tools and services for educators and learners to use in school or at home. One challenge for educators is to determine how best to work with these technology-led businesses to improve learning outcomes cost-efficiently and effectively.

Technology can contribute to foundational skills in several ways. It provides new content to users, thus improving access to learning and teaching resources. Importantly, it contributes to changing pedagogical practices, ushering in an era of learning that is more student-centered.

Software that enables self-paced learning and that tailors teaching to individual students is an important new trend. In its simplest form, self-paced learning occurs when students progress at their own speed through a learning program, some moving faster than others toward more complex material. Adaptive software takes this a step further, directing students through individualized learning pathways. For example, students having more difficulty than others with a particular concept are given more detailed explanations and more exercises for practice. Further, the software forwards individualized data to teachers so they can target specific students for additional tutoring or more advanced teaching. This promotes more inclusive learning cost-effectively. Progress in machine learning and artificial intelligence will make this type of software more sophisticated. As it disseminates, it will change the role of educators from teacher to mentor.

Job-relevant skills in a technology-driven economy

Job-relevant skills are of two types. Transversal skills, which are transferable across occupations and sectors, include interpersonal skills, the ability to think critically, and the ability to solve problems. They are acquired throughout one's education and life experience. Specialized skills, by contrast, relate to a particular occupation (such as teaching), task (coding), or knowledge area (anthropology). They are typically acquired through technical and vocational education and training (TVET), higher education, and work experience. Specialized skills are likely to depreciate quickly, particularly in a time of fast-evolving technology, and thus require regular updating and upgrading. With more automation and machine learning, higher-order specialized skills applicable to nonroutine tasks will be particularly valuable.

TVET and higher education systems alike face a complex set of challenges. They must expand to accommodate the rising number of graduates, as well as adults seeking to upgrade their skills or retrain. At the same time, they need to improve the relevance of the training and education they provide to respond to fast-changing labor market demand.

Stronger links between TVET and higher education can bring progress toward this goal. To better respond to labor market demand, the People's Republic of China, for example, is transforming many of its universities into polytechnics, and Indonesia is expanding its network of polytechnics. Credit transfer systems are developing to enable TVET graduates to pursue higher education—allowing, for example, a technician to become an engineer—and a university student to choose a more vocationally oriented track. This is an important step toward expanding skillsets in the whole workforce. However, these efforts must be embedded in a comprehensive approach that provides opportunities for experienced workers to upgrade their skills. It involves, for instance, a framework for recognizing prior learning and developing programs for working adults.

Strengthening linkages between firms, universities, and vocational schools is essential to make higher education and TVET systems more responsive to technological change. Traditional approaches remain relevant, such as involving industry partners in the design and delivery of TVET programs and promoting workplace learning. New technologies provide opportunities for deeper and broader partnerships. Online collaborative platforms, for example, can facilitate development of joint projects, including applied research, between schools and enterprises.

Leveraging new technologies for job-relevant skills and learning to relearn

Machine learning and big data analysis can help assess and more closely monitor in real time the evolution of occupations and their task content and required skillsets. However, it requires copious data and works only for sectors and occupations well represented on professional networking and job search platforms. JobKred in Singapore has developed this kind of tool. By mining data and using other sources of information, it assesses the types of skills in demand at any given time for specific occupations. It also provides individualized career guidance to users based on their current skillsets and recommends education or training programs to match them to job requirements. As Asia and the Pacific become better connected, these services can improve labor market intermediation and address the problem of asymmetric information.

With fast-evolving technology rapidly depleting skills, learning to relearn is becoming the new normal. A major implication of lifelong learning is that education and training have to be interwoven with full-time work, so content must be provided in a format that is short, convenient, and mobile. Shorter online education and training programs are emerging in response to this growing demand. So-called “nanodegrees” were developed following the mixed results of massive open online courses. These nanodegrees develop skillsets for targeted professions, incorporating user experience and acknowledging the need to transform content to make it as easy as possible to assimilate. New initiatives—such as the Gnowbe in the US and Singapore, and Funzi in Finland—expand on the concept of short, convenient, and mobile learning with their “mobile microlearning” model, which relies on gamification, short videos tailored to modern attention spans, quizzes interspersed in learning materials, and learners’ social interaction.

Fast-changing labor market demand will increasingly require individuals to learn, unlearn, and relearn. Digital technologies, if adapted to local needs, can be powerful tools for individualized and therefore more inclusive learning at different stages of life.

Labor regulations and social protection

New technologies are transforming the ways work is organized. Because digital technologies in particular allow some types of work to be done remotely, they have great potential to accelerate the rise of part-time, on-call, or temporary employment—arrangements the International Labour Organization calls nonstandard forms of employment. While such forms grant employers flexibility and allow workers to pursue new opportunities in the labor market, perhaps while reconciling work with the demands of home life, they often offer little job security. For some workers it can mean cycling between short-term jobs and unemployment beset by worries over when they will next find work and be paid. Such workers may also have meager social security coverage and face greater occupational safety and health risks. Finally, they are less likely to join a union.

Well-designed labor regulation that takes into account associated aspects of social protection systems is an important element of the policy response to spread the benefits of new technologies. Labor regulation includes legislation to protect employees by establishing rules for hiring and firing; setting some wages, in particular minimum wages; regulating work hours and conditions, not least to protect health and safety; and promoting equal opportunity. By extension, labor regulation includes the social protection elements most often tied to work such as health care, income replacement when a job is lost, and help in finding a new job through information and other support from public and private sources.

The key policy challenge today is that labor regulations and social protection systems now current globally were designed for an era when the expected norm was full-time employment with a single company over the long term. This assumption never described most labor markets in developing Asia, however, and, where it is a reasonably accurate description, new technologies will likely bring widespread changes to the world of work. The prospect of a worker remaining in one job with a single employer over the long term looks less and less likely for large groups of workers.

While a detailed examination of current labor regulations and social protection systems—and how they need to evolve—is beyond the scope of this chapter, the concept of "protected mobility" seems an appropriate guiding principle (Auer 2005). A central aspect of this is to ensure that a highly mobile labor market—and one dealing out more frequent spells of unemployment—has mechanisms that protect worker incomes.

First, labor regulations must avoid two extremes: one that leaves workers with too little protection, and the other that imposes high labor costs that only encourage firms to automate. Using cross-country panel data on manufacturing industries, Hasan, Mitra, and Sundaram (2013) found more restrictive labor regulations associated with higher capital intensity in manufacturing, especially in developing economies and in sectors that either require more frequent labor adjustment or, like garments and footwear, are labor intensive and employ more unskilled workers.

Second, at a time when job security will likely erode, any temptation to restrict job dismissals through blunt means must be avoided. The Centre for Business Research Labour Index database at the University of Cambridge, which covers 22 economies in developing Asia, reports that employers must obtain prior permission from the state to dismiss an individual in India, Indonesia, and, since 2008, the People's Republic of China. Such requirements can make layoffs very cumbersome and costly for firms, effectively raising the cost of hiring labor in the first place. In general, policy makers should be guided by the principle of protecting workers rather than protecting jobs. In developing countries, transitioning workers to more productive sectors and firms, especially from informal to formal employment, is essential to creating good jobs. Theory and evidence both support the conclusion that restricting dismissals undermines workers' welfare when a better alternative is severance pay or unemployment insurance (Ranjan, Hasan, and Eleazar, 2018).

Third, even severance pay has its drawbacks as workers enter periods of unemployment.[10] Policy makers, especially in middle-income countries, should consider unemployment insurance tailored to developing country circumstances. Such systems can function alongside more traditional public works programs, such as India's Mahatma Gandhi National Rural Employment Guarantee Act, which provides to the needy 100 days of wage employment annually on public works. Worldwide, and especially in advanced economies, unemployment insurance systems more effectively provide adequate income protection without imposing large efficiency costs (Vodopivec 2013). The catch is that such unemployment insurance systems are demanding, both financially and administratively. They therefore need to be tailored to the developing economy capacities (Box 2.4.1). Fortunately, digital technologies allow biometric identification, as in India's Aadhaar system, initiated in 2008 and now covering 1.2 billion people. As they also allow digitized administrative records that can be shared securely and accurately, they hold great promise for building the administrative capacity required to manage a modern system of unemployment benefits. Other large-scale digital ID initiatives in Asia include Indonesia's e-KTP card, Malaysia's MyKad, and Pakistan's NADRA.

Fourth, minimum wages are an important way for policy makers to ensure that less-skilled workers enjoy a decent standard of living and to counter inequality. Good design principles are crucial in setting minimum wages. They need to avoid being either too generous or too meager, and they should rise in line with productivity gains. A rule of thumb is for minimum wages to be 30%–40% of the median wage, or 25%–35% of the mean wage (IMF 2016). Different minimum wages for different locations should accurately reflect differences in the cost of living. At the same time, governments must resist pressure to introduce different minimum wages for different sectors or categories of workers. The more types of minimum wage there are, the more likely lobbyists and special interest groups will interfere and keep the market from playing its vital role in allocating resources.

Fifth, rather than create regulatory barriers to nonstandard forms of employment such as part-time contract labor, it may be better to regulate more neutrally. These workers need social protection too, requiring that social security systems

2.4.1 Adapting unemployment insurance to developing economy realities

In developed countries, unemployment insurance provides income support to workers who have lost their jobs. Systems require both workers and employers to contribute. Once a worker has met certain minimum requirements for length of employment and amount contributed, they qualify for job-loss benefits. Benefits are typically 40%–75% of average earnings and can be collected for a prescribed period, typically 6 months in the US, on the condition that the recipient actively seeks new employment. Studies show that such systems allow job-seekers to smooth consumption while looking for new work. While unemployment insurance may hinder economic efficiency if recipients slow their job search, it has the positive effect of giving workers time to find more suitable reemployment. Moreover, unemployment insurance acts as an automatic macroeconomic stabilizer by contributing to aggregate demand during recessions.

In developing countries, however, unemployment insurance systems are rare. Where they exist, they typically cover only a small fraction of the formal workforce, excluding agricultural and informal workers entirely. The systems are most common in Latin America, though the PRC has one for urban workers. Obstacles for developing countries are large informal sectors and little of the administrative capacity needed to ensure that contributions come as required from both workers and enterprises, and to accurately track workers and confirm their eligibility.

To successfully adapt unemployment insurance systems to developing country realities, governments should do several things: Relax eligibility criteria by permitting informal work without terminating benefits. Rely initially only on worker and employer contributions to finance the system through unemployment insurance savings accounts, as tried in several Latin American countries, in which unused savings merge with retirement accounts. Transition to more sophisticated systems by moving on from simple unemployment insurance savings accounts to a hybrid version, such as the one Chile introduced in 2002. These hybrids are initially funded from worker contributions and subsequently through a "solidarity" fund, partly financed through employer contributions in lieu of paying into existing severance pay systems, and through general taxes, especially as economically vulnerable workers are brought into the system.

Source: ADB based on Robalino and Weber (2013) and Vodopivec (2013).

be adapted to increase coverage. Advisable adaptations include lowering thresholds required for minimum hours, earnings, or duration of employment; making systems more flexible regarding the contributions required to qualify for benefits; allowing interrupted contribution; and making benefits more portable.

Tax and expenditure policies

Public finance must be the main source for investments in education and training, especially to benefit the economically disadvantaged and those displaced by new technology, and for funding social protection systems. Figure 2.4.2 shows many regional economies spending much less on social protection than do advanced economies. Augmenting social protection expenditure will require governments to raise more revenue. The share of government revenue in GDP is low in many Asian countries—in 2016 about 10 percentage points below the OECD average of 25%. Most government revenue is tax revenue, which can be increased by broadening the tax base, improving tax administration, and making taxes more progressive, which also addresses income inequality.

2.4.2 Public social protection expenditure, 2015 or latest available year

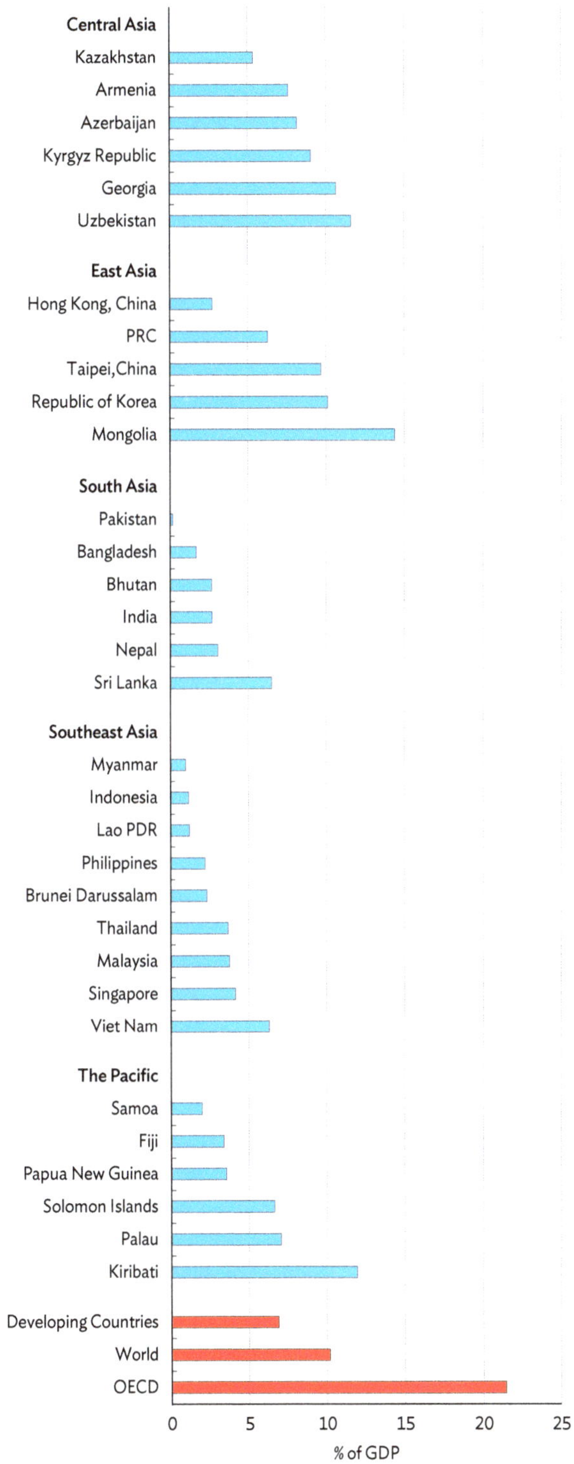

GDP = gross domestic product, Lao PDR = Lao People's Democratic Republic, OECD = Organisation for Economic Co-operation and Development, PRC = People's Republic of China.

Note: Data are from 2015, except 2014 for Bangladesh, Bhutan, India, the Kyrgyz Republic, Pakistan, and Uzbekistan; 2012 for the Lao PDR; 2012 for Malaysia; 2011 for Myanmar; and 2010 for Taipei,China.

Source: International Labour Organization. World Social Protection Report Data. http://www.social-protection.org/gimi/gess/Wspr.action (accessed 2 March 2018).

2.4.3 Personal income tax, 2014 or latest available year

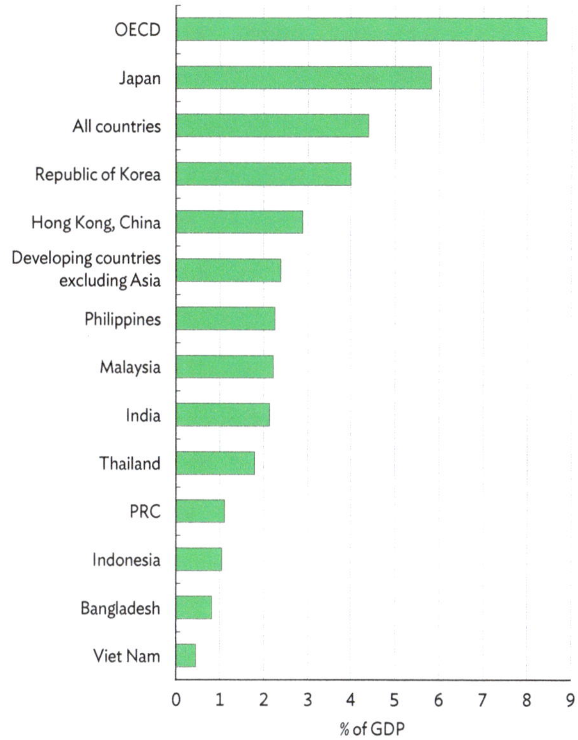

GDP = gross domestic product, OECD = Organisation for Economic Co-operation and Development, PRC = People's Republic of China.

Notes: Simple averages are given for all countries, OECD, and developing countries excluding Asia. Personal tax revenue uses 2014 figures, except 2015 for OECD; 2013 for Bangladesh, India, and the PRC; and 2004 for Viet Nam.

Sources: International Monetary Fund. World Revenue Longitudinal Dataset. https://data.world/imf/world-revenue-longitudinal-dat; Organisation for Economic Co-operation and Development. Revenue Statistics. https://stats.oecd.org/Index.aspx?DataSetCode=REV (both accessed 2 March 2018).

Broadening the tax base

The tax base can be broadened by reining in various exemptions, deductions, and incentives. And, despite tax rates comparable with the world average (though below the OECD average), personal income tax collection is low in Asia (Figure 2.4.3). One reason is relatively high exemption thresholds, and another is slow graduation to the top personal income tax rates (ADB 2012). Tax concessions also keep collection low.

Improving tax administration

Government revenue can be increased by improving tax administration. In the Philippines, for example, weak tax administration is a constraint on government revenue (ADB 2009). Complicated tax systems with many rates, exemptions, deductions, and concessions increase the cost of tax administration and of monitoring compliance, while creating opportunities for tax avoidance and tax planning, which are seen to favor higher-income taxpayers because they generally have more scope for shifting income to avoid higher rates. Unfair tax systems can inhibit willingness to pay taxes. Strengthening governance and institutions is key to improving tax collection, and digital technologies can help (Box 2.4.2).

2.4.2 Goods and services tax in India facilitated using technology

Governments are increasingly using digital technologies to improve tax compliance and enforcement. Digitization can broaden the tax base, reduce administrative costs, improve transparency, ease the compliance burden, and incentivize tax compliance.

On 1 July 2017, India rolled out its goods and services tax (GST), a landmark tax reform that replaced its numerous central government and state taxes with a simplified and unified tax system designed to create a single Indian market. The GST is expected to cut red tape, curb corruption, lubricate domestic trade, broaden the tax base, and increase tax revenue.

All GST filings are handled electronically. GST is implemented through the GST Network, a web-based "one-stop solution" for all India's indirect tax requirements. The GST Network is the information technology backbone for the GST, providing a common portal where taxpayers can file tax returns and tax authorities can match input credits with the liability declared by suppliers and issue notices. India's Income Tax Act, as amended on 1 July 2017, likewise requires taxpayers to be registered with the 2008 Aadhaar program, India's biometric identification system, to file income tax returns. Aadhaar, in turn, is mandated by law to be linked to individual bank accounts. Banks will eventually be required to freeze unlinked accounts as part of the wider government effort to trace tax evasion and formalize the underground economy.

Under this new digital tax regime, the government can put India on a path toward a system with more transparency and greater participation in the formal economy. Mandatory electronic tax filing can better ensure administration at arm's length by minimizing taxpayers' personal interaction with tax officials. Increased digitization is further expected to broaden the tax base and lessen tax evasion. A survey using GST data helped the government add 3.4 million new indirect taxpayers as of December 2017 (Government of India 2018).

Making taxes more progressive

The progressive orientation of fiscal revenue systems can be enhanced through taxes on property, inheritance, and capital gains. They can make resource mobilization more equitable at a relatively low economic cost. Taxes levied on immovable property are widely viewed as a fiscal source tailored for local government. Because such taxes are underused in most parts of the world, including in developing Asia, they offer scope for strengthening fiscal resources, particularly for local governments.

Taxes on property include annual taxes on land and property, stamp duties or property transfer taxes, development fees, betterment levies, estate duties or inheritance taxes, and capital gains taxes on property transfers. An attractive feature of property tax is that, among broadly collected taxes, it has the least adverse effect on growth. In addition, property tax is progressive because it is proportional to property value.

Another inherently progressive tax is inheritance tax, which currently exists in only four economies in the region (ADB 2015b). This levy taxes the transmission of wealth (and hence inequality) across generations but has little effect on work incentive. The capital gains tax similarly targets the rich, who tend to own more capital, and does not adversely affect incentives, as the tax is usually levied on gains realized from investments.

Corporate income taxes are similarly low in some Asian economies, partly because of tax incentives to attract investment and to spare activities seen as having social or economic merit. However, income taxes are less progressive if tax incentives go to the high-income special interests who often lobby for concessions. Moreover, such incentives are often inefficient because they simply subsidize activities firms would have undertaken anyway. Thus, tax collection can be increased by broadening the corporate tax base. On a related issue, there have been many articles in the press about taxing robots. Many people worry that extreme automation will destroy countless jobs without replacing them with comparable jobs, causing unprecedented labor displacement. As that proposal is controversial, a more practical option to consider might be to reform policies that subsidize capital, such as tax deductions for interest paid on loans, to raise the cost of capital and thereby buoy demand for labor.

The full agenda is broader

As noted above, governments are tasked with responding to technology and its effects on the labor market. At the same time, they stand to benefit by embracing new technology. From tax compliance and enforcement to smart cities, health care, and education, there is tremendous potential for more efficient and effective delivery of public services. However, governments need to create an environment that enables technology adoption through a two-pronged strategy. As they complete the necessary support infrastructure, they should support research and development and also innovation. In both cases, government involvement is both direct and indirect.

The public sector is directly responsible for providing basic infrastructure such as energy supply and transport. Similarly, given the central role the internet plays in new technologies, developing a nationwide broadband backbone and other ICT infrastructure is essential. Even when parts of the infrastructure are provided by the private sector, the government still has a role to play, whether in allocating space on the spectrum, ensuring competition among providers, or enforcing minimum standards and interoperability. Particularly important, to address inclusion and poverty reduction, is to ensure that service providers cover the “last mile” to the homes, farms, and businesses of the poorest customers. The technological infrastructure that receives the fewest headlines but is the most critical for inclusion and poverty reduction is in remote and lagging regions, where there is little financial incentive for private provision. Technological innovations cannot help areas that lack connectivity. This is especially true for rural areas, where new technologies have considerable potential for raising productivity and earnings in agriculture (Box 2.4.3).

The general view among economists is that the private sector tends to leave a lot of necessary research and development to the public sector, considering it a public good. Government can directly fund research or create an environment that is conducive to private sector innovation. Government-supported research can be conducted in universities or in publicly funded research centers, or by private entities that receive grants or fiscal incentives to undertake research and development. Private sector innovation, meanwhile, requires regulation to protect personal data and privacy, an effective system of intellectual property protection, and the means to ensure that large technology firms abide by the norms of fair competition. Finally, technology startups need adequate capital to get their business off the ground.

Developing Asia has historically relied on abundant labor to support export-led growth. Now it is poised to leverage its expanding middle class to usher in a new era of consumption-driven growth. With the right policies, new technologies can play a key role in this transition.

2.4.3 Technology for agriculture, Asia's biggest employer

Agriculture will remain a top employer in Asia for some time to come. Even if workers continue to leave agriculture at the same rate as in 2000–2015, in 2030 the sector will still employ 21% of the workforce in Bangladesh, 43% in the Lao People's Democratic Republic, and 28% in Myanmar. It is therefore vital that productivity and earnings in the sector be raised to tackle the challenge of worsening inequality in the region.

Productivity can be enhanced, and food security safeguarded, by further extending the use of proven technologies such as mechanization, high-yielding crop varieties, and improved irrigation, fertilizer, and pesticide.

Fourth Industrial Revolution technologies can improve productivity even further. Bioinformatics—combining computer science, biology, math, and engineering to analyze biological data—allows the development of even better crop varieties using modern agricultural biotechnology and genomics (Xue et al. 2008). Dramatic productivity gains can be achieved through precision agriculture, which prescribes exact quantities of seed, fertilizer, pesticide, water, and tillage for individually managed plots as small as 1 square meter using field or remote sensors (Mulla and Miao 2016). Pesticides can be administered by drone, and manual control of drip irrigation can be automated.

Fourth Industrial Revolution technologies may initially benefit mainly larger and better-off farmers, taking time to spread. Precision agriculture is only gradually becoming the norm even in developed economies, with 60% of farmers in Europe and North America expecting current trends in adoption to continue until most farmers use the practice by 2030 (Corsini et al. 2015).

However, some new technologies have potential to benefit smallholder farmers in developing Asia today. Relatively accessible and cheap ICT technologies can cost-effectively help farmers improve production practices, better connect with markets, and narrow the gap between farm gate prices and retail prices—a gap that, for rice in the Philippines, can equal the farm gate price. Branding and marketing can be enhanced. Hazelnut producers in Bhutan use digital data collection to trace produce and verify plant health and best practices, as well as to improve supply chains. Similarly, the Digital India campaign brings villages online to promote knowledge-intensive agriculture, financial inclusion, and rural entrepreneurship (Lele 2017). In the PRC, the Hunan Agri-Telecom Platform uses text messages to send farmers market and other information, and the E-Price App uses the internet, cloud computing, and smartphones to disseminate prices (Singh et al. 2011).

Any technology that provides to farmers an otherwise scarce or expensive resource helps to spur rural growth from the bottom up. Sharing tractors Uber style can help, as can electronic payment of fertilizer subsidies and e-extension to reach remote areas veterinarians and agronomists rarely visit.

Of course, such ICT-based interventions are no silver bullet. They require affordable access to mobile phones and the internet. Meanwhile, internet penetration in Pakistan, for example, is estimated at 15.5%, less than half of the PRC rate of 53.2% (ADB 2017d). Such digital divides pose significant barriers to smallholder farmers. And, in the end, farm gate prices can never be generous where basic transportation and storage infrastructure is weak.

Endnotes

1 Most references to productivity in this chapter are to labor productivity. Growth in output per worker has three main sources: capital accumulation, which provides to workers more equipment to work with; technological change, which usually introduces new types of equipment and machines but includes better ways of managing the shop floor and the firm more generally; and better skills, which are acquired not only through education and training but also from experience. It is widely accepted that technological change is the main driver of increases in productivity.

2 Similar results emerge from a 10-sector decomposition of changes in average labor productivity into structural change and within-sector productivity components.

3 GVCs are also known by various terms, such as global supply chains, international production networks, and production fragmentation. GVCs give rise to offshoring, vertical specialization, trade in value added, second unbundling, and trade in tasks.

4 When labor force surveys or population censuses are unavailable for any given year, total employment as well as occupation-industry shares are interpolated or extrapolated.

5 Employment changes over the decade between 2005 and 2015 are studied to abstract from cyclical factors.

6 Based on ILOSTAT data on employment in developing Asia, which includes 38 economies with employment estimates from the International Labour Organization: Afghanistan; Armenia; Azerbaijan; Bangladesh; Bhutan; Brunei Darussalam; Cambodia; the People's Republic of China; Fiji; Georgia; Hong Kong, China; India; Indonesia; Kazakhstan; the Republic of Korea; the Kyrgyz Republic; the Lao People's Democratic Republic; Malaysia; Maldives; Mongolia; Myanmar; Nepal; Pakistan; Papua New Guinea; the Philippines; Samoa; Singapore; Solomon Islands; Sri Lanka; Taipei,China; Tajikistan; Thailand; Timor-Leste; Tonga; Turkmenistan; Uzbekistan; Vanuatu; and Viet Nam.

7 An efficiency correction is used by constructing a measure of total factor productivity for each country and each year in the dataset using the Penn World Tables, release 9.0 (Feenstra, Inklaar, and Timmer 2015). A concern is that the contribution of trade and technology to changes in jobs is sensitive to the choice of the efficiency correction. Alternative estimates of total factor productivity, including those developed by Inklaar and Diewert (2016), suggest that the results do not qualitatively change.

8 Methodology and data used in this section do not allow manual tasks to be disaggregated into routine and nonroutine.

9 Why were wages stagnant for so long, even as new technology improved labor productivity? Wage growth depends not only on how much output expands per worker, but also on how workers' share in output evolves. This is partly determined by the nature of the technology, but there are other factors: the extent of competition in product markets, workers' bargaining power, the relative mobility of capital versus labor, and even social norms. While unions are one source of worker bargaining power, Bessen (2015) highlighted another: the skills workers possess and their experience. In US cotton mills in the early 19th century, technology was constantly improving, continually changing the skills needed to operate machinery. Because of this, experience did not boost workers' bargaining power. Only when the technology standardized and skill certification became possible did experience translate into bargaining power. If their wages did not improve, workers could move to other firms happy to pay them more.

10 There are several reasons. First, many workers entitled to severance pay fail to receive it. Second, payouts are unrelated to the time unemployed. Third, unless severance pay is very generous, which can impose serious efficiency costs, it is rarely sufficient. Data from World Bank *Doing Business* surveys show that some countries in developing Asia, notably Indonesia and Sri Lanka, require very generous severance pay. By contrast, the few developed countries that rely on mandatory severance pay do not require it to be very generous. These economies do, however, provide unemployment insurance.

Background papers

Bertulfo, D., E. Gentile, and G. de Vries. Forthcoming[a]. Robots and Labor Demand: Cross-Country Evidence. *ADB Economics Working Paper Series*. Asian Development Bank.

——. Forthcoming[b]. The Employment Effects of Technological Innovation and Participation in Global Value Chains: Evidence from Asia. *ADB Economics Working Paper Series*. Asian Development Bank.

Campbell, D. Forthcoming. Work and Social Protection in the 4th Industrial Revolution. Unpublished.

Chun, N. and H. Tang. 2018. Do Information and Communication Technologies Empower Female Workers? Firm-Level Evidence from Vietnam. *ADB Economics Working Paper Series*. Asian Development Bank.

Flaminiano, J. P., S. Khatiwada, R. Molato, and M. K. Veloso. Forthcoming. Technology and New Occupations: Evidence from Asia. *ADB Economics Working Paper Series*. Asian Development Bank.

Khatiwada, S. and O. Velarde. Forthcoming. Does Rising Productivity Threaten Employment? Evidence from Asia. *ADB Economics Working Paper Series*. Asian Development Bank.

Khatiwada, S., C. Lennon, and S. Zilian. Forthcoming. Technology and Jobs: Task Intensity of Occupations in Asia. *ADB Economics Working Paper Series*. Asian Development Bank.

Ranjan, P., R. Hasan, and E. Eleazar. 2018. Labor Market Regulations in the Context of Structural Transformation. *ADB Economics Working Paper Series*. Asian Development Bank.

References

Acemoglu, D. and D. Autor. 2011. Skills, Tasks and Technologies: Implications for Employment and Earnings. In O. Ashenfelter and D. Card, eds. *Handbook of Labor Economics*. Elsevier B.V.

Acemoglu, D. and P. Restrepo. 2017a. Robots and Jobs: Evidence from US Labor Markets. *NBER Working Paper* No. 23285. National Bureau of Economic Research.

——. 2017b. The Race between Machine and Man: Implications of Technology for Growth, Factor Shares and Employment. *NBER Working Paper* No. 22252. National Bureau of Economic Research.

——. 2018. Artificial Intelligence, Automation and Work. *NBER Working Paper* No. 24196. National Bureau of Economic Research.

Acosta, P., T. Igarashi, R. Olfindo, and J. Rutkowski. 2017. *Developing Socioemotional Skills for the Philippines' Labor Market. Directions in Development—Human Development*. World Bank.

ADB. 2009. *Philippines: Critical Development Constraints.* Asian Development Bank.
——. 2012. *Asian Development Outlook: Confronting Rising Inequality in Asia.* Asian Development Bank.
——. 2015a. A Smarter Future: Skills, Education, and Growth in Asia. In *Key Indicators for Asia and the Pacific 2015.* Asian Development Bank.
——. 2015b. *Making Money Work: Financing a Sustainable Future in Asia and the Pacific.* Asian Development Bank.
——. 2017a. *Meeting Asia's Infrastructure Needs.* Asian Development Bank.
——. 2017b. *Asian Economic Integration Report 2017: The Era of Financial Interconnectedness.* Asian Development Bank.
——. 2017c. *Aid for Trade in Asia and the Pacific: Promoting Connectivity for Inclusive Development.* Asian Development Bank.
——. 2017d. *Key Indicators for Asia and the Pacific 2017.* Asian Development Bank.
ADB and BPS. 2011. The Informal Sector and Informal Employment in Indonesia. *Country Report 2010.* Asian Development Bank and Badan Pusat Statistik (Statistics Indonesia).
Anandan, R., R. Sipahimalani, S. Saini, A. Bharadwaj, R. Beattie, D. Kim, and S. Aryasomayajula. 2017. *E-Conomy Sea Spotlight 2017: Unprecedented Growth for Southeast Asia's $50b Internet Economy.* Google-Temasek e-Conomy SEA.
Asia Pacific Foundation of Canada. 2017. 2017 Survey of Entrepreneurs and MSMEs in Viet Nam: Building the Capacity of MSMEs through Technology and Innovation. https://apfcanada-msme.ca.
Auer, P. 2005. Protected Mobility for Employment and Decent Work: Labour Market Security in a Globalised World. *Employment Strategy Paper* No. 2005/1. International Labour Organization.
Autor, D. H. 2015. Why Are There Still So Many Jobs? The History and Future of Workplace Automation. *Journal of Economic Perspectives* 29(3).
Autor, D. H. and D. Dorn. 2013. The Growth of Low-Skill Service Jobs and the Polarization of the US Labor Market. *American Economic Review* 103(5).
Autor, D. H., F. Levy, and R. J. Murnane. 2003. The Skill Content of Recent Technological Change: An Empirical Exploration. *Quarterly Journal of Economic* 118(4).
Autor, D. H. and A. Salomons. 2017. Does Productivity Growth Threaten Employment? Paper prepared for the ECB Forum on Central Banking.
Bangko Sentral ng Pilipinas. 2013. *Results of the 2013 Survey of Information Technology – Business Process Outsourcing (IT-BPO) Services.*
Bessen, J. E. 2015. *Learning by Doing: The Real Connection between Innovation, Wages, and Wealth.* Yale University Press.
——. 2017. Automation and Jobs: When Technology Boosts Employment. *Law and Economics Research Paper* No. 17-09. Boston University School of Law.

Blockchain Research Institute. 2018. The Block Chain Revolution. https://www.blockchainresearchinstitute.org/about-1/.

Chadha, R. 2016. Social Commerce Counts for 30% of Digital Sales in Southeast Asia. https://www.emarketer.com/Article/Social-Commerce-Counts-30-of-Digital-Sales-Southeast-Asia/1014830.

Chang, J. H., G. Rynhart, and P. Huynh. 2016. ASEAN in Transformation: How Technology is Changing Jobs and Enterprises. *Bureau for Employers' Activities Working Paper* No. 10. International Labour Organization.

Chen, G. and S. Hamori. 2011. Formal and Informal Employment and Income Differentials in Urban China. *Journal of International Development* 25(7).

Corsini, L., K. Wagner, A. Gocke, and T. Kurth. 2015. *Crop Farming 2030: The Reinvention of the Sector*. Boston Consulting Group.

Dasgupta, S., R. Bhula-or, and T. Fakthong. 2015. Earnings Differentials between Formal and Informal Employment in Thailand. *ILO Asia-Pacific Working Paper Series*. International Labour Organization.

Durlak, J. A., R. P. Weissberg, A. B. Dymnicki, R. D. Taylor, and K. B. Schellinger. 2011. The Impact of Enhancing Students' Social and Emotional Learning: A Meta-Analysis of School-Based Universal Interventions. *Child Development* 82(1).

Dweck, C. S. 2007. *Mindset: The New Psychology of Success*. Ballantine Books.

Estudillo, J. P., Y. Sawada, and K. Otsuka. 2006. The Green Revolution, Development of Labor Markets, and Poverty Reduction in the Rural Philippines, 1985–2004. *Agricultural Economics* 35.

Fanggidae, V., M. P. Sagala, and D. R. Ningrum. 2016. On-Demand Transport Workers in Indonesia: Toward Understanding the Sharing Economy in Emerging Markets. In *Transformations in Technology, Transformations in Work*. JustJobs Network Inc.

Farole, T. and Y. Cho. 2017. Bangladesh Jobs Diagnostics. *Jobs Series* No. 9. World Bank.

Feenstra, R. C., R. Inklaar, and M. P. Timmer. 2015. The Next Generation of the Penn World Table *American Economic Review* 105(10).

Felipe, J., A. Mehta, and C. Rhee. 2018. Manufacturing Matters... but It's the Jobs That Count. *Cambridge Journal of Economics*.

Ford, M. and V. Honan. 2017. The Go-Jek Effect. In Jurriens, E. and R. Tapsell, eds. *Digital Indonesia: Connectivity and Divergence*. ISEAS–Yusof Ishak Institute.

Frey, C. B. and M. Osborne. 2017. The Future of Employment: How Susceptible Are Jobs to Computerisation? *Technological Forecasting and Social Change* 114(C).

Frey, C. B. and E. Rahbari. 2016. Do Labor-Saving Technologies Spell the Death of Jobs in the Developing World. Paper prepared for the 2016 Brookings Blum Roundtable.

Go-Jek. 2017. "Go-Jek's Impact for Indonesia." *Product Tech Blog* (blog), 30 August. https://blog.gojekengineering.com/gojeks-impact-for-indonesia-1d506d2146b1.

Government of India, Ministry of Finance. 2018. *Economic Survey 2017–2018*. New Delhi.

Graetz, G. and G. Michaels. Forthcoming. Robots at Work. *Review of Economics and Statistics*.

Gunatilaka, R. 2008. Informal Employment in Sri Lanka: Nature, Probability of Employment, and Determinants of Wages. *ILO Asia-Pacific Working Paper Series*. International Labour Organization.

Hasan, R., D. Mitra, and A. Sundaram. 2013. The Determinants of Capital Intensity in Manufacturing: The Role of Factor Market Imperfections. *World Development* 51.

IBM Q Network. What is Quantum Computing. https://www.research.ibm.com/ibm-q/learn/what-is-quantum-computing/.

IMF. 2016. Cross-Country Report on Minimum Wages. *IMF Country Report* No. 16/151. International Monetary Fund.

Inklaar, R. and W. E. Diewert. 2016. Measuring Industry Productivity and Cross-Country Convergence. *Journal of Econometrics* 191(2).

International Federation of Robotics. 2016. *World Robotics Report 2016*.

International Trade Center. 2017. *New Pathways to E-Commerce: A Global MSME Competitiveness Survey*.

Irfan, M. 2008. Pakistan's Wage Structure, During 1990/1991 to 2006/2007. *Working paper*. Pakistan Institute of Development Economics.

Jacobs, J. 1969. *The Economy of the Cities*. Random House.

JakPat. 2015. "Indonesian Online Seller Survey Report." *Jajak Pendapat App* (blog), 9 March. https://blog.jakpat.net/indonesian-online-seller-survey-report/.

Jia, P., A. Park, and Y. Du. 2018. *Robots, Automation, and Jobs in Chinese Manufacturing Firms*. Unpublished.

Klemp, S. 2017. "Digital in Southeast Asia in 2017." *We are Social* (blog), 16 February. https://wearesocial.com/special-reports/digital-southeast-asia-2017.

Lee, S. Y. 2016. Biotechnology: What It is and How It's About to Change Our Lives. https://www.weforum.org/agenda/2016/12/what-is-biotechnology-how-will-it-change-our-lives.

Lele, U. 2017. How Technology is Transforming the Lives of India's Farmers. https://www.weforum.org/agenda/2017/10/india-fourth-industrial-revolution-farming/.

Lin, J. 2011. Technological Adaptation, Cities, and New Work. *Review of Economics and Statistics* 93(2).

Llamas, C. 2017. Who's Winning the Philippines' E-Commerce Arena: Local or International Players. http://www.marketing-interactive.com/whos-winning-the-philippines-e-commerce-arena-local-or-international-players/.

Los, B., M. P. Timmer, and G. J. de Vries. 2015. How Important Are Exports for Job Growth in China? A Demand Side Analysis. *Journal of Comparative Economics* 43(1).

Malabuppha, T. 2017. Thailand E-Commerce Market: What to Expect in 2017. https://www.pricezagroup.com/2017/thailand-e-commerce-market-expect/.

Maligalig, D. S., S. Cuevas, and A. Rosario. 2009. Informal Employment in Bangladesh. *ADB Economics Working Paper Series* No. 155. Asian Development Bank.

Mann, K. and L. Püttmann. 2017. *Benign Effects of Automation: New Evidence from Patent Texts.* University of Bonn. Working paper.

ManpowerGroup. 2016. *Skilled Talent: It's at Your Fingertips. As Organizations Report the Highest Talent Shortage since 2007, Employers Look to Develop Their Own Workforces to Fill in-Demand Role.* News release.

Marcolin, L., S. Miroudot, and M. Squicciarini. 2016. The Routine Content of Occupations: New Cross-Country Measures Based on PIAAC. *Trade Policy Papers* No. 188. Organisation for Economic Co-operation and Development.

Mayer, J. 2017. *Robots, Industrialization, and Industrial Policy.* Paper submitted for the Multi-year Expert Meeting on Enhancing the Enabling Economic Environment at all Levels in Support of Inclusive and Sustainable Development, and the Promotion of Economic Integration and Cooperation.

McCarthy, J. 2007. What is Artificial Intelligence. http://jmc.stanford.edu/articles/whatisai/whatisai.pdf.

McKinsey Global Institute. 2016. *Digital Globalization: The New Era of Global Flows.* McKinsey & Company.

——. 2017a. *Jobs Lost, Jobs Gained: Workforce Transitions in a Time of Automation (Executive Summary).* McKinsey & Company.

——. 2017b. *Jobs Lost, Jobs Gained: Workforce Transitions in a Time of Automation.* McKinsey & Company.

Mcmillan, M., D. Rodrik, and I. Verduzco-Gallo. 2014. Globalization, Structural Change, and Productivity Growth, with an Update on Africa. *World Development* 63.

Mulla, D. and Y. Miao. 2016. Precision Farming. In Thenkabail, P. S., ed. *Land Resources Monitoring, Modeling, and Mapping with Remote Sensing.* Taylor & Francis Group.

Nguyen, C. V. 2013. The Impact of Minimum Wages on Employment of Low-Wage Workers. *Economics of Transition* 21(3).

OECD. 2013a. *OECD Skills Outlook 2013: Further Results from the Survey of Adult Skills.* Organisation for Economic Co-operation and Development Publishing.

——. 2013b. *PISA 2012 Results: Ready to Learn.* Vol. III. Organisation for Economic Co-operation and Development Publishing.

——. 2015. *Skills for Social Progress: The Power of Social and Emotional Skills.* Organisation for Economic Co-operation and Development Publishing.

——. 2016a. *Skills Matter: Further Results from the Survey of Adult Skills, OECD Skills Studies.* Organisation for Economic Co-operation and Development Publishing.

——. 2016b. *Skills for a Digital World.* Background Paper for Ministerial Panel. Directorate for Science, Technology and Innovation Committee on Digital Economy Policy.

Philippine Statistics Authority. 2017. *2016 Occupational Wages Survey (OWS).*

Polanyi, M. 1966. *The Tacit Dimension.* University of Chicago Press.

PricewaterhouseCoopers. 2016. *They Say They Want a Revolution: Total Retail 2016.*

——. 2017. *UK Economic Outlook.*

Reijnders, L. S. M. and G. J. de Vries. 2017. *Trade, Technology and the Rise of Non-Routine Jobs.* Groningen Growth and Development Centre, mimeo.

Robalino, D. A. and M. Weber. 2013. Designing and Implementing Unemployment Benefit Systems in Middle and Low Income Countries: Beyond Risk-Pooling vs Savings. *IZA Journal of Labor Policy* 2(1).

Schwab, K. 2017. *The Fourth Industrial Revolution.* World Economic Forum.

Singh, V. K., A. Singh, R. Chand, and C. Kushwaha. 2011. Role of Bioinformatics in Agriculture and Sustainable Development. *International Journal of Bioinformatics Research* 3(2).

Statista. 2018. The Statistics Portal. https://www.statista.com/statistics/268136/top-15-countries-based-on-number-of-facebook-users/.

Timmer, M. P., E. Dietzenbacher, B. Los, R. Stehrer, and G. J. de Vries. 2015. An Illustrated User Guide to the World Input–Output Database: The Case of Global Automotive Production. *Review of International Economics* 23(3).

Timmer, M. P., A. A. Erumban, B. Los, R. Stehrer, and G. J. de Vries. 2014. Slicing up Global Value Chains. *Journal of Economic Perspectives* 28(2).

UNCTAD. 2017. Robots, Industrialization and Inclusive Growth. In *Trade and Development Report 2017: Beyond Austerity: Towards a Global New Deal.* United Nations Conference on Trade and Development.

UNESCO. 2014. Skills for Holistic Human Development. *Asia-Pacific Education Policy Brief* 2. United Nations Educational, Scientific and Cultural Organization.

United States Government, The White House. 2016. *Economic Report of the President.*

Unni, J. 2005. Wages and Incomes in Formal and Informal Sectors in India. *The Indian Journal of Labour Economics* 48(2).

Vodopivec, M. 2013. Introducing Unemployment Insurance to Developing Countries. *IZA Journal of Labor Policy* 2(1).

Winston, P. 2010. *Artificial Intelligence.* Massachusetts Institute of Technology OpenCourseWare.

World Bank. 2016. *World Development Report 2016: Digital Dividends.*

Xue, J., S. Zhao, Y. Liang, C. Hou, and J. Wang. 2008. Bioinformatics and Its Applications in Agriculture. Paper presented at the International Conference on Computer and Computing Technologies in Agriculture. Beijing, PRC. 18–20 October.

Yap, S. 2016. A Quick Ride out of Poverty, Thanks to Ride-Sharing Apps. *Channel News Asia.* 3 October. https://www.channelnewsasia.com/news/asia/a-quick-ride-out-of-poverty-thanks-to-ride-sharing-apps-7816034.

These are the labor force surveys from government statistical agencies used in this study.

Government of Bangladesh. Bangladesh Bureau of Statistics. Labour Force Survey 2005–2006.

——. Labour Force Survey 2010.

——. Labour Force Survey 2013.

——. Quarterly Labour Force Survey 2015–2016.

Government of India. National Sample Survey Office. National Sample Survey—Employment and Unemployment Survey (NSS-EUS) 1999–2000.

——. National Sample Survey—Employment and Unemployment Survey (NSS-EUS) 2004–2005.

——. National Sample Survey—Employment and Unemployment Survey (NSS-EUS) 2011–2012.

Government of Indonesia. Badan Pusat Statistik—Statistics Indonesia. National Labor Force Survey (SAKERNAS) 2000.

——. National Labor Force Survey (SAKERNAS) 2005.

——. National Labor Force Survey (SAKERNAS) 2008.

——. National Labor Force Survey (SAKERNAS) 2010.

——. National Labor Force Survey (SAKERNAS) 2014.

Government of Nepal. Central Bureau of Statistics. Labor Force Survey 1998–1999.

——. Labor Force Survey 2008.

Government of Pakistan. Bureau of Statistics. Labor Force Survey 2001–2002.

——. Labor Force Survey 2003–2004.

——. Labor Force Survey 2012–2013.

Government of Sri Lanka, Department of Census and Statistics. Labor Force Survey 2004.

——. Labor Force Survey 2006.

——. Labor Force Survey 2012.

——. Labor Force Survey 2014.

Government of Thailand, National Statistics Office. Labor Force Survey 2000.

——. Labor Force Survey 2005.

——. Labor Force Survey 2010.

Government of the Philippines, Philippine Statistics Authority. Labor Force Survey 2001.

——. Labor Force Survey 2004.

——. Labor Force Survey 2009.

——. Labor Force Survey 2013.

——. Labor Force Survey 2015.

——. Labor Force Survey 2016.

Government of Viet Nam, General Statistics Office. Labor Force Survey 2007.

——. Labor Force Survey 2013.

——. Labor Force Survey 2015.

3

ECONOMIC TRENDS AND PROSPECTS IN DEVELOPING ASIA

CENTRAL ASIA

- ARMENIA
- AZERBAIJAN
- GEORGIA
- KAZAKHSTAN
- KYRGYZ REPUBLIC
- TAJIKISTAN
- TURKMENISTAN
- UZBEKISTAN

Armenia

Growth jumped to 7.5% in 2017, following near-zero growth in 2016, on stronger demand both at home and abroad. Inflation returned, at 1.0%, and the current account deficit widened slightly to equal 2.5% of GDP. Growth is projected to moderate to 4.0% in 2018 and 4.2% in 2019, as inflation remains below 3.0% and the current account deficit widens further toward 3.0% of GDP. Continued fiscal consolidation is critical to reduce high public debt.

Economic performance

Strong expansion in industry and services boosted growth to 7.5% in 2017 from a negligible 0.2% in 2016. On the supply side, industry excluding construction expanded by 10.4%, double the 4.8% rate in 2016, with gains in most subsectors. Growth in services accelerated to 10.4% from 4.0%, reflecting strong recovery in consumption. Buffeted by poor weather, agriculture declined by 4.0%. Construction grew by 3.1%, after 4 years of contraction, on higher private construction and government investment (Figure 3.1.1).

On the demand side, consumption and investment propelled growth. Private consumption rose by an estimated 6.7%, following a 1.2% decline in 2016, on higher lending and remittances. Public consumption expanded by 6.3%, up from 4.1% in 2016, despite fiscal consolidation. Investment rose by 7.8%, reversing an 8.7% decline in 2016, with higher inventories and an estimated 4.0% increase in fixed capital formation, including higher government spending. The deficit in net exports widened as imports grew faster than exports.

Average annual inflation was 1.0% in 2017, reversing 1.4% deflation in 2016. Prices rose by 4.0% for food but declined by 1.8% for other goods and 1.3% for services (Figure 3.1.2). The year-on-year inflation rate reached 2.6% in December 2017, within the target band of 2.5%–5.5% set by the Central Bank of Armenia.

Monetary policy was relaxed last year to support growth. The central bank reduced its policy interest rate by 25 basis points to 6.0% in February 2017. The banking sector remains sound, well capitalized, and profitable. A sixfold increase in minimum bank capital to AMD30 billion, required since January 2017, induced consolidation in Armenia's banking

3.1.1 Supply-side contributions to growth

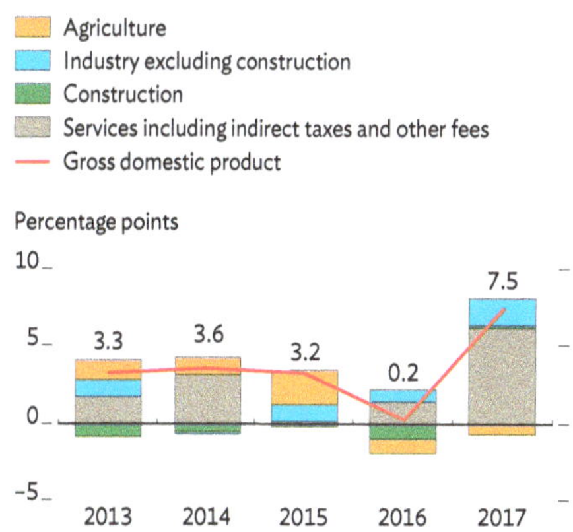

Source: National Statistical Service of the Republic of Armenia. http://www.armstat.am (accessed 2 March 2018).

3.1.2 Inflation

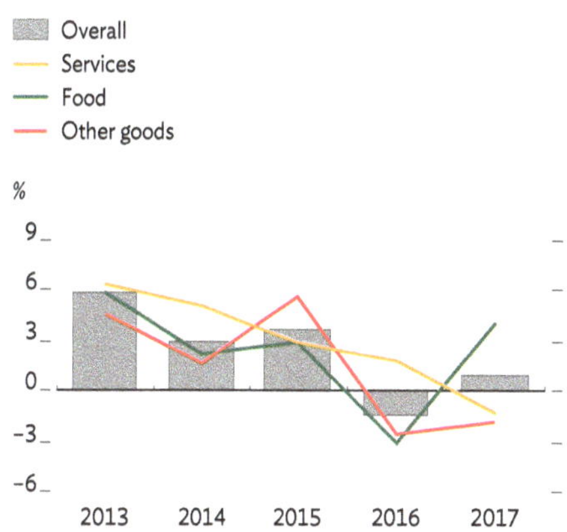

Source: National Statistical Service of the Republic of Armenia. http://www.armstat.am (accessed 2 March 2018).

This chapter was written by Grigor Gyurjyan of the Armenia Resident Mission, ADB, Yerevan.

system, improving efficiency and financial soundness indicators. Broad money growth accelerated to 18.5% from 17.5% in 2016, while credit to the economy expanded by 16.5%, well above the 6.0% increase in 2016.

Fiscal policy, on the other hand, was less expansionary in 2017 as the government began much-needed fiscal consolidation to help cut the ratio of public debt to GDP. The budget deficit narrowed to 4.8% of GDP from 5.5% in 2016 but remained outside the 2.8% target (Figure 3.1.3).

Higher tax revenue from strong growth, a broader tax base, and improved revenue administration lifted revenue by 5.6% in 2017, as expenditure grew by 3.8%. Because they trailed GDP growth, however, both fell as shares of GDP, revenue to 22.2% from 23.1% a year earlier and expenditure to 27.0% from 28.5%. Higher revenue allowed the government to raise planned capital expenditure during the year by 0.8% of GDP.

Public debt rose to equal 58.8% of GDP at the end of 2017 from 56.6% a year earlier (Figure 3.1.4). External public debt rose by 14.4% to reach 47.7% of GDP, while domestic public debt increased by 12.6% to reach 11.1% of GDP.

The current account deficit widened to an estimated 2.5% of GDP from 2.3% in 2016 as a significant worsening of the trade deficit offset higher earnings from services, income, and personal transfers (Figure 3.1.5).

The trade deficit widened to 11.1% of GDP from 8.9% in 2016. Exports rose by an estimated 22.3%, reflecting strong external demand for agricultural products, manufactured goods, and commodities from traditional markets and some new ones. However, imports surged by about 27.0% as economic growth spurred demand for consumer and capital goods.

After 3 years of decline, remittances, measured as the net inflow of private noncommercial transfers through banks, rose by 2.2% to $731.5 million in 2017. Remittances from the Russian Federation jumped by 22.2%, more than offsetting net outflows to other countries (Figure 3.1.6).

Gross international reserves stood at $2.3 billion at the end of 2017, cover for 5.4 months of imports (Figure 3.1.7). The Armenian dram depreciated slightly in both real and nominal effective terms.

Economic prospects

Growth is projected to return to trend, slowing sharply to 4.0% in 2018 and then improving slightly to 4.2% in 2019 (Figure 3.1.8). These projections assume a continuing favorable external environment and the acceleration of structural reform to improve governance and promote private investment and exports.

On the supply side, industry and services are expected to support growth, as are agriculture and construction to

3.1.3 Fiscal indicators

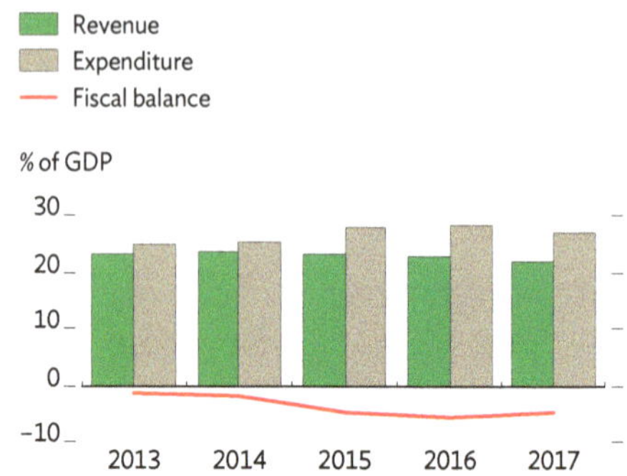

Sources: Ministry of Finance. http://www.minfin.am; National Statistical Service of the Republic of Armenia. http://www.armstat.am (accessed 2 March 2018).

3.1.4 Public debt

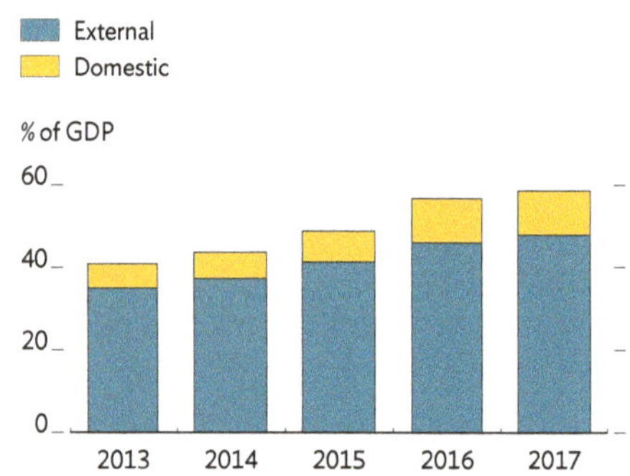

Sources: Ministry of Finance. http://www.minfin.am; National Statistical Service of the Republic of Armenia. http://www.armstat.am (both accessed 2 March 2018).

3.1.5 Current account components

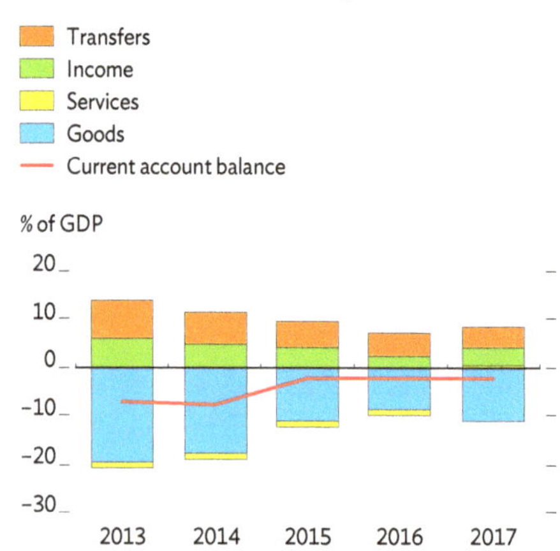

Sources: Central Bank of Armenia. http://www.cba.am (accessed 2 March 2018); ADB estimates.

a lesser extent. Agriculture should recover from declines in 2016 and 2017 with better weather, the government's provision of subsidized loans to food processors and to farmers for hail nets and drip irrigation systems, and its efforts to promote greenhouses by, for example, reducing gas tariffs. In addition, the government is introducing a pilot program for agro-insurance. Expansion in industry excluding construction will likely moderate after the jump in 2017 but remain above 5% thanks to external demand for processed foods, minerals, textiles, and footwear. Growth in services is projected somewhat higher than trend at 5.0%–5.5%, reflecting anticipated gains in consumption and expansion in finance, transportation, hotels, and information and communications services.

On the demand side, consumption, investment, and higher exports should all support growth. Despite projections for further increases in remittances, growth in private consumption is expected to moderate in 2018 in response to higher inflation, and then rise slightly in 2019 as inflation slows. Investment should benefit from higher government capital spending and steady private investment in export-oriented industries.

Monetary policy will likely tighten in 2018 to combat rising inflationary pressures before returning to a more accommodative stance in 2019. Average annual inflation is projected to accelerate to 2.7% in 2018—reflecting higher excise taxes for fuel, liquefied gas, beverages, and cigarettes, as well as increased customs duties since January 2018 for about 200 items under the Customs Code of the Eurasian Economic Union—and then moderate to 2.2% in 2019.

Fiscal consolidation is set to continue in 2018 and 2019, to put the ratio of public debt to GDP on a downward path. To maintain macroeconomic stability, reduce debt-related vulnerability, and contain fiscal risk, the 2018 budget envisages the fiscal deficit narrowing further to 2.7% of GDP, mainly through modest rises in revenue and expenditure and constraints on wage and pension outlays. Tax changes that took effect in January 2018—including higher rates for income and excise taxes and a lower ceiling for small firms and individual proprietors eligible to use simplified taxation instead of value-added and profit tax—are expected to support fiscal consolidation over the medium term. The downside is that fiscal tightening and higher inflation could worsen the poverty rate somewhat, reversing improvement over the past 3 years.

The current account deficit is projected to widen to equal 3.2% of GDP in 2018 before narrowing again to 2.8% in 2019 (Figure 3.1.9).

Trade expansion is expected to slow in 2018, with import growth continuing to outpace export growth. Increased import payments for consumer and capital goods, partly from the higher customs duties since January, are projected to

3.1.6 Remittances and their sources

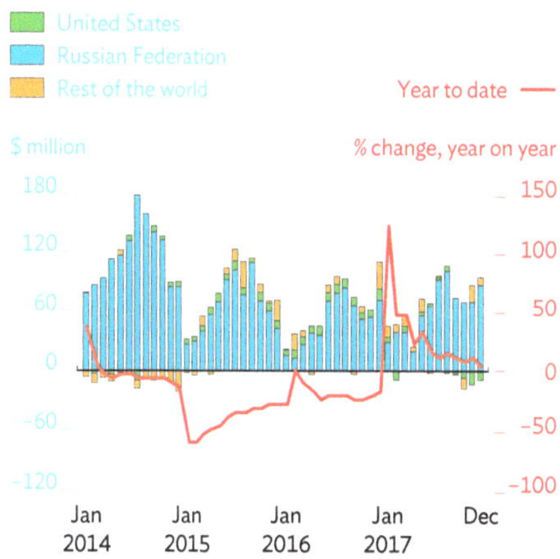

Source: Central Bank of Armenia. http://www.cba.am (accessed 2 March 2018).

3.1.7 Reserves and effective exchange rates

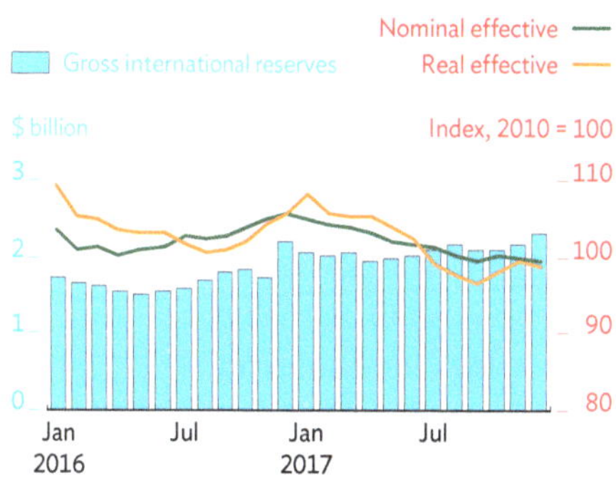

Sources: Central Bank of Armenia. http://www.cba.am; International Monetary Fund. International Financial Statistics online database (accessed 2 March 2018).

3.1.8 GDP growth

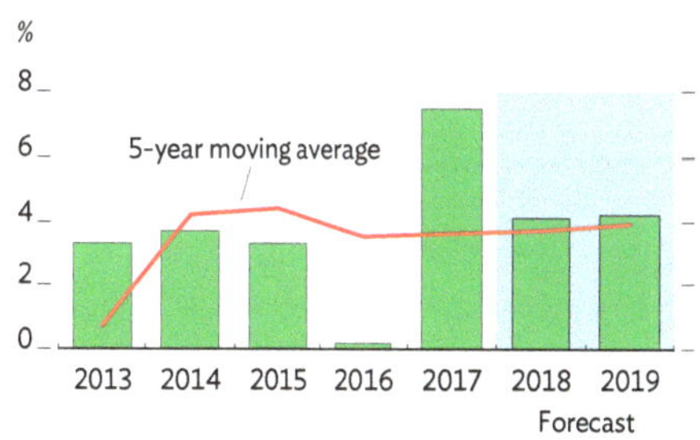

Sources: National Statistical Service of the Republic of Armenia. http://www.armstat.am (accessed 2 March 2018); ADB estimates.

offset sustained growth in exports of agricultural products, textiles, precious and other nonferrous metals, and gemstones. Accordingly, the trade deficit is expected to widen, offset partly by higher earnings from services, income, and personal transfers. The current account deficit will likely be financed mainly by foreign direct investment and other private capital flows, along with modest public sector borrowing.

3.1.1 Selected economic indicators (%)

	2018	2019
GDP growth	4.0	4.2
Inflation	2.7	2.2
Current account balance (share of GDP)	-3.2	-2.8

Source: ADB estimates.

Policy challenge—fiscal consolidation while promoting growth

Armenia's public and publicly guaranteed external debt rose sharply during the global financial crisis of 2008–2009 and has since continued to grow. The ratio of public debt to GDP jumped from 16.4% in 2008 to 40.6% a year later. In 2017, it reached 58.8%, near the 60% legal ceiling. Fiscal consolidation to reduce the debt ratio is thus the government's top priority over the medium term. At the same time, higher growth and growth-friendly fiscal reform are essential to rebuild fiscal health and make debt reduction sustainable, especially with a $500 million eurobond due for repayment in 2020.

The authorities view economic growth as a counterbalance to fiscal consolidation. Growth could benefit substantially from further institutional and regulatory strengthening to improve the investment climate, from productivity-enhancing structural reform (for agriculture in particular), and from the expansion of current initiatives that support sectors with export potential, such as food processing, textiles, mining, information technology, and tourism.

Measures addressing both revenue and expenditure are essential for fiscal consolidation, as are steps to minimize inevitable constraint on growth. Broadening the tax base and enhancing revenue administration, along with measures to rationalize spending and improve efficiency, should eventually balance the budget. The government's digital transformation strategy, to be approved in 2018, aims to establish a united digital environment in all spheres of state administration to enhance efficiency and transparency, thereby improving the business environment.

The introduction in January 2018 of higher personal income taxes and excises on gasoline, diesel fuel, and tobacco promises to boost revenues. On the expenditure side, a stronger foundation for growth can emerge from spending that prioritizes productive activities. Growth may continue to accelerate even as fiscal policy tightens if the government improves budget efficiency by reallocating expenditure in favor of high-return investment projects and reforming public financial management in general. The government's commitment to developing a systematic approach to preparing,

3.1.9 Current account balance

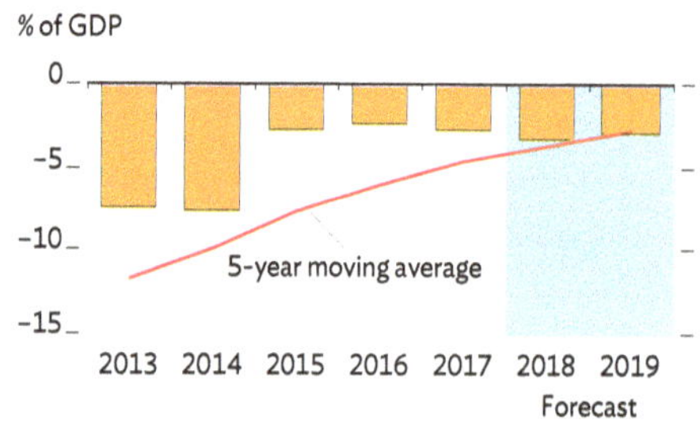

Sources: Central Bank of Armenia. http://www.cba.am; National Statistical Service of the Republic of Armenia. http://www.armstat.am (both accessed 2 March 2018); ADB estimates.

implementing, and managing public–private partnerships, with legislation scheduled for 2018, stands to promote private participation in public investment projects, maximize synergy between the two sectors, and help sustain growth.

Fiscal regulation limits the budget deficit to 3% of average GDP over the previous 3 years (equivalent to 2.8% of GDP in 2017) if public debt outstanding exceeds 50% of the previous year's GDP, with an absolute cap on debt at 60%. Changes to this fiscal rule, which take effect during the 2018 budget cycle, allow the government more flexibility to respond to the business cycle and prioritize capital expenditure. Under the revised fiscal rule, if public debt exceeds 40% of GDP, the deficit in the state budget should be less than capital expenditure. If debt exceeds 50% of GDP, current expenditure must rise more slowly than recent GDP growth. If debt exceeds 60% of GDP, current expenditure is further restricted and may not exceed domestic revenue. With total spending thus linked more closely to the size of budget deficit, and with tighter restrictions on current outlays, the government should find it easier to reallocate expenditure toward growth-enhancing programs, in particular capital projects.

Azerbaijan

Recession ended in 2017 as higher oil prices and gains in services and agriculture offset a decline in industry and returned the current account balance to surplus. Inflation accelerated slightly to 12.9%. Growth is forecast to reach 1.7% in 2018 and 2.0% in 2019 as reviving oil prices allow higher public investment, stabilize the exchange rate and contain inflation, and maintain the current account surplus. Fiscal consolidation is needed to sustain sovereign wealth resources.

Economic performance

Expansion in services and agriculture stabilized the economy in 2017. Growth returned at 0.1%, following the sharp 3.1% contraction in 2016.

On the supply side, industry shrank by 3.6% in 2017, less than the 5.9% fall in 2016, with a smaller decline in construction (Figure 3.2.1). Mining dropped by 4.6%, reversing 0.7% growth in 2016 as oil output fell by 5.6% and gas by 3.0%. This reflected a gradual decline in production to avoid sharp decreases in future years as limited reserves become depleted. Construction fell by 1.5%, improving on a 22.9% plunge in 2016, thanks to work on the Shah Deniz gas field and the Southern Gas Corridor pipeline, as well as projects for power distribution, education, and agriculture. Agriculture expanded by 4.2%, up from 2.6% in 2016 as crop production rose by 6.1% on gains in cotton, fruit, and sugar beets. Services grew by 3.5%, following a 0.7% decline in 2016, with increases in tourism and transportation.

On the demand side, higher oil prices and exchange rate stability (Figure 3.2.2) helped consumption grow by 4.4%. Investment fell by 2.6%, more than the 0.9% decline in 2016, because of lower oil revenues. Net exports rose by 7.1%, however, reversing a 12.0% drop in 2016 as exports outpaced imports.

Inflation accelerated to 12.9% from 12.4% in 2016, reflecting the lagged effect of currency devaluation and a rise in fuel and electricity tariffs in December 2016, although the pace of inflation slowed toward the end of the year (Figure 3.2.3). Prices rose by 16.4% for food, 11.6% for other goods, and 9.3% for services.

Fiscal policy was generally expansionary as the state budget deficit widened to equal 1.6% of GDP, up from 0.4% in 2016 (Figure 3.2.4). Revenue fell to 23.5% of GDP from 29.0%, reflecting smaller transfers from the State Oil Fund of Azerbaijan (SOFAZ), the sovereign wealth fund.

3.2.1 GDP growth by sector

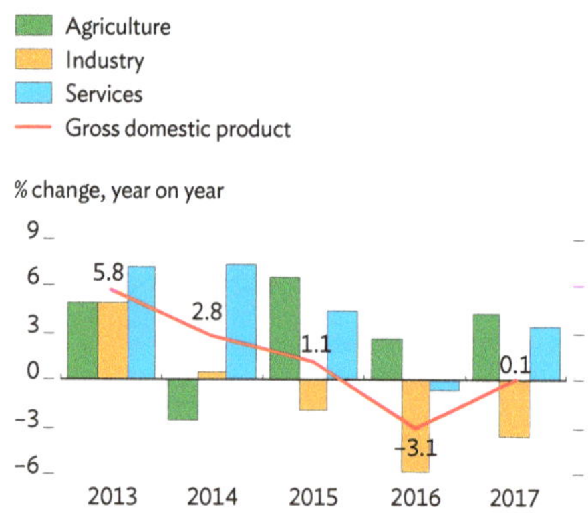

Source: State Statistical Committee of the Republic of Azerbaijan.

3.2.2 Exchange rate and average crude oil price

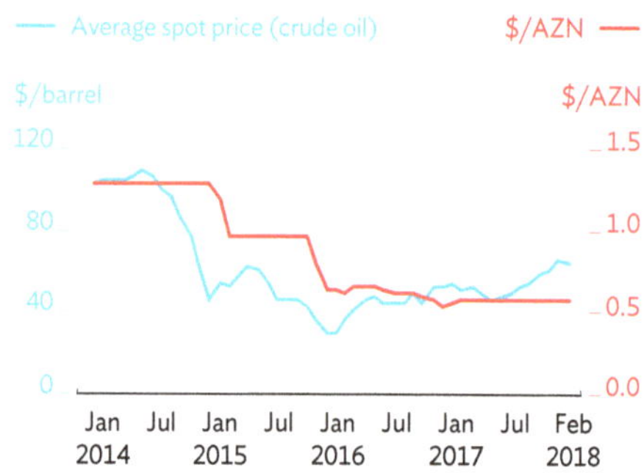

Note: An increase in the exchange rate indicates a depreciation.

Sources: Central Bank of the Republic of Azerbaijan; Haver Analytics (accessed 19 March 2018).

This chapter was written by Nail Valiyev of the Azerbaijan Resident Mission, ADB, Baku.

The authorities have been reducing transfers from the fund since 2013 to alleviate fiscal dependence on oil revenues, with a further 20% cut in 2017. Tax revenue rose by 9.2% on gains in income tax, value-added tax on imports, and customs duties. Expenditure declined to 25.1% of GDP from 29.4% in 2016, with social expenditure representing 38% of total outlays. Official statistics report that public and publicly guaranteed debt equaled 22.8% of GDP at the end of 2017.

Monetary policy aimed to maintain price stability while preventing a post-devaluation slump. The Central Bank of Azerbaijan kept the policy interest rate at 15.0% in 2017. Broad money grew by 9.0%, reversing a 2.0% decline in 2016 (Figure 3.2.5). Net international reserves rose by 34.2% as a recovery in oil prices helped limit the continuing depreciation of the Azerbaijan manat to 7.7% against the US dollar. However, credit to the economy fell by 35.7%. Dollarization remains extensive, with 72.3% of deposits in foreign currency, reflecting weak confidence in the manat. This constrains lending to the economy, as households, who receive 38% of all loans, prefer to borrow in manat. Nonperforming loans grew by 10.4%, reaching 13.8% of total bank lending.

The current account balance recorded an estimated surplus equal to 5.5% of GDP, reversing a deficit of 3.6% in 2016. With higher oil prices, the trade surplus reached 16.4% of GDP. Exports grew by 17.1%, having dropped by 15.2% in 2016. Imports declined by 2.5%, less than the 7.9% decrease in 2016, as lower imports for the oil sector and restrictions on government imports offset a rise in other imports. Inward worker remittances nearly doubled to $1.0 billion. As higher oil prices helped limit manat depreciation, the central bank boosted reserves to $5.3 billion from $4.0 billion in 2016. SOFAZ expanded its assets by $2.7 billion to $35.8 billion at the end of 2017 (Figure 3.2.6).

3.2.3 Monthly inflation

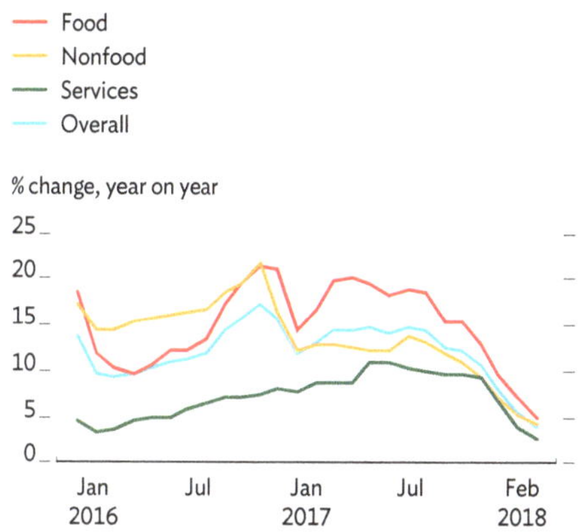

Sources: State Statistical Committee of the Republic of Azerbaijan; Haver Analytics (accessed 19 March 2018).

3.2.4 Fiscal balance

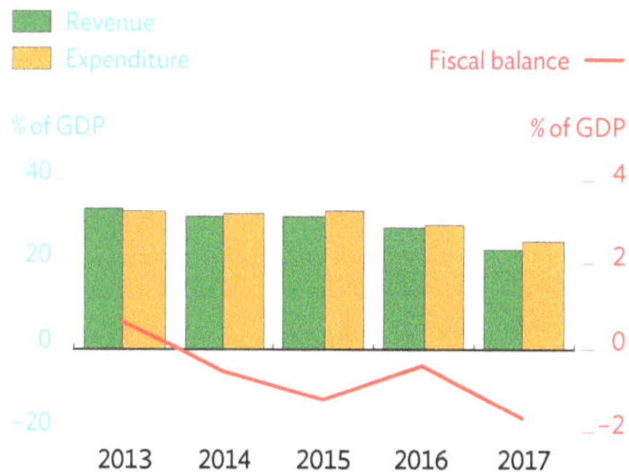

Source: Ministry of Finance of the Republic of Azerbaijan.

Economic prospects

Growth is forecast to reach 1.7% in 2018 on a rebound in construction and accelerate further to 2.0% in 2019 as industry begins to expand (Figure 3.2.7). Private consumption is expected to rise as the exchange rate stabilizes and economic activity improves, with higher public investment boosting the non-oil economy.

On the supply side, industry is forecast to contract by 0.5% in 2018 with a further drop in oil production, though the launch of the Shah Deniz II gas field in the second half of the year will offset some of the decline. In 2019, industry is expected to grow by 3.0% as gas production from Shah Deniz II expands. A planned doubling of public investment, notably on infrastructure and public housing, is expected to boost construction by 6.0% in 2018, after which expansion

3.2.5 Contributions to money supply growth

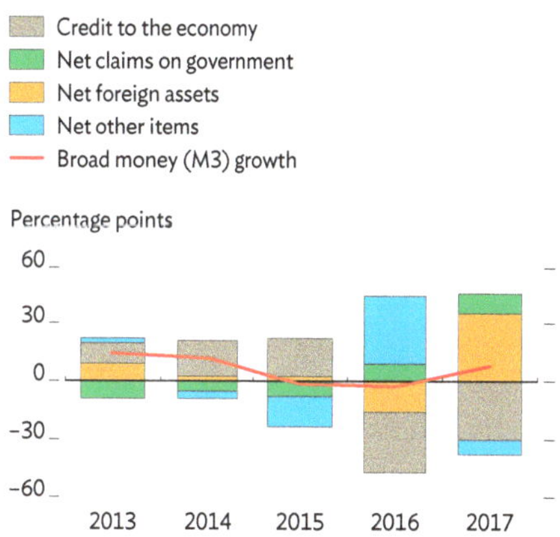

Source: Central Bank of the Republic of Azerbaijan.

should slow to a more sustainable 3.0% in 2019 with the Southern Gas Corridor nearly completed. Import substitution programs should provide further impetus to agriculture, which is expected to expand by 5.0% annually in the next 2 years. Services are projected to grow by 2.0% in both 2018 and 2019, reflecting modest gains in retail trade, transportation, and tourism thanks to a more competitive exchange rate and the construction of moderately priced hotels.

On the demand side, higher incomes and a more stable currency should raise private consumption in both 2018 and 2019. Higher government spending will boost public investment, particularly in infrastructure and to help meet demand for housing. Increased gas production, especially in 2019, should expand net exports.

Inflation is projected to decelerate to 7.0% in 2018, as exchange rate stability improves, and rise to 8.0% in 2019 with higher economic growth and a possible increase in utility tariffs (Figure 3.2.8). Combatting inflation will remain a key challenge, requiring coordinated monetary and fiscal policies.

Fiscal policy is expected to support growth, with additional SOFAZ transfers financing a major expansion in public investment. Including these transfers, the central budget deficit is projected to narrow to 1.5% of GDP in 2018 and 0.8% in 2019—though without transfers the deficit would widen from 7.1% of GDP in 2017 to 13.5% in 2018 and 12.8% in 2019. Stronger growth and higher oil prices are expected to boost revenues, as will higher customs duties and excise taxes that took effect in early 2018. With higher SOFAZ transfers, revenue is forecast to reach 32.8% of GDP in 2018 but decline to 30.3% in 2019. Expenditure is also projected to rise sharply, to 34.2% of GDP in 2018 as investment spending doubles, then ease to 31.1% in 2019.

Over the next 2 years, monetary policy is expected to remain tight to curb inflation. Increased oil earnings should tame volatility in the foreign exchange market, and the central bank may intervene to prevent any significant depreciation of the manat and thereby limit inflationary pressures. Banking is expected to remain highly dollarized, and with improved exchange rate stability the private sector may be more willing to borrow in foreign currency, boosting lending.

The current account surplus is forecast to widen to equal 6.9% of GDP in 2018 before returning to 6.2% in 2019 as the Shah Deniz II gas field begins operation, and with oil prices projected to remain above $60/barrel (Figure 3.2.9). Imports are forecast to decline by 6.0% in 2018, constrained by higher customs duties on machinery and cars, and show little change in 2019. Exports are projected to grow by 13.0% in 2018 with higher oil prices and then contract by 3.5% in 2019 with lower oil production and a forecast small decline in oil prices. The services deficit is projected to narrow by 7.4% in 2018 and 12.5% in 2019 as imports of construction-related services

3.2.6 State oil fund assets and central bank reserves

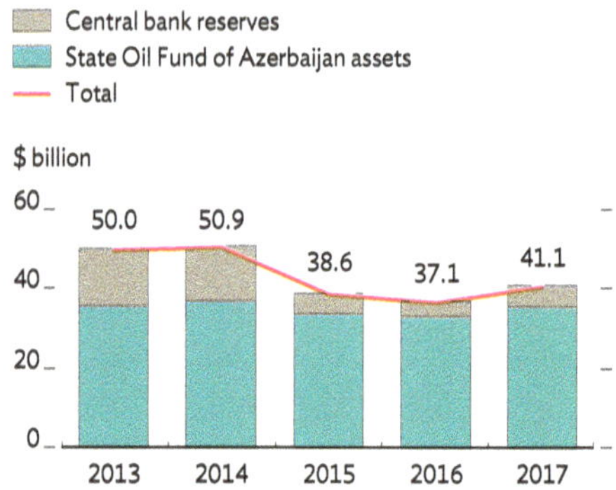

Sources: Central Bank of the Republic of Azerbaijan; State Oil Fund of Azerbaijan. http://www.oilfund.az (accessed 20 March 2018).

3.2.1 Selected economic indicators (%)

	2018	2019
GDP growth	1.7	2.0
Inflation	7.0	8.0
Current account balance (share of GDP)	6.9	6.2

Source: ADB estimates.

3.2.7 GDP growth

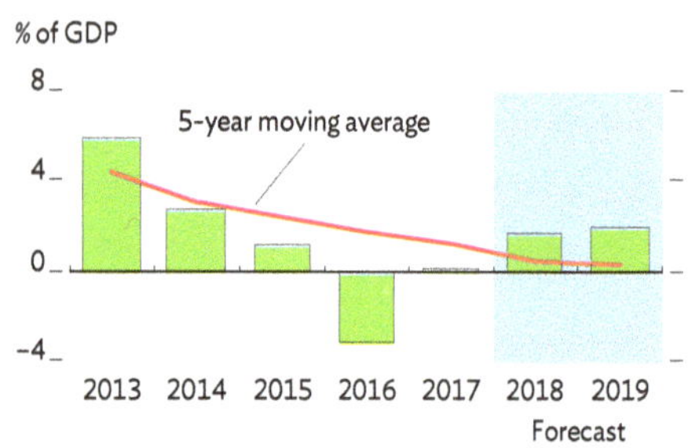

Sources: Central Bank of the Republic of Azerbaijan; ADB estimates.

decline while receipts from transportation and tourism improve. However, profit repatriation by foreign hydrocarbon companies will likely keep the income balance in deficit.

Policy challenge—fiscal consolidation to sustain sovereign wealth resources

Hydrocarbon revenues have long supported growth and development in Azerbaijan. To establish a strong financial position and preserve resources for future generations, the government created SOFAZ in 1999 as the country's sovereign wealth fund. It has been a significant source of financing for public investment, either directly or through transfers to the state budget. Thanks to the government's boosting of non-oil revenues, transfers from SOFAZ have steadily eased from 50.7% of budget revenues in 2014 to 37.1% in 2017. To promote good governance in the oil and gas sector, Azerbaijan established in April 2017 the Extractive Industries Transparency Commission under SOFAZ leadership.

SOFAZ assets slid from $37.1 billion in 2014 to $33.6 billion in 2015 as large transfers continued despite a fall in revenues caused by declines in oil prices and export volumes. To stop the drawdown, the government cut transfers by 6.3% in 2016 and a further 20% in 2017, helping restore SOFAZ assets to $35.8 billion at the end of 2017. Yet the return on SOFAZ investments weakened from 4.5% in 2007 to 1.9% in 2017. Over the past 5 years, annualized returns on SOFAZ investments have averaged 2.4%. By comparison, the real return on Norway's Oil Fund investment portfolio averaged 9.2%.

With a recovery in oil prices, the 2018 budget calls for a 51% rise in SOFAZ transfers to cover a 19.7% increase in spending. Although SOFAZ is projected to have a net income of $1.1 billion in 2018, further large transfers in the event of other revenue shortfalls could put pressure on SOFAZ assets. Along with central bank reserves, SOFAZ assets are important in determining the country's sovereign credit rating. Ensuring good quality and growth in fund assets is therefore important to maintain and improve Azerbaijan's creditworthiness, toward keeping moderate the cost of borrowing for development.

In December 2016, the government adopted a strategic road map that calls for rules-based SOFAZ transfers, ending the link between transfers and oil prices. This entails setting SOFAZ budget transfers in line with a medium-term fiscal framework that provides clear revenue targets and expenditure limits to ensure fiscal sustainability. Beyond this reform, strengthening the broader economy and improving tax administration would increase non-oil revenue, thereby reducing the need for SOFAZ budget transfers, as could more efficient public investment management. In addition, SOFAZ could identify ways to boost earnings in its investment strategy.

3.2.8 Annual inflation

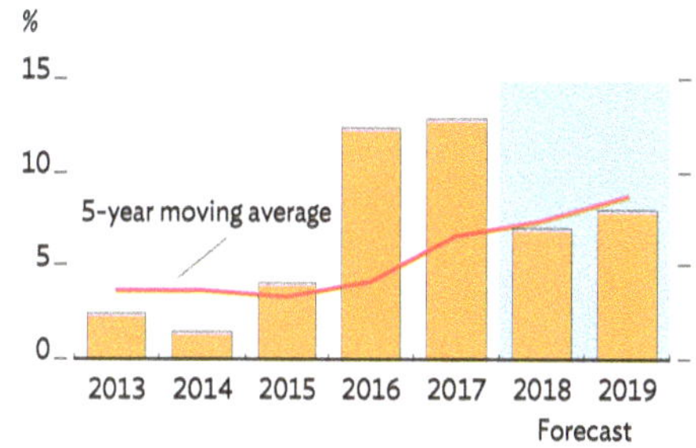

Sources: Central Bank of the Republic of Azerbaijan; ADB estimates.

3.2.9 Current account balance

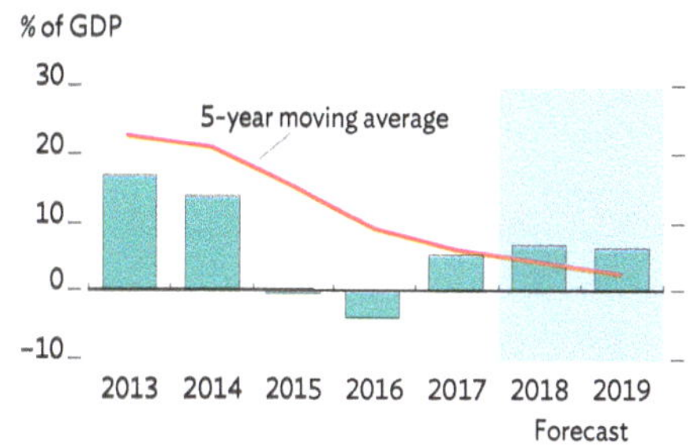

Sources: Central Bank of the Republic of Azerbaijan; ADB estimates.

Georgia

Strong gains in services, consumption, and investment boosted growth to an estimated 5.0% in 2017. Coupled with higher excise taxes and import prices, this tripled inflation to 6.0%. Export expansion helped narrow the current account deficit. Growth is projected to reach 4.7% in 2019, following a dip to 4.5% in 2018, on strong investment and exports. Greater diversification in service exports would support growth.

Economic performance

Growth rose to an estimated 5.0% from 2.8% in 2016, reflecting improvement in services and gains in private consumption, public investment, and net exports. On the supply side, services expanded by 5.5%, up from 2.4% in 2016 on robust growth in finance, up 9.0%, and hospitality services, with hotel and restaurant activity up 11.2% and transportation up 7.3%. Industry expanded by 5.6%, less than the 6.0% rise in 2016, with gains of 11.1% in construction and 6.8% in mining. Agriculture shrank by 2.7%, reversing 0.3% growth in 2016 as investment in the sector declined (Figure 3.3.1).

On the demand side, a 6.0% rise in consumption, including a 7.2% gain in private consumption, boosted expansion. Also supporting growth were a 2.6% pickup in investment as capital projects expanded and a sharp 41.6% rise in net exports, reflecting stronger demand in Georgia's main trading partners.

Average inflation accelerated to 6.0% from 2.1% in 2016, reflecting higher excise taxes and import prices, faster growth, and the lagged effects of currency depreciation in 2016. Prices rose notably for alcoholic beverages and tobacco by 17.1%, transport 15.1%, and food 6.8%. The year-on-year inflation rate in December was 6.7%, up from 1.8% a year earlier (Figure 3.3.2). In February 2018, annual inflation slowed to 2.7%.

Fiscal policy remained expansionary in 2017 despite curbs on current spending. The budget deficit narrowed to 0.9% of GDP from 1.4% in 2016, as tax collections that exceeded expectations and current outlays that fell short created room to expand capital expenditure while containing public debt (Figure 3.3.3). Revenue rose to the equivalent of 28.7% of GDP from 28.4% in 2016. Expenditure was 29.6% of GDP, versus 29.8% in 2016. Public debt declined to 42.3% of GDP at the end of 2017 from 44.6% a year earlier.

3.3.1 GDP growth by sector

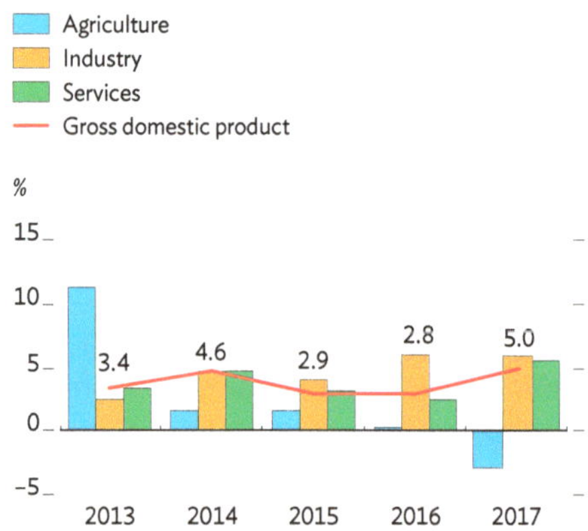

Source: National Statistics Office of Georgia. http://www.geostat.ge (accessed 21 March 2018).

3.3.2 Monthly inflation

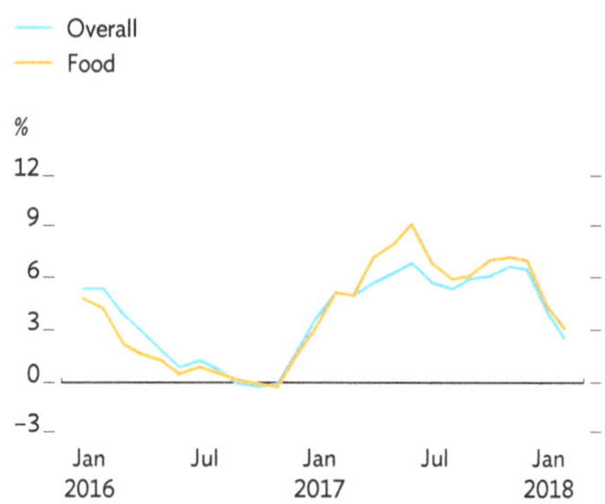

Source: National Statistics Office of Georgia. http://www.geostat.ge (accessed 8 March 2018).

This chapter was written by George Luarsabishvili of the Georgia Resident Mission, ADB, Tbilisi.

Monetary policy aimed for balance between combating inflation and supporting growth. The National Bank of Georgia, the central bank, raised the policy rate by 0.75 percentage points to 7.25% in two steps toward the end of 2017 to restrain inflation caused by unexpectedly vigorous expansion. Higher interest rates helped slow broad money growth to 14.8% from 20.2% in 2016, as private credit grew by 15.6% (Figure 3.3.4).

The Georgian lari fell by another 6.0% against the US dollar and 8.2% against the euro in 2017. It depreciated by 2.4% in nominal effective terms and by 2.2% in real terms (Figure 3.3.5), improving competitiveness and boosting exports. However, the lari started appreciating in early 2018.

Banks remained profitable and well capitalized as the central bank stiffened minimum capital requirements and started requiring banks to hold enough liquid assets to pass a stress test. Bank profits rose by 5.6%, and nonperforming loans remained below 4.0%. A central bank program to reduce dollarization helped cut foreign currency loans to 58.4% of the total from 63.9% at the end of 2016 and decrease foreign currency deposits to 63.6% from 69.8% a year earlier, thereby boosting growth in domestic currency deposits (Figure 3.3.6). Monetary tightening pushed the average lending rate to 16.2% from 14.4% in 2016, while the average deposit rate was little changed at 4.8% (Figure 3.3.7). A new deposit insurance system took effect at the start of 2018.

The current account deficit narrowed to the equivalent of 9.0% of GDP from 12.8% in 2016 thanks to strong growth in exports of goods and tourism-related services. Exports rose by 29.1%, and 9.4% growth in imports reflected hefty foreign direct investment. Although tourism boosted service receipts by 30.0%, the repatriation of higher profits and dividends weakened the income account. Remittance earnings rose by 19.8% to $1.4 billion. Gross reserves increased to $3.1 billion from $2.8 billion in 2016, including central bank purchases of $130 million. Public and publicly guaranteed external debt fell to the equivalent of 33.1% of GDP at the end of 2017 from 35.2% a year earlier.

Economic prospects

Growth is forecast to decelerate to 4.5% in 2018, with slower growth in services, and then rise to 4.7% in 2019 on higher consumption, public investment, and net exports (Figure 3.3.8). On the supply side, industry is forecast to expand by 5.4% in 2018 and 5.8% in 2019, with strong growth in construction and a rebound in utilities. Services are projected to grow by 4.5% in 2018 and 4.8% in 2019 on further gains in tourism and finance. With continued help from government programs, agriculture is expected to expand by 2.1% in 2018 and 3.7%

3.3.3 Fiscal indicators

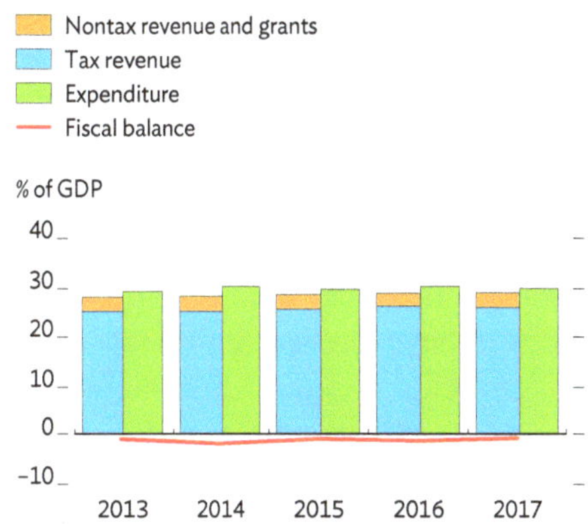

Sources: International Monetary Fund. www.imf.org; Ministry of Finance of Georgia. www.mof.ge (both accessed 20 March 2018).

3.3.4 Contributions to M3 broad money growth

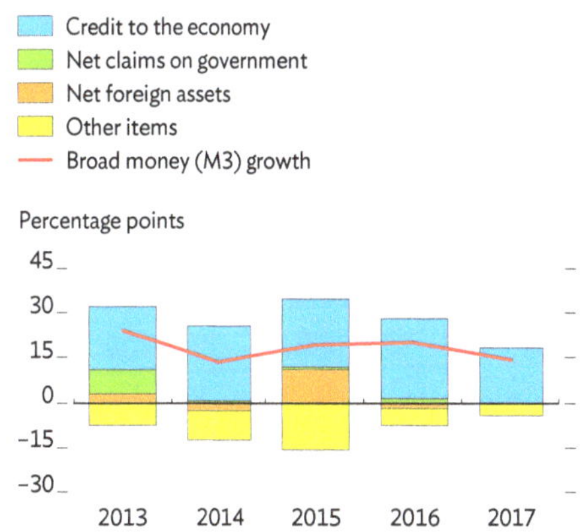

Source: National Bank of Georgia. https://www.nbg.gov.ge (accessed 20 March 2018).

3.3.5 Exchange rate

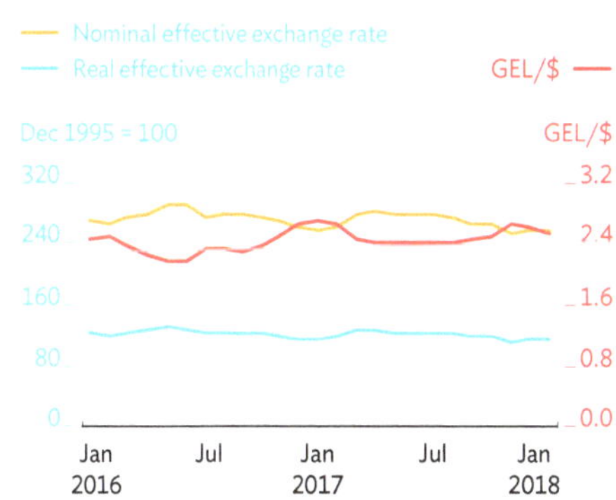

Source: National Bank of Georgia. https://www.nbg.gov.ge (accessed 20 March 2018).

in 2019. Pension and capital market reforms planned for the second half of 2018 should support growth by boosting savings and investment. Further support should come from anticipated reforms to upgrade infrastructure, improve arrangements for public–private partnership, promote trade integration, and strengthen public procurement. A downside risk to the forecast is weaker exports if Georgia's trading partners underperform. By contrast, a stronger external environment could accelerate growth beyond current projections.

Inflation is projected to slow to 3.5% in 2018 as the impact of one-time increases in excise taxes wanes (Figure 3.3.9). A further slowing toward 3.0% is projected for 2019 as fiscal discipline, supported by Georgia's current arrangement with the International Monetary Fund, promises to stabilize prices. Growth above expectations could boost inflation, however, as could energy or food price increases above current forecasts or currency depreciation if US monetary policy tightens faster than expected.

Fiscal policy is expected to remain tight, with the budget deficit limited to about 1.0% of GDP in both 2018 and 2019. With revenues forecast to decline slightly as a percentage of GDP, outlays will likely be held to 30.0% of GDP in 2018 and 29.5% in 2019 as curbs on wage payments and better targeting of social benefits constrain current expenditure.

Monetary policy is expected to move more toward supporting growth in 2018 as inflation slows. Broad money is projected to continue growing by about 15% a year in 2018 and 2019, reflecting similar growth in private credit. Foreign exchange interventions will likely be limited to smoothing exchange rate fluctuations.

The current account deficit is forecast to widen to 9.5% of GDP in 2018 on increased capital spending and narrow to 8.5% in 2019 with continued strong performance in exports and tourism (Figure 3.3.10). Exports of goods and services are projected to grow by 13.5% in 2018 and 15.0% in 2019 as the external environment improves further. Imports of goods and services are expected to rise by 9.5% in 2018 and 11.0% in 2019 with higher investment. Remittances should equal or exceed last year's $1.4 billion, helped by global recovery. Gross reserves are forecast to reach $3.3 billion in 2018 and $3.6 billion in 2019 on higher capital inflows and in response to increased reserve requirements for foreign currency bank deposits, though the share of foreign currency deposits should continue declining (Figure 3.3.11). Public and publicly guaranteed external debt is projected to increase slightly, to 42.7% of GDP at the end of 2018 and 42.8% a year later.

3.3.1 Selected economic indicators (%)

	2018	2019
GDP growth	4.5	4.7
Inflation	3.5	3.0
Current account balance (share of GDP)	-9.5	-8.5

Source: ADB estimates.

3.3.6 Foreign currency loans and deposits

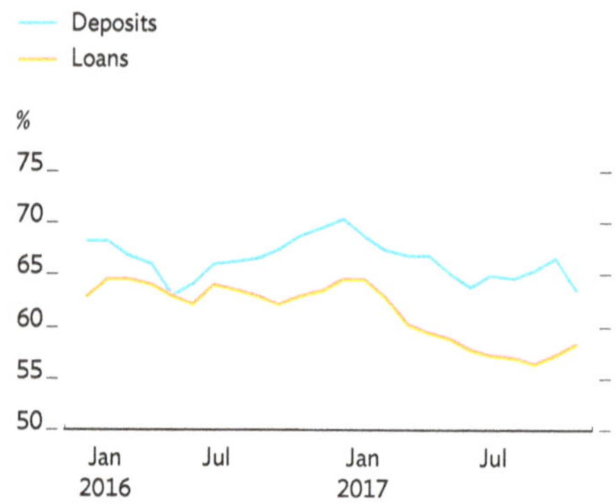

Source: National Bank of Georgia. https://www.nbg.gov.ge (accessed 20 March 2018).

3.3.7 Interest rates

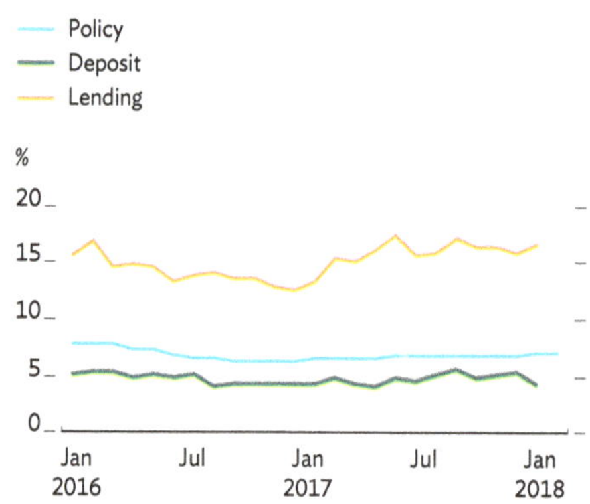

Source: National Bank of Georgia. https://www.nbg.gov.ge (accessed 20 March 2018).

3.3.8 GDP growth

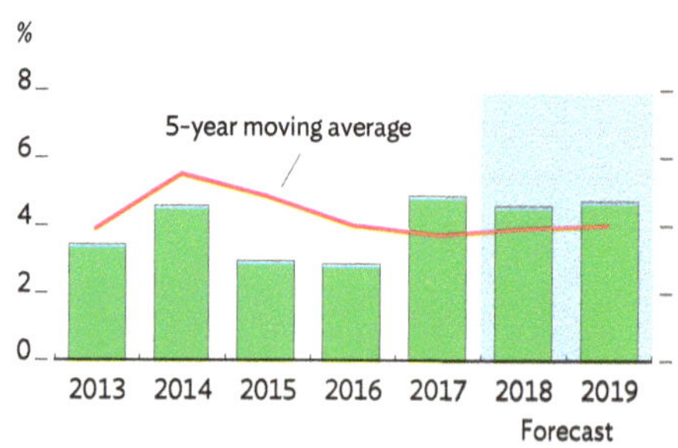

Source: *Asian Development Outlook* database.

Policy challenge—making service exports more diverse and sophisticated

Georgia's exports are highly concentrated, rendering the country vulnerable to small changes in external markets. Exported goods are mostly raw materials and intermediate manufactured goods with little value added. Meanwhile, exports of services exceed those of goods, more than doubling from 2007 to 2017, and are better able to withstand external shocks. Tourism comprises 53% of all service exports, with more sophisticated categories such as information and computer services providing only a small share.

While Georgia has relatively well-developed traditional services for travel and transport, thanks to its booming tourist trade, it needs to diversify into higher-value exports such as business, information, and computer services. Achieving this requires regulatory and tax reform to create a more supportive climate for their expansion.

Toward this objective, the government has strengthened the environment for developing information and computer services by providing extensive e-services in public financial management, health and education, state procurement, and real asset inventory maintenance using up-to-date eCloud and secure blockchain technologies. These services have facilitated activity, particularly for business and information services, supporting service exports and trade integration. In addition, developments in information and communication technology (ICT) have proved useful in prioritizing government investments, attracting talent to the service sector, and strengthening university–industry collaboration in research and development, thereby heightening business sophistication. Georgia's Innovation and Technology Agency has helped create a modern innovation ecosystem by supporting the application of innovative technologies in business. A government program called Produce in Georgia offers new firms expertise and funding to boost production capacity. Georgia's Export Credit Agency provides guarantees and insurance to export-oriented firms.

Services will also benefit from a one-stop shop for licenses, permits, and other government services for businesses that enhances the transparency of governance, the quality of public services, and government accountability. The government also plans to cut and simplify taxes for small and medium-sized enterprises, which could boost investment, particularly for export-oriented firms.

Recently negotiated free trade agreements with the European Union and the People's Republic of China promise to support the diversification and sophistication of Georgia's service exports by lowering nontariff barriers to trade in high-value services. The recently established Entrepreneurship

3.3.9 Inflation

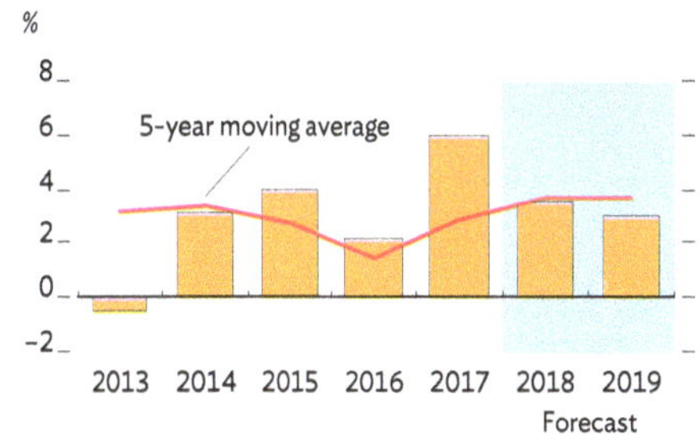

Source: *Asian Development Outlook* database.

3.3.10 Current account components

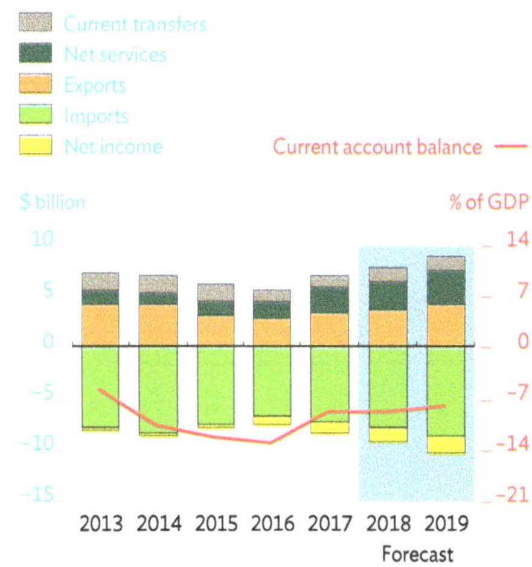

Sources: National Bank of Georgia. https://www.nbg.gov.ge (accessed 20 March 2018); ADB estimates.

3.3.11 Gross international reserves

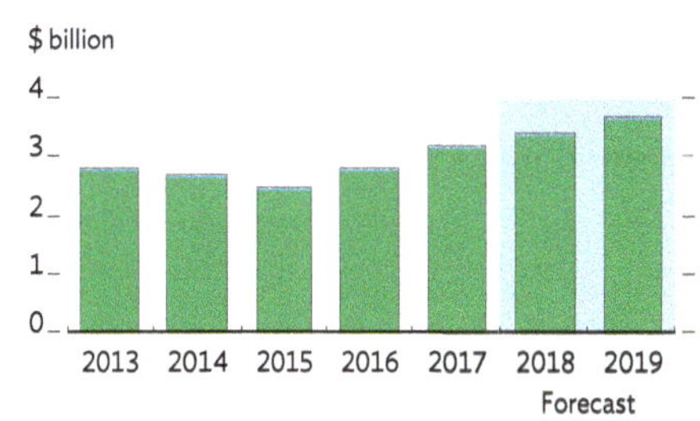

Sources: National Bank of Georgia. www.nbg.gov.ge; International Monetary Fund. www.imf.org (both accessed 20 March 2018); ADB estimates.

Development Agency is helping firms understand and meet the requirements of free trade agreements, thus promoting exports.

Georgia can do more, however, to develop business services linked to new technology. Possible measures include increasing investment in ICT-enabled commerce, the emerging internet of things, and the nascent use of virtual reality. Harnessing technological innovation and sophistication, it can also strengthen business process outsourcing, finance and insurance services, digital transactions, and blockchain technologies, in which Georgia already has some capacity.

Further progress can come from efforts to create an innovative environment in ICT-based business services with value-adding business intelligence, know-how, and data analytics. Strong ICT can boost productivity in the service sector and help create high-value jobs by providing readily accessible electronic services.

Georgia would benefit from better connectivity and improved education, as greater computerization and a highly educated and skilled workforce are essential for developing higher value products and services. Also helpful would be export promotion agencies and programs to expand the ability of firms to export through improvements in knowledge, productivity, and technology skills. In addition, programs that fill gaps in trade financing and make resources available to export-oriented firms can help meet the need for financing in a more contemporary service sector.

Kazakhstan

Growth rebounded to 4.0% in 2017 on sharply higher oil and mineral production. Exchange rate stability trimmed inflation to 7.4%, and export growth halved the current account deficit to 3.0% of GDP. More moderate expansion in industry, despite further gains in oil and mineral output, is projected to slow growth to 3.2% in 2018 and 3.5% in 2019. Inflation will ease further if higher oil export prices keep the exchange rate stable. Expanding the private sector would promote growth.

Economic performance

Growth recovered in 2017, most noticeably in the first half, when economic activity rose by 4.3% over weak performance in the first half of the previous year. Growth continued but at a slower pace in the second half, averaging 4.0% for the entire year, up from 1.1% in 2016.

On the supply side, industry, excluding construction, propelled growth, rising by 7.1% after a 0.4% decline in 2016 (Figure 3.4.1). By subsector, oil production rose by 10.5% on higher prices and expansion at the Kashagan field, and coal output rose by 6.0%, iron ore by 6.9%, and other minerals by 8.2%. Manufacturing grew by 5.1%, with metallurgy up 5.9%, food processing 4.1%, refined oil 5.1%, chemicals 7.2%, machinery 5.6%, and construction materials 3.7%. Meanwhile, services revived from 0.9% growth in 2016 to 2.7%, with trade up 3.2%, transport and logistics 4.8%, and finance 0.5%. Construction growth slowed steeply to 1.9% from 7.4% in 2016 with the completion of Expo 2017 in Astana and refinery plant modifications, and despite the continuation of programs to build infrastructure and housing and to expand oil production. Growth in agriculture almost halved to 2.9% from 5.4% as expansion in crop production slowed to 2.2% from 7.5% in 2016. Livestock production, by contrast, rose by 3.9%, up from 2.8% a year earlier.

On the demand side, data for the first 9 months of the year showed significantly higher net exports as the main source of growth. Export volume expanded by 0.8%, reversing a 5.2% decline in the period a year earlier, while import volume fell by 6.5%. Private consumption expanded by 1.4%, up from 1.0% in the same period of 2016, and public consumption by 1.8%, down from 2.7%. Investment growth accelerated to 2.5% from 1.3% a year earlier, with fixed capital formation rising by 3.9%.

This chapter was written by Zhanat Murzakulova of the Kazakhstan Resident Mission, ADB, Astana.

3.4.1 Supply-side contributions to growth

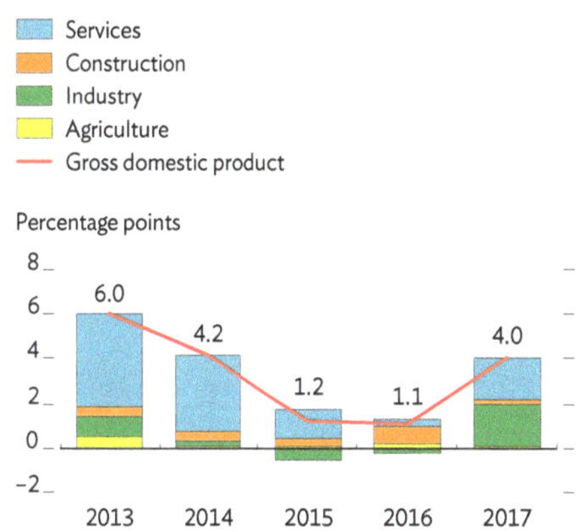

Source: Republic of Kazakhstan. Ministry of National Economy. Committee on Statistics.

3.4.2 Monthly inflation

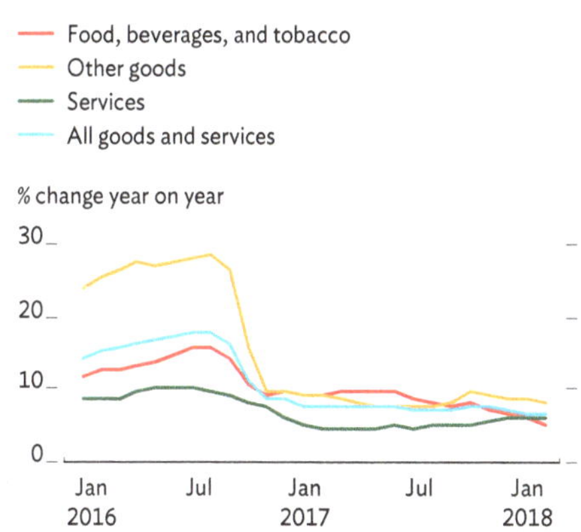

Source: Haver Analytics (accessed 9 March 2018).

A relatively stable exchange rate almost halved inflation to 7.4% in 2017 from 14.6% in 2016, despite higher increases at the beginning of the year and in the third quarter caused by periodic shortages of vegetables, meat, and gasoline. Prices rose by 8.6% for food, 8.4% for other goods, and 5.1% for services. The year-on-year inflation rate in December 2017 was 7.1% (Figure 3.4.2), reflecting a rise of 8.9% for goods other than food, including sharp increases for diesel fuel at 31.8%, gasoline 17.6%, coal 14.9%, and liquefied gas 8.6%. Large price hikes for vegetables and meat raised food prices by 6.5%, while increases for utilities, road and air transportation, and miscellaneous items boosted prices for services by 5.9%.

Fiscal policy supported growth, as the government maintained development programs for infrastructure, housing, and agriculture while allocating funds equal to 4.6% of GDP to support a large troubled bank. State budget revenue equaled 22.4% of GDP, reflecting a 13.1% rise in tax revenue and a 54.6% increase in transfers from the National Fund of the Republic of Kazakhstan, the sovereign wealth fund, in part to support the domestic banking system. Budget expenditure rose by nearly a third to equal 25.2% of GDP, reflecting outlays for bank recapitalization and increases for wages and salaries, state pensions, and education and training programs. The budget deficit equaled 2.8% of GDP, up from 1.6% in 2016. Public debt reached 25.7% of GDP, with external debt at 8.9% of GDP (Figure 3.4.3).

Monetary policy targeted inflation while maintaining a flexible exchange rate. As inflation came within the 6%–8% target, the National Bank of Kazakhstan, the central bank, reduced the base interest rate from 12.00% to 10.25% in three steps from February to August. It maintained this rate for the rest of 2017, despite greater pressure on the exchange rate and higher inflation in the second half, but reduced it to 9.75% in January 2018 and 9.50% in March. The central bank intervened periodically in 2017 to limit exchange rate volatility, injecting $620.5 million and helping limit dollarization to 48%–50% of the deposit base (Figure 3.4.4). It provided to five large banks the equivalent of 1.3% of GDP to boost their capital and strengthen the financial sector, providing subordinated debt convertible into central bank shares. Broad money contracted by 1.7% during the year, reflecting a small decline in total credit (Figure 3.4.5). The central bank reported nonperforming loans to have risen from 6.7% of all loans at the start of 2017 to 9.3% at the end of the year. A recent Standard & Poor's report estimates, however, the ratio much higher at 25%–30%.

The current account deficit narrowed sharply to the equivalent of 3.0% of GDP from 6.5% in 2016. With higher oil prices, particularly since July, full-year merchandise exports rose by 32.2% and imports by 13.1%, nearly doubling the trade surplus to $17.5 billion from $9.2 billion a year earlier.

3.4.3 Fiscal indicators

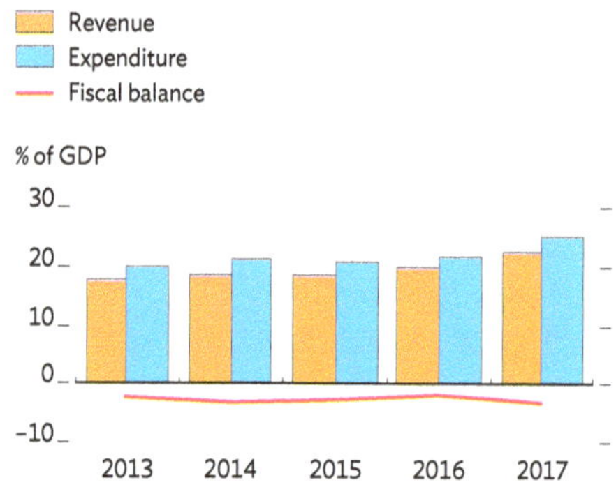

Sources: Ministry of Finance; Ministry of Economy; National Bank of the Republic of Kazakhstan.

3.4.4 Dollarization in the banking system

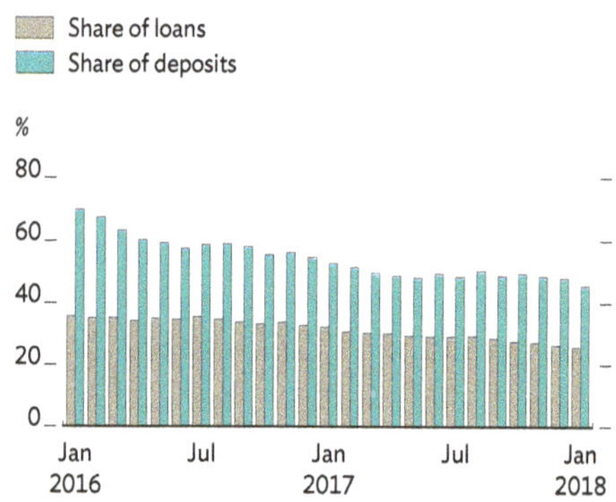

Source: National Bank of the Republic of Kazakhstan.

3.4.5 Growth in monetary aggregates

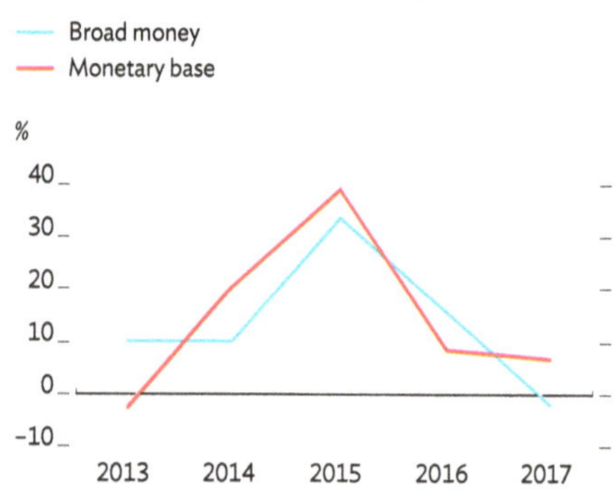

Source: National Bank of the Republic of Kazakhstan.

Higher profit repatriation nevertheless boosted the income deficit by 33.5%. Net international reserves rose by 3.6% to \$30.2 billion (19.1% of GDP), while sovereign wealth fund assets declined by 4.7% to \$58.3 billion (36.9% of GDP) at the end of 2017 (Figure 3.4.6). External debt, which is mostly private, reached at year-end 105.9% of GDP if counting intercompany debt, or 39.8% excluding it (Figure 3.4.7).

Economic prospects

Kazakhstan's recovery remains fragile. Growth is forecast to slow to 3.2% in 2018 as expansion in industry moderates and then improve to 3.5% in 2019 with slightly faster growth in capital formation and construction (Figure 3.4.8).

On the supply side, industry is projected to grow by 5.0% in 2018 and 4.5% in 2019, driven by oil production and mining. Some support will come from the government's industrialization policy and measures to promote manufacturing to make the subsector more competitive and achieve wider diversification. Construction will benefit from state programs and is likely to expand by 3.6% in 2018 and 4.2% in 2019. Agriculture is projected to grow by 3.0% in both years thanks to government efforts to raise productivity, diversify crop production, boost livestock, and promote exports of processed agricultural goods. Services growth is forecast at 2.5% in 2018 and 3.0% in 2019, with greater business activity supporting transport, logistics, trade, and real estate.

On the demand side, small wage increases are expected to limit expansion in private consumption to 2.2% in 2018 and 2.6% in 2019. Government efforts at fiscal consolidation will limit growth in public consumption to 1.0% in both years. However, government programs to boost manufacturing and establish a digital economy should raise investment by 5.0% in 2018 and 6.0% in 2019. Net exports in real terms are forecast to grow by 8.0% in 2018 and 6.0% in 2019, as higher oil exports and government policies to promote exports other than oil should help growth in exports outpace imports.

Inflation is projected to slow to 6.8% in 2018 and 6.2% in 2019, assuming a stable exchange rate, with the 12-month inflation rate to December falling to 6.2% in both years (Figure 3.4.9). Food price inflation is expected to ease to 7.5% in 2018 and 6.5% in 2019 thanks to government action to control the prices of critical foodstuffs, as well as its stabilization funds and measures to support domestic food production. Government efforts to prevent fuel shortages, limit monopoly pricing, and support competition are likely to slow price increases for other goods to 8.0% in 2018 and 7.0% in 2019 and to limit inflation in services to 5.0% each year.

Fiscal policy over the next 2 years is expected to be less expansionary, with the budget deficit falling to the equivalent

3.4.6 Foreign currency reserves and oil fund assets

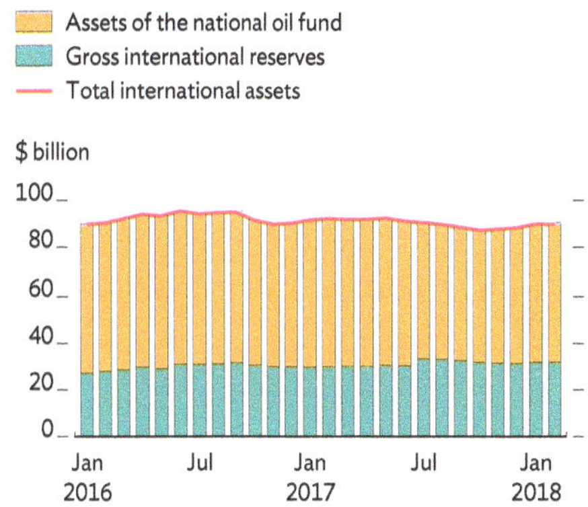

Source: National Bank of the Republic of Kazakhstan.

3.4.7 External debt

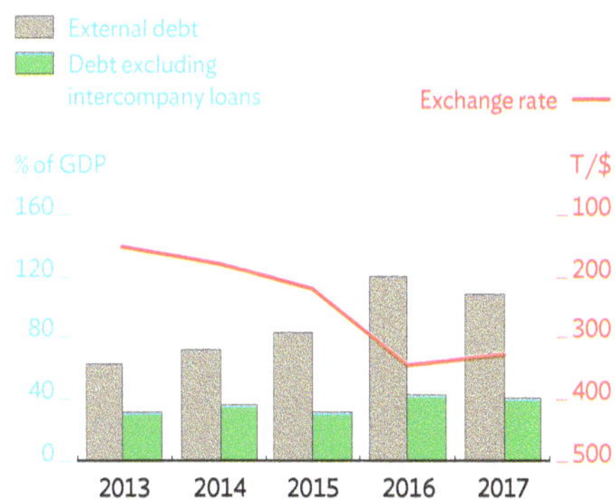

Sources: National Bank of Kazakhstan; ADB estimates.

3.4.8 GDP growth

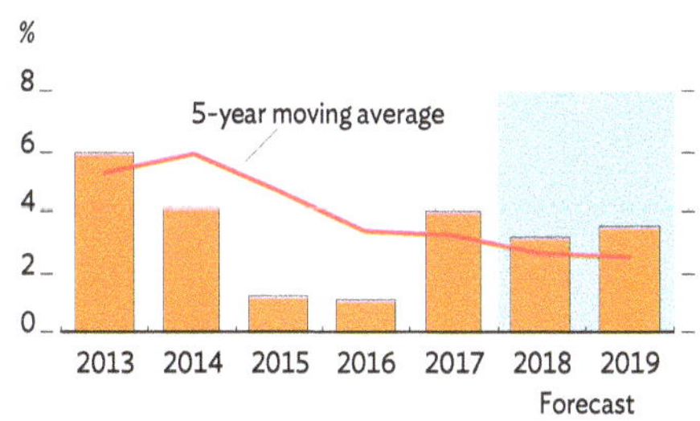

Source: *Asian Development Outlook* database.

of 1.1% of GDP in 2018 and 1.0% in 2019 as the non-oil deficit narrows to 7.1% in 2018 and 5.9% in 2019. Discretionary targeted transfers to the budget from the sovereign wealth fund will be eliminated in 2018, and, to conserve fund assets and promote fiscal consolidation, the annual guaranteed transfer will be scaled back from the current $8 billion to $6 billion in 2020. A new tax code that took effect early in 2018 aims to collect more taxes by improving administrative procedures, reducing distortions, and creating a more predictable tax environment, while providing support to small and medium-sized enterprises, agriculture, and geological exploration for petroleum and mineral wealth. A study by Standard & Poor's predicted that the new tax code would broaden the tax base and increase revenues by an estimated 3.0% of GDP. With sovereign wealth fund transfers shrinking, revenue is forecast to equal 18.0% of GDP in 2018 and 17.7% in 2019. Expenditure is forecast at 19.1% of GDP in 2018 and 18.7% in 2019, with no further outlays for bank recapitalization but continued spending on industrialization, infrastructure, housing, and agriculture. Public debt is projected to decline to 25.0% of GDP at the end of 2018 and 24.0% a year later.

Monetary policy over the next 2 years is expected to focus on reducing inflation. Broad money growth is projected at 2.0% annually, as efforts to drain excess liquidity will limit the expansion of credit to the private sector. Exchange rate policy will likely aim to limit volatility using targeted market interventions. The extent of nonperforming loans will probably remain substantial and continue to constrain lending.

The current account deficit is projected to widen to equal 3.3% of GDP in 2018 and 3.4% in 2019 as recovering private consumption boosts imports (Figure 3.4.10). Exports are projected to grow by 9.0% in 2018 on higher oil prices and, with somewhat lower prices in 2019, by 5.0% that year as operations at Kashagan continue to boost oil production and manufacturing exports grow steadily. Imports are forecast to expand by 9.1% in 2018 and 11.1% in 2019 on higher domestic demand and likely currency depreciation caused by lower oil prices in 2019, which will expand the deficit on services as well. The deficit in the income account is expected to widen by 14.0% in 2018, as higher oil prices boost profit repatriation, and narrow by 3.2% in 2019, as oil prices decline. Net international reserves are projected to reach $31.3 billion in 2018 and $32.4 billion in 2019, while sovereign wealth fund assets rise to $59.5 billion at the end of 2018 and $60.7 billion a year later, reflecting smaller transfers to the budget. External debt is projected to fall to the equivalent of 96.0% of GDP at the end of 2018 and 90.0% a year later.

3.4.9 Inflation

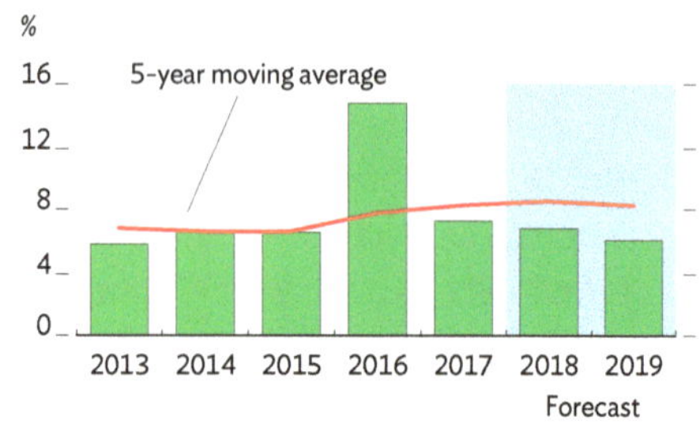

Source: *Asian Development Outlook* database.

3.4.1 Selected economic indicators (%)

	2018	2019
GDP growth	3.2	3.5
Inflation	6.8	6.2
Current account balance (share of GDP)	-3.3	-3.4

Source: ADB estimates.

3.4.10 Current account balance

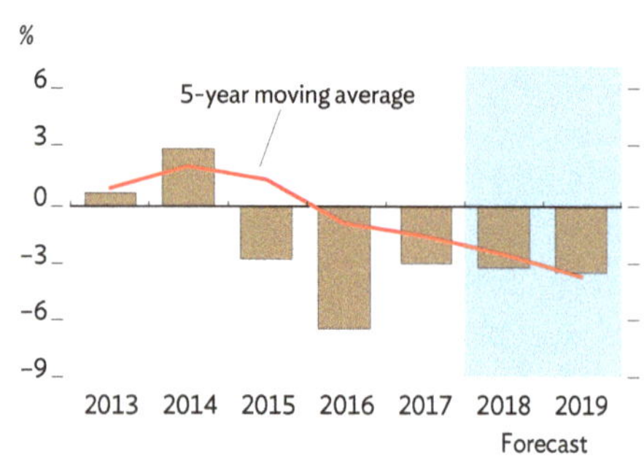

Source: *Asian Development Outlook* database.

Policy challenge—privatization and public–private partnership for private sector growth

With the adoption of a new development strategy and of a strategic plan for 2025 in early 2018, the government aims to shift from resource-driven growth to growth propelled by higher productivity and technology, in line with the so-called industry 4.0 programs now under way in many countries. The goal is to develop an export-oriented economy with higher value added to products and better integration into global value chains. The new development strategy prioritizes the privatization of state-owned enterprises and the development of public–private partnership (PPP) to support private sector expansion and sustain higher GDP growth.

The government aims to reduce its share of output, including value added by public enterprises, from the current 18% of GDP to 15% by the end of 2020, and to boost the GDP share of small and medium-sized enterprises from its current 27%. Since the start of the privatization effort in 2016, the government has sold 367 entities with a combined value of $500 million, and it aims to privatize 900 entities by 2020. Most valuable will be components of the state-owned Samruk-Kazyna holding company that are functional monopolies or face limited competition, including shares in the national railway, oil and gas fields, airlines, and energy and metal producers. Privatization is an important element of ongoing structural reform, as it attracts new foreign direct investment outside the oil sector and supports capital market development if pursued transparently and efficiently.

The government also plans to support private activity through PPP. This modality has traditionally been used to leverage fiscal resources by sharing the costs of infrastructure projects with private firms in areas where they can bring expertise and innovation. In Kazakhstan, such projects are intended to save budget resources while supporting the development of private firms. PPP activity is currently limited, however, comprising 116 contracts with a total value of $430 million. Most are in education, with 45 contracts, and healthcare, with 27. The government is considering new PPP projects worth $5.2 billion, equal to 3.2% of GDP. They will include the recently agreed, long-standing project to construct a new ring road around Almaty.

The success of PPP will depend on creating an enabling environment by undertaking bankable projects through a transparent bidding and selection process. In addition, an efficient risk-sharing framework must be created to allow private firms to secure their rights through contract enforcement and efficient dispute resolution. Also needed is a way to monitor and assess project performance and terminate projects as needed. This will require an appropriate legal and regulatory environment, supportive advisory services, and greater capacity in government to execute long-term contracts and manage operational risks, including uncertainty.

Establishing an enabling environment will allow PPPs to provide a wide range of investment projects that the government cannot undertake alone as it pursues fiscal consolidation. However, success will depend on developing capital markets and the rest of the financial system—in particular domestic capital markets, the weakness of which remains a key obstacle to economic growth. Access to finance remains limited, with the extent of financial intermediation narrow and its sophistication low. Sizable nonperforming loans further limit credit availability. An efficient banking sector requires better supervisory and regulatory enforcement. Private sector expansion will thus require financial deepening and a wider range of financial services to fund private investment.

Kyrgyz Republic

Growth improved to 4.6% from 4.3% in 2016, reflecting gains in industry, along with higher government spending and remittance earnings. Inflation accelerated to 3.2%, and the current account deficit narrowed to 4.8% of GDP from 11.6% in 2016. Growth is projected to moderate to 3.5% in 2018 before recovering to 4.0% in 2019. The government is promoting economic diversification through digitalization.

Economic performance

Growth accelerated to 4.6% from 4.3% in 2016 as strong gains in industry offset slower growth in services and agriculture (Figure 3.5.1). On the supply side, industry expanded by 9.3%, up from 7.1% in 2016, with large increases of 78.4% in mining, 7.6% in manufacturing, and 10.1% in electricity generation. Growth in construction slowed to 7.1% from 9.3% in 2016, despite slightly faster growth in fixed capital investment, mostly in construction for mining, energy generation, and transport. Agriculture expanded by 2.2%, less than the 2.9% rise in 2016, with crops up by 2.5% and animal husbandry by 2.0%. Services rose by 2.6%, down from 3.4% in 2016, as growth in wholesale and retail trade slowed to 3.5% from 8.0% a year earlier.

On the demand side, growth found support from higher public consumption and investment linked to election spending and a modest rise in private consumption that reflected a 24% improvement in remittance earnings (Figure 3.5.2).

Average inflation accelerated to 3.2% from 0.4% in 2016, while the year-on-year inflation rate to December reached 3.7% (Figure 3.5.3). Higher inflation reflected price increases of 2.7% for food, 4.0% for alcoholic beverages, 3.2% for other goods, and 6.9% for services. Inflation would likely have been higher if the average value of the Kyrgyz som against the US dollar had not appreciated by 1.5% during the year (Figure 3.5.4).

The government managed to narrow the fiscal deficit to 3.2% of GDP from 4.4% in 2016 despite election-related spending. Revenue rose to the equivalent of 28.7% of GDP from 27.4% in 2016, while expenditure rose slightly but remained equal to 31.8% of GDP. With the smaller deficit and currency appreciation, external government debt fell to 56.0% of GDP from 56.6% in 2016. Domestic debt equaled less than 6% of GDP.

3.5.1 GDP growth by sector

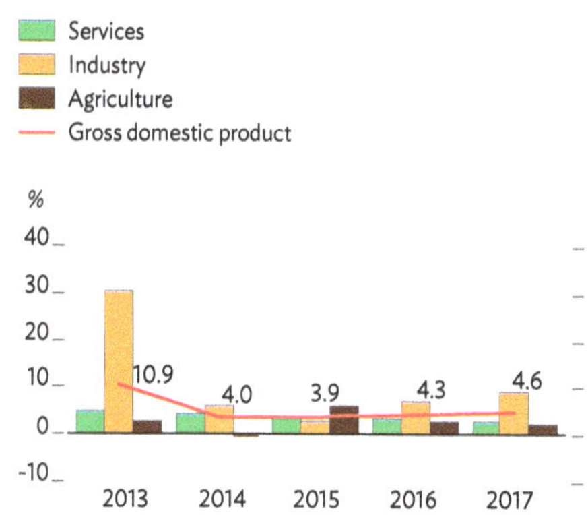

Source: National Statistics Committee of the Kyrgyz Republic. http://www.stat.kg (accessed 14 March 2018).

3.5.2 Remittances

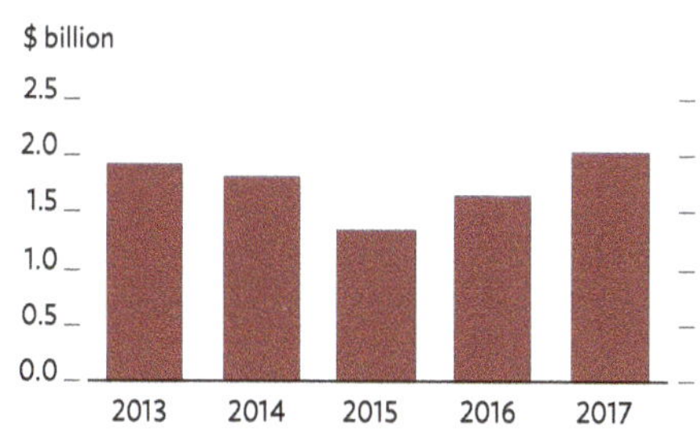

Source: National Bank of the Kyrgyz Republic. http://www.nbkr.kg (accessed 14 March 2018).

This chapter was written by Gulkayr Tentieva of the Kyrgyz Resident Mission, ADB, Bishkek.

Monetary policy remained cautious in 2017, with the National Bank of the Kyrgyz Republic, the central bank, intervening on currency markets only to smooth excess volatility. It kept the policy interest rate at 5.0%. The average deposit interest rate declined by 0.2 percentage points to 4.4%, while the average lending rate fell by 2.1 percentage points to 16.2%. Deposits rose by 10.4% and credit by 13.1%, while broad money grew by 17.9%, slightly more than the 14.6% growth in 2016. At the end of 2017, the incidence of nonperforming loans was 7.6%, down from 8.8% in 2016. However, dollarization remained extensive at the end of 2017, with 39.5% of loans and 49.8% of deposits in foreign currency.

The current account deficit is estimated to have narrowed to 4.8% from 11.6% in 2016, reflecting some improvement in the trade balance. Trade rose by 12.5% as exports expanded by 14.4% on gains in gold and agricultural products, and as higher demand for oil products, construction materials, textiles, and consumer goods lifted imports by 11.4%. By the end of 2017, international reserves had risen by $0.2 billion to reach $2.2 billion, or cover for 4.4 months of imports. With a decline in private debt and currency appreciation, external debt including government-guaranteed and private debt is estimated to have fallen to equal 94.9% of GDP at the end of 2017, down significantly from 103.2% a year earlier (Figure 3.5.5).

Economic prospects

Growth is projected to slow to 3.5% in 2018, reflecting an expected decline in output from the Kumtor, the main mine in the important gold-mining industry (Figure 3.5.6). Recovery to 4.0% is expected in 2019 with some improvement in the domestic economy and continued growth in the region.

On the supply side, growth should come from agro-processing, light industry, and, to some extent, construction. On the demand side, higher remittances will raise household incomes, bolstering private consumption. Over the longer term, the country should benefit from increased foreign trade and the free movement of labor, capital, and services provided by membership in the Eurasian Economic Union (EEU).

Inflation is forecast to accelerate to 4.0% in 2018 and 4.5% in 2019 with continued growth and higher tariffs required by EEU membership. However, inflation could worsen with depreciation of the som in response to weakness in the currencies of Kazakhstan and the Russian Federation.

The central bank is expected to maintain a flexible exchange rate and continue to limit interventions to smooth excessive exchange rate volatility. Monetary policy will likely stay focused on maintaining price stability in view of the expected rise in inflation.

3.5.3 Monthly inflation

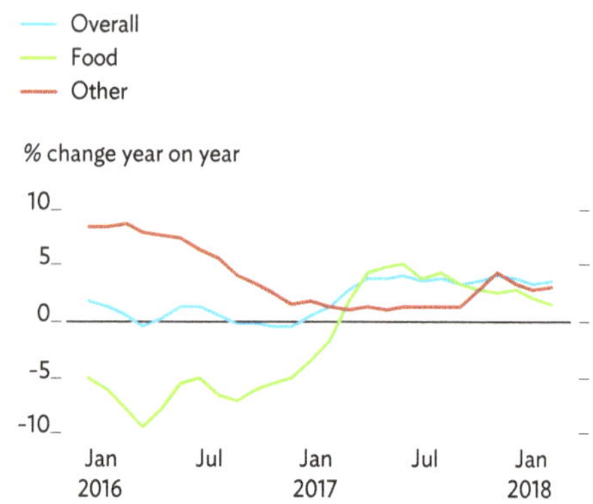

Source: National Bank of the Kyrgyz Republic. http://www.nbkr.kg (accessed 14 March 2018).

3.5.4 Exchange rate

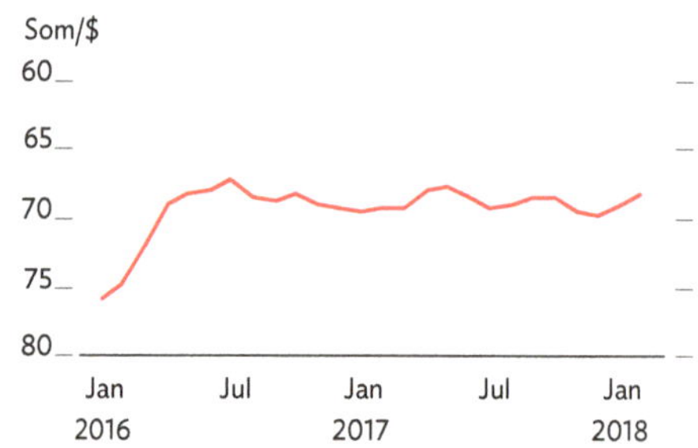

Source: National Bank of the Kyrgyz Republic. http://www.nbkr.kg (accessed 5 March 2018).

3.5.5 External debt

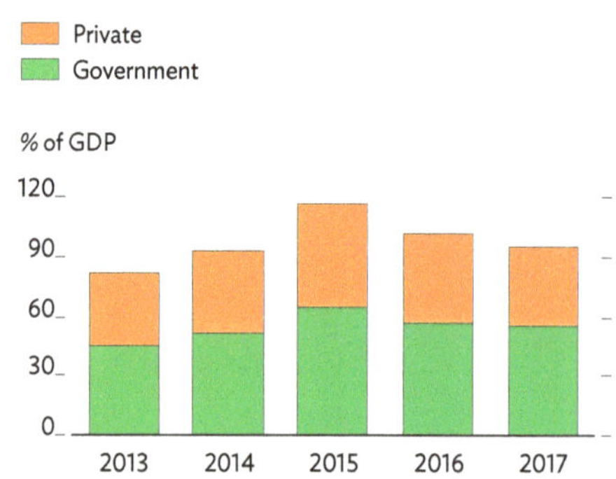

Note: Government debt is both government and government-guaranteed debt.

Sources: Ministry of Finance; National Statistics Committee. http://www.stat.kg; National Bank of the Kyrgyz Republic. http://www.nbkr.kg (both accessed 20 February 2018).

The fiscal deficit is projected to narrow to equal 2.5% of GDP in 2018 and 2019 as the government restrains expenditure while improving tax policy and administration. Tax revenue could rise if EEU accession yields more customs revenue than now forecast. Fiscal consolidation remains a priority to rebuild government finances and ensure debt sustainability. Consolidation will likely involve rationalizing expenditure by reforming public wages, cutting subsidies, and improving the targeting of the social benefits. The government aims to raise revenue as well by broadening the tax base and strengthening tax and customs administration. External public debt is projected to equal 55.0% of GDP at the end of 2018 and 56.0% a year later.

The current account deficit is expected to widen to 12.0% in 2018 and then narrow to 10.0% in 2019 (Figure 3.5.7). Export growth is projected to slow to 8.0% in 2018 with lower gold exports and then recover to 14.0% in 2019 with higher exports of agricultural products and textiles. Infrastructure projects are expected to boost imports by 12.0% in 2018 and 11.0% in 2019. Remittances will likely rise by a further 25%–30% in 2018 and 2019, reflecting advantages to Kyrgyz migrant workers from the EEU treaty. International reserves are forecast to remain at $2.2 billion in 2018 and reach $2.3 billion at the end of 2019. The outlook for exports and the current account balance could worsen with weak demand from EEU trade partners and because of Kyrgyz products' poor compliance with EEU veterinary and agricultural standards.

While debt sustainability has improved, vulnerability to external and domestic risks persists. The Kyrgyz Republic is considered at moderate risk of debt distress because of continuing vulnerabilities regarding currency stability and possible deterioration in the fiscal balance. With public external debt now equal to 56% of GDP, total external debt could, barring shocks, be less than 96% of GDP by the end of 2019.

Policy challenge—promoting diversification through digitalization

The Kyrgyz Republic is a small, landlocked country with limited natural resources and a narrow economic base. Worker remittances and gold exports have been its main income sources. Remittances from Kazakhstan and the Russian Federation have averaged about 25% of GDP during the past 5 years, while gold production has been estimated to provide on average 8.7% of GDP and 30% of export earnings. With limited opportunities for growth in these areas, the Kyrgyz Republic needs to diversify its economy and find new income sources.

3.5.1 Selected economic indicators (%)

	2018	2019
GDP growth	3.5	4.0
Inflation	4.0	4.5
Current account balance (share of GDP)	-12.0	-10.0

Source: ADB estimates.

3.5.6 GDP growth

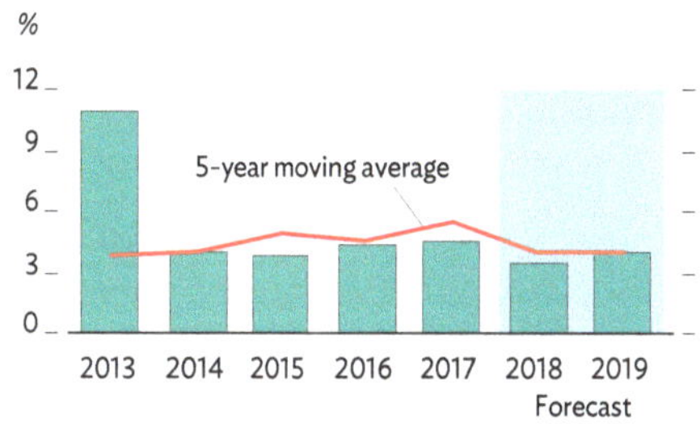

Sources: National Statistics Committee of the Kyrgyz Republic. http://www.stat.kg (accessed 14 March 2018); ADB estimates.

3.5.7 Current account balance

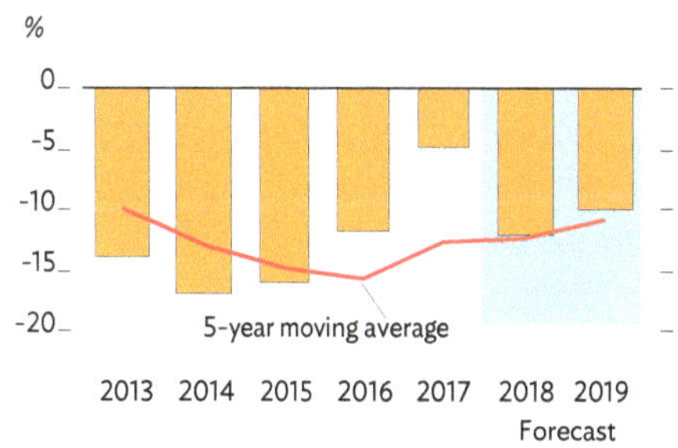

Sources: National Bank of the Kyrgyz Republic. http://www.nbkr.kg (accessed 14 March 2018); ADB estimates.

A key obstacle to further development has been the country's lack of advanced business facilities, including poor connectivity. According to the *Global Competitiveness Report 2017–2018*, in which the Kyrgyz Republic ranks 102 out of 137 countries, it ranks particularly low in innovation at 127 and business sophistication at 126. It also lags in technological readiness at 102 and infrastructure at 109. With technological innovation dramatically reshaping the global environment and information flows becoming increasingly important, improving the country's poor digital environment is essential for developing new sources of income and employment.

To respond to these challenges, the government introduced the Taza Koom program of support for sustainable development through digitalization and innovation. It involves creating a countrywide fiber-optic network to improve internet access in even the most remote areas, increase digital transactions, and strengthen public service delivery to communities and firms. The goal is to encourage a shift toward higher-tech and innovative activities that can support better-paying jobs. The program aims to improve public administration and the delivery of services such as education and health care, heighten transparency in the public sphere to fight corruption (as the name suggests), and reduce the transaction costs that firms incur to meet registration and other regulatory requirements and to pay taxes.

Taza Koom's current action plan covers the year beginning in August 2017. It includes projects on information infrastructure, cyber security to enable a cashless economy, and the streamlined delivery of services by regional and municipal governments. Its digital infrastructure project is laying fiber-optic lines, expanding access to mobile high-speed internet and the applications available, and providing means to achieve a more fault-tolerant network with improved data transmission. Another project aims to ensure the availability of information in multiple languages, including Kyrgyz.

While the Taza Koom program has the potential to advance diversification through digitalization, additional measures would help achieve this goal.

One would be to accelerate reform to improve the business climate by addressing problems with contract enforcement, reliable electricity supply, resolving insolvency, and paying taxes—all areas where the country ranks especially low, at 100 or worse among 190 countries covered in the most recent World Bank *Doing Business* survey.

Others would be to improve the management of public investment, encourage private investors to fill supply gaps in infrastructure for energy and other areas, and increase job training so that workers can satisfy the skills requirements of new jobs. Also helpful would be reform to trade policies that would maximize benefits from preferential arrangements accorded by the Kyrgyz Republic's trading partners.

Tajikistan

Growth rose to 7.1% in 2017 as the external environment strengthened and public investment continued. Inflation accelerated to 6.7%. Lower imports and higher exports and remittances moved the current account into surplus. Growth is projected to slow to 6.0% in 2018 with tighter fiscal policy and continued weakness in banking, recovering to 6.5% in 2019. Higher infrastructure spending will likely return the current account to a deficit. Tajikistan needs to expand productive employment.

Economic performance

Growth accelerated to 7.1% from 6.9% in 2016, reflecting higher exports and remittances as conditions improved abroad and ambitious public investment continued (Figure 3.6.1).

On the supply side, industry growth accelerated to 21.3% from 16.0% in 2016 with gains in mining at 22.5%, manufacturing 22.7%, and electricity generation 16.7% (Figure 3.6.2). Aluminum production plunged by 22.0% because input supplies were unstable and production facilities were under renovation. Gold extraction increased by 11.2%. Agriculture rose by 6.8%, up from 5.2% in 2016 as favorable weather and additional cultivated area boosted cotton production by 35.8%. Higher remittances increased disposable income by 10.0% and retail trade by 6.6%, reversing the service sector's 0.3% contraction in 2016 with 1.8% growth.

On the demand side, higher public spending helped expand investment by 4.1%, while private consumption rose by 2.4%. Net exports improved by 8.6% as higher output and external demand boosted exports while import substitution further reduced imports.

Inflation accelerated to 6.7% from 6.1% in 2016 as bank recapitalization fueled liquidity despite tight monetary policy (Figure 3.6.3). Prices rose by 7.7% for food, 4.4% for other goods, and 7.7% for services. Continued depreciation of the Tajik somoni by 12% fueled inflation, as did a 15% hike in average electricity tariffs in October. Flat global food prices and slow credit growth kept inflation from rising faster.

Fiscal policy aimed to contain current spending, though higher infrastructure outlays and weak revenues widened the budget deficit to the equivalent of 2.5% of GDP from 1.7% in 2016 (Figure 3.6.4). Revenue equaled 31.0% of GDP, down from 32.1% in 2016 as further declines in imports caused shortfalls in collections of value-added tax, excises, and customs duties—despite better tax administration. Expenditure equaled 33.5% of GDP, near the 33.8% recorded in 2016, despite fiscal consolidation

3.6.1 GDP growth by sector

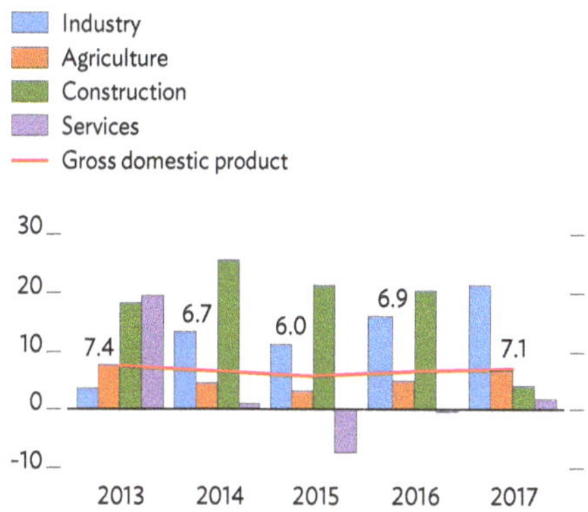

Source: Tajikistan State Statistical Agency.

3.6.2 Supply-side contributions to growth

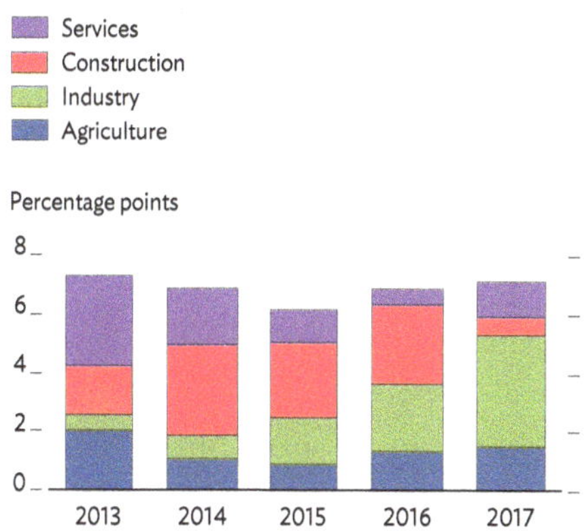

Source: Tajikistan State Statistical Agency.

This chapter was written by Muhammadi Boboev of the Tajikistan Resident Mission, ADB, Dushanbe.

and efforts to control costs while maintaining social programs and using foreign finance to expand capital spending. Public and publicly guaranteed external debt jumped to 40.3% of GDP from 32.7% in 2016 because of currency depreciation and new borrowing, in particular a $500 million eurobond offering to finance a major infrastructure project (Box 3.6.1). Domestic debt reached 11.1% of GDP as troubled banks were shored up with Treasury securities issued in exchange for assets. With public debt breaching several indicative limits, the International Monetary Fund decided in November 2017 to reclassify Tajikistan's debt distress level from low to high.

Monetary policy aimed to limit currency depreciation and combat inflation. To stem depreciation, the National Bank of Tajikistan, the central bank, restrained money growth while continuing to require that all remittances in rubles be converted to somoni and that banks immediately sell to it half of the rubles converted. Moreover, in February 2017, all Tajiks were required to register their foreign accounts. To mitigate expectations of devaluation, the central bank unified official and market exchange rates on 24 May 2017. It liberalized gold trading domestically while tightening foreign exchange controls. These measures helped stabilize the exchange rate after May and reduce the share of deposits in foreign currency from 62.5% at the end of 2016 to 56.6% a year later.

To curb inflation, the central bank raised its refinancing rate from 11.0% to 12.5% in February 2017 and again to 16.0% in March, when it also increased reserve requirements and the interest rate on liquidity support loans. The authorities expanded sales of central bank securities and Treasury bills to the equivalent of 12.4% of GDP, up from 7.9% in 2016, to sterilize the impact on liquidity of the ruble conversion requirement and bank recapitalization. The central bank introduced new monetary policy instruments, including overnight and intraday lending facilities and overnight deposits. In a move toward inflation targeting, it established a medium-term inflation goal of 7% ±2 percentage points, while improving its communication of monetary policy decisions.

Broad money grew by 21.8%, slowing from 37.1% in 2016 as credit to the private sector plunged by 18.8% because of weak demand for loans, financial sector difficulties, and a sharp slowdown from 71% to 21% in the growth of reserve money, meaning currency in circulation plus bank reserves (Figure 3.6.5). Nonperforming loans fell from 54.0% of the total at the end of 2016 to 36.5% a year later. The average return on assets improved to 0.4% from –28% in 2016, and on equity to 1.5% from –20.7% (Figure 3.6.6). Higher minimum capital requirements and stronger supervision cut the number of microfinance organizations by 7.7%. Meanwhile, two large systemic banks remained troubled despite having received a 5-year government loan in 2016 to bolster their capital; resolution plans have yet to be approved.

3.6.1 Tajikistan's $500 million eurobond financing for the Rogun hydropower project

Tajikistan started the 3,600-megawatt Rogun hydropower project in the 1980s, but the collapse of the Soviet Union halted construction, and debates postponed its resumption for many years. The government views the project as crucial to resolving Tajikistan's winter electricity deficit and turning the country into a regional energy supplier. Recent project assessments have concluded that Rogun would meet international efficiency standards with some design modifications, including measures to mitigate adverse environmental effects. A contract for $3.9 billion to build the project was approved in July 2016, and construction restarted in October 2016.

With limited fiscal resources, the government decided to finance the project in part through an initial issue of $500 million in eurobonds, which required obtaining a sovereign credit rating. Rated B3 by Moody's Investors Service and B– by Standard & Poor's, Tajikistan raised $500 million with 10-year bonds paying a fixed interest rate of 7.125%. Fund managers bought 84% of the bonds and hedge funds 9%, with 38% of purchases from the US, 35% from the euro area, and 24% from the United Kingdom.

3.6.3 Sources of inflation

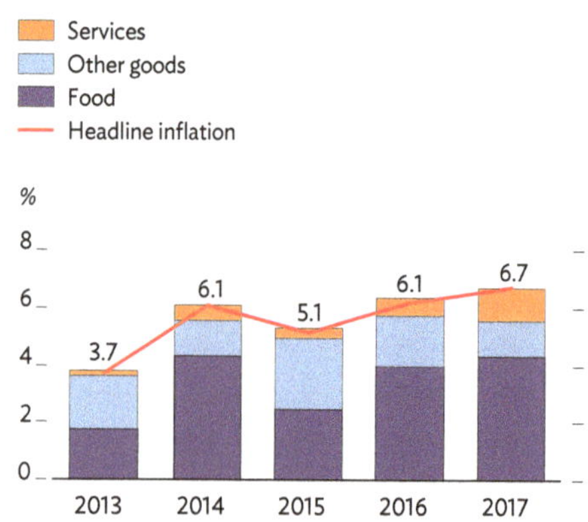

Source: Tajikistan State Statistical Agency.

The current account is estimated to have achieved a surplus equal to 3.0% of GDP, reversing a deficit of 3.8% in 2016 as imports continued to fall and a better external environment boosted exports and remittances. The trade deficit narrowed to $1.8 billion from $2.1 billion in 2016 as exports rose by 9.4%, up from 0.8% in 2016, and imports fell by 8.5%, albeit less than the 11.5% decline in 2016. With economic recovery in the Russian Federation, remittances rose to $1.7 billion in the first 9 months of 2017 from $1.4 billion in the same period of 2016. Gross international reserves nearly doubled to $1.2 billion thanks to the improved trade position, purchases of domestically produced gold, and proceeds from the eurobond issue (Figure 3.6.7).

3.6.4 Fiscal balance and public debt

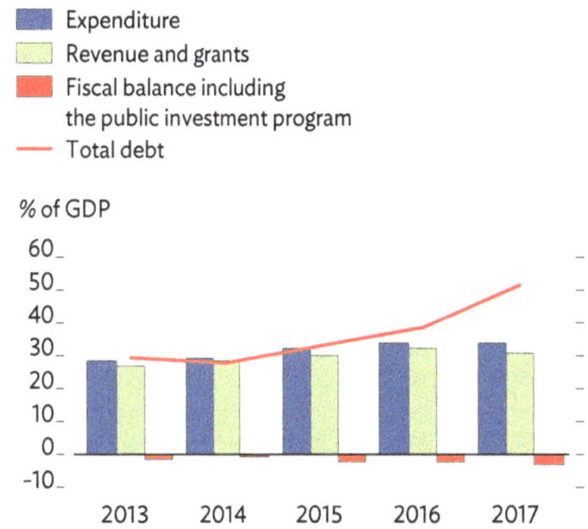

Sources: National Bank of Tajikistan; Tajikistan State Statistical Agency.

Economic prospects

Growth is forecast to moderate to 6.0% in 2018, despite further improvements in the external environment, as fiscal tightening to address the high ratio of public debt to GDP constrains public investment and a weak banking sector limits credit growth, curbing private investment. Growth is expected to recover to 6.5% in 2019 on gains in manufacturing and mining, higher remittances, and the expanded replacement of imports with local alternatives.

On the supply side, industry is forecast to expand in 2018 and 2019 as construction on the Rogun hydropower project continues and mining posts gains. In addition, the opening of the Tajik segment of a gas pipeline from Turkmenistan to the People's Republic of China should expand manufacturing. Agriculture is expected to rise modestly, barring an unusually dry winter. Higher remittances should boost services moderately.

On the demand side, consumption should expand, reflecting higher remittances and expected hikes in public sector wages. However, fiscal consolidation and weak credit expansion will limit growth in investment. Net exports are forecast to rise as exports expand and domestic production increasingly replaces imports.

Inflation is projected to accelerate to 7.5% in 2018 as liquidity is spurred by further sizable bank recapitalization, public salary and electricity tariff hikes, and modest somoni depreciation. Despite higher remittances in 2019, inflation will likely moderate to 7.0% (Figure 3.6.8).

Over the next 2 years, fiscal policy is expected to remain tight, with the budget deficit projected to remain at 2.5% of GDP in 2018 and 2019, consistent with the approved fiscal strategy for 2017–2020. Slower growth and constrained imports are projected to limit revenue to 30.2% of GDP in 2018 and 30.9% in 2019. Expenditure is forecast to equal to 32.7% of GDP in 2018 and 33.4% in 2019, with accelerated debt repayment and demands for public spending forecast to raise outlays. Expenditure could be higher with additional recapitalization of troubled banks, a cleaning of arrears at state-owned enterprises, or faster currency

3.6.5 Monetary indicators

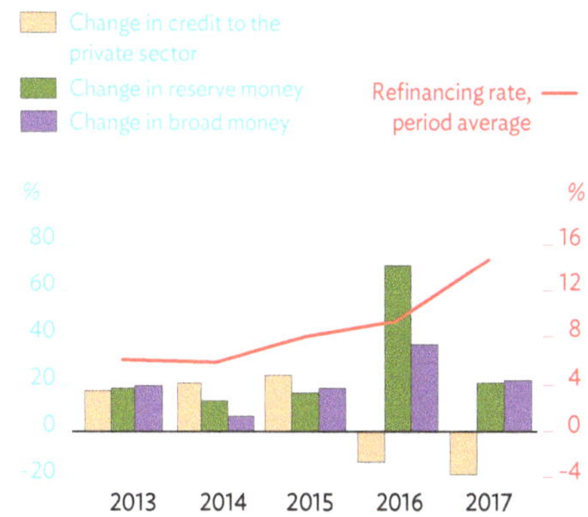

Sources: National Bank of Tajikistan; Tajikistan State Statistical Agency.

3.6.6 Indicators of banking system soundness

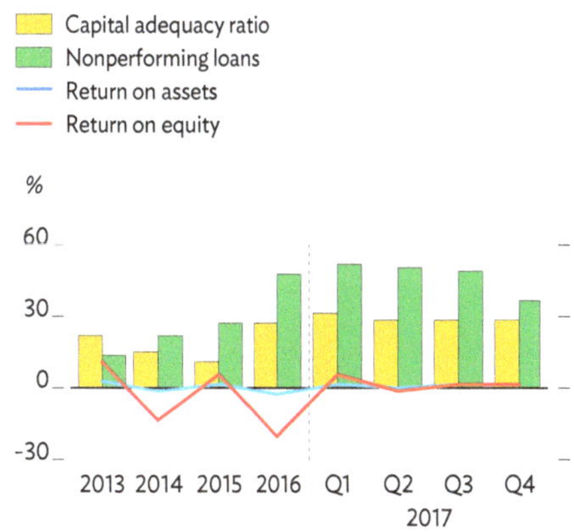

Q = quarter.

Source: National Bank of Tajikistan.

depreciation. Any of these developments would add to public debt, as would further eurobond placements to finance large infrastructure projects.

Monetary policy is expected to focus in 2018 and 2019 on lowering inflation while avoiding an economic slowdown. Broad money is projected to expand moderately with some reserve accumulation, higher foreign exchange deposits, and further support for local currency lending. Weak demand and continued high nonperforming loans should limit growth in private credit. The central bank may adjust the refinancing rate if needed to contain inflation. With a more flexible exchange rate to support inflation targeting, rate changes can do more to absorb external shocks, albeit at the cost of greater fluctuation.

Despite expectations of higher remittances (Figure 3.6.9), the current account surplus is forecast to narrow to 1.1% of GDP in 2018 and return to a deficit in 2019, at 3.0%, as higher spending on the Rogun hydropower project worsens the deficit in services (Figure 3.6.10). Higher electricity and mining output will contribute to projected export growth of 15.0% in 2018 and 20.0% in 2019 as the launch of the first and the second Rogun generators expand industry. Even with efforts at import substitution, imports are expected to grow by 5.0% in 2018 and 10.0% in 2019, powered by further gains in remittances and higher capital spending. With imports recovering and construction of the Rogun project accelerating, little increase in gross international reserves is expected.

3.6.7 Gross international reserves

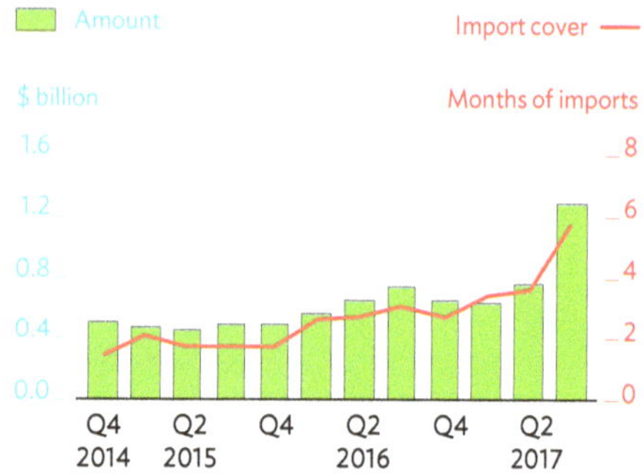

Q = quarter.
Source: National Bank of Tajikistan.

3.6.8 Inflation

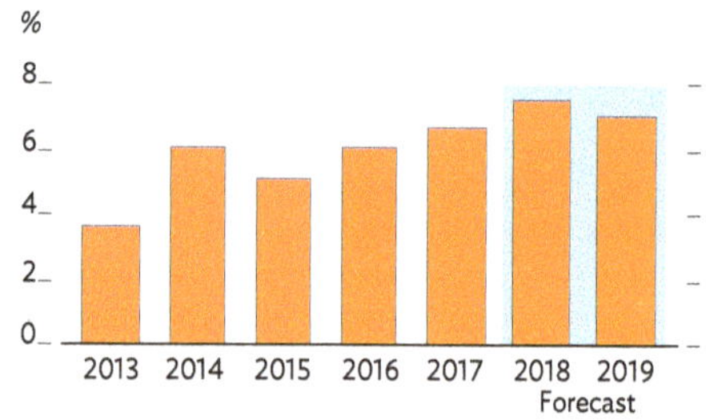

Sources: Tajikistan State Statistical Agency; ADB estimates.

Policy challenge—promoting productive employment

Despite average growth of 7.2% from 1997 through 2016, Tajikistan is not creating enough jobs. Annually from 1991 to 2016, the working-age population increased by 3.0% but employment rose by only 0.7%. Economic growth has come largely from improved labor productivity and higher domestic consumption financed by remittances from Tajik migrant workers. Meanwhile, large-scale labor migration not only boosted household income and purchasing power but also took the spotlight off domestic job creation.

Since 2013, both labor migration and remittances have fallen significantly, despite some recovery in 2017, heightening pressure to create jobs for young entrants into the labor market and returning migrant workers. Growth in jobs must supplement higher labor productivity in the years ahead.

A report last year to the Ministry of Economic Development and Trade suggested that some 900,000 productive jobs—jobs able to lift households out of poverty—needed to be created in the 10 years to 2025 to reduce the 2025 poverty rate to 18% from the current 30%, based on a national poverty line set at TJS175.2 per month. More than two-thirds of these jobs, about 660,000,

3.6.9 Remittances and GDP growth

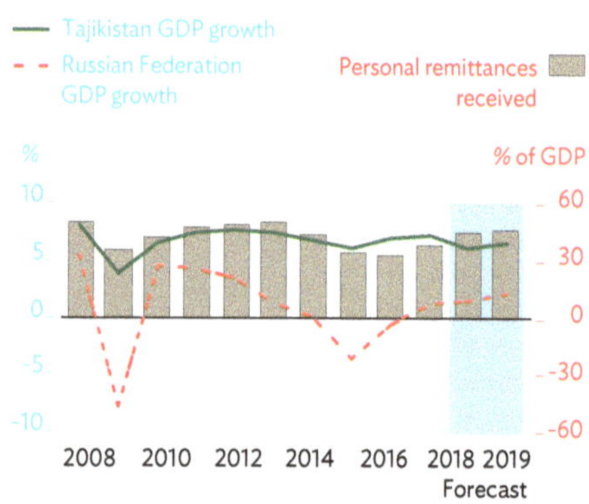

Sources: World Bank, *World Development Indicators online database*; National Bank of Tajikistan; ADB estimates.

are needed for the large number of young people entering the labor force in the coming years. A further 233,000 jobs are needed for the working poor whose current incomes fall below the poverty line. Providing these jobs will require upgrades to current employment through productivity gains from on-the-job training and workplace reorganization, along with workers shifting to new and more productive jobs elsewhere in the economy.

Remittances are currently forecast to rise. If migrants begin returning again at the rate observed in 2016, however, additional jobs will be needed to meet the poverty objective. The estimates last year, which did not directly address the impact of returning migrants, suggest that an additional 280,000 productive jobs are needed by 2025 to provide work for them. Because migrants earn more on average than domestic workers, replacing their previous income would require creating an even larger number of productive jobs.

Tajikistan's National Development Strategy to 2030 lists productive employment as a key objective, and steps have been taken to expand jobs. The Decent Work Country Program, 2015–2017 reportedly created 100,000 jobs annually, but mainly seasonal work in agriculture. Reform to the technical and vocational education and training system is currently upgrading facilities, providing new competency-based curricula and learning materials, developing an in-service teacher training plan, and strengthening sector management. To encourage self-employment, 2018 has been declared a year of tourism development and folk crafts.

The percentage of Tajikistan's population of working age is projected to continue rising to 2030. Benefiting from this demographic dividend requires structural reform to boost growth and create more high-quality jobs. This includes additional measures to improve the business climate, such as further reducing and consolidating the number of official bodies with inspection powers, creating a healthier banking sector to facilitate lending, and streamlining procedures for issuing construction permits, paying taxes, and enforcing contracts. Strengthening local value chains and helping small and medium-sized enterprises improve their productivity and earnings can further promote productive employment. Assessing demand for various skills and using that information to improve job training can match workforce skills to market demand.

Measures to raise educational attainment, improve training, and reform regulation would boost productivity, enabling firms to pay higher wages. Additional infrastructure would also help, as would measures to improve the quality of education spending and outcomes. Clearing administrative obstacles to economic activity, such as requirements for multiple licenses and permits, would support economic expansion and job creation. Finally, incentives are needed to promote job creation in the formal sector, perhaps by reviewing current taxes and labor regulations.

3.6.1 Selected economic indicators (%)

	2018	2019
GDP growth	6.0	6.5
Inflation	7.5	7.0
Current account balance (share of GDP)	1.1	-3.0

Source: ADB estimates.

3.6.10 Current account balance

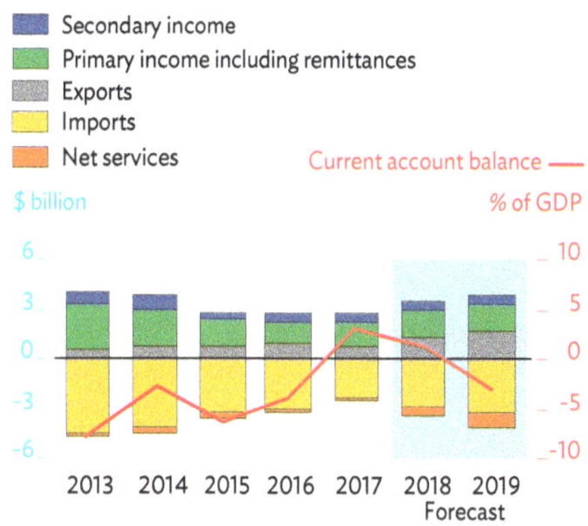

Sources: International Monetary Fund; National Bank of Tajikistan; ADB estimates.

Turkmenistan

Growth accelerated to 6.5% in 2017 from 6.2% a year earlier, with higher gas production, expansionary credit policy, and support for activity outside the large hydrocarbon economy. Price and cash controls held inflation to 8.0%. Improved energy prices boosted exports and trimmed the current account deficit to 11.5% of GDP. Stable growth is projected this year and next, with higher energy output. Post-secondary education reform is crucial for economic diversification.

Economic performance

The government reported growth at 6.5% in 2017, up from 6.2% a year earlier, as hydrocarbon prices improved somewhat in the second half of the year, having languished since 2014 (Figure 3.7.1). Faster growth reflected increased gas production, an expansionary credit policy for private firms, and considerable government support for the economy aside from hydrocarbons to produce goods able to substitute for imports.

On the supply side, the hydrocarbon economy expanded by 4.3%, reversing 4.8% contraction in 2016, but growth came mainly from the non-hydrocarbon economy, which expanded by 7.4%, albeit less than the previous year's 11.5% increase. Industry grew by 5.5%, up from 1.2% in 2016 with better performance in hydrocarbons (Figure 3.7.2). Services expanded by 8.9%, less than the 11.0% recorded in 2016, reflecting gains of 9.4% in trade, 11.1% in transport and communications, 1.3% in construction services, and 9.0% in other services. Agriculture was reported as expanding by 5.0%, reflecting higher output of cotton, wheat, and other crops, but down from 12.0% growth in 2016.

On the demand side, growth found support from public investment, higher export earnings, rising domestic consumption, and expanded production of goods that could substitute for imports. While public investment expanded, its share of GDP fell to 41% from 47% in 2016.

Average annual inflation was reported at 8.0% (Figure 3.7.3). To bring prices for utilities and public transportation closer to cost-recovery levels, the government gradually cut subsidies and increased tariffs, which had been very low. Also boosting prices were higher import

3.7.1 GDP growth

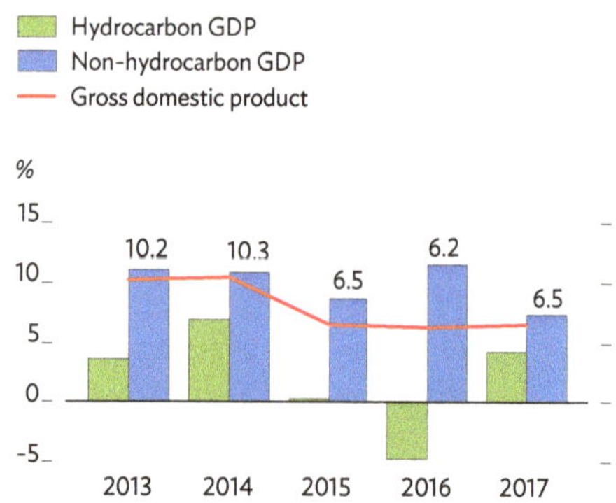

Sources: International Monetary Fund. 2017. *Regional Economic Outlook, Middle East and Central Asia*; ADB estimates.

3.7.2 GDP growth by sector

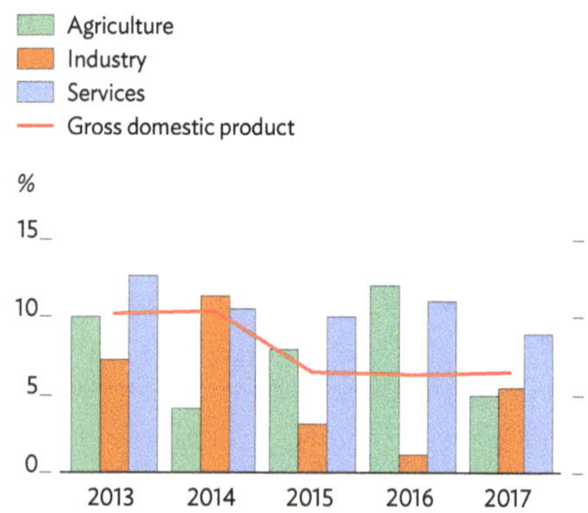

Sources: International Monetary Fund. 2017. *Regional Economic Outlook, Middle East and Central Asia*; ADB estimates.

This chapter was written by Jennet Hojanazarova of the Turkmenistan Resident Mission, ADB, Ashgabat.

duties and steep depreciation of the Turkmen manat on the parallel market (the official rate remained steady at TMT3.5). The government maintained administrative price controls for basic commodities and supported the production of import substitutes to ensure ample supplies on the domestic market and contain inflation. The Central Bank of Turkmenistan kept strict control of cash in circulation, promoting noncash payments and restricting foreign exchange conversion. Even as credit to the private sector accelerated to 21.0% from 16.5% in 2016, growth in total credit slowed to 18.0% from 24.0% a year earlier.

The state budget deficit is estimated to have narrowed to the equivalent 0.9% of GDP from 1.3% in 2016 (Figure 3.7.4). However, this excludes extra-budgetary operations that would double the deficit if brought on budget. Revenues, which fell in 2015 and 2016 with lower hydrocarbon receipts, were estimated at 12.2% of GDP, reportedly 1.8% above planning assumptions. Expenditure was reported at 13.1% of GDP, reflecting spending cuts that kept outlays 3.6% below budget. Most budget outlays went for social programs, along with a 10.0% rise in salaries, pensions, and stipends. To achieve government targets, state-owned enterprises took on debt for development projects, but less than in previous years. Meanwhile, government debt, all external, is estimated to have risen to equal 25.9% of GDP from 23.9% at the end of 2016.

Since 2015, the current account has recorded large deficits because of low hydrocarbon prices and heavy investment that has boosted imports. Foreign direct investment (FDI) was estimated at 12.0% of GDP in 2016 (Figure 3.7.5), and the United Nations Conference on Trade and Development estimated in 2017 that Turkmenistan remained among the top five FDI recipients among economies in transition to a market economy. With higher gas exports to the People's Republic of China and energy price recovery in the second half of the year, the current account deficit narrowed to 11.5% of GDP from a high of 21.0% in 2016. The International Monetary Fund estimated foreign exchange reserves sufficient to pay for more than 20 months of imports of goods and services.

Economic prospects

Growth is forecast to remain at 6.5% in 2018 and accelerate slightly to 6.7% in 2019, with an improved outlook for energy prices and an expected rise in hydrocarbon output and exports. Public investment to fulfill sector and regional plans under the President's socioeconomic development program for 2018–2024 will remain an important source of growth.

On the supply side, industry will continue as the main growth driver, with higher external demand for hydrocarbons boosting output. Industry is projected to grow by 8%–10% in

3.7.3 GDP growth and inflation

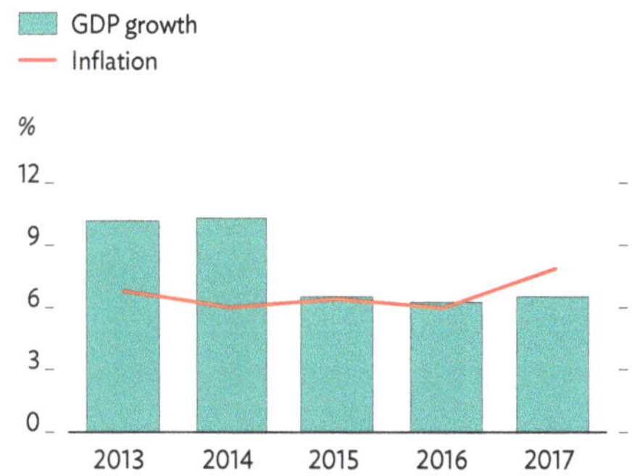

Sources: International Monetary Fund. 2017. *Regional Economic Outlook, Middle East and Central Asia*; ADB estimates.

3.7.4 Government fiscal balances

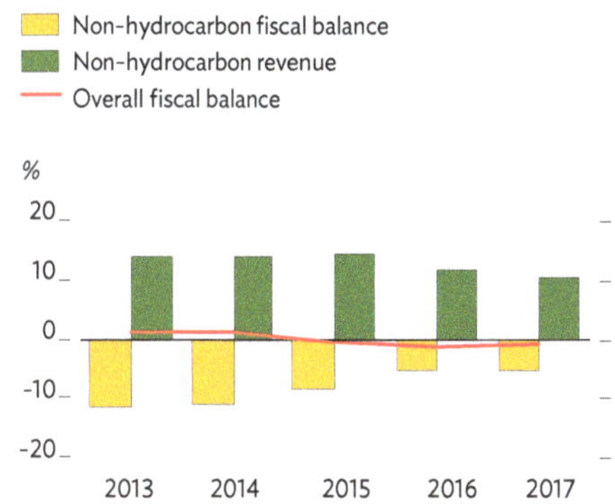

Note: Fiscal data refer to general government. Non-hydrocarbon fiscal balance and revenue are percentages of non-oil gross domestic product, and the overall fiscal balance is a percentage of total gross domestic product.

Sources: International Monetary Fund. 2017. *Regional Economic Outlook, Middle East and Central Asia*; ADB estimates.

3.7.5 Foreign direct investment

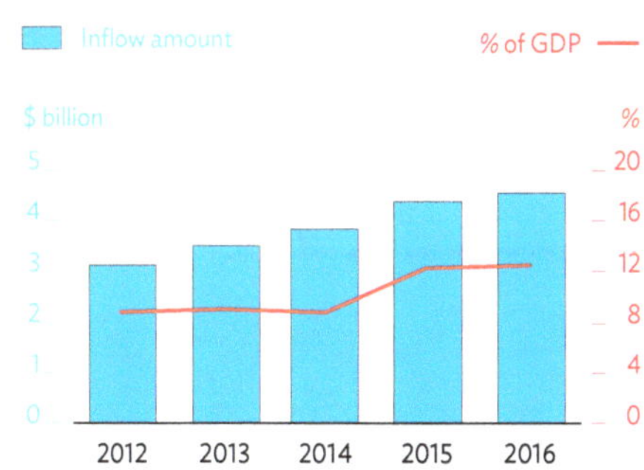

Sources: United Nations Conference on Trade and Development. 2017. *World Investment Report*; United Nations Statistics Division. National Accounts Main Aggregates Database. https://unstats.un.org/unsd/snaama/ (accessed 9 March 2018); ADB estimates.

2018 and 2019, and services by double-digit rates. With planned measures to boost sector productivity, agriculture is projected to grow by 7%–8% annually during this period.

The President's program for 2018–2024 envisages major industrial projects in mining, chemicals, and metallurgy, as well as to develop regional social infrastructure. The program stipulates further reforms to facilitate the transition to a market economy, spur private activity, and create jobs in the regions away from the capital. The program includes measures to create special economic zones, upgrade and improve the labor code, and reform land and tax codes. To reduce public sector dominance in the economy and provide greater scope for the private sector, the program aims to speed the transformation of public enterprises into joint stock companies and private firms.

Average annual consumer inflation is likely to remain at 8.0% in 2018 and 2019, assuming no further currency depreciation. The government will continue to support import substitution, with annual growth in credit to private firms projected at 18%. At the same time, price controls and stringent foreign exchange regulations will be maintained to limit inflation. Credit expansion is expected to permit broad money growth at around 10% annually. As the manat has appreciated strongly in real terms since its last devaluation in January 2015, further devaluation is possible.

The state budget is projected to achieve near balance in 2018 and 2019, reflecting higher oil and gas receipts from increased exports, as well as additional income and revenue from expansion in the non-hydrocarbon economy (Figure 3.7.6). Despite measures to streamline public investment, the government will continue to support social programs and invest in infrastructure in the regions. Government debt is expected to reach 30.2% of GDP in 2018 and 35.0% in 2019 (Figure 3.7.7). Because this debt is all external and the ratio is likely to rise further, careful monitoring and debt management will be important.

With the improved outlook for hydrocarbon prices and output, the current account deficit is projected to narrow to about 9% of GDP in 2018 and 8% in 2019 (Figure 3.7.8). The government is expected to finance the deficit through foreign borrowing and FDI, mainly for the hydrocarbon sector, with new FDI continuing to equal about 7% of GDP in 2018.

Policy challenge—post-secondary education reform to strengthen labor

Turkmenistan needs a highly skilled and technically qualified labor force to diversify the economy, develop a more innovative private sector, and enable productive and well-paid jobs for a growing workforce.

3.7.1 Selected economic indicators (%)

	2018	2019
GDP growth	6.5	6.7
Inflation	8.0	8.0
Current account balance (share of GDP)	-9.0	-8.0

Source: ADB estimates.

3.7.6 Fiscal indicators

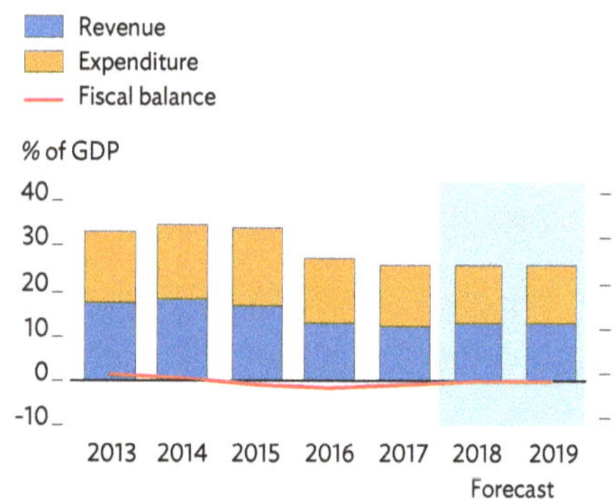

Sources: International Monetary Fund. 2017. *Regional Economic Outlook, Middle East and Central Asia*; ADB estimates.

3.7.7 External government debt

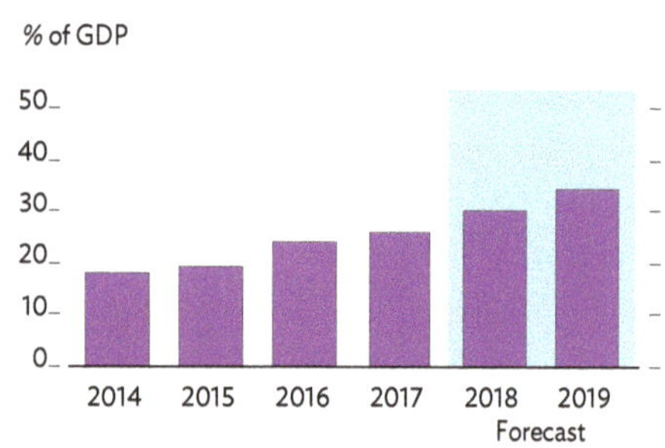

Sources: International Monetary Fund. 2017. *Regional Economic Outlook, Middle East and Central Asia*; ADB estimates.

Current development programs stress the importance of education and training for economic and industrial transformation. Various reforms to education have been introduced in recent years: substantial investments in education infrastructure, higher outlays for education, the creation of new higher education institutions, a transition to compulsory 12-year education requiring the completion of secondary school, and new learning programs and curricula at all levels to align the education system with international norms. Turkmenistan is introducing a multitier system that awards bachelor's, master's, and doctoral degrees in conformity with the Bologna Process, a series of European ministerial meetings and agreements to ensure comparable standards for higher-education qualifications.

However, great potential exists for further enhancement, especially in higher education and technical and vocational training, to meet international standards and align graduates' knowledge and skills with the requirements of a more diversified economy. This is especially important because of rapid population growth and relatively high youth unemployment, most recently estimated by the International Labour Organization at 19.5% in 2015, reflecting in part a skills mismatch between labor supply and demand.

The country's tertiary gross enrollment ratio is under 10%, well below the average of 26% in Central and West Asia and 35% worldwide, as reported in the United Nation's *Human Development Report 2016* (Figure 3.7.9). According to a 2015 study by the European Training Foundation, about 5% of secondary school graduates in Turkmenistan typically continue to local university, partly because places in state-funded universities are limited. Another 5% of graduates continue to vocational education and training. Some graduates seek tertiary education abroad, but many of these foreign-trained professionals choose to pursue careers abroad.

Secondary school graduates thus dominate the domestic workforce, whose expertise does not keep pace with technological change and innovation. Agriculture is the sector providing the most employment, at 43.3% in 2016, but most of these jobs are low-skill and low-wage. Conditions for jobs in services, providing more than 30% of employment, are similar. Government plans to diversify the economy and foster private sector innovation highlight the importance of boosting workforce skills and productivity through high-quality and inclusive education that is consistent with the needs of a modern information economy. Indeed, failure to address the pervasive shortage of skilled professionals could be a major obstacle to diversification.

Greater investment in post-secondary and vocational education would promote agriculture with higher value added and help develop high-tech industries outside of

3.7.8 Current account balance

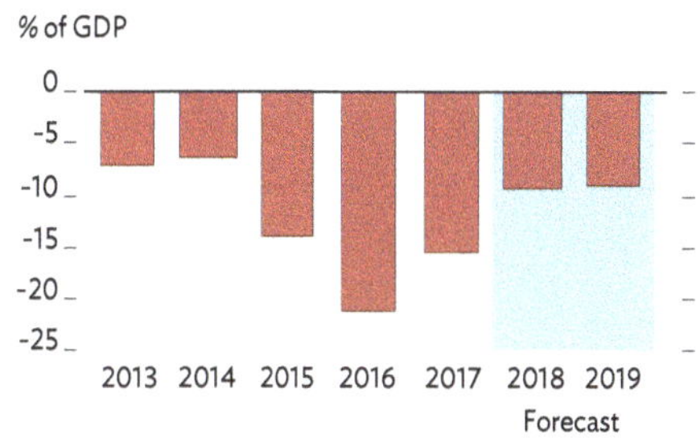

Sources: International Monetary Fund. 2017. *Regional Economic Outlook, Middle East and Central Asia*; ADB estimates.

3.7.9 Average tertiary gross enrollment ratio, 2010–2015

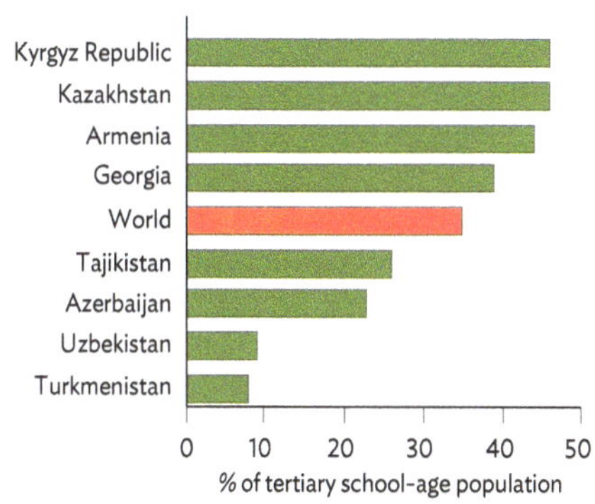

Source: United Nations Development Programme. 2016. *Human Development Report.*

the hydrocarbon economy, including services. It would entail the expansion and comprehensive modernization of higher education and vocational programs at all levels. While spending for education has reportedly increased, it remains low by international standards, equal to about 3% of GDP in 2010–2014, according to the *Human Development Report 2016*. Post-secondary education receives less than 15% of Turkmenistan's education spending and needs greater support.

Increased expenditure, both from government sources and through public–private partnerships, should aim to improve the quality, equity, and relevance of higher education and focus on strengthening research and development to create knowledge and foster innovation. Vocational education must be linked with labor market policies, employment services, and entrepreneurship. Also needed are stronger professional collaboration with regional and international education networks and Turkmenistan's participation in international surveys and rankings such as the Global Competitiveness Index, Global Innovation Index, and Human Capital Index. This would allow better assessment of the economy's skill requirements and the ability of the education system to meet them.

Uzbekistan

Growth slowed to 5.3% in 2017, and inflation jumped to 14.4%, both reflecting steep currency devaluation that required adjustment across the economy. The current account surplus reached 2.8% of GDP. An improving external outlook is expected to boost exports, nudging growth to 5.5% in 2018 and 5.6% in 2019 as inflation stays high with anticipated wage, pension, and utility increases. Public financial management needs to be strengthened.

Economic performance

The government reported that growth slowed steeply to 5.3% from 7.8% in 2016. This occurred as output and private consumption moderated in the wake of a large devaluation in September to reconcile the official exchange rate with the parallel currency market. The devaluation cut the US dollar value of the Uzbek som by 48% as part of wide-ranging and unprecedented reform to remove price and exchange rate distortions, improve public services, and make official statistics more transparent and reliable. Although necessary and long awaited, the reforms forced up prices and interest rates, triggering a credit crunch and moderating household consumption.

On the supply side, growth came mostly from services, which expanded by 6.9%, down from 9.3% in 2016 (Figure 3.8.1). While transport and communications accelerated to 8.9% from 7.1% in 2016, slower growth in private consumption slashed expansion in trade, food, and accommodation to 3.9% from 13.4% in 2016. Growth in industry, excluding construction, moderated to 4.6% from 5.0% a year earlier, with weaker mining and quarrying. Construction growth, hit by higher import and credit costs, halved to 5.6% from 12.5% in 2016. Expansion in agriculture slowed to 2.0% from 6.6% in 2016 as prices for imported inputs nearly doubled in som terms, raising production costs and prices for purchasers. Meanwhile, the cheaper som and stronger growth in neighboring countries helped reenergize external demand for fruit and vegetables, boosting total sales.

On the demand side, net exports and investment propelled growth, partly offsetting weaker consumption. Gross capital formation grew by 7.1%, down from 9.6% in 2016 despite

3.8.1 Supply-side contributions to growth

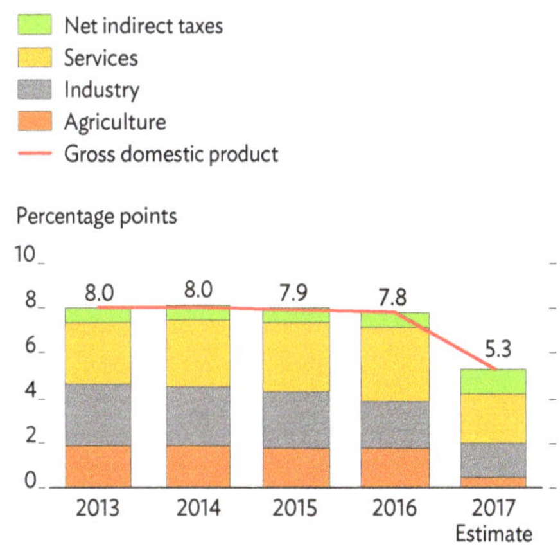

Sources: State Statistics Committee; ADB estimates.

3.8.2 Broad money and inflation

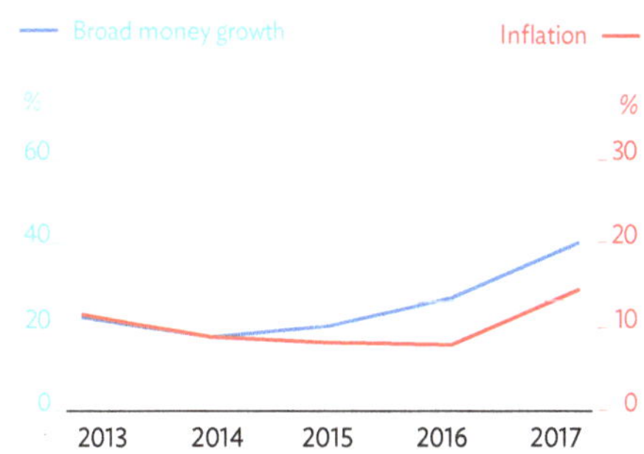

Source: International Monetary Fund.

This chapter was written by Iskandar Gulamov of the Uzbekistan Resident Mission, ADB, Tashkent.

higher government spending on social infrastructure, including housing and health facilities. Foreign investment also rose, reportedly by 28.3%, mostly into metallurgy and petrochemicals, including the construction of a large facility to process gas at Kandym in western Uzbekistan. A 15.0% rise in exports supported expansion, but growth in consumption slowed to 3.2% from 8.6% in 2016 as private consumption decelerated to 2.5% from 11.3% in 2016, offsetting a 5.7% rise in government consumption.

The government reported inflation soaring to an average of 14.4% in 2017 from 5.7% in 2016. Two factors contributed to the increase: the impact of devaluation on import prices and production costs and, statistically, an expanded list of goods and services used to monitor prices and estimate the consumer price index (CPI). In addition, the authorities have made progress toward entering the enhanced General Data Dissemination System, an International Monetary Fund initiative (Box 3.8.1).

Food prices rose by 15.9% as meat and poultry prices jumped by 30%, contributing 6.5 percentage points to the CPI increase. Other goods rose by 16.0%, adding another 5.7 points. Prices for gasoline, most of it imported, rose by 39.7% in the 12 months to November 2017, contributing 0.5 points. Rising production and debt-service costs prompted utilities to raise tariffs by 7.1%, adding 0.4 points. In response to rising prices, the government established a special fund under the Ministry of Finance to procure critically needed goods and distribute them to vulnerable groups.

While detailed fiscal data are not yet available, the augmented budget including the balance in the Fund for Reconstruction and Development is expected to record a deficit equal to around 3% of GDP in 2017. The weaker som strained the balance sheets of major taxpayers, particularly state-owned enterprises, prompting additional tax holidays and exemptions announced in the second half of 2017. While devaluation probably increased receipts for some items, such as value-added tax, revenue declined overall. At the same time, expenditure rose, though continued downsizing of the public sector offset some of the rise in outlays as the government shielded vulnerable groups and strategic industries from some consequences of reform. The Fund for Reconstruction and Development balance probably moved into deficit as it provided increased support to commercial banks and financing to undertake various development initiatives. In response, the government sought budget assistance from multilateral development banks in mid-2017.

Beginning in the second half of 2017, the Central Bank of the Republic of Uzbekistan tightened monetary policy to limit money growth and stem inflation. In the first half, bank assets grew by 26% as credit expanded by 34%.

3.8.1 Recent changes in economic data management

A new government prioritized in 2017 improving its distribution of economic and social data in a bid to enhance economic planning with more reliable data and to make public administration more accountable. Senior government officials had openly questioned previous reports, suspecting that GDP growth rates were overstated and inflation underreported. The government further initiated reform to national income accounting and CPI methodology. Since February 2018, a revised CPI methodology that aligns with international standards is used to measure inflation. The government describes its release of 2017 GDP growth at 5.3% and CPI inflation at 14.4% as "true" estimates. The national statistics office did not, however, provide revised historical data for these indicators.

To improve data availability, the government lifted nondisclosure requirements and declassified such key economic data as the volume and composition of international reserves. In addition, the government introduced sweeping institutional changes in the national statistics office to improve its capacity to manage data. The authorities have also decided to join the International Monetary Fund's enhanced General Data Dissemination System, and they expect to post by May 2018 a national summary data page with key economic, financial, and social statistics.

Broad money excluding foreign currency deposits grew by 15%, creating strong inflationary pressures. In June, the central bank responded by hiking its policy rate from 9.0% to 14.0%, triggering a 4.7% decline in broad money excluding foreign currency deposits in the second half of the year and slowing annual money expansion to 9.0%. If foreign currency deposits are included, broad money grew by 40.2% in 2017 (Figure 3.8.2).

While preparing for exchange rate reform, the government injected $0.6 billion into several large state-owned commercial banks. The International Monetary Fund noted that, while most banks benefited from upward revaluation of their foreign exchange assets and liabilities, some of these gains might be only notional as they mirrored valuation losses in state-owned enterprises, which had large foreign exchange exposure to banks and external lenders.

An improving external environment promoted higher exports of goods and services, helping widen the current account surplus to the equivalent of an estimated 2.8% of GDP from 0.1% in 2016 (Figure 3.8.3). External demand improved with economic recovery in the Russian Federation and Kazakhstan, as well as higher global energy prices. New export and investment agreements were reached with key trade partners during the year, and Uzbek competitiveness improved with devaluation. Government sources reported exports of goods and services up by 15.0%, led by foodstuffs, metals, and machinery. Imports of goods and services rose by 7.2% on higher imports of metals and energy products. Som depreciation cut growth in imports of capital goods and equipment, the biggest item on the import list, to 0.7%.

Economic recovery in the Russian Federation, including demand linked to preparations for the 2018 FIFA World Cup in June and July, helped raise remittances by 22% in the first 9 months of 2017 over the same period in 2016. While detailed data are not available, foreign direct investment is believed to have risen modestly, in line with Uzbekistan's improved investment climate. The government reported gross foreign reserves worth $28.1 billion at the end of 2017, cover for 28 months of merchandise imports (Figure 3.8.4). External debt rose to an estimated 49.0% of GDP at the end of 2017 from 21.3% in 2016, reflecting the impact of devaluation and some additional foreign borrowing.

Economic prospects

Growth is forecast to accelerate to 5.5% in 2018 and 5.6% in 2019 with further improvement in the external outlook that should boost export demand and foreign investment, particularly from the Russian Federation (Figure 3.8.5). On the supply side, investment in capital-intensive industry

3.8.3 Current account components

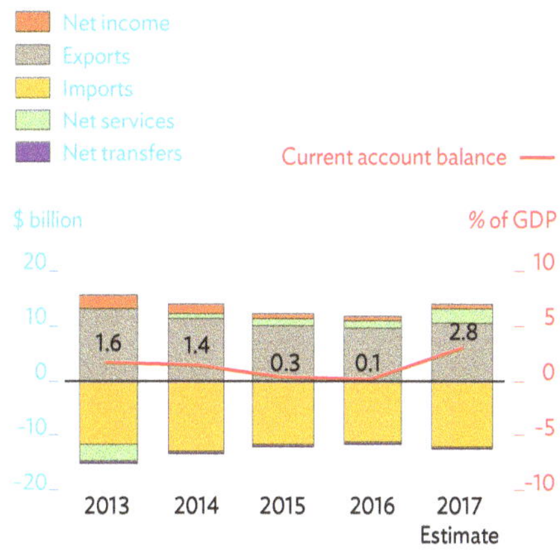

Sources: International Monetary Fund; ADB estimates.

3.8.4 Gross international reserves

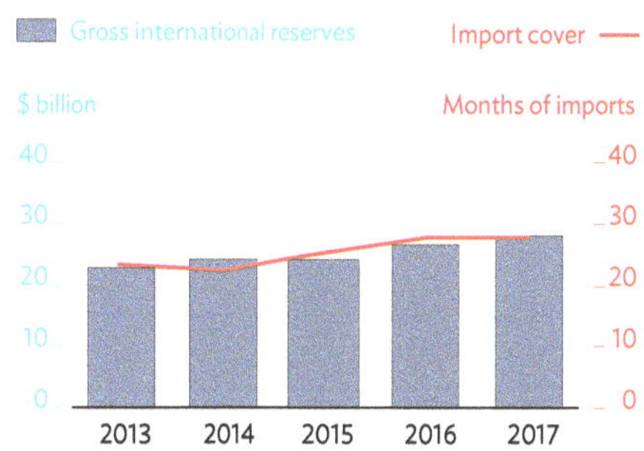

Sources: International Monetary Fund; ADB estimates.

3.8.5 GDP growth

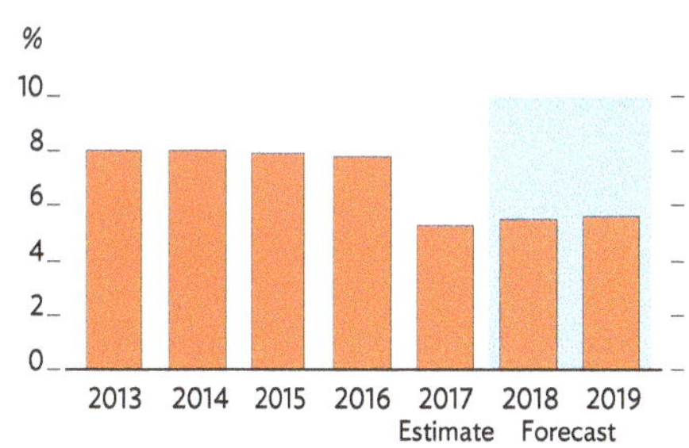

Source: *Asian Development Outlook* database.

is expected to remain a key driver of growth, with improving external demand sustaining growth in industry at around 5.0% in 2018 and 2019. Private consumption should rise with higher remittances, planned real increases in wages and pensions, and targeted social support. This, along with expansion in electronic banking, should keep growth in services at around 7.0% in both years. Agriculture is expected to grow by 4.5% in 2018 and 4.8% in 2019 as horticulture expands and reform takes hold. On the demand side, rising investment, both domestic and foreign, will promote growth. Reflecting improvements in the business climate and public administration, domestic investment should buoy agriculture, trade, and services. Foreign investment will benefit from realistic exchange rates and, from early 2019, the first global listing of Uzbekistan's sovereign debt. Nevertheless, 2018 will be a challenging year, with substantial downside risk to the forecasts from lagged effects of devaluation on living costs and household incomes.

Inflation is projected to accelerate further to 16.0% in 2018 before slowing to 14.0% in 2019 (Figure 3.8.6). Inflationary pressures will persist following the 2017 devaluation and come as well from higher government spending on promised annual increases in wages and pensions. In addition, state-owned utilities will continue raising tariffs to shore up their financial viability, service debt, and finance operations. Inflation rose sharply in early 2018, with the CPI up by 2.7% month on month in January and 1.1% in February. Managing inflation will remain a tough policy challenge, requiring closely coordinated monetary and fiscal policies. Fiscal consolidation—to include tightening internal controls, limiting off-budget operations, and hardening budget constraints on state-owned enterprises—will be especially important to attain price stability.

Broad money including foreign currency deposits is projected to grow by 25% in 2018 and 20% in 2019. Limited bank capital and high interest rates in 2018 will continue to make access to credit a challenge. Closer to 2019, increases in bank capital—as banks comply with new capital requirements to be imposed on 1 January 2019—should support credit growth. The central bank is expected to expand its sterilization of foreign exchange and limit its accumulation of official reserves.

The budget deficit including the Fund for Reconstruction and Development balance is forecast to narrow slightly to 1.1% of GDP in 2018 and 1.0% in 2019 (Figure 3.8.7). Budget revenue is set to rise modestly, reflecting improved collection and an expanding private sector. This will offset higher spending on ambitious new development initiatives. In 2018, the government aims to strengthen the social sector by expanding health care, education, and scientific research while supporting the private sector with tax privileges and customs exemptions.

3.8.1 Selected economic indicators (%)

	2018	2019
GDP growth	5.5	5.6
Inflation	16.0	14.0
Current account balance (share of GDP)	0.5	0.1

Source: ADB estimates.

3.8.6 Inflation

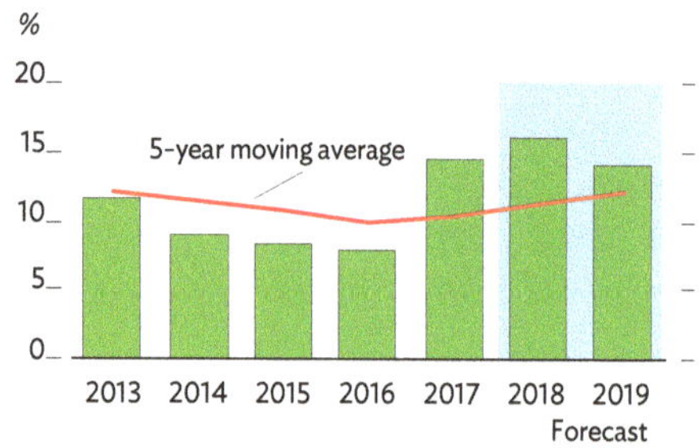

Source: *Asian Development Outlook* database.

3.8.7 Augmented fiscal balance

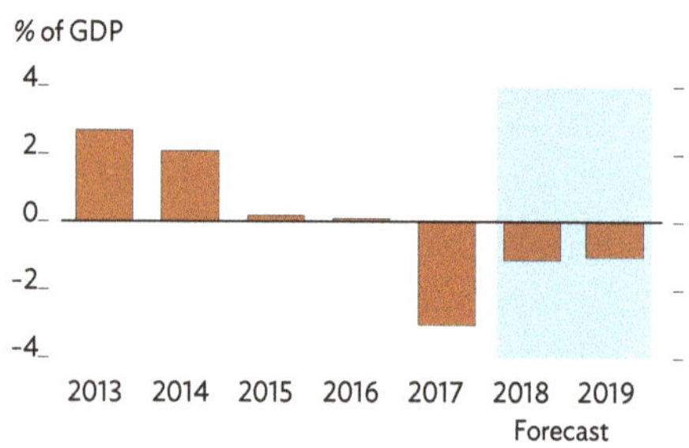

Source: *Asian Development Outlook* database.

The current account surplus is forecast to narrow to 0.5% of GDP in 2018 and 0.1% in 2019 (Figure 3.8.8). Exports of goods are projected to rise by 8.0% in 2018 and 10.0% in 2019, reflecting continued growth in the Russian Federation and economic recovery in Kazakhstan, which will boost exports of Uzbek fruit and vegetables. Imports of goods are projected to rise gradually, by 4.0% in 2018 and 8.0% in 2019, with demand coming mostly from industry and government, notably for oil, chemicals, and capital goods. If the exchange rate remains stable and foreign borrowing for state development programs is modest, external debt is likely to decline to the equivalent of 40.7% of GDP in 2018 and 33.6% in 2019. Foreign currency reserves are projected to reach $29.0 billion by the end of 2018 and $29.5 billion a year later.

3.8.8 Current account balance

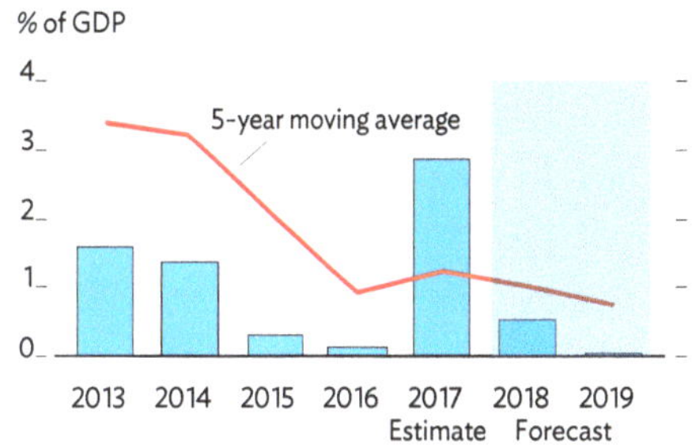

Source: *Asian Development Outlook* database.

Policy challenge—strengthening public financial management

Uzbekistan's landmark reform package of 2017, though necessary, has raised living costs, slashed credit to the private sector, and undermined the viability of many large state-owned enterprises, which were ill-prepared for a market-based exchange rate. There were strong expectations of a commensurate fiscal response to mitigate social risks, promote the private sector, and sustain the delivery of public services, as evidenced by an unprecedented review of the 2018 state budget in December 2017. However, two key factors have limited the capacity of the budget to respond effectively: eroding finances, as rising outlays and a decline in revenues from weak commodity prices worsened indebtedness, and fragmentation of the budget framework with the transfer of capital expenditures for state development programs to a new off-budget fund. While global commodity prices are projected to rebound and restore revenue with help from planned tax reform, fiscal fragmentation remains a serious concern because it undermines government efforts to decentralize and make public spending more efficient.

Public financial management must be strengthened to cope with a persistent fiscal deficit, mounting needs for financing (including foreign borrowing), new development programs, and ongoing fiscal decentralization. A rationalized, consolidated, and forward-looking system of public financial management would strengthen fiscal policy by clearly informing policy makers on the resources available, the constraints on their use in addressing desired objectives, and options that would support economic stabilization.

Much remains to be done to make public spending more efficient. More bottom-up planning for the medium term would enable the budget to better take into account the costs of strategies for developing particular sectors while providing clear priorities for decision making.

The government is gradually introducing computerized accounting systems in ministries, departments, and agencies. This will make information for monitoring and decision making more comprehensive while strengthening the ability of these entities to assess their use of resources. What is ultimately needed is a coherent and comprehensive internal control framework that goes beyond ensuring the legality of transactions. Another need is an effective internal audit system covering all government agencies. In 2018, the government submitted a draft procurement law to Parliament, but it describes only a general platform for public procurement without comprehensively going into procurement practices. Additional legislation is thus required to align domestic procurement with internationally accepted practice. On a more positive note, the government established a single oversight body to make basic procurement data readily available and provide an institutional focus for improving public procurement.

Finally, the government must improve its management of reform. This requires drawing on all available resources inside and outside of government, and on implementing global best practices, especially after the substantial downsizing of the public sector that took place in 2017. In addition, successful reform will require effective communication about proposed measures and their motivations to citizens, government employees, development partners, and investors, both domestic and international.

EAST ASIA

- HONG KONG, CHINA
- MONGOLIA
- PEOPLE'S REPUBLIC OF CHINA
- REPUBLIC OF KOREA
- TAIPEI,CHINA

Hong Kong, China

Growth accelerated in 2017, propelled by a strong external environment and solid domestic demand. A tight labor market and recovering inbound tourism should sustain robust growth this year and next, though some moderation is expected. Inflation will rise on higher global prices, and the current account surplus will narrow slightly on stronger imports. Integrating the Guangdong–Hong Kong–Macao Bay Area poses challenges commensurate with its vast opportunities in the years ahead.

Economic performance

After lackluster growth at 2.1% in 2016, the economy revived to grow by 3.8% in 2017. Robust domestic demand, especially healthy private spending, continues to be a main growth driver. Growth in private consumption improved by nearly threefold from 2016, fueled by higher incomes and upbeat economic sentiment, and contributed 3.6 percentage points to GDP growth (Figure 3.9.1). Government consumption and inventory restocking each added 0.3 percentage points. From contraction in 2016, gross fixed capital formation expanded by 4.2% last year and contributed 0.9 percentage points to growth, supported by buoyant construction. Trade benefited from stronger global growth, with exports of goods and services expanding by 5.5% and imports by 6.3%, such that net exports shaved 1.3 percentage points from GDP growth (Figure 3.9.2). On the supply side, construction and services were the primary drivers, construction up by 3.9% and services by 3.5% on stronger growth in import and export trades, transportation, and finance.

Consumer price inflation slowed to 1.5% in 2017, continuing a 3-year easing trend. Limited external or internal pressure on prices, especially for food, housing, or utilities, subdued inflation for most of the year, as did a government subsidy to reduce school tuition fees (Figure 3.9.3). After falling by 23% in October, the volume of residential property sales jumped by 58% by year-end. As of January 2018, average home prices had risen month on month for 22 consecutive months (Figure 3.9.4).

The current account surplus widened to equal 4.2% of GDP in 2017 from 4.0% the previous year. This reflected higher net primary income and a wider service surplus, only partly offset by a larger trade deficit. Net capital flows turned positive as

This chapter was written by Benno Ferrarini and Marthe Hinojales of the Economic Research and Regional Cooperation Department, ADB, Manila.

3.9.1 Demand-side contributions to growth

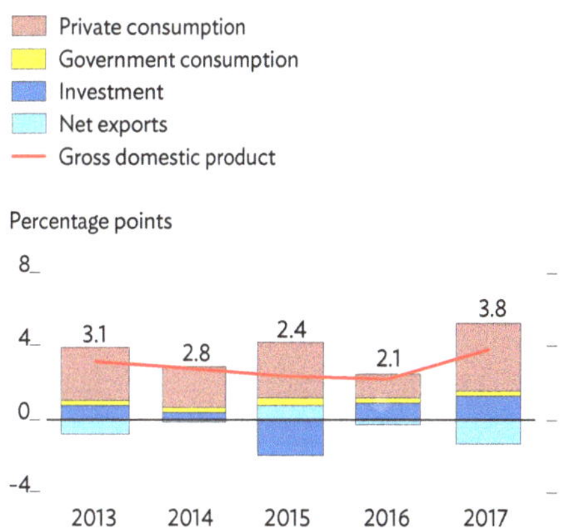

Source: CEIC Data Company (accessed 1 March 2018).

3.9.2 External trade

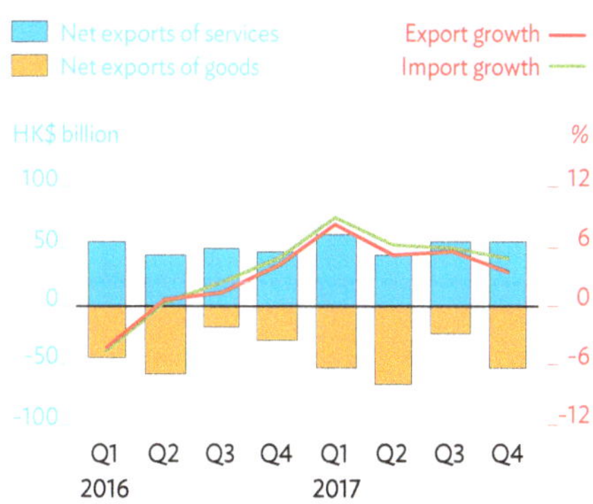

Q = quarter.

Source: CEIC Data Company (accessed 28 February 2018).

net inflows of portfolio investment increased. Meanwhile, the overall balance of payments surplus widened to 9.4% of GDP in 2017, and gross official reserves rose by the end of 2017 to $431.4 billion, or cover for 8.1 months of imports.

The government revised its budget surplus estimate for fiscal year 2017 (FY2017, ended 31 March 2018) to 5.2% of GDP from its original estimate of 0.6% (Figure 3.9.5). Revenues from land premium and stamp duties exceeded expectations owing to robust property and stock markets. Government expenditure is estimated to be less than budgeted because of lower disbursements under some social programs, notably living allowances for seniors and low-income working families.

Following the US federal funds rate, the Hong Kong Monetary Authority adjusted its benchmark base rate 3 times last year, finally to 1.75%. To satisfy the strong market demand, additional Exchange Fund Bills were issued, resulting in an HK$80 billion reduction in interbank liquidity. Lending remained buoyant, however, as commercial banks lagged in adjusting their prime rates. Domestic credit grew by 15.5%, double the 7.3% increase in 2016, and growth in broad money (M2) supply accelerated to 10.0%. In March, the monetary authority further raised the base rate by 25 basis points to 2.0%. A wide interest rate spread between the US and Hong Kong, China pushed the local dollar toward the weak end of its US dollar peg band, causing it to fall in March 2018 to its lowest value since 2007. Net equity fund inflows rose substantially, in contrast with largely negative flows in the preceding 2 years. On the stock market, the Hang Seng Index gained 36.0%, compared with a scant 0.4% gain in 2016 (Figure 3.9.6).

Economic prospects

GDP growth is expected to moderate to 3.2% in 2018 and further to 3.0% next year, still buttressed by domestic demand (Figure 3.9.7). Favorable employment and wage conditions, and income effects from last year's buoyant asset and property markets, will prop up consumer sentiment, while intensive construction, in particularly on government infrastructure megaprojects, will push up capital spending. Private investment could also rise on business optimism. The composite purchasing managers' index climbed further into expansionary territory, reaching 51.7 in February 2018, the sixth consecutive month of expansion. Most businesses expect their order volumes to increase in the short term, particularly in financial services and retail, the latter benefitting from higher inbound tourism (Figure 3.9.8). Some moderation in demand from the People's Republic of China (PRC) is expected, but shipments to other regional economies will remain solid, underpinning recovery in exports. On the supply side, services will continue

3.9.3 Inflation

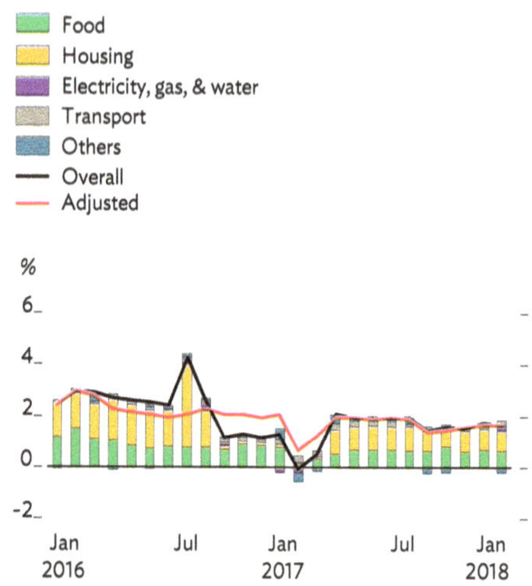

Note: Adjusted inflation refers to the rate once the effects of temporary subsidies by the government are removed.
Source: CEIC Data Company (accessed 3 March 2018).

3.9.4 Property market indicators

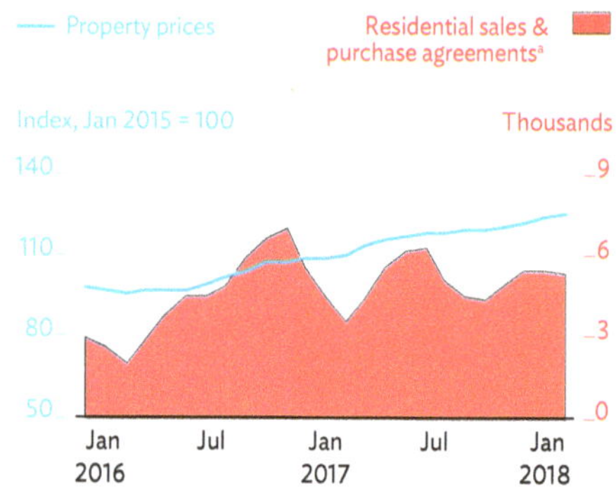

[a] 3-month moving averages.
Source: CEIC Data Company (accessed 13 March 2018).

3.9.5 Fiscal indicators

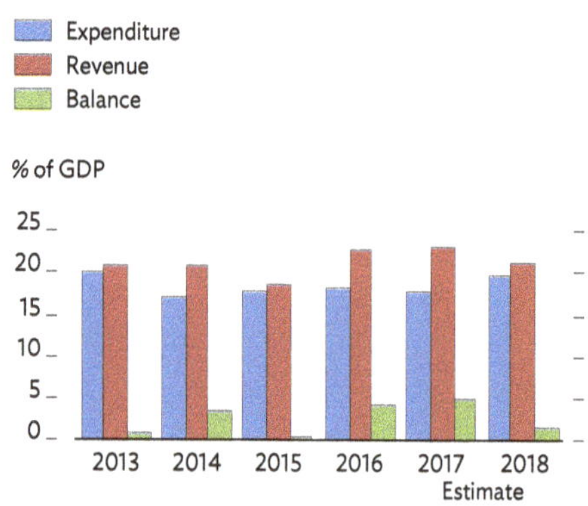

Note: Years are fiscal years ending 31 March of that year.
Sources: The Government of the Hong Kong Special Administrative Region of the PRC. The 2017–2018 Budget, and other years. http://www.budget.gov.hk; Hong Kong Monetary Authority; *Asian Development Outlook* database.

to be the main driver of growth, supported by trade-related and professional services and benefitting especially from strengthening business and investment ties with the PRC and opportunities arising in the Guangdong–Hong Kong–Macao Bay Area, discussed below.

Headline inflation has been slowly inching up since October 2017, after successive quarters of above-trend economic growth. Weakness in the US dollar and some upward pressure from import costs contributed. Inflation will likely reach 2.2% in 2018 because of higher import costs, as well as rising rents that reflect high demand for commercial space, and a more rapid increase in wages stoked by the tight labor market. However, higher interest rates will exert downward pressure on consumption and prices. Inflation is expected to decelerate slightly to 2.1% in 2019 in line with an anticipated easing of global oil prices.

The FY2018 fiscal surplus is forecast to dip to 1.7% of GDP. Budgetary expenditure is slated to rise by 17.6%, as the government ramps up spending on social welfare, education, health care, and family allowances, while increasing investment in innovative and creative industries, including through a startup fund. Budgetary revenue is projected to fall by 1.3%, however, mainly as a result of anticipated lower receipts from land premium and salary taxes resulting from a one-off tax concession and adjustments to tax bands, marginal tax rates, and certain allowances and deductions.

Improving global demand, and recovery in tourist arrivals that began in the second half of last year, should offer some support to exports of goods and services in 2018. However, the strong exports of last year are unlikely to replay this year, given slower growth in demand from the PRC and uncertainty spawned by rising global trade protectionism. Higher demand for capital goods and construction materials, supported in part by expected renminbi depreciation, should continue to boost imports and widen the trade deficit. The services account will post a growing surplus as tourist numbers grow and exports of business and financial services expand, particularly in 2019 when a new trade and investment agreement between the Association of Southeast Asian Nations and Hong Kong, China takes effect. In sum, the current account surplus is forecast to narrow to 3.9% this year and further to 3.5% in 2019.

Hong Kong, China remains the world's largest offshore renminbi clearing center, with a share of global renminbi payments standing above 70% in 2017. The offshore renminbi business enjoys support from the July 2017 launch of Bond Connect, which links bond markets in the PRC and Hong Kong, China, and by an expansion of the Renminbi Qualified Foreign Institutional Investor quota, which allows overseas investors to participate in PRC financial markets through Hong Kong, China. Further, heightened regional and international

3.9.1 Selected economic indicators (%)

	2018	2019
GDP growth	3.2	3.0
Inflation	2.2	2.1
Current account balance (share of GDP)	3.9	3.5

Source: ADB estimates.

3.9.6 Stock market

Source: Bloomberg (accessed 2 March 2018).

3.9.7 GDP growth

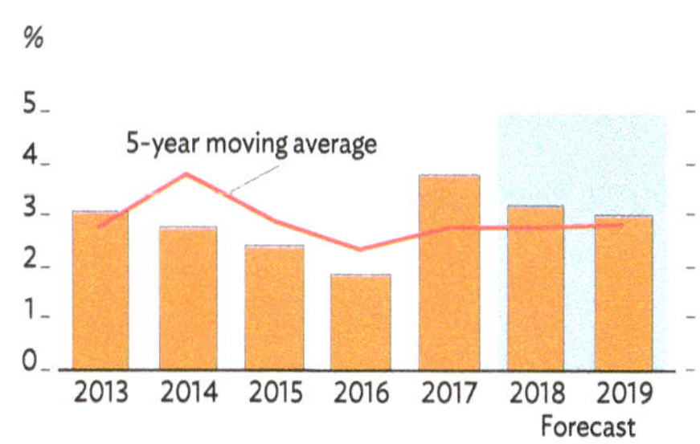

Source: *Asian Development Outlook* database.

cooperation under the PRC-led Belt and Road strategy should boost the super-intermediary role that Hong Kong, China plays in the offshore renminbi business.

The main risk to the outlook would be abrupt monetary tightening in the US, given local interest rate links to US monetary policy through the exchange rate peg. This could cause a sharp correction in the property market, which is already a downside domestic risk owing to sky-high prices. Tightened capital controls in the PRC on overseas investments may further depress property prices, with corresponding wealth effects hitting private consumption. While tax reform in the US will induce some repatriation of funds and banking outflows, strong infrastructure and sophisticated financial markets will keep Hong Kong, China highly attractive to international businesses. Lastly, worsening trade friction could undermine this regional trading hub. In any case, Hong Kong, China is well positioned to face the challenges posed by these risks, with sizeable external reserves and ample fiscal reserves estimated to equal 41.0% of GDP at the end of March 2018.

3.9.8 Business tendency surveys

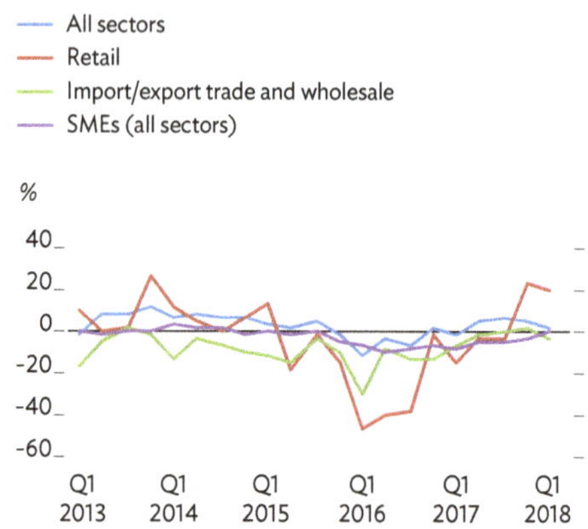

Notes: Except for the SME index, indicators represent the net balance of expected quarter-on-quarter changes in business situation. A positive reading denotes a likely upward trend in business situation.

The SME variable represents the distance of the quarter's SME headline index from the 50-threshold mark, where a negative number represents predominantly pessimistic sentiment.

Sources: CEIC Data Company (accessed 22 January 2018); Standard Chartered Hong Kong SME Leading Business Index, Standard Chartered and Hong Kong Productivity Council.

Policy challenge—integrating the Guangdong–Hong Kong–Macao Bay Area

An ambitious cross-boundary vision, covered by the Government of the PRC in its Thirteenth Five-Year Plan, 2016–2020, aims to deepen the economic integration of nine cities in Guangdong Province with Hong Kong, China and Macao, China to create a metropolitan agglomerate called the Guangdong–Hong Kong–Macao Bay Area. The ambition for the Bay Area—set out in a 2017 framework agreement—is to improve its productivity and global competitiveness and forge a global industrial, commercial, and financial cluster like those surrounding Tokyo Bay and San Francisco Bay (Figure 3.9.9).

To this end, the Bay Area hopes to leverage the comparative advantage of each of the 11 cities and exploit their synergies. In particular, it will confirm Hong Kong, China as the premier international shipping, financial, and commercial services platform bridging PRC business with the rest of the world. Further, the initiative presents an opportunity for Hong Kong, China to progressively integrate its service sector with those of the other Bay Area cities. Rather than face competition from their growing service industries, Hong Kong, China stands to benefit from easier access to their vast labor resources. Increased mobility under a joint Bay Area regulatory framework will address labor market mismatches, helping to alleviate shortages in Hong Kong, China in industries such as construction and tourism, and boosting employment opportunities created by Shenzhen firms expanding into Hong Kong, China.

3.9.9 Economic size of global bay areas, 2016

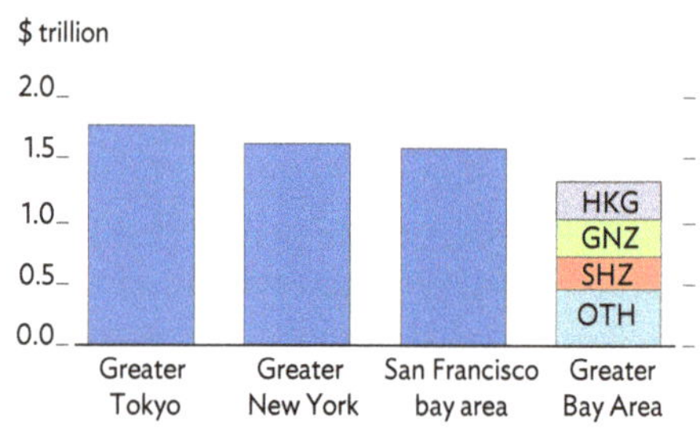

HKG = Hong Kong, China, GNZ = Guangzhou, OTH = the 8 cities of Zhuhai, Foshan, Zhongshan, Dongguan, Huizhou, Jiangmen, Zhaoqing, and Macau, China, SHZ = Shenzhen.

Sources: KPMG; Fung Business Intelligence.

Important challenges lie ahead. The Bay Area comprises three customs territories, each with its own administrative, economic, and social systems. Connectivity within the Bay Area having been improved through massive investments in infrastructure, the focus now is to explore further integration through strategic dialogue across jurisdictions and the progressive dismantling of their regulatory silos. Progress will require close governmental coordination to harmonize rules and practices and to pool customs administrations to ease clearance for cross-boundary flows of people, goods, and services and to allow the seamless integration of production and supply chain transactions. Governments should coordinate boundary controls to facilitate sustainable worker flows. The political and social implications of increased labor mobility, especially in lower-skilled segments, will have to be carefully managed to minimize local resentment of migrants. Also of crucial importance will be the portability of social security and harmonization of tax systems, with a particular focus on migrant and frontier workers. Looking ahead, easing labor market imbalances in Hong Kong, China through migration requires the resolution of its long-standing housing shortage.

Mongolia

The economy revived in 2017 from slowing growth in previous years. Growth will remain solid in 2018 and 2019, albeit with slight moderation, thanks to large investments in mining. Inflation will rise in 2018 before decelerating modestly in 2019, and the current account deficit will narrow considerably in 2018 before widening somewhat in 2019. Urban air pollution, especially in winter, poses an urgent and complex policy challenge.

Economic performance

GDP growth accelerated to 5.1% in 2017 from 1.2% in 2016, mainly on a surge in coal exports and large investments tied to underground development at the Oyu Tolgoi copper and gold mine. Gross capital formation was a major driver of growth, increasing by 36.2% as fixed capital investments resumed, adding 10.6 percentage points to growth. Despite a fall in government consumption in line with fiscal consolidation efforts, overall consumption rose, adding 1.8 percentage points to growth, as household consumption recovered with increased income from agriculture. Exports rose by 13.4%, mainly because coal exports more than doubled. However, increased mining investments pushed up imports substantially, such that a decline in net exports subtracted 7.3 percentage points from growth (Figure 3.10.1).

A fall in copper concentrate quality at the Oyu Tolgoi mine lowered mining production by 6.9% in 2017. This was despite a 32.7% increase in coal production driven by favorable prices. Strong recovery in manufacturing—in particular coal washing, cement production, and meatpacking—helped industry contribute 0.2 percentage points to growth notwithstanding subdued mining production and a decline in construction. Large mining-related investments and imports underpinned expansion in the transport, wholesale, and retail industries, making the service sector the main driver of growth, with a contribution of 4.3 percentage points. Despite a drought affecting vegetables and staple crops, agriculture added 0.6 percentage points as livestock herds continued to grow (Figure 3.10.2).

Average consumer price inflation accelerated to 4.3% in 2017 from 1.1% in 2016 as pass-through from a 24.8% depreciation of the Mongolian togrog in 2016 began to affect

This chapter was written by Declan Magee and Amar Lkhagvasuren of the Mongolia Resident Mission, ADB, Ulaanbaatar.

3.10.1 Demand-side contributions to growth

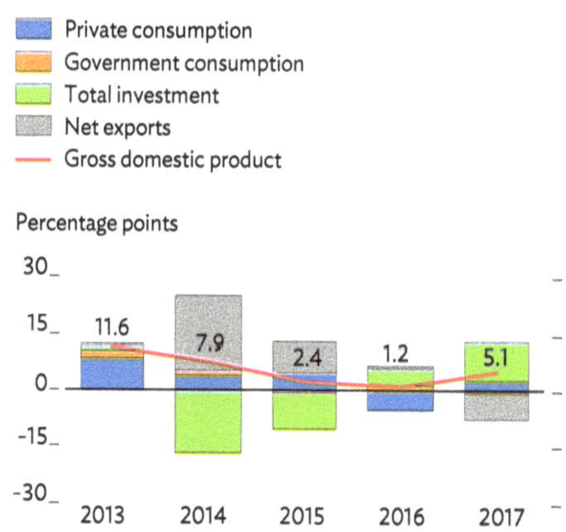

Source: National Statistical Office of Mongolia. 2018. *Monthly Statistical Bulletin*. January. http://www.nso.mn.

3.10.2 Supply-side contributions to growth

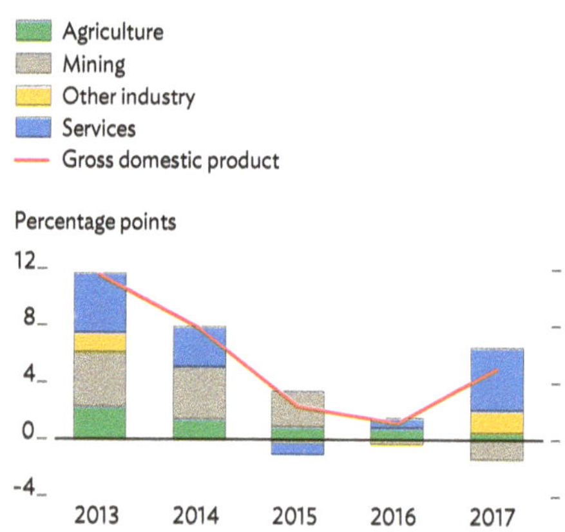

Source: National Statistical Office of Mongolia. 2018. *Monthly Statistical Bulletin*. January. http://www.nso.mn.

import prices, drought in the summer reduced supplies and boosted prices for vegetables and other foods, and higher excise taxes on vehicles pushed up transport costs. Core inflation excluding food and energy was substantially higher in the second half of 2017, and even higher in January 2018 at 8.8% year on year, indicating intensifying pressure on prices (Figure 3.10.3).

In line with the government's commitments under an agreement with the International Monetary Fund Extended Fund Facility, the budget deficit was slashed to the equivalent of 3.9% of GDP from 15.3% in 2016 (Figure 3.10.4). Fiscal consolidation reduced budgetary expenditure by 5.4% despite continued inclusion of formerly off-budget spending in the budget, while higher receipts from taxes on external trade and connected activities lifted budget revenue by 35.8%. Even with stronger revenue performance, the authorities withdrew savings from the Fiscal Stability Fund, estimated to equal 2.1% of GDP, to finance normal budgetary operations. This negated the purpose of the fund, which is insurance against revenue shortfalls arising from natural disasters or commodity price shocks. Deficit financing, currency depreciation, and a rising share of external debt in total public debt pushed up interest payments on government debt to 12.9% of total expenditure in 2017 from 10.4% in 2016.

A surge in repatriated profits from mining widened the current account deficit by 62.6% to equal 10.2% of GDP in 2017 (Figure 3.10.5). Nevertheless, a sharp recovery in foreign direct investment (FDI), including the reinvestment of a record share of mining profits—as well as financial support from multilateral development partners and better terms of trade—allowed the country to refinance a major part of its external debt. Net foreign liabilities dropped by 78.1% to $412 million, and gross reserves more than doubled to $3.0 billion, or cover for 5.5 months of imports. These developments pushed the value of the togrog up by 2.5% against the US dollar. This will allow the Bank of Mongolia, the central bank, to pay off a portion of its short-term, high-interest foreign liabilities, which amounted to 15.4% of GDP in December 2017. Public debt including central bank foreign liabilities declined to the equivalent of 99.1% of GDP (Figure 3.10.6).

As pressure eased on the balance of payments, the central bank lowered its policy rate by 3.0 percentage points in two steps in 2017 and by a further percentage point in March this year. Net domestic credit fell by 2.8% as government borrowing dropped significantly, but broad money growth surged by 24.2% as the net foreign liabilities of the banking system declined. The nonperforming loan ratio remained elevated, officially at 8.5% of the total but likely higher if not for loan classification, forbearance, and reporting problems. A review of bank asset quality was completed in 2017, and a bank

3.10.3 Inflation and exchange rate

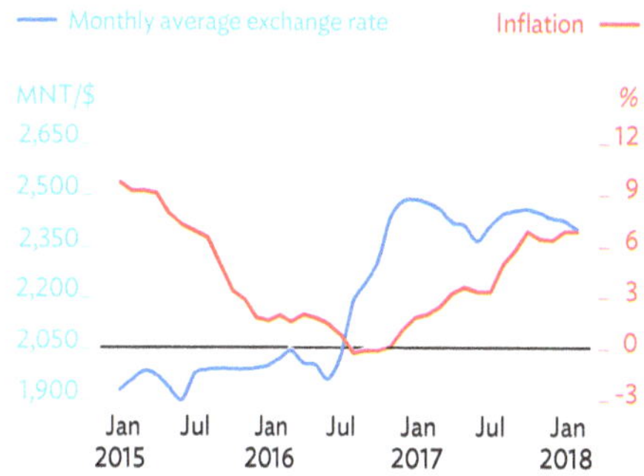

Source: Bank of Mongolia. http://www.mongolbank.mn.

3.10.4 Fiscal indicators

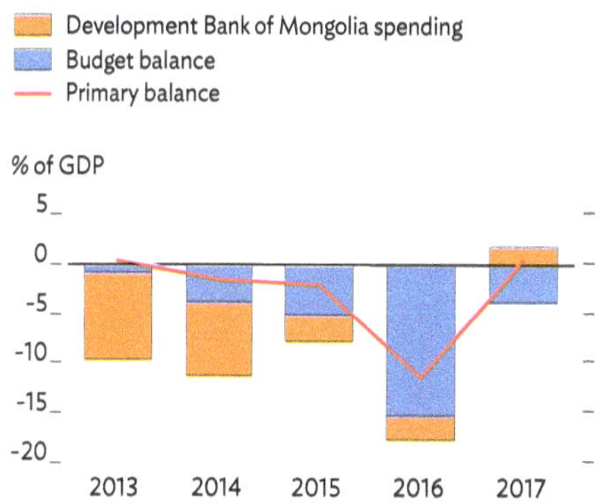

Sources: Ministry of Finance. http://www.mof.gov.mn; Bank of Mongolia. http://www.mongolbank.mn.

3.10.5 External indicators

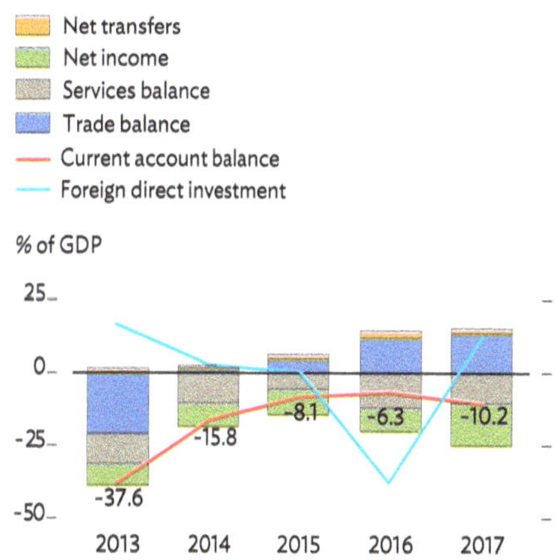

Source: Bank of Mongolia. http://www.mongolbank.mn.

recapitalization plan is being implemented, requiring banks to meet stiffer capital adequacy requirements by the end of 2018 (Figure 3.10.7).

Economic prospects

Growth is forecast to decelerate slightly to 3.8% this year before rising again to 4.3% in 2019, supported by FDI anticipated to exceed $1 billion annually this year and next to develop the Oyu Tolgoi underground mine (Figure 3.10.8). The quality of copper concentrate from the open-pit mine is expected to improve significantly. The contribution to growth from coal mining and related activities will be smaller in 2018, as transportation bottlenecks limit expansion in coal exports, but larger again in 2019 as they are alleviated. On the whole, the contribution of mining to growth is projected to turn positive in 2018 and rise higher in 2019. The service sector will remain the driver of growth, though its contribution will be lower in 2018 as coal transport declines, recovering in 2019. Crop production is projected to return to normal in 2018 after the drought in 2017, helping agriculture recover. Manufacturing will grow at a slower rate than in 2017, with cement and food processing playing prominent roles. Construction is set to recover in line with higher mining investments.

Consumption growth will be supported in both 2018 and 2019 by rising government expenditure, higher incomes, and strengthening consumer confidence linked to mining activity. Investment will grow in both years but at a diminishing pace as FDI inflows remain stable. The decline in coal exports in 2018 will likely be compensated by increased copper concentrate exports, but with imports expected to remain robust, net exports should be negative in both years.

Average inflation will accelerate to 8.0% in 2018 and ease to 7.0% in 2019 (Figure 3.10.9). Rising domestic demand and international oil and food prices will, with the effect of looser monetary policy in 2017, drive inflation higher in 2018. These effects will be less pronounced in 2019 as oil prices and domestic demand subside.

Fiscal policy will be more expansionary in 2018 and 2019. The budget deficit is projected to equal 6.4% of GDP in 2018 and 5.1% in 2019 as expenditure on social insurance, welfare, and equipment increases—and because reform to ease reporting requirements and the tax burden for small and medium-sized enterprises is likely to reduce budget revenue.

The trade surplus will narrow slightly in 2018 with rising imports related to FDI but widen again in 2019 on rising coal exports. The large service deficit will remain broadly constant in 2018 and 2019 as service payments rise with higher FDI-induced imports, and the deficit in the income account will remain high but lower than the one-off peak caused by

3.10.6 Public debt

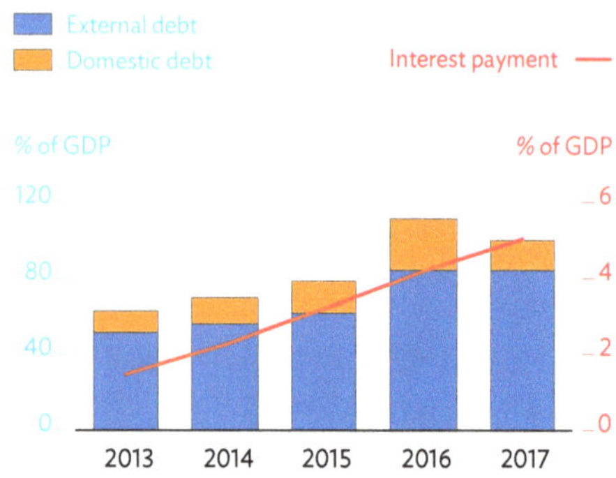

Note: Includes Bank of Mongolia's short-term liabilities.
Sources: Ministry of Finance. http://www.mof.gov.mn; Bank of Mongolia. http://www.mongolbank.mn.

3.10.7 Banking indicators

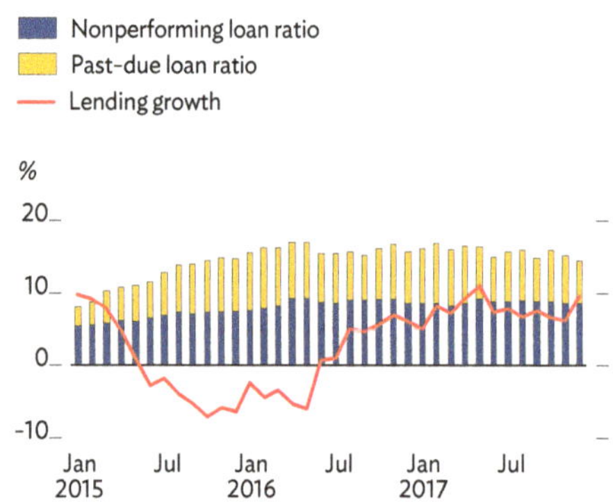

Source: Bank of Mongolia. http://www.mongolbank.mn.

3.10.8 GDP growth

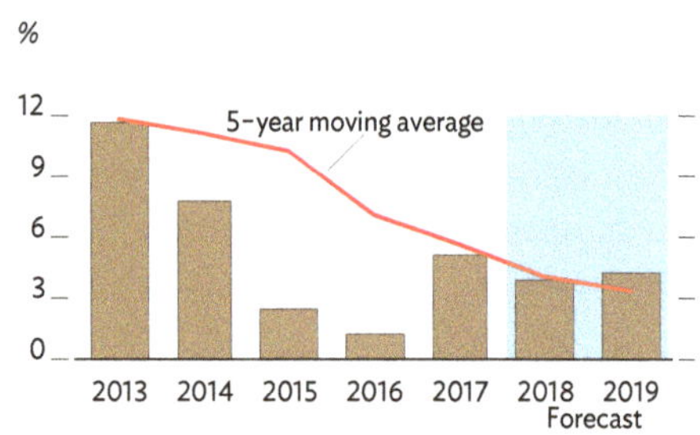

Source: *Asian Development Outlook* database.

3.10.1 Selected economic indicators (%)

	2018	2019
GDP growth	3.8	4.3
Inflation	8.0	7.0
Current account balance (share of GDP)	-6.3	-7.0

Source: ADB estimates.

profit repatriation in 2017. Thus, the current account deficit will narrow to 6.3% of GDP in 2018 before widening slightly to 7.0% in 2019.

Downside risks to the outlook would include lower coal and copper prices, disruptions to the successful implementation of the program supported by the International Monetary Fund, higher meat prices, interruptions to Oyu Tolgoi production or investment, and worsening financial instability arising from the bank restructuring program. Upside risks to growth would be higher commodity prices and a possible deal on large infrastructure projects tied to existing mining production.

3.10.9 Inflation

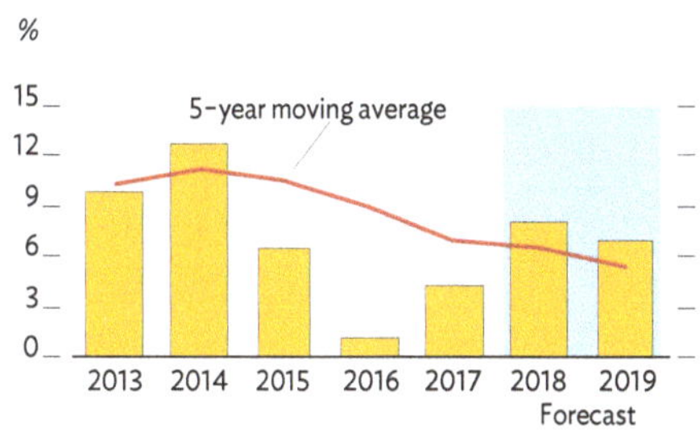

Source: *Asian Development Outlook* database.

Policy challenge—reducing the high cost of air pollution in Ulaanbaatar

Ulaanbaatar is the coldest national capital in the world and the most polluted city in wintertime. Pollutant concentrations in the coldest months can average 20 times recommended guidelines from the World Health Organization, with daily levels up to 80 times higher (Figure 3.10.10). The annual economic cost of pollution through premature death and higher hospitalization is estimated by the Millennium Challenge Corporation in the US to equal 8%–13% of Mongolian GDP. Poor families are especially exposed as they are more likely to live and work in the most polluted areas and often cannot afford medical care. With poverty rates estimated to have risen from 2014 to 2016 by 8.0 percentage points to 29.6% nationwide and by 8.4 percentage points to 24.8% in Ulaanbaatar mainly due to the worsening economic situation in this period, the number of people vulnerable to pollution has increased significantly. Thus, pollution both increases economic costs and deepens inequality.

High pollution has both human and natural causes. Increasingly frequent harsh winters and summer droughts worsen conditions for herders, stoking migration to cities. Ulaanbaatar has grown by more than 30% since 2007 to a population of 1.5 million, expected to hit 1.9 million by 2025. Close to 60% of city residents live in vast informal developments and rely on raw coal or refuse burned in inefficient stoves for heating and cooking, which generate 80% of pollution in Ulaanbaatar. Exacerbating the problem are the use of highly polluting coal-fired boilers for heating, combined heat and power plants, the growing number of vehicles, and mountains that trap polluted air in winter.

The National Program for Reducing Air and Environmental Pollution, 2017–2025 aims to strengthen regulations on fuel quality, ban raw coal in Ulaanbaatar by 2019, and improve access to higher-quality energy sources by subsidizing the use of electricity and cleaner fuels. It includes longer-term

3.10.10 Average concentration of pollutants in Ulaanbaatar

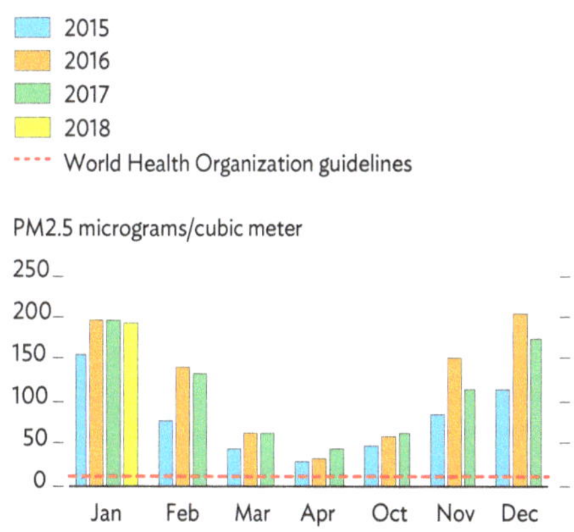

PM2.5 = small particulate matter that penetrates deep into the lungs.

Sources: Department of Weather and Environment Analyses; World Health Organization.

plans to improve energy efficiency, broaden access to clean energy sources, improve public transport, provide affordable housing, and strengthen urban planning and development. The program is estimated to cost $4 billion, of which $1.8 billion targets air pollution, with the remainder focused on land and water pollution. Only 4.5% has reportedly been secured. Development partners have committed to funding parts of the program, but the government will need to create the right conditions to attract additional financing. Success requires careful analysis of sustainability and cost-effectiveness to ensure resource allocation to activities with impact and the sustainability of measures such as fuel subsidies.

Meanwhile, improving conditions in rural areas would be better than forcing people out of the city or restricting migration, which might well exacerbate unplanned urban expansion and pollution. Finally, the national program must be immune to political changes to ensure its uninterrupted implementation.

People's Republic of China

Growth accelerated in 2017 on robust consumption and rising exports. It will decelerate in 2018 and 2019 as macroeconomic policy is carefully tightened to put the economy on a more sustainable growth path. Inflation will stir but remain low in 2018 and 2019, and the current account surplus will trend downward. A key policy challenge is to reform personal income tax and social security contributions to enhance tax revenue and reduce income inequality.

Economic performance

GDP growth accelerated slightly from 6.7% in 2016 to 6.9% in 2017, reversing the declining trend since 2011, when the impact of stimulus initiated by the government in late 2008 faded out (Figure 3.11.1). Although monetary and fiscal policies tightened somewhat toward the end of 2017, robust domestic consumption and surprisingly strong external demand supported growth and facilitated further economic rebalancing toward consumption and services. Ranked the second largest economy in the world, the People's Republic of China (PRC) contributed a third of global economic growth in 2017.

On the supply side, services remained the main driver of growth, accelerating to 8.0% from 7.7% in 2016 and contributing 4.0 percentage points to GDP growth (Figure 3.11.2). Rapid expansion in transportation, information transmission and technology, and leasing and business services offset moderation in financial and real estate services. The contribution of industry to growth fell to 2.5 percentage points as the sector, which includes mining and construction in addition to manufacturing, experienced growth deceleration from 6.3% in 2016 to 6.1%. Export, consumer, and high-tech industries continued to do well, but construction weakened in conjunction with moderating property prices and sales. On the positive side, the capacity utilization rate in manufacturing improved to 77%, the highest in 5 years and close to the international norm of 80%, thanks to increases in production and restrictions under the government's supply-side policy reform program that cut production capacity. The share of services in nominal GDP increased to 51.6%, while that of industry eased to 40.5%.

These developments, which reflect rebalancing from heavy industry toward services and consumption, continued a trend toward lower energy consumption per unit of GDP, tamping

3.11.1 Economic growth

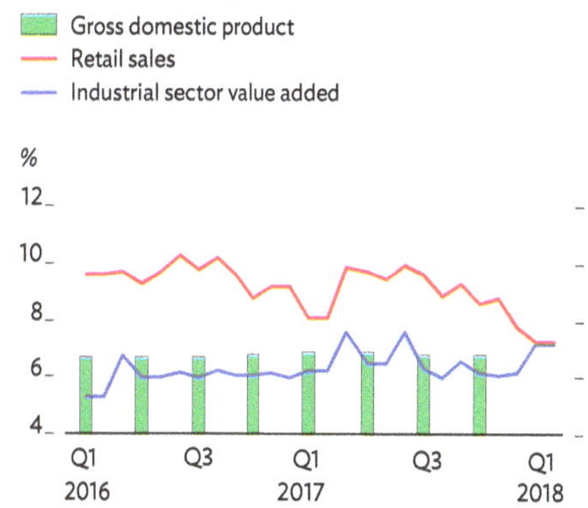

Q = quarter.

Note: GDP data for the first quarter of 2018 are not yet available.

Source: National Bureau of Statistics.

3.11.2 Supply-side contributions to growth

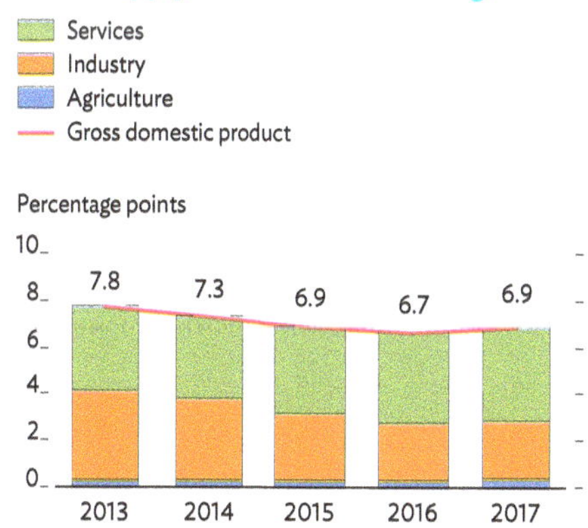

Source: National Bureau of Statistics.

This chapter was written by Jurgen Conrad, Dominik Peschel, and Jian Zhuang of the People's Republic of China Resident Mission, ADB, Beijing.

it down by another 3.7% in 2017. Strong service sector growth kept the labor market buoyant, with 13.5 million new urban jobs created in 2017, significantly above the government's target of 11 million. The ratio of urban job openings to job seekers increased again to 1.22 in the fourth quarter of 2017, the highest since 2001. Ongoing investment and normal weather accelerated agriculture growth from 3.3% in 2016 to 3.9% in 2017, but the sector's share in GDP declined further from 8.6% to 7.9%.

On the demand side, consumption grew by an estimated 8.0%, and its contribution to GDP growth, at 4.1 percentage points, again surpassed that of investment at 2.2 points (Figure 3.11.3). Consumption growth found support in higher household disposable income, which grew by 7.3% in real terms, and rising government social spending. For the ninth successive year, rural households saw real income increase faster than did urban residents, though urban households still earned 2.7 times more than their rural counterparts (Figure 3.11.4). Reflecting these trends, retail sales in rural areas rose faster than in cities.

Investment growth decelerated to an estimated 4.6% year on year, owing to a slowdown in real estate investment as purchase restrictions—including quotas and larger down-payment requirements—were implemented in more and more cities. Nevertheless, property sales continued to outpace new property completed, shrinking the housing overhang, measured by floor space awaiting sale, by 15.3% in line with the objectives of the government's ongoing supply-side reform (Figure 3.11.5). Growth in infrastructure investment accelerated slightly on continued government support, notably through public–private partnership. Growth in manufacturing investment stabilized as investment in general and transportation equipment recovered, and as investment in automobiles and in information technology hardware accelerated, but investment in other manufacturing remained constrained by excess capacity and high corporate debt.

Boosted by strong demand from developed and developing economies alike for both capital- and labor-intensive goods since late 2016, the contribution of net exports to GDP growth jumped to 0.6 percentage points, reversing a drag of 0.6 percentage points in 2016. This sharp turnaround was critical for GDP growth acceleration in 2017 in the face of weakening investment.

Consumer price inflation averaged 1.6% in 2017, down from 2.0% in 2016, mainly from a 1.4% decline in food prices (especially for pork, vegetables, and eggs), which account for one-third of the official consumer price basket (Figure 3.11.6). Base effects, favorable weather, and improved supplies were key reasons. Prices for services increased by 3.0%, however, on rising labor and education costs, and as price deregulation pushed up health and elder care expenses, raising core inflation excluding energy and food from 1.6% in 2016 to 2.2% in 2017.

3.11.3 Demand-side contributions to growth

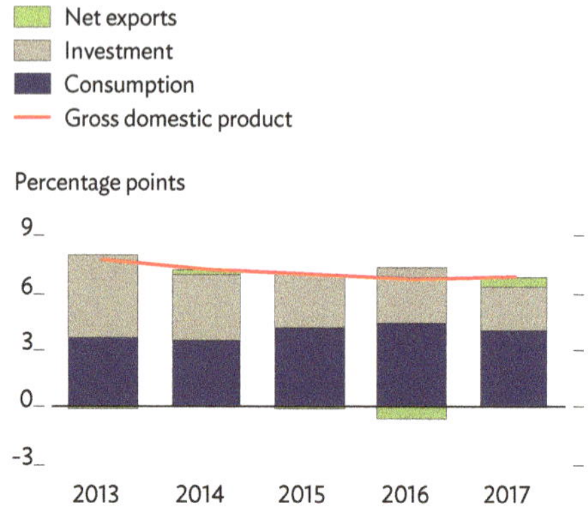

Source: National Bureau of Statistics.

3.11.4 Per capita income

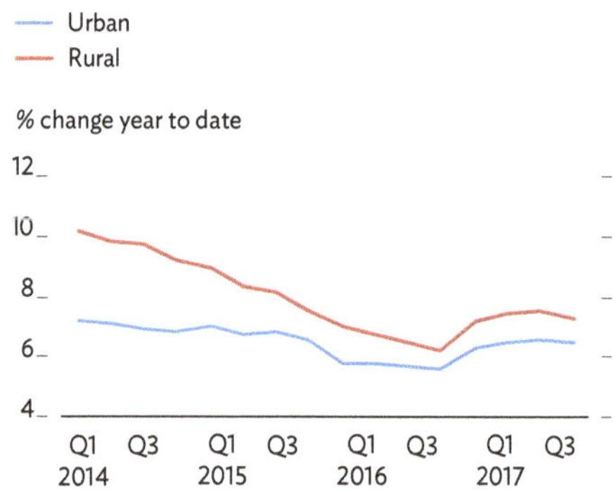

Q = quarter.
Source: National Bureau of Statistics.

3.11.5 Real estate market

Sources: National Bureau of Statistics; National Development and Reform Commission; ADB estimates.

Supported by rising commodity prices and a strong recovery in prices for upstream industrial products, the producer price index climbed by 6.3% in 2017 after falling by an average of 2.4% year on year from 2012 to 2016. Industry profit soared by 21.0% in 2017, skyrocketing by nearly 60% in the materials subsector, allowing these industries to service their debt and reduce borrowing. These outcomes arguably arose from production ceilings imposed on industries with excess capacity and high indebtedness, such as coal, steel, aluminum, iron, and cement. Capping their output aimed to raise prices and thereby their profitability to achieve a stated objective of supply-side reform.

Housing prices rose by 5.6% in 2017, slowing from 10.1% growth in 2016 with the expansion of restrictions on housing purchases and regulations tightening access to mortgages.

Both monetary policy and financial regulations were tightened in 2017. Regulatory tightening aimed to curb speculative investment and contain enterprise debt, while ensuring adequate financing to the rest of the economy to support the government's growth objective. The People's Bank of China, the central bank, reduced liquidity in the interbank market, forcing up interbank interest rates. The benchmark 7-day rate rose from 2.5% on average in January 2017 to 2.9% in December 2017 (Figure 3.11.7). Similarly, the weighted average lending rate increased year on year to the fourth quarter of 2017 by 0.4 percentage points to 5.7%. In line with higher interest rates and tighter regulation, credit to nonbank financial institutions grew more slowly in 2017 than in 2016 as banks reduced investment in bonds and other financial instruments issued by nonbank borrowers. Corporate bond issuance took a hit as outstanding volume grew by only 2.5%, down steeply from 20.8% in 2016. The bond market thus became a collateral victim of the government's deleveraging efforts.

All in all, broad money (M2) expanded by only 8.2% in 2017, down from 11.3% in 2016 and reflecting slower expansion in net domestic credit (Figure 3.11.8). However, total social financing, a broader credit aggregate that includes not only bank credit but also financing to households and enterprises from nonbank financial institutions and the capital market, grew by 12.0%, only 0.8 percentage points less than in 2016. Within total social financing, bank loans outstanding grew by 12.7%, up from 12.6% in 2016, while trust loans, a well-regulated type of nonbank credit, grew even faster. Meanwhile, regulatory tightening slowed growth in intercompany loans channeled through banks.

The consolidated central and local government budget ran a deficit equal to 3.7% of GDP in 2017, slightly below the 3.8% reached in 2016. Consolidated budget revenues grew faster in 2017 than in 2016, mainly on higher revenues from taxes on individual income and, in particular, on profits, reflecting

3.11.6 Monthly inflation

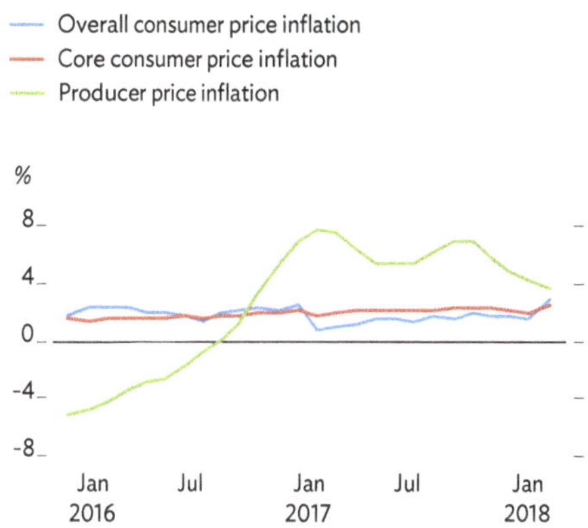

Source: National Bureau of Statistics.

3.11.7 Policy and interbank market interest rates

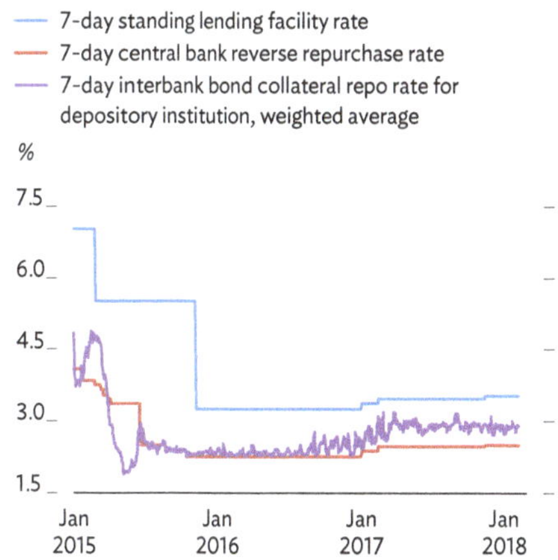

Sources: People's Bank of China; National Interbank Funding Center.

3.11.8 Growth of money supply and total social financing

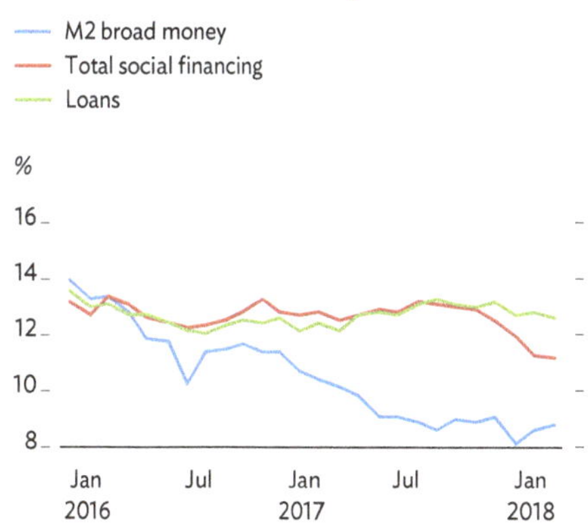

Sources: People's Bank of China; ADB estimates.

high personal income and profit growth. As a percentage of GDP, however, revenues declined further from 21.5% in 2016 to 20.9%, which is low for a country at the income level of the PRC. Similarly, expenditure growth increased in nominal terms but fell as a share of GDP to 24.6%, partly because of slow progress toward bringing off-budget spending on budget. Timely data on off-budget activity are not available, but it has been sizeable for years as local government budget revenues have failed to keep pace with rising social and infrastructure spending needs.

Exports increased in 2017 by 11.4% in US dollar terms, and imports by 16.4%, reversing declines in 2015 and 2016. Exports increased more than initially expected, mainly on vigorous demand from the US, the euro area, Japan, and Southeast Asia. The trade surplus shrank by 3.6%, and the deficit in services trade widened, causing the current account surplus to narrow further to the equivalent of 1.4% of GDP in 2017 from 1.8% in 2016 (Figure 3.11.9). Strong economic growth and a weakening US dollar moderated net capital outflow despite some relaxation of capital controls, and official reserves remained broadly stable at $3.2 trillion.

Amid some volatility, the renminbi strengthened against the US dollar by 4.7% in 2017, mainly reflecting US dollar weakness, and it appreciated by 0.6% in nominal effective terms against a trade-weighted basket of currencies. This aligned with the government objective to keep the exchange rate "basically stable." Taking inflation into account, the renminbi strengthened by 1.0% in real effective terms (Figure 3.11.10).

Economic prospects

After an uptick in 2017, GDP growth is expected to return to its moderating trajectory. Strong momentum from 6.8% growth in the last quarter of 2017 is expected to spill over into 2018, supported by a favorable global economic environment, pushing growth to 6.6%, above the official target of 6.5% (Figure 3.11.11). As in 2017, faster growth in the first half of the year will be followed by slight moderation in the second half as momentum fades. The forecast assumes that the government sustains moderate tightening in both monetary and fiscal policy over the forecast period, aiming for a more sustainable growth rate. To improve the quality of growth, government policy is expected to focus on three priorities announced in December 2017 and reconfirmed at the National People's Congress in March 2018: heading off financial risk, controlling environmental pollution, and using targeted intervention to eliminate poverty. These policies will initially dampen growth, especially in 2019 when their full impact will be felt. Growth is therefore forecast to slow further to 6.4% in 2019. As in the past, the government can be expected to counter any

3.11.9 Current account balance

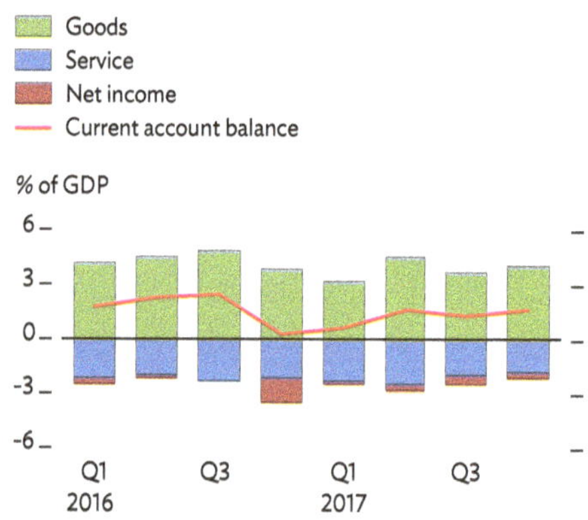

Q = quarter.

Sources: State Administration of Foreign Exchange; ADB estimates.

3.11.10 Exchange rates

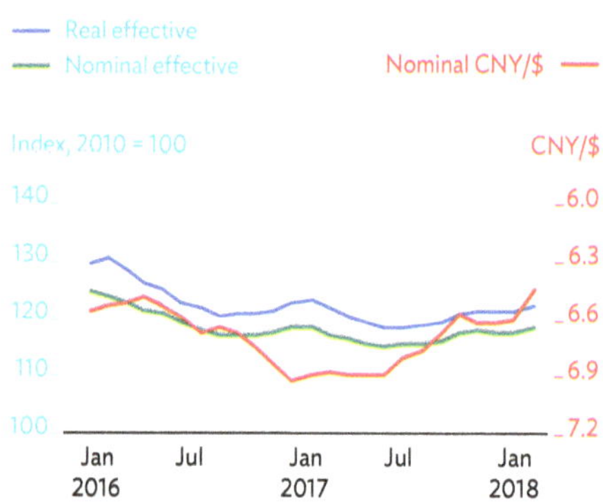

Sources: Bank for International Settlements; State Administration of Foreign Exchange.

3.11.11 GDP growth

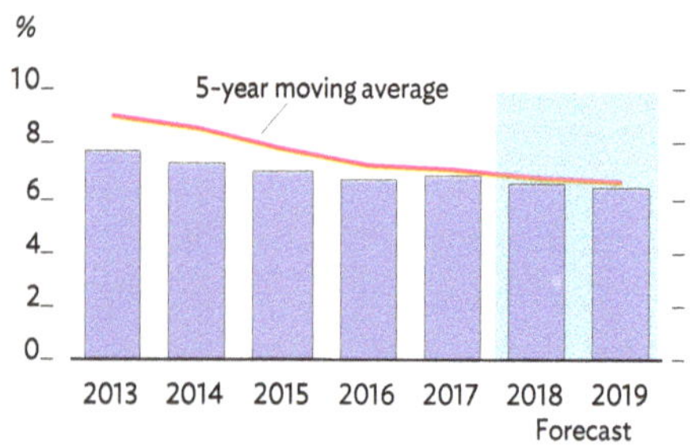

Source: *Asian Development Outlook* database.

external shocks with fiscal and monetary policies as necessary to achieve its growth target. That said, the National People's Congress signaled in March 2018 a rising tolerance on the part of the government for moderately lower growth as long as labor market stability is maintained.

On the demand side, consumption will remain the main driver of growth in 2018 and 2019, with its contribution to growth continuing to rise. Support will again come from higher government social spending, high wage growth backed by a tight market for skilled blue-collar workers, and rising consumer confidence. The consumer confidence index reached 115.6 in 2017, its highest since 1994, as employment expectation improved and personal incomes increased, raising households' propensity to spend. These trends are expected to continue to the forecast horizon.

Investment is projected to continue its decelerating trend, its share of GDP shrinking but remaining above 40%, which is still very high from an international perspective. Real estate investment growth will weaken further in response to purchase restrictions in more cities, though available housing stocks in larger cities are already low and demand remains strong, harboring an upside risk to the forecast. Excess capacity and high debt will continue to limit investment in heavy industry, and enterprises that pollute the environment will face additional constraints on investment (and production) imposed by the government as part of ongoing structural reform.

Government investment in infrastructure will remain sizeable, but its growth rate is projected to decline, the government having already started to streamline infrastructure spending both on and off budget to control growth in local government debt. As bond yields drive up financing costs, constraints are stiffening as well on government-owned policy banks, which have provided heavily subsidized loans on a large scale for infrastructure projects, shantytown reconstruction, and social housing. As a result, infrastructure investment growth has already weakened since December 2017, scuttling several major infrastructure projects that had been pursued as public–private partnerships. These developments cannot be fully compensated by stronger investment in emerging industries, consumer-oriented industries, and services because most of them are less capital intensive. However, investment in export-oriented industries may increase, especially if the surge in exports continues. This possibility harbors an upside risk to the forecast.

The trend in exports and imports over the forecast period should be a continuation from 2017, tempered by the pattern of growth in the major industrial economies—the US, the euro area, and Japan—which is expected to accelerate in 2018 and moderate in 2019. As in 2017, high commodity prices, robust domestic demand, and a still large share of final assembly

3.11.1 Selected economic indicators (%)

	2018	2019
GDP growth	6.6	6.4
Inflation	2.4	2.3
Current account balance (share of GDP)	1.3	1.2

Source: ADB estimates.

of manufactures will keep growth in imports above that of exports in 2018. The major contribution of net exports to growth in 2017 is expected to unwind in 2018 and 2019. With a slightly larger deficit in the services account—resulting from more outbound tourism, study abroad, and intellectual property royalties encouraged by service sector liberalization—the current account surplus should slip further to equal 1.3% of GDP in 2018 and 1.2% in 2019.

On the supply side, services will remain the main driver of growth, even if contributions from financial intermediation and real estate continue to weaken. The service sector still has huge catch-up potential in the PRC, given its GDP share in 2017 of just 51.6%, or 10–15 percentage points below the share of services in other economies at a similar income level. Such potential, particularly in health care, education, entertainment, tourism, internet, leasing, and commercial services, is expected to be unleashed gradually as urbanization progresses and the government continues to deregulate banking, security, and insurance activities, gradually opening them to private and foreign investors. Constrained by high debt and cooling real estate, growth in traditional manufacturing industries and construction will decelerate further in 2018 and 2019, though strong performances are expected from consumer- and export-oriented industries and emerging high-technology subsectors.

Consumer price inflation is projected to increase to 2.4% in 2018 and 2.3% in 2019 because food prices, which declined in 2017, have normalized and price inflation for services remains elevated (Figure 3.11.12). Apart from volatile food prices, key drivers of inflation continue to be strong consumer demand for other commodities and services, higher wages, and continued price deregulation, particularly for health care. Some spillover from higher producer prices is expected despite tenuous linkage experienced in 2017, arguably caused by the lagged effect of producer price inflation on the consumer price index.

3.11.12 Inflation

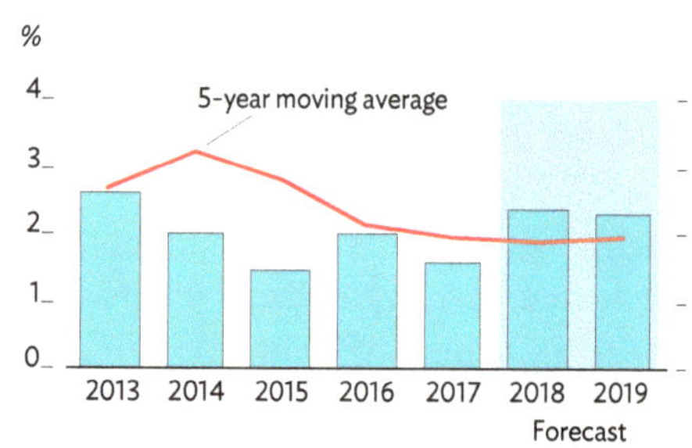

Source: *Asian Development Outlook* database.

Monetary policy is likely to continue its balancing act, reining in speculative nonbank credit and containing state-owned enterprise debt while ensuring credit to areas prioritized for economic development or unduly encumbered by difficulty in obtaining bank loans. No money supply targets were set for 2018, which augments flexibility for policy makers. Short-term policy interest rates are likely to rise moderately in the remainder of 2018 in response to rising inflationary pressure and the central bank's sustained focus on deleveraging and reducing financial risk. Although regulatory tightening was responsible for a sharp decrease in bond financing, it remains to be seen if the government will take action to revive this important channel of finance to the real economy.

Fiscal policy will remain "proactive," as the government recently reconfirmed at the National People's Congress.

However, support may be a bit weaker over the forecast period than in 2016 and early 2017, with a slightly lower budget deficit target than in 2017 and renewed efforts to bring under control off-budget borrowing by local governments. Budget deficits will be financed increasingly by bonds issued by local governments, the central government having set higher quotas to give local government more room to finance infrastructure on-budget. Within the consolidated budget, transfers from the center to local governments will increase to institute across the country unified standards of public service delivery, which many local governments cannot finance without greater support. The government is expected to make more visible efforts to reform property and personal income taxes by advancing legislation, but no increase in revenues will materialize within the forecast period. Revenues may be raised and deficits reduced if local governments are allowed to sell assets, including shares in local state-owned enterprises to repair their balance sheets, rather than rely on budgetary support.

Further improvement in the global trade outlook harbors an upside risk to the forecast, while lower commodity prices would pose a downside risk, as they could undercut recently strong export demand from commodity-exporting economies. Other downside risks include heightened global trade protectionism, which could undercut PRC exports and investment, and renewed large capital outflows if interest rate hikes in the US stoke expectations of dollar appreciation (Figure 3.11.13). However, these risks seem to be moderate over the forecast period. At this stage, there are no signs that the US dollar will appreciate significantly in the short run, so there is little incentive to move capital out of the PRC. In any case, strong finances position the PRC well to manage any such risks and limit their impact on growth.

A domestic downside risk to the forecast would be a deepening slowdown in investment growth, though the government would have the necessary monetary and fiscal tools to stabilize investments, if needed. Another domestic risk is that regulatory tightening could cause liquidity shortages and drive weaker financial institutions into bankruptcy, engendering systemic instability. However, the likelihood of such a risk materializing remains low, considering that substantial progress has been made in reducing financial flows between banks and nonbanks and in making intermediation channels more transparent. Further, the central bank has acknowledged that mitigating risk exposure in the financial system would likely reduce bank liquidity, thereby hurting weaker banks and making investment financing less available. It has stated that it stands ready to avert these outcomes by providing liquidity as needed.

3.11.13 Official reserves and capital flows

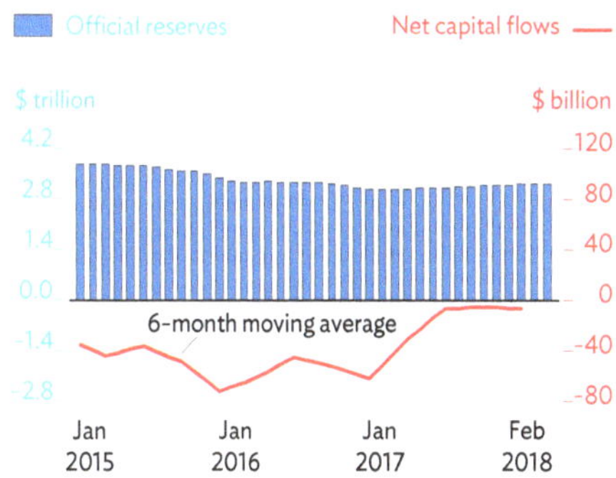

Sources: People's Bank of China; State Administration of Foreign Exchange.

Policy challenge—tax reform to raise revenue and narrow income inequality

The PRC has made substantial progress with fiscal reform over recent years, but tax revenues has been declining as a ratio of GDP (Figure 3.11.14). The combination of falling tax revenue and rising expenditure has translated into rising budget deficits, public debt, and contingent liabilities.

International experience shows that the ratio of tax revenue to GDP tends to increase as countries grow richer. This reflects better administration and collection, as well as a more comprehensive social contract to provide a broader range of high-quality public services. However, the ratio of tax revenue to GDP in the PRC, excluding social security contributions, was only 17.5% in 2017, after peaking at 18.6% in 2012 and 2013. By comparison, in 2014, the ratio was 25% on average in the advanced economies of the Organisation for Economic Co-operation and Development (OECD) and 21% in the 10 emerging economies in the Group of 20 (G20).

The stagnation of tax revenue in the PRC can be explained by heavy dependence on indirect taxes, whose growth has slowed following value-added tax reform that eased the tax burden for enterprises in the service sector. Indeed, direct taxes in the PRC make only a small contribution to tax revenue equal to 5% of GDP, compared with 11% in the OECD countries and 7%–8% in the G20 emerging economies. The lackluster collection of direct taxes reflects mainly low receipts of personal income taxes, equal to 1.4% of GDP and much lower than the OECD norm of 8.4%. This suggests that there is substantial potential in the PRC to raise more revenue from personal income taxes. Another issue is that the tax system in the PRC does little to narrow income inequality, which remains a big concern for the country. The difference between Gini coefficients, the usual measure of inequality, before and after taxes and transfers is only 3% in the PRC, compared with over 30% in OECD countries.

Three main reasons explain the low contribution of personal income taxes to revenue and their limited use to address inequality. First, a high standard personal exemption of CNY42,000, or twice the average annual national wage, narrows the income tax base such that fewer than 20% of wage earners pay it. Second, the top marginal rate of 45% applies only to income above CNY960,000, which is the highest bracket of income distribution and almost 35 times the average annual national wage. In contrast, in OECD countries, the personal exemption is only one quarter of the average annual national wage, and the top marginal rate starts to apply at around 4 times the average. Third, personal income is not taxed on a consolidated basis but according to a multicategory system that subjects income from different sources to different

3.11.14 Tax revenue

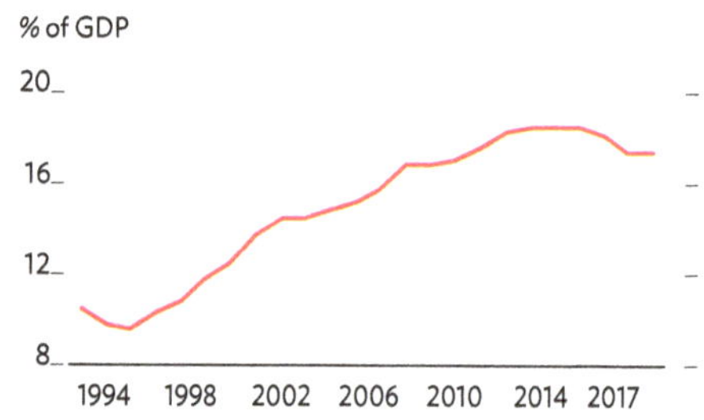

Sources: National Bureau of Statistics; Ministry of Finance.

tax schedules. Depending on the category, income from some sources is taxed at progressive rates (as are wages and salaries), while others are taxed at a flat rate (rental and lease income, among others) or even tax-exempt (interest on savings deposits and bonds).

Taxes on wage income are rendered even less progressive by the highly regressive structure of social security contributions. A flat and slightly different contribution rate is applied to employees' gross wages in each province and locality. Nationwide, the rate averages 11%. The social security contribution base to which the contribution rate applies is the employee's salary in the previous year, except for those earning below a threshold, who must pay a fixed minimum amount, and those earning above a threshold, who pay a fixed maximum amount. The lower threshold is generally set at 60% of the previous year's average local wage, and the top threshold at 300% of that wage. As the earnings of about 30% of urban workers are below the lower threshold, these low-income workers effectively make social security contributions higher than 11% of their income. Meanwhile, for the top earners, the effective rate is lower than 11%. Indeed, the tax bite on low incomes is substantial and grows as income falls. This is not only regressive, because it worsens inequality, but potentially a disincentive for low-income workers to enter formal employment. This barrier to entry is further exacerbated by employer social security contributions that are relatively high, almost 35% of payroll on the average, more than double the 16% average in the 10 advanced economies in the G20 and substantially more than the 25% norm in the European Union.

These issues suggest to the government a future direction for tax reform. First, adjustment to the standard personal allowance that, for example, replaces it with a well-calibrated tax credit, could significantly broaden the personal income tax base and make it more progressive. Second, a good complement to the first reform would be to simplify the tax rate structure with fewer income categories such that higher rates capture more income from upper-middle earners. Third, levying social security contributions on the actual income of all earners, without thresholds, would make them much less regressive. Further, by removing regressive taxation as a disincentive to seeking formal wage employment, social security reform could make both personal income tax and social security receipts more buoyant.

These reforms will likely be initiated within the forecast period and gradually help raise revenue, address inequality, and strengthen labor market flexibility and enterprise competitiveness over the long term. At the 19th Party Congress in October 2017 and the National People's Congress in March 2018, the PRC leadership confirmed the need to comprehensively reform personal income taxes and social security contributions.

Republic of Korea

Robust global expansion spurred exports and investment, pushing growth in 2017 higher than expected. Supported by domestic consumption and external demand, growth will slow marginally in 2018 and 2019. Inflation will remain low and stable, and the sizable current account surplus will narrow slightly. Youth unemployment needs to be tackled by improving conditions for smaller businesses, to make the jobs they offer more attractive.

Economic performance

GDP expanded by 3.1% in 2017, up from 2.8% in 2016 as political uncertainties in the first half of the year dissipated with the election of a new government in May, which improved domestic demand, and as relations warmed with the People's Republic of China (PRC), the largest trade partner of the Republic of Korea (ROK). GDP grew at a slower pace of 2.8% in the first half of the year as consumption stagnated and export growth weakened, though investment growth was strong at 12.0% (Figure 3.12.1). Growth picked up in the second half of the year, reaching 3.3% as both public and private consumption strengthened after the election of the new government, a supplementary budget was implemented, and investment growth sustained its momentum. The recovery was strongly supported by an improving global economy and accommodative domestic monetary and fiscal policies.

Investment expanded by 8.6%, the highest annual growth rate since 2000, and was the major source of GDP growth, contributing 3.0 percentage points (Figure 3.12.2). The investment surge was driven by a rebound in machinery and equipment investment driven in turn by stronger exports, especially of semiconductors and other information technology (IT) products. Construction investment grew by 7.6% in 2017 from 10.3% a year earlier, mainly on account of strong residential construction, which grew by 14.9%.

Consumption grew by 2.8% in 2017, slower than in the previous year but adding 1.8 percentage points to growth. Private consumption rose rapidly as the consumer sentiment index breached the 100-point threshold at midyear. Unemployment remained unchanged from 2016 at 3.7%. Exports grew for a second straight year on strong global demand for semiconductors and petrochemicals. Meanwhile, a fall in visitor arrivals from the PRC reduced service exports.

This chapter was written by Cindy Castillejos-Petalcorin, Donghyun Park, and Shu Tian of the Economic Research and Regional Cooperation Department, ADB, Manila.

3.12.1 Half-yearly GDP growth

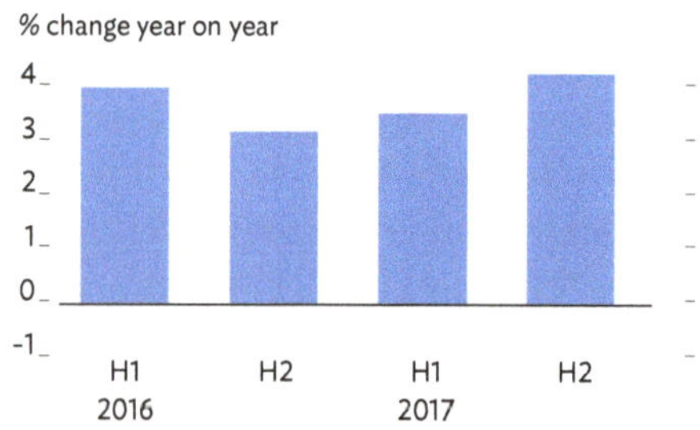

GDP = gross domestic product, H = half.

Source: Bank of Korea, Economic Statistics System, http://ecos.bok.or.kr (accessed 31 March 2018).

3.12.2 Demand-side contributions to growth

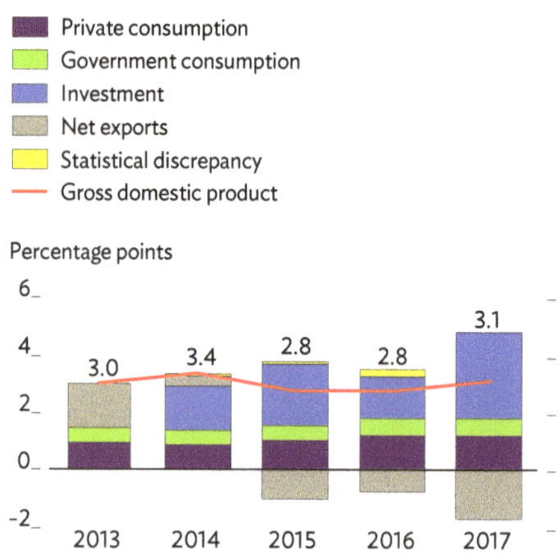

Source: Bank of Korea, Economic Statistics System, http://ecos.bok.or.kr (accessed 31 March 2018).

With export growth outpaced by import growth fueled by demand for production inputs, net exports declined, subtracting 1.7 percentage points from growth (Figure 3.12.3).

On the supply side, industry expanded by 4.6% in 2017 and contributed 1.6 percentage points to GDP growth. In tandem with growth in merchandise exports, manufacturing grew by 4.3%, while construction remained strong thanks to expanded civil works projects. Services grew more modestly for a second consecutive year as wholesale and retail trade weakened with fewer tourist arrivals from the PRC, but the sector still contributed 1.1 percentage points to growth. Agriculture recovered in the second half of the year from avian influenza and unfavorable weather, posting positive growth for the year.

Inflation averaged 1.9% in 2017, up from 1.0% in 2016, and for most of the year stayed below the 2.0% target set by the Bank of Korea, the central bank (Figure 3.12.4). A spike in food and utility prices contributed to inflation, but core inflation excluding food and energy eased from 1.9% in 2016 to 1.5%.

Monetary policy continued to support growth against a backdrop of benign inflation. With its first rate increase since June 2016, the central bank raised its benchmark policy rate in November 2017 from 1.25% to 1.50%, signaling a gradual normalization of monetary policy. To mitigate potential financial risk associated with household debt—which grew to equal 83.1% of GDP at the end of September 2017, with mortgages accounting for more than 40%—the government increased capital gains tax on owners of multiple homes, tightened loan limits, and restricted the rapid resale of new apartments.

Fiscal policy remained expansionary in 2017 as the estimated budget deficit equaled 2.0% of GDP, raising government debt from 38.3% of GDP in 2016 to 39.6%. Boosted by the strong economy, revenue surpassed the government target for a third straight year. Expenditure grew more strongly, however, as civil works and social welfare spending rose and a $10 billion supplementary budget for job creation programs was enacted in July.

Customs data indicate that merchandise exports rebounded by 15.8% last year in US dollar terms, with exports to all major markets growing robustly. Exports to the PRC, which receives a quarter of total exports, expanded by 14.2% after 3 years of decline. Exports to the US increased after a drop in 2016, and those to two other major markets, Southeast Asia and the European Union, both grew by double digits. Strengthened domestic demand and recovering global commodity prices pushed up merchandise imports by 17.8%, a turnaround from the previous year.

The current account surplus shrank to the equivalent of 5.1% of GDP in 2017 as the merchandise trade surplus narrowed and the service deficit widened. There was an

3.12.3 Merchandise exports and imports

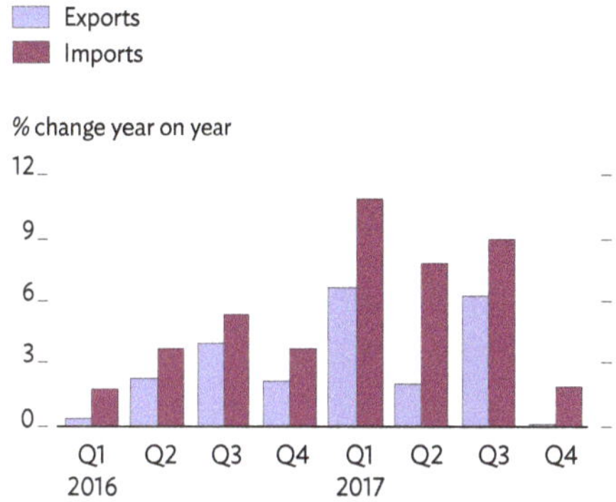

Q = quarter.

Source: Bank of Korea, Economic Statistics System, http://ecos.bok.or.kr (accessed 2 February 2018).

3.12.4 Monthly inflation

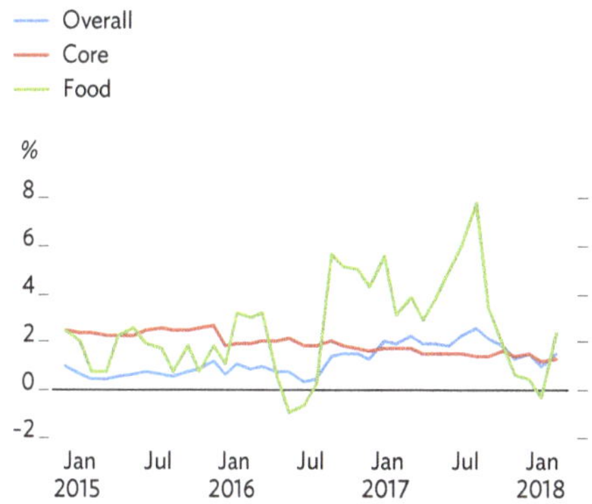

Source: CEIC Data Company (accessed 13 March 2018).

3.12.1 Selected economic indicators (%)

	2018	2019
GDP growth	3.0	2.9
Inflation	1.9	2.0
Current account balance (share of GDP)	4.9	4.8

Source: ADB estimates.

increase in inbound foreign direct investment. Portfolio flows remained positive as inflows of equity investment rose by 62.3% to $33.9 billion, pushing up the Korea Composite Stock Price Index by 29% to record highs at the end of December. The ROK won appreciated by 8.9% against the US dollar in 2017, more than any other major Asian currency, and by 3.7% in real effective terms. It rose another 10.6% against the dollar in the first 45 days of 2018 (Figure 3.12.5).

3.12.5 Exchange rates

Source: CEIC Data Company (accessed 13 March 2018).

Economic prospects

GDP growth is projected at 3.0% in 2018 and 2.9% in 2019, allowing the ROK to reach the milestone per capita income of $30,000, cementing its status as a developed economy (Figure 3.12.6). The economy will be buoyed by robust exports as growth in global and domestic demand continues. Private consumption will receive a boost from the Pyeongchang 2018 Olympic Winter Games and the likely revival of tourist arrivals from the PRC, as well as from positive consumer sentiment (Figure 3.12.7).

Investment growth is expected to moderate in 2018 and 2019. Housing construction and civil works are expected to slow because of restrictions intended to stabilize housing prices and cuts to the government's social overhead capital budget, which funds infrastructure spending. Investments in IT machinery and equipment are also likely to moderate in line with the global IT business cycle.

Exports of goods and services are projected to grow strongly this year on healthy global demand, especially for high-technology products, despite higher US tariffs on washing machines and steel. Improved diplomatic relations with the PRC will further support exports. Merchandise import growth will likely moderate along with lower investment growth, but rising consumption and a higher oil import bill will temper the slowdown. Imports will exceed exports, trimming the trade surplus, but net service receipts will improve with the likely return of PRC tourists, keeping the current account surplus sizeable at the equivalent of 4.9% of GDP in 2018 and 4.8% in 2019.

Moderate price increases in January point to waning inflation, but sustained expansion of domestic demand, a large hike in the minimum wage, and higher global oil prices will drive inflation to an average of 1.9% this year and 2.0% next year. With inflation below the central bank target, monetary policy will be geared primarily toward supporting economic growth. The central bank kept the interest rate unchanged at 1.5% at its February 2018 meeting and, with consumer debt high, is unlikely to raise rates to avoid exacerbating the burden on households.

3.12.6 GDP growth

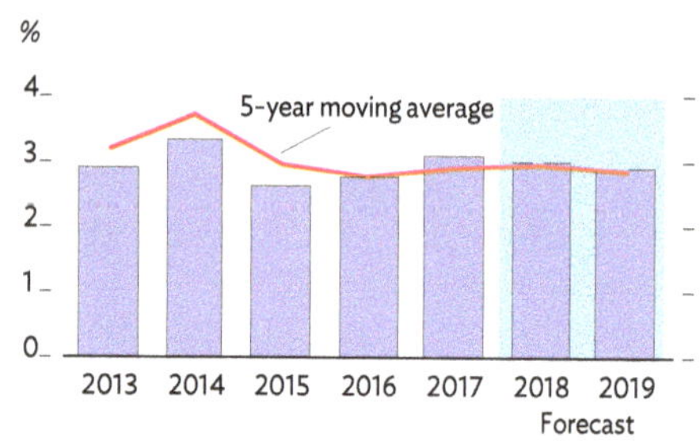

Source: *Asian Development Outlook* database.

3.12.7 Consumer confidence

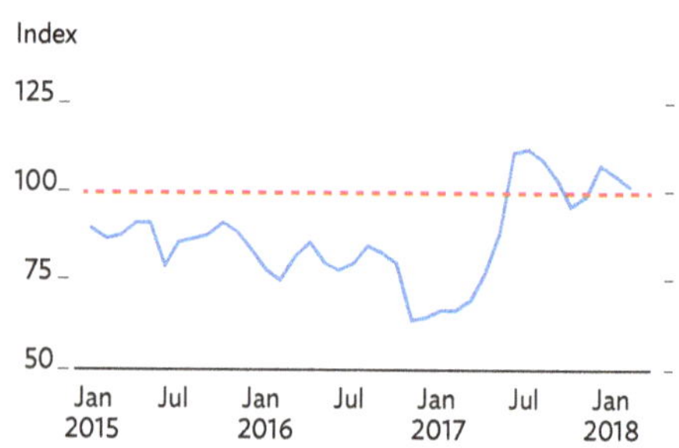

Note: A reading below 100 means that more respondents answered negatively than positively.

Source: Bank of Korea, Economics Statistic System, http://ecos.bok.or.kr (accessed 31 March 2018).

Fiscal policy will remain expansionary with the budget deficit remaining at 2.0% of GDP in 2018 and 2019. The budget for fiscal 2018 (ending on 30 September 2018) includes a record $385 billion in expenditure, a 4.6% increase from last year as social and welfare spending grows. Revenue will also be higher with the top corporate tax rate raised in December from 22% to 40% and the top individual income tax rate up from 25% to 42%.

Risks to the forecasts are broadly balanced. Unexpectedly strong global growth is an upside risk as it would raise demand for ROK exports, while slower global growth is a downside risk, especially if global IT business downcycles lower than expected. The easing of political tensions on the Korean Peninsula would support growth. Downside risks include faster normalization of monetary policy than expected in the major industrial economies, especially in the US, which could undermine domestic financial stability. High and growing household debt exacerbates the risk, which would be further magnified if asset prices were to fall (Figure 3.12.8).

An ongoing review of the KORUS bilateral trade agreement between the ROK and the US adds a degree of uncertainty to a generally favorable external environment. Progress has been slow, but a breakthrough came in late March when a tentative agreement was reached allowing improved market access to the ROK for US automobile makers and reducing the quota for exports of ROK steel to the US, in return for the continued exemption of the ROK from tariffs on steel imports from the US. Although the prolongation of negotiations means little impact in the short term, the export-oriented ROK economy will be hard hit if protectionism gains further ground. Recent appreciation of the ROK won could, if continued, render some manufactures less competitive, but the effect is likely to be contained as demand overseas for semiconductors and some other key exports is not highly price sensitive. In any case, with ample foreign exchange reserves at $389.3 billion and substantial fiscal strength, the ROK is well placed to meet any risk that materializes.

3.12.8 Credit to households and house price

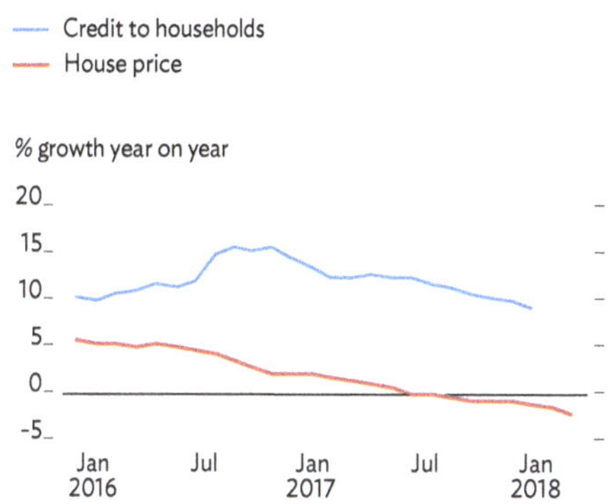

Note: House price is the deposit for a 2-year lease on an apartment under the *jeonse* system.

Source: CEIC Data Company (accessed 8 February 2018).

Policy challenge—tackling youth unemployment

Youth unemployment has been worsening in the ROK, in contrast with the improving trend in the rest of the Organisation for Economic Co-operation and Development (OECD)—this despite the ROK overall unemployment rate being lower than the OECD average (Figure 3.12.9). In December 2017, the unemployment rate for the 25–29 age group, encompassing young people first entering the workforce after completing university and military service, rose from

3.12.9 Unemployment rate for population aged 15–24

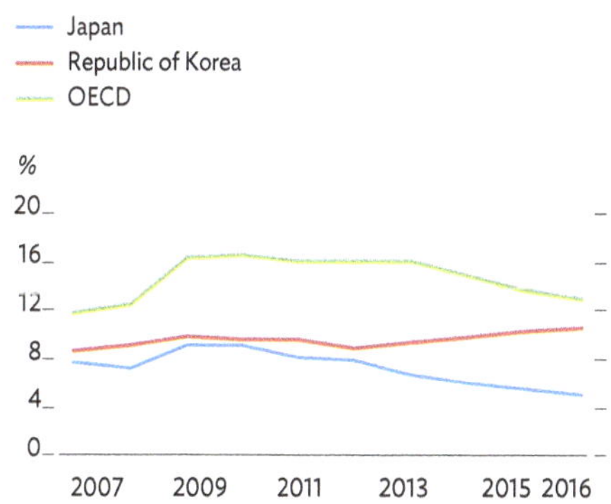

OECD = Organisation for Economic Co-operation and Development.

Source: OECD Labor statistics (accessed 24 January 2018).

5.7% in 2000 to a 17-year record high of 9.6%, almost 3 times the overall unemployment rate of 3.3%. Unemployment in the 15–29 age group rose to 9.2%, also a 17-year high (Figure 3.12.10).

The increase in youth employment reflects in part weaker economic performance since the global financial crisis of 2008–2009 and a rising population of young job seekers, but also structural issues in the ROK labor market. While the first two factors will be alleviated by economic and demographic trends in the coming years, a proactive policy is needed to address two entrenched labor market deficiencies.

First, labor market inflexibility means low turnover for secure, well-paid jobs, mostly in larger corporations, and few good prospects for young job seekers. Second, small and medium-sized enterprises (SMEs) offer lower wages and benefits than large corporations or the public sector but provide 80% of private sector employment. OECD data show that, owing to these structural issues, young ROK workers enjoy less job security and earn less than other age groups (Figure 3.12.11). The problem is not a lack of skills, as the unemployed in the ROK are better educated than the OECD average. Rather, unsatisfactory working conditions at SMEs prompt young adults to spend many years preparing for secure public sector jobs rather than seek immediate employment in an SME. Indeed, 45.2% of young job seekers remained economically inactive in 2017 as they prepared for public sector job examinations, and 32.5% of new hires at SMEs quit their jobs within a year (Figure 3.12.12). As a result, SMEs face the twin problems of labor shortage and skills mismatch, reflected in their high vacancy rate of 12.6% in the first half of 2017, nearly 3 times the 4.6% rate for large companies.

ROK demographics are among the fastest-changing in the world and may eventually alleviate the youth unemployment problem. The twentysomething cohort is still expanding despite an aging population overall, but it will peak in 2019 by some estimates and start to decline. As in Japan, the ROK will likely experience an abundance of jobs for younger workers over the medium term. In the short term, however, tackling youth unemployment requires concerted efforts to address the twin problems of low job quality and high expectations in a largely university-educated young population.

The government plans to reduce youth unemployment by creating public sector jobs. However, the capacity of the public sector to absorb the rising number of job seekers is limited, and government employment should reflect demand for government services, not unemployment.

3.12.10 Unemployment of youth population

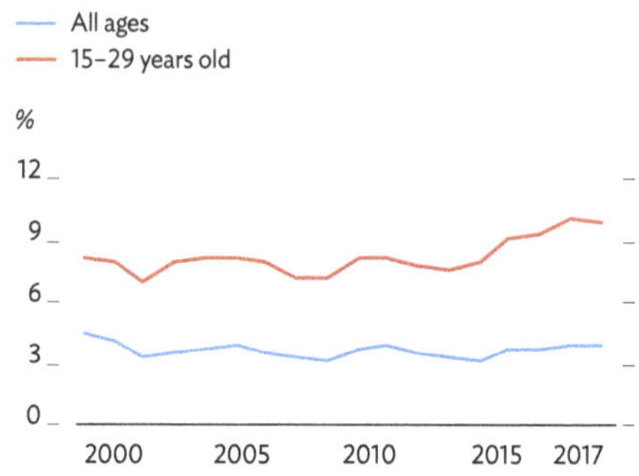

Source: Korea Development Institute.

3.12.11 OECD job quality, 2012

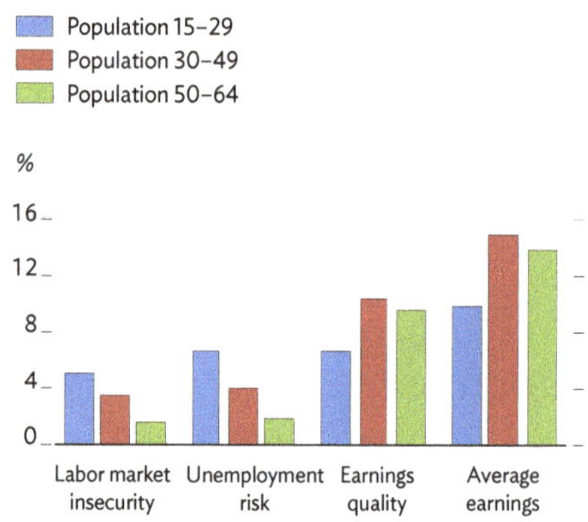

OECD = Organisation for Economic Co-operation and Development.

Notes: Higher values reflect better job quality. Average earnings are gross hourly earnings in constant dollars. Earnings quality is the gross earnings per hour in constant dollars adjust for an inequality aversion factor. Labor market insecurity is the expected monetary loss on becoming unemployed as a percentage of previous earnings. Unemployment risk is the probability of becoming and staying unemployed.

Source: OECD labour statistics (accessed 24 January 2018).

This points to the need for a more dynamic and competitive SME sector. A promising avenue is to improve the business environment, and thereby make SMEs more productive, by reducing regulatory barriers that protect established firms and restrict entry. Increased competition and productivity are essential to improve wages and benefits for young employees.

Boosting entrepreneurship would also help to mitigate youth unemployment. The government should support entrepreneurship training, coaching, and mentoring programs; provide some financial support for aspiring entrepreneurs; and promote angel funds and venture capital. It could also facilitate the provision of employment services—such as skills training and matching job seekers to jobs—to mitigate market failures arising from information asymmetry and skills mismatch. Finally, developing a more diverse and flexible education system that includes technical and vocational training would provide abilities tailored to diverse business demands and mitigate the problem of skills mismatch.

3.12.12 Employment exam preparation of economically inactive youth in 2017 by sector

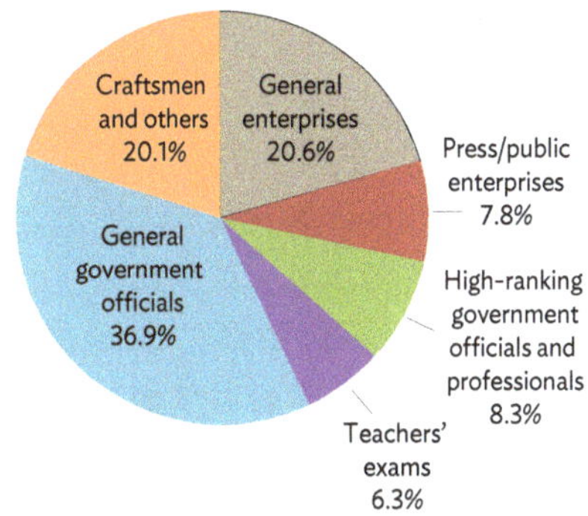

Source: Statistics Korea (accessed 24 January 2018).

Taipei,China

Strong external demand and rising consumption lifted the growth rate in 2017, while soft food prices halved inflation. Growth is expected to be stable in 2018 and 2019, sustained by robust domestic demand and an improving global economy, with moderately higher inflation and a shrinking current account surplus. Better remuneration for talented, highly skilled labor may be key to making human capital more competitive and enabling growth driven by innovation.

Economic performance

GDP growth reached a 3-year high of 2.9% in 2017, the rate doubling annually for a second time since 2015 as exports surged and private consumption expanded (Figure 3.13.1). Supported by strengthening global trade, especially higher demand for consumer electronics, merchandise exports reversed shrinkage by 1.8% in 2016 to increase by 13.2% in 2017, the highest growth rate since 2010. Electronic components, information and communication devices, and audio-video products were the drivers of export growth, rising by double digits. Exports to the People's Republic of China, accounting for 28% of the total, soared by 20.4%, up from 0.6% in the previous year, while those to the US, the second largest market, recovered from stagnation to expand by 10.2%. Merchandise imports increased by 12.4% on expansion in domestic demand and rising prices for imported raw material. Net exports, having subtracted from growth in the previous 2 years, added 2.0 percentage points to economic growth in 2017.

Private consumption rose as a tightening labor market lowered the unemployment rate to 3.8%, pushed wages up by 2.7%, and, with the help of higher asset prices, engendered a positive consumer outlook. Despite lower government consumption in 2017, total consumption contributed 1.1 percentage points to growth. Capital formation stagnated in the face of larger government infrastructure outlays as investment in machinery and equipment declined, shaving 0.3 percentage points off growth.

On the supply side, the service sector was the main driver of GDP growth in 2017, contributing 1.4 percentage points. Industry added another 1.3 points, while agriculture contributed only 0.1 points despite being the fastest-growing sector. Services were buoyed by tourist arrivals, which continued to rise, albeit at a slowing rate, as higher numbers from Southeast Asia

This chapter was written by Xuehui Han and Nedelyn Magtibay-Ramos of the Economic Research and Regional Cooperation Department, ADB, Manila.

3.13.1 Demand-side contributions to GDP growth

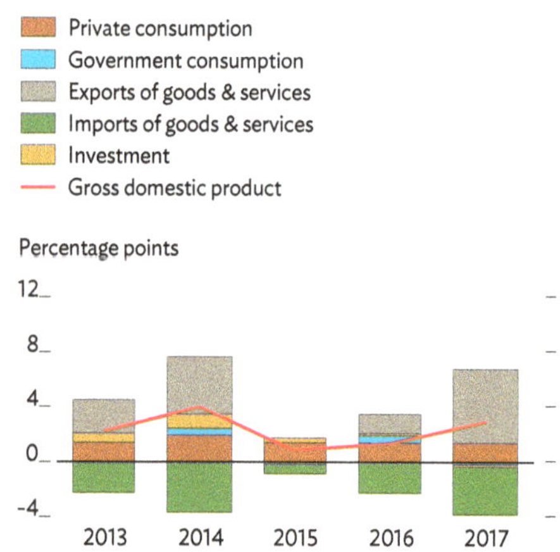

Source: Haver Analytics (accessed 15 March 2018).

3.13.2 Tourist arrivals

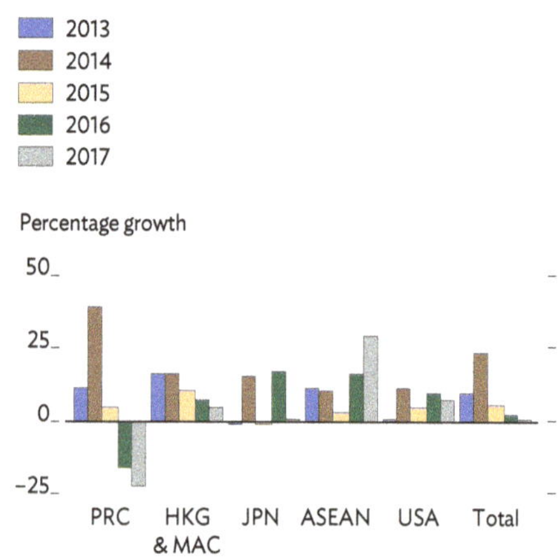

ASEAN = Association of Southeast Asian Nations, HKG = Hong Kong, China, JPN = Japan, MAC = Macau, China, PRC = People's Republic of China, USA = United States.

Source: Haver Analytics (accessed 15 March 2018).

compensated for a steeply declining trend in arrivals from the People's Republic of China (Figure 3.13.2).

Headline inflation halved to 0.6% in 2017 from 1.4% in 2016 as food prices eased under fair weather (Figure 3.13.3). Core inflation excluding food and energy increased marginally to 0.7% from 0.6%, and the wholesale price index rose by 0.9%. Tame inflation allowed the central bank to hold its policy rate at 1.38%. Broad money grew by 3.6%, the same rate as in 2016, with outstanding credit to the private sector rising by 6.1% and the net foreign assets of the banking system declining by 3.5%.

To stimulate the economy and drive industrial transformation, the government began in 2017 to implement its Forward-Looking Infrastructure Development Program. Higher infrastructure expenditure and a 2.2% decline in revenue are estimated to have raised the budget deficit to 0.9% of GDP from 0.3% in 2016.

The current account surplus widened to the equivalent of 14.7% of GDP in 2017 from 13.7% in 2016 as the trade surplus grew, and gross foreign exchange reserves increased by 4.0% to cover 16.8 months of imports. The local dollar appreciated by 6.3% against the US dollar in 2017, but it depreciated by 6.4% in nominal effective terms and 3.4% in real effective terms, taking relative prices into account (Figure 3.13.4).

3.13.3 Inflation

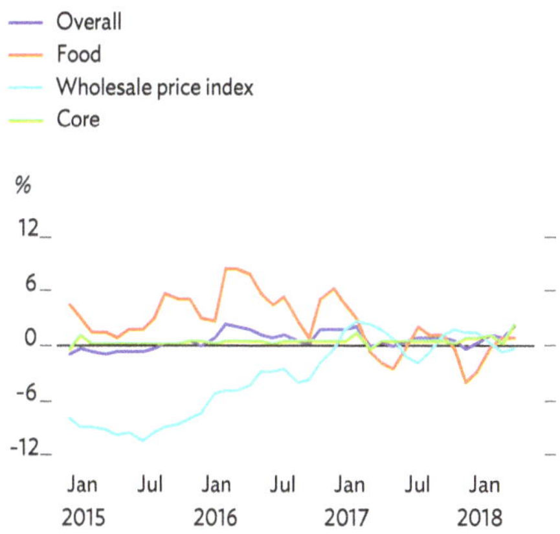

Source: CEIC Data Company (accessed 16 March 2018).

3.13.4 Exchange rates

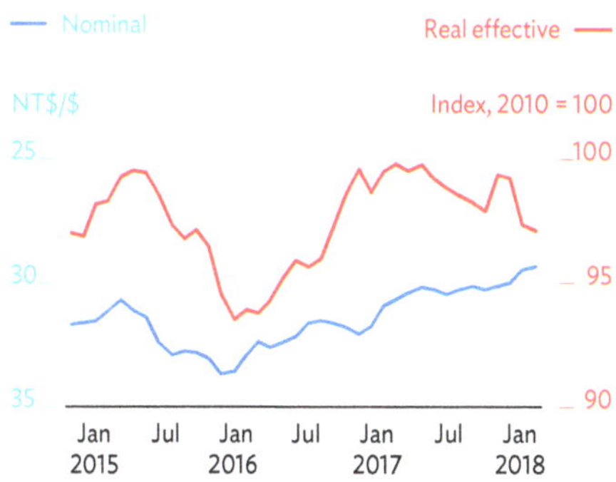

Source: Haver Analytics (accessed 15 March 2018).

Economic prospects

GDP growth is forecast unchanged at 2.9% in 2018 and down marginally at 2.8% in 2019, sustained by rising private consumption, robust public investment, and global expansion. Private consumption will be boosted by a 3.0% public sector wage increase at the beginning of 2018, which history teaches will be followed by private sector wage increases in the second half of the year and in 2019.

Investment is projected to rise on the strength of public outlays, which are slated to increase by 2.1% in 2018 and 0.8% in 2019. Industries referred to as new policy industries—smart machinery, green energy technology, biotech, industrial agriculture, defense, and recycling—will claim the largest share of budgetary spending, along with the Asian Silicon Valley program, which aims to turn Taipei,China into a startup destination for innovative young Asians. Infrastructure investment is budgeted to increase by 13.1% in 2018, with the Forward-Looking Infrastructure Development Program absorbing 19.5% of the total.

Private investment in semiconductors, artificial intelligence equipment, and electronic devices used in cars will likely continue to grow, as these industries display strong expansion in the manufacturing purchasing managers' index for January 2018. Reconstruction following an earthquake in Hualian in February 2018 should further lift investment. However, the

3.13.1 Selected economic indicators (%)

	2018	2019
GDP growth	2.9	2.8
Inflation	1.1	1.1
Current account balance (share of GDP)	10.0	9.0

Source: ADB estimates.

dampening impact of an increase in the corporate tax rate from 17% to 20% is expected to hold private investment relatively stable in 2018 and 2019.

This year's fiscal deficit is expected to shrink to the equivalent of 0.8% of GDP. A further decline is expected in 2019. Government expenditure is budgeted to rise by 3.3% in 2018, while revenue is slated to grow by 3.6% on rising incomes. Low and declining government debt, which fell to the equivalent of 33% of GDP in 2017 from 36% in 2016, leaves substantial scope for higher expenditure, if desired, to further boost the economy.

Inflation is forecast to trend slightly higher to 1.1% in both 2018 and 2019 on strong domestic consumption and investment, reflecting as well a low base effect. Given the tame inflation forecast, the authorities are not expected to change current monetary policy, and the current central bank policy rate will likely be maintained at least to the end of 2018.

Exports will be driven higher by better economic conditions in developed economies, but imports too are expected to rise strongly on robust private consumption and public investment, aided by the strength of the local currency against the US dollar. Net exports will thus contribute little to GDP growth this year and next. The trade surplus is projected to trend downward, narrowing the current account surplus to 10.0% of GDP in 2018 and 9.0% in 2019, despite a likely increase in net receipts from services.

Downside risks to the outlook include tourism hit harder by the February earthquake than foreseen. External risks are trade tensions caused by rising protectionism, such as tariffs the US might apply directly or indirectly to products from Taipei,China, and unexpectedly high interest rates in the US that could reduce capital flows into Taipei,China. That said, higher rates in the US simultaneously constitute an upside risk to projections, as they could drive down the value of the local dollar against the US dollar, thereby making exports more competitive.

Policy challenge—making human capital more competitive

Taipei,China has suffered declining competitiveness in human capital, measured by higher education attainment and training and labor market efficiency. The Global Competitiveness Index compiled by the World Economic Forum tracked scores for Taipei,China in these areas declining since 2012, especially for labor market efficiency (Figure 3.13.5). If continued, this trend is likely to cause a further slide in business sophistication, one of two key predictors for an economy aspiring to be driven by innovation. Although the Taipei,China score for competitiveness in innovation, the other predictor, rose in the same period, continued good performance in innovation cannot be sustained

3.13.5 Global competitiveness scores

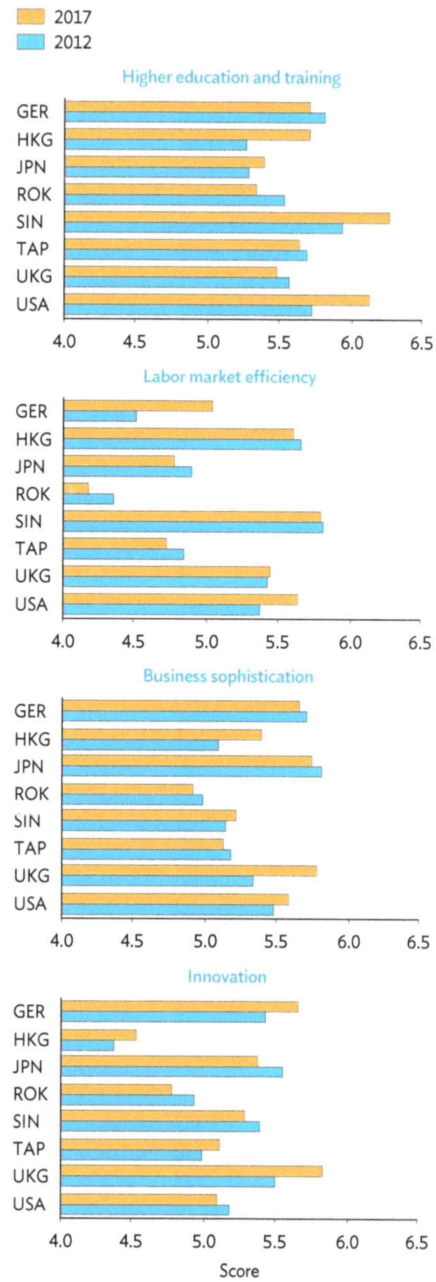

GER = Germany, HKG = Hong Kong, China, JPN = Japan, ROK = Republic of Korea, SIN = Singapore, TAP = Taipei,China, UKG = United Kingdom, USA = United States.

Note: Scale ranges from 1 (worst) to 7 (best), primarily as evaluated by business leaders responding to the Executive Opinion Survey conducted by the World Economic Forum. The index of higher education and training measures secondary and tertiary enrollment rates, as well as the quality of education. The index of labor market efficiency measures cooperation in labor–employer relations, flexibility of wage determination, and country capacity to retain talent, among other things. The business sophistication index measures local supplier quantity and quality, the state of cluster development, value chain breadth, and the extent of marketing, among other things. The innovation index measures capacity innovation, quality of scientific research institutions, company spending on research and development, and university-to-industry research and collaboration, among other things.

Source: World Economic Forum. 2013 and 2018. *The Global Competitiveness Report. 2012–2013* and *2017–2018*.

if the declines for education and labor market efficiency persist. To meet demand brought on by progress in innovation, there must be progress in the recruitment and training of talent.

The government has acknowledged that labor and talent shortages will challenge growth potential in Taipei,China. It has taken steps to attract foreign talent, including legislation to relax regulations on visas, residency, health insurance, taxes, and retirement benefits. However, these measures have to be complemented by policies that allocate to talented workers a larger share of the prosperity generated by economic growth.

Data on the evolution of real wages by skill category and productivity growth are not available, forestalling a robust examination of compensation for talented workers, but indications are that real wages for this group of workers have not kept pace with rising prosperity. Real wages actually declined in 3 of the 6 years from 2012 to 2017 (Figure 3.13.6). Average real wage growth by sector did not fare any better. It reached 4.5% only in electronic components and was below 2.0% in 44 of 48 categories measured. Surprisingly, real wage growth rates for professionals working in information and communication services and scientific technology services—the backbone of the impressive export performance—were both a mere 0.06%. Moreover, the growth rate of the average annual real wage (or total wages earned divided by the number of workers) was higher than growth in GDP per capita only in 2015, when economic performance was particularly weak as exports fell sharply. This indicates that growth in wage income lagged growth in other forms of income, creating incentives for talented workers to seek employment abroad.

These trends point to inadequate rewards for skilled human capital, which could partly reflect labor market rigidity that suppresses signals regarding supply and demand for talented workers. Without government intervention to create the right incentives to reward talent better, competitiveness in human capital may suffer, preventing progress in technology and innovation, creating incentives for talented workers to seek employment abroad.

The government has addressed labor market concerns by setting minimum wages, encouraging labor force participation, and providing favorable benefit packages in the public sector—action that has been helpful but insufficient. The labor market needs to be more flexible and transparent, especially under current tight market conditions reflected in a low unemployment rate below 4%. In addition to speeding up current pension reform to improve mobility, insurance, and retirement benefits for talented workers, the government should ensure that real wages and benefits clearly reflect demand for skilled and talented labor. One step in this direction would be to include all benefit information explicitly and clearly in the compensation package, for job seekers to see. A better remuneration package can also stem the flow of talented workers seeking employment overseas.

3.13.6 Growth in real wages and GDP per capita

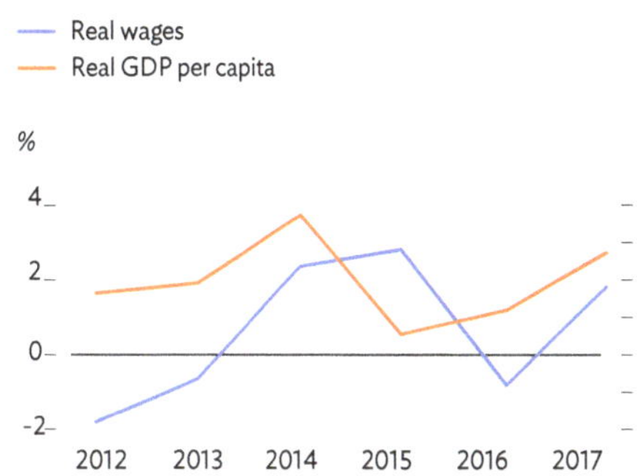

GDP = gross domestic product.
Source: CEIC Data Company (accessed 15 March 2018).

SOUTH ASIA

AFGHANISTAN ■

BANGLADESH ■

BHUTAN ■

INDIA ■

MALDIVES ■

NEPAL ■

PAKISTAN ■

SRI LANKA ■

Afghanistan

Economic growth inched up to 2.5% in 2017 as security and political challenges continued to weigh heavily on the economy. Good progress on domestic revenue collection was insufficient to counter declining grants. The outlook is tempered by continuing security concerns and possible political instability with elections scheduled over the next 2 years. Economic growth, job creation, and reducing reliance on foreign aid will depend heavily on attracting private investment.

Economic performance

As in 2016, a tenuous political situation and worsening security limited economic growth in 2017. GDP growth accelerated marginally to 2.5% from 2.4% in 2016 (Figure 3.14.1). Agriculture, industry, and services all grew. Wheat production was lower in 2017 than in 2016 for lack of precipitation. Instead, a sharp 16.6% rise in fruit production and a near doubling in current prices of value added in fruit helped to drive growth in agriculture.

Domestic investment remained steady, equal to 18.5% of GDP. Private investment is estimated at only 8.0% of GDP in 2017, reflecting a lack of confidence in political and security conditions. Public investment, measured as spending from the government development budget, increased by 8% in nominal terms over 2016 as the execution rate improved from 54% that year to 67% in 2017 with better budget planning, simplified execution rules, and more authority delegated to line ministries.

The United Nations Office on Drugs and Crime reported an 87% increase in opium production in 2017 to a record high of about 9,000 tons. The area under poppy cultivation jumped by 63% over the previous year, and a 15% improvement in opium yield per hectare contributed to the sharp rise. The farm-gate value of opium rose by more than half to hit $1.4 billion, equal to 7% of Afghanistan's licit GDP.

Consumer inflation peaked at 7.5% year on year in May 2017 but dropped to 3.1% in December (Figure 3.14.2). Volatility in inflation came from swings in food prices with the temporary closure of border crossings with Pakistan, which affected food imports. Food inflation was highest in June at 10.9% but eventually dropped to 4.6% in December. Average inflation stood at 5.0% in 2017, up from 4.4% in 2016, and was driven by food price inflation, which averaged 7.0%. Nonfood inflation averaged 3.2%, unchanged from the average a year earlier.

3.14.1 GDP growth by sector

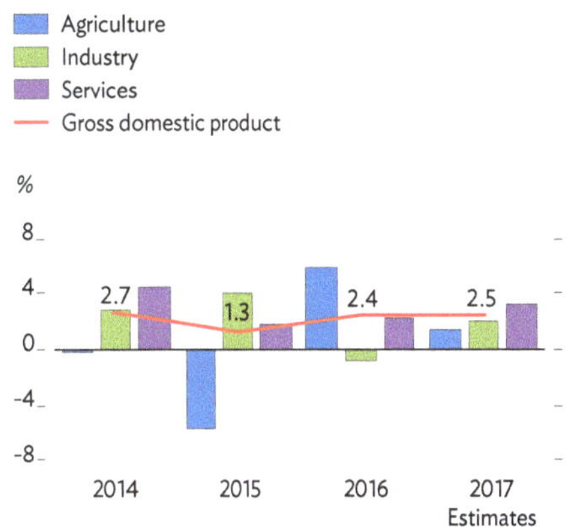

GDP = gross domestic product.

Note: Years are fiscal years ending on 21 December of the same calendar year.

Sources: World Bank. *World Development Indicators* (accessed 9 March 2018); ADB estimates.

3.14.2 Inflation

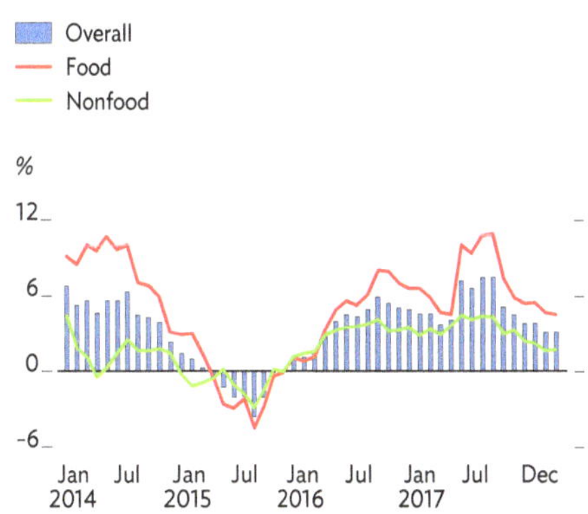

Sources: Central Statistical Office; ADB estimates.

This chapter was written by David Oldfield and Fatima Catacutan of the Central and West Asia Department, ADB, Manila.

Domestic revenue collection rose by 11.2% to AF169 billion in 2017 and exceeded the target set under an arrangement with the International Monetary Fund Extended Credit Facility. Despite the increase, domestic revenue remains low at less than 12% of GDP. Grants comprise an estimated 56% of budget revenue, or 15.6% of GDP. While government efforts have broadly succeeded in maintaining fiscal and external stability, efforts to set a budget for 2018 point to growing tension between, on the one hand, expanding security and development spending and, on the other, ensuring that financing arrangements are consistent with continued macroeconomic stability.

Growth in broad money supply (M2) fell to 4.1% in 2017 from 9.7% in 2016, with lending to the private sector sluggish and growth in currency in circulation slowing (Figure 3.14.3). Demand for credit was weak in light of the fragile security situation and poor macroeconomic conditions. Moreover, banks are cautious about extending credit because of the high share of nonperforming loans, about 12% of the total in December 2017, and the difficulty of evaluating credit risk in the uncertain investment environment. Deposit dollarization remains high at 62%.

Following short-lived appreciation in 2016, the afghani depreciated only slightly in 2017 despite a slowdown in official grant inflows, increased contractual payments in the second half of the year, and escalating political tensions (Figure 3.14.4).

The current account surplus including net transfers is estimated to have narrowed from the equivalent of 7.1% of GDP in 2016 to 4.5% in 2017 because of higher imports and lower official grants (Figure 3.14.5). Excluding grants of $7.9 billion, the current account would be a very large deficit equal to 30.8% of GDP. The merchandise trade deficit widened to $6.7 billion. Exports rose from $0.6 billion in 2016 to $0.7 billion in 2017 but remained far too weak to fund imports. Exports were boosted by the commencement of an air corridor linking Afghanistan and India that facilitated higher sales of Afghan fruit.

Gross international reserves rose to $8.2 billion in 2017 from $7.6 billion in 2016, providing cover for 13 months of imports (Figure 3.14.6). Given the country's weak external position, government policy strictly limits external borrowing. External debt is manageable, falling to the equivalent of 6.1% of GDP in 2017 from 6.3% a year earlier.

Economic prospects

The outlook is for subdued GDP growth in 2018 and 2019. Growth is projected to remain at 2.5% in 2018 and 2019 (Figure 3.14.7). The security and political situations are the two crucial determinants of the economic outlook, other important factors being agriculture and the amount of foreign aid. Security is unstable, particularly in Kabul, with high-profile terror attacks

3.14.3 Monetary indicators

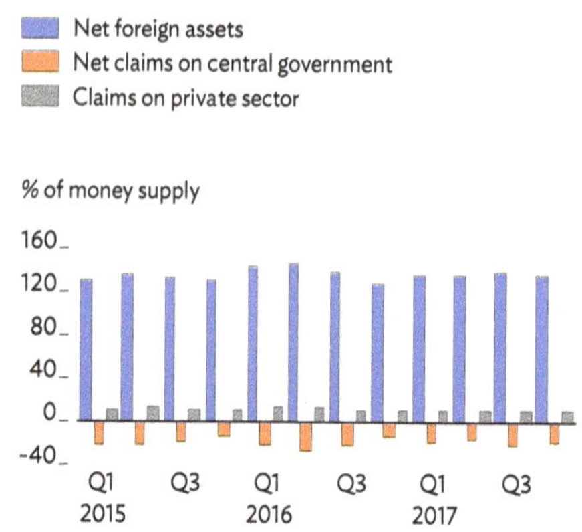

Q = quarter.

Source: International Monetary Fund. *International Financial Statistics* (accessed 26 March 2018).

3.14.4 Nominal exchange rate

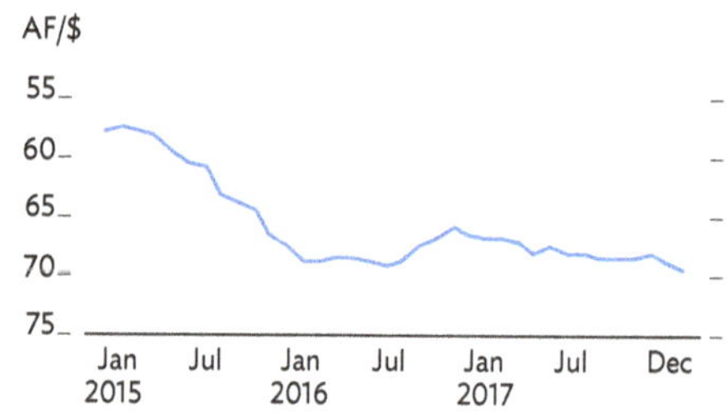

Sources: Da Afghanistan Bank. http://www.centralbank.gov.af/ (accessed 8 March 2018); ADB estimates.

3.14.5 Current account balance

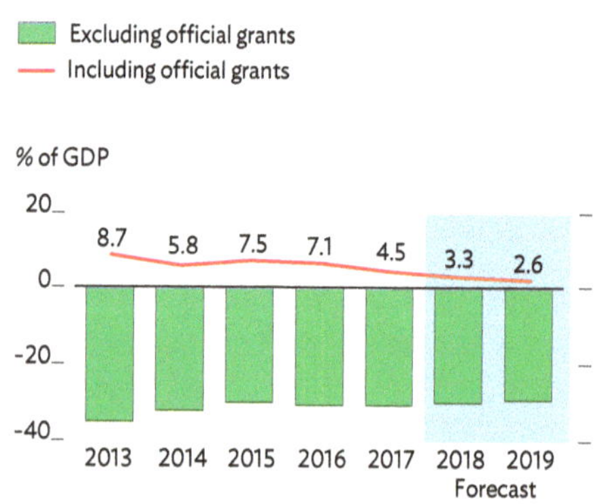

Note: Years are fiscal years ending on 21 December of the same calendar year.

Sources: International Monetary Fund. *IMF Country Report* No. 14/128, 16/252, 17/144, 17/377; ADB estimates.

in late 2017 and early 2018. The country is likely to experience greater political uncertainty from friction within the National Unity Government. Parliamentary elections are scheduled for 2018 and a presidential election in 2019, which could cause businesses to adopt a wait-and-see approach.

Precipitation was scarce in late 2017 and early 2018. If it does not pick up, agriculture could be affected, at least in the first harvest of 2018. Progress on structural reform under the Extended Credit Facility program should help to boost economic activity in 2018–2019 and beyond. However, declining grants may diminish public investment.

Inflation is forecast to remain at 5% in 2018 and 2019, barring major shocks such as greatly intensified insurgent activity or a significant increase in returnees from Pakistan. Food price inflation may spike if agricultural output suffers under extended dry weather. The afghani–US dollar exchange rate has been relatively stable recently, and the central bank is expected to prevent undue volatility and keep an orderly managed float for the afghani.

Setting the 2018 budget follows a new process that is more in line with international standards. It presents a medium-term expenditure framework with estimates for revenue and expenditure for the budget year and the next 3 years. The budget now consolidates the operating and development budgets, eliminates carryover of previous year commitments, and is more realistic than past budgets, which overestimated expenditure.

Budget revenue including grants for 2018 is forecast to decline from 26.5% of GDP in 2017 to 24.3% in 2018 and 22.5% in 2019. Domestic revenue in 2018 is targeted to reach 11.7% of GDP, with tax reform and improved administration, and then rise further to 11.8% in 2019. Higher domestic revenue will not compensate, however, for the decline in grants. Grants are projected to provide 54% of budget revenue in 2018, falling to less than 50% in 2019 as the declining trend continues.

Expenditure is budgeted to rise to AF377 billion in 2018, a 4.4% increase and equal to 25.4% of GDP. In 2019, expenditure is forecast to fall to 25.0% of GDP with declining grants. The stress caused by the decline in grants is evident in the projected 2018 budget deficit of AF16 billion, or 1.1% of GDP.

The current account surplus including grants is forecast to shrink to 3.3% of GDP in 2018 and 2.6% in 2019 as grants decline and imports remain high. Exports are forecast to grow by about 20% in 2018 and 25% in 2019. Exports of fruits and medicinal plants in particular have potential for high growth rates with the new Afghanistan–India air corridor and the opening of the first phase of Chabahar port in Iran in late 2017. Chabahar opened a new transit route linking Afghanistan, India, and Iran. The port and the trilateral agreement on the International Transport and Transit Corridor should facilitate higher exports from Afghanistan in the coming years.

3.14.6 International reserves

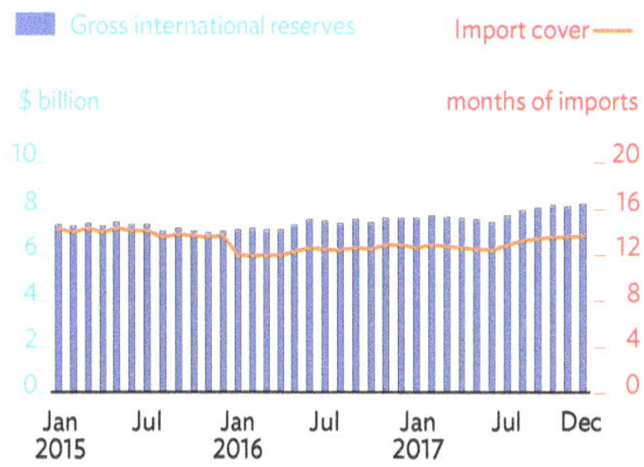

Sources: International Monetary Fund. *International Financial Statistics* (accessed 15 February 2018); Da Afghanistan Bank. http://www.centralbank.gov.af/ (accessed 8 March 2018).

3.14.1 Selected economic indicators (%)

	2018	2019
GDP growth	2.5	2.5
Inflation	5.0	5.0
Current account balance (share of GDP)	3.3	2.6

Source: ADB estimates.

3.14.7 GDP growth

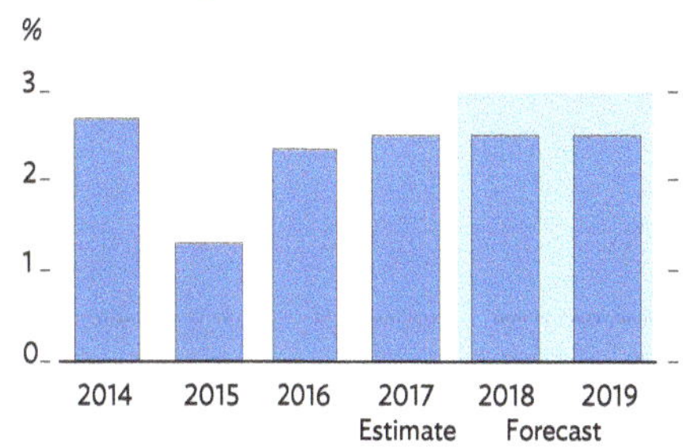

Note: Years are fiscal years ending on 21 December of the same calendar year.

Sources: International Monetary Fund; World Bank. *World Development Indicators* (accessed 9 March 2018); ADB estimates.

Policy challenge—boosting private investment

Afghanistan has attracted very little private investment, estimated to equal 8.0% of GDP, well below the South Asia average of 20.8%. This shortcoming is a major constraint on economic growth, job creation, and reducing dependence on foreign aid.

Poor security is the fundamental cause of low investment, having stymied large foreign investment in mining projects for years, but other factors have also been deterrents, especially for smaller investors: political tensions since 2014, the dearth of infrastructure, corruption and bureaucratic red tape, shortages of technical and managerial skills, and deficiency in upholding the rule of law, particularly on commercial and investment matters.

Despite these impediments, Afghanistan can appeal as a frontier economy. The risks are high, but the rewards can be as well. High-risk countries affected by violence can attract sizeable investments because they frequently have untapped resources, large reconstruction needs, and unmet consumer demand. Afghanistan fits this profile.

Clearly, investment will not meet full potential until the security situation improves, but measures can be taken now to begin to attract more private investment and build toward a brighter future. To begin, a coordinated government approach is needed to move the country forward by raising investors' confidence. The government will also need to continue efforts to create a better environment for investment and economic activity (Box 3.14.1). The legal and regulatory framework has improved but is still developing and incomplete. This is particularly evident in mining, which is expected to be a key driver of growth in the medium term.

A targeted and systematic strategy to promote investment and investor services could reap benefits in the short and medium term. This could include creating investment opportunities for companies with experience operating in conflict-affected countries, investors in neighboring countries who are familiar with local conditions, and the Afghan diaspora, which has played a large role in developing the economy since the fall of the Taliban regime in 2001.

Finally, the government should maintain its efforts toward regional cooperation. Connectivity and open trade with neighbors can attract more private investment as regional markets become more open. On top of the commercial benefits of regional cooperation, a peace dividend would give neighboring countries a greater stake in peace and stability in Afghanistan through economic links and opportunities.

3.14.1 Private investment

Measures to attract more private investment include the following:

- fair and peaceful elections for the National Assembly and the presidency;
- effective efforts to address notable deficiencies in the legal and regulatory framework such as registering property, enforcing contracts, and resolving insolvency;
- upholding the rule of law and ensuring the consistent application of tax laws, commercial laws, and regulations;
- continued progress against corruption;
- efficient implementation of infrastructure projects under the National Infrastructure Plan investment pipeline; and
- greater investment in technical and vocational training.

Bangladesh

Growth exceeded expectations despite slower export expansion and declining remittances. Inflation eased, but the current account fell into deficit. Growth is expected to moderate in fiscal 2018 as growth in agriculture and services slows. Inflation will edge up and the current account deficit widen. Sustained high growth demands an expanded industrial base and a diversified export basket, which depend in turn on filling large infrastructure deficits and implementing policy reform.

Economic performance

GDP grew by 7.3% in fiscal year 2017 (FY2017, ended 30 June 2017), edging up from 7.1% a year earlier (Figure 3.15.1). The pickup mainly reflected acceleration in private consumption expenditure, despite falling remittances, and continued growth in public infrastructure investment. Private investment rose marginally. With faster expansion in import volume while exports stagnated, net exports subtracted from growth. At $1.7 billion, foreign direct investment equaled less than 1.0% of GDP.

On the supply side, agriculture grew by 3.0%, up from 2.8% the year before. Despite staple crop losses to heavy rain and prolonged flooding, good performance in other subsectors—horticulture, animal husbandry, forestry, and fishing—buoyed agricultural output overall. Industry growth slowed to 10.2% from 11.1% largely on weaker growth in medium- and large-scale manufacturing as garment production stagnated. Services growth accelerated to 6.7% from 6.3%, mainly on higher growth in wholesale and retail trade and in transport services.

Despite food inflation trending higher during the year as weather induced rice shortages, average inflation decelerated to 5.4% from 5.9% as nonfood inflation slowed. This reflected the conservative monetary policy of Bangladesh Bank, the central bank, and a stable exchange rate. Inflation rose to 5.9% year on year in June 2017, from 5.5% a year earlier, as food inflation accelerated to 7.5% from 4.2% and nonfood inflation decelerated to 3.7% from 7.5% (Figure 3.15.2).

Growth in broad money slowed in FY2017 to 10.9%, well below the monetary program target of 15.5% (Figure 3.15.3). The slowdown came mainly from a sharp decline in net credit to the government as it turned to borrowing more through the

This chapter was written by Jyotsana Varma, Soon Chan Hong, Md. Golam Mortaza, and Barun K. Dey of the Bangladesh Resident Mission, ADB, Dhaka.

3.15.1 Supply-side contributions to growth

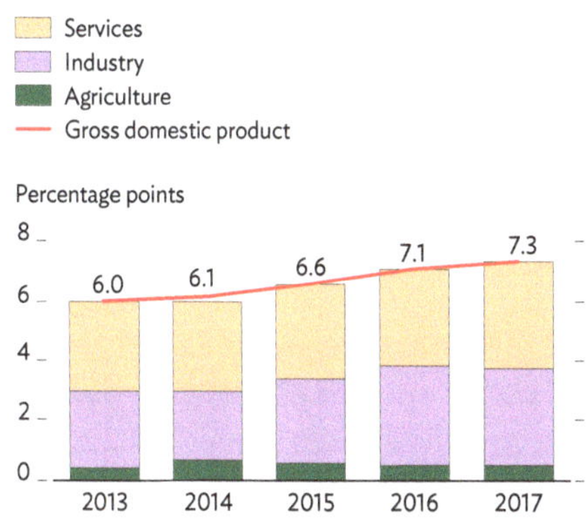

Note: Years are fiscal years ending on 30 June of that year.
Sources: Bangladesh Bureau of Statistics. http://www.bbs.gov.bd; ADB estimates.

3.15.2 Monthly inflation

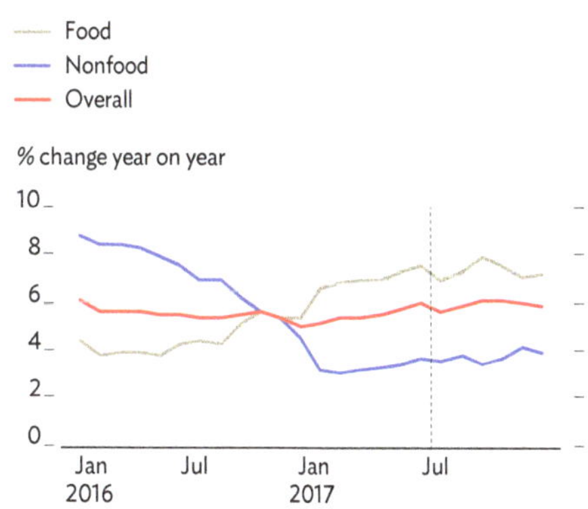

Note: Dotted line denotes the end of fiscal 2017.
Source: Bangladesh Bank. 2018. *Monthly Economic Trends*. February. http://www.bb.org.bd.

sale of national savings certificates. Private credit growth was close to its target of 16.5% as private investment picked up. Expansion in net foreign assets slowed on a smaller increase in central bank foreign exchange reserves.

The central bank kept its repo and reverse repo policy rates unchanged in FY2017, but ample liquidity in the banking system meant that interest rates continued to decline (Figure 3.15.4). The call money rate remained stable under easing liquidity pressure. The weighted average yield on 91-day Treasury bills declined to 3.7% in June 2017 from 4.0% a year earlier. Banks' weighted average lending rate eased to 9.6% from 10.3% in the same period, while the weighted average deposit rate declined to 4.8% from 5.4%, narrowing banks' interest rate spread by 0.2 percentage points to 4.7 points. Nonperforming loans in state-owned commercial banks continued to be a major issue as, despite remedial policies, their gross prevalence increased to 29.3% of all loans at the end of September 2017 from 25.2% a year earlier.

Budget revenue as a share of GDP remained very low at 10.2%, continuing to constrain a more rapid pace of development even as it rose slightly from 10.0% in the previous year. Tax collection by the National Board of Revenue grew by 19.0% in FY2017 but still fell short of the high budget target. Nontax revenue collection was below target. Expenditure was lower than budgeted and declined to equal 13.2% of GDP from 13.8% a year earlier. Strengthened monitoring of public spending through a new integrated budget and accounting system helped moderate current spending, curb public spending as a share of GDP, and make it more effective. The budget deficit declined to the equivalent of 3.0% of GDP in FY2017 from 3.8% in FY2016, well below the 5.0% budget target (Figure 3.15.5).

Exports grew marginally in FY2017, by 1.7%, down from 8.9% a year earlier. Garment exports grew by a scant 0.2%, down from 10.2% in FY2016. The slump reflected much weaker demand in major markets in the euro area and the US, as well as an infrastructure deficit that kept exporters from filling some orders. Other exports grew rapidly at 8.5%.

With stepped-up domestic demand, growth in import payments accelerated to 9.0% from 5.9%, reflecting solid increases in most categories: food, investment and consumer goods, and crude oil and petroleum products. Growth in intermediates for the garment industry, however, were modest.

Despite expanded employment overseas, worker remittances fell by 14.5% in FY2017. The decline mostly reflected economic adjustment to low oil prices in the Gulf, which hosts most Bangladeshi migrant workers, that depressed wages and employment. Another factor was a rise in remittances through unofficial channels.

3.15.3 Growth of monetary indicators

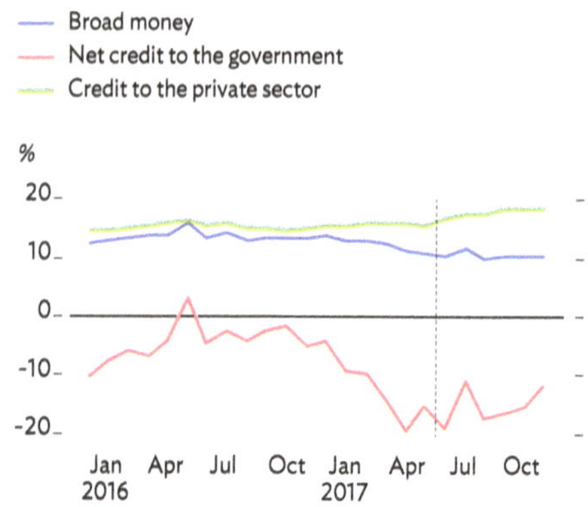

Note: Dotted line denotes the end of fiscal 2017.

Source: Bangladesh Bank. 2018. *Major Economic Indicators: Monthly Update*. February. http://www.bb.org.bd.

3.15.4 Interest rates

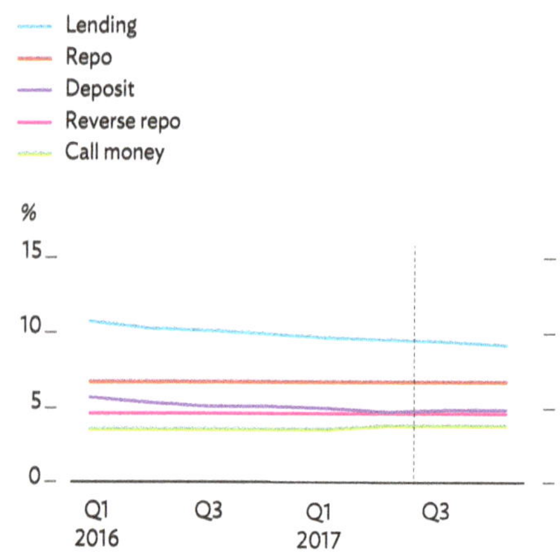

Q = quarter.

Note: Dotted line denotes the end of fiscal 2017.

Source: Bangladesh Bank. 2018. *Major Economic Indicators: Monthly Update*. February. http://www.bb.org.bd.

3.15.5 Fiscal indicators

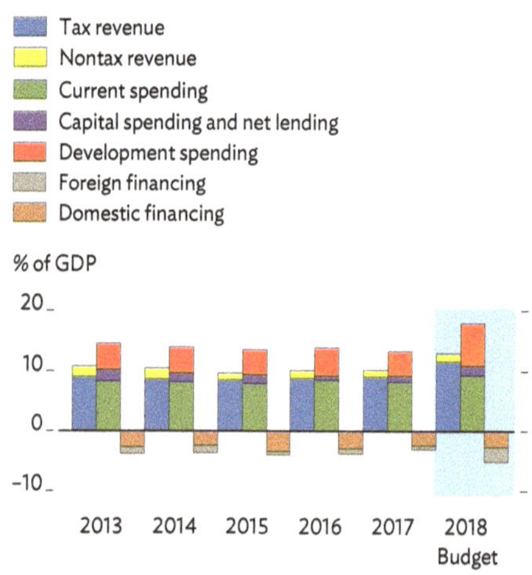

Note: Years are fiscal years ending on 30 June of that year.

Source: *Asian Development Outlook* database.

The current account fell into deficit in FY2017 by $1.5 billion, equal to 0.6% of GDP, which reversed a surplus of $4.3 billion in FY2016. The downturn reflected a $3.0 billion widening of the trade deficit and a $2.1 billion fall in remittances, as well as continued small deficits in the service and primary income accounts (Figure 3.15.6). The surplus in the combined capital and financial accounts nevertheless rose to $4.5 billion, which lifted gross foreign exchange reserves in the central bank by $3.2 billion to $33.4 billion at the end of June 2017, providing nearly 8 months of import cover.

The Bangladesh taka depreciated against the US dollar by 2.7% in nominal terms in the year to the end of June 2017 (Figure 3.15.7). Taking into account differences in inflation, the taka appreciated by 2.4% in real effective terms, eroding competitiveness.

The Dhaka Stock Exchange broad index rose by 25.5% over the year to June 2017, reaching 5,656.1 points as the price–earnings ratio rose to 15.7 from 14.6 (Figure 3.15.8). Market capitalization rose by 19.3% in the period, but it remains relatively small, equivalent to 19% of GDP. Only four new companies were listed in FY2017. While stock prices on the exchange increased broadly in line with those in other emerging markets in Asia over FY2017, net foreign portfolio investment surged to $458 million from $139 million in FY2016.

3.15.6 Current account components

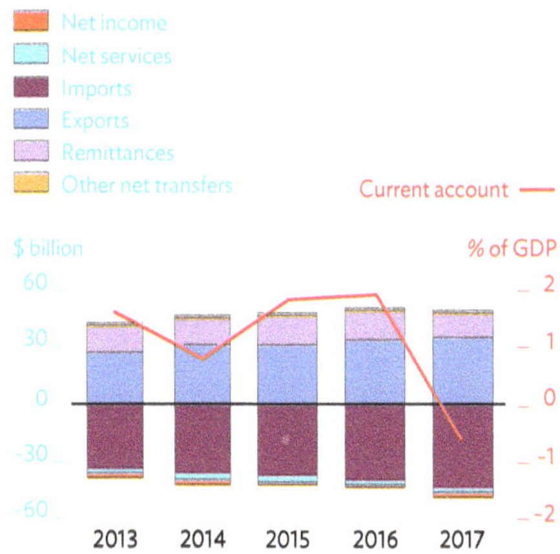

Note: Years are fiscal years ending on 30 June of that year.

Sources: Bangladesh Bank. 2017. *Annual Report 2016–2017.* https://www.bb.org.bd; ADB estimates.

3.15.1 Selected economic indicators (%)

	2018	2019
GDP growth	7.0	7.2
Inflation	6.1	6.3
Current account balance (share of GDP)	-2.2	-1.9

Note: Years are fiscal years ending on 30 June of that year.

Source: ADB estimates.

Economic prospects

GDP growth is expected to moderate to 7.0% in FY2018 as consumption demand slackens despite a rebound in worker remittances (Figure 3.15.9). Remittance beneficiaries are likely to adopt a cautious approach to spending, repaying debt incurred in recent years of remittance declines. Private investment is nevertheless expected to edge up with support from an accommodative credit policy, and public investment will expand as the authorities seek to speed the implementation of infrastructure projects. Export performance is expected to strengthen on projected higher growth in the euro area and the US. However, net exports will not add to growth, as imports are expected to expand strongly with substantial restocking of food grains, rising fuel requirements, and a steady increase in imports of capital goods.

Broadly favorable global growth and trade prospects are expected to continue in FY2019. With a further strengthening of exports and remittances, GDP growth that year is expected to firm to 7.2%. A marked stepping up of budget revenue mobilization could fuel a somewhat stronger advance in investment and therefore growth, but FY2019 budget policies will become known only when announced later.

On the supply side, agriculture growth is expected to moderate to 2.3% in FY2018 from 3.0% last year because it

3.15.7 Exchange rates

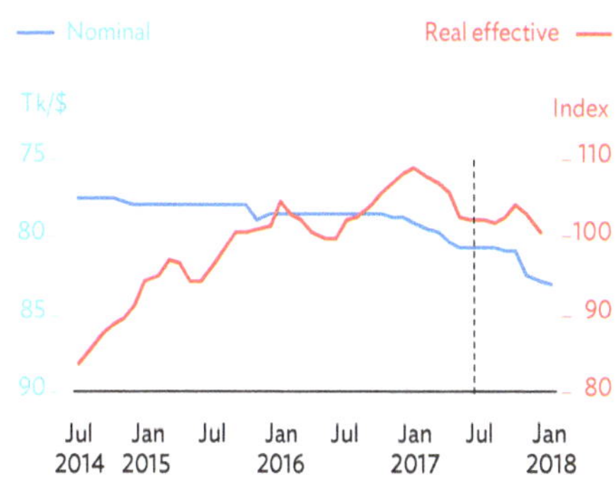

Note: Dotted line denotes the end of fiscal 2017.

Source: Bangladesh Bank. 2018. Monthly Economic Trends. February. http://www.bb.org.bd.

is from a higher base and prolonged flooding again hindered the planting of the wet monsoon rice crop. Industry growth is forecast to pick up slightly to 10.4%, underpinned by higher exports. Expansion in services is likely to slow to 6.4% from 6.7% in the previous year as consumer spending moderates and growth in agriculture income slows.

In FY2019, agriculture growth is projected to be slightly higher at 2.5% as higher rice prices encourage farmers to plant more of the staple crop. With an expected improvement in domestic and external demand, industry growth will likely be stronger at 10.6%, as services edge up to 6.5%.

Inflation is expected to accelerate to average 6.1% in FY2018. Food inflation averaged just over 7% year on year in the first half because of crop losses from the flooding, but it eased from a peak of 7.9% in September 2017 to 7.1% in December with imports of food grains and the arrival in markets of a newly harvested crop. Rice prices will nevertheless remain higher than last year. Nonfood inflation has remained broadly stable, averaging 3.5% in the first half of the year, but is expected to be higher in the second half because of anticipated upward adjustments to natural gas and electricity prices, higher global oil prices, and taka depreciation.

Inflation is projected to edge up to 6.3% in FY2019 because of further increases in natural gas and electricity prices and continued taka depreciation. However, normal weather and projected stability in global oil prices should temper price pressures compared with this year.

The monetary policy statement for the second half of FY2018 (January–June 2018) focuses on monetary and prudential policies to moderate high import growth in the first half toward a sustainable trend and to contain a possible rise in inflationary expectations reflecting higher food and energy prices. The central bank kept the main policy repo rate unchanged at 6.75% and decided to intensively supervise credit flows to ensure their quality and composition appropriate for productive use, rather than resort to broader restrictions on credit. The declining trend in government borrowing from banks allowed the central bank to adjust earlier monetary targets to accommodate slightly higher growth in credit to the private sector, at 16.8% in the second half of FY2018 after overshooting its target in the first half. A likely decline in net foreign assets will keep broad money growth a bit lower than originally projected.

Exports rebounded by 7.4% in the first 8 months of FY2018, up from 2.7% growth in the same period a year earlier as garment sales accelerated to 8.7% growth from 2.8% (Figure 3.15.10). Given stronger projected growth in the euro area and the US, exports are expected to increase by 7.0% in FY2018. With a continued favorable global outlook, export growth is projected at 9.0% in FY2019.

3.15.8 Dhaka stock exchange indicators

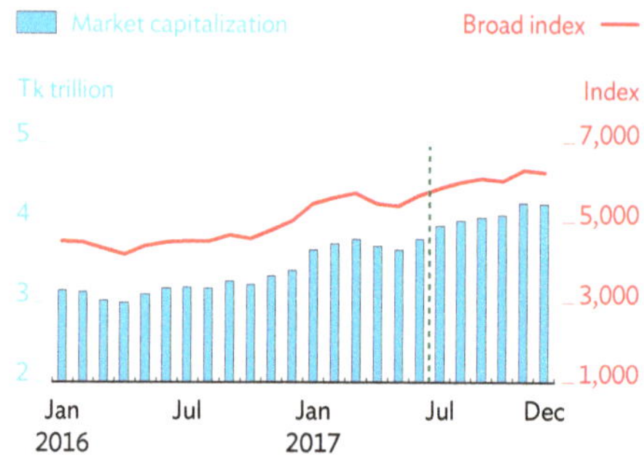

Note: Dotted line denotes the end of fiscal 2017.

Source: Dhaka Stock Exchange. 2017. *Monthly Review.* December.

3.15.9 GDP growth by sector

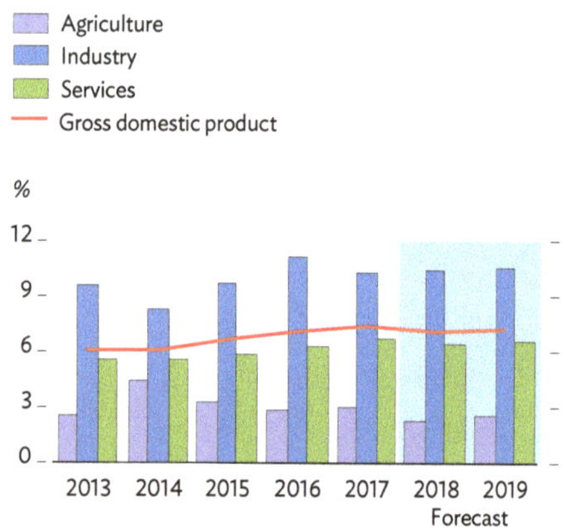

GDP = gross domestic product.

Note: Years are fiscal years ending on 30 June of that year.

Sources: Bangladesh Bureau of Statistics. http://www.bbs.gov.bd; ADB estimates.

3.15.10 Exports growth

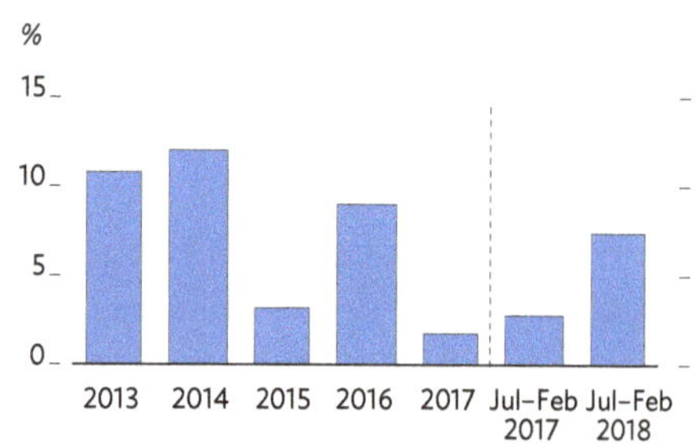

Notes: Years are fiscal years ending on 30 June of that year. Dotted line denotes the end of fiscal 2017.

Sources: Export Promotion Bureau, Bangladesh. *Export performance*, various issues.

Import payments rose strongly, by 25.8% in the first half of FY2018, with a sharp rise in imports of food grains, capital goods, and fuel and other intermediates. Taking into account food grain restocking in the first half and central bank policy measures, imports in the second half are forecast to moderate to 17.0% growth in FY2018 and 14.0% in FY2019.

Worker remittances rebounded to expand by 16.6% in the first 8 months of FY2018, reflecting reduced bank fees and charges and 1 million workers going abroad in 2017, the highest number in about a decade (Figure 3.15.11). As the dynamics of the recovery stabilize, remittances are expected to grow by 10.0% in FY2018 and by 9.0% in FY2019.

Despite rising remittances and exports, the current account deficit is expected to widen further to equal 2.2% of GDP in FY2018 as import demand rises (Figure 3.15.12). With monetary policy beginning to moderate import demand, the FY2019 current account deficit is projected lower, at 1.9% of GDP.

The taka depreciated by 4.3% against the US dollar in February 2018 from the same period last year and is expected to depreciate further in response to the large current account deficit. To avoid excessive volatility in the foreign exchange market, the central bank sold $1.1 billion to meet demand for foreign currency in this period. By December 2017, the taka had depreciated by 6.8% in real effective terms from a year earlier, indicating a gain in competitiveness.

The FY2018 budget, announced in June 2017, projected that revenue growth at 31.8% would outpace spending growth at 26.2%. Annual development spending was slated to grow by 38.5% to accelerate the implementation of some large infrastructure projects including the Padma Bridge, Dhaka Metro Rail, Rooppur Nuclear Power Plant, Payra Port, and coal-fired power plants at Rampal and Matarbari. Revenue was projected to rise to equal 13.0% of GDP, and public spending 18.0%, both significant increases from the previous year. Attaining these large increases will be challenging, and shortfalls on both sides of the ledger are likely to yield a deficit on target at 5.0% of GDP. In the first 7 months of FY2018, revenues grew by 15.3% and development program implementation by 33.4%.

The ratio of government debt to GDP has declined slightly over time and is quite low for developing Asia. External debt amounted to 11.4% of GDP in FY2017, reflecting the government's continued preference for concessional external borrowing. Domestic debt amounted to 15.7% of GDP.

The outlook is subject to downside risks. The current account deficit may deteriorate further if policies to rein in import demand do not succeed. Failure to boost revenues and tap foreign financing could unduly limit spending on needed infrastructure. Political uncertainty ahead of national elections expected by December 2018 could undermine consumer and

3.15.11 Remittances growth

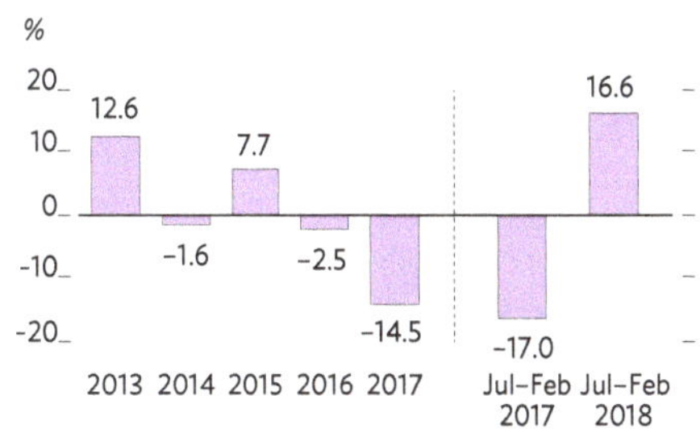

Note: Years are fiscal years ending on 30 June of that year.
Source: Bangladesh Bank.

3.15.12 Current account balance

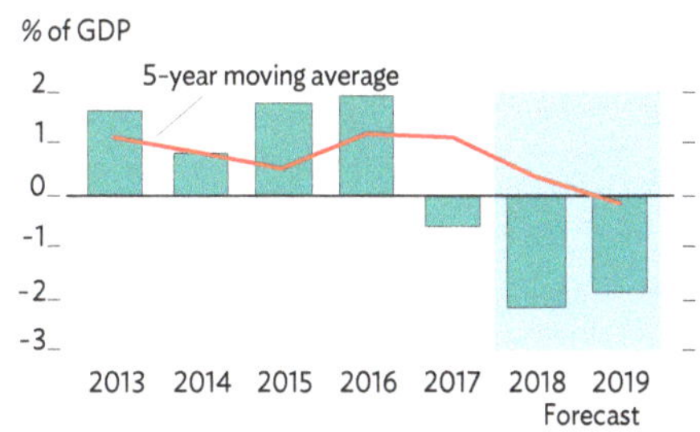

GDP = gross domestic product.
Note: Years are fiscal years ending on 30 June of that year.
Sources: Bangladesh Bank. 2017. *Annual Report 2016–2017.* https://www.bb.org.bd; ADB estimates.

3.15.13 Trends in exports and remittances

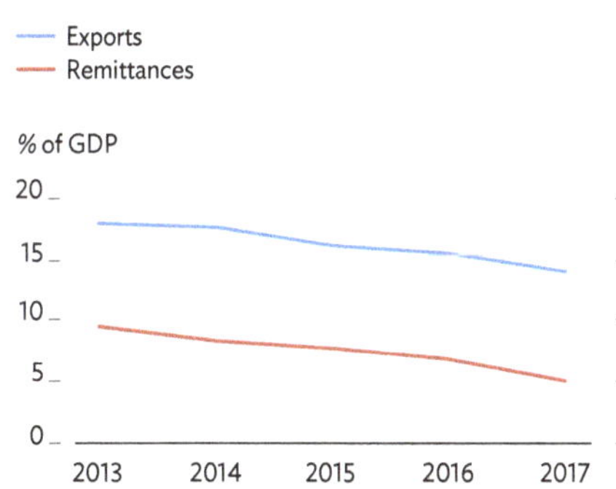

Note: Years are fiscal years ending on 30 June of that year.
Sources: Export Promotion Bureau, Bangladesh; Bangladesh Bank; and ADB estimates.

investor confidence. Fiscal risks from the influx of displaced people from Myanmar appears minimal considering the assistance provided by international relief agencies and others. Finally, unfavorable weather is always a risk.

Policy challenge—economic diversification for sustained high growth

Exports and remittances have historically served Bangladesh well by fostering rapid economic growth, but in more recent years their contributions to growth have weakened (Figure 3.15.13). This points to the need for new drivers of growth. Diversifying exports away from readymade garments, now accounting for over 80% of the total, would broaden the export basket, enhance resilience, and underpin continued high economic growth. Promoting labor-intensive manufacturing in general would help expand industry to meet growing demand in the domestic market.

Bangladesh has good potential in several industries: leather and footwear, light engineering, electronics, pharmaceuticals, furniture, shipbuilding, jute products, food processing, automobiles, and rubber goods. These industries could leverage the country's large supply of low-cost labor and advantageous location to garner participation in various stages of global value chains and enter new markets. Some of these products would enjoy a sizeable domestic market. Having recently experienced quick success in exporting software and other information and communication technology products, Bangladesh can expect to become a player in this fast-growing field.

However, the World Bank ranked Bangladesh 177 out of 190 economies in *Doing Business 2018*. To translate potential into concrete development outcomes, this poor ranking shows, the country needs to improve its business environment and thereby reduce costs. The Bangladesh Investment Development Authority is implementing a detailed action plan of business reform to correct deficiencies across all indicators.

Bangladesh has significant infrastructure deficits, ranking near the bottom globally in commercial access to basic infrastructure such as electricity, roads, and railways. In its *Global Competitiveness Report 2017–2018*, the World Economic Forum ranked Bangladesh 111 out of 137 economies in the quality of its infrastructure—behind India, Pakistan, and Sri Lanka (Figure 3.15.14). Major ongoing investments in the government's Annual Development Programme aim to relieve the most severe bottlenecks. Bangladesh needs to improve its trade infrastructure and logistics. It lags its peers in efficiently connecting production centers to ports that serve domestic and global markets (Figure 3.15.15). Current infrastructure

3.15.14 Infrastructure quality 2017–2018

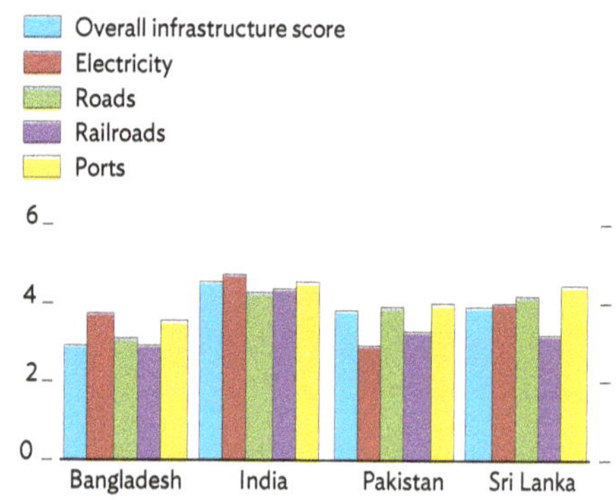

Source: World Economic Forum. 2017. *The Global Competitiveness Report 2017–2018.*

3.15.15 Logistics performance

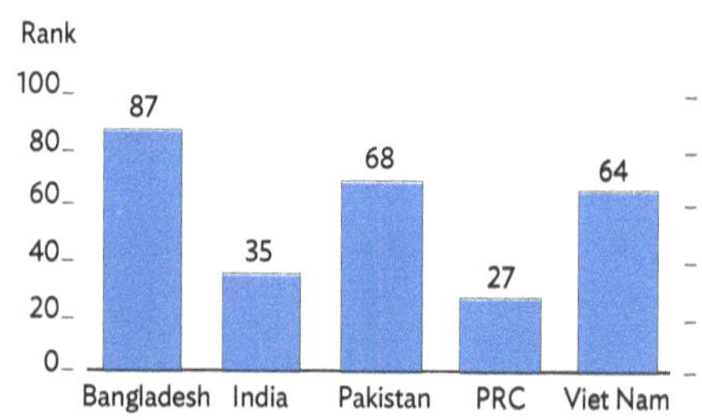

PRC = People's Republic of China.

Note: Rank 1 = best, 160 = worst.

Source: World Bank. *The Logistics Performance Index and Its Indicators 2016.*

investment, equal to about 3% of GDP, is grossly inadequate and needs to be raised to 6%–8% to put the country on a higher growth path.

Further, the tax system requires broad reform. The implementation of the new value-added tax law, which was deferred again last year, needs to be accomplished without delay to generate the additional revenue that is essential for infrastructure investment. To foster greater productivity and competitiveness in domestic manufacturing, import tariffs need to be lowered and rationalized. More attention to strengthening bank performance would expand access to finance for the private sector.

Bangladesh faces an acute shortage of personnel with the technical and managerial skills needed to diversify the economy and make it more competitive globally. Meeting these needs will require the government to boost resources and programs devoted to training in this critical area.

Finally, most economic activity is concentrated in and around Dhaka and Chittagong. To ensure balanced regional development and take advantage of its natural endowments, Bangladesh is promoting economic zones that provide serviced industrial land and infrastructure to attract investors and spur efforts to diversify the manufacturing base. Two such zones, the Mirsarai Economic Zone near Chittagong and the Shreehatta Economic Zone near Sylhet, are expected to begin operations in the near future. A comprehensive development plan for the Southwest Bangladesh Economic Corridor has been prepared to advance government plans to establish economic corridors.

Bhutan

Growth edged up in fiscal 2017 on moderate advances in industry and services. Inflation pushed slightly higher, and the current account deficit narrowed. The outlook is for continued strong, stable growth, but the delayed completion of two large hydropower plants has postponed a sharp upturn that was forecast earlier. Despite sustained economic progress, youth unemployment has been worsening. The government is responding with a range of new programs and policies.

Economic performance

Strong growth strengthened a bit more in fiscal year 2017 (FY2017, ended 30 June 2017) as industry and services were the main drivers of expansion to 7.5% from 7.3% in the previous year (Figure 3.16.1). Growth in agriculture slackened a bit because of destructive rains in the wet monsoon. Industry growth edged up to 7.7% as construction on hydropower plants continued and projects under the Eleventh Five Year Plan, 2013–2018 approached completion. Electricity generation improved, particularly at the large Tala Hydropower Plant, on better water flow during the year. Services were up by 9.2% with growth acceleration in tourism and hospitality services and with expanded retail and wholesale trade.

On the demand side, growth in GDP was lifted by sustained increases in fixed capital investment and consumption. However, the major contributor to expansion in FY2017 was the pronounced contribution of net exports as export volume markedly increased, particularly of electricity and minerals, while import volume declined, largely reflecting scaled-down needs for materials used to build hydropower plants (Figure 3.16.2).

Inflation was higher and volatile in FY2017 but finally held to an average of 4.3%, up from 3.3% in the previous year (Figure 3.16.3). The pickup in inflation largely reflected higher food prices, both in India— the major source of supply—and domestically because of excessively heavy monsoon rains, distribution problems, and the imposition of import restrictions on vegetables. While overall inflation hovered at around 5% year on year in the second half of FY2017, it fell to 3.3% in December 2017, reflecting the impact of the lower import prices following the implementation of India's goods and services tax.

3.16.1 Supply-side contributions to growth

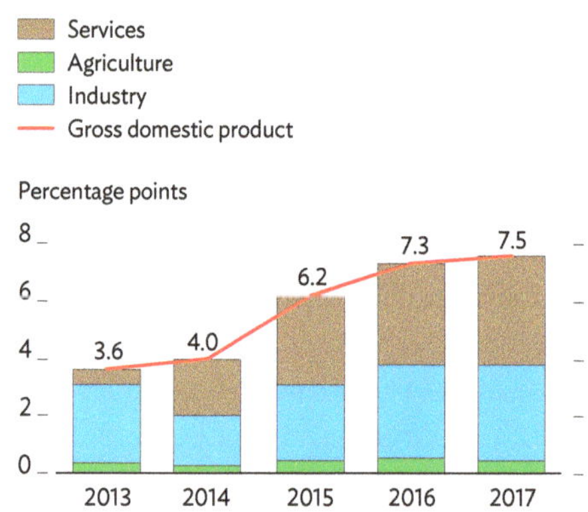

Note: Years are fiscal years ending on 30 June of that year.
Sources: National Statistics Bureau. National Accounts Statistics 2017. http://www.nsb.gov.bt; ADB estimates.

3.16.2 Demand-side contributions to growth

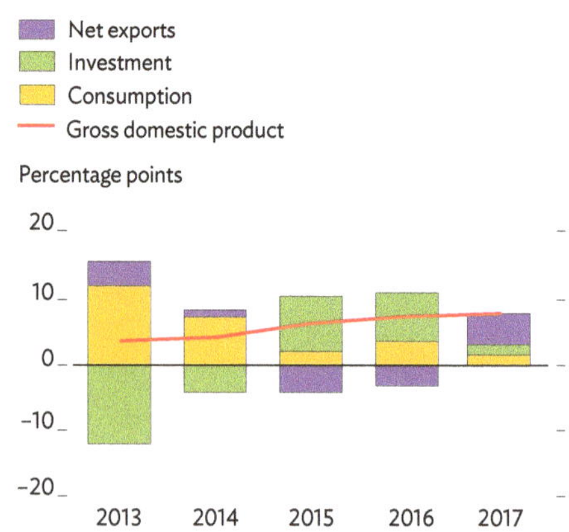

Note: Years are fiscal years ending on 30 June of that year.
Sources: National Statistics Bureau. National Accounts Statistics 2017. http://www.nsb.gov.bt; ADB estimates.

This chapter was written by Kanokpan Lao-Araya and Tshewang Norbu of the Bhutan Resident Mission, ADB, Thimphu, and Danileen Parel, consultant, South Asia Department, ADB, Manila.

Fiscal performance was expansionary with expenditure growing by an estimated 25.9%, mainly on stepped-up capital expenditure (Figure 3.16.4). Government resources grew by 13.9%, amounting to just over 30% of GDP. The budget deficit widened to the equivalent of 4.1% of GDP from 1.1% in the previous year, with about 85% of the deficit financed by domestic sources.

Monetary policy aimed to manage credit to avoid overheating yet foster rapid and inclusive economic growth. Domestic credit expanded by 29.5% in FY2017, reflecting the need to finance most of the larger budget deficit but also a 15.4% increase in credit to the private sector. Broad money growth doubled to 31.5%, roughly in line with expanded domestic credit (Figure 3.16.5). Net foreign assets in the banking system grew only marginally.

The current account deficit narrowed markedly in FY2017 but remained high at the equivalent of 23.0% of GDP, the improvement coming mostly from a narrower trade deficit (Figure 3.16.6). Nearly two-thirds of the improvement in the trade account came thanks to larger exports as hydropower sales to India improved by volume and fetched higher prices, and as exports of mineral products and base metals expanded to Bangladesh and Nepal. The rest of the improvement in the trade account came from a 3.4% decline in imports as the import intensity of investment and consumption spending fell slightly.

The services deficit shrank as receipts from tourists paying in both Indian rupees and convertible currency raised the travel surplus. The primary income deficit widened with growth in interest payments on external debt. Secondary income remained in surplus despite a decline in grants owing to the receipt of an excise duty refund from the Government of India for the previous fiscal year.

Gross international reserves declined slightly, by 3.6% to $1.1 billion, or cover for 12.2 months of merchandise imports (Figure 3.16.7). Indian rupee reserves increased to the equivalent of 5.2 months of imports from 4.3 months. This change is reflected in a decline in the share convertible currency reserves to 64% of total reserves. This shift in reserve currency composition was decided based on an assessment of Bhutan's reserve management strategy.

Government external debt increased by about 8% to $2.5 billion in FY2017, mainly on higher borrowing for hydropower projects, which now amounts to 69.2% of all external debt (Figure 3.16.8). The external debt ratio nevertheless improved to equal 102.5% of GDP, down from 111.5% because GDP continued to grow rapidly. Debt servicing temporarily increased to take about a quarter of export earnings, from just 14.5% in the previous year, because Bhutan repaid a currency swap received from the Reserve Bank of India in FY2016.

3.16.3 Inflation

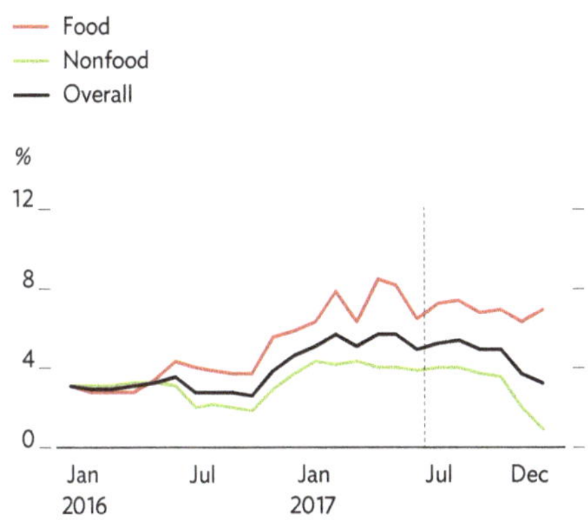

Note: Dotted line denotes the end of fiscal 2017.

Source: National Statistics Bureau. Monthly Consumer Price Index Bulletin. January 2018. http://www.nsb.gov.bt.

3.16.4 Fiscal indicators

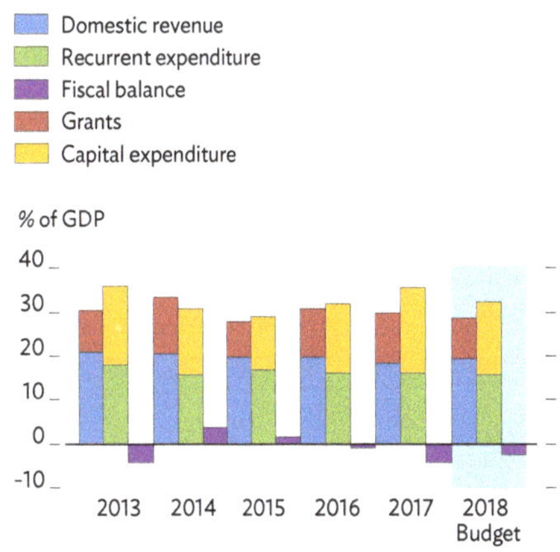

Note: Years are fiscal years ending on 30 June of that year.

Source: Ministry of Finance. National Budget Financial Year 2017/18. http://www.mof.gov.bt.

3.16.5 Monetary indicators

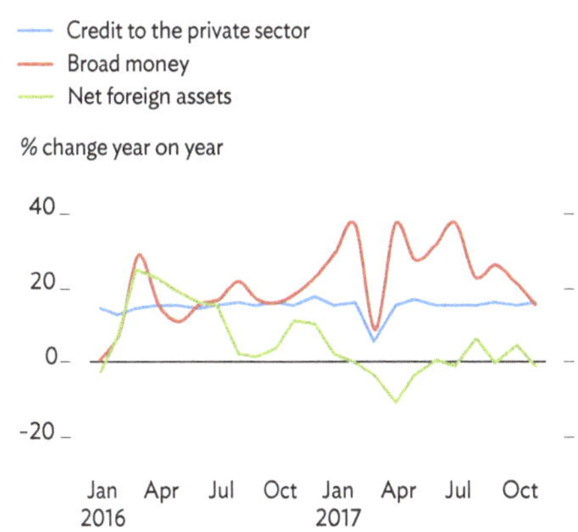

Source: Royal Monetary Authority of Bhutan. Monthly Statistical Bulletin February 2018. http://www.rma.org.bt.

Economic prospects

Growth is projected to remain strong in the forecast period, albeit moderating to 7.1% in FY2018 before picking up again to 7.4% in FY2019. Services are expected to be the main driver of the economy as wholesale and retail businesses and tourism continue to expand. Growth in industry is forecast to moderate because the final stages of construction will slow a bit at two large hydropower plants, Punatsangchhu I and II. Industry growth will strengthen slightly in FY2019 because of the expected commissioning of the Mangdechhu Hydropower Plant in September 2018, which will bolster electricity production and exports.

Agriculture, a relatively small sector, is expected to grow faster in FY2018 than last year on the assumption of normal weather and on government efforts to introduce new crops, improve productivity, and channel additional credit to agriculture as part of its agenda for financial inclusion.

Fiscal policy is expected to be less expansionary to the forecast horizon as capital expenditure falls off with the end of the current 5-year plan. Elections are set for both the National Council and the House of Representatives this year, and the formulation of the new government is expected in November 2018. Parliamentary endorsement of a new 5-year plan will follow.

The government projects the budget deficit narrowing to the equivalent of 2.5% of GDP in FY2018 as resources expand on royalties from hydropower plants and tourism, and with additional revenues from a higher power tariff. The deficit is expected to shrink further to 0.4% of GDP in FY2019 despite an expected decline in grants, mainly thanks to revenue from the operation of the Mangdechhu Hydropower Plant and capital expenditure bottoming out before the new plan goes fully into effect.

Inflation is projected at 4.6% in FY2018 and 5.4% in FY2019, broadly in line with expected price trends in India. Goods and services tax (GST) reform adopted by India in July 2017 benefits Bhutan through lower import prices because export sales are zero rated under the GST. However, India has announced that it will raise guaranteed minimum support prices for certain agricultural goods, which may create inflationary pressures in FY2019. Monetary policy will remain accommodative, placing stronger emphasis on financial inclusion and on financial deepening to better channel credit to productive sectors.

Fuels were not subject to India's GST levy, but from October 2017, the Government of India agreed to exempt its federal excise duty of 17% on petrol and 14% on diesel on export sales to Bhutan. The Government of Bhutan decided to pass on the full benefit of these exemptions to the public without imposing any offsetting local taxes, as it did in connection with the July adoption of India's GST.

3.16.1 Selected economic indicators (%)

	2018	2019
GDP growth	7.1	7.4
Inflation	4.6	5.4
Current account balance (share of GDP)	−22.2	−18.8

Source: ADB estimates.

3.16.6 Current account components

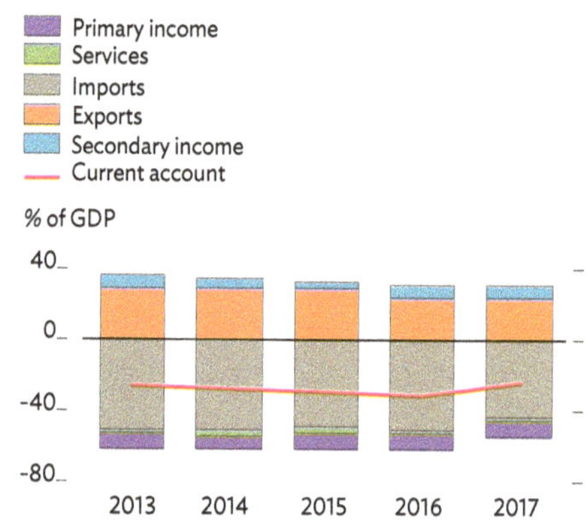

Note: Years are fiscal years ending on 30 June of that year.
Sources: Royal Monetary Authority of Bhutan. Monthly Statistics. January 2018; Annual Report FY2016/17. http://www.rma.org.bt.

3.16.7 Gross international reserves

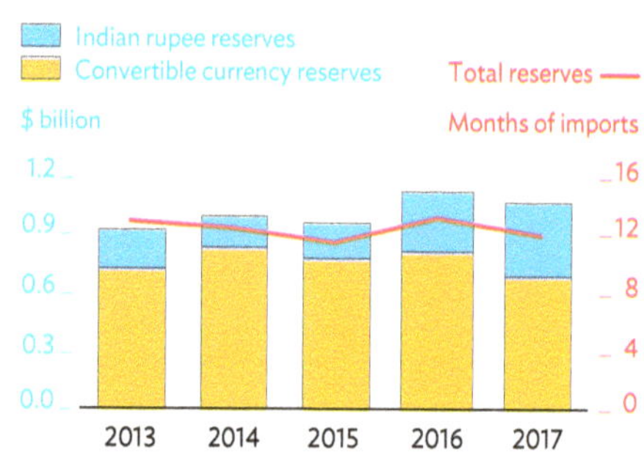

Note: Years are fiscal years ending on 30 June of that year.
Source: Royal Monetary Authority. Monthly Statistical Bulletin. February 2018. http://www.rma.org.bt.

Although prospective budget revenues are foregone with the decisions to pass all GST benefits on to the public, and with delays in finishing the two large hydropower projects, the government expects to make up for the losses by various means, including tax revision, expenditure savings, and the pursuit of additional grants.

The current account deficit is projected to narrow slightly but remain high at the equivalent of 22.2% of GDP in FY2018, falling to 18.8% in FY2019. Imports will increase in FY2018, after a dip last year, as construction on hydropower plants continues and as lower import prices encourage consumer spending and imports. The lower current account deficit in FY2019 reflects some easing in import growth and higher electricity exports from the new Mangdechhu Hydropower Plant.

3.16.8 External debt

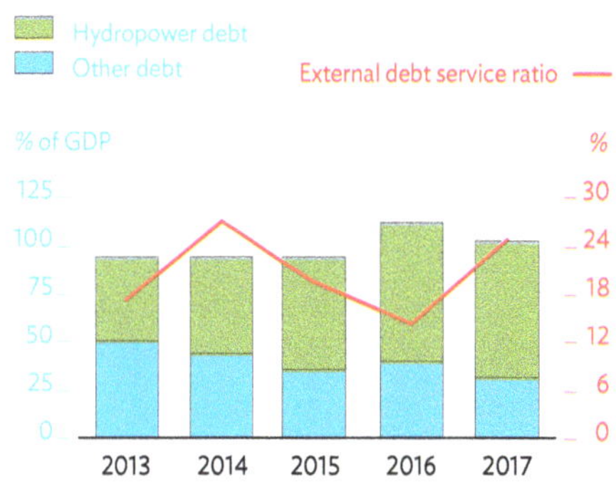

Notes: Years are fiscal years ending on 30 June of that year. The external debt service ratio excludes external debt service for loans received through an overdraft facility provided by India.

Source: Royal Monetary Authority of Bhutan. Monthly Statistical Bulletin. February 2018. http://www.rma.org.bt.

Policy challenge—employing youth through training and cottage industries

Although Bhutan has enjoyed remarkable economic progress, growth has not brought commensurate job creation for new entrants into the labor force. Youth unemployment has been increasing, afflicting 4,813 young participants in the labor force in 2016, or 13.2%, which is several times the overall unemployment rate of 2.1% (Figure 3.16.9).

The causes of high unemployment among the young are many: a mismatch between the skills the young possess and those that employers demand, a preference for office jobs over manual or temporary work, limited absorption capacity in the job market and particularly in the public sector, and family support granted to young people while unemployed, sapping their motivation to pursue financial independence.

Solutions to youth unemployment are likewise multidimensional. The government initiated a targeted youth engagement program in January 2017 that aims to facilitate direct employment both domestically and overseas, offer entrepreneurship development and training to promote self-employment and promote livelihood. In addition, a development partner is preparing a project that aims to support the government's effort to reduce youth unemployment by expanding and modernizing skills development programs in five technical training institutes, enhancing vocational orientation for secondary school students, and forging performance-based apprenticing partnerships with the private sector.

Cottage and small industries (CSIs) employ on average almost five workers per enterprise. In 2017, such enterprises employed 92,322 workers, or over 26% of the labor force. The government has therefore identified the CSI sector as having great potential for generating youth employment opportunities.

3.16.9 Unemployment rate

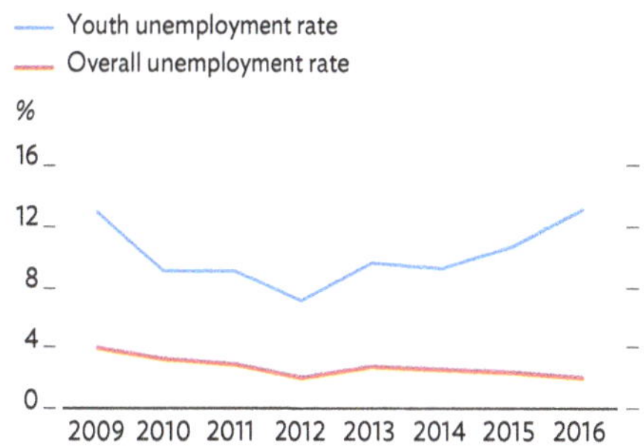

Source: Ministry of Labour and Human Resources. Labor Force Survey Report 2016. http://www.molhr.gov.bt.

Various reforms are being undertaken to foster CSI startups. Limited finance is a problem because high interest rates and onerous collateral requirements substantially restricted the ability of CSI entrepreneurs to borrow capital for startup and expansion. To improve access to finance, programs and institutions are being launched to provide collateral-free loans guaranteed by the government to qualified CSI applicants, among them are CSI banks created by the Royal Monetary Authority. In addition, economic development policy in 2017 required financial institutions to devote at least 20% of their lending portfolio to priority sectors, including CSIs.

Policies to develop economic clusters have been initiated to allow CSIs to benefit from common infrastructure to lower costs and thereby enhance their efficiency and productivity. Because CSI development involves multiple government agencies to handle its various issues, the Department of Cottage and Small Industries under the Ministry of Economic Affairs will need to play an active role in coordinating the implementation of the new initiatives.

India

Economic growth slowed to 6.6% in fiscal 2017 as landmark tax reform encountered transitory headwinds. Inflation eased, and the current account deficit widened but remained modest. After 2 years of moderating growth, the economy is projected to rebound on stronger domestic demand, aided by measures to spur rural incomes, a modest uptick in investment as firms and banks strive to improve their balance sheets, and an improved business environment.

Economic performance

The government launched the long-awaited goods and services tax (GST) on 1 July 2017, paving the way for a more integrated and efficient national economy, bolstered competitiveness in manufacturing, and a wider tax base. Teething issues in the initial months affected mainly small and medium-sized enterprises and exporters facing higher compliance burdens and short of working capital because input tax refunds were delayed. Headwinds came as well from the lingering effects of demonetization in November 2016, when the government suddenly withdrew legal tender status from high-denomination banknotes but experienced delays introducing new ones.

On balance, transitional forces weighed on economic growth (Figure 3.17.1), which according to initial estimates slowed to 6.6% in fiscal year 2017 (FY2017, ended 31 March 2018). Lower growth also reflected subdued performance in agriculture, which grew by 3.0%. Food grain production only marginally exceeded a good harvest a year earlier, but livestock and fisheries, which provide 41% of agricultural value added, grew at robust rates.

Growth in industry slowed to 4.8% in FY2017 from 6.8% in FY2016, primarily because manufacturing growth weakened to 5.1% from 7.9% a year earlier. Manufacturing in the first half of FY2017 was affected by demonetization, which especially affected the informal sector. Next, firms cut back production to clear inventories before the introduction of the GST, then small and medium-sized enterprises in particular experienced difficulties in adjusting to the new tax regime. Manufacturing growth stepped up by quarter, however, finally reaching 7.6% in the second half of FY2017. The rebound was lifted by robust performances in automobiles and auto components, electronic products, and pharmaceuticals, though textiles, apparel, rubber, and plastics continued to contract.

3.17.1 Supply-side contributions to growth

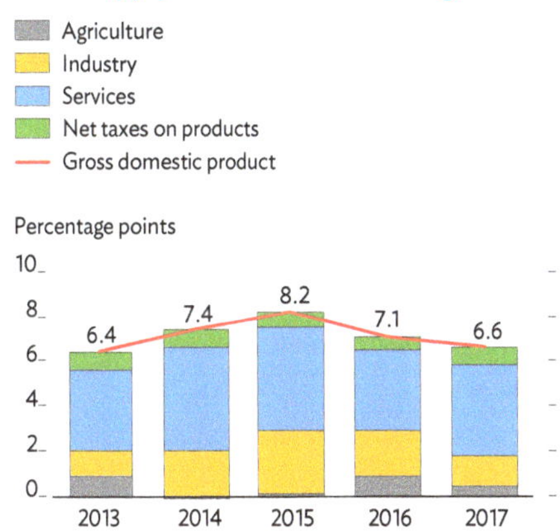

Note: Years are fiscal years ending on 31 March of the next year.

Source: Ministry of Statistics and Programme Implementation. http://www.mospi.nic.in (accessed 9 March 2018).

This chapter was written by Abhijit Sen Gupta of the India Resident Mission, ADB, New Delhi.

Growth in construction more than tripled from 1.3% in FY2016 to 4.3% in FY2017, aided by impetus given to affordable housing and robust public spending on infrastructure in the first half of the year. Mining slowed, notably as production of coal and crude oil weakened.

Services grew by 8.3%, mainly on improved growth in finance, real estate, trade, hotels, transportation, and communication services. Financial services were buoyed by a healthy revival in credit growth in the second half of FY2017 that reflected an uptick in economic activity but also a base effect from a sharp fall in credit growth in the aftermath of demonetization. Strong growth in transportation services came from expansion in air passengers and cargo and in railway freight, as well as robust growth in sales of commercial vehicles. Government services including public administration, defense, and "other services" registered robust growth.

Private consumption growth slowed to 6.1% in FY2017, the lowest in 5 years (Figure 3.17.2). Rural consumption dipped because of weak prices for agricultural produce for much of the year, a slowdown in rural wage growth, and the lingering effects of demonetization. Government consumption grew by 10.9%, by contrast, on higher pensions. Gross fixed capital formation expanded by 7.6% after only sluggish growth in the first half, picking up in the second half aided by strong production of capital goods. Valuables, comprising gold and precious stones, rose sharply as falling interest rates made saving in financial assets less attractive. After growing at a robust rate in the initial months of FY2017, the pace of central government capital expenditure moderated under fiscal pressure. Private investment remained lackadaisical as it continued to be afflicted by stress on corporate balance sheets and by low capacity utilization at about 72%. Weak credit growth to industry and infrastructure also curbed investment.

Although inflation averaged less than 4.0% in FY2017, it picked up steadily from the second quarter (Figure 3.17.3). Food inflation reversed a deflationary trend in the first quarter and neared 5.0% at the end of FY2017 on price spikes for sugar and vegetables. Prices for pulses contracted, by contrast, following a bumper harvest. With oil prices increasing by over 20% in FY2017, the government reduced excise duty to moderate some of the pass-through to domestic prices. Nevertheless, fuel inflation more than doubled from the previous year to 6.2% in FY2017, with sharp increases for cooking gas and kerosene. Core inflation started inching up steadily from August 2017, driven by a rise in housing allowances of government employees and higher taxes on services under the GST.

Subdued inflation in the first quarter of FY2017 allowed the Reserve Bank of India, the central bank, to reduce policy rates by 25 basis points in FY2017, for a cumulative decline of 200 basis points since January 2015 (Figure 3.17.4).

3.17.2 Demand-side contributions to growth

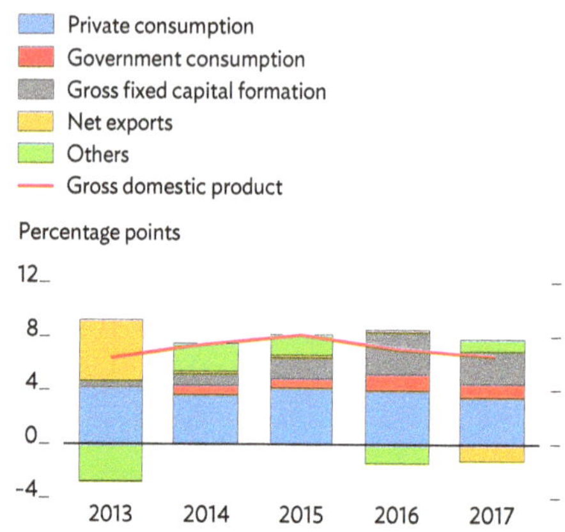

Note: Years are fiscal years ending on 31 March of the next year.

Sources: Ministry of Statistics and Programme Implementation. http://www.mospi.nic.in and CEIC Data Company (accessed 9 March 2018).

3.17.3 Inflation

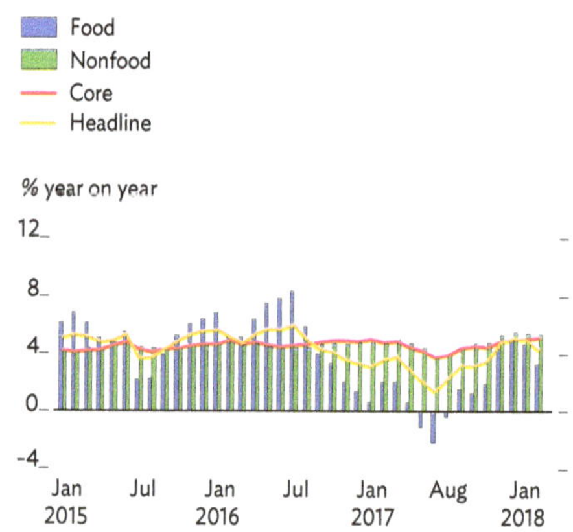

Sources: CEIC data company (accessed 14 March 2018); ADB staff estimates.

3.17.4 Policy interest rates

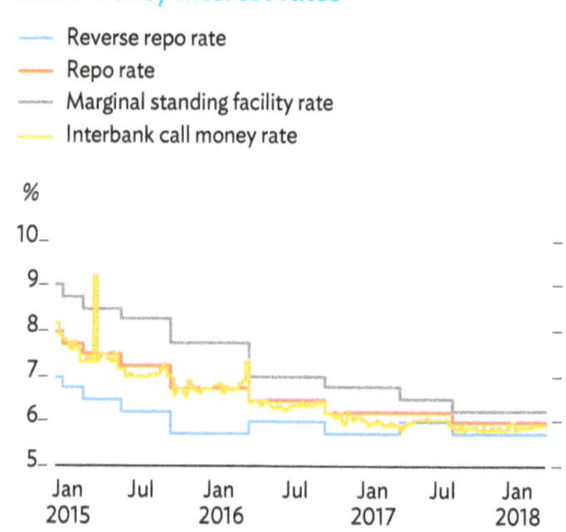

Sources: Bloomberg and CEIC Data Company (accessed 15 March 2018).

The steady declining trend in credit growth over the past 6 years bottomed out in FY2017 with 7.0% growth (Figure 3.17.5). A sign of recovery was credit growing by 9.0% in the second half of FY2017, up from 6.0% in the first half on a pickup in credit to services, notably wholesale and retail trade, transportation, and professional services. Credit to industry remained subdued, however, with credit to medium- and large-scale industries continuing to contract. Retail loans, including housing and personal loans, have remained strong, signaling robust consumer demand. Deposit growth moderated considerably, partly because of declining interest rates but also reflecting a base effect following a surge in deposits in the wake of demonetization in 2016.

Banks continued to hold a lot of stressed assets as their nonperforming loans proliferated to 10.2% of the total in September 2017 from 9.6% in March 2017 (Figure 3.17.6). Over the same period, restructured stressed advances fell from 2.5% to 2.0%, taking all stressed assets up marginally from 12.1% to 12.2%. Although, public banks continue to hold the bulk of nonperforming loans, private banks acquired them at a faster pace in the first half of FY2017. The health of the banking sector could improve with recent efforts toward resolving major insolvency cases expeditiously and the implementation of a bank recapitalization plan, though further reform to strengthen bank governance is needed.

Fiscal consolidation slowed with the central government revising up its fiscal deficit for FY2017 from a target equal to 3.2% of GDP to 3.5%, unchanged from the FY2016 outcome (Figure 3.17.7). Nevertheless, the government reiterated its commitment to fiscal consolidation by targeting a fiscal deficit equal to 3.3% of GDP in FY2018, 3.1% in FY2019, and 3.0% in FY2020.

The fiscal overrun partly reflected a shortfall in nontax revenue as profits and dividends from public sector enterprises including the central bank weakened, as well as lower telecom license fees and spectrum usage charges. Direct tax revenues were buoyant as personal income tax collection benefiting from improved compliance, and as corporate tax revenue exceeded targets.

The indirect tax system was completely overhauled when the government introduced the GST (a value-added tax) in July 2017. GST revenue has been robust, though with some decline in November and December 2017 as the government reduced tax rates for many commodities. Improved economic activity and better compliance restored GST revenue to pre-November levels starting in January 2018. Revenue from excise taxes on goods that remain outside the GST moderated a bit as the government reduced rates to contain the pass-through of global prices to retail prices. The target for revenue from disinvestment in state-owned enterprises for FY2017 was exceeded for the first time in many years.

3.17.5 Bank credit

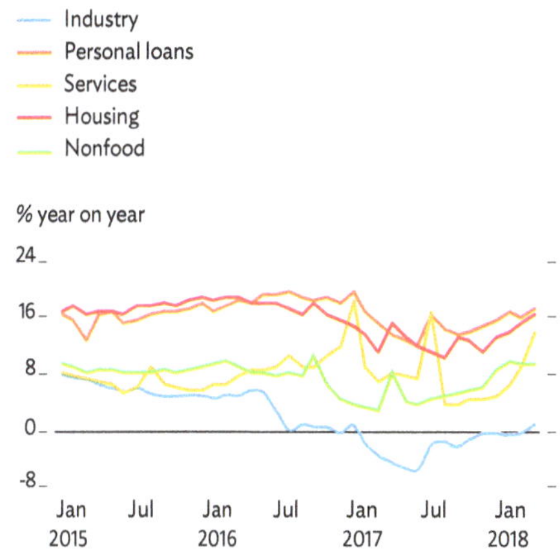

Sources: Bloomberg and CEIC Data Company (accessed 15 March 2018).

3.17.6 Nonperforming and restructured loans

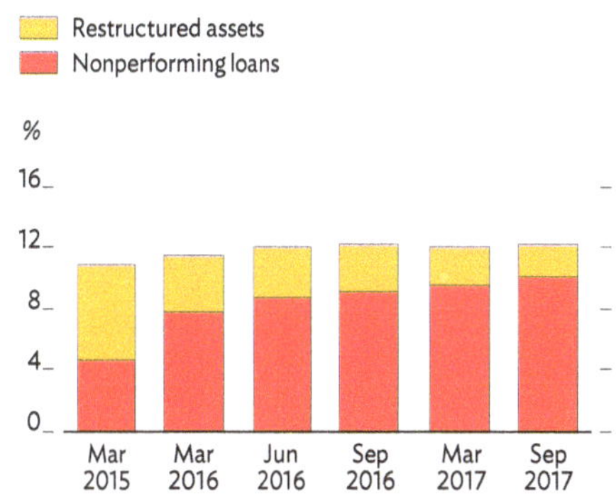

Source: Reserve Bank of India. http://www.rbi.org.in.

3.17.7 Federal budget indicators

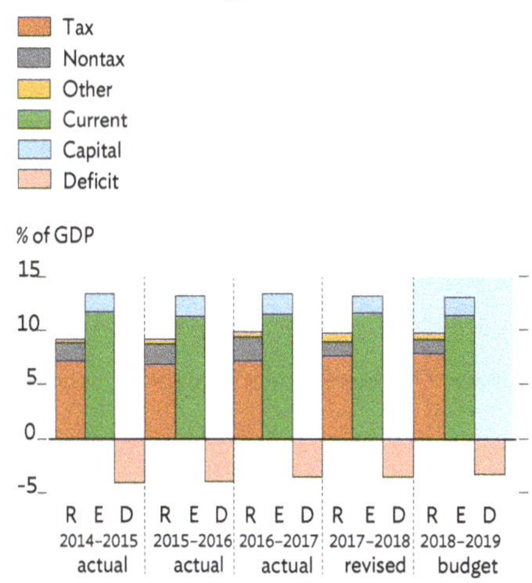

R = revenue, E = expenditure, D = deficit financing.

Note: Years are fiscal years ending on 31 March of the next year.

Source: Ministry of Finance Union Budget 2016–2018. http://indiabudget.nic.in.

The quality of expenditure deteriorated in FY2017 as capital expenditure contracted by 3.9% and current expenditure increased by 15.0%, the upsurge being payments higher than expected to states for revenue losses from the rollout of the GST, as well as larger pension payouts and interest payments. After growing at a healthy rate in the first half of the year, capital expenditure slowed in the second half as fiscal pressures mounted.

After 2 years of weakness, imports picked up sharply in FY2017 to grow by 21.0% (Figure 3.17.8). Much of this increase was driven by 26.9% growth in oil imports from steep price increases but also an uptick in volume. Gold imports surged by 42.4% on robust local demand and a transitory bump in the first half, when taxes on gold were adjusted downward to align with the GST, which made imports from certain countries attractive, depending on the terms of bilateral trade agreements with India. Imports other than oil or gold also increased at a robust pace, driven by a strong currency and the pickup in economic activity in the second half.

Export growth was more muted during the year at 11.0%. Exports of refined petroleum grew by nearly 20% after 3 years of contraction. Healthy growth in exports of automobiles, auto parts, chemicals, and iron and steel propelled growth in exports overall, despite contraction in exports of apparel and precious stones. The surplus in services grew by 15.6%, mainly on improved travel services, even as software service exports stagnated. Remittances expanded, helped by improved growth in the advanced economies and higher oil prices, which boosted growth prospects in oil-producing countries. A continued rise in net outflows of investment income dragged on invisibles. On balance, the FY2017 current account deficit is estimated to equal 2.0% of GDP.

Net foreign direct investment (FDI) inflows, which crossed the $35 billion mark in the previous 2 years, are estimated to have dipped to $30 billion, equal to 1.2% of GDP in FY2017. While the service sector remained the major recipient of FDI in FY2017, FDI flows into manufacturing and construction have increased. By contrast, net portfolio inflows tripled to $23 billion over the previous year, mainly on debt flows (Figure 3.17.9). The stock market was driven largely by local investor sentiment, rising by 14% in FY2017 but underperforming the 21% gain in emerging markets across Asia (Figure 3.17.10). Strong capital flows kept the Indian rupee stable in FY2017, trading in a narrow range around ₹64.70 to the dollar (Figure 3.17.11). India's reserve holdings increased by $50 billion in FY2017 to exceed $420 billion (Figure 3.17.12).

3.17.8 Trade indicators

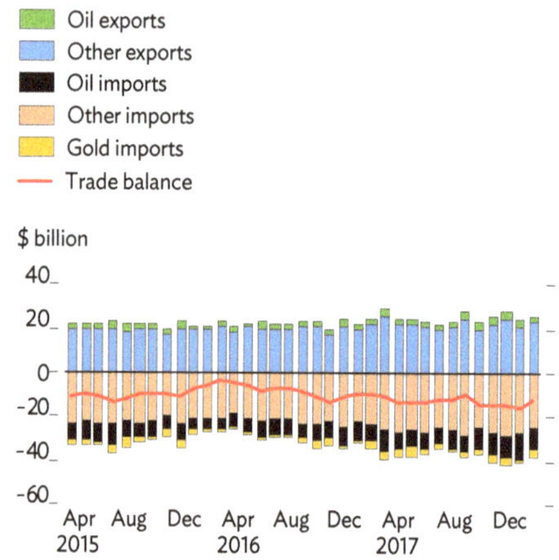

Note: Years are fiscal years ending on 31 March of the next year.

Sources: CEIC Data Company (accessed 1 April 2018); ADB estimates.

3.17.9 Portfolio capital flows

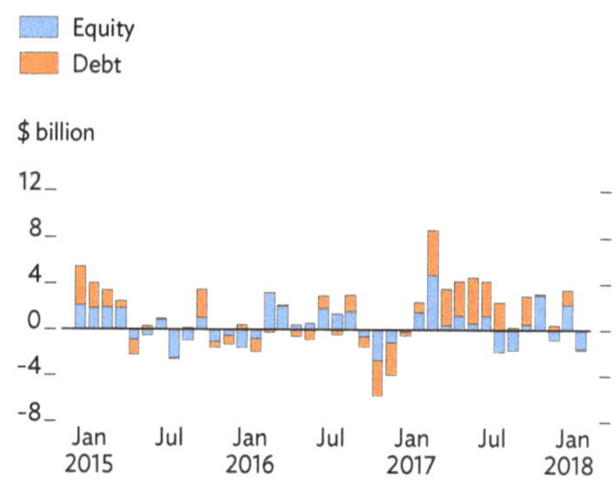

Source: Security and Exchange Board of India.

3.17.10 Stock price indexes

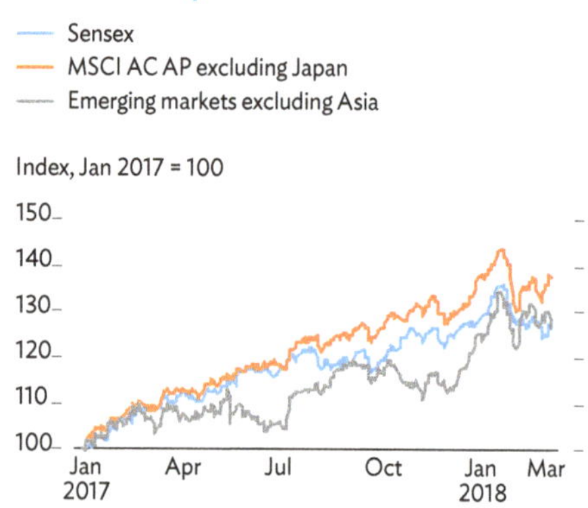

Source: Bloomberg (accessed 15 March 2018).

Economic prospects

Consumption is expected to remain an important growth driver in FY2018. Farmers should enjoy more purchasing power with an announced budget policy to spur rural incomes with higher food-procurement prices, agriculture market reform, crop insurance, and investment in irrigation and logistics. Stronger rural wages augur well for rural consumption, but urban consumption will be less dynamic with only moderate growth in urban wages and employment. Strong retail lending and a positive wealth effect from stock market gains may, however, boost some urban consumption, as may higher salaries for employees of some state governments in FY2018 following an earlier hike for central government employees. The deferment of central government fiscal consolidation will allow government consumption to increase, providing an impetus to growth.

Investment growth has been sluggish over the past 7 years but is showing nascent signs of recovery. The central bank's industrial outlook survey showed business expectations in the last quarter of 2017 reaching their highest in nearly 3 years (Figure 3.17.13). Moreover, there has been a steady increase in the portion of respondents expecting capacity utilization to improve in coming quarters, which can spur investment. Measures to hasten the resolution of banks' nonperforming loans and the implementation of the plan for comprehensive bank recapitalization may allow banks to raise their lending volumes. Finally, higher production and imports of capital goods indicate an investment revival. However, any rebound in investment is expected to be muted in view of the high proportion of leveraged companies and a sharp drop in announcements of new projects in the second half of 2017 (Figure 3.17.14). Similarly, public capital expenditure is likely to be modest, with the central government targeting an increase that trails the pace of nominal growth.

A healthy monsoon and various government initiatives to improve farm productivity will help agriculture grow at a robust rate. Various outlook surveys indicate some improvement in manufacturing and services. The Nikkei purchasing managers' indexes for both manufacturing and services improved significantly from July 2017 to January 2018 on strong growth in new orders, with the manufacturing index reaching a 5-year peak in December 2017 (Figure 3.17.15). The Nomura composite leading index for India reached a 7-year high in the fourth quarter of FY2017, suggesting a strong pickup in nonagricultural GDP growth.

Improved growth prospects for the advanced economies in 2018 should bolster exports of goods and tradeable services, but they will likely be offset by higher imports on account of anticipated increases in oil prices and domestic demand. Negative net exports will therefore drag on growth but less so than in FY2017.

3.17.1 Selected economic indicators (%)

	2018	2019
GDP growth	7.3	7.6
Inflation	4.6	5.0
Current account balance (share of GDP)	–2.2	–2.4

Note: Years are fiscal years ending on 31 March of the next year.

Source: ADB estimates.

3.17.11 Exchange rates

Source: Bloomberg (accessed 5 March 2018).

3.17.12 International reserves

Source: CEIC Data Company (accessed 15 March 2018).

In sum, growth is forecast to pick up to 7.3% in FY2018 on improved rural consumption, a modest uptick in private investment, and less drag from net exports. Urban consumption growth will remain stable, and impetus from public investment modest. Growth is expected to pick up further to 7.6% in FY2019 as efforts to strengthen the banking system and continued corporate deleveraging are likely to bolster private investment. Also set to catalyze growth are benefits from the GST as it mitigates geographic fragmentation and adds revenue to the exchequer, as well as further progress on fiscal consolidation and reform to promote FDI.

Inflation has inched up since July 2017. Its future prospects are molded by several factors. With global oil prices forecast to increase by 19.7% in 2018, decontrolled prices for fuels are expected to go up. This will spill over into transportation and add some 30 basis points to inflation. The outlook for food prices is shaped by an interplay of various factors. The proposed increase in procurement prices will add to inflation, though the impact will depend on the size of the proposed increase. Any strengthening of rural wages may affect retail food prices. However, prospects for a good monsoon, only modest increases in global food prices, and government efforts to improve agriculture supply management promise to mitigate the rise in food inflation. Core inflation could inch up as accelerated economic activity allows producers to pass their rising input costs on to consumers. Household inflation expectations turned higher in December 2017 from a year earlier. In sum, inflation is likely to average 4.6% in FY2018, rising to 5.0% in FY2019 with further firming of global commodity prices and strengthening of domestic demand (Figure 3.17.16).

Prospects for policy stimulus remain limited. The deferment of fiscal consolidation, upside risks to inflation, and expected hikes in US interest rates in 2018 squeeze maneuvering room for policy rate cuts to stimulate growth. At the same time, the odds of a rate hike are low with the central bank indicating tolerance for slightly higher inflation and recognition of the need to nurture recovery. Consequently, the status quo is likely to hold in FY2018, albeit with some risk of monetary tightening.

The pace of central government fiscal consolidation moderated as the fiscal deficit target for FY2018 was revised to 3.3% of GDP from 3.0%. Yet revenue prospects are robust thanks to the GST and progress on other reform, with gross tax revenue expected to grow by 16.7% in FY2018. Tax buoyancy, or the ratio of revenue growth to nominal GDP growth, is expected to increase to 1.4, well above the 5-year average of 1.2. Improved compliance is projected to boost personal income tax collection by almost 20%. Meanwhile, weakness in corporate balance sheets and reduced corporate tax rates will moderate

3.17.13 Industrial outlook survey

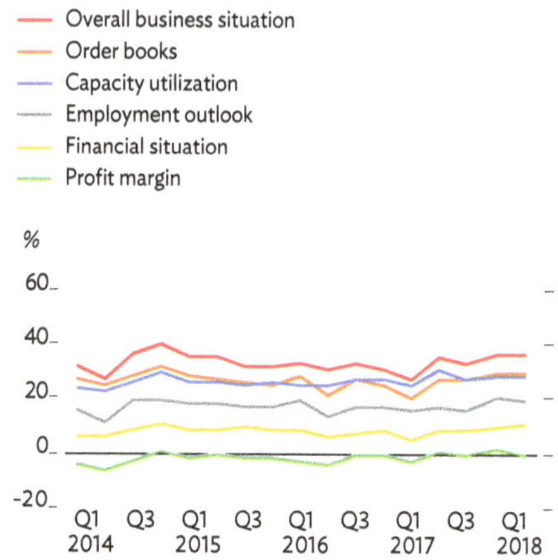

Q = quarter.

Notes: Years are fiscal years, Q1 refers to data for April–June.

Source: Reserve Bank of India.

3.17.14 New investment projects

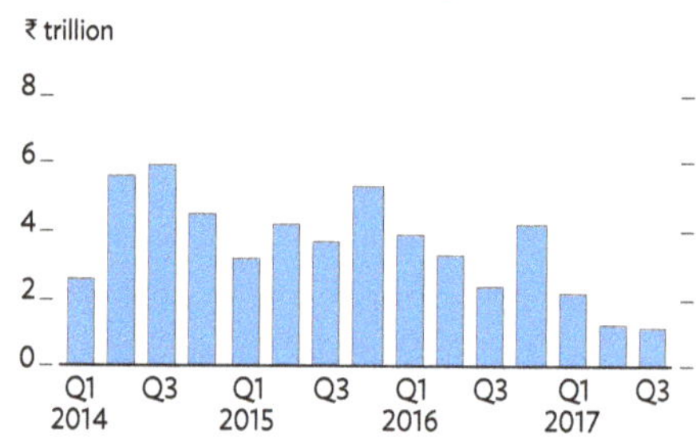

Q = quarter.

Note: Years are fiscal years ending on 31 March of the next year.

Source: Centre for Monitoring Indian Economy.

growth in corporate tax collection. Indirect tax collection is expected to rise by more than 19% in FY2018 with a substantial increase in compliance under the GST. Dividends from public sector enterprises and revenue from auctions of telecom spectrum are forecast to grow at modest rates. Disinvestment and strategic sales are expected to raise Rs800 billion, equal to 0.4% of GDP.

Expenditure quality will be unchanged with both capital and current expenditure forecast to expand by about 10.0% in FY2018. Capital outlays on infrastructure are projected to see significant increases for roads and highways, railways, shipping, and telecommunications, with a major part of the increases to be funded by the internal resources of public enterprises in these sectors. Additional funds have been budgeted for some flagship irrigation and housing schemes. Among current expenditures, the food subsidy is forecast to increase by 20.7%, reflecting the government's decision to hike procurement prices. The government also announced a state-funded health insurance program that will insure 100 million families. Expenditure targets are hostage to any significant increase in oil prices, considering that fuel subsidies are budgeted in line with FY2017 results. Any shortfall in revenue or increase in current expenditure is likely to curb capital expenditure, as has happened in past years.

Refined petroleum exports will rise with higher oil prices, and price recovery for other commodities will bolster commodity exports. With GST-induced disruption waning, exports could get a lift in FY2018. Robust external demand driven by growth in the advanced economies stands to strengthen exports of merchandise and tradeable services, though any new measures to restrict trade could dampen growth. Export growth overall is expected at 8.0% in FY2018, down from FY2017. Higher commodity prices and rising domestic demand will likely propel imports of petroleum and other products, and higher imports of capital goods are expected as investment revives. A relatively strong currency will make imports attractive.

Growth in imports is expected to accelerate to 11.0% in FY2018, again lower than in FY2017. Remittances will rise with improved growth prospects in the advanced economies and, with the rise in oil prices, in oil exporters, where a significant number of Indian workers are employed. On balance, the current account deficit is expected to equal about 2.2% of GDP. It will be comfortably financed by stable capital inflows, as India remains an attractive destination for FDI because of its healthy growth prospects, improved ease of doing business, and liberalizing investment regime, with more than 90% of FDI coming through automatic approval routes. A buoyant equities market and a stable currency are expected to bolster portfolio flows.

3.17.15 Purchasing managers' indexes

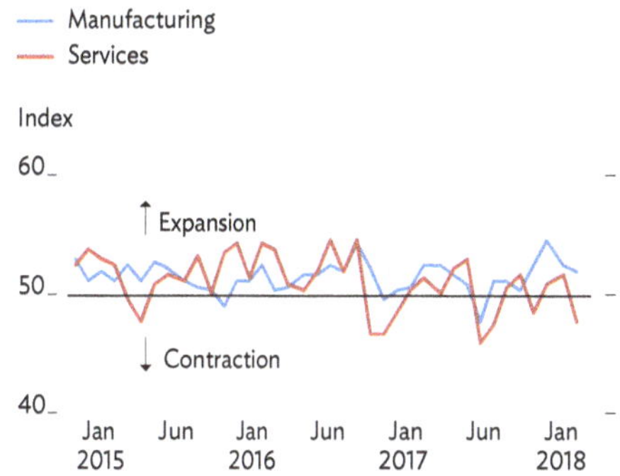

Note: Nikkei, Markit.

Source: Bloomberg (accessed 15 March 2018).

3.17.16 Inflation forecast

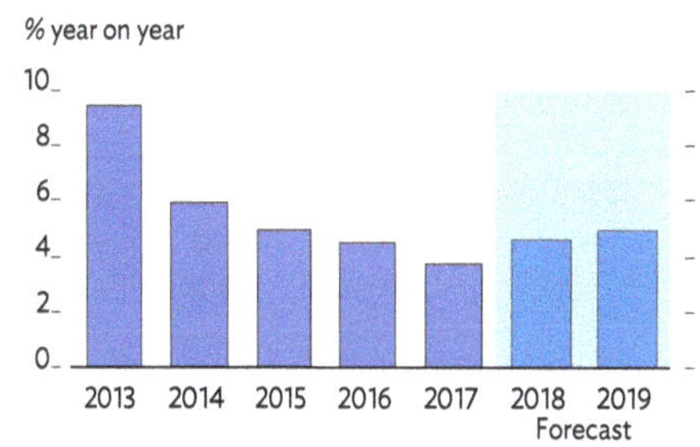

Sources: CEIC data company (accessed 14 March 2018); ADB estimates.

In FY2019, export growth is expected to average 9.0% as advanced economies continue to grow at a healthy rate and domestic competitiveness improves. At the same time, import growth is projected to slow to 10.0% as a drop in oil prices balances the increase in imports arising from higher domestic aggregate demand. The current account deficit is forecast to widen to the equivalent of 2.4% of GDP.

Policy challenge—reviving investment as a growth driver

The share of gross fixed capital formation in GDP declined steadily from 34.3% in FY2011 to 28.5% in FY2017. This decline reflected tepid growth of investment in recent years as average annual growth in investment more than halved to 5.3% in FY2012–FY2017 from 12.8% in FY2003–FY2011. This decline poses challenges for future growth, given the strong relationship between investment growth and GDP growth in India (Figure 3.17.17).

3.17.17 Investment and gross domestic product growth

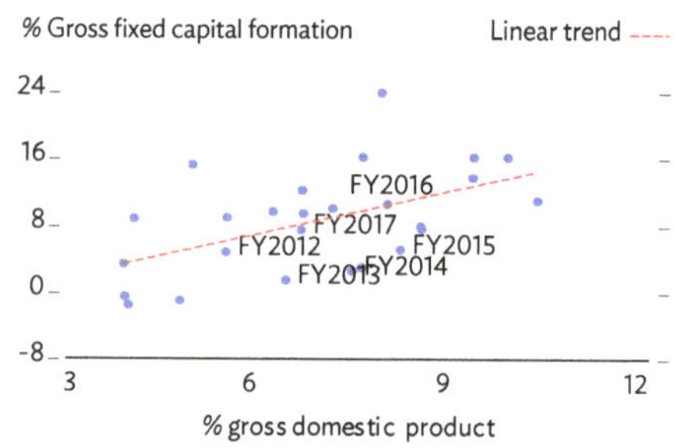

Sources: Ministry of Statistics and Programme Implementation. http://www.mospi.nic.in and CEIC Data Company (accessed 9 March 2018).

The robust rate of investment growth in FY2003–FY2011 was driven by the healthy balance sheets of corporations, households, and public institutions; strong external demand reflected in double-digit export growth; and robust expansion in bank credit. In contrast, the slowdown over the past 6 years reflected worsening stress on corporate and bank balance sheets, excess industrial capacity, weak external demand, tepid household investment, and fiscal limitations. Moreover, during the initial years of this period, India experienced some macroeconomic stress in the form of high inflation, elevated fiscal deficits, and high current account deficits.

In the past 6 years, the share of private corporate investment in GDP has stagnated to 11% to 12% (Figure 3.17.18). Reinvigorating corporate investment which has been undermined by the twin balance sheet problem would require progress on multiple fronts. While stress on corporate balance sheet remains high with interest coverage ratios remaining low, corporations have been deleveraging, as reflected in lower interest expenses in recent quarters. Corporate leverage is expected to ease further as firms sell assets and their earnings increase with improved demand. This could pave the way for firms to undertake fresh investments. Reviving corporate investment would hinge as well on reigniting the lending cycle, which has slowed in response to the rising prevalence of stressed assets in the banking system. The implementation of the bankruptcy act and a large recapitalization plan could speed the resolution of stressed assets and bolster credit growth, but more needs to be done to strengthen banks.

3.17.18 Gross fixed capital formation by institution

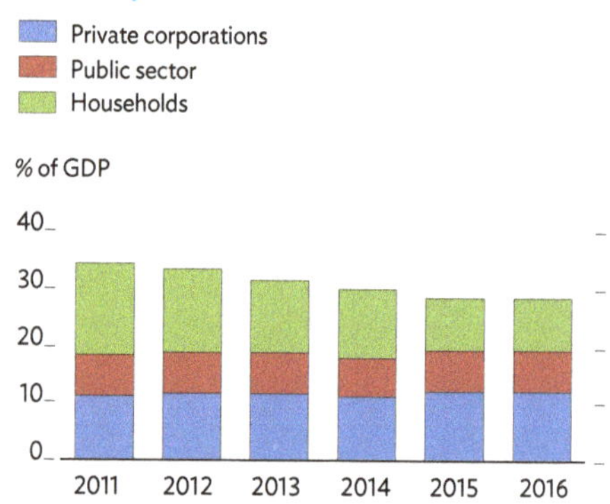

Sources: Ministry of Statistics and Programme Implementation. http://www.mospi.nic.in and CEIC Data Company (accessed 9 March 2018).

Since FY2012, deceleration in consumer price inflation has outpaced declines in nominal interest rates, steadily pushing up real interest rates and thereby discouraging investment. India's formal adoption of a flexible inflation-targeting framework will help contain inflation expectations and pave the way for lower inflation and interest rates in the years ahead.

Much of the decline in investment has been a decline in household and small enterprise investment from the equivalent of 15.7% of GDP in FY2011 to 9.1% in FY2016. A large part of this drop can be attributed to a near halving of investment in dwellings and buildings in the same period, from 12.8% of GDP to 6.6%, reflecting challenging conditions in real estate including low returns, a large unsold inventory, and legal disputes between buyers and developers. Government measures to improve transparency and accountability in the sector by, for example, enacting the Real Estate (Regulation and Development) Act in 2016, promise to help speed dispute resolution and redress, and so protect home buyers and boost investment in housing. The impetus given to affordable housing is expected to support the sector's revival. Further, by conferring infrastructure status on affordable housing, the government has enabled the sector to benefit from lower borrowing rates, tax concessions, and increased inflows of foreign and private capital.

According to a survey conducted by the Centre for Monitoring Indian Economy in December 2017, issues related to land acquisition and securing environmental and other clearances stalled ₹4.3 trillion of the surveyed projects, of which about 60% were government projects (Figure 3.17.19). These structural bottlenecks need to be alleviated to ensure that current projects are completed in a timely way. Another impediment to investment is low capacity utilization. According to a central bank survey of order books, inventories, and capacity utilization, capacity utilization fell to less than 72% in the third quarter of FY2017 from 83.2% in the fourth quarter of FY2010, reflecting subdued domestic demand and tepid exports. Excess capacity in industry must be resolved to increase investment opportunities.

Finally, in recent years, public investment has been constrained by efforts to rein in the fiscal deficit. Fiscal health can be restored by improving revenue generation and rationalizing expenditure. Recent efforts, including demonetization and the implementation of the GST, aim to formalize more of the economy and improve tax compliance, which promises to bolster tax revenue and provide funds to buttress capital expenditure. At the same time, better targeting of subsidies using digital technology would help contain expenditure on subsidies and free up resources for capital expenditure. Finally, the resources of the public sector enterprises can be tapped to strengthen public investment.

3.17.19 Projects abandoned, shelved, or stalled

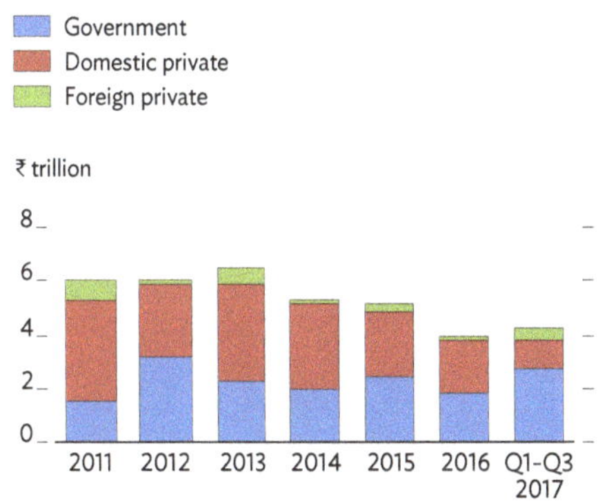

Q = quarter.

Note: Years are fiscal years ending on 31 March of the next year.

Source: Centre for Monitoring Indian Economy.

Maldives

Strong growth in tourism and an expansion in construction pushed growth higher in 2017. Inflation stayed low with help from subsidies, and the current account deficit moderated but remained high. The outlook is for modest growth, low inflation, and a narrower current account deficit. To foster economic inclusion and lower large income disparities, the government is working to boost the development of micro, small, and medium-sized enterprises on outer atolls.

Economic performance

Using revised calculations (Box 3.18.1), GDP growth accelerated to 6.5% in 2017 from 6.2% in 2016, driven by a rebound in tourism and buoyed by continued strong growth in construction (Figure 3.18.1). After lackluster expansion in the previous 2 years, growth in tourist arrivals nearly doubled to 8.0% in 2017, mainly reflecting improved economies in the major markets. Arrivals from Europe jumped by 12.4%, accounting for nearly 70% of the increase (Figure 3.18.2). Other factors were the government's intensive marketing campaign, four major airlines launching flights from Europe and Asia, and the opening of several resorts.

Arrivals from Asia, the second largest market, grew by only 2.5%, mainly because of a 5.5% decline in visitors from the People's Republic of China, which remains a major market providing just over a fifth of arrivals. Bed-night occupancy increased sharply by 10.8%. However, growth in tourism services output was only 4.2% and in tourist goods and services tax collection only 5.5%, suggesting more moderate growth in income.

Construction continued in 2017 despite an estimated cutback in Public Sector Investment Program spending by 17%. The cutback is consistent with construction increasing by an estimated 5%, down from 17% a year earlier. However, bank lending to the private sector for construction and real estate rose by 35% from 28% a year earlier, pointing to robust private construction, as do imports of construction materials that are estimated to increase by 26%, up from 19% in 2016.

Fisheries prospered with higher international fish prices and strong demand from export markets in Asia and Europe. The value of fish exports is estimated to have increased by 40% in 2017 following a 2% decline a year earlier. Growth in other areas, such as financial and social services, was modest.

3.18.1 Supply-side contributions to growth

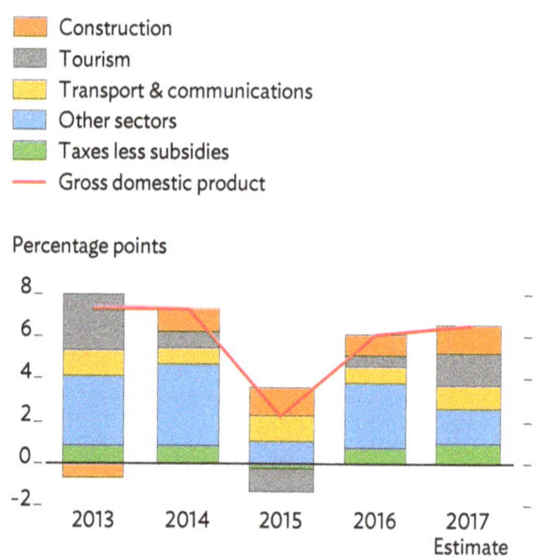

Source: Maldives Monetary Authority. 2018. *Monthly Statistics*. February. http://www.mma.gov.mv.

3.18.2 Tourism indicators

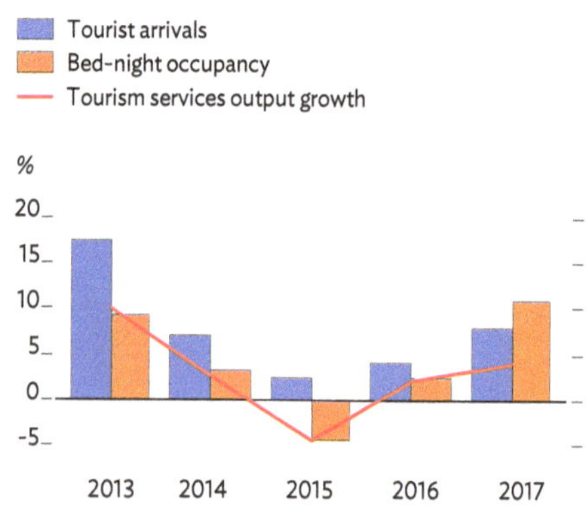

Note: 2017 data on tourism services output growth is an estimate.

Source: Maldives Monetary Authority. 2018. *Monthly Statistics*. February. http://www.mma.gov.mv.

This chapter was written by Masato Nakane of the South Asia Department, ADB, Manila; and Macrina Mallari and Remedios Baes-Espineda, consultants, South Asia Department, ADB, Manila.

Inflation accelerated in the first half of 2017 after subsidies on major staples started being removed in the third quarter of 2016 and as global prices rose for petroleum products and food. Inflation braked in the second half after the government imposed price cuts and controls on major staples and amended the Export Impact Act to reduce import duty on fuel, which allowed lower electricity rates. Despite inflation averaging near 4.0% in the first half, for the whole of 2017 it averaged only 2.8% (Figure 3.18.3).

With inflation low, the Maldives Monetary Authority maintained an accommodative stance and kept policy rates unchanged. Growth in credit to the private sector accelerated to 14.4% from 10.4% a year earlier, with the bulk of credit going to tourism, construction, and real estate and commerce. Bank lending to state-owned enterprises expanded by 11.4% but remained small compared with private sector credit. Rates charged to private borrowers averaged about 10% per annum.

Fiscal reprioritization in 2017 aimed to manage the ballooning deficit by cutting current expenditure by 6.4% and capital expenditure by 22.3%, such that total spending fell by 12.2% in 2017 following an 18.0% increase in 2016. Revenue growth in 2017 picked up slightly to 12.0%. Preliminary official estimates yield a budget deficit equal to 2.0% of GDP, well below 10.4% a year earlier (Figure 3.18.4). Data on budget borrowing indicate a somewhat higher deficit, however, at 6.2% of GDP.

Government external debt escalated to $1.1 billion in 2017 as the Maldives issued its first international sovereign bond in June and November. The $250 million bond had a 5-year maturity and a coupon of 7%. Proceeds will finance development projects. Government domestic debt increased by 2.7% in 2017 to Rf27.2 billion, or 37.9% of GDP. At the end of 2017, total public debt was estimated at Rf43.8 billion or 61.1% of GDP (Figure 3.18.5).

The 2017 current account deficit is estimated at a large 21.7% of GDP despite improving by 2.8 percentage points (Figure 3.18.6). The trade deficit remained very high. Improvement in the current account deficit was supported by a marked fall in the secondary income deficit from 2016. Worker remittances increased and amounted to over 8% of GDP, reflecting a continuing need for expatriate labor, including in tourism. The welcome improvement in income from tourism was largely offset by larger service payments, which were substantial. Financial inflows, mainly direct investment and portfolio capital, were sufficient to cover the current account deficit and boost gross international reserves to $586.1 million. Of this, usable reserves come to $206.4 million, or cover for only a little more than a month of imports (Figure 3.18.7).

Economic prospects

Sustained tourism recovery and vibrant construction will propel growth in 2018 and 2019. Prospects for tourism appear bright with high growth forecast in the main tourist markets in Europe

3.18.1 GDP statistics revised

The National Bureau of Statistics has revised the national accounts for 2003–2015. The new GDP series uses 2014 for benchmarks and prices, updated from 2003, and presents data using market prices. The new series features statistical, conceptual, and methodological revisions. Under the new procedures, average rebased nominal GDP from 2003 to 2015 is higher by about 11% annually, with 2014 GDP revised up by as much as 20%. Real GDP growth rates for the 2003 and 2014 series show a similar pattern, but the 2014 series is somewhat more volatile. Average annual growth in real GDP in 2003–2015 was 5.9% using the 2003 series and 5.0% using the 2014 series. As a share of GDP, tourism increased moderately from 22.5% under the 2003 series to 25.2% under the 2014 series. There were more sizeable changes in industry share of GDP: Wholesale and retail trade tripled to 9.4% in the 2014 series, construction fell by just over half to 4.9%, and public administration declined by just less than half to 7.7%. Some sectors saw very slight change in GDP share: manufacturing at 1.5%, education at 3.0%, and health and social work at 2.7%.

3.18.3 Inflation

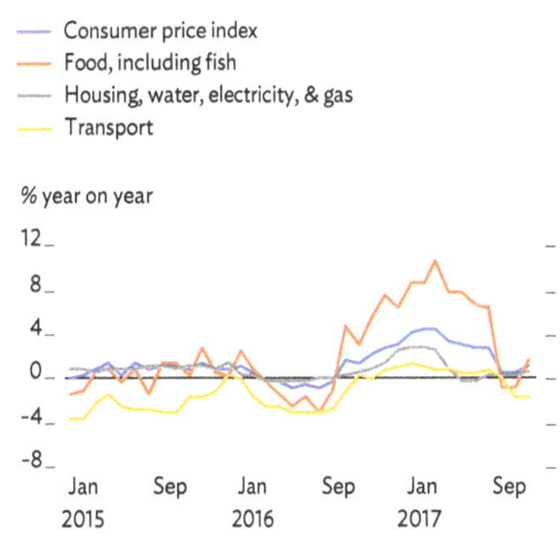

Source: Maldives Monetary Authority. 2018. *Monthly Statistics*. February. http://www.mma.gov.mv.

and in the People's Republic of China. Growth in tourism will be supported as well by the new air routes opened from Europe and Asia last year, the expected completion of a new runaway at Velana International Airport by mid-2018, the opening of 30 new resorts, the construction of several new regional airports, and persistent marketing initiatives of Travel Trade Maldives.

After cuts in 2017, the government plans to reaccelerate Public Sector Investment Program spending in the next 2 years. This is reflected in an increase in capital expenditure of nearly 25% in the approved budget for 2018. Major projects include developing 6,000 homes in Malé and other islands, building regional airports and hospitals, improving water supply and sewerage, and constructing roads and bridges.

Spending is slated to increase by 12.0%, with a 6.4% increase in current expenditure and a 23.9% increase in capital expenditure. Revenue and grants are projected to increase by 7.6% on an increase in tax revenue by nearly 12%, four-fifths of it from the goods and services tax and taxes on business profit. The government aims to hold the 2018 budget deficit to the equivalent of 3.2% of GDP, with 70% of it externally financed. It may be difficult to limit current spending as projected, however, because increases of only 2% for wages and salaries and for general expenses are small in an election year, and subsidies may require more spending. To achieve projected capital spending, the budget deficit may double to 6.5% of GDP.

Following strong growth in 2017, fisheries are poised for continued rapid expansion through new value-added products. Spillover from the projected growth in tourism and construction on related sectors—transport, communications, and wholesale and retail trade—will further underpin solid growth. GDP is projected to grow by 6.7% in 2018 and 6.8% in 2019.

Despite nearly 20% higher oil prices projected for 2018 and a continued rise in food prices, prevailing government price ceilings and budget allocations for food and electricity subsidies are projected to keep average inflation at 3.1% in 2018, moderating to 3.0% in 2019 as commodity prices ease.

The trade deficit will still weigh heavily on the current account balance, given the expected expansion in construction and higher oil prices. Imports are projected to increase by 11.2% in 2018 and taper to 10.8% in 2019. Favorable economic conditions in trading partners are expected to drive export growth to 12.0% this year and 11.8% in 2019. Projected strong growth in tourism will boost the service balance in the next 2 years and help narrow the current account deficit, which is projected to equal 17.3% of GDP in 2018 and 17.1% in 2019.

Risks to the outlook are the large external debt, low foreign exchange reserves, high dependence on shock-prone foreign borrowing and tourism, and escalating political tensions, especially in light of the 2018 presidential elections.

3.18.4 Fiscal indicators

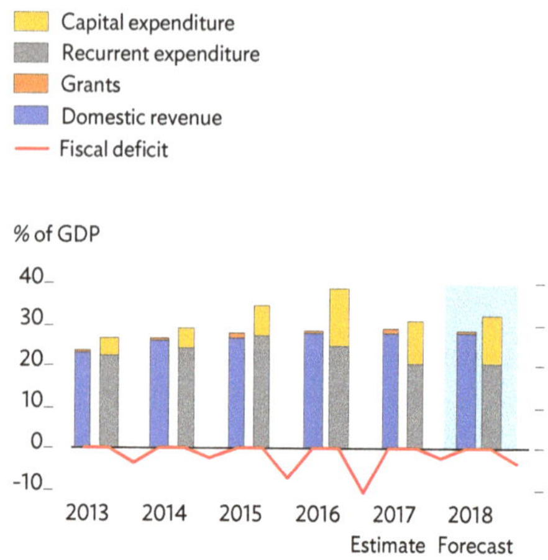

Source: Maldives Monetary Authority. 2018. *Monthly Statistics*. February. http://www.mma.gov.mv.

3.18.5 Public debt

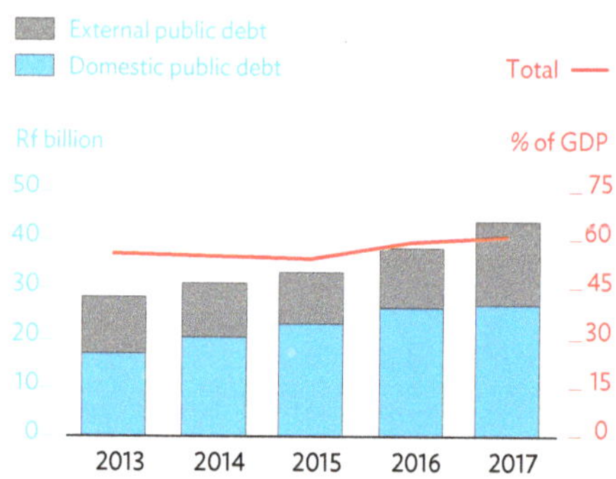

Source: Maldives Monetary Authority. 2018. *Monthly Statistics*. February. http://www.mma.gov.mv.

3.18.6 Balance of payments

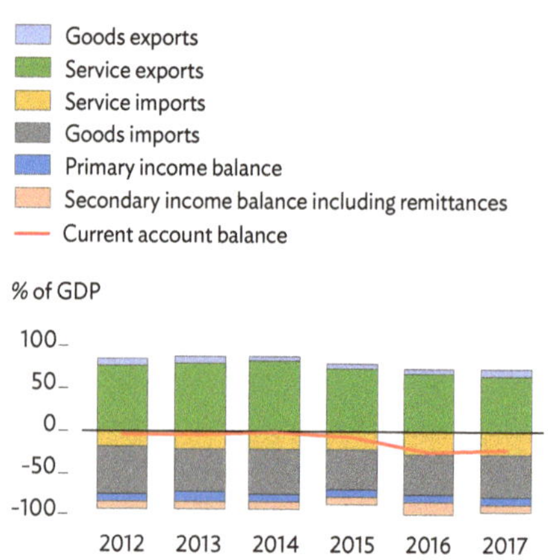

Source: Maldives Monetary Authority. 2018. *Monthly Statistics*. February. http://www.mma.gov.mv.

Policy challenge—expanding micro, small, and medium-sized enterprises

Fostering rapid growth in micro, small, and medium-sized enterprises (MSMEs) is, as articulated in the National Framework for Development, 2009–2013, an important vehicle for economic inclusion and reducing large income disparities between the capital at Malé and outlying atolls, where poverty incidence is high.

The government has undertaken a number of efforts to support MSMEs and address challenges to their growth. The Ministry of Economic Development heads the consolidation of initiatives into a more holistic approach to private sector promotion and development. A law on small and medium-sized enterprises (SMEs) enacted in 2013 paved the way for establishing business centers to provide development services to SMEs. These centers now operate in the country's six regions with assistance from development partners. In addition, the state-owned Business Center Corporation was set up in 2017 to implement SME development programs, including one to improve the operation and management of the business centers.

To address the large unmet credit needs of SMEs, which in 2012 were estimated at $15 million–$30 million, the government and its development partners have created several loan programs for them. In addition, the Maldives Monetary Authority created two institutions that have proven effective in helping small enterprises obtain financing: the Credit Guarantee Scheme which reduces risk for lenders, and the Credit Information Bureau, which helps lenders evaluate borrowers' creditworthiness.

Significant progress has been made over the years, but challenges continue to beset MSMEs, particularly in accessing finance. In *Doing Business 2018*, the World Bank ranks Maldives 133 in 190 economies surveyed globally, and second lowest among South Asian peers for ease in accessing credit (Figure 3.18.8).

A clearer and more inclusive strategy is required for developing MSMEs. The business center network needs to be strengthened, and the range of services updated to accommodate the varying needs of MSME customers across the atolls, particularly regarding help on financial literacy. Substantially increasing the line of credit offered by the Bank of Maldives to lenders would widen access to financing. Access to credit would improve if bank branches had greater presence on the atolls, microfinance lending were available through island community and village cooperatives, and information technology were leveraged to reach MSMEs in far-flung areas. The government should establish a long-term master plan for MSME development to guide policy and set benchmarks for improving services to them.

3.18.1 Selected economic indicators (%)

	2018	2019
GDP growth	6.7	6.8
Inflation	3.1	3.0
Current account balance (share of GDP)	-17.3	-17.1

Source: ADB estimates.

3.18.7 Gross international reserves

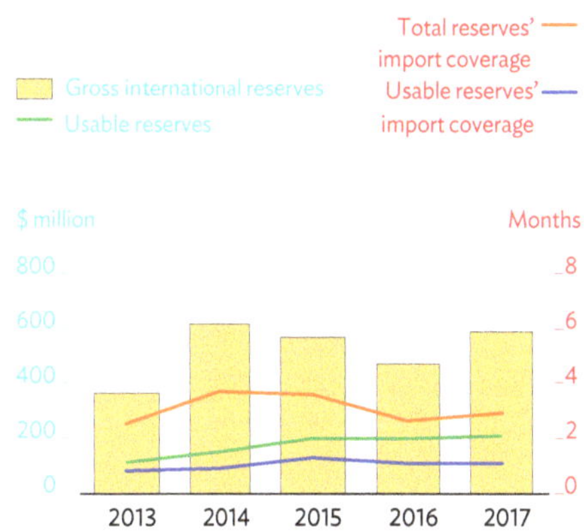

Source: Maldives Monetary Authority. 2018. *Monthly Statistics*. February. http://www.mma.gov.mv.

3.18.8 Rank in ease of access to credit

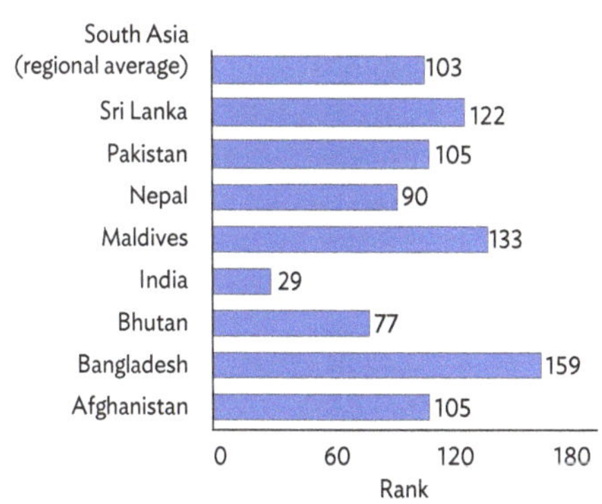

Note: Rank is of 190 countries. Lower rank means easier access to credit.

Source: The World Bank. 2018. *Doing Business 2018*. http://www.doingbusiness.org/~/media/WBG/DoingBusiness/Documents/Annual-Reports/English/DB2018-Full-Report.pdf.

Nepal

Growth accelerated from a low base in fiscal 2017 on a favorable monsoon, normalized trade flows, and an expansive fiscal policy. The outlook is for only moderate growth this year and next, given delayed project implementation and limited capacity in governments under a new federal structure. Weak remittances and export competitiveness will widen the current account deficit. Commercialized agriculture could raise farm productivity and boost farmers' income.

Economic performance

The economy grew by an estimated 6.9% in fiscal year 2017 (FY2017, ended 15 July 2017), recovering from stagnation in the previous year in the wake of devastating earthquakes in 2015 (Figure 3.19.1). The rebound reflected the normalization of disrupted trade from February 2016, better management of electricity supply, and a favorable monsoon that enabled better harvests. Paddy production, which supplies nearly 7% of GDP, increased to 5.2 million tons, for a gain of nearly 21%. Construction revived as materials flowed more easily across the southern border, post-earthquake reconstruction gained some momentum, and manufacturing output grew markedly thanks to improved electricity supply. Services, which supply 53% of GDP, expanded notably, reviving from a dismal performance in FY2016 in the aftermath of earthquakes further hindered by disrupted trade and supply. Among services, wholesale and retail trade, hotels and restaurants, transport, and tourism expanded markedly.

On the demand side, consumption dominated higher spending in FY2017. Fixed investment was also strong, however, growing by 27.2% to account for about a third of GDP. Private investment increased markedly in construction, hotels, hydropower, and aviation, while public fixed investment rose by 16.1% to equal nearly 6% of GDP.

Inflationary pressures subsided with increased domestic production, particularly of agricultural products, and with normalized trade and subdued inflation in neighboring India, the main source of supplies, to whose currency Nepal maintains a fixed exchange rate. Average annual inflation moderated to 4.5% in FY2017 from 9.9% a year earlier. Food inflation, which accounts for 44% of the consumer price basket, slowed more than nonfood inflation, reflecting high crop yields and relative ease in transporting supplies (Figure 3.19.2).

3.19.1 Supply-side contributions to growth

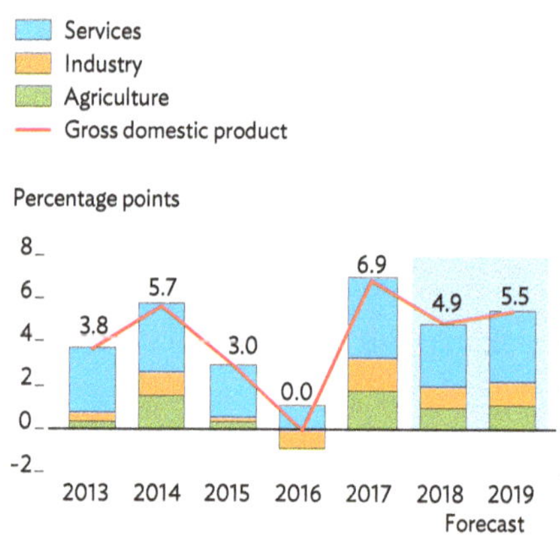

Note: Years are fiscal years ending on 15 July of that year.

Sources: Central Bureau of Statistics. 2017. *National Accounts of Nepal 2016/17.* http://cbs.gov.np/; ADB estimates.

3.19.2 Monthly inflation

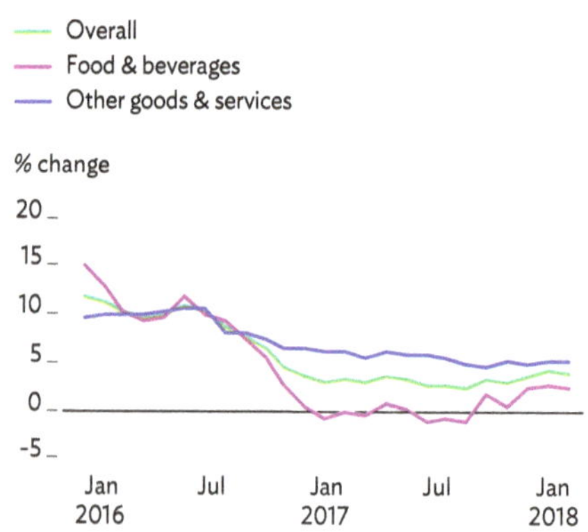

Source: Nepal Rastra Bank. 2018. *Recent Macroeconomic Situation.* http://www.nrb.org.np.

This chapter was written by Manbar Singh Khadka and Neelina Nakarmi of the Nepal Resident Mission, ADB, Kathmandu.

Fiscal policy was expansionary in FY2017. Very large increases in recurrent and capital expenditures widened the budget deficit to 5.4% of GDP from 0.3% a year earlier (Figure 3.19.3). Data from Nepal Rastra Bank, the central bank, show about 60% of the deficit financed by domestic sources. Though government expenditure has mounted, poor execution of the capital budget is reflected in large budget shortfalls. Lack of project readiness has engendered implementation delays. Reflecting a surge in imports, customs duties provided a major boost to budget revenue, which increased by 26.4% to equal 23.4% of GDP in FY2017. Government external debt equated to only 15.9% of GDP, indicating low risk of debt distress. The prevalence of official concessional borrowing with long maturity means that payments needed to service external debt are modest.

Broad money (M2) supply increased by 15.5% in FY2017, slowing from an increase of 19.5% in FY2016 with a smaller increase in net foreign assets. Credit to the private sector grew by 18.0% on revived economic activity and investment, but excessive lending for real estate and the hire purchase of vehicles induced a liquidity crunch. Consequently, deposit and lending rates alike increased by about 300 basis points over the year even as inflation fell markedly (Figure 3.19.4).

The Nepalese rupee appreciated against the US dollar in FY2017 in both nominal and real effective terms. Nominal appreciation was by 4.4% in the fiscal year to mid-July 2017, in line with Indian rupee appreciation. In real effective terms, meanwhile, the Nepalese rupee has appreciated rapidly in recent years because inflation in Nepal has exceeded that of its trade partners, weakening export competitiveness.

With large purchases of capital goods, construction materials, and telecommunication equipment and devices, imports surged in FY2017 while export earnings increased only slightly. This widened Nepal's traditionally large trade deficit to the equivalent of 34.5% of GDP. Increases in worker remittances and other transfers, and a recovery in tourism, held the current account deficit to $95.7 million, amounting to only 0.4% of GDP but reversing a $1.3 billion surplus in FY2016 (Figure 3.19.5). Nevertheless, continued capital and financial inflows boosted gross foreign exchange reserves by nearly 8% to $10.5 billion, providing 11.4 months of cover for imports of goods and services (Figure 3.19.6).

Economic prospects

The economy will likely grow by 4.9% in FY2018, slowing from 6.9% in FY2017 mainly with the elimination of a low base effect for comparison. Paddy production is expected to be 5.1 million tons, a drop of 1.5% from FY2017 because floods in August 2017 affected the transplant of paddy seedlings. The output of other

3.19.3 Fiscal indicators

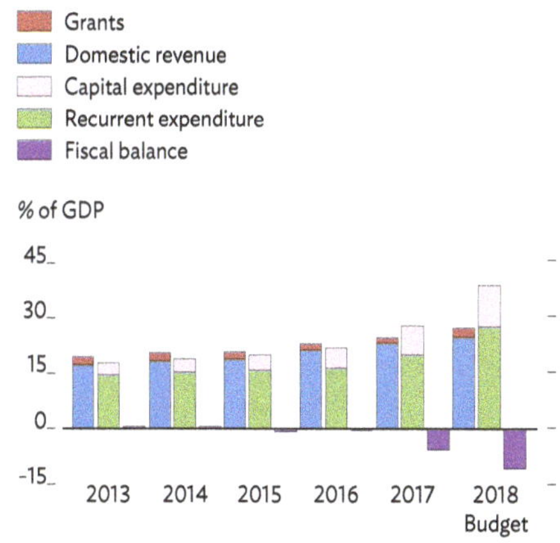

Note: Years are fiscal years ending on 15 July of that year.
Source: Ministry of Finance. Budget Speech 2018.

3.19.4 Credit to the private sector and M2 growth

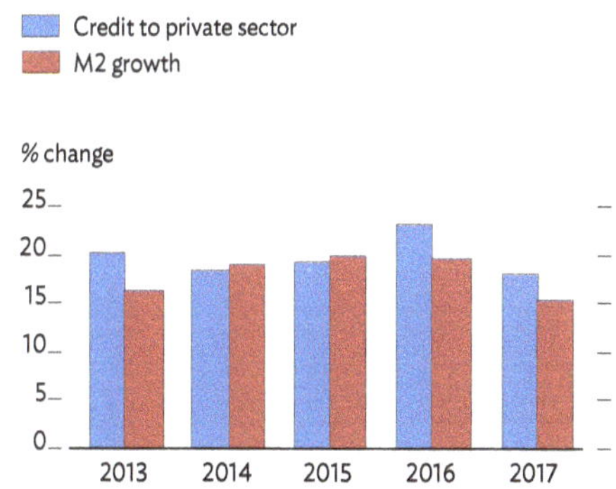

Note: Years are fiscal years ending on 15 July of that year.
Source: Nepal Rastra Bank. 2018. *Recent Macroeconomic Situation.* http://www.nrb.org.np.

3.19.5 Current account components

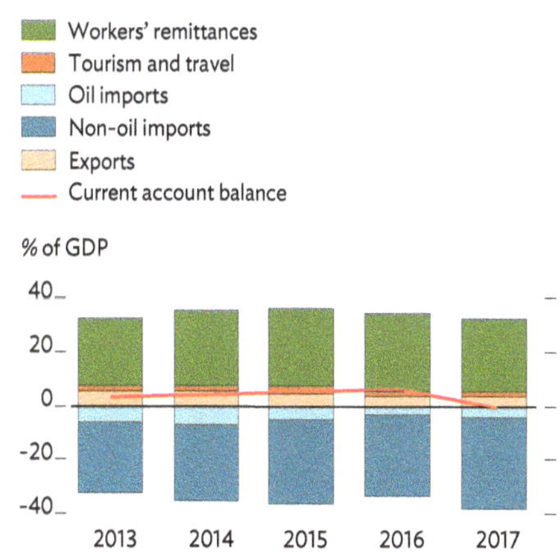

Note: Years are fiscal years ending on 15 July of that year.
Source: Nepal Rastra Bank. 2018. *Recent Macroeconomic Situation.* http://www.nrb.org.np.

major summer crops will likely increase, and agriculture is anticipated to grow by 3.0%.

Industry will probably grow by 6.4% in FY2018. Though capacity utilization has improved, long-standing challenges tied to inadequate investment and structural bottlenecks will limit the pace of growth. Construction will expand with further acceleration in post-earthquake reconstruction and in response to the huge need for physical infrastructure, in particular office buildings in the provinces with continued implementation of fiscal federalism. Manufacturing will benefit from better electricity supply. Services will likely grow by 5.5%, supported by expansion in wholesale and retail trade, financial intermediation, and travel and tourism.

Growth in government expenditure and an uptick in investment will drive growth in FY2018. The FY2018 budget envisages a deficit equal to 10.6% of GDP, but it will likely materialize as only 6.7% as capital expenditure underperforms allocation. Even with troubled implementation, capital spending surged by 37.3% in the first half over the year-earlier period (Figure 3.19.7). Election expenditures and fiscal transfers to local and provincial governments have further buoyed spending.

Growth in private consumption will remain subdued with only a moderate rise in remittances in the wake of a decline in outward migration to major destination countries (Figure 3.19.8). The trade deficit will widen in FY2018, mainly reflecting an uptick in investment and higher oil prices. Inadequate infrastructure, a lacking competitive environment in major markets, and currency appreciation in real effective terms are some of the factors hindering the competitiveness of goods exports. The current account deficit is projected to widen to the equivalent of 3.5% of GDP, well up from 0.4% a year earlier because of the slow rise in remittances.

Average annual inflation will rise to a still modest 5.5% in FY2018 from 4.5% in FY2017. Inflation averaged 3.5% in the first 6 months of FY2018, below the 5.8% result in the year-earlier period. Higher government expenditure, including disbursement of relief grants to earthquake and flood victims, will intensify inflationary pressure in the second half of the year.

Monetary policy aims to contain inflation by maintaining growth in broad money supply at 18.0%. Net foreign assets will rise at a slower pace, given the restrained growth in remittances and the rising trade deficit. Increased domestic borrowing to fund the budget deficit is affecting the availability of funds loanable to the private sector, thereby exerting upward pressure on nominal and real interest rates.

GDP growth is projected at 5.5% in FY2019, assuming a normal monsoon, better supply of farm inputs, and the acceleration of ongoing megaprojects. The 456-megawatt

3.19.6 Gross international reserves and exchange rate

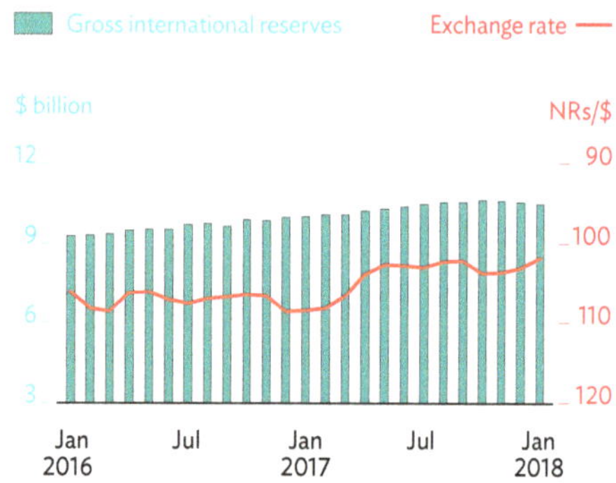

Source: Nepal Rastra Bank. 2018. *Recent Macroeconomic Situation*. http://www.nrb.org.np.

3.19.1 Selected economic indicators (%)

	2018	2019
GDP growth	4.9	5.5
Inflation	5.5	6.0
Current account balance (share of GDP)	–3.5	–5.8

Note: Years are fiscal years ending on 15 July of that year.
Source: ADB estimates.

3.19.7 Mid-year capital expenditure

Note: Years are fiscal years ending on 15 July of that year.
Sources: Ministry of Finance, Budget speech various years; Financial Comptroller General Office.

Upper Tamakoshi Hydropower Project will likely begin contributing to the national grid in FY2019, making Nepal self-sufficient in electricity during the rainy season. Increased generation of hydroelectricity from independent power producers will further strengthen the nation's power supply. Nepal will nevertheless have to rely on power imports from India to close its deficiency during the dry season.

Average annual inflation will stay moderate at 6.0% in FY2019, assuming a favorable harvest, moderate increase in oil prices, and modest increase in Indian inflation. The current account deficit is expected to widen further to equal 5.8% of GDP as remittances weaken and the trade deficit widens on higher economic growth.

Downside risks to the outlook in FY2019 arise from limited experience and capacity in all three tiers of government. The budget deficit may widen on account of weak capacity to mobilize revenue in newly empowered provincial and local governments.

3.19.8 Migrant workers and remittance

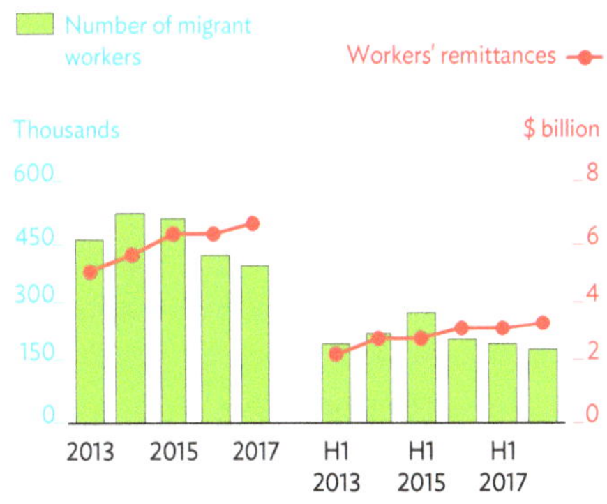

H = half.

Note: Years are fiscal years ending on 15 July of that year.

Sources: Department of Foreign Employment; Nepal Rastra Bank.

Policy challenge—commercializing agriculture to boost productivity

Agriculture in Nepal suffers from long-standing challenges posed by limits on the adoption of new technology, the availability of farm inputs, and market linkages, all hindering farm productivity. Stagnant farm productivity is a major concern since it hinders livelihood improvement for much of the population (Figure 3.19.9). To boost farm productivity and farmers' income, the government has prioritized the commercialization of agriculture with contract and cooperative farming promoted through various policy documents: the Trade Policy, 2009; Fourteenth Three-Year Plan, FY2017–FY2019; and Agriculture Development Strategy, 2015–2035. Notably, a policy for agribusiness promotion was enacted a decade ago to promote mass-scale and high-quality production, but neither farm productivity nor exports of promising agricultural products increased (Figure 3.19.10).

Prospects for commercialization in agriculture have suffered for lack of an appropriate legal framework, compounded by bottlenecks strangling the supply of modern inputs. New legislation and better-defined responsibilities in contract farming are essential for the successful cultivation of several niche crops such as tea, coffee, ginger, and large cardamom, which have great export potential through contract farming.

Under the contract farming modality, a sponsoring firm provides farm inputs and technical and extension services to farmers. In exchange, the contracted farmers supply agriculture produce in an agreed quantity within an agreed

3.19.9 Productivity of major cereal crops

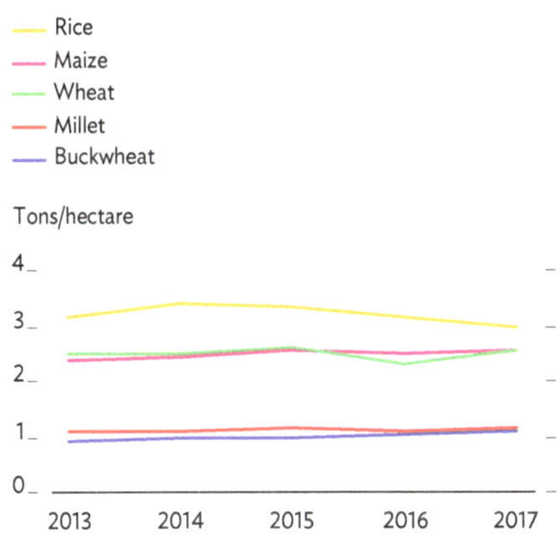

Note: Years are fiscal years ending on 15 July of that year.

Source: Ministry of Agricultural, Land Management, and Cooperatives.

timeframe. Farmers are guaranteed predetermined prices for their produce, and they need not worry about market access. This approach facilitates the mass production of high-quality produce able to meet the exacting requirement of agro-processing firms.

Initiatives crucial to progress would enact legislation enabling agribusiness promotion, conduct appropriate research, provide adequate extension support to farmers, and formulate and implement a national strategy on land consolidation to achieve appropriate farm size. Moreover, farmer empowerment depends on a revitalized cooperative movement. In this regard, the roles of local and provincial governments under the new federal governance structure will be decisive in implementing effective programs that raise productivity, export production, and farmers' income.

A lack of credit is a constraint on expanding commercial farming and agribusiness. The emphasis should therefore be on developing credit facilities that offer appropriate terms for farming through formal banking channels. The ongoing construction of postal roads and the Mid-Hill Highway running from east to west across the country are expected to improve market linkages and enable progress. Similarly, major irrigation efforts such as Sikta Project and that Rani Jamara Kulariya Project promise, if completed with no further delay, to greatly facilitate commercial agriculture in Nepal.

3.19.10 Export growth rate of competitive agro commodities

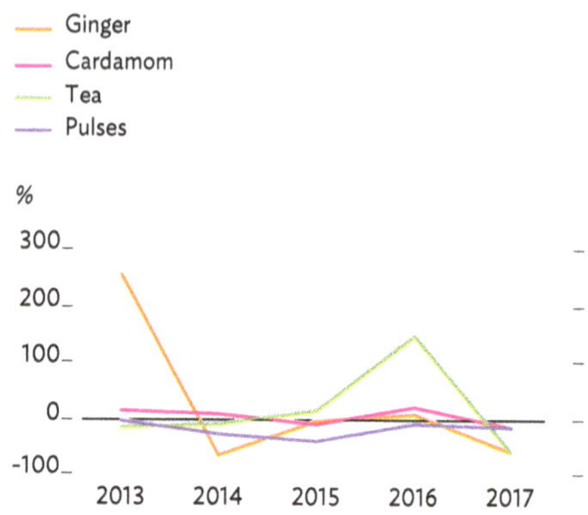

Note: Years are fiscal years ending on 15 July of that year.
Source: Nepal Rastra Bank. 2018. *Current Macroeconomic and Financial Situation*, various years. http://www.nrb.org.np.

Pakistan

Growth picked up in fiscal 2017 to 5.3% as services grew, agriculture rebounded, and consumer and investment demand strengthened. However, a fiscal lapse and continued weak exports caused large budget and current account deficits and a loss of foreign exchange reserves. The outlook is for wider current account deficits and moderating growth. Addressing fiscal and external imbalances and revitalizing exports are challenges now and following elections in 2018.

Economic performance

GDP growth in fiscal year 2017 (FY2017, ended 30 June 2017) accelerated to 5.3% on continued strong growth in services at 6.0%, led by wholesale retail and trade, and on a rebound in agriculture (Figure 3.20.1). The strong performance was underpinned by expansion in manufacturing, construction on major infrastructure investments, and higher consumer spending.

Expenditure on private consumption, providing about 80% of GDP, grew by 8.6% and remained the largest contributor to growth in FY2017 (Figure 3.20.2). Faster growth in fixed investment, at 8.3%, reflected larger public investment, while private investment grew by only 4.1%, restrained by substantial infrastructure deficits, especially for electric power supply. The deficits are being addressed, especially by investment in energy, including under the China–Pakistan Economic Corridor (CPEC) project. A number of projects, especially in power supply, are already completed or nearly so, with financing from government development expenditure, multilateral development banks, and CPEC resources. The large increase in the volume of imports in the face of stagnant exports pushed net exports substantially lower during the year.

To support growth now enabled by improved energy supply, the State Bank of Pakistan, the central bank, maintained its policy rate at 5.75% in FY2017, which facilitated a 13.7% increase in money supply. Credit to the private sector grew by 16.8%, the largest such expansion in recent years. The average interest rate on new lending to the private sector was, at 7.25%, little changed from a year earlier.

Average inflation in FY2017 reached 4.2%, higher by 1.3 percentage points than in the previous year, when global prices were highly favorable to Pakistan, especially for oil (Figure 3.20.3). Food inflation averaged 3.8%, though shortages of some perishable products sometimes pushed prices higher.

3.20.1 Supply-side contributions to growth

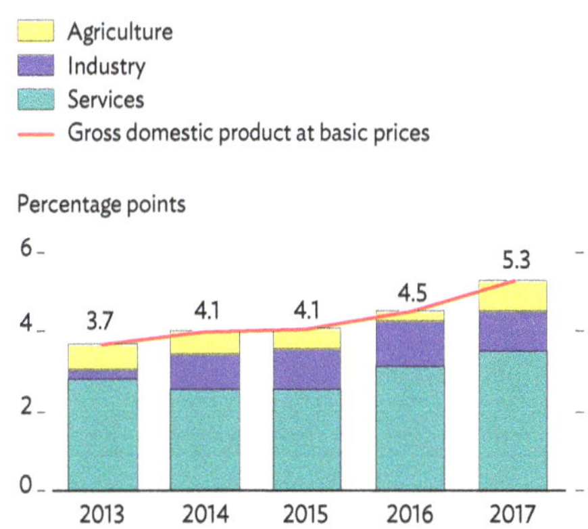

Note: Years are fiscal years ending on 30 June of that year.
Source: Ministry of Finance. *Pakistan Economic Survey 2016–17.* http://www.finance.gov.pk.

3.20.2 Demand-side contributions to growth

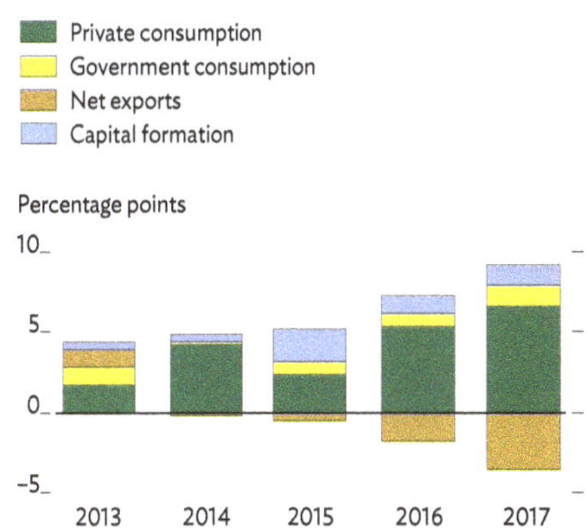

Note: Years are fiscal years ending on 30 June of that year.
Source: Ministry of Finance. *Pakistan Economic Survey 2016–17.* http://www.finance.gov.pk.

This chapter was written by Guntur Sugiyarto and Farzana Noshab of the Pakistan Resident Mission, ADB, Islamabad.

Strong domestic demand was evident as core inflation, which leaves out food and energy, increased to an average of 5.2% from 4.2% in FY2016.

The consolidated federal and provincial budget deficit climbed to 5.8% of GDP in FY2017, well above the target of 3.8% and the 4.5% outcome a year earlier (Figure 3.20.4). This larger deficit came as revenue collection slowed and development expenditure rose. Tax revenue grew by only 8.4%, down from the 21.3% gain in the preceding year. Only higher nontax revenue allowed the ratio of total revenue to GDP to increase, and only marginally to 12.5%. The weaker tax performance reflected various tax incentives for agriculture and exporters and new revenue measures that were less than effective. A sharp increase in total expenditure by 17.3% was underpinned by a nearly 30% surge in development expenditure, which was more pronounced at the provincial level than at the federal. About 70% of the deficit was financed through domestic bank borrowing, with the central bank providing the bulk of the credit.

Total public debt equaled 67.2% of GDP in FY2017, essentially unchanged from a year earlier and continuing to breach the Fiscal Responsibility Debt Limitation Act ceiling of 60%. Public external debt and liabilities rose to 20.6% of GDP, while the ratio of domestic debt to GDP declined marginally to 46.6%. The cost of external debt servicing rose again to 2.0% of GDP after having declined to 1.6% in the preceding 3 years.

A surge of imports was the main reason the current account deficit widened significantly in FY2017 to $12.4 billion, equal to 4.1% of GDP and well up from 1.7% a year earlier (Figure 3.20.5). The trade deficit reached $26.6 billion as imports increased by 17.6% on large increases for oil at much higher prices, liquefied natural gas, investment goods, and food. Exports were essentially unchanged, but this was a marked improvement over the 8.8% decline recorded in FY2016. An increase in the combined service and primary income deficit reflected in part lower receipts from the US Coalition Support Fund. Workers' remittances, the major offset to persistently large trade deficit, fell by 2.8% to $19.4 billion after significant annual increases for over a decade (Figure 3.20.6).

Financial inflows increased to $10.4 billion, mainly on government borrowing. To fill the current account financing gap, foreign exchange reserves were drawn down by $2.0 billion, leaving $16.1 billion, or cover for only 3 months of imports of goods and services (Figure 3.20.7).

Economic prospects

GDP growth is expected to accelerate to 5.6% on strong prospects for large-scale manufacturing and crop harvests for a second year in a row, continued buoyant domestic demand, including from CPEC and other infrastructure investments,

3.20.3 Inflation

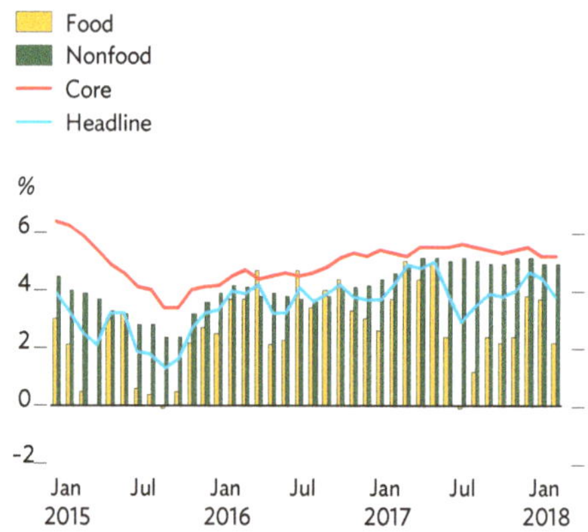

Source: State Bank of Pakistan. *Economic Data*. http://www.sbp.org.pk (accessed 22 March 2018).

3.20.4 Government budget indicators

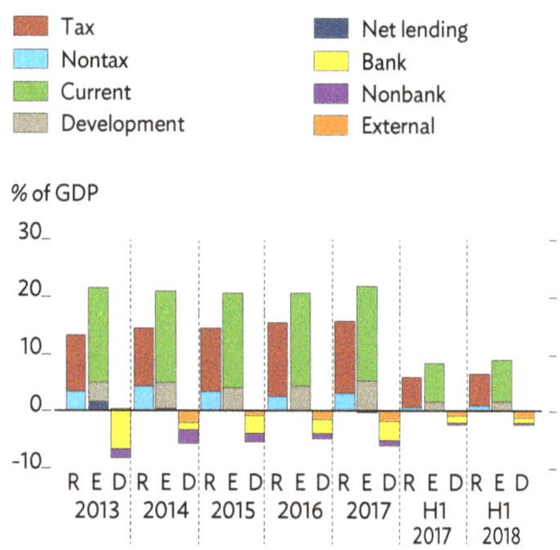

R = revenue, E = expenditure, D = deficit financing.

Note: Years are fiscal years ending on 30 June of that year.

Sources: Ministry of Finance. *Pakistan Economic Survey 2016–2017; Pakistan Summary of Consolidated Federal & Provincial Budgetry Operations, 2016–17.*

3.20.5 Current account components

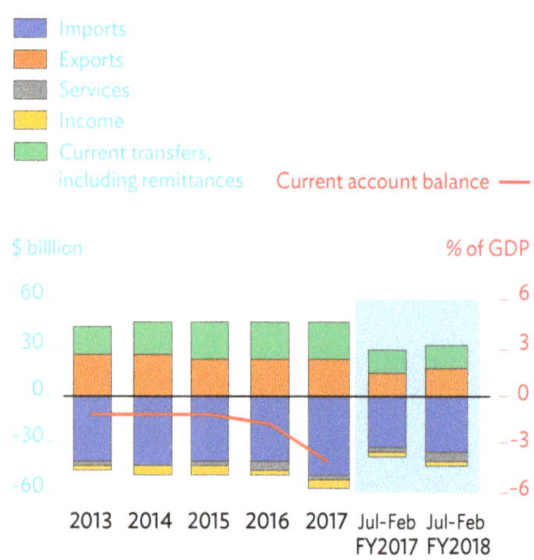

Note: Years are fiscal years ending on 30 June of that year.

Source: State Bank of Pakistan. *Economic Data*. http://www.sbp.org.pk (accessed 28 March 2018).

strengthened economic growth globally that will revive exports, much improved power supply, and commodity prices that are still broadly favorable despite a further double-digit increase in the oil price. GDP growth is expected to adjust downward in FY2019 to 5.1% as balance-of-payment constraints seem to outweigh improvements to supply-side factors such as better security and energy supply. While the budget deficit may moderate slightly in FY2018 from a year earlier, spillover from higher investment expenditure is expected to widen the current account deficit. Securing adequate financing to contain the drawdown in foreign exchange reserves is a concern.

Growth in FY2018 is being led by large-scale manufacturing, which expanded by 6.3% in the first 7 months of FY2018 from 3.6% in the same period last year. This improvement was largely from solid expansion in cement, iron, and steel products that reflects higher demand from construction on public infrastructure projects. Higher domestic demand was indicated by sharp expansion in consumer goods such as automobiles and electronics. Recovery in engineering, petroleum products, and rubber also contributed to growth, which is expected to continue in light of a favorable demand outlook.

Provisional estimates for major winter crops suggest strong agriculture in FY2018 for a second year in a row, supported by increased cultivated area, fertilizer use, and credit. However, the wheat crop is expected to be slightly below target with reduced sown area.

Food inflation was 2.2% in the first 8 months of FY2018, well below that in the year-earlier period, as abundant agricultural supplies held headline inflation to 3.8% even as nonfood inflation rose to 5.0%. Currency depreciation and the transmission of rising international oil prices to the domestic market are expected to boost inflation in the second half of the year, generating average inflation at 4.5% for all of FY2018. Inflation is projected to accelerate marginally to 4.8% in FY2019, reflecting increases in global oil prices and Pakistan rupee depreciation against major currencies.

The central bank raised its policy rate by 25 basis points to 6.00% in its January 2018 monetary policy statement and maintained it there (Figure 3.20.8). While credit growth slowed in the first 8 months of FY2018 from the year-earlier period, demand pressures have kept imports high, and the resulting steady drawdown of foreign exchange reserves indicates a need for policy tightening. Other concerns were the rise in global oil prices and a firming outlook for higher interest rates in the US and global capital markets. In a departure from past policy, the central bank has permitted greater flexibility in determining the Pakistan rupee–dollar exchange rate since December 2017, and by the end of March 2018 the rupee had depreciated by 9.2% (Figure 3.20.9). Flexibility in determining the rate will help mitigate eroded competitiveness indicated in recent years by rupee appreciation in real effective terms.

3.20.6 Remittances

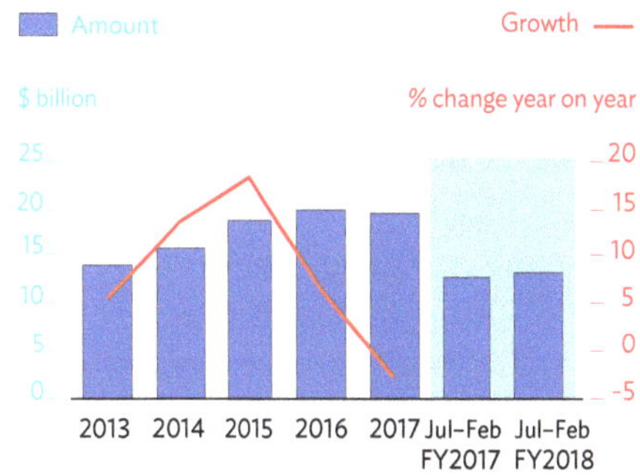

Note: Years are fiscal years ending on 30 June of that year.
Source: State Bank of Pakistan. *Economic Data.* http://www.sbp.org.pk (accessed 28 March 2018).

3.20.7 Gross international reserves

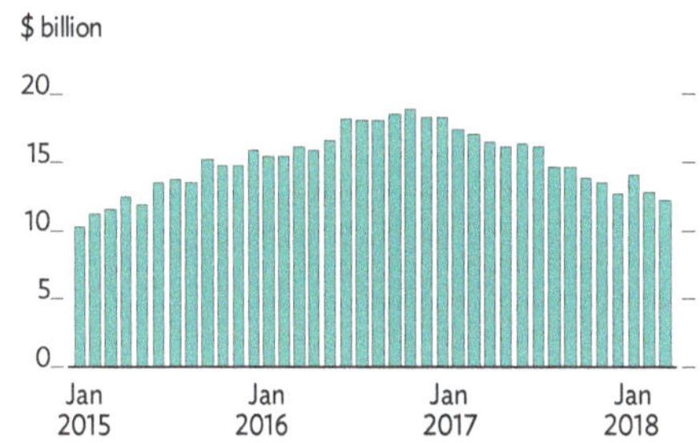

Source: State Bank of Pakistan. *Economic Data.* http://www.sbp.org.pk (accessed 26 March 2018).

3.20.8 Interest rates

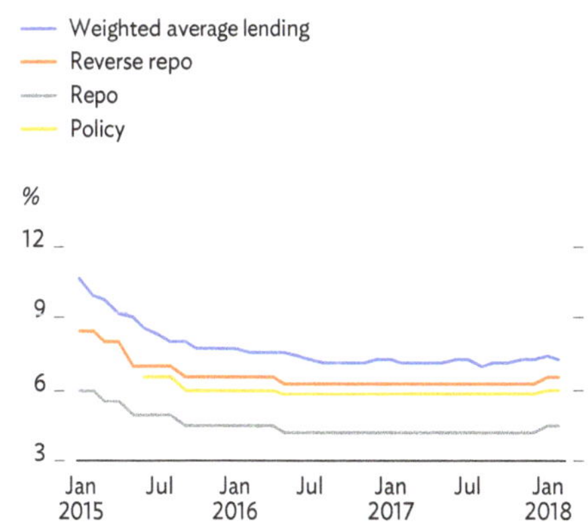

Sources: State Bank of Pakistan. *Economic Data.* http://www.sbp.org.pk (accessed 26 March 2018); *Monetary Policy Information Compendium January 2018.*

The consolidated government budget for FY2018 envisages a fiscal deficit equal to 4.1% of GDP, much narrower than the 5.8% deficit in FY2017. Higher tax collection and further rationalization of current expenditure are expected to allow capital expenditure of 6.3% of GDP while meeting the fiscal deficit target.

Budget expenditure grew by 14.0% in the first half of FY2018 on increases in both current and development expenditures. Tax collection rose by 16.4%, and total revenue including nontax revenue by nearly 20%. Higher tax revenue and $2.5 billion in proceeds from a $1.0 billion *sukuk* bond and a $1.5 billion eurobond issued in November 2017 contained government domestic borrowing for budgetary support. If this momentum continues in the second half of the year, the budget deficit may be held below 5.8% of GDP.

The current account remained under pressure in the first 8 months of FY2018 as the deficit rose to $10.8 billion, or 4.8% of estimated GDP for the period, from $7.2 billion in the year-earlier period. The deficit expanded on larger imports that widened the trade deficit despite a strong revival in exports. Remittances, the traditional offset to the trade deficit, grew by 3.4% in the period, reversing a decline a year earlier, but had only a limited impact on the current account. Net financial inflows increased by about 14% from the year-earlier period. Filling the financing gap required a drawdown of $3.9 billion in foreign exchange reserves to $12.2 billion (Figure 3.20.10).

Exports revived to grow by 12.2% in the first 8 months of FY2018. Large increases in food exports (mainly sugar and rice), readymade garments and knitwear, leather manufactures, and chemical and pharmaceutical products accounted for the bulk of the rebound.

Despite new regulatory duties, imports grew by 17.3% in the first 8 months of FY2018, slightly faster than in the comparable period of FY2017 to meet sustained domestic demand and the continued large import needs of infrastructure projects reflected in double-digit growth in machinery, metals, and vehicles. Imports of petroleum products were especially large because of higher prices, accounting for a third of the rise in imports.

In the remainder of FY2018, the current account deficit should be reined in by the lagged effects of adjustments to regulatory duties, currency depreciation and credit tightening in January, and the favorable external environment for exports. However, with increased seasonal spending on infrastructure projects, the current account deficit will likely edge up a bit to equal 4.9% of GDP. The amount of foreign financing available in the final months of FY2018 will determine any further pressure on foreign exchange reserves. The preliminary projection for the current account deficit in FY2019 is

3.20.1 Selected economic indicators (%)

	2018	2019
GDP growth	5.6	5.1
Inflation	4.5	4.8
Current account balance (share of GDP)	-4.9	-4.5

Note: Years are fiscal years ending on 30 June of that year.
Source: ADB estimates.

3.20.9 Exchange rates

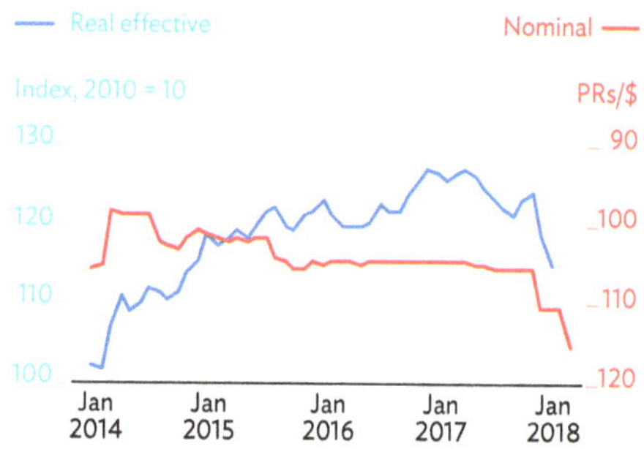

Source: State Bank of Pakistan. *Economic Data*. http://www.sbp.org.pk (accessed 26 March 2018).

3.20.10 Capital and financial account balance

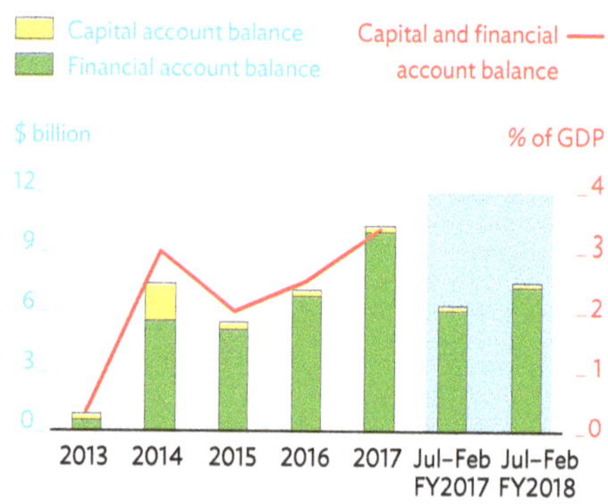

Note: Years are fiscal years ending on 30 June of that year.
Source: State Bank of Pakistan. *Economic Data*. http://www.sbp.org.pk (accessed 28 March 2018).

4.5% of GDP, with somewhat slower growth but continued implementation of CPEC projects. Successfully financing these large investments will require the government to pursue real structural reform.

Policy challenge—revitalizing exports

Declining exports pose a major challenge to the sustainability of external accounts. Exports grew on average by 10.7% per annum from FY2004 to FY2011, peaking at $25.4 billion at the end of the period. Exports then fell by an average of 2.6% per annum to $21.9 billion in FY2017 (Figure 3.20.11). Over the past decade, exports as a share of GDP have contracted significantly, from 11.2% in 2007 to 7.2% in 2017, far below the 28% average in developing Asia. Clearly, the circumstances that caused exports to deteriorate have undermined economic growth, beyond directly worsening the country's external position.

Various structural weaknesses undermine Pakistan's trade performance. In particular, weak logistics and trade facilitation, including customs procedures, add to transaction costs. In *Doing Business 2018*, the World Bank ranked Pakistan 171 out of 189 economies in ease of trading across borders. Further, business in general suffers under a tax structure with multiple taxes and high rates. The time required to prepare and pay taxes disadvantages business in Pakistan more than in peer developing economies. A simple average of most favored nation applied tariff rates stood at a high 12.1% in 2016. In addition, the overvalued domestic currency is thought to hold down exports. The Pakistan rupee has appreciated by 20% in real effective terms since FY2011, as exports fell by 17%.

Evidence suggests that supply-side factors—including workforce skills, the business environment, and infrastructure factors, especially power supply and logistics—significantly limit export performance. To address these issues, the government is preparing a medium-term framework on trade policy that will be implemented over the next 5 years. It aims to revitalize exports by promoting investment and resolving trade facilitation, e-commerce, and tariff issues. These reforms are steps in the right direction and align with large CPEC investments now improving infrastructure and connectivity. Both efforts are essential to facilitate Pakistan's integration into global value chains and production networks.

In addition, the government should consider other reforms: greater exchange rate flexibility, enforcing industrial compliance with quality control and other standards, operationalizing a national single window for trade, skills development that aligns with industry demand, and instituting legal and institutional frameworks to support new industries such as information and communication technology services.

3.20.11 Compounded annual growth of exports

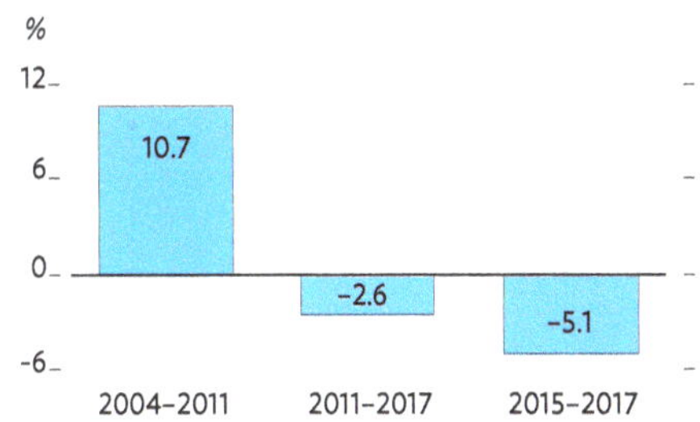

Note: Years are fiscal years ending on 30 June of that year.
Source: ADB computation based on State Bank of Pakistan data.

Sri Lanka

Growth in 2017 slowed to a new low since 2001 as agriculture contracted and industry and services slackened. Inflation surged briefly, and the current account deficit widened. The outlook is for gradually improving growth as structural reform addresses major fiscal and external imbalances. Dealing with the weak performance of state-owned enterprises is a major component of the revenue-based fiscal consolidation needed to achieve durable and inclusive growth.

Economic performance

Growth slowed dramatically to 3.1% in 2017 as bad weather shrank output from agriculture for a second year (Figure 3.21.1). Weaker growth in industry and services contributed to the slowdown. The ratio of revenue to GDP continued to improve as fiscal consolidation aligned with the government's economic program, supported by the International Monetary Fund (IMF), to reduce fiscal and external vulnerabilities. Monetary tightening brought growth in credit to the private sector to a more sustainable rate of 14.7%, following 21.9% expansion in 2016.

On the supply side, rice production declined by 4.0% in 2017, while the production of oil-yielding fruit dropped by 19.5% and of vegetables by 16.5%. Tea production finally rebounded after a 3-year decline but remained below potential. In sum, agriculture contracted by 0.8% but improved on a much larger 3.8% drop in 2016. Industry, which provides about 30% of value added, grew by 3.9%, well below expansion at 5.8% a year earlier. Textiles, apparel, and leather, which make up half of exports, grew by 5.7%, having strengthened in the second half of the year following the restoration of privileges under the European Union's Generalised Scheme of Preferences Plus (GSP+). However, growth in construction plunged to 3.1%, following 8.3% expansion a year earlier, as growth in fixed investment slowed.

Services, which provide just over 60% of value added, expanded by 3.1%, well below their 4.7% performance in 2016. Growth came from accommodation, finance, real estate, health care, and other personal services. These gains were partly offset, however, by contraction in public administration and mere 0.9% expansion in the important transportation sector, down from 5.5% growth in 2016.

3.21.1 GDP growth by sector

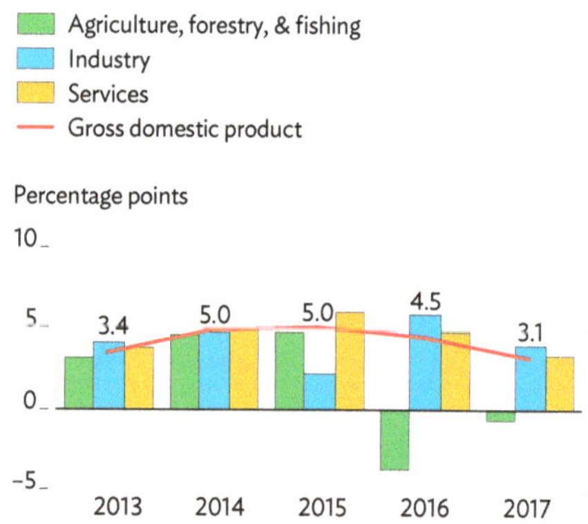

Source: Department of Census and Statistics of Sri Lanka. http://www.statistics.gov.lk/ (accessed 20 March 2018).

3.21.2 Demand-side contributions to growth

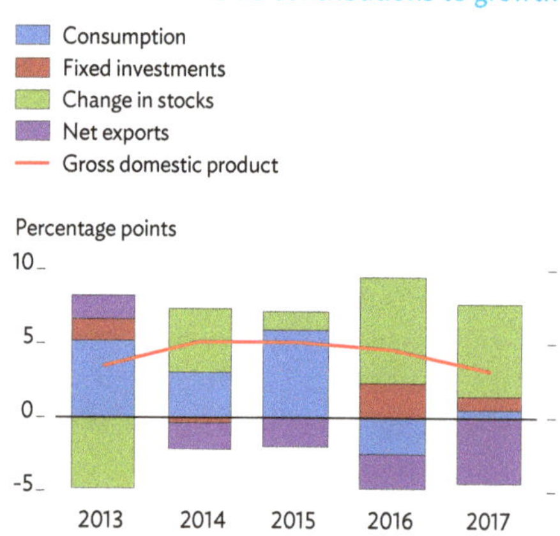

Source: Department of Census and Statistics of Sri Lanka. http://statistics.gov.lk.

This chapter was written by Utsav Kumar, Nimali Hasitha Wickremasinghe, and Savindi Jayakody of the Sri Lanka Resident Mission, ADB, Colombo.

On the demand side, preliminary data for 2017 indicate that private consumption grew by 1.3%. However, government consumption contracted markedly under fiscal consolidation, limiting the contribution of total consumption to growth (Figure 3.21.2). The slowdown in fixed investment also limited its contribution to growth. Net exports dragged growth lower than a year earlier on a larger volume of imports. Increased inventories again buoyed growth but much of this is probably statistical discrepancies in the estimates.

Inflation was 7.3% year on year to December 2017, averaging 7.7% for the year. An increase in the value-added tax (VAT) rate from 11% to 15% in November 2016 contributed to inflationary pressures, but the main driver was high food inflation pushed up by weather-induced supply shortages to average 11.3% from to 3.1% in 2016 (Figure 3.21.3). Nonfood inflation moderated substantially during the year on weaker demand to average 4.9%, as did core inflation. Then overall inflation and its components converged at just over 3% in February 2018 from a year earlier. This marked fall reflected both improved supply, indicated by price deflation month on month, and a large base effect.

The revenue ratio is estimated to have improved to 15.3% of GDP in 2017 as tax collection benefited from an increase in the value-added tax rate from 11% to 15% (Figure 3.21.4). Higher interest costs drove current expenditure marginally higher to equal 15.8% of GDP. With continued government attempts to rationalize expenditure, current expenditure excepting interest is estimated to have been contained at 10.2% of GDP. Public investment is estimated to have fallen marginally to 4.9% of GDP from 5.0% in 2016. Expenditure targets were not achieved because floods and landslides necessitated unanticipated expenses to assist farmers and other affected families and to reconstruct damaged infrastructure. Despite this, the primary balance recorded a surplus over the first 10 months of 2017, for the first time in 63 years. The fiscal deficit in 2017 is estimated to have narrowed to the equivalent of 5.2% of GDP from 5.4% in 2016. Early estimates indicate a small increase in the ratio of government debt to GDP in 2017 from 78.8% in 2016 (Figure 3.21.5).

Monetary tightening begun in 2016 continued in early 2017. The Central Bank of Sri Lanka raised policy rates by 25 basis points in March 2017—to 7.25% for the standing deposit facility and 8.75% for the standing lending facility—to calm rising inflation that stemmed from the increase in VAT rate and higher food prices (Figure 3.21.6). As a result, growth in credit to the private sector decelerated from 21.9% in December 2016 to 14.7% in 2017 as monetary tightening took hold (Figure 3.21.7). Then, given marked improvement in inflation in the early months of 2018 and lackluster growth in the economy, the Monetary Board on 3 April decided to reduce the standing lending facility rate by 25 basis points to 8.50%.

3.21.3 Inflation

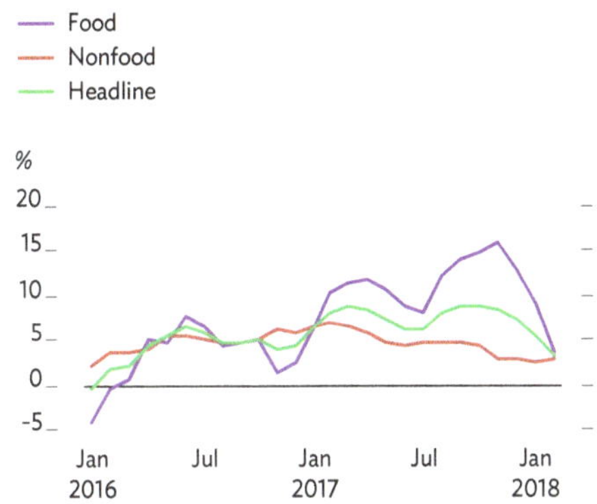

Source: Department of Census and Statistics of Sri Lanka. http://statistics.gov.lk.

3.21.4 Government finance

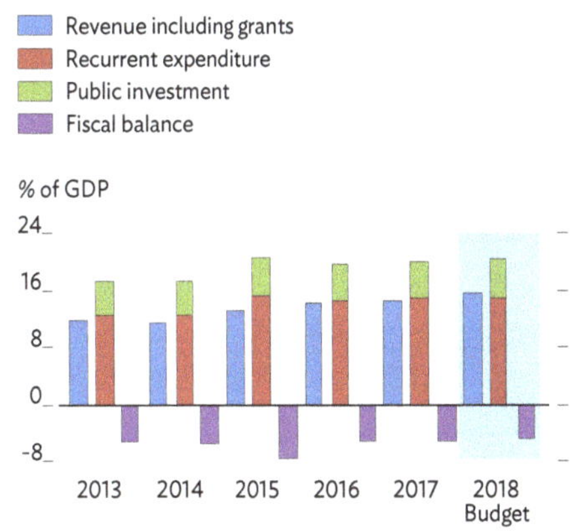

Sources: Ministry of Finance; Budget speech 2018.

3.21.5 Government debt

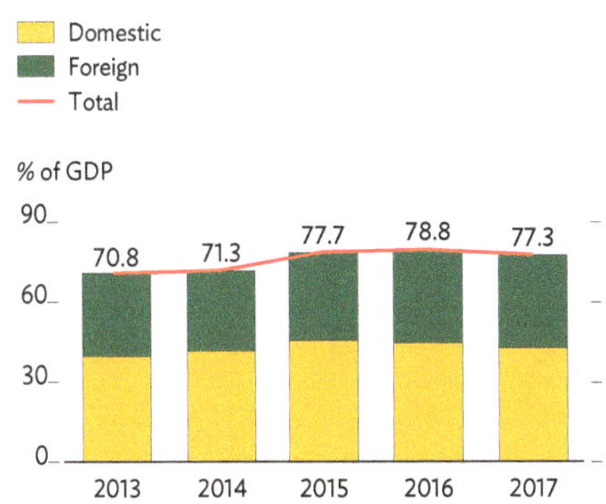

Note: 2017 is to the end of September.

Sources: Central Bank of Sri Lanka. *Monthly Economic Indicators*. http://www.cbsl.gov.lk; ADB estimates.

Exports grew by 10.2% in 2017, supported by tea and garments. Higher prices and volume expanded tea exports by 20.5% in 2017, accounting for a quarter of the increase. Garments, Sri Lanka's major export, saw exports drop in the first half of the year but pick up to grow by 3.0% as the restoration of GSP+ took effect. Imports expanded by 9.4% mainly on higher oil import volumes for thermal electric power generation necessitated by drought and on higher international prices. Rice imports expanded to meet a shortfall in domestic production. Fuel imports accounted for 54% of import growth, and rice imports 16%.

As political uncertainty worsened in the Middle East and the region sought to replace migrants with domestic workers, especially in the skilled labor category, outward migration from Sri Lanka continued to decline. Remittances were, at $7.1 billion, 1.1% lower than 2016. Tourist arrivals increased by 3.2% to reach 2.1 million, and earnings reached $3.6 billion (Figure 3.21.8). With a higher trade deficit and reduced invisible earnings, the current account deficit widened to the equivalent of 3.0% of GDP from 2.4% in 2016.

Sri Lanka issued two international bonds in 2017, one raising $1.5 billion and the other $515 million. Inflows strengthened by $293 million on receipts from China Merchants Group in December 2017, the first payment on the long-term lease of Hambantota Port, and by the release of the fourth tranche of the ongoing IMF program. Gross official reserves increased by $2.0 billion to $8.0 billion at the end of December 2017, sufficient to cover 4.6 months of imports (Figure 3.21.9). The Sri Lanka rupee depreciated by 2.0% in 2017 to end the year at SLRs152.8 to the dollar, but appreciated by 3.4% in real effective terms (Figure 3.21.10).

3.21.6 Deposit and lending rates

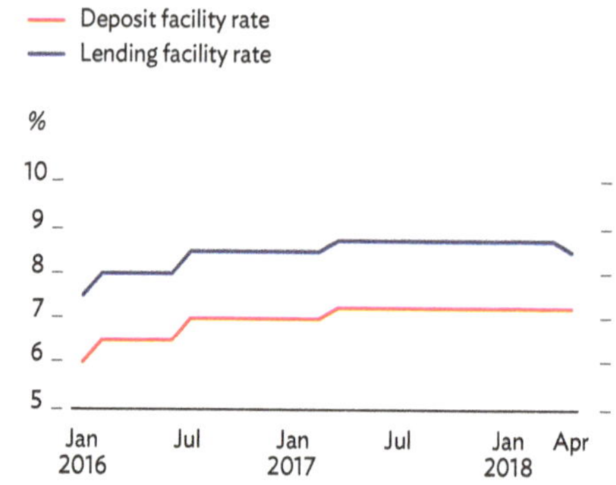

Source: Central Bank of Sri Lanka. http://www.cbsl.gov.lk.

3.21.7 Interest rate, credit, and money growth

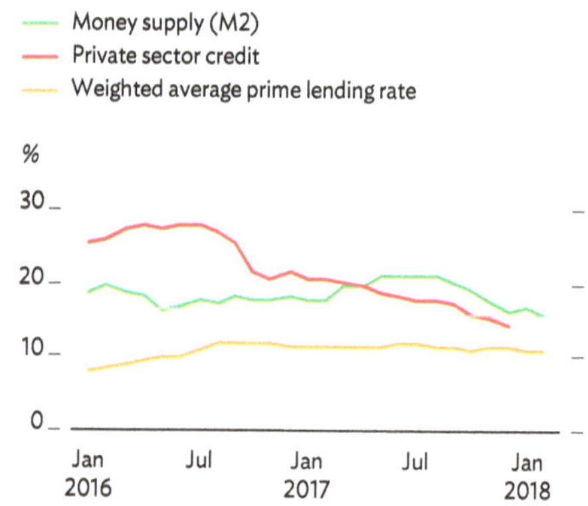

Sources: Central Bank of Sri Lanka. Weekly Economic Indicators, various issues.

Economic prospects

Growth over the next 2 years will depend on agriculture and the political climate as elections approach. Assuming normal weather in 2018 and 2019, agriculture is expected to rebound to 6.0% growth in 2018 and recover fully in 2019, expanding by 5.6%.

Industry will benefit from recovery in agriculture as demand expands and agro-industry recovers in 2018. Apparel will benefit from continued strong global growth and GSP+. Construction will expand on continuing government projects and new private sector ventures, mainly hotels and apartments, and with construction starting on buildings in the large Colombo Port City financial center project. Industry is expected to expand by 3.9% 2018 and 4.5% in 2019.

Growth in services is forecast at 3.7% in 2018 and 4.6% in 2019 on higher demand as rural areas recover, continued growth in financial services and tourist arrivals, and a small

3.21.8 Current account components

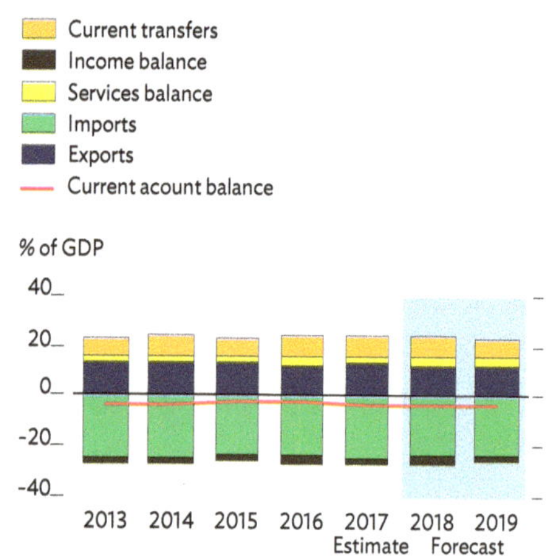

Sources: Central Bank of Sri Lanka. *Annual Report 2016*; ADB estimates.

expansion in public administration and professional services. Tight policy will constrain government spending, and private investment may take time to pick up. On the other hand, government remedial action on several fronts and a reform-oriented budget should improve the business climate and attract new investment. On balance, growth is forecast to rebound to 4.2% in 2018 and reach 4.8% in 2019.

Food inflation is expected to abate as agriculture recovers under normal weather. By February 2018, food inflation had dropped to 3.2% year on year from 7.3% in December 2017 as overall inflation settled at a low of 3.0%, mainly reflecting a high base effect. Inflation is projected to average 5.2% in 2018 and slow further to 5.0% in 2019. The introduction of automatic pricing formulas for oil and electricity in 2018, and greater currency depreciation as foreign reserves are built up to meet debt service requirements, are likely to exert inflationary pressures.

Revenue collection is expected to continue to improve with the new Inland Revenue Act that went into effect at the beginning of April 2018. It seeks to increase tax revenue by eliminating many exemptions, reducing the tax-exempt threshold for small and medium-sized enterprises, bringing most corporations under the higher 28% rate, and introducing new taxes, notably one on capital gains. Tax revenue is expected to increase by 800 basis points to equal 14.3% of GDP in 2018 as total revenue including nontax revenue and grants amounts to 16.3% of GDP. Expenditure is budgeted to be marginally higher at 21.1% of GDP, up from 20.6% in 2017. The increase covers higher interest payments and budgeted public investment. Meanwhile, current expenditure excluding interest is expected to be marginally lower than in 2017. The budget targets a deficit equal to 4.8% of GDP.

A major challenge for the government is the bunching in 2018–2024 of $22 billion in debt repayments, with $4.2 billion due in 2019. The new Liability Management Act enables the central bank to borrow above the limits of the appropriation bill for debt repayment, a practice not previously allowed. In addition, proceeds from the Hambantota Port deal are expected to be set aside for debt repayment. The government plans to issue $2 billion in sovereign bonds and $3 billion in Sri Lanka development bonds in 2018. In March 2018, the central bank called for proposals to raise a foreign currency term financing facility of up to $1 billion to fund budgetary expenditure.

Exports are projected to expand moderately by 6.5% in 2018, still driven by apparel and tea, and by 6.0% in 2019. The rupee is likely to come under pressure in 2018 from the need to provide for debt repayment. It depreciated by 1.7% in the first 3 months of 2018. A hands-off approach helped to maintain reserves at $7.9 billion to the end of February 2018.

3.21.9 Gross official reserves

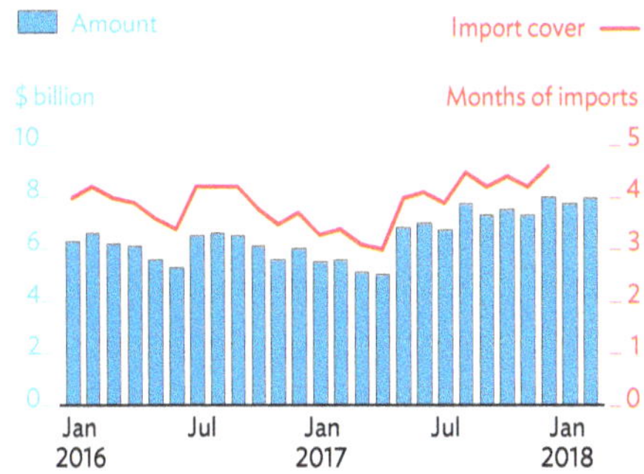

Source: Central Bank of Sri Lanka. http://www.cbsl.gov.lk.

3.21.10 Exchange rates

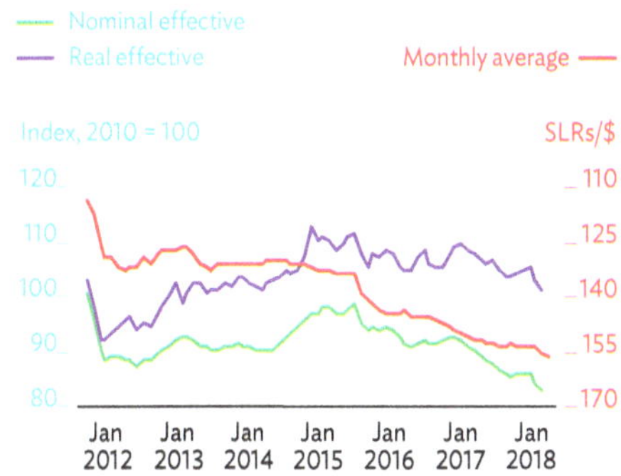

Source: Central Bank of Sri Lanka. http://www.cbsl.gov.lk.

3.21.1 Selected economic indicators (%)

	2018	2019
GDP growth	4.2	4.8
Inflation	5.2	5.0
Current account balance (share of GDP)	-2.7	-2.5

Source: ADB estimates.

Imports are expected to expand moderately as oil import volumes drop with normal rainfall enabling hydropower generation. Import growth, mainly to supply construction and the apparel industry, is forecast at 5.5% in 2018 and 6.0% in 2019. The current account deficit is projected to equal 2.7% of GDP in 2018 and 2.5% in 2019.

The outlook has downside risks. Weather is an obvious concern. With local government elections in February 2018 having dealt the ruling coalition an unexpected setback, political uncertainty could damage investor confidence and undermine the reform agenda. An unexpectedly large rise in global interest rates or volatility in capital markets could sharply limit planned borrowing and increase its cost.

Policy challenge—reforming state-owned enterprises

State-owned enterprises (SOEs) are estimated to account for some 17% of economic activity in Sri Lanka, their dominating presence spanning infrastructure services, banking and insurance, hotels, media, salt production, plantations, and livestock.

While finance SOEs are profitable, the sector loses money as a whole. Publicly guaranteed debt including SOE debt is estimated at the equivalent of 4.2% of GDP. Additional SOE financial obligations were estimated to equal 11.9% of GDP at the end of 2016. SOE demand for financing thus potentially crowds out credit to the private sector. Continued losses undermine fiscal consolidation and divert resources from productive developmental needs. Weak SOE finances and their lack of high-quality public service delivery constrain productivity and growth.

Under the ongoing program with the IMF, statements of corporate intent signed for the five largest SOEs are expected to enhance oversight and financial discipline. An outcome of these statements is a requirement that fuel and electricity come under an automatic pricing mechanism, which the cabinet is expected to approve in 2018. The government's approach under its Vision 2025 economic program is to improve SOE governance structures by enhancing accountability and to restructure them to make them commercially viable, in part through cost-reflective pricing and targeted subsidies to the poor to ensure equity.

The government is considering a proposal to set up a state-owned holding company along the lines of Singapore's Temasek Holdings. Critical to its success would be an appropriate regulatory framework, a governance structure, accountability mechanisms, an adequate pool of technocrats, and arm's length distance from politics.

Worldwide, SOE reform is inevitably intertwined with politics. SOE reform in Sri Lanka, first initiated in the 1990s, has since been carried out only sporadically and in line with the economic policy of the government of the day. Given the efficiency, fiscal, and distributional implications of an underperforming SOE sector, continued SOE reform is essential beyond the life of the IMF program. Meaningful and sustained SOE reform depends on building a political consensus and ring-fencing the reform process from change in the political order.

Equally important is that future reform draw upon lessons from past experience. It must avoid institutional lapses such as the divesture of Lanka Marine Services, a provider of bunker fuel. Following a complaint filed by the Committee on Public Enterprises that there were irregularities in the privatization process that benefited a private holding company, the Supreme Court in 2009 reversed the privatization and ordered that the enterprise be reverted to state ownership. Experience with the use of management contracts for plantations has been similarly problematic, partly because short contract duration disincentivizes investment to enhance productivity.

The liberalization of the telecom sector in the late 1990s offers several positive lessons. In 1997, the government initiated reforms in the sector with the sale through competitive bidding of its 35% stake in Sri Lanka Telecom. An employee share ownership plan was instituted to counter anticipated trade union resistance, with union members encouraged to study similar privatization processes. Privatization was accompanied by the setting up of the Telecommunications Regulatory Commission as an independent regulator to pursue reform to make the industry more competitive. Competition, contestability, and regulation oriented toward competition were crucial to successful reform in the industry.

Ownership change is not a panacea for underperforming SOEs. What may matter more toward improving performance is to institutionalize incentives while strengthening accountability and governance. Four elements are likely to be critical to SOE reform: efficient state provision of public services that takes into account their cost, a competitive business environment, independent regulators, and fully transparent SOE finances.

SOUTHEAST ASIA

- BRUNEI DARUSSALAM
- CAMBODIA
- INDONESIA
- LAO PEOPLE'S DEMOCRATIC REPUBLIC
- MALAYSIA
- MYANMAR
- PHILIPPINES
- SINGAPORE
- THAILAND
- VIET NAM

Brunei Darussalam

With a rise in global oil prices, the economy seems to have posted marginally positive growth in 2017, for the first time in 5 years. Growth should strengthen this year to 1.5% and next year to 2.0%. Inflation will likely edge up but continue to be low, and the current account will continue to post substantial though narrowing surpluses. Enhancing domestic competition is key to diversifying the economy.

Economic performance

GDP is estimated to have grown by 0.8% in 2017, following 4 years of economic contraction (Figure 3.22.1). Last year's turnaround to marginal growth was underpinned by increased government consumption and a recovery in fixed investment.

Government expenditure on consumption, which had declined by 6.5% in 2016, rose by 10.2% in the first 9 months of last year over the same period a year earlier. It is likely to have kept up that pace in the last quarter as higher international oil prices boosted government revenue. Data for the first 3 quarters of 2017 suggest that a recovery in investment is under way, with fixed investment growing by 11.0% year on year. Even as higher oil prices boost export revenue, export volumes of goods and services continued to decline, dragging on GDP growth.

By sector, contraction in agriculture persisted for a second year in a row, but industry and services reversed 2016 declines and posted marginally positive growth (Figure 3.22.2). Growth in services such as hotels and restaurants, and transportation, is estimated to have been positive last year, reversing declines in 2016.

Deflation that began in 2014 stretched into 2017 as the consumer price index slipped by 0.2%. Prices continued to ease last year for many consumer goods and services. These declines more than offset price increases for transportation, education, food and beverages, and communication.

The US dollar value of customs-based merchandise exports, mostly crude oil and liquefied natural gas, increased by an estimated 13.6% in 2017, reversing a 22.5% decline in 2016 (Figure 3.22.3). Higher global oil and gas prices lifted export receipts, offsetting the decline in the volume of exports. Meanwhile, the US dollar value of customs-based imports, bolstered by purchases of machinery and transport equipment and of consumer goods, rose even faster, by 19.5%. Despite the stiff rise in the import bill, the trade surplus widened, further

This chapter was written by Shikha Jha and Pilipinas Quising of the Economic Research and Regional Cooperation Department, ADB, Manila.

3.22.1 GDP growth

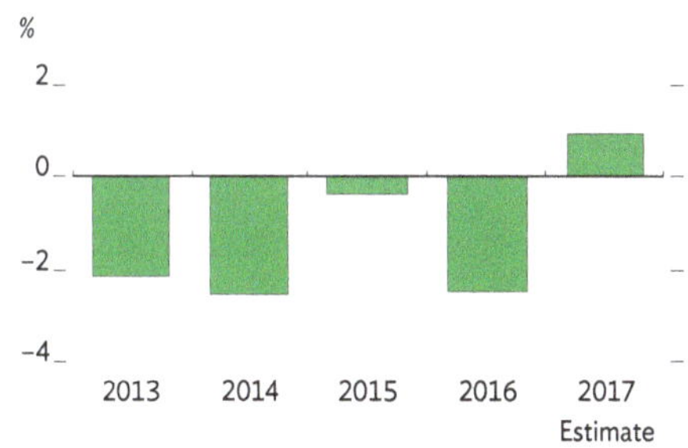

Source: *Asian Development Outlook* database.

3.22.2 Sectoral growth

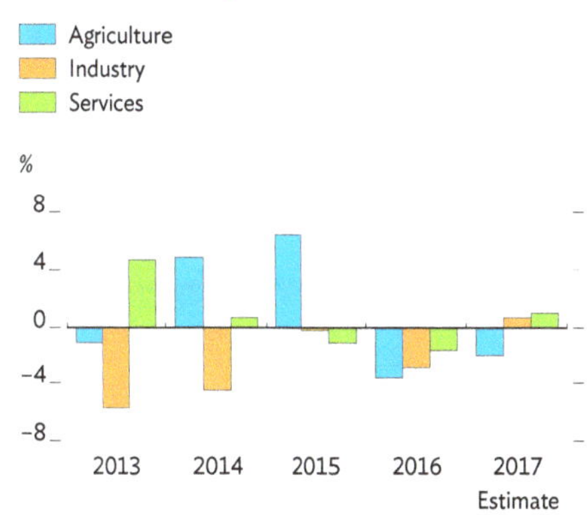

Sources: CEIC Data Company (accessed 16 March 2018); ADB estimates.

building up the current account surplus from the equivalent of 15.5% of GDP in 2016 to an estimated 19.0% in 2017.

Government revenues began to shrink in 2014, as energy prices declined, and continued to slump in fiscal year 2016 (FY2016, ended 31 March 2017), but are estimated to have risen by a fifth in FY2017 (Figure 3.22.4). At the same time, fiscal expenditure dropped from B$6.1 billion in FY2016 to a budgeted B$5.3 billion in FY2017, narrowing the fiscal deficit.

The Brunei dollar maintained parity with the Singapore dollar. In May 2017, the monetary authority deregulated bank lending rates, allowing banks to price their loans freely. Additionally, the monetary authority deregulated interest rates for term deposits in banks. In August 2017, banks loosened the required debt service ratio, which weighs borrowers' monthly debt obligations against monthly income, to encourage consumers to borrow to buy durable goods.

3.22.3 Merchandise trade

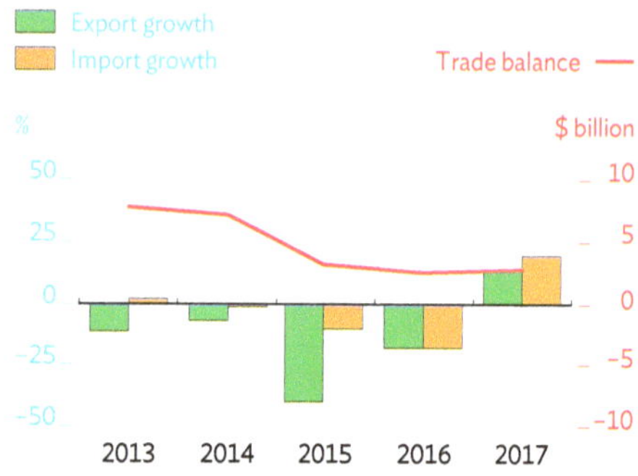

Sources: CEIC Data Company (accessed 16 March 2018); Brunei Darussalam Ministry of Finance.

Economic prospects

A favorable economic outlook for the major industrial economies and higher global oil prices this year and next should help Brunei Darussalam build on last year's turnaround and post GDP growth at 1.5% in 2018 and 2.0% in 2019.

On the demand side, investment is expected to continue to recover and support growth in both years. Government and private consumption should expand modestly, supported by rising oil and gas revenue, higher lending to households, and a better business environment.

By sector, industry is likely to accelerate from marginally positive growth last year to 1.9% this year and 2.5% next. Within industry, gas output could rise, though crude oil output will remain constrained by commitments to internationally agreed production cuts. Meanwhile, industry aside from oil and gas will continue to develop. A margarine plant began operations late last year, for example, and is expected to earn export receipts.

Construction will continue to support growth. Dredging, jetting construction, and installation works are well under way at the planned oil refinery and aromatics cracker on Pulau Muara Besar. Several road and bridge projects linking the capital to outer districts are also under construction and due for completion this year and next. Construction on an ammonia and urea plant continues, with production expected by 2021. Service sector output is forecast to maintain growth this year much as last year before inching up to 1.3% in 2019.

With growth edging up, prices should keep deflation at bay. The consumer price index will stabilize with marginally positive change both this year and next, in line with government policy to subsidize many consumer items (Figure 3.22.5).

As growth strengthens, imports will rise strongly. Yet, the current account will remain in surplus both this year and next,

3.22.1 Selected economic indicators (%)

	2018	2019
GDP growth	1.5	2.0
Inflation	0.1	0.1
Current account balance (share of GDP)	14.0	14.0

Source: ADB estimates.

3.22.4 Fiscal indicators

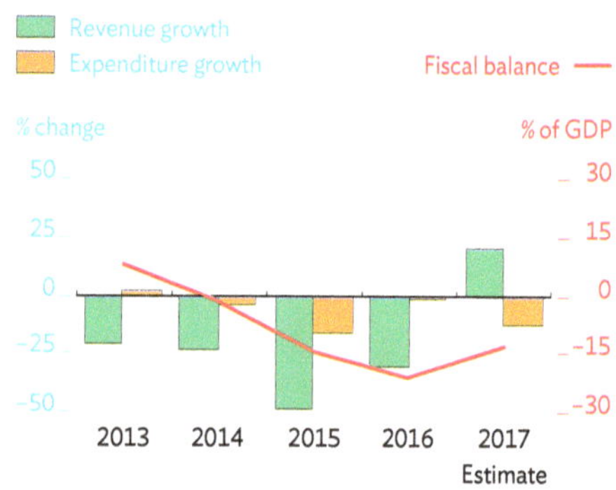

Note: Years are fiscal years ending 31 March of the next year.

Sources: CEIC Data Company (accessed 16 March 2018); ADB estimates.

though far below the surpluses recorded when global oil and gas prices were higher. In the forecast period, the current account surplus as a percentage of GDP will be narrower than in 2017.

Policy challenge—enhancing domestic competition

In recent years, a lack of domestic competition in the private sector has emerged as a constraint on the government's efforts to encourage investment away from petroleum and thereby diversify the economy. This is one observation that underscores the need for a sound policy on domestic competition and, importantly, its vigorous implementation.

Brunei Darussalam has moved up in the World Bank *Doing Business* ranking of 190 economies, from 72 in 2017 to 56 in 2018, but it is still behind Singapore, Malaysia, and Thailand in protecting the rights of minority shareholders and contract enforcement. Similarly, Brunei Darussalam's ranking in the *Global Competitiveness Report 2017–2018* of the World Economic Forum improved—to 46 out of 137 economies, from 58 out of 138 the previous year—but it ranks 51 in the extent of domestic competition, trailing Singapore in first place, Malaysia at 19, Indonesia at 39, and Thailand at 48 (Figure 3.22.6). It ranks 104 in terms of the intensity of local competition, 102 in the extent of market dominance, and 89 in having an effective antimonopoly policy.

Encouragingly, in January 2015 the government passed its first national competition law, the Competition Order, which discourages market manipulation and cartel practices while prohibiting anticompetitive agreements and mergers, as well as abuse of dominant power. Complementing that initiative, the Companies Act was amended to strengthen the rights of minority shareholders in May 2017, and the Competition Commission of Brunei Darussalam was established in August 2017 to oversee the implementation of the Competition Order, including passing judgments on anticompetitive cases and imposing penalties on violators. The Competition and Consumer Affairs Department was formed to serve as the commission's investigative and administrative arm and to carry out advocacy campaigns, receive complaints, and conduct market reviews.

Enacting legislation and setting up institutions are only the first steps toward bringing about stronger domestic competition. Transparent implementation of laws is a much more formidable challenge but necessary to reap their benefits. A key requirement is well-trained and professionally competent personnel to interpret legislation and to enforce it transparently and effectively. Building such human capacity should be the next priority, to ensure that recent policy initiatives bring about much stiffer competition, to the benefit of the whole country.

3.22.5 Inflation

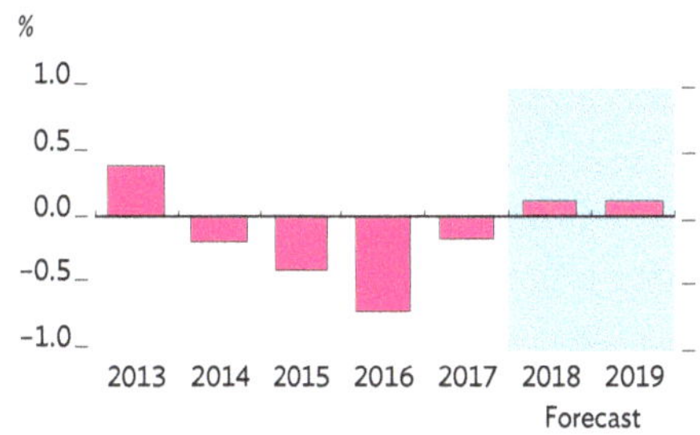

Source: *Asian Development Outlook* database.

3.22.6 Global competitiveness index rankings, 2017

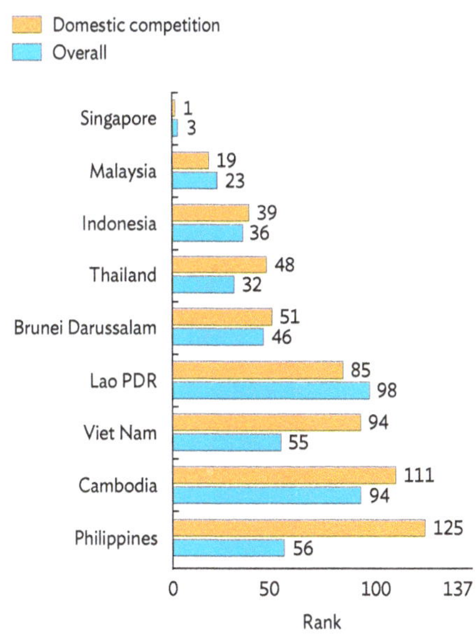

Lao PDR = Lao People's Democratic Republic.
Source: World Economic Forum. The Global Competitiveness Index Historical dataset 2007–2017. http://reports.weforum.org/global-competitiveness-index-2017-2018/downloads/.

Cambodia

The economy last year featured strong growth, stable inflation, and a narrowing current account deficit. Growth momentum will likely be sustained this year and next. Inflation will edge up, and the current account deficit will widen before narrowing in 2019. Rising wages require that other costs of doing business be cut to maintain competitiveness with peer economies. Great potential exists in simplifying cumbersome business procedures.

Economic performance

Robust exports, buoyant tourism, and strong foreign direct investment (FDI) enabled Cambodia to sustain GDP growth at an estimated 7.0% in 2017, unchanged from the previous 2 years (Figure 3.23.1).

Merchandise export growth moderated from 10.1% in 2016 to an estimated 9.3% last year, despite an impressive rise in shipments of electrical goods, automobile components, bicycles, and milled rice—but not garments, the largest category by far. Service exports improved, helped by an 11.8% rise in tourist arrivals that more than doubled the 5.0% growth rate in 2016. Preliminary data show FDI rising by an impressive 21.5% last year to reach $2.7 billion (Figure 3.23.2).

By sector, a mild slowdown in industry was offset by faster growth in services and agriculture. Industry grew by an estimated 9.7% in 2017, slightly down from 10.5% in 2016. Construction seems to have moderated but still grew robustly, as indicated by 36.0% growth in imports of construction materials and a 27.0% increase in construction projects approved. Helped by accelerating growth in tourism, services expanded by an estimated 7.1% last year, up from 6.8%. Agriculture grew by an estimated 1.7%.

Even as high growth was sustained and international oil prices rose, inflation averaged 2.9% last year, about the same rate as in 2016 despite prices for food, weighted at 43.3% in the consumer price index, easing thanks to better harvests.

The current account deficit excluding official transfers is estimated to have narrowed to the equivalent of 10.9% of GDP last year from 11.2% in 2016 as net service exports improved (Figure 3.23.3). Robust official transfers and buoyant FDI inflows more than compensated for the current account deficit, enabling gross foreign exchange reserves to rise from $6.7 billion at the end of 2016 to $8.8 billion a year later, sufficient to cover 6 months of imports. Reserves are greater than the country's external debt of $6.7 billion, equal to 30.1% of GDP in 2017.

3.23.1 Supply-side contributions to growth

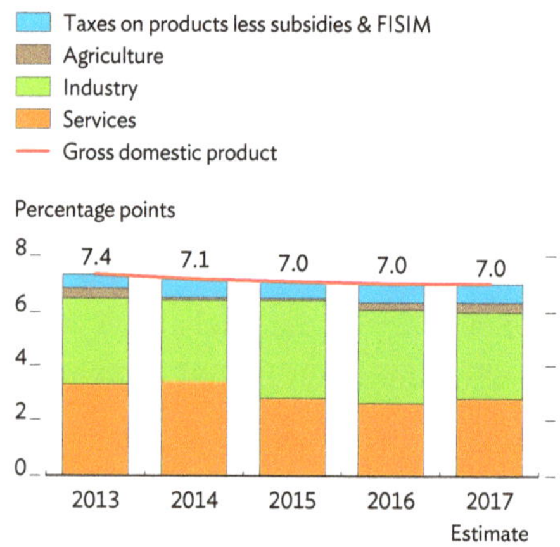

FISIM = financial intermediation services indirectly measured.

Sources: National Institute of Statistics; ADB estimates.

3.23.2 Foreign direct investment

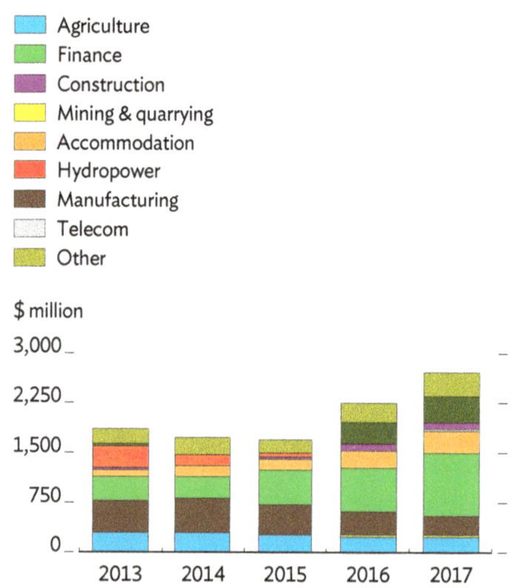

Source: National Bank of Cambodia.

This chapter was written by Jan Hansen and Poullang Doung of the Cambodia Resident Mission, ADB, Phnom Penh.

The 2017 budget had planned for a fiscal deficit equal to 4.3% of GDP, rather higher than the 2.8% outturn in 2016. However, preliminary data show actual expenditure was 19.3% below budget because of sluggish disbursement and delays in recording public capital spending financed by development partners. Meanwhile, revenue rose faster than planned, narrowing the fiscal deficit to 0.9% of GDP.

The National Bank of Cambodia, the central bank, maintained a stable exchange rate of KR4,050 to the US dollar. It reined in growth in bank credit to the private sector to 18.5% last year, from an average of 27.0% annually over the preceding 3 years, and continued the phased implementation of higher minimum capital requirements and a liquidity coverage ratio for banks.

3.23.3 Current account balance

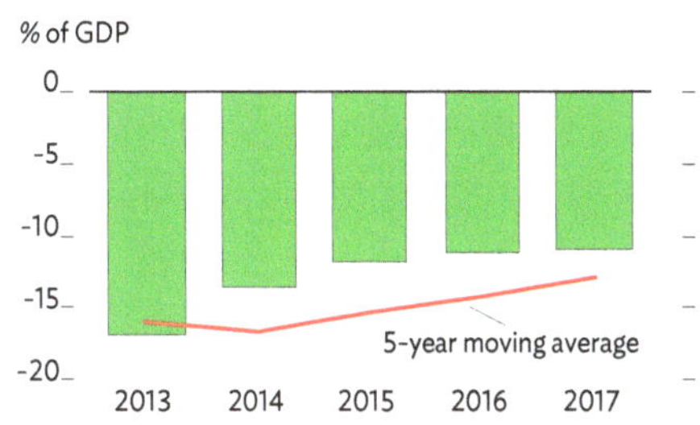

GDP = gross domestic product.
Sources: National Bank of Cambodia; ADB estimates.

Economic prospects

With continued strength in the global economy, the outlook for Cambodia this year and next remains positive. Growth is forecast at 7.0%, sustained by robust expansion in exports, strong FDI inflows, solid tourist arrivals, and buoyant domestic demand (Figure 3.23.4).

By sector, industry is likely to continue to grow by around 9.6%, with a slowdown in garments and footwear offset by stronger growth in emerging industries: electrical parts, automobile components, bicycles, milled rice, and rubber. That said, the continued rapid rise since 2013 in Cambodia's minimum wage for garment manufacturing is a matter of concern, as it may erode export competitiveness in an industry that accounts for nearly 80% of the country's manufacturing output. Turning to other sectors, growth in services should remain at 7.1%, as in 2017, with continued buoyancy in tourism. Agriculture should post around 1.8% growth.

Inflation is forecast to rise to 3.2% this year and 3.5% in 2019 with continued strong GDP growth and international food and oil prices trending higher (Figure 3.23.5). However, local food prices, which matter the most to poor households, should continue to be subdued, barring adverse weather.

The trade deficit is expected to remain substantial as import costs rise for imported oil and other needs in a fast-growing economy. The expected rise in tourism receipts promises, however, to cushion the current account deficit somewhat. Meanwhile, higher FDI inflows and official concessionary loans from abroad should be more than adequate to finance the current account deficit, even building up foreign reserves to about $10.0 billion by the end of 2018.

Fiscal policy is expected to be more expansionary this year than last, while monetary policy will continue to focus on maintaining a stable exchange rate and improving financial regulation and supervision. The 2018 budget plans to raise the fiscal deficit to the equivalent of 5.1% of GDP, with revenue planned at 17.9% of GDP and expenditure at 23.0% (Figure 3.23.6).

3.23.4 GDP growth

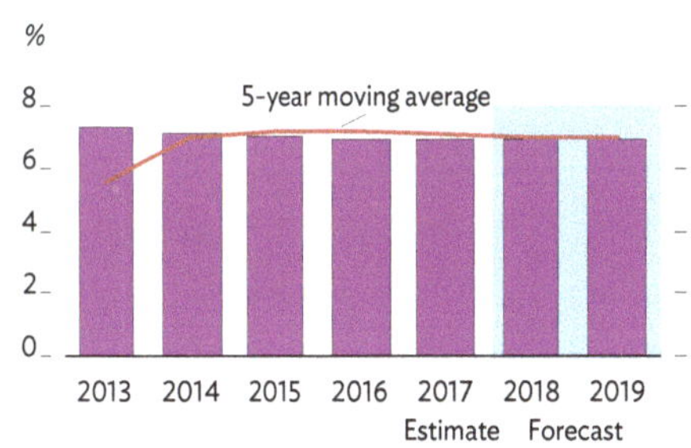

Source: *Asian Development Outlook* database.

3.23.5 Inflation

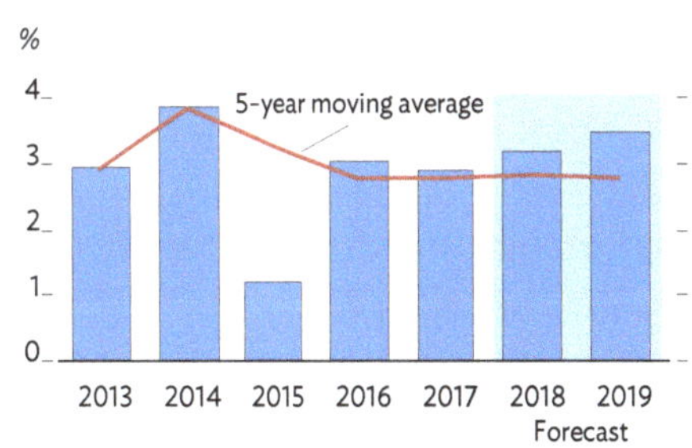

Source: *Asian Development Outlook* database.

3.23.1 Selected economic indicators (%)

	2018	2019
GDP growth	7.0	7.0
Inflation	3.2	3.5
Current account balance (share of GDP)	-11.1	-10.8

Source: ADB estimates.

External risks to the outlook could be interest rates tightening in the US faster than anticipated, heightened volatility in international financial markets, or an unexpected hike in oil prices. A domestic risk is potential uncertainty in the approach to national elections in July 2018.

Policy challenge—simplifying business procedures

Rapidly rising wages and an emerging shortage of skills to fill a wide range of jobs and professions are eroding Cambodia's competitiveness in manufacturing for export. If the country fails to implement policies to bring down other costs of doing business, it will jeopardize its rapid growth and its ability to diversify the economy over the medium to long term. Policy makers should consider vastly simplifying the processes and procedures required to do business. This would cut costs and help keep the country's manufacturing and services internationally competitive.

The World Bank's *Doing Business 2018* report ranks Cambodia 135 out of 190 countries surveyed, far behind many of its neighbors and peers. Indeed, the country is near the bottom of the ranking in three areas: starting a business, getting construction permits, and enforcing contracts (Figure 3.23.7). Moreover, Cambodia's ranking in these three areas has stagnated since 2011. Policy makers should expeditiously streamline procedures and processes in these areas to reduce the cost of doing business.

The government would be well advised to constitute a special task force with representatives from government ministries, public agencies, and the private sector. The task force would review procedures and suggest ways to simplify or remove excessive procedures and paperwork now required to register a business, obtain construction permits, and enforce commercial contracts. It could consider creating a single window to streamline procedures and unify fees for opening a business, thereby reducing costs.

Creating such a single window would build on progress Cambodia has made since 2015 toward making it easier to start a business. The country has simplified company name checks, streamlined tax registration, eliminated the requirement to publish information in the official gazette, and introduced online business registration.

Meanwhile, the judicial system is not seen as effective in resolving commercial disputes. The interpretation and enforcement of commercial law could be improved by developing and rolling out decrees and guidelines on implementation, conducting awareness campaigns about business needs, and training authorities in the central and provincial governments to improve their uptake of these materials. Commercial courts should be established to resolve commercial disputes and enable speedier contract enforcement.

3.23.6 Fiscal indicators

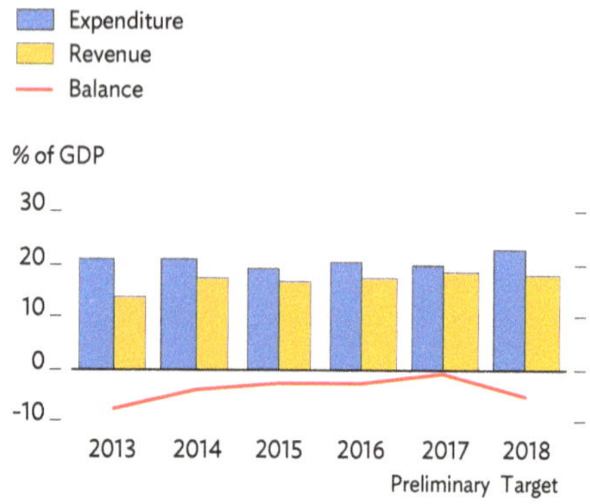

Sources: Ministry of Economy and Finance; ADB estimates.

3.23.7 Doing business indicators, 2018

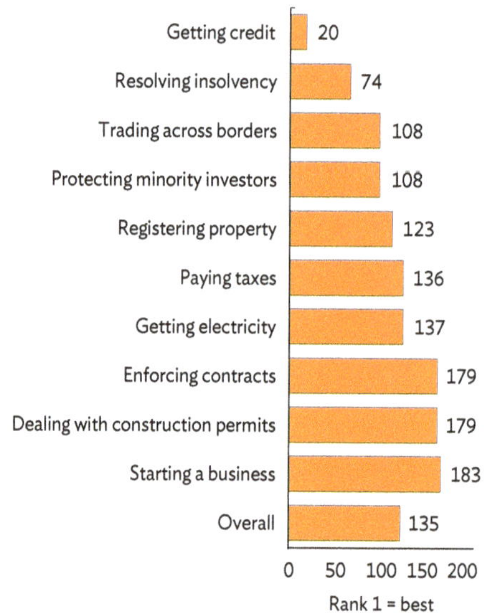

Source: World Bank. 2018. *Doing Business 2018.*

Indonesia

Supported by an export turnaround, strengthening investment, and robust consumption, economic growth picked up last year. Inflation rose slightly, and the current account deficit narrowed marginally. Growth should firm up on higher investment and private consumption. The current account deficit will likely widen, and inflation remain within the central bank's target range. Early experience demonstrates how smart solutions can help to better manage the country's rapid urbanization.

Economic performance

GDP growth edged up to 5.1% last year from 5.0% in 2016, driven by renewed acceleration in export growth, stronger investment, and private consumption encouraged by a robust job market (Figure 3.24.1). Exports of goods and services, having contracted for 2 consecutive years in 2015 and 2016, rose last year by 9.1% at constant prices, providing fresh impetus to the economy. Data on the balance of payments show the US dollar value of merchandise exports rising last year for the first time since 2011, recording hefty 16.9% growth that benefited from a pickup in global trade and higher international commodity prices. Export earnings accelerated for primary commodities such as coal, palm oil, natural gas, and rubber and for manufactured products such as textiles, metal goods, and electrical appliances.

Supported by higher public infrastructure spending and stronger private investment, fixed capital formation accelerated by 6.2% from 4.5% growth in 2016 (Figure 3.24.2). Aside from strong growth in the construction of buildings, investment in machinery and equipment grew by 9.5%, its highest since 2012.

Robust growth in private consumption at 5.0%, as in 2016, reflected solid job growth and low inflation. Of the 2.6 million jobs added, 1 million were created by manufacturing enterprises in the formal sector, mostly in Java. The average real wage for regular employees in manufacturing increased by 7.9%. Public consumption rebounded from contraction in 2016 with a 2.1% rise as government spending normalized in 2017 after substantial cuts in the revised budget for 2016.

By sector, industry grew by 4.1%, improving slightly on 3.8% in 2016 with a better performance in construction as infrastructure projects under state-owned enterprises and the government accelerated (Figure 3.24.3). Within industry, growth in manufacturing remained stable at 4.3%, as in the previous 2 years, with robust growth in food and beverages and, after

This chapter was written by Emma Allen and Priasto Aji of the Indonesia Resident Mission, ADB, Jakarta.

3.24.1 Demand-side contributions to growth

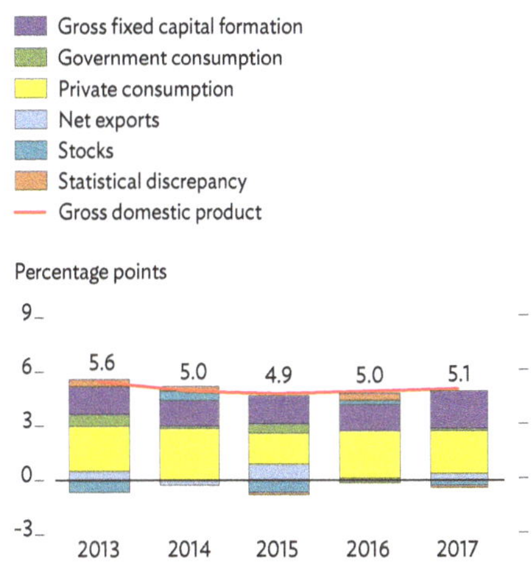

Source: CEIC Data Company (accessed 15 March 2018).

3.24.2 Contributions to fixed investment growth

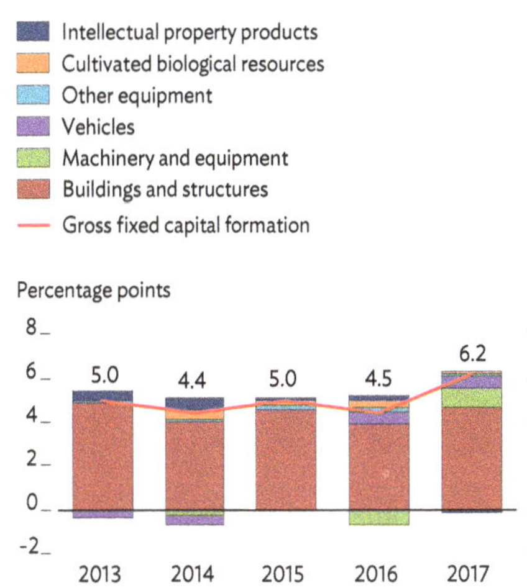

Source: CEIC Data Company (accessed 15 March 2018).

2 years of contraction, a turnaround in textiles and apparel. Agriculture posted a 3.8% increase, slightly higher than the 3.4% growth in 2016. Services maintained the 2016 growth rate at 5.7% to provide nearly half of GDP growth. Growth in logistics and information and telecommunication technology strengthened, while rapidly rising tourist arrivals boosted trade, hotels, and restaurants, despite an eruption of Mount Agung volcano in Bali.

Headline inflation averaged 3.8% in 2017, slightly up from 3.5% in 2016, with hikes for administered tariffs on electricity and other energy supply more than offsetting price moderation for most other products (Figure 3.24.4). Food inflation was tamer than in previous years with better production and supply management. Core inflation has been declining since 2015, largely reflecting stability in the exchange rate and inflation expectations.

Merchandise imports rose by 16.1% in 2017, less than the 16.9% rise in merchandise export earnings reported above. Imports supported new infrastructure projects, particularly in electricity generation (Figure 3.24.5). The net result was a merchandise trade surplus of $18.9 billion, slightly higher than the $15.3 billion surplus in 2016. The current account deficit thus narrowed marginally to the equivalent of 1.7% of GDP last year from 1.8% a year earlier (Figure 3.24.6). In the financial account, net portfolio capital inflows grew by 8.8%, and inflows of FDI reached $23.1 billion. The overall balance of payments surplus edged up to $11.6 billion, taking foreign exchange reserves up to $130.2 billion, or cover for 8.3 months of imports and repayment of official debt (Figure 3.24.7). Meanwhile, the Indonesian rupiah remained relatively stable in 2017, depreciating marginally by 0.6% against the US dollar.

Indonesia's external debt in 2017 remained moderate at $352.2 billion, equal to 34.8% of GDP. External debt is 86.1% long term, 51.3% of it public and 48.7% of it private. Total public debt rose to the equivalent of 29.0% of GDP in 2017 from 28.3% in 2016 because of a higher fiscal deficit and slight rupiah depreciation, but it remains low by international standards and well below the legal threshold of 60% of GDP. Debt denominated in foreign currency is only one-third of total public debt, but foreign ownership of public debt is higher, with nonresidents holding 39.8% of rupiah-denominated government bonds in 2017.

The fiscal deficit last year is estimated to have equaled 2.5% of GDP. Performance improved on higher revenue and expenditure outcomes, with revenue supported by structural factors and spending quality enhanced. Thanks to efforts to broaden the tax base and improve tax administration, higher tax revenues—excluding those paid during the 9-month tax amnesty that concluded on 31 March 2017—raised the ratio of tax to GDP from 9.5% in 2016 to 9.8% in 2017. Capital expenditure achieved 92.8% of the budget target, the highest in 3 years (Figure 3.24.8).

With moderate inflation, Bank Indonesia, the central bank, lowered its policy interest rate, the 7-day reverse repo, by 25 basis points twice last year, in August and September. The rate has

3.24.3 Supply-side contributions to growth

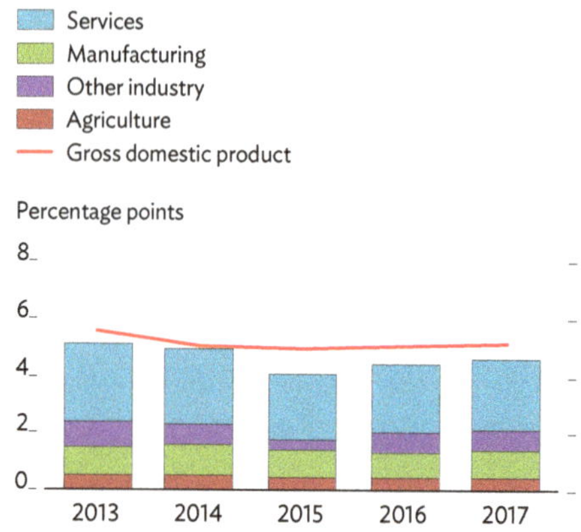

Source: CEIC Data Company (accessed 15 March 2018).

3.24.4 Monthly inflation

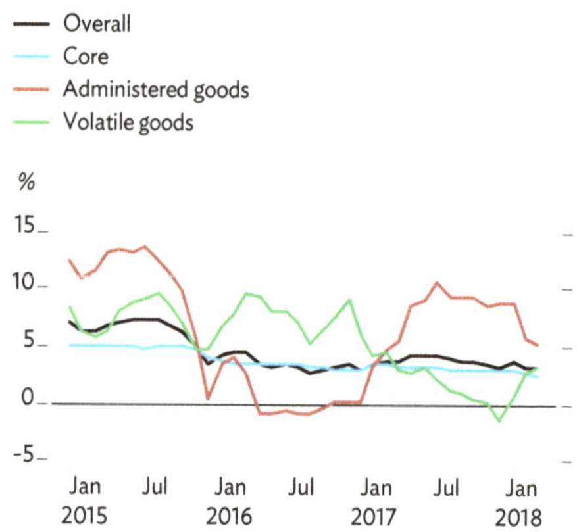

Source: CEIC Data Company (accessed 15 March 2018).

3.24.5 Merchandise trade

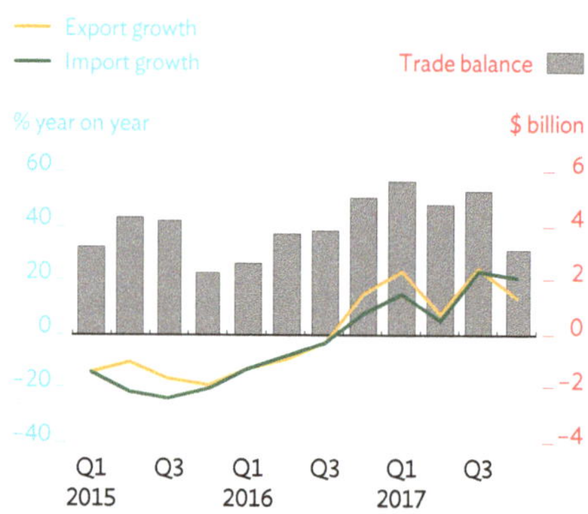

Q = quarter.

Source: CEIC Data Company (accessed 15 March 2018).

since been maintained at 4.25%, with the bank deposit rate down to 3.5% and the bank lending rate to 5.0%. Subdued credit growth in 2017 slightly lowered the ratio of loans to deposits.

Economic prospects

Growth is forecast higher, at 5.3% both this year and next, with continued strength in investment and private consumption more than offsetting expected moderation in export growth. The government's commitment to boosting infrastructure and improving the business environment should support stronger investment. Public investment is expected to peak in 2018, especially for projects in energy and transport and those tied to the 2018 Asian Games in Jakarta and Palembang in August. Several large projects implemented by state-owned enterprises are scheduled for completion this year and next. Annual growth in total investment should stay well above 6% over the next 2 years. Positive business sentiment encouraged by structural reform may be partly offset by some private investors adopting a wait-and-see stance as regional elections in 2018 and a national election in 2019 approaches. Credit growth is expected to accelerate at a moderate pace this year and next from its subdued 8.2% increase last year (Figure 3.24.9). Nonbank financing from the capital market has become increasingly important to investment growth.

A gradual improvement in private consumption is expected, supported by continued job growth and low inflation. Consumer confidence remains elevated, with higher-income households set to consume more services, especially in travel and communications. Lower-income households will receive a boost from growth in formal employment outside of agriculture and from the continued expansion of government social assistance programs. Although the pace of retail and vehicle sales has moderated, elections this year and the next should boost private consumption (Figure 3.24.10). The net effect of falling sales in traditional stores and rapidly growing sales online is still inconclusive.

Construction is seen to draw support from simpler procedures for licensing and land acquisition, as well as the fast-tracking of several national strategic projects. The latest purchasing managers' index shows improving vigor in manufacturing. Services associated with the digital economy are expected to take off. Barring bad weather, agriculture should post stronger growth, although the peak of the harvest season may be delayed from the first quarter to the second.

Even as growth strengthens, assuming stable domestic energy prices, inflation is forecast to be 3.8% this year and to edge up to 4.0% in 2019. Both rates are well within the central bank inflation target for 2018 at 3.5% ±1.0 percentage point. Pressure on food prices should ease with continued improvement in food distribution channels across the country and with imports of selected foods. In the first 2 months of 2018, inflation fell to 3.2% year on year.

3.24.6 Current account components

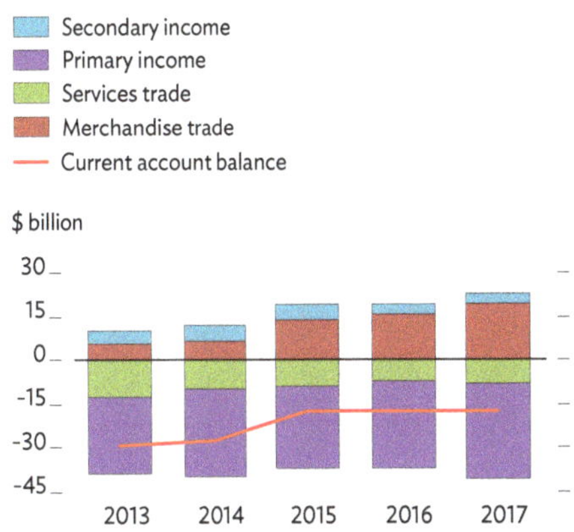

Source: CEIC Data Company (accessed 15 March 2018).

3.24.7 Gross international reserves and exchange rate

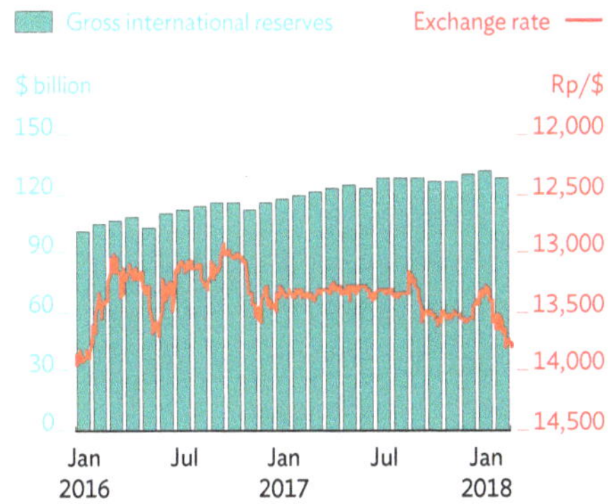

Sources: CEIC Data Company; Bloomberg (both accessed 15 March 2018).

3.24.8 Actual capital expenditures

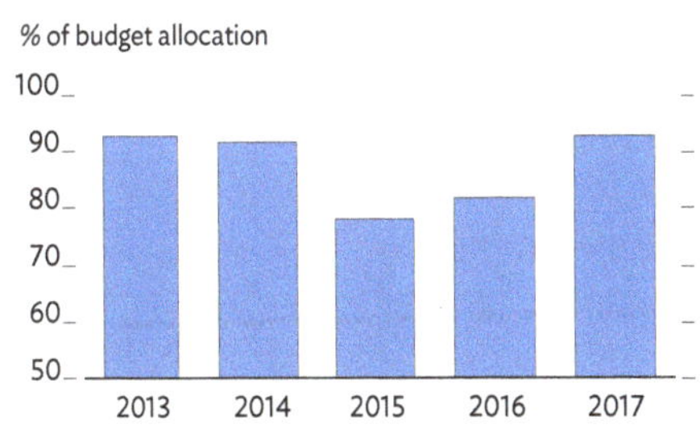

Sources: Bank Indonesia; Ministry of Finance.

On the balance of payments, export growth is expected to moderate as commodity prices and overseas demand stabilize. Imports should remain strong, buoyed by demand for capital goods to support rising public and private investment, thus narrowing the trade surplus and, consequently, widening the current account deficit to the equivalent of 2.2% of GDP this year and next.

The 2018 budget sets a higher revenue target than last year and a lower target for expenditure growth. The fiscal deficit target is 2.2% of GDP. Measures to broaden the tax base and improve compliance should, along with gains in nontax income, translate into higher revenue over the next 2 years. Revenue may improve further with the tax office gaining better access to bank financial data under recent international agreements instituting the automatic exchange of information. Improving the quality and efficiency of spending are priorities in 2018, with a particular emphasis on capital and social assistance expenditure. In February 2018, the Ministry of Social Affairs reported that disbursement of social spending in the year to date had doubled over the year-earlier period.

External risks to the outlook include capital outflows and resulting pressure on the rupiah as the normalization of monetary policy proceeds in the advanced economies, shifts in trade policy in export markets, and escalating geopolitical tensions in East Asia. Domestic risks could emanate from revenue shortfalls or expenditure delays affecting the 2018 budget. The Indonesian crude price is now about $60 per barrel, far higher than the assumption in the 2018 budget of $48 per barrel. If domestic fuel prices are not adjusted in line with rising global crude oil prices, pressure on the budget could undermine development spending.

3.24.1 Selected economic indicators (%)

	2018	2019
GDP growth	5.3	5.3
Inflation	3.8	4.0
Current account balance (share of GDP)	-2.2	-2.2

Source: ADB estimates.

3.24.9 Growth of commercial banks credit

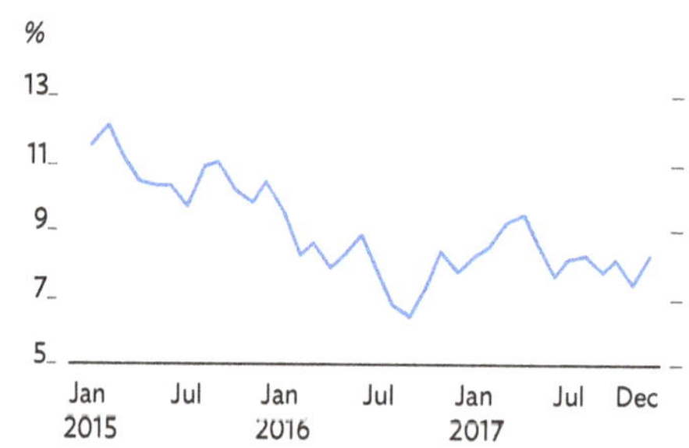

Source: CEIC Data Company (accessed 15 March 2018).

Policy challenge—scaling up smart solutions to address urban challenges

Indonesia is urbanizing rapidly. More than half of its population of 262 million live in urban areas, with up to two-thirds projected to live in cities by 2035 (Figure 3.24.11). Partly because urbanization has been rapid, it has lacked sound planning or adequate financing, straining basic service delivery and the environment. Only one in three urban households has access to decent water (Figure 3.24.12). Only one in hundred is connected to a sewerage system, which poses high risks to public health. Floods and landslides account for more than 60% of natural disasters in Indonesia, the impact of which is exacerbated by insufficient urban drainage systems and poor municipal waste management. Less than 10% of urban commuters travel to work by public transport, and inadequate transport facilities contribute to congestion and significant economic losses.

The core challenge of upgrading urban services boils down to finding innovative ways to plan and finance urban development. The government has ambitious plans to improve urban services.

3.24.10 Retail sales growth

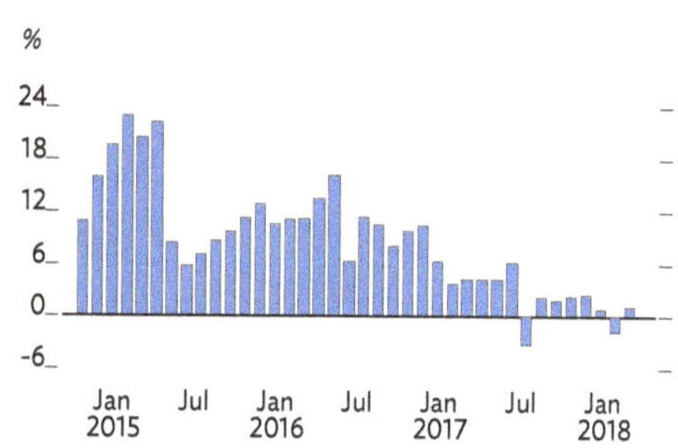

Source: CEIC Data Company (accessed 15 March 2018).

In the national medium-term development plan for 2015–2019, the "100-0-100" target aims to provide access to clean water to 100% of urban households, reduce urban slums to zero, and provide access to improved sanitation to 100% of urban residents. Other national strategic projects for urban development include investments in mass rapid transit systems and in expanding the broadband network to all cities and districts. This opens up several opportunities to use smart solutions that tap technology to address urban challenges and optimize the benefits enabled by agglomeration and economies of scale.

The government is already experimenting with the use of smart solutions to tackle urban challenges in a few cities. For better urban planning, technology solutions provide an opportunity to map and analyze sprawl, land-use changes, and events such as floods. In Palembang, satellite imagery is improving land-use planning and decisions on where to locate urban infrastructure and facilities. This will facilitate the sharing of solid waste disposal and wastewater treatment plants across district boundaries.

Bandung is strengthening urban governance with information and communication technology. An *e-mah warga* is a public information kiosk designed to capture grassroots data from neighborhood *kampungs* to improve asset management and service delivery. It can provide real-time data when infrastructure breaks down, for example, while collecting dynamic and transparent information on welfare needs as they emerge.

To bridge the urban services gap and strengthen delivery systems, wireless sensors and financial technology can be deployed for better mapping of properties and payment of public utility bills. In Jambi City on Sumatra, data on the location and condition of septic tanks will feed into an interactive map to schedule desludging. An auto-debiting system is planned for desludging services, billing either communities or individual households. These innovations have potential to reduce costs, strengthen local revenue, and improve the creditworthiness of local governments.

Encouraging as these few examples of good practice in using smart solutions to manage urban challenges may be, scaling up such solutions to cover most major urban areas in a vast country will require massive investment. Here, too, innovative financing solutions should be actively pursued. One option would be for local governments to access domestic capital markets by issuing municipal bonds. Similarly, utility providers could use pooled municipal debt obligations to raise funds to finance smart solutions for urban utility provision.

Such approaches would encourage good governance and transparency in local governments and urban utility providers. Over time, this can attract private participation in the financing and provision of urban services. With the right policies and investments, Indonesia can thus use smart solutions to turn its cities into promoters of innovative and inclusive growth.

3.24.11 Population projections

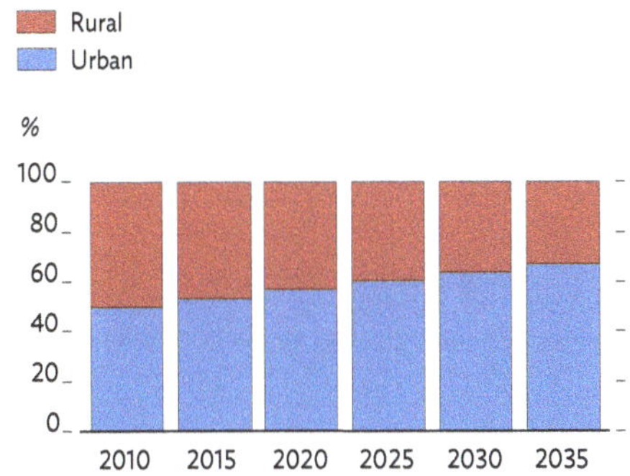

Source: Badan Pusat Statistik. 2013. *Indonesia Population Projection*.

3.24.12 Access to clean water and decent water, urban households

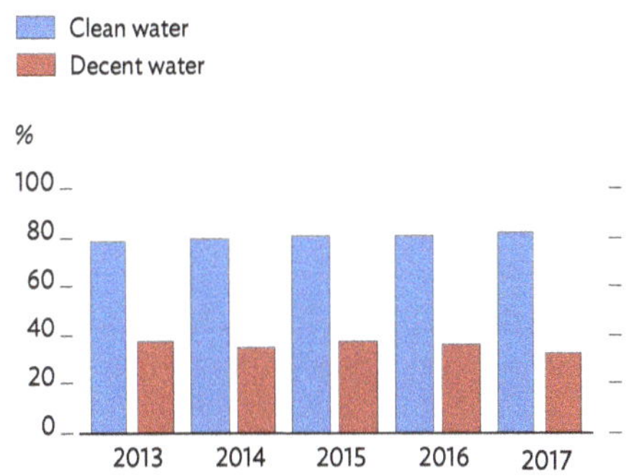

Notes: Clean water consist of packaged water, refill water, pipe, and water from other sources (i.e., artesian well/pump, protected well, and protected spring) with distance to the nearest final disposal site of faeces ≥ 10 meters. Decent water consist of pipe, rain water, and water from other sources with distance to the nearest final disposal site of faeces ≥ 10 meters.

Source: Badan Pusat Statistik. 2017. *Welfare Statistics*.

Lao People's Democratic Republic

Economic growth held up well last year at 6.8%. Inflation hit an 8-year low, and the current account deficit narrowed. Growth is likely to be sustained this year and accelerate in 2019. Inflation is forecast to edge up, and the current account deficit to worsen. Large current account and fiscal deficits are immediate concerns for the policy makers, and a medium-term challenge is to address a widening skills gap.

Economic performance

Despite a new government ban on logging exports, tighter credit, subdued international mineral prices, and lower tourist arrivals, GDP growth in 2017 came in at 6.8%, slightly lower than the 7.0% figure for 2016 (Figure 3.25.1).

By sector, a slowdown in industry was offset by acceleration in services, while growth in agriculture was unchanged from 2016. Despite a hefty 24.8% rise in electricity generation, industry growth slowed from 12.0% in 2016 to 9.5% last year as persistently subdued global mineral prices dragged down mining and metal production. Meanwhile, growth in services accelerated from 4.7% in 2016 to 6.2% last year as growth in wholesale and retail trade, and in information and communications, more than offset a slowdown in tourism business caused by a 7.5% decline in tourist arrivals largely traceable to tightened visa requirements.

Even as the economy grew apace and international oil prices rose sharply in 2017, buoyant agricultural production drove down food prices and kept a lid on inflation. Average inflation halved from 1.6% in 2016 to 0.8% last year, the lowest since 2009 (Figure 3.25.2).

The current account deficit narrowed from the equivalent of 14.1% of GDP in 2016 to an estimated 13.0% last year, as 16.1% growth in merchandise exports outpaced a 13.6% rise in imports and net service exports stood at $360 million. On the capital account, net foreign direct investment inflows, mostly for large hydropower projects, surged from $2.1 billion in 2016 to $2.8 billion last year. This more than offset $1.4 billion in net outflows of portfolio capital, yielding a balance of payments surplus of $165 million that helped foreign exchange reserves improve from $815 million in 2016 to $980 million at the end of 2017. Even with this improvement, reserves were sufficient to

3.25.1 Supply-side contributions to growth

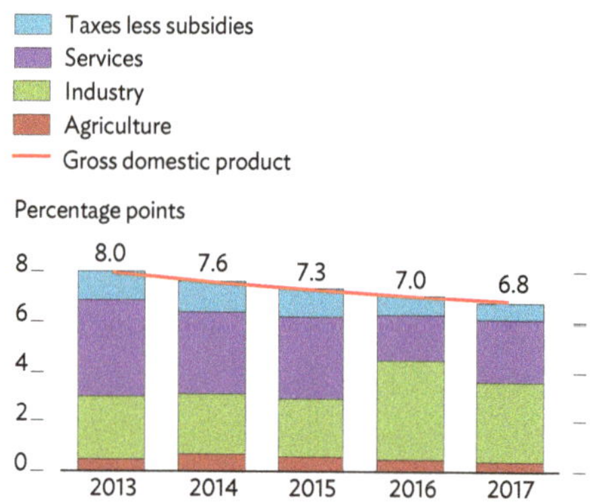

Sources: Lao Statistics Bureau; *Asian Development Outlook* database.

3.25.2 Monthly inflation

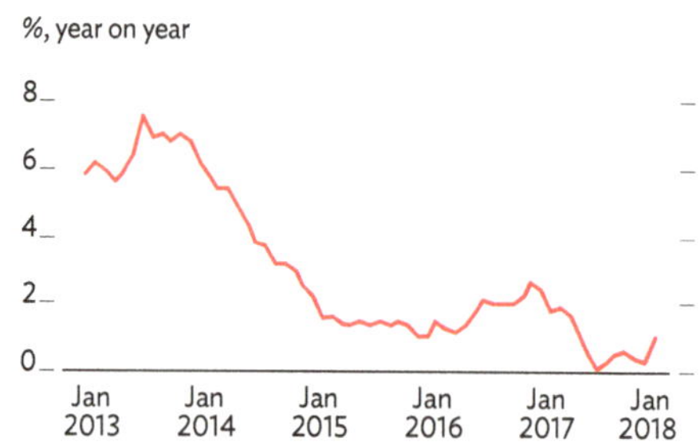

Sources: Bank of the Lao People's Democratic Republic; CEIC Data Company (accessed 19 March 2018).

This chapter was written by Rattanatay Luanglatbandith and Soulinthone Leuangkhamsing of the Lao PDR Resident Mission, ADB, Vientiane.

cover only 1.3 months of imports. Meanwhile, external public and publicly guaranteed debt rose to the equivalent of 49.1% of GDP last year from 46.6% at the end of 2016.

Despite government efforts to consolidate its finances, the fiscal deficit reached 4.8% of GDP in 2017 from 4.6% a year earlier (Figure 3.25.3). Revenue fell short of the budget target but still rose from 15.8% of GDP in 2016 to 16.7%. Meanwhile, expenditure rose from 20.5% to 21.7%, capital expenditure being exempted from austerity measures that constrained current expenditure. Credit growth slowed last year to an estimated 15.0% from 20.9% in 2016, and the ratio of loans to deposits in the banking system stabilized at 103%.

3.25.3 Fiscal balance

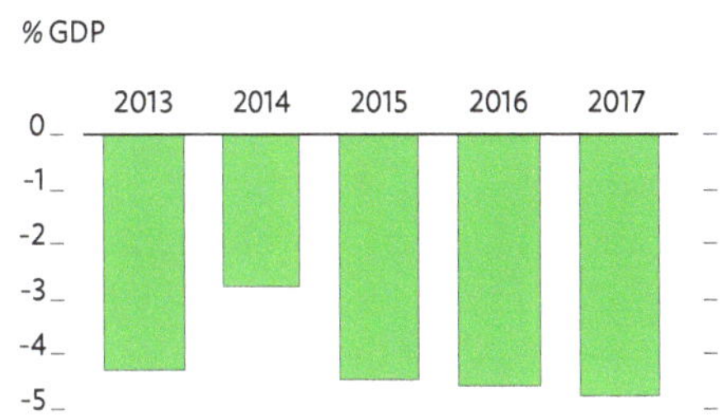

Sources: Ministry of Finance; *Asian Development Outlook* database.

Economic prospects

Growth is expected to continue at 6.8% in 2018, as the industry slowdown that began last year persists but is compensated by slightly higher growth in services, then pick up to 7.0% in 2019 (Figure 3.25.4). As some hydropower projects now under construction come online in 2019, notably the 1,300-megawatt Xayaburi dam, industry should reverse its declining trend. Meanwhile, barring more bad weather, agriculture should continue to grow by about 3.0%, and growth in services is forecast to strengthen mildly as tourist arrivals recover from last year's huge decline.

As growth momentum is maintained, inflation is expected to rally from last year's dip but remain moderate at 2.0%–2.5% (Figure 3.25.5). This is despite a forecast rise in international oil prices and possible depreciation of the Lao kip in response to the continued precarious state of the balance of payments situation.

The current account deficit is projected to expand to the equivalent of 14.9% of GDP in 2018 as higher inflation and international oil prices drive up the import bill and moderating export growth brings in less revenue. As new hydropower projects come online, electricity exports should pick up in 2019, pushing the current account deficit down to the equivalent of 13.7% of GDP (Figure 3.25.6). On the capital account, net inflows of foreign direct investment are expected to equal 16% of GDP in 2018 and 15% in 2019.

Continued failure to meet fiscal deficit targets in recent years is a matter of concern. The government seems to remain committed to paring the fiscal deficit to the equivalent of 4.3% of GDP this year and 4.0% in 2019. However, this would require large cuts to public expenditure and higher revenue achieved through improved tax administration and higher taxes on natural resource industries.

Regarding monetary policy, the government is likely to continue to let the kip depreciate gradually while retaining current interest rate caps over the next 2 years.

3.25.1 Selected economic indicators (%)

	2018	2019
GDP growth	6.8	7.0
Inflation	2.0	2.5
Current account balance (share of GDP)	-14.9	-13.7

Source: ADB estimates.

3.25.4 GDP growth

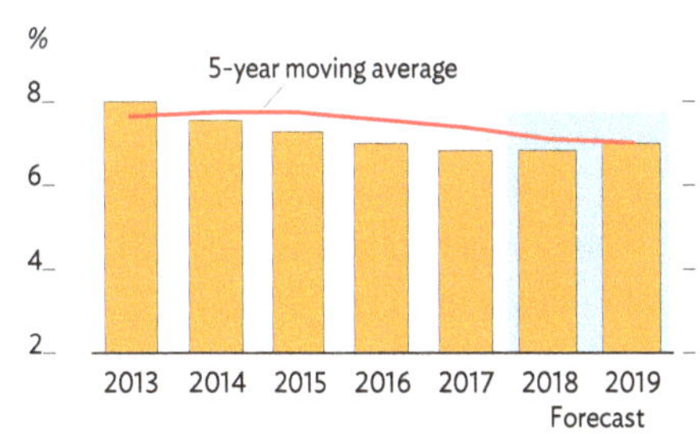

Source: *Asian Development Outlook* database.

3.25.5 Inflation

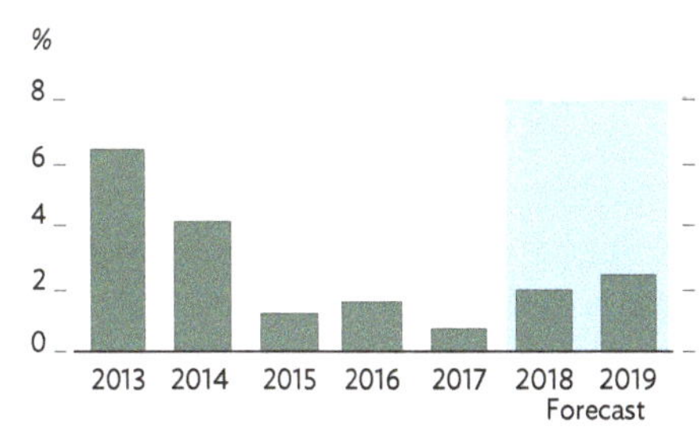

Source: *Asian Development Outlook* database.

Broad money supply is expected to grow by about 20% annually this year and next, with annual credit growth at about 17%.

External risks to the outlook would include an unexpectedly large slowdown in trade and heightened instability in financial markets, either globally or within the region. A bigger risk could stem from domestic conditions if government efforts to consolidate its finances continue to falter, threatening debt distress even as foreign exchange reserves barely cover normal imports.

3.25.6 Current account balance

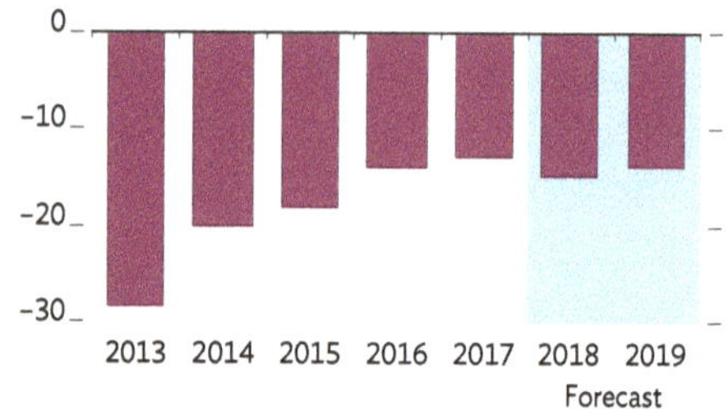

Source: *Asian Development Outlook* database.

Policy challenge—addressing the skills gap

Building on the country's graduation in 2011 to lower-middle-income status, the government now aspires to reach upper-middle-income status by 2030. Among the many constraints that could frustrate the achievement of this milestone, the emergence of huge skills gap merits special mention. A World Bank report found in 2014 that 36% of firms faced a shortage of highly skilled workers, while 44% cited a shortage of workers with medium skills as a bottleneck, and 47% reported business constrained by a shortage of even unskilled workers. Part of the problem is a mismatch between the skills that young people acquire in schools and those in demand in the labor market. Among the 14,000 graduates from technical education and vocational training institutions following the 2016–2017 school year, most were accountants or electricians, for which there is very limited demand (Figure 3.25.7). Meanwhile, despite severe shortages of architects, engineers, electronics specialists, masons, mechanics, and carpenters, enrollment in these areas continues to languish.

The worsening skills gap reflects lower enrollment and completion rates in schools and colleges. Although the Lao People's Democratic Republic is now close to achieving universal primary education, the enrollment rate in lower secondary school is only 74%, in upper secondary school a paltry 41%, and in tertiary education about 20%. Compounding low enrollment and completion rates is the low quality of education at all levels.

Improving access to post-primary education would require greater resources to hire more teachers, as well as to provide financial assistance to children from poorer families. Improving the quality of education is difficult, as greater resources alone cannot enhance quality. Comprehensive efforts to address a range of issues would be needed to improve the quality of education: modernizing the curriculum, training teachers, forging a stronger partnership between educational institutions and industry, granting more autonomy to educational institutions, and improving governance across the education sector.

3.25.7 TVET graduates by sector, school year 2016–2017

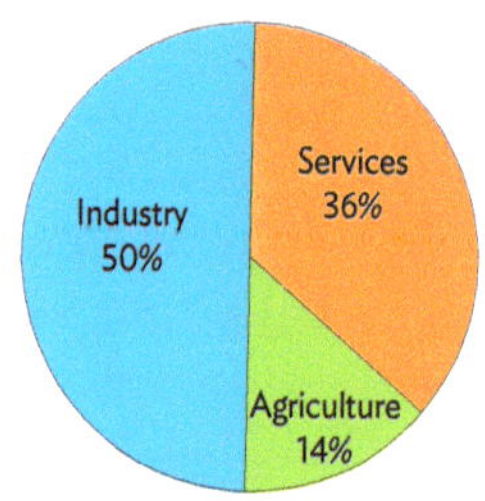

TVET = technical and vocational education and training.

Note: Most graduates in services are in accounting and secretarial services, hospitality and food processing, business administration, tourism, and information and communication technology. Most graduates in agriculture are in farming and livestock breeding, followed by environmental industries. In industry, most the graduates are in electricity supply, surveying and land management, automobile technology, information technology for business, and auto mechanics.

Source: Ministry of Education and Sports.

Malaysia

An export rebound and strong domestic demand accelerated GDP growth to 5.9% last year. Inflation edged up, and the current account surplus widened. Growth is seen to moderate to 5.3% this year and 5.0% next, with inflation subsiding and the current account surplus narrowing marginally. The country can move up the value chain and become a high-tech economy by implementing its strategy to strengthen workforce skills and technical capacity.

Economic performance

A revival in exports and robust domestic demand helped GDP growth accelerate from 4.2% in 2016 to 5.9% last year. Exports of goods and services rose in real terms by 9.6% after near stagnation in 2016, when exports edged up by only 1.1%. Merchandise exports soared by 13.7% in US dollar terms, reversing 5.2% contraction in 2016, on sharp upturns for global trade and commodity prices. Malaysia is highly open to trade, with a ratio of trade to GDP at 131%—fourth in Asia after Hong Kong, China; Singapore; and Viet Nam in that order—so the turnaround in merchandise exports breathed new life into the economy (Figure 3.26.1).

Growth in domestic demand was well distributed across the economy (Figure 3.26.2). Private consumption rose by 7.0%, improving on 6.0% growth recorded in 2016 with help from higher growth in wage income amid a tight labor market, and public consumption rose by 5.4% from a scant 0.9% in 2016. Stronger export demand encouraged private investment into several large projects to expand capacity in manufacturing and services. At the same time, public investment turned around 3 years of decline with a small gain that brought growth in total investment to 6.2%.

All sectors performed well, but manufacturing stood out for its contribution to GDP growth. Production rose by 6.0%, driven by 8.0% growth in electrical and electronic equipment manufacturing, which comprises 25% of manufacturing and 40% of external trade. Growth in industry as a whole accelerated to 4.9% from 4.2% in 2016. Services, which provide more than half of GDP, saw growth accelerate to 6.2% from 5.6% in 2016 on expansion in transport, telecommunications, business services, and e-commerce. Agriculture, which provides 9.0% of GDP, posted 7.2% growth, reversing 5.1% contraction in 2016 on the strength of higher commodity prices and favorable weather.

3.26.1 Trade in goods and services, 2017

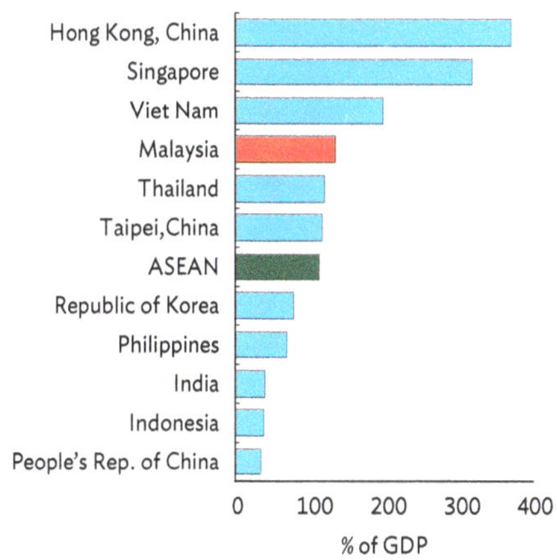

ASEAN = Association of Southeast Asian Nations.

Notes: Trade openess is the ratio of total trade in goods and services as a share of GDP. The average for ASEAN, weighted by current GDP in US dollars, excludes the Lao People's Democratic Republic.

Sources: CEIC Data Company (accessed 16 March 2018); General Statistics Office of Viet Nam.

3.26.2 Demand-side contributions to growth

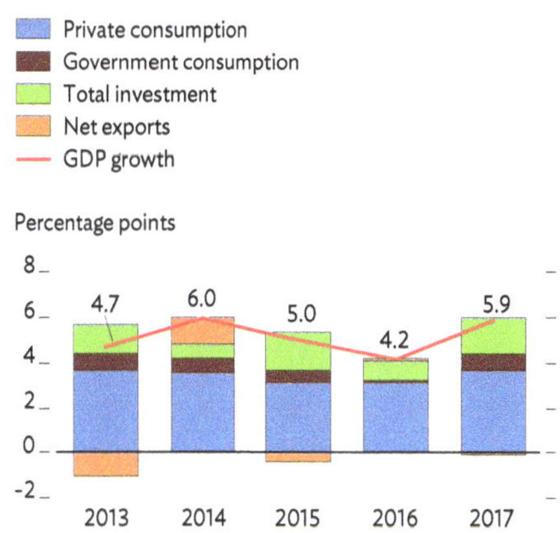

Sources: Haver Analytics; Bank Negara Malaysia. 2018. Monthly Highlights and Statistics. February. http://www.bnm.gov.my (accessed 16 March 2018).

This chapter was written by Valerie A. Mercer-Blackman and Shiela Camingue-Romance of the Economic Research and Regional Cooperation Department, ADB, Manila.

With stronger growth came higher inflation. Transport prices climbed by 13.2% as fuel and lubricant costs spiked early in the year, and as adjustments to controlled prices shifted from a monthly to a weekly basis and were finally aligned with international oil prices. Despite little change in other prices, including for food, headline inflation reached 3.8% in 2017 from 2.1% in 2016, well above the 2.4% average over the previous 10 years. Meanwhile, core inflation, excluding the more volatile categories, moderated to 1.8% from 2.8% in 2016 (Figure 3.26.3).

The current account surplus expanded slightly, further strengthening Malaysia's already ample external buffers. Merchandise imports rose by 14.0%, slightly outpacing 13.7% export growth. Because exports grew from a larger base, though, the trade surplus widened from the equivalent of 8.3% of GDP in 2016 to 8.7%, while the current account surplus rose to 3.0% of GDP from 2.4% in 2016 (Figure 3.26.4). The capital account was broadly in balance as net inbound direct foreign investment, equal to 0.9% of GDP, offset net outflows in other areas. Gross external reserves thus rose to $102 billion at the end of 2017, which is cover for 7.3 months of retained imports and a sum greater than the country's short-term external debt.

With the strong rebound in growth, the federal government program of fiscal consolidation proceeded apace, the fiscal deficit for the year estimated at 2.9% of GDP, a notch below the deficit in 2016 (Figure 3.26.5). Government expenditure fell slightly last year as a percentage of GDP, with current expenditure in particular down in line with government efforts to rationalize subsidies. Meanwhile, revenue rose a bit to reach 17.4% of GDP. Buoyant revenue from individual income tax and general sales tax raised nonenergy tax revenue slightly to an estimated 13.1% of GDP in 2017. Improvement from 11.1% in 2010 illustrates the success of government efforts to shift away from dependence on revenue from oil and gas.

Monetary policy continued to support growth in 2017 as Bank Negara Malaysia, the central bank, kept its policy interest rate unchanged at 3.0%. Then, in January this year, it raised the policy rate by 25 basis points to preclude possibly importing volatility from abroad and prevent the buildup of risk from interest rates staying too low for too long. Broad money (M3) grew by 4.7% in 2017, a slightly higher pace than in the previous 2 years.

Economic prospects

Strong external demand in 2017 fueled expansion in domestic demand in 2018. Having carried over into the first part of 2018, this growth momentum should moderate later in the year to a sustainable pace closer to potential growth. Real export growth should slow too as global trade growth moderates from

3.26.3 Monthly inflation

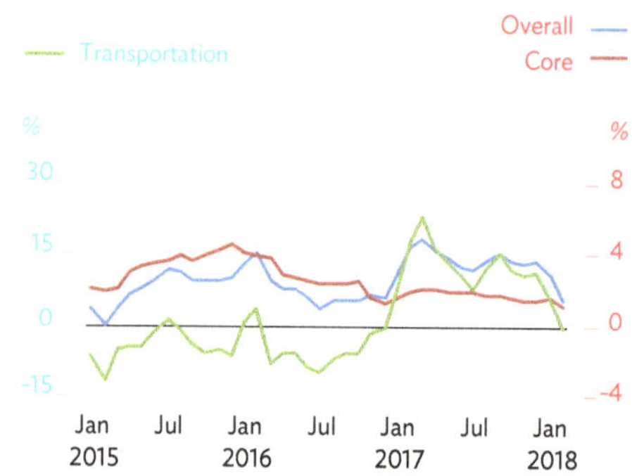

Sources: Haver Analytics; Bank Negara Malaysia. 2018. Monthly Highlights and Statistics. February. http://www.bnm.gov.my (accessed 16 March 2018).

3.26.4 Current account components

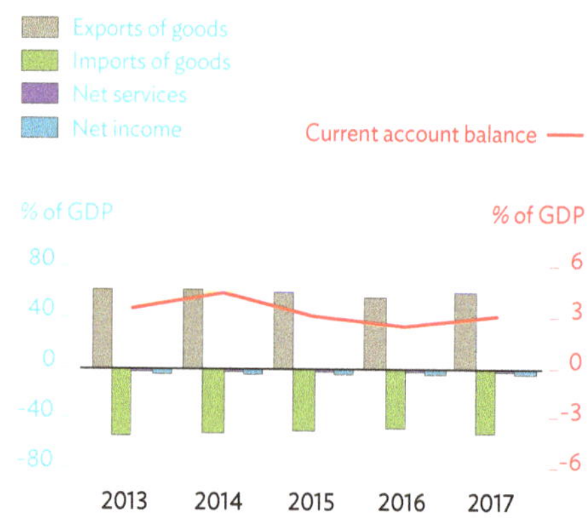

Sources: Haver Analytics; Bank Negara Malaysia. 2018. Monthly Highlights and Statistics. February. http://www.bnm.gov.my (accessed 16 March 2018).

3.26.5 Fiscal performance

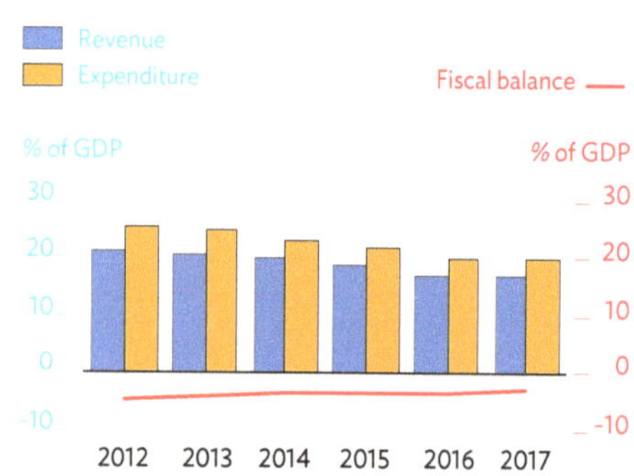

Sources: Haver Analytics; Bank Negara Malaysia. 2018. Monthly Highlights and Statistics. February. http://www.bnm.gov.my (accessed 16 March 2018).

last year's rebound, which was especially notable in electronics. GDP growth is forecast at 5.3% this year and 5.0% in 2019 (Figure 3.26.6).

Stable employment and wages should keep household consumption growing just below the 2017 rate—a view confirmed by upbeat consumer sentiment indicators. Private investment is likely to rise by 8.7%, only moderately short of 9.3% expansion last year as business sentiment remains positive (Figure 3.26.7). Makers of electrical and electronic equipment, for example, are expanding capacity as their products find new applications in automobiles, medical equipment, and aerospace. Construction on two large infrastructure projects, the East Coast Rail Link and a petrochemical complex in Johor, will continue into 2019. The plan is to start building the Kuala Lumpur–Singapore high-speed rail link by the end of 2019.

Inflation should decelerate following last year's one-off upward adjustment to fuel and transport prices. It is projected at 2.6% in 2018, in line with the 10-year average, and 1.8% in 2019 as oil prices subside.

On the balance of payments, moderating export growth is expected to slow import growth by half as demand falls for manufacturing inputs. However, imports of construction materials and of machinery and equipment should be strong in 2019 as investment in large infrastructure projects picks up. The current account is forecast to narrow to the equivalent of 2.4% of GDP this year and 2.1% in 2019.

Fiscal consolidation will remain a government priority. Reform to tax administration and measures to encourage tax compliance are likely to push revenue a little higher this year and next. As expenditure rationalization continues, the ratio of expenditure to GDP should decline slightly from an estimated 20.3% last year. The fiscal deficit is thus seen to decline steadily from the equivalent of 2.9% of GDP last year. The federal government's success in reaching its fiscal deficit target, equal to 1.0% of GDP by 2020, will depend on how effectively reform is implemented.

Following a policy rate hike in January 2018, monetary policy will likely complement fiscal consolidation toward managing aggregate demand with an eye to easing the economy back to its potential growth rate of about 5.0%. Bank Negara Malaysia, the central bank, has reiterated its intention to balance risks as a more upbeat outlook for domestic growth threatens higher inflation. Meanwhile, it is strengthening macroprudential oversight. Household debt as a share of GDP is a high 80% but has started to decline. More than half of this debt is mortgages granted according to relatively stringent requirements, so they enjoy a good repayment record.

3.26.6 Annual GDP growth

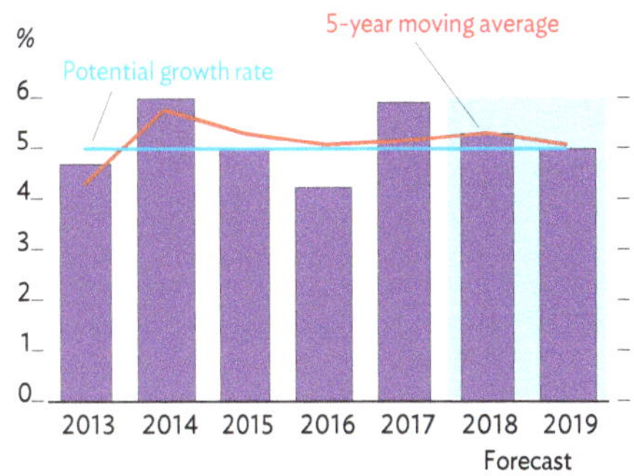

Source: *Asian Development Outlook* database.

3.26.1 Selected economic indicators (%)

	2018	2019
GDP growth	5.3	5.0
Inflation	2.6	1.8
Current account balance (share of GDP)	2.4	2.1

Source: ADB estimates.

3.26.7 Consumer and business confidence indexes

Q = quarter.

Source: Haver Analytics (accessed 22 March 2018).

One risk to the outlook would be dampened business confidence in export-oriented firms in response to rising protectionist sentiment abroad. Another would be volatility in financial markets. Malaysia has sufficient buffers, however, to counter any foreseeable risk.

Policy challenge—becoming a high-tech economy

Malaysia is set to become a high-income country in the next few years. Building on that milestone, the country aspires to move up the regional and global production network and supply chain to become a high-tech economy. Realizing that aspiration is not preordained. One of the biggest challenges will be to produce the kind of products and services that will transform Malaysia into a knowledge economy. The country's manufacturing industry is already highly integrated into global value chains. Malaysia is opening up its service sector, meanwhile, as part of the integration process with its partners in the Association of Southeast Asian Nations (ASEAN). However, to compete with a new set of high-income peers, Malaysia will have to add more value by moving into more complex stages of high-technology production. These stages include, on the upstream side, research and development and product conceptualization and, on the downstream side, logistics and the commercialization of high-tech goods and services (Figure 3.26.8).

Today, the more complex segments of the production processes in which Malaysia participates are handled abroad. For Malaysia to capture more of these segments, it needs a critical mass of highly skilled workers. Achieving this would require Malaysia to improve the quality of general education and of its technical and vocational training institutions, as well as provide more opportunities for workers to upgrade their capabilities on the job and thereby master the technology underlying the more complex stages of production.

Secondary education in Malaysia underperforms the average in the Organisation for Economic Co-operation and Development. As indicated by the scores of Malaysian 15-year-olds in tests conducted in 2015 by the Programme for International Student Assessment, it also trails its ASEAN partners Singapore and Viet Nam (Figure 3.26.9). The labor force is becoming more technology-ready, but this trend can be strengthened with more and better training on the job. In its *Global Competitiveness Report 2017–2018*, the World Economic Forum ranked Malaysia 46 out of 137 countries for technology-readiness, considerably below the Republic of Korea, which ranked 29 and has already achieved high-tech economy status. Malaysia trailed even more in higher education and training,

3.26.8 Moving up the electronics value chain

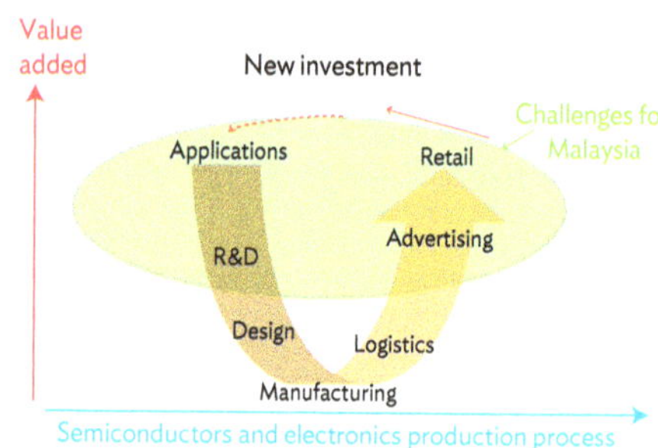

Source: ADB based on Idtech Report.

3.26.9 Math and reading scores in selected economies, 2015

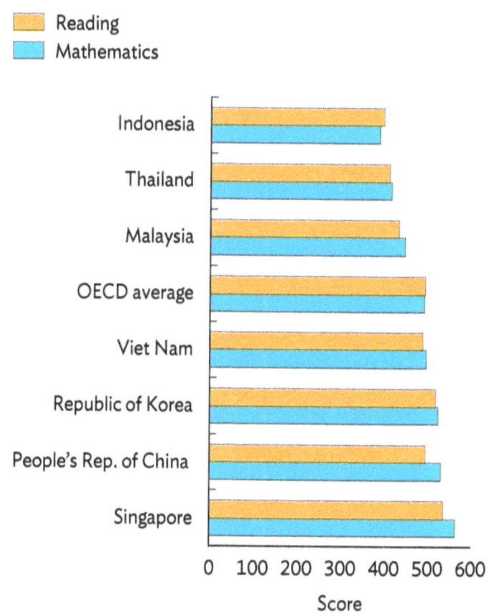

OECD = Organisation for Economic Co-operation and Development.

Note: The Programme for International Student Assessment assesses middle-schoolers in 72 countries. Mathematics measures the ability of a 15 year-old to formulate, employ, and interpret mathematics to describe, predict, and explain phenomena. Reading measures capacity to understand, use, and reflect on written texts to achieve goals, develop knowledge and potential, and participate in society. Only four urban centers were tested in the People's Republic of China, and sample selection similarly renders the results for Malaysia less than completely comparable.

Source: Programme for International Student Assessment, 2015 results: http://ww.oecd.org/pisa.

ranked 45 with the Republic of Korea at 25. Such comparative indicators underscore the need for Malaysia to strengthen its education system and opportunities for on-the-job training if it hopes to climb up the production value chain and become a high-tech economy.

Aware of those challenges, the government adopted in early 2018 a strategy to tackle them and enable the domestic production of more sophisticated goods and services. The three pillars of the strategy are selective investment targeting, which favors foreign investors willing to transfer technology and train workers while discouraging those seeking only a low-cost production base; the creation of digital free-trade zones to facilitate e-commerce and equip smaller enterprises with digital technology; and pursuing a consultative policy dubbed National Industry 4.0, which, among other things, aims to build factories of the future and enhance entrepreneur and worker capacity in product conceptualization, design, usage, marketing, and distribution. Effective implementation of the strategy is critical to the realization of Malaysia's aspiration to become a high-tech economy over the long term.

Myanmar

GDP growth picked up in fiscal 2017 to 6.8%. Inflation eased, and the current account deficit widened. With continued economic reform, growth should be sustained this year and accelerate next year. Inflation will likely edge up and the current account deficit widen further. By pursuing reform to improve the business environment, policy makers can sustain the sizable foreign direct investment needed over the medium term to finance the current account deficit.

Economic performance

In fiscal year 2017 (FY2017, ended 31 March 2018), economic growth quickened to the equivalent of an estimated 6.8% in FY2017, up from 5.9% in FY2016. Data on demand-side components of GDP are limited, but support appears to have come from stronger agriculture, growth in exports, and robust private consumption, with investment continuing to soften.

By sector, agriculture, which provides about 30% of GDP, turned around with better weather to post growth estimated at 3.5%, reversing drought-induced contraction in FY2016. The industry and service sectors maintained strong growth estimated to exceed 8.0%. Robust manufacturing drove industrial output higher, while services benefitted from buoyant tourism and strengthening domestic consumption.

Merchandise exports are estimated to have grown by 15.0% in FY2017 in US dollar terms, reversing 0.3% contraction in the previous year. Exports were driven by rice shipments estimated at 2.8 million tons, the highest in half a century, and high demand for garments. Earnings from service exports appear to have remained buoyant, with the Ministry of Hotels and Tourism reporting international tourist arrivals up by 18.0% last year to reach 3.4 million (Figure 3.27.1). Private consumption seems to have remained strong, supported by higher purchasing power for urban residents and more commercial activity in the private sector. Investment growth may have softened, however, as investors awaited clarity on a new company law expected in August 2018.

Even as growth picked up, inflation slowed to an estimated 5.3% from 6.8% in FY2016, reflecting mainly lower food inflation with recovery in agriculture (Figure 3.27.2). Subdued international grains prices, slower monetary expansion, and a stable exchange rate helped keep the lid on inflation, which nevertheless began edging up in September 2017.

3.27.1 Tourism indicators

Note: Data refer to calendar year. Tourist arrivals include border tourism.

Sources: Central Statistical Organization; Ministry of Hotels and Tourism.

3.27.2 Inflation

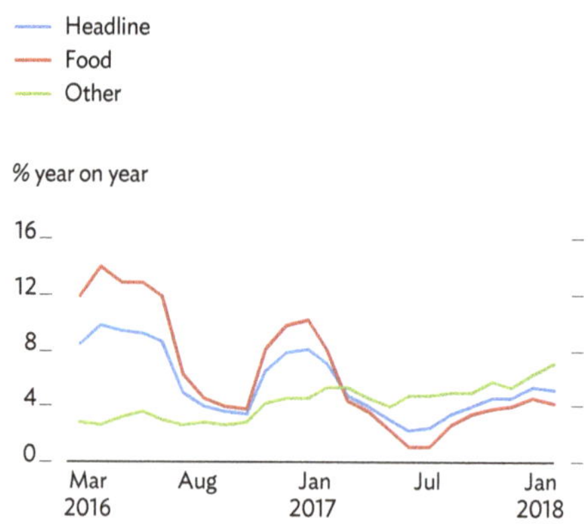

Source: Central Statistical Organization.

This chapter was written by Yumiko Tamura of the Myanmar Resident Mission, ADB, Nay Pyi Taw; Thiam Hee Ng of the Southeast Asia Department, ADB, Manila; and Marthe Hinojales of the Economic Research and Regional Cooperation Department, ADB, Manila.

Growth in merchandise imports is estimated to have accelerated fivefold to 12.0% from 2.4% growth in FY2016 on strengthening domestic consumption and demand for capital goods to supply infrastructure projects, widening the trade deficit. With higher service exports only partly offsetting the expanding trade deficit, the current account deficit is estimated to have widened to the equivalent of 5.0% of GDP in FY2017 from 3.9% a year earlier. After depreciating by more than 10% from June to December 2016, the Myanmar kyat was stable throughout 2017 (Figure 3.27.3).

Credit growth slowed to an estimated 21.2% in FY2017 from 25.5% in FY2016, according to an International Monetary Fund report published in March 2018, as growth in the money supply slowed to an estimated 16.5% from 19.4%, reflecting monetary policy intended to rein in inflation. Meanwhile, the fiscal deficit is estimated to have widened to the equivalent of 3.5% of GDP in FY2017 from 2.5% in FY2016 as the government increased spending on electric power infrastructure, health care, education, and social welfare.

3.27.3 Exchange rate

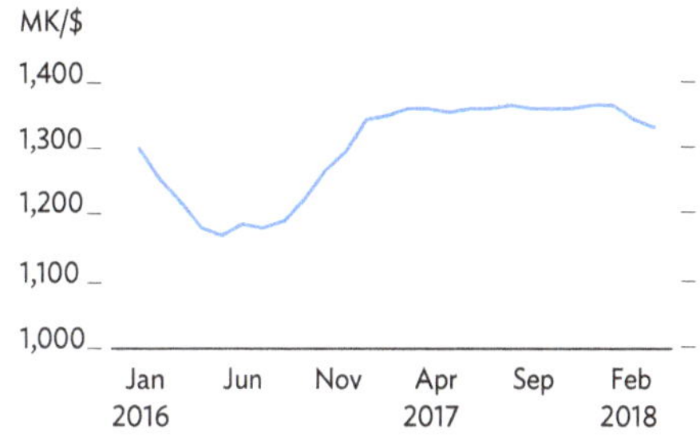

Source: CEIC database.

Economic prospects

With continued strong global growth, the external economic environment should remain favorable. The economy is so far little affected by the situation in Northern Rakhine. Demand generated in Myanmar by foreign direct investment (FDI) should continue to support growth. GDP growth is projected at an annualized 6.8% in the 6 months from April to September 2018, before Myanmar adopts a new fiscal year in October 2018 (Figure 3.27.4). Growth is forecast at 7.2% in FY2019 (ending 31 September 2019).

Agriculture is forecast to continue to grow robustly, assuming normal weather and favorable commodity prices. Signs indicate improved conditions for manufacturing, with the Nikkei purchasing managers' index rising in February 2018 to 52.6, well above the threshold of 50.0 indicating expansion (Figure 3.27.5). Growth in industry is therefore projected to strengthen both this year and next. Services should expand further with solid growth in tourism and information technology services.

Higher growth will likely stoke inflation, as will an expected rise in international oil prices. Inflation is thus forecast to accelerate to 6.2% this year before moderating slightly to 6.0% in FY2019. The current account deficit is forecast to widen to the equivalent of 5.4% of GDP in FY2018 and 5.5% in FY2019. An improved external environment will help export growth, but it will likely be outpaced by import growth needed to support public investments in infrastructure and continuing FDI.

The fiscal deficit is projected to remain near 4.0% of GDP over the next 2 years as public spending increases to support the socioeconomic development agenda. While revenue collection has improved, requiring less financing of the fiscal deficit by the Central Bank of Myanmar in recent years, public financial management needs to be strengthened.

3.27.4 GDP growth

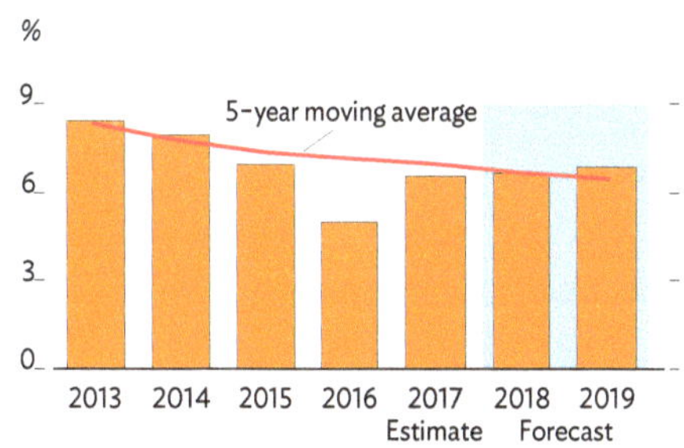

Note: From 2013 to 2017, years are fiscal years ending 31 March of the next year; 2018 covers April–September; in 2019, the fiscal year ends 31 September of the year.

Sources: International Monetary Fund; ADB estimates.

3.27.5 Nikkei manufacturing purchasing managers' index

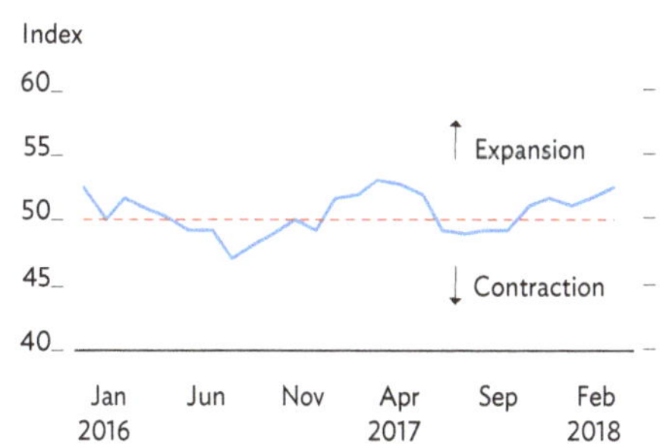

Sources: IHS Markit; Bloomberg.

The positive economic outlook depends on Myanmar augmenting limited public resources by effectively engaging development partners, foreign investors, and the domestic private sector to help finance its staggering infrastructure requirements, narrow regional socioeconomic disparities, and support the long-term development agenda. This will require legal, regulatory, and institutional reform to create a more enabling environment for doing business.

A risk to the outlook would be lackluster progress on economic reform. Although measures have been introduced to deepen the capital market and better regulate banks, a substantial agenda of economic, social, and institutional reform remains.

3.27.1 Selected economic indicators (%)

	2018	2019
GDP growth	6.8	7.2
Inflation	6.2	6.0
Current account balance (share of GDP)	-5.4	-5.5

Note: From 2013 to 2017, years are fiscal years ending 31 March of the next year; 2018 covers April–September; in 2019, the fiscal year ends 31 September of the year.

Source: ADB estimates.

Policy challenge—sustaining foreign direct investment to support growth

FDI is crucial to Myanmar over the medium term to finance its persistent current account deficit and support growth. The recent trend of import growth outpacing export growth is likely to persist for some time, widening the trade deficit. Although remittances and development assistance can cushion the growing trade deficit, substantial current account deficits will remain and need to be financed sustainably. With underdeveloped capital markets, Myanmar cannot hope to attract sizable portfolio capital inflows in the near future. FDI will therefore have to be the main source of financing for the current account deficit. As Myanmar has favorable demographics thanks to a large and youthful population, FDI can help tap the country's potential for export-oriented production of labor-intensive goods.

Although Myanmar has liberalized policy in recent years to attract more FDI, a composite FDI regulatory restrictiveness index that considers countries' limits on foreign equity holdings, screening and approval mechanisms, and controls on capital repatriation by foreign enterprises seems to suggest that Myanmar's FDI regulations are more restrictive than in most peer economies in Southeast Asia (Figure 3.27.6). Moreover, in *Doing Business 2018*, the World Bank ranks Myanmar at 171 of 190 economies, though it ranks better on some specifics, notably obtaining construction permits, paying taxes, and registering property. These points underscore the need for the country to liberalize its FDI regulations and improve the business environment.

Encouragingly, progress in December 2017 toward enacting a new company law can assure foreign investors that corporate reform will continue. Similarly, a government initiative to formulate a 238-point economic policy agenda, set out in the draft Myanmar Sustainable Development Plan, should keep investors engaged. Building on these initiatives, policy makers should implement reform expeditiously and effectively to buoy investor confidence and attract sizable FDI in the years to come.

3.27.6 Foreign direct investment regulatory restrictiveness index, 2016

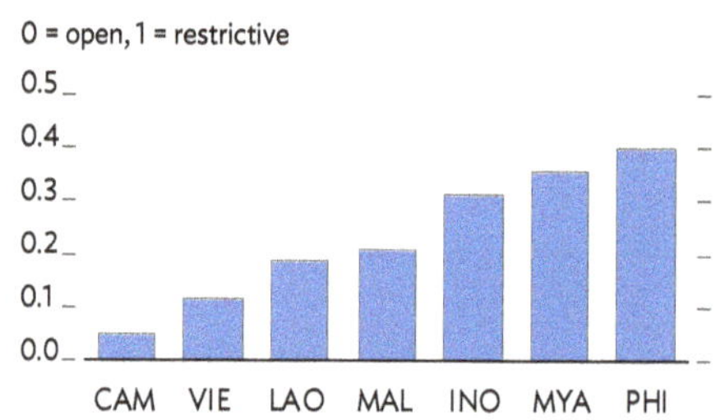

CAM = Cambodia, INO = Indonesia, LAO = Lao People's Democratic Republic, MAL = Malaysia, MYA = Myanmar, PHI = Philippines, VIE = Viet Nam.

Source: Organisation for Economic Co-operation and Development.

Philippines

Broad expansion in aggregate demand, helped by higher export growth, underpinned strong economic growth last year. Inflation picked up, and the current account posted a marginal deficit. Accelerated investment should offset moderation in exports this year and next, enabling higher growth. Inflation will edge up, and the current account will remain in deficit. Strengthened project planning and implementation capacity is crucial to the success of an ambitious public infrastructure program.

Economic performance

Robust domestic demand, upheld by higher export growth, helped GDP grow by 6.7% in 2017 (Figure 3.28.1). This was marginally slower than 6.9% in 2016, partly because of a high base effect following election spending in 2016. Domestic investment grew by 9.0% last year, down from a striking 23.7% rise in 2016. Fixed investment, accounting for a large share of domestic investment, continued to increase, by 10.3% last year on top of hefty 25.2% growth in 2016, to equal 25.2% of GDP in 2017, the highest percentage in over a decade (Figure 3.28.2). Fixed investment in industrial machinery, transport equipment, and public construction were particularly strong.

Supported by higher employment and remittances from overseas Filipinos, household consumption grew by 5.8% last year, easing from a 7.0% rise in 2016. With 2.4 million jobs created last year, the unemployment rate fell from 6.6% in January 2017 to a low of 5.3% in January 2018. Remittances from overseas rose by 5.3% to $31.3 billion, equal to 10.0% of GDP. Government consumption moderated from 8.4% growth in 2016 to 7.3% last year, though in the second half government expenditure—including national health insurance, education services, and cash transfers to poor families—accelerated by 11.2% over the year-earlier period.

Growth in exports of goods and services nearly doubled in real terms from 10.7% in 2016 to 19.2% last year (Figure 3.28.3). With a rebound in global electronics trade, growth in merchandise exports more than doubled from 9.2% in 2016 to 20.7%. Electronics, mainly semiconductors, accounted for three-fourths of the expansion in merchandise exports, other notable items including processed food, furniture, machinery and transportation equipment, and agricultural and mineral products.

3.28.1 Demand-side contributions to growth

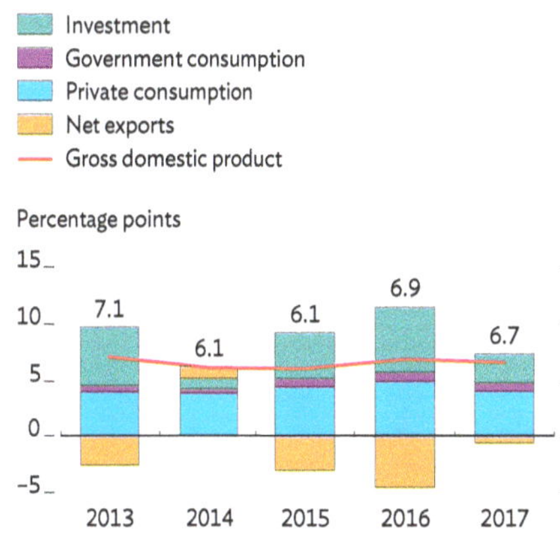

Source: CEIC Data Company (accessed 16 March 2018).

3.28.2 Fixed investment

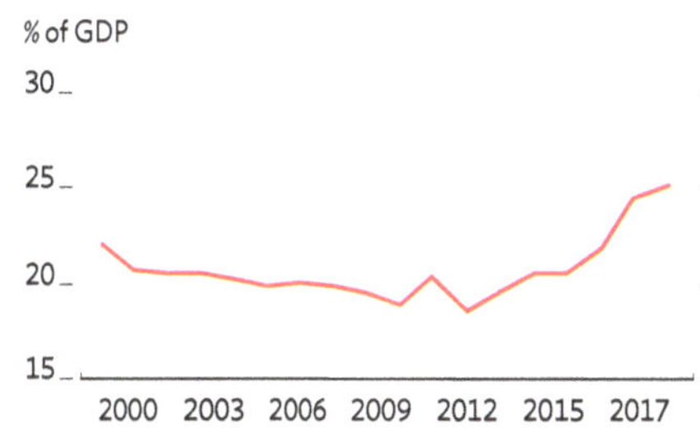

Source: CEIC Data Company (accessed 16 March 2018).

This chapter was written by Aekapol Chongvilaivan and Teresa Mendoza of the Philippines Country Office, ADB, Manila.

By sector, agriculture recovered from dry weather caused by El Niño to grow by 3.9% last year, reversing a 1.3% decline in 2016 (Figure 3.28.4). Rice and corn production rebounded. Industry output rose by 7.2%, moderating from 8.4% growth in 2016, to provide one-third of GDP expansion. Buoyant domestic demand and higher export growth spurred 8.6% growth in manufacturing, the highest in 4 years. Manufacturing expansion extended across food processing, electronics, construction materials, furniture, communication, transportation, and office equipment. Growth in construction more than halved to 5.4% from 13.7% in 2016, largely from moderation in private investment.

Broad expansion in services eased from 7.4% in 2016 to 6.7%, but the sector still provided nearly 60% of the expansion in GDP. Trade, finance, business process outsourcing, and real estate services all grew, as did accommodation and restaurants on higher tourism.

Strong growth, higher international fuel prices, and depreciation of the Philippine peso pushed headline inflation to 3.2% last year from 1.8% in 2016, with notably higher prices for fuel, meat, and fish. Inflation remained within the target of 2%–4% set by Bangko Sentral ng Pilipinas, the central bank.

A 12.8% rise in merchandise exports in US dollar terms was outpaced by 14.2% growth in merchandise imports. Brisk growth in manufacturing pushed up imports of raw materials, parts, and components, while stronger domestic demand pushed up imports of consumer and capital goods. Higher international fuel prices boosted the import bill for oil and petroleum products. The result was a trade deficit of $41.2 billion, equal to 13.1% of GDP and expanded from 11.7% in 2016 (Figure 3.28.5). Strong rises in remittances from overseas Filipinos and service exports, mainly business process outsourcing and tourism, partly offset the merchandise trade deficit to yield a current account deficit of only $2.5 billion, equal to 0.8% of GDP but up from 0.4% in 2016. Foreign direct investment inflows reached $10.0 billion in 2017, a 21.4% increase over 2016 (Figure 3.28.6). The balance of payments deficit equaled 0.3% of GDP, up from 0.1% in 2016 partly because of higher portfolio capital outflows. Gross international reserves rose to $81.6 billion in 2017, providing 8.0 months of cover for imports of goods and services and income payments. On average, the peso depreciated in 2017 by 5.8% from its year-earlier value against the US dollar.

With inflation still modest and the external payments position comfortable, monetary policy remained accommodative. The central bank reduced the 20% reserve ratio required of financial institutions by 1 percentage point in March 2018. It maintained its policy overnight reverse repurchase rate at 3.0%. In a near replay of 2017, money supply (M3) rose by 12.8% year on year in January 2018, and bank credit to the private sector rose by 16.5%.

3.28.3 Trade in real goods and services

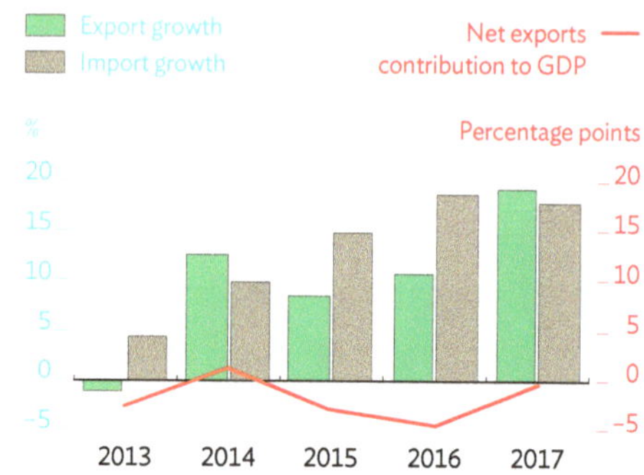

Source: CEIC Data Company (accessed 16 March 2018).

3.28.4 Supply-side contributions to growth

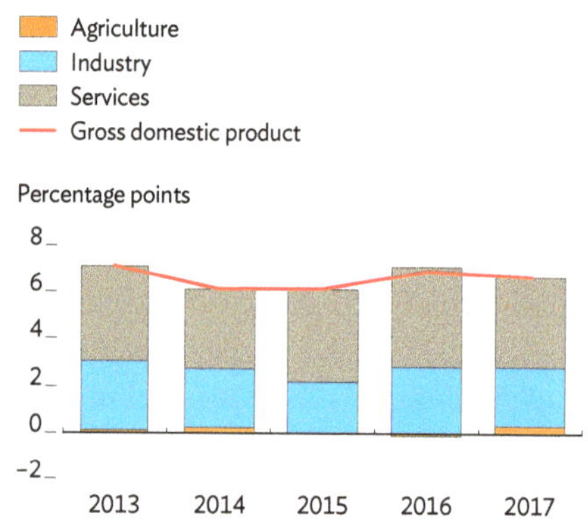

Source: CEIC Data Company (accessed 16 March 2018).

3.28.5 Current account components

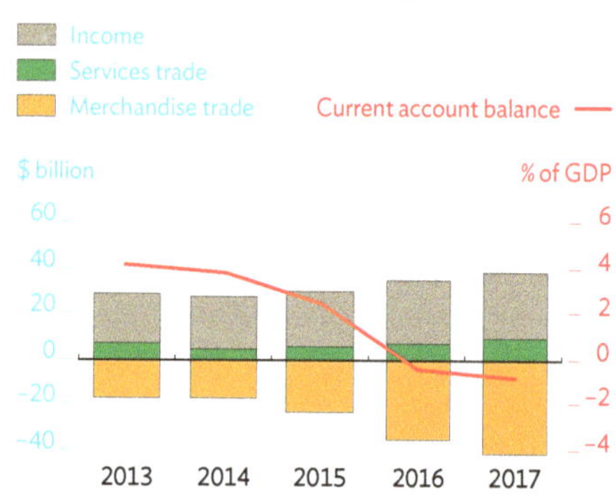

Source: CEIC Data Company (accessed 16 March 2018).

The fiscal deficit in 2017 equaled 2.2% of GDP, below the statutory ceiling of 3.0% and down from 2.4% in 2016. Rising revenue helped the ratio of revenue to GDP rise to 15.7% last year from 15.2% in 2016. Tax collection, providing 91% of revenue, rose by 13.6% to equal 14.2% of GDP, improving from 13.7% in 2016. Meanwhile, government expenditure rose by 10.8% last year, taking the ratio of expenditure to GDP to 17.9% from 17.6% in 2016. Infrastructure spending—mostly on roads, flood control and irrigation, and school buildings—rose by 15.4% to account for a fourth of the increase in total expenditure.

3.28.6 Foreign direct investment net inflows

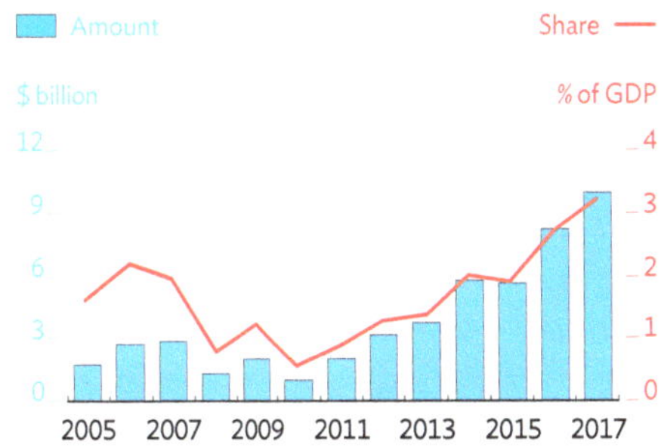

Source: CEIC Data Company (accessed 16 March 2018).

Economic prospects

Strengthening domestic demand will underpin growth in 2018 and 2019. Investment will be supported by large public infrastructure projects such as national and provincial roads, railways, airports, and the Philippines' first mass transit subway. Export growth will likely moderate from last year's rebound. Low unemployment and steady remittances will continue to support private consumption. GDP growth is thus forecast to strengthen to 6.8% this year and 6.9% next (Figure 3.28.7).

An accommodative fiscal policy is likely to continue this year and next. The 2018 budget raises expenditure by 12.4% over last year, with two-thirds allocated to regions outside of Metro Manila. Allocations for the provinces are 25% higher than in 2017 and are earmarked for rural development and job creation toward improving rural incomes. The budget for infrastructure is a quarter higher, equal to 6.1% of GDP, up from 5.4% in 2017. The government recently approved free tuition in all state universities and colleges under the Universal Access to Quality Tertiary Education Act, 2017 and free irrigation for smallholder farmers under the Free Irrigation Service Act, 2018.

The government is mobilizing more revenue to allow for higher investment in infrastructure and social services while keeping the fiscal deficit within 3.0% of GDP in the medium term. It thus targets the ratio of revenue to GDP in the 2018 budget to rise to 16.3% from 15.7% last year. Early progress toward achieving the revenue target was made in December 2017 with the approval of the Tax Reform for Acceleration and Inclusion law, the first phase of government's comprehensive tax reform program. The law is projected to yield ₱90 billion in additional revenue in 2018 and ₱144 billion in 2019. Further augmentation of tax revenue is anticipated as the government pursues succeeding phases of comprehensive tax reform.

Remittances from overseas Filipinos are expected to continue to support household consumption. From the fiscal side, a cut in the personal income tax should boost disposable income and consumption among taxpayers, but an increase in excise taxes on petroleum products and a few other commodities could be a counterweight restraining household

3.28.7 GDP growth

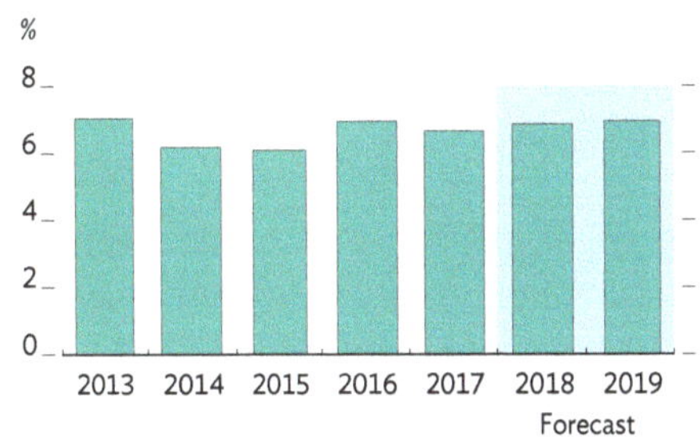

Source: *Asian Development Outlook* database.

3.28.8 Purchasing managers' index

Source: Bangko Sentral ng Pilipinas. 2018. *Philippines Selected Economics and Financial Indicators.* http://www.bsp.gov.ph/statistics/keystat/sefi.pdf.

consumption. On balance, strong household consumption is seen continuing this year and next.

Several signs point to strengthening private investment. Imports of capital goods rose by 16.9% year on year in January 2018, while bank credit to businesses increased by 18.1% in the same month. The government is improving the investment climate by streamlining procedures for doing business in national and local agencies alike, including for business registration and applications for permits. In December 2017, Fitch Ratings upgraded the Philippine rating for long-term foreign currency credit to BBB from BBB–, which should reinforce market confidence. A business outlook survey conducted by the central bank in the first quarter of 2018 found sentiment upbeat in response to strong domestic demand and the expected increase in public infrastructure spending.

By sector, services will continue to provide much of GDP growth as broad expansion continues. The purchasing managers' index in January 2018 reached its highest since May 2016 with improving readings for services, trade, and manufacturing (Figure 3.28.8). Manufacturing will continue to expand on robust domestic demand and exports. The manufacturing production index rose by 21.9% year on year in January 2018 on strong growth in food and beverages, construction materials, and some export-oriented products. Construction will benefit largely from public infrastructure projects, but it is notable that building permits for privately constructed commercial and office buildings expanded by 23.2% year on year in the fourth quarter of 2017.

As growth strengthens, inflation is projected to pick up to 4.0% in 2018, using a consumer price index series based on 2006. Inflation in the first 2 months of this year accelerated to 4.2% using that series but slowed to 3.7% using a new series rebased on 2012 (Figure 3.28.9). Inflation largely reflected a rise in global oil and food prices and peso depreciation. Higher excises on fuel, sugar-sweetened beverages, and cigarettes since January 2018 could contribute to inflation, but mitigation measures are under way. The government is moving away from restrictions on the volume of rice imports toward tariffs on rice imports to help augment domestic supply and contain domestic rice prices. Inflation is forecast at 3.9% in 2019, with upward adjustment to monetary policy rates anticipated in line with tightening monetary policy globally (Figure 3.28.10).

Import growth is expected to outpace export growth in light of robust domestic demand. The expected widening of the merchandise trade deficit this year and next should mean a wider but still modest current account deficit, contained by a further rise in remittances and service exports, notably in business process outsourcing and tourism. Improving business sentiment points to a continued uptrend in foreign direct investment.

3.28.1 Selected economic indicators (%)

	2018	2019
GDP growth	6.8	6.9
Inflation	4.0	3.9
Current account balance (share of GDP)	-1.0	-1.4

Source: ADB estimates.

3.28.9 Monthly inflation

Source: CEIC Data Company (accessed 16 March 2018).

3.28.10 Inflation

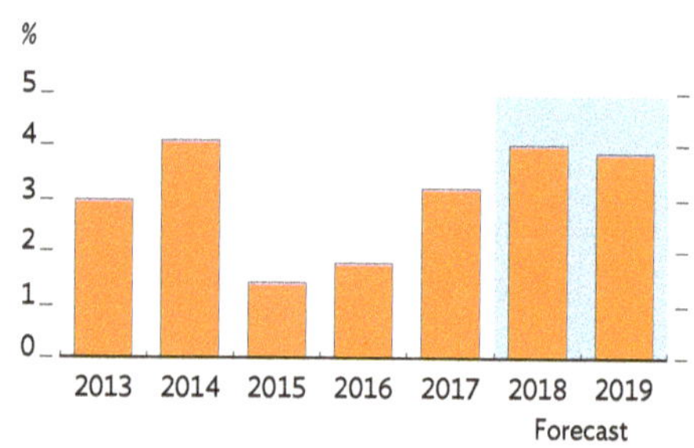

Source: *Asian Development Outlook* database.

External risks to the outlook would be heightened volatility in international financial markets or a revival of protectionist trade policies around the world. However, a strong external payments position appears to make the Philippines resilient under any foreseeable external shock. External debt trended down to the equivalent of 23.3% of GDP in 2017. National government debt has moderated to 42.1% of GDP and is denominated mostly in local currency (Figure 3.28.11).

3.28.11 National government debt

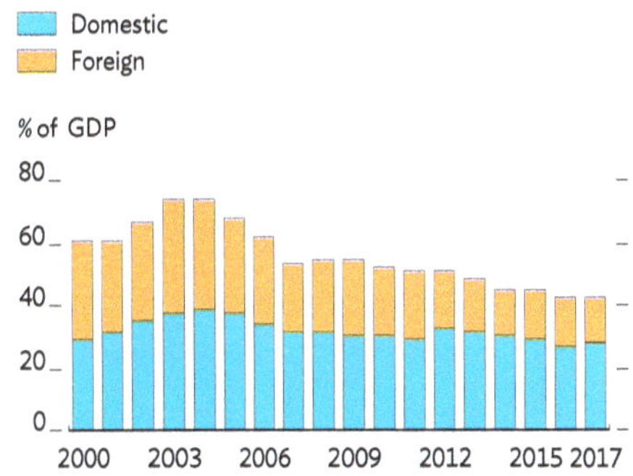

Source: CEIC Data Company (accessed 16 March 2018).

Policy challenge—enhancing the government's absorptive capacity for infrastructure development

The Philippine government has embarked on a massive infrastructure program worth \$160 billion–\$180 billion from 2017 to 2022, called "Build Build Build." The program aims to address infrastructure bottlenecks that have long constrained Philippine competitiveness globally and its long-term growth prospects. Under the program, public infrastructure spending is targeted to rise from 4.5% of GDP in 2016 to 7.3% by 2022. The program has already gathered momentum, with public spending on infrastructure estimated to rise by nearly a percentage point of GDP last year to reach 5.4%. This is a remarkable achievement for the first year. However, considering the wide array of infrastructure projects under the program, the challenge for the government is to ensure that government departments, and other implementing agencies have the adequate absorptive capacity to roll out and implement such large and complex projects.

Encouragingly, efforts are already under way to enhance the absorptive capacity of government agencies, including their technical and institutional capabilities for project readiness and budget execution. Initiatives include a proposed shift from a multiyear budget system to an annual cash-based system effective in January 2019 with a view to improving budget execution. A budget reform bill is being pursued in the legislature to institutionalize improvements in the financial management, budgeting, accountability, and result-orientation of the budget process and public spending.

Building on these recent initiatives, concerted efforts on three fronts should help further enhance the absorptive capacity of government agencies: making interagency coordination more cohesive; fostering stronger partnership between government agencies, the private sector, and development partners; and strengthening the skills of staff in implementing public agencies.

The timely completion of infrastructure projects requires more cohesive interagency coordination in planning and budgeting bodies and in sectoral government departments and line agencies. A project facilitation, monitoring, and innovation task force was established in June 2017 to expeditiously address bottlenecks constraining infrastructure projects at every step in the project cycle, from planning and approval to implementation and monitoring. Building on this initiative, the task force has potential to serve as a center for interagency coordination and strategic planning for infrastructure development.

Another way to expand absorptive capacity in public sector bodies would be to strengthen partnerships between the government, the private sector, and development partners. The private sector and development partners can bring in technical support, innovation, and new ideas for project preparation and implementation.

Finally, there is an urgent need to augment technical capacity within agencies. Some projects such as long-span bridges and tunnels are technically complex and beyond previous experience in the Philippines. These projects need to be pursued with international best practices, knowledge, and innovation. Capacity-building takes time but is indispensable. As many infrastructure projects are already being prepared and implemented, the government may facilitate on-the-job training and transfer of knowledge and best practices from experts.

Singapore

After a sharp pickup in 2017, GDP growth will slow only slightly in 2018 and 2019, supported by strong but moderating exports of manufactures. Inflation will rise on higher food prices and excise taxes but remain moderate, while the current account surplus will expand along with GDP. A key policy issue is improving corporate capacity to innovate to ensure that it stays competitive in the digital age.

Economic performance

GDP growth accelerated to 3.6% in 2017 from 2.4% in 2016 on robust performances in manufacturing and services. Manufacturing grew by 10.1%, the highest rate since 2010, as strong electronics and precision engineering clusters outweighed weakness notably in biomedicine and transport. Manufacturing expansion lifted the contribution of industry to GDP growth to 1.4 percentage points, despite contraction in construction by 8.4% (Figure 3.29.1). Services expanded by 2.8%, double their rate in 2016 owing to a strong result from finance and insurance, and from transportation and storage. The sector contributed 1.9 percentage points to GDP growth.

On the demand side, the main sources of growth in 2017 were exports, investments, and consumption (Figure 3.29.2). Real exports of goods and services grew by 4.1%, driven largely by exports of machinery and transport equipment and of chemical products. Imports also grew at a faster rate of 5.2%, however, turning net exports negative and shaving 0.7 percentage points off growth. Investment contributed 2.4 percentage points to growth as firms accumulated inventory in expectation of stronger demand in the first half of 2018—and despite fixed capital outlays falling as infrastructure spending slumped. Private consumption grew by 3.1% on a modest rise in wages, and government spending rose by 4.1%, notably on social services. Combined consumption contributed 1.5 percentage points to growth.

After 2 consecutive years of deflation, the consumer price index rose by 0.6% in 2017 as prices increased for transportation, education, and food, which together account for over 40% of the index. Inflation was tempered by lower rents and utility prices. Transportation costs, the largest contributor to inflation, rose on higher prices for gasoline and parking,

3.29.1 Contributions to growth by industry

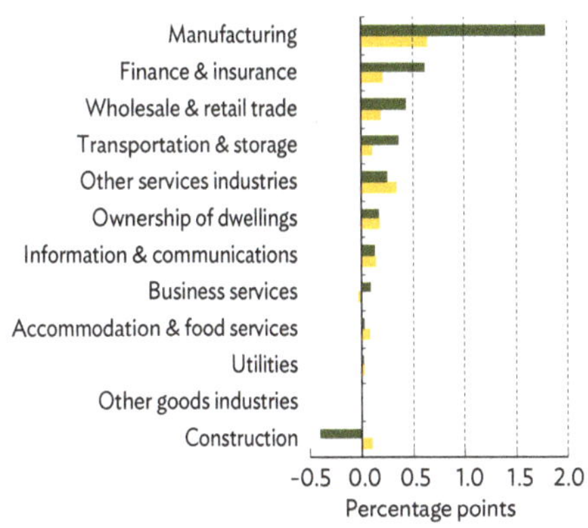

Source: Ministry of Trade and Industry. Economic Survey Singapore 2017 (accessed 14 February 2018).

3.29.2 Demand-side contributions to growth

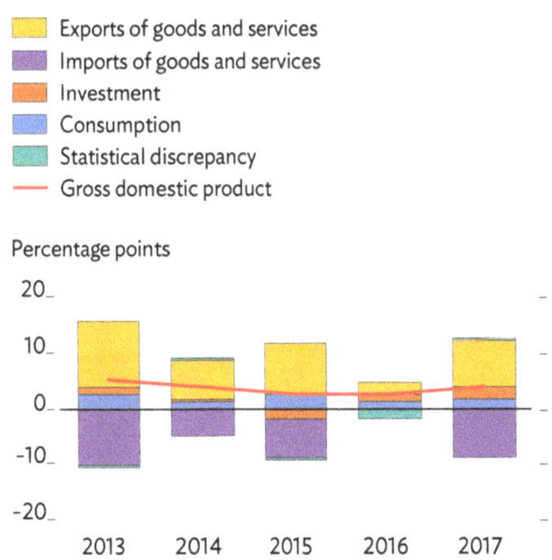

Source: Ministry of Trade and Industry. Economic Survey Singapore 2017 (accessed 14 February 2018).

This chapter was written by Minsoo Lee and Mai Lin Villaruel of the Economic Research and Regional Cooperation Department, ADB, Manila.

and with the expiry of a road tax rebate. Core inflation, which excludes private road transport and accommodation, edged up to average 1.5% in 2017 from 0.9% in 2016 (Figure 3.29.3).

The trade surplus rose to equal 26.2% of GDP in 2017 (Figure 3.29.4). Merchandise exports increased by 9.3%, mainly as exports of petroleum products surged to reverse a decline in 2016, with higher sales to Hong Kong, China; Indonesia; and the People's Republic of China. Merchandise imports increased by 12.4%, with crude oil, electronics, specialized machinery, and pharmaceuticals imports growing rapidly. The net services deficit widened, narrowing the current account surplus to the equivalent of 18.8% of GDP. Net foreign exchange reserves rose, however, as net capital outflows in 2016 turned to net inflows (Figure 3.29.5).

The Monetary Authority of Singapore (MAS) has maintained its policy band for the nominal effective exchange rate since April 2016. On average in 2017, the Singapore dollar appreciated in nominal effective terms by 0.5%, within this band, while rising against the US dollar by a fractional 0.04% (Figure 3.29.6). The 3-month Singapore interbank offered rate, typically the reference to price home loans, rose to 1.50% in December 2017 from 0.97% in December 2016 in tandem with a rise in the US federal funds rate. Nevertheless, outstanding loans and advances increased by 5.6%, and money supply (M2) grew by 3.2%, down from 8.0% in 2016.

The budget surplus widened to equal 2.1% of GDP in fiscal year 2017 (FY2017, ended 31 March 2018). Operating revenue grew by 9.0%, with stamp duty collections rising substantially on a recent property market pickup. Government expenditure including special transfers rose by 3.5%, but development expenditure declined by 5.8%. The surplus came largely from the transfer by MAS and two investment funds of a portion of their investment income to the budget, the MAS contribution amounting to S$4.6 billion. The budget deficit excluding these transfers narrowed to equal 1.1% of GDP.

Economic prospects

Growth is expected to moderate to 3.1% in 2018 and 2.9% in 2019. Manufacturing will continue to be the main driver of growth but less than in 2017. Business sentiment in manufacturing remains optimistic, but the purchasing managers' index for electronics, which contribute 30% of manufacturing output, has edged down, indicating moderation in production and exports (Figures 3.29.7). Weakness in construction is expected to ease with the implementation of public projects and civil engineering works. Services will remain strong domestically as the government continues to boost health care and other social spending.

3.29.3 Inflation

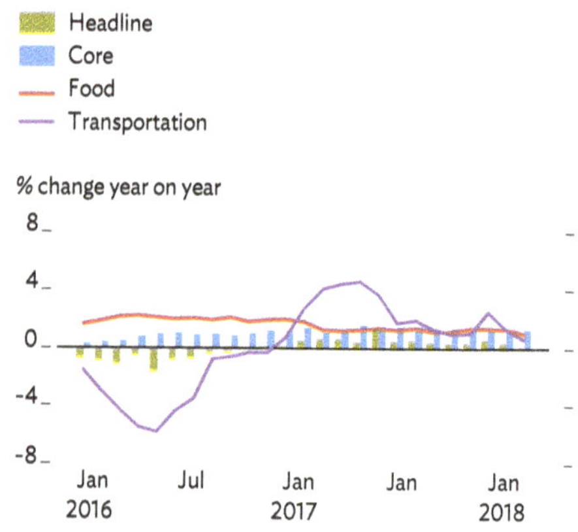

Source: CEIC Data Company (accessed 9 March 2018).

3.29.4 Merchandise trade

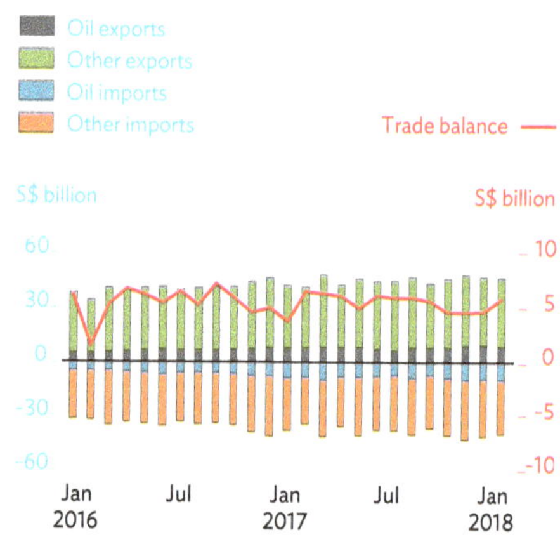

Source: CEIC Data Company (accessed 9 March 2018).

3.29.5 Balance of payments

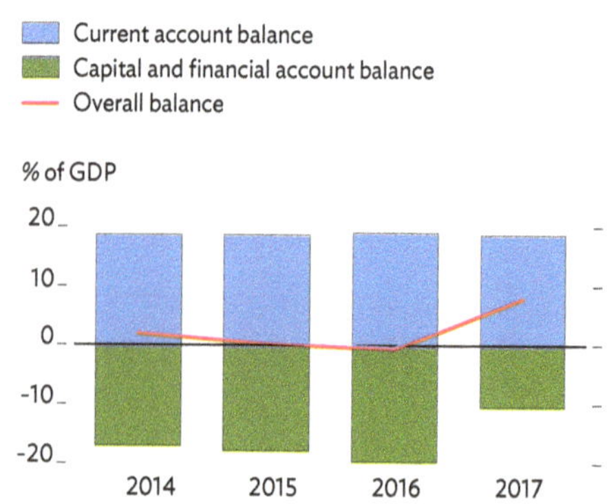

Source: Ministry of Trade and Industry. Economic Survey Singapore 2017 (accessed 14 February 2018).

Domestic demand will support the economy in 2018 and 2019 as the government increases spending on social services, safety nets, and infrastructure including rail lines. The contribution of private consumption to growth will likely moderate, however, as the labor market gradually slackens and wage growth slows. Private investment will improve, with spending expected to amount to 2.3% of GDP. The seasonally adjusted trend in exports since the beginning of the year points to moderating export growth, while imports are expected to increase as domestic demand grows. On balance, though, net exports will contribute to growth this year and in 2019. Trade is expected to post surpluses in both years. With rising net service receipts as well, the current account surplus should expand marginally to 19.0% of GDP in 2018 and stay there in 2019.

Inflation moderated a tad in January 2018. Soft rental housing and labor markets will dampen prices this year and next as rising food and oil prices and a 10% increase in the tobacco excise push prices higher. On balance, inflation is projected to rise to 0.9% in 2018 and 1.4% in 2019, when a carbon tax will be introduced. Considering its modest inflation forecast, MAS will likely intervene to dampen the pace of interest rate rises as US rates increase.

The FY2018 budget emphasizes securing Singapore's development through innovation, a high-quality living environment, and the pursuit of a caring and cohesive society. Fiscal policy will be expansionary in FY2018. Expenditure including transfers is slated to rise to equal 19.2% of GDP, 1.3 percentage points higher than in FY2017, and operational revenue is projected at 15.6% of GDP, for a deficit equal to 3.6% of GDP, which will be financed largely by contributions from investment earnings (Figure 3.29.8).

External risks to the outlook would include surprisingly sluggish growth in the major industrial economies and a faster slowdown in the People's Republic of China than expected. Meanwhile, Singapore's highly open economy is vulnerable to protectionist policies. Further, rising inflation risks in the US could push up US interest rates more than expected, upsetting capital flows and raising local interest rates. A domestic downside risk is that tax hikes may reduce consumer spending more than expected. However, with sufficient reserve buffers, Singapore is well positioned to contain the impact of any risk to economic growth that may materialize.

Policy challenge—sustaining competitiveness in the digital age

In its *Global Competitiveness Report 2017–2018*, the World Economic Forum ranked Singapore third among 137 economies for institutions and policies that support overall

3.29.6 Exchange rates

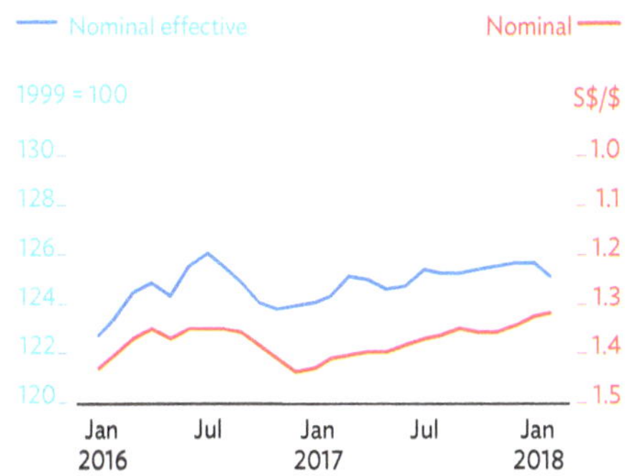

Sources: CEIC Data Company and Haver Analytics (accessed 9 March 2018).

3.29.7 Manufacturing purchasing managers' index

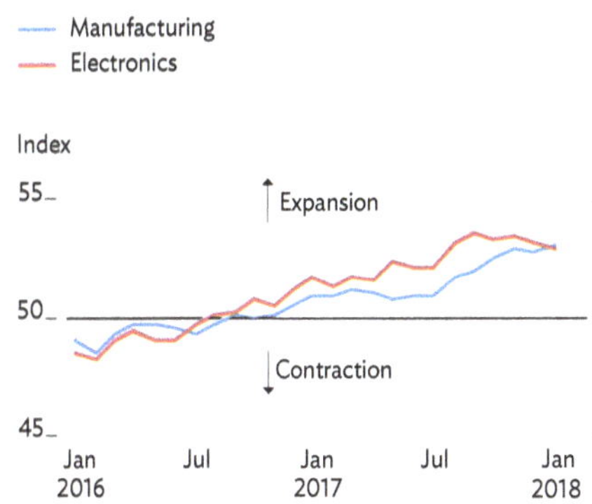

Source: CEIC Data Company (accessed 9 March 2018).

3.29.8 Fiscal indicators

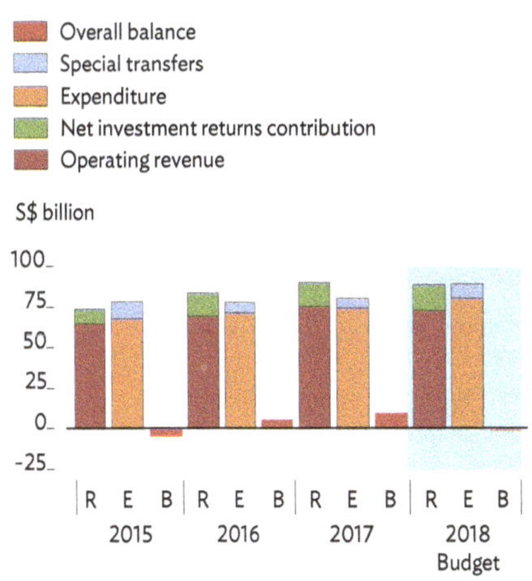

R = revenue, E = expenditure, B = balance.

Note: Years are fiscal years ending 31 March of the next year.

Source: Ministry of Finance (accessed 21 February 2018).

competitiveness but only 20th for its capacity to innovate and 18th for business sophistication. The forum's executive opinion survey identified insufficient capacity to innovate as the second biggest problem in doing business in Singapore. At the same time, new information technologies generate new products and business models that disrupt established business norms and require specialized skills that are lacking in the local workforce. Although businesses recognize the importance of digital transformation for growth and productivity, impediments to digital transformation remain in the form of skills gaps and fear of change. A policy challenge is to encourage businesses to adapt to new smart technologies and to train workers in new skills.

To this end, Singapore has invested significantly in research and development for innovation in digital industries since 2000. This investment amounts to 14.1% of budgetary expenditure annually, equal to 2.3% of GDP (Figure 2.29.9), ranking Singapore just behind the US. The government has launched 23 industry transformation maps (ITMs) that equip each industry with a road map for skills development, innovation, investment in new technologies with high value added, and collaboration with partners. ITMs provide companies with industry-specific financial and logistical assistance to achieve these goals. In addition, the FY2018 budget has a package of incentives including tax and licensing fee reductions for the commercial use of intellectual property and assistance to resolve firms' inhibitions against digital transformation.

The government has launched several initiatives, including its SkillsFuture platform, toward improving Singaporean firms' capacity to innovate. They provide opportunities to deepen skills through subsidized education and training that responds to constantly evolving needs. The Capability Transfer Programme, meanwhile, improves the transmission of skills from foreign specialists to local workers. These programs should be complemented by public-private collaboration to design training approaches—such as skills-based internship programs, competitive incentives packages, and advocacy plans—that can encourage participation and help retain trained workers. The ITMs should be properly communicated to the private sector, and businesses should be encouraged through logistical support and financial incentives under various government initiatives to craft digitally enabled and data-driven business models. To ensure firms' full participation, the government should design safeguards for risks to cybersecurity and data privacy, provide guarantees against damages if risks materialize, and formulate policies, guidelines, and explicit agreements on how data can be used, to minimize the risks inherent in sharing proprietary data.

3.29.1 Selected economic indicators (%)

	2018	2019
GDP growth	3.1	2.9
Inflation	0.9	1.4
Current account balance (share of GDP)	19.0	19.0

Source: ADB estimates.

3.29.9 Research and development expenditure

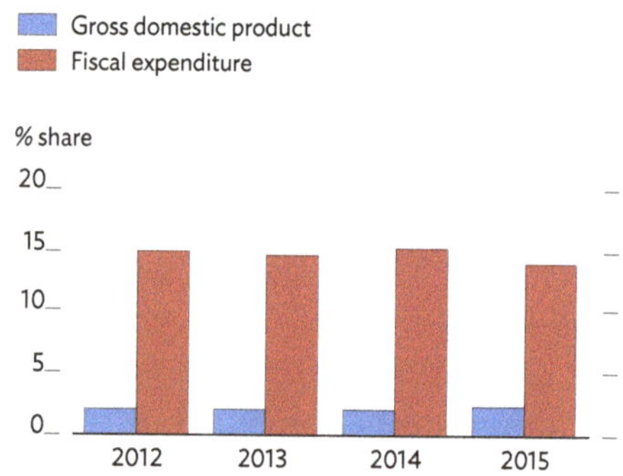

Sources: Ministry of Finance Budget FY2018; Ministry of Trade and Industry. Economic Survey Singapore 2017; Singapore Statistics (all accessed 20 February 2018).

Thailand

Helped by a turnaround in exports and agriculture, economic growth improved last year to 3.9%. Inflation remained low, and the current account surplus swelled. Annual GDP growth is likely to inch up to 4.0% this year and 4.1% next, as inflation stirs mildly and the current account surplus narrows. A worsening skills shortage needs to be addressed to reinvigorate growth and achieve the goals of the government's Thailand 4.0 development strategy.

Economic performance

Driven by strengthening external demand and reviving agriculture, GDP growth improved from 3.3% in 2016 to 3.9% in 2017 (Figure 3.30.1). Exports of goods and services rose last year by 5.5% at constant prices, improving on 2.8% growth in 2016. Strong recovery in global trade and a pickup in commodity prices fueled impressive 9.7% growth in the dollar value of merchandise exports, up from 0.1% growth in 2016. While exports of agricultural products such as rice and rubber rose by a hefty 20.0%, exports of manufactures such as electronics, chemicals, and automobile parts and components accelerated by 10.3%. Service exports performed well in 2017 as tourist arrivals grew by 8.8% to reach 35.4 million.

Strong demand drew down large inventories built up in 2016. However, fixed investment has yet to recover from years in the doldrums, posting only feeble 0.9% growth last year (Figure 3.30.2). Private investment showed faint signs of recovery, while public investment, which had grown by 28.4% in 2015 and 9.5% in 2016, declined by 1.2% last year as a new government procurement act caused delays in procurement and project implementation. Meanwhile, with slightly higher spending on machinery and equipment, private investment grew by 1.7%, improving on 0.5% growth in 2016. Private consumption expanded by 3.2%, slightly up from 3.0% in 2016. This was supported by a 3.9% increase in farm income as higher harvests offset weaker prices. However, high household debt remained a drag on private consumption.

By sector, agriculture grew by 6.2% on better weather, strongly reversing a decline of 2.5% in 2016. The service sector was another big contributor to GDP growth, expanding by 5.3% to outpace the 4.6% rise in 2016. Surging tourist numbers helped fuel strong growth in the hotel and restaurant industries, which expanded by 8.5%. Growth in manufacturing continued to be feeble at 2.5% last year, only marginally higher than the 2.3% growth in 2016. Meanwhile, construction contracted by 2.3% as the implementation of public infrastructure projects slowed.

This chapter was written by Thiam Hee Ng of the Southeast Asia Department, ADB, Manila.

3.30.1 Supply-side contributions to growth

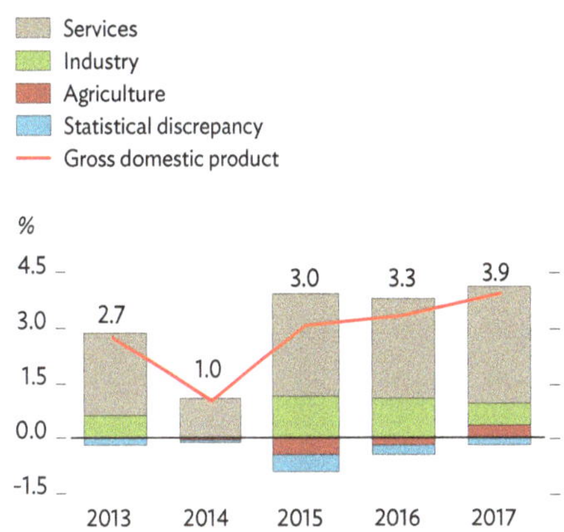

Source: National Economic and Social Development Board. http://www.nesdb.go.th (accessed 8 March 2018).

3.30.2 Fixed investment growth

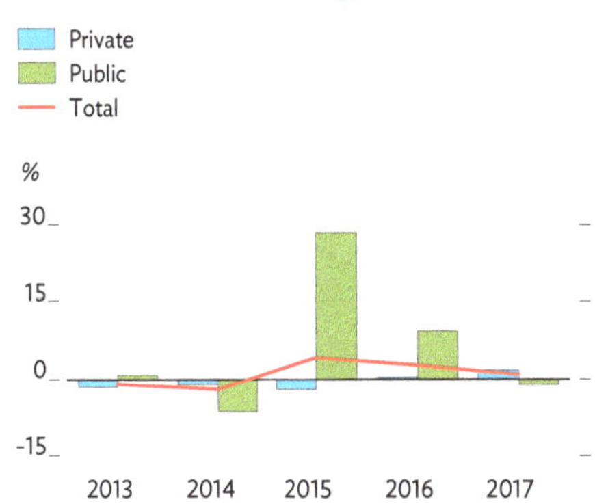

Source: National Economic and Social Development Board. http://www.nesdb.go.th (accessed 8 March 2018).

Despite better growth, inflation remained well under control, with headline inflation reaching only 0.7% last year, up from 0.2% in 2016. This largely reflected ample excess capacity in manufacturing. Fuel prices increased in line with global oil prices, but food prices remained quite stable as production rebounded.

Turning to the balance of payments, rising merchandise exports were accompanied by strong import growth at 14.4% (Figure 3.30.3). The higher imports were mostly raw materials and intermediate goods needed to support the expanded production of electronics for export. Despite the strong imports, the trade balance continued to post a large surplus of $31.9 billion, equal to 7.0% of GDP in 2017, albeit smaller than the 2016 surplus of $36.5 billion, or 8.9% of GDP. Net service exports continued to show impressive growth at 23.0% in 2017, though down slightly from 25.9% growth in 2016. The current account balance thus posted a surplus of $49.3 billion, equal to 10.8% of GDP. The financial account showed a deficit of $19.1 billion because of large investments abroad. In sum, already high international reserves continued to rise, reaching $202.6 billion at the end of 2017, sufficient to cover 11.1 months of imports or 3.3 times the country's short-term foreign debt.

The large current account surplus and strong interest in baht-denominated bonds from foreign investors helped to drive appreciation of the Thai baht by 3.9% against the US dollar in 2017. The stock market also had a good run in 2017, with the Stock Exchange of Thailand index up by 14% partly on greater interest from foreign investors and expectations of further baht appreciation.

Despite low inflation, the Bank of Thailand, the central bank, kept its policy interest rate unchanged at 1.5% throughout 2017 as the economy showed signs of picking up (Figure 3.30.4). On the fiscal front, policy mildly supported growth with a fiscal deficit that was only marginally higher than in 2016. That said, to boost domestic consumption, the government approved an aid package worth B42 billion in August 2017 that entitled 11.4 million low-income people to receive welfare smartcards that gave them a monthly allowance for consumer goods and subsidized their use of public transportation.

Actual government expenditure in fiscal year 2017 (FY2017, ended 30 September 2017) was 95.6% of the budgeted figure, or equal to 18.1% of GDP. Actual revenue turned out to be 80.5% of the budget, or 15.2% of GDP, slightly lower than the 16.6% recorded in FY2016. A one-off boost to revenue in FY2016 from the auction of the fourth generation telecommunication spectrum may have pushed down the ratio of revenue to GDP. Adjusting for changes in the government's off-budget cash account, the overall fiscal deficit in FY2017 was equal to 2.7% of GDP, as in FY2016 (Figure 3.30.5). Public debt remained manageable at the equivalent of 41.2% of GDP.

3.30.3 Trade indicators

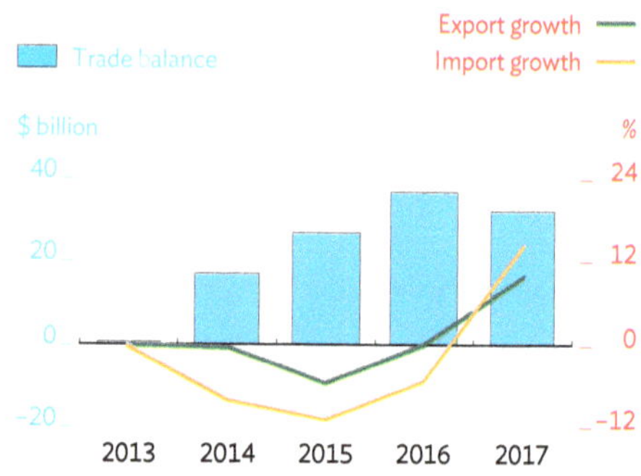

Source: Bank of Thailand. http://www.bot.or.th (accessed 8 March 2018).

3.30.4 Inflation and policy interest rate

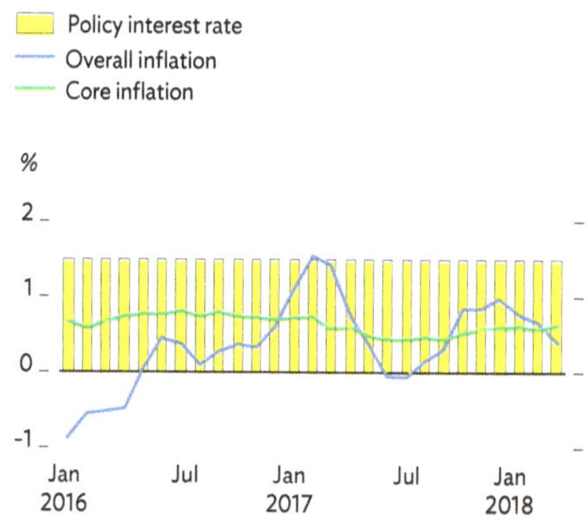

Sources: Bank of Thailand. http://www.bot.or.th; CEIC Data Company (both accessed 8 March 2018).

3.30.5 Fiscal balance

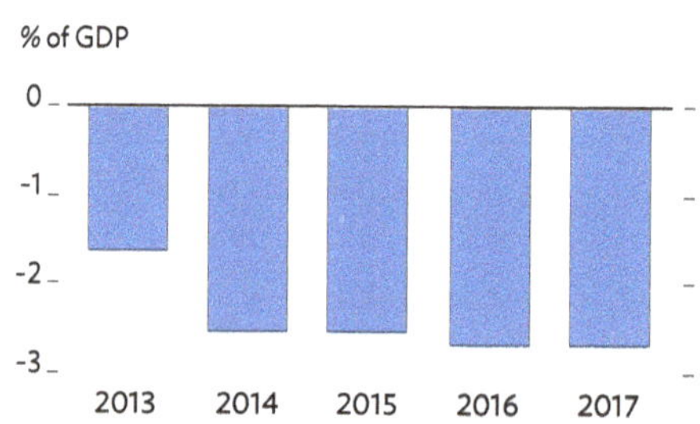

Note: Fiscal balance as a percentage of GDP is for the fiscal year, which ends on 30 September of that year, with GDP recalculated for the fiscal year.

Source: Bank of Thailand, http://www.bot.or.th (accessed 8 March 2018).

Economic prospects

As global trade growth moderates this year and next, export demand should grow at a more modest pace than last year, especially for electronics. Agriculture growth, having turned positive last year, is likely to stabilize at a much lower growth rate. The slack in growth thus created will likely be compensated by a surge in public investment, especially in big-ticket infrastructure projects, as domestic consumption and private investment play complementary roles. Annual GDP growth is thus seen to inch up to 4.0% this year and a shade higher next year (Figure 3.30.6).

Public investment is expected to rebound after its lackluster performance in 2017, with B900 billion in infrastructure projects planned under the Transport Infrastructure Action Plan, 2017 for double-tracking railways, extending mass rapid transit lines, and expanding highways. Most of the projects are expected to be implemented in 2018 and 2019. Further, five large projects in the Eastern Economic Corridor selected for fast-tracking are targeted for approval by the end of this year and implementation immediately through public–private partnership. Major infrastructure upgrades in the corridor aim to expand a deep seaport and improve its links to business parks, airports, the capital, and adjacent coastal areas. The implementation of public investment projects is expected to be smoother than in the past as government agencies become more familiar with a new procurement system introduced last year.

Private investment is also expected to pick up, albeit modestly, as capacity utilization tightens in some sectors after the huge drawdown of inventories in recent years. Last year's rise in export demand has pushed up utilization in some key industries to where new investment in machinery and equipment is warranted to expand capacity. The implementation of big public infrastructure projects, especially in transportation, could spur private investment in construction. The business outlook is more optimistic, prompting sharply higher applications for investment promotion support from the Board of Investment.

Domestic consumption is forecast to pick up slightly. Consumer confidence has improved, reaching in January 2018 the highest level in 3 years. Government aid packages implemented in recent years to help low-income farmers and others are expected to maintain their spending levels. A hike effective on 1 April 2018 in the daily minimum wage, by B5–B22 or 2%–7% depending on the sector, should help sustain private consumption. Household debt is high but seems to have peaked. Growth in public consumption is expected to accelerate with a supplemental budget to support local communities and agriculture reform.

The stellar performance from tourism is expected to continue (Figure 3.30.7). Government promotion of tourism as market economies overseas strengthen should continue to support higher tourist arrivals. The Tourism Authority of Thailand projects

3.30.1 Selected economic indicators (%)

	2018	2019
GDP growth	4.0	4.1
Inflation	1.2	1.3
Current account balance (share of GDP)	8.0	7.5

Source: ADB estimates.

3.30.6 GDP growth

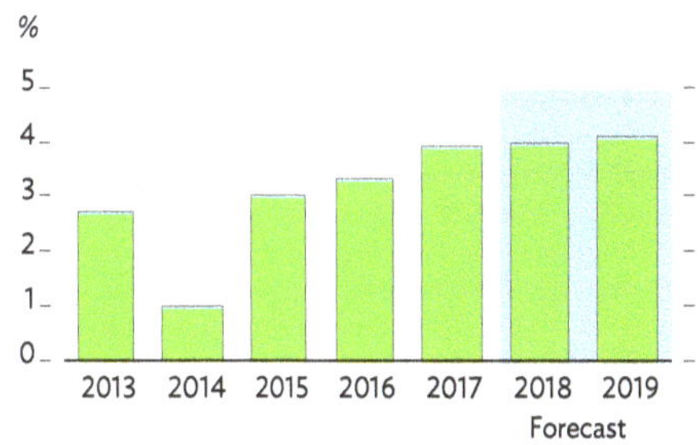

Source: *Asian Development Outlook* database.

3.30.7 Tourism indicators

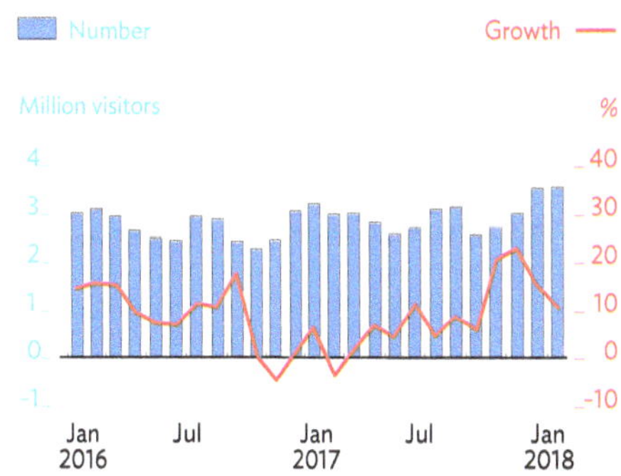

Source: Bank of Thailand. http://www.bot.or.th (accessed 8 March 2018).

arrivals to reach 37 million this year. More investment will be needed to meet tourist demand.

Higher growth and a consequent tightening in the labor market could push up inflation, as will higher global fuel prices. Inflation is thus forecast to edge up but remain modest at 1.2% this year and 1.3% next (Figure 3.30.8). Food prices will likely be kept in check with the recovery in agricultural production. The higher minimum wage is projected to have a minimal effect on inflation.

Looking again at the balance of payments, merchandise export growth is expected to moderate this year and next after its strong performance in 2017. While baht appreciation and weaker global demand for electronics will somewhat dampen prospects for merchandise exports, net service exports should be positive as tourist arrivals continue to rise. Merchandise import growth is projected to outpace exports on increased demand for raw materials and intermediate goods needed to support large infrastructure projects and higher manufacturing for export. The trade surplus should thus shrink, narrowing the current account surplus from 10.8% of GDP last year to 8.0% this year and 7.5% next year (Figure 3.30.9). Portfolio and FDI inflows are expected to increase, for a smaller financial account deficit. International reserves will remain more than ample to cover normal imports and to service short-term debt.

With continued low inflation and a comfortable balance of payments, ample scope exists for monetary easing, even after allowing for an expected hike in US interest rates. Last year, the central bank left its policy interest rate unchanged and the baht free to appreciate. Further large portfolio inflows could push the baht up further, threatening to hinder export competitiveness. Manageable public and external debt means there is scope to stimulate growth through higher fiscal deficits in the near term.

External risks to the economic outlook would include a disappointing global economic recovery. A domestic risk is possible delay in implementing the government's ambitious public infrastructure investment program, as most of the large Eastern Economic Corridor projects are expected to be financed through public–private partnership, requiring negotiations with private firms that could take longer than expected. Finally, uncertainty regarding the timing of the next general election may affect recovery in private investment.

3.30.8 Inflation

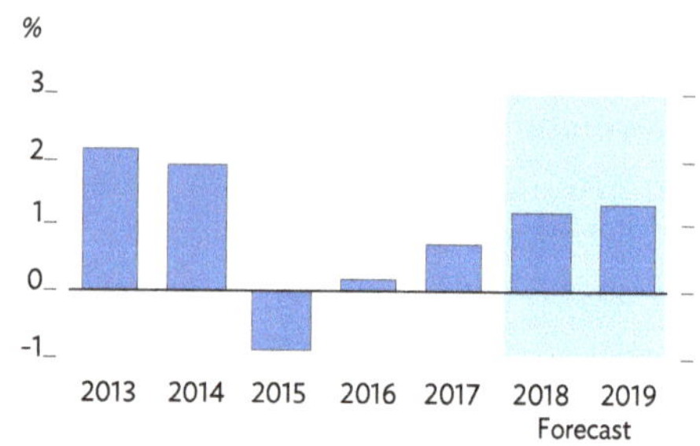

Source: *Asian Development Outlook* database.

3.30.9 Current account balance

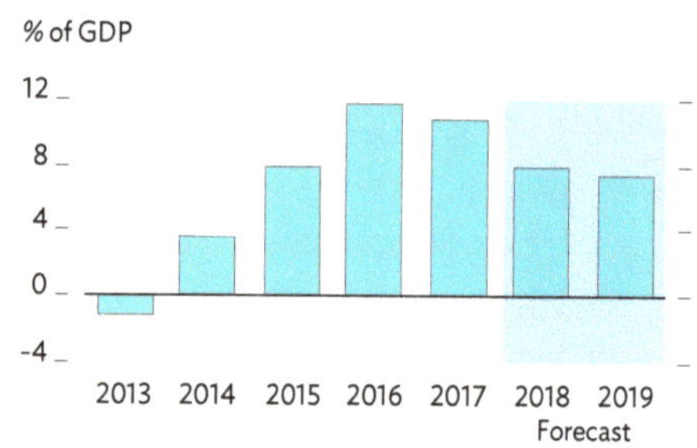

Source: *Asian Development Outlook* database.

Policy challenge—upgrading skills to support Thailand 4.0

Thailand has embarked on an ambitious economic reform program known as Thailand 4.0 to accelerate growth over the long run to 5%–6%. The initial emphasis of the program is on upgrading five existing business clusters: the next generation of automobiles, smart electronics, medical and wellness tourism, agriculture and biotechnology, and food for the future. Ultimately, these upgraded clusters are expected to evolve into five new industries: robotics, aviation and logistics, biofuel and biochemical, digital technology, and medical technology.

The Eastern Economic Corridor (EEC) is in the provinces of Chachoengsao, Chonburi, and Rayong, whose strong industrial base was the basis for their selection for this pilot geographic project under Thailand 4.0. The EEC targets B1.7 trillion in public and private investment over the next 5 years to upgrade infrastructure and industry.

Among the many factors needed for the program to succeed, the most critical is upgraded workforce skills. Policy to enhance workforce skills in support of Thailand 4.0 divides into three areas: enhancing the quality of secondary education; promoting the study of science, technology, engineering, and mathematics in higher education institutions; and forging stronger collaboration between educational institutions and the private sector.

A large share of secondary school students lack basic skills in mathematics, reading, and science. Test results from the Programme for International Student Assessment 2015 showed more than 50% of Thailand's 15-year-old students do not have basic reading skills or proficiency in mathematics, and 47% lack basic scientific knowledge (Figure 3.30.10). Enhancing the quality of secondary education across almost all subjects is thus crucial to ensure that students possess the basic skills necessary to succeed in tertiary education.

Further, universities are not turning out enough graduates in science, technology, engineering, and mathematics. Less than 20% of tertiary students are enrolled in science or engineering (Figure 3.30.11). Greater cooperation between local educational institutions and universities abroad can help boost the number of students with the technical skills needed for Thailand 4.0. Recognizing this, Thailand has opened up education in the EEC to foreign educational institutions. Carnegie Mellon University, for example, is collaborating with King Mongkut's Institute of Technology Ladkrabang to expand research and education in new digital technologies.

Finally, greater collaboration between the private sector and higher education and technical and vocational education and training institutions can help Thailand move away from a current education system driven by supply toward one that responds to demand. These partnerships can help ensure that the training and education students receive equip them to meet the demands of industry, thus making them more employable.

Education reform needs time to translate into upgraded skills in the young workforce. In the meantime, to fill the skills gap, skilled personnel may need to be recruited from abroad. Incentives may be able to entice back highly skilled Thais working abroad. Encouragingly, the government is offering tax incentives to foreign executives and specialists in companies situated in the EEC.

3.30.10 Proficiency of 15-year-olds by skill

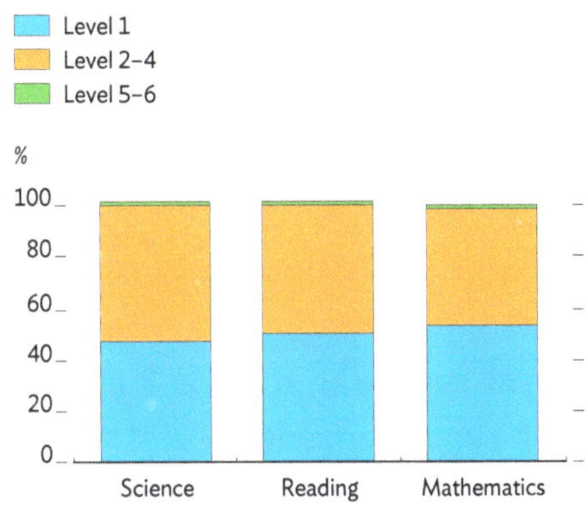

Note: Level 1 is the lowest proficiency, level 6 the highest, with level 2 considered basic understanding.

Source: Organisation for Economic Co-operation and Development. 2016. *PISA 2015 Results Volume I: Excellence and Equity in Education.*

3.30.11 Share of enrollment in tertiary education, 2014

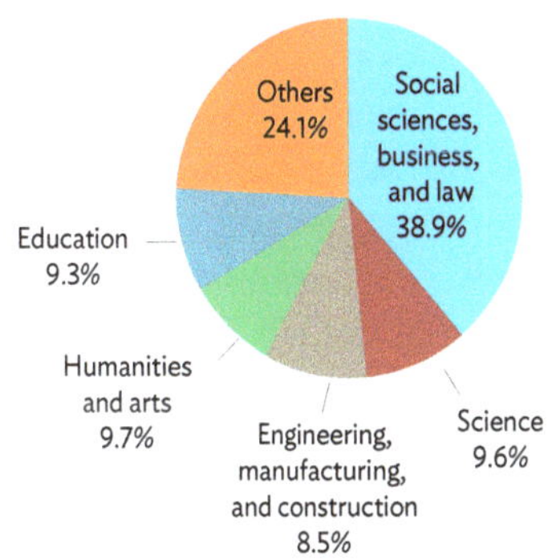

Note: Others include services, health and welfare, agriculture.

Source: World Bank. World Development Indicators online database (accessed 9 January 2018).

Viet Nam

Driven by rising foreign direct investment, vigorous export growth, strengthening agriculture, and robust domestic demand, GDP growth is expected to accelerate from 6.8% last year to 7.1% this year, then ease back to 6.8% in 2019. Inflation will edge up but remain modest, and the current account surplus will narrow. Closing the country's widening skills gap is key to remaining attractive to foreign investors and sustaining growth.

Economic performance

Growth accelerated from 6.2% in 2016 to 6.8% in 2017, its highest rate since before the global financial crisis of 2008–2009. A hefty rise in exports, a strong increase in investment, and buoyant private consumption underpinned growth last year (Figure 3.31.1).

A rebound in global trade, especially in electronics, helped merchandise exports rise by a whopping 21.2%, measured in dollar value. Another boost to aggregate demand came from the 9.8% growth in domestic investment lifted by high foreign direct investment (FDI) and rapid credit growth. Registered FDI surged by 47.0% in 2017 to reach nearly $36 billion, while disbursed FDI jumped by 10.8% to a record $17.5 billion. As the consumer confidence index rose to a high 117, private consumption increased by 7.4%, more than offsetting slight moderation in public consumption caused by continued fiscal consolidation. Reflecting buoyant private consumption, retail sales grew by 10.9% in 2017 to a record $129.6 billion, equal to 58.6% of GDP.

By sector, industry and construction increased by 8.0% as the rebound in aggregate demand helped the sector shrug off a 7.1% contraction in mining to improve upon its 7.6% rise a year earlier. Within industry, manufacturing rose by 14.4%, led by strong export-oriented manufacturing, especially of electronics, telecommunication products, and textiles. These performances more than offset mild moderation in construction growth from 10.0% in 2016 to 8.7% last year, caused largely by banks tightening standards for credit to real estate.

Coupled with strong domestic demand and a record 29.1% rise in international tourist arrivals, services posted 7.4% growth, up from 7.0% in 2016. Thanks to better weather and strong export demand, output from agriculture, forestry, and fisheries grew by 2.9% last year, more than twice the pace in 2016.

Strengthened aggregate demand put pressure on prices, as did higher international oil prices and continued upward adjustment to government-administered fees for public education and health care. Thus, even as food prices moderated, inflation

3.31.1 Demand-side contributions to growth

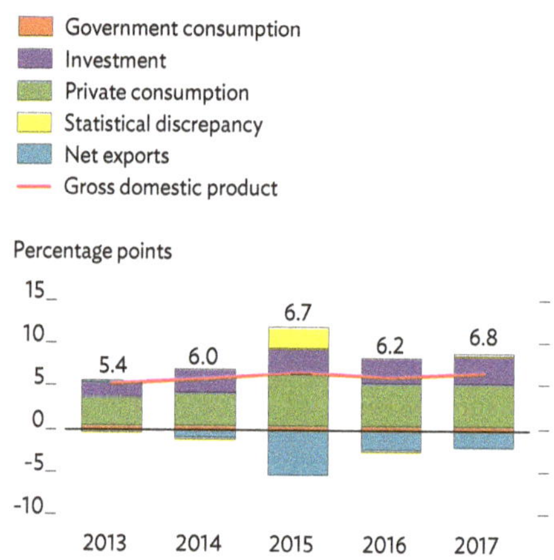

Source: General Statistics Office of Viet Nam.

3.31.2 Inflation

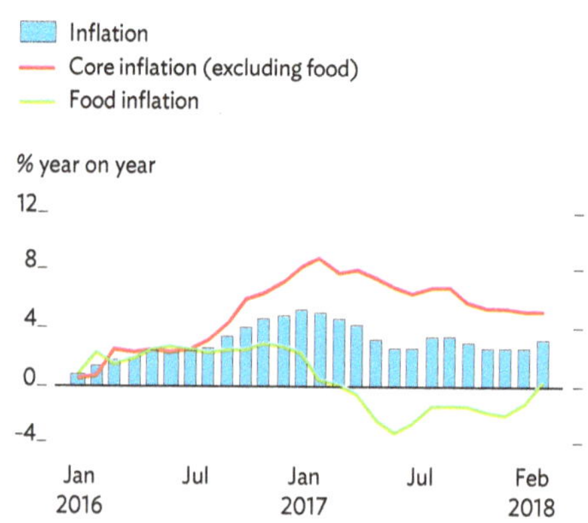

Source: General Statistics Office of Viet Nam.

This chapter was written by Aaron Batten, Chu Hong Minh, and Nguyen Luu Thuc Phuong of the Viet Nam Resident Mission, ADB, Ha Noi.

edged up to 3.5% in 2017 from 2.7% in 2016, still below the 4.0% government target (Figure 3.31.2).

Supported by a large trade surplus estimated at $11.6 billion and stable remittances, the current account surplus was estimated to equal 2.9% of GDP, little changed from 2016. A 21.2% rise in merchandise exports was led by 31.0% expansion for mobile phones and components, which now comprise 21% of all exports. Imports grew even faster at 22.3%. Imports of telephone parts jumped by 53.2%, while those of other electronic components picked up by 35.0%. This reflected Viet Nam's growing integration in regional supply chains. Meanwhile, buoyant domestic consumption drove imports of consumer goods higher by 17.0%.

The capital account recorded a surplus estimated to equal 8.9% of GDP, bolstered by strong FDI disbursements and an estimated $1.9 billion in portfolio capital inflows as the government relaxed restrictions on foreign ownership of domestic businesses. While small by regional standards, last year's portfolio capital inflow was a sevenfold increase over 2016. Surpluses in the current and capital account balances added up to an overall balance of payments surplus estimated to equal 5.6% of GDP (Figure 3.31.3).

The strengthening balance of payments allowed the State Bank of Viet Nam, the central bank, to increase foreign reserves to an estimated 3.0 months of import cover, up from 2.6 months at the beginning of the year. The Viet Nam dong was stable, depreciating by 1.2% against the US dollar during the year (Figure 3.31.4).

With inflation rising but still moderate and an improving balance of payments, the central bank cut policy interest rates in July 2017 by 25 basis points, taking the refinancing rate down to 6.25% and the discount rate down to 4.25%. Average commercial bank lending rates consequently fell by 0.5–1.0 percentage points during the year. Declining lending rates and improving consumer and investor sentiment helped to stimulate credit growth to an estimated 18.0% in 2017, meeting the government target. Broad money (M2) supply increased by an estimated 16.0% year on year (Figure 3.31.5).

Efforts to rein in the fiscal deficit began to pay dividends in 2017. The official budget deficit narrowed to equal an estimated 3.5% of GDP, down from 4.3% in 2016. Revenue grew by 12.5% to equal 24.8% of GDP, up slightly from 24.5% in 2016. The rise in revenue was broad in that collections rose from personal income, corporate income, and value-added tax alike. Meanwhile, expenditure grew by 9.3%, exceeding budgeted growth by 2.0 percentage points. Public debt including government debt guarantees fell to equal an estimated 61.3% of GDP by year-end from 63.6% a year earlier.

Progress in divestment from state-owned enterprises picked up in 2017 but still fell short of the target. The government sold equity stakes in 39 state-owned enterprises, against a target of 44. These sales generated receipts of $1.0 billion, the highest divestment receipts in a single year since the divestment program began in 2013. A factor pushing up receipts was a

3.31.3 Balance of payments indicators

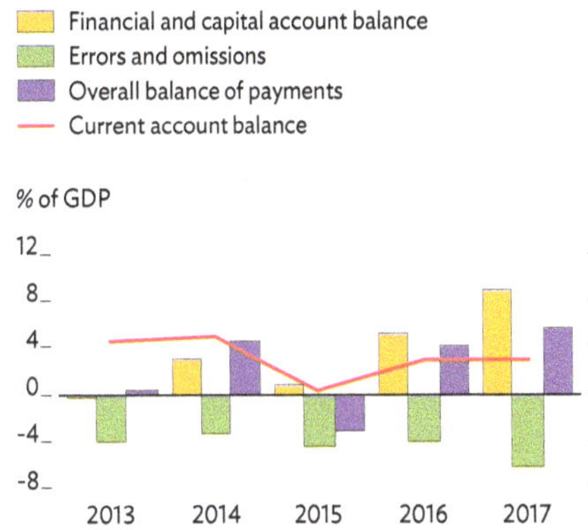

Sources: State Bank of Viet Nam; International Monetary Fund; ADB estimates.

3.31.4 Exchange rate

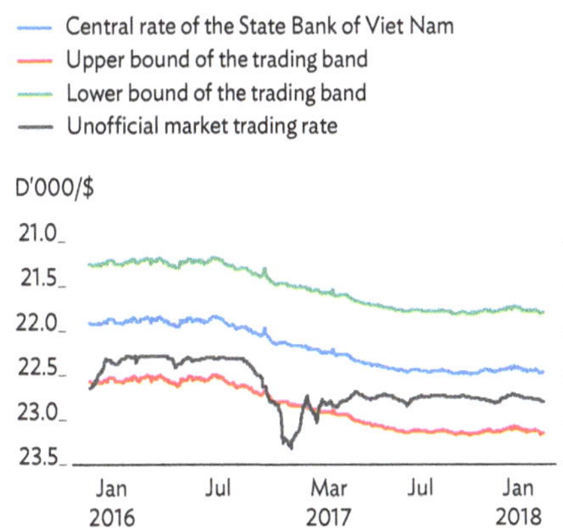

Sources: State Bank of Viet Nam; ADB observations.

3.31.5 Credit and money supply growth

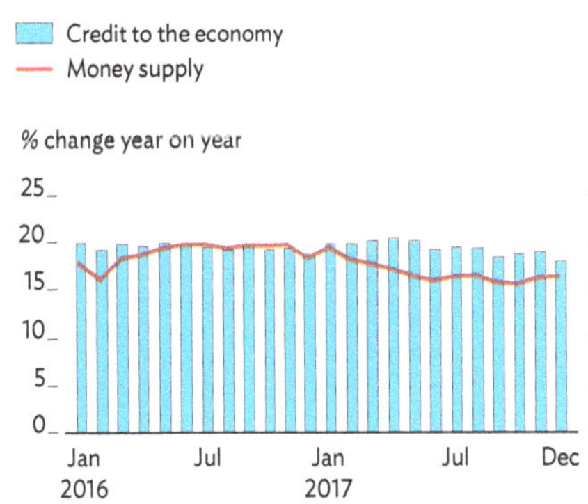

Sources: State Bank of Viet Nam; ADB estimates.

strong performance by the stock market, which saw the share price index rise by a whopping 48% last year, taking stock market capitalization to nearly 75% of GDP.

Less progress was made in resolving banks' nonperforming loans (NPLs). The NPL ratio reportedly fell to 2.3% of all outstanding loans at the end of 2017, only marginally lower than the 2.5% recorded at the end of 2016. This reflected in part the continued transfer of NPLs from banks to the state-owned Viet Nam Asset Management Company (VAMC). Meanwhile, NPLs held by both the VAMC and banks, combined with potential bad debts, stood at an estimated 7.9% of outstanding loans at the end of 2017, down from 10.1% in 2016. A National Assembly resolution effective from August 2017 that grants to the VAMC additional powers to resolve NPLs is hoped to accelerate NPL resolution in the coming years.

3.31.6 GDP growth

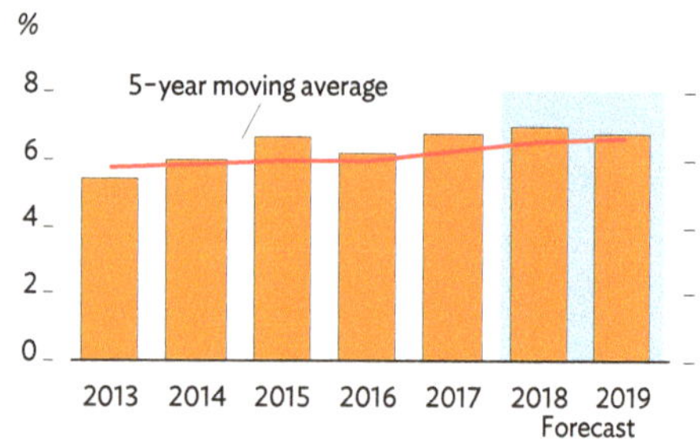

Source: *Asian Development Outlook* database.

Economic prospects

GDP growth is forecast to accelerate to 7.1% in 2018 before easing to 6.8% in 2019 (Figure 3.31.6). Growth will be led by vigorous export expansion, rising domestic consumption, strong investment fueled by FDI, and strengthening agriculture.

Robust private consumption is expected to be supported by rising incomes and stable inflation. Prospects for private investment are bright. Business sentiment remains buoyant, as indicated in December 2017 by upbeat business survey results and in February 2018 by the Nikkei purchasing managers' index (Figure 3.31.7). Private investment is projected to benefit from Viet Nam having risen 14 places in the World Bank's *Doing Business* rankings for 2018. The number of newly established enterprises hit a record high of 126,859 in 2017, up by 15.2% from 2016. The government target is for an additional 135,000 new enterprises in 2018.

By sector, solid FDI should enable industry to maintain strong growth momentum. Continued strengthening in the US and the euro area will further boost manufacturing over the next 2 years. Construction is projected to pick up in 2018 and 2019, benefitting from last year's record FDI commitments and disbursements (Figure 3.31.8). The service sector is projected to sustain growth in 2018 and 2019, with tourist arrivals forecast to rise by 15%–20% in 2018 and bank lending to grow by 17%–18%. Agriculture is expected to continue to pick up over the next 2 years, growing in 2018 in line with the government target of 2.8%–3.0%.

Inflation is projected to edge up but remain broadly stable, averaging 3.7% this year and rising to 4.0% in 2019 as strong domestic demand and high bank lending are partly offset by stable domestic food and transportation costs and smaller increases in administered prices for education, health care, electricity, and water. Any significant rise in global oil prices would have a particularly significant impact on inflation by lifting transport and energy prices, which have been depressed over recent years. In the first 3 months of 2018, headline inflation averaged 2.8%.

3.31.7 Purchasing managers' index

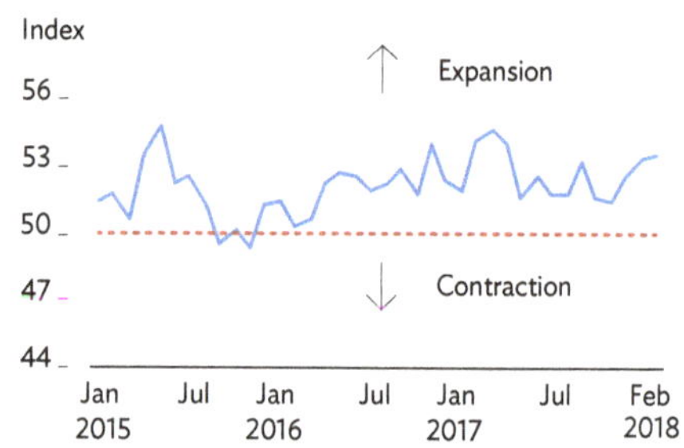

Note: Nikkei, Markit.
Source: Bloomberg (accessed 15 March 2018).

3.31.8 Foreign direct investment

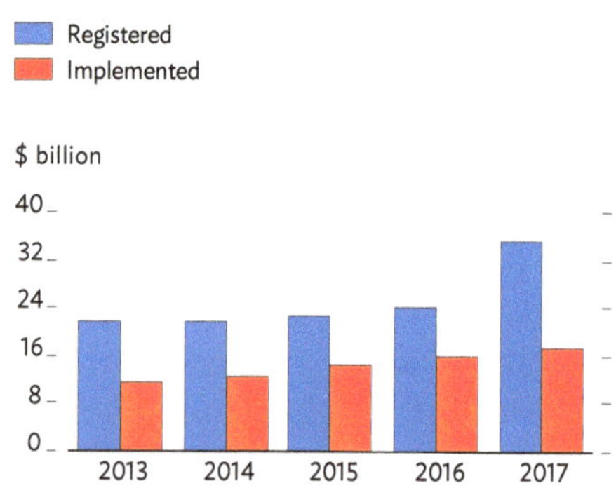

Source: General Statistics Office of Viet Nam.

The current account surplus is projected to narrow to 2.5% of GDP this year and 2.0% in 2019 (Figure 3.31.9). Merchandise exports are forecast to rise by 15%–20% in 2018 and 2019. Remittances are likely to remain strong thanks to improving global prospects and a stable exchange rate. Rising exports will be partly offset by faster import growth driven by rising global oil prices, strengthening domestic consumption, and higher imports of intermediate inputs for export-orientated manufacturing. Strong FDI and portfolio inflows should bolster the capital account balance and further strengthen the balance of payments.

Monetary policy needs to strike a balance between supporting economic growth and managing inflation. Credit growth is projected to remain high, as in 2017, aided by interest rate cuts late last year. Lending interest rates may rise if inflation edges toward 4.0%.

On the fiscal front, the government has set a fiscal deficit target for 2018 equal to 3.7% of GDP, seeking to encourage capital investment to support growth while consolidating finances to sustain macroeconomic stability. The budget for 2018 emphasizes capital expenditure by increasing its share of total spending to 26.0% in 2018, up from a low of 21.0% in 2016.

Vulnerability in the financial sector to unresolved NPLs and undercapitalized banks poses a domestic risk to the outlook, as does unexpectedly rapid credit growth, though a resolution newly passed by the National Assembly and revision to the Law on Credit Institutions should remove some legal impediments to effective NPL resolution and bank restructuring. Meanwhile, any rise in trade protectionism, such as through the prospect of higher US tariffs on steel and aluminum, would hit Viet Nam hard. Significant reliance on the Republic of Korea for FDI and trade exposes Viet Nam to possible risks from geopolitical tensions. Heightened global financial volatility or disruption of capital flows would have significant spillover into the domestic market.

3.31.1 Selected economic indicators (%)

	2018	2019
GDP growth	7.1	6.8
Inflation	3.7	4.0
Current account balance (share of GDP)	2.5	2.0

Source: ADB estimates.

3.31.9 Current account balance

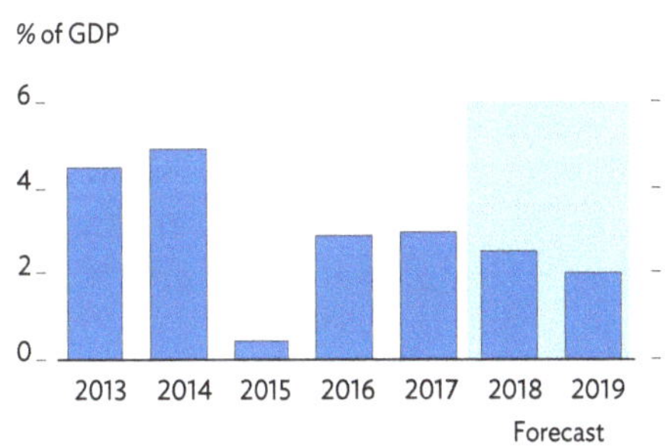

Source: *Asian Development Outlook* database.

Policy challenge—closing the skills gap

Viet Nam has an abundance of efficient labor working for relatively low wages. This attracts large FDI inflows especially for labor-intensive export-oriented manufacturing. Since 2012, manufacturing has absorbed on average 400,000 workers per year (Figure 3.31.10).

However, a skills gap is emerging as an obstacle to FDI absorption and to business more generally. In its *Global Competitiveness Report 2017–2018*, the World Economic Forum cited an "inadequately educated workforce" as the second-biggest constraint on doing business in Viet Nam (Figure 3.31.11). Similarly, a World Bank survey of employers found that filling vacancies for jobs that require higher skills was a major challenge for most firms, with 70%–80% of managerial and technical applicants reported as being underqualified.

3.31.10 Employment by sector

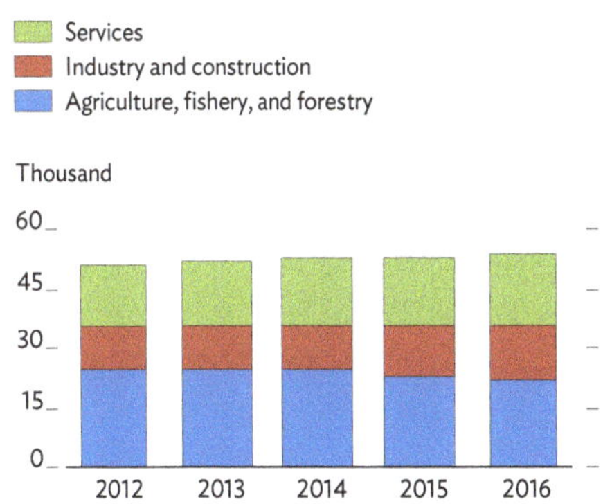

Note: 2016 data is preliminary.

Source: General Statistics Office of Viet Nam.

To address these skills gaps, Viet Nam needs to prioritize three sets of initiatives toward strengthening its universities and its technical and vocational education and training (TVET) system: expanding access, improving quality, and streamlining governance.

Expanding access is key. Viet Nam's labor force is growing rapidly. From 38 million in 2000, it is projected to reach 56 million by 2020. Despite significant increases in funding, the current supply of places offered in TVET institutions is inadequate to meet the needs of this workforce. Currently, just 20% of workers nationwide hold formal university or vocational qualifications (Figure 3.31.12).

Second is the need to improve quality. The Programme for International Student Assessment has found that secondary school students in Viet Nam substantially outperform their peers in Southeast Asia, including those in much richer countries such as Thailand and Malaysia, in some tasks. However, more progress is needed in developing the capacity of higher-education students for critical thinking, problem solving, and people-management skills in real world settings. Reflecting this, Viet Nam's ranking for the perceived quality of its higher education systems in the *Global Competitiveness Report 2017–2018* slipped by one spot to 84 out of nearly 140 countries surveyed. Meanwhile, Viet Nam ranked only 120 for the quality of its management schools, its lowest ranking across all index subcomponents. These results reveal an urgent need to match curriculums better with industry needs. Although reform has brought some progress in recent years, public universities and some TVET institutions are still hampered by insufficient autonomy and outdated curriculums, while private universities are restricted from expanding their enrollment. All in all, a stronger and more consistent partnership between the government and the private sector is needed to upgrade higher education toward international benchmarks and prepare students for future workplaces.

Finally, there is a need to streamline university and TVET governance. Effective management is complicated by fragmentation of responsibility among the 13 line ministries and 63 provincial governments that administer some 2,000 institutions. While accreditation has been compulsary for all institutions since 2005, enforcing common standards has been difficult in practice. Fragmentation has likewise made it difficult to develop coordinated strategies toward achieving national policy targets or to adopt jointly agreed standards and responsibilities among training providers.

As changes in education and training can take a generation to yield results, the time to modernize university and TVET systems is now. This will ensure that inadequate worker skills do not become a bottleneck constraining the country's future growth and development.

3.31.11 Doing business: Most problematic factors

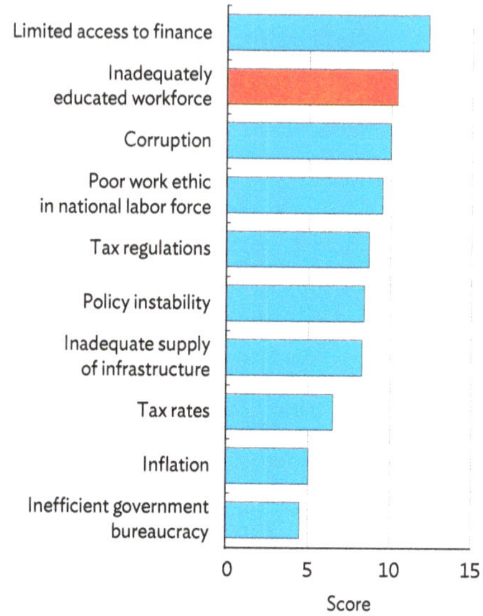

Note: From a list of factors, respondents to the survey were asked to select and rank the five most problematic factors for doing business in their country.

Sources: Global Competitiveness Index 2017-2018; International Monetary Fund. 2017. *World Economic Outlook database*. April.

3.31.12 Share of trained workers, 15 years and above

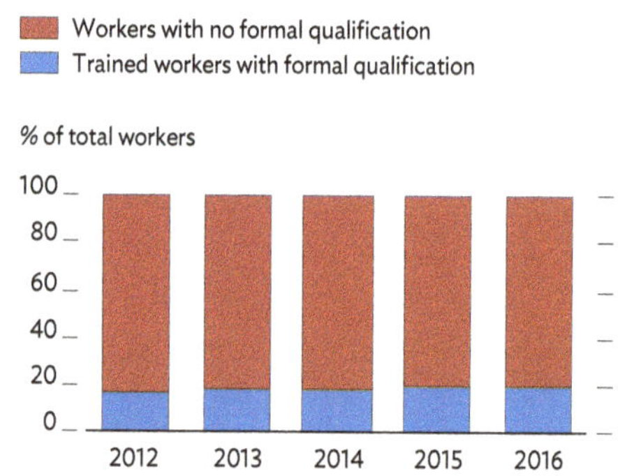

Source: General Statistics Office of Viet Nam.

THE PACIFIC

- FIJI
- PAPUA NEW GUINEA
- SOLOMON ISLANDS
- TIMOR-LESTE
- VANUATU
- NORTH PACIFIC ECONOMIES
- SOUTH PACIFIC ECONOMIES
- SMALL ISLAND ECONOMIES

Fiji

Growth recovered in 2017, after a steep slowdown in the wake of Cyclone Winston, on reconstruction spending, improved agricultural output, and continuing growth in tourism. Reconstruction is expected to end in 2018, allowing resources to be reallocated toward improving economic infrastructure, especially roads. Recent experience with storm damage illustrates the need to mainstream climate resilience in investment decisions.

Economic performance

The economy grew by 3.9% in 2017 with recovery in agriculture, continued growth in tourist arrivals, and reconstruction following Cyclone Winston in February 2016 (Figure 3.32.1). The government supported housing reconstruction through its Help for Homes program, and the statutory pension fund allowed storm-hit contributors to draw down their pensions to rehabilitate their homes. These initiatives contributed to growth in construction during the year. Despite rainfall below average, sugarcane production increased by 18.2% from the 2016 harvest (Figure 3.32.2).

Tourism continued to be an important driver of growth, with visitor arrivals setting yet another record. Significant growth in visitor arrivals from New Zealand and North America—the latter by 16.2% but from a smaller base—led 6.4% growth in arrivals overall (Figure 3.32.3). Last year also saw recovery in arrivals from Australia, Fiji's largest market. This contributed to 5.8% growth in accommodation and food services in 2017, reversing a decline of 6.3% in 2016. Other sectors that grew faster during the period were manufacturing, electricity, finance and insurance, and real estate.

Consumption continued to grow strongly in 2017, with new vehicle sales higher by 8.7%, value-added tax collections by 14.3%, and residential electricity consumption by 9.0%. Increased consumption was fueled by commercial bank lending for consumption, which increased by 12.2%, and by remittances, which grew by 1.7%.

Inflation slowed to 3.3%, with 2.4 percentage points coming from a 26.1% increase for alcoholic beverages, tobacco, and other intoxicants as excise duties on alcohol and tobacco were hiked by 15 percentage points and supply-side constraints affected kava prices (Figure 3.32.4). Transport prices rose by 1.8%, and restaurants and hotel prices by 3.1%, with a tax increase on service turnover and a new environmental levy.

3.32.1 GDP growth

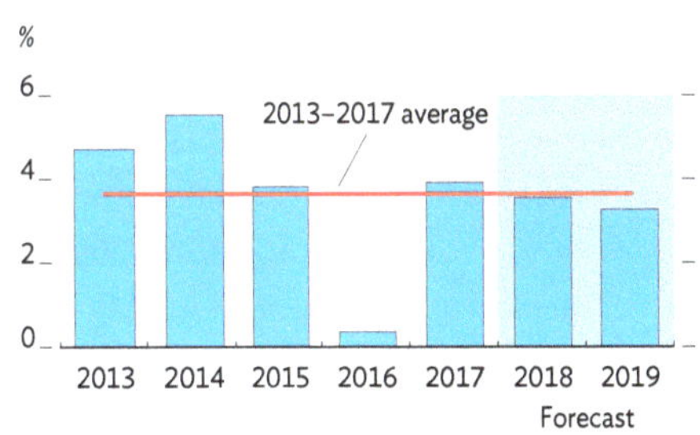

Sources: Fiji Bureau of Statistics; ADB estimates.

3.32.2 Sugarcane production

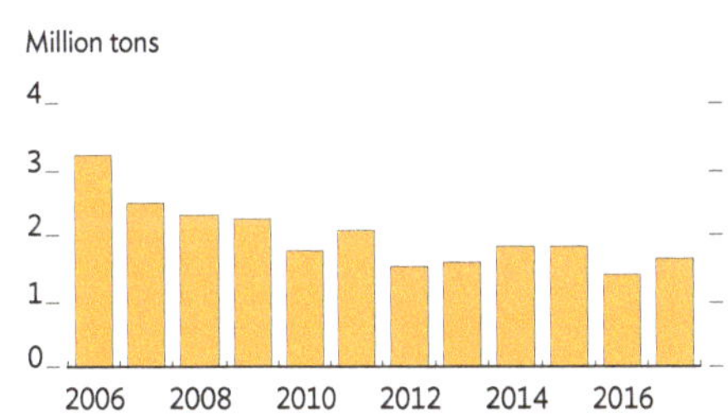

Sources: Fiji Sugar Corporation; ADB estimates.

This chapter was written by Shiu Raj Singh of the South Pacific Subregional Office, ADB, Suva.

Housing costs rose by 2.3%, and all other components of the consumer price index were either stable or down.

The deficit for fiscal year 2017 (FY2017, ended 31 August 2017) was equal 2.3% of GDP, significantly smaller than the 4.1% deficit in FY2016 during the immediate aftermath of Cyclone Winston (Figure 3.32.5). The improved fiscal position was assisted by lower capital expenditure than expected because of delays affecting reconstruction. At the end of July 2017, public debt equaled 46.7% of GDP, of which about one-third was foreign debt.

Monetary policy remained accommodative as the policy interest rate stayed at 0.5% throughout 2017, keeping commercial interest rates historically low. Liquidity improved significantly, largely from increased foreign reserves. Broad money increased by 6.1% during the year. Average rates for time deposits of more than 24 months firmed to 3.21%, or 26 basis points higher than in 2016. However, the weighted average commercial bank lending rate fell from 5.80% to 5.66%. Private sector credit increased—albeit more slowly than in 2016—by 11.6% to the equivalent of 71.7% of GDP. Lending for investment grew by 25.0% during the year with increased lending to real estate and for building and construction.

The current account deficit is estimated at the equivalent of 5.2% of GDP in 2017, marginally higher than in the previous year. Higher imports of mineral fuels and miscellaneous manufactured goods offset higher exports, mainly of sugar, molasses, and mineral water. Foreign currency reserves stood at $1.11 billion at the end of the year, sufficient to cover 5.5 months of retained imports of goods and nonfactor services.

3.32.3 Visitor arrivals

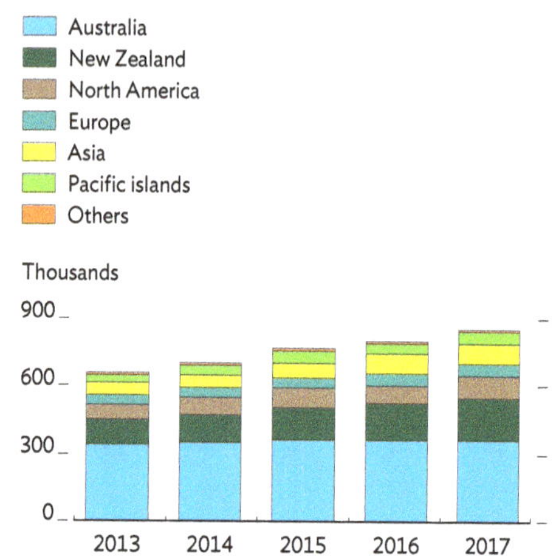

Source: Fiji Bureau of Statistics.

3.32.1 Selected economic indicators (%)

	2018	2019
GDP growth	3.6	3.3
Inflation	3.0	3.0
Current account balance (share of GDP)	-5.0	-4.8

Source: ADB estimates.

Economic prospects

With cyclone reconstruction tailing off, growth is projected to decelerate to 3.6% in 2018. All sectors are expected to grow, however, with major contributions from public administration, wholesale and retail trade, manufacturing, agriculture, accommodation and food services, and construction. High investment lending in 2017 and a number of ongoing tourism investments suggest that the private sector will generate higher tourism numbers. Growth at 3.3% in 2019 will be well distributed, with tourism, agriculture, and construction expected to be the major contributors.

The government has announced several infrastructure developments over the next 2 years. While capital expenditure will likely continue to be constrained by limited implementation capacity in government agencies, public infrastructure investments are expected to facilitate additional private construction able to support growth over the next couple of years. The government aims to improve implementation capacity through a number of reform initiatives and partnerships with the private sector.

3.32.4 Inflation

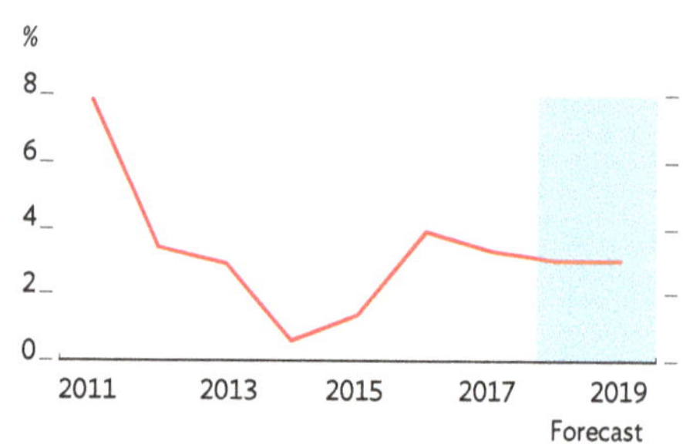

Note: Inflation in 2011 is in reference to 2005 prices, and from 2012 to 2016 in reference to 2011.

Sources: Fiji Bureau of Statistics; ADB estimates.

Tourism is on track for another record year, with benefits from new direct flights to Japan and increased flights to Singapore and San Francisco. Inward remittances are expected to continue growing in 2018 in tandem with higher exports of athletic talent and seasonal labor, as well as military deployments on peacekeeping missions (Figure 3.32.6).

Inflation is expected to moderate in 2018 and 2019. Rising international prices for fuel and food and higher taxes on alcoholic beverages and tobacco are expected to be offset by lower domestic food prices as agriculture recovers from the impacts of Cyclone Winston.

Exports are expected to grow strongly as agriculture, especially tree crops, recover from cyclone damage. With higher earnings from tourism and remittances, the current account deficit is forecast to narrow to 5.0% of GDP in 2018 and 4.8% in 2019.

3.32.5 Fiscal balance

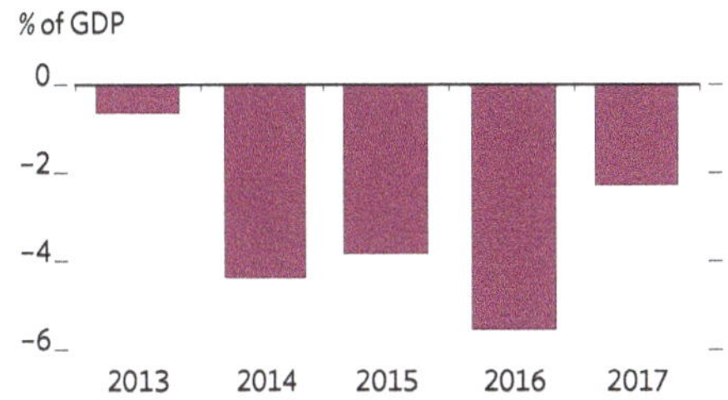

Note: Calendar years from 2013 to 2014 but fiscal years (ending on 31 July of that year) from 2015 to 2017.
Source: Fiji Ministry of Economy.

Policy challenge—building resilience under climate change

Like other Pacific island nations, Fiji is extremely vulnerable to tropical cyclones, droughts, tsunamis, storm surges, and flooding. Most recently, Cyclone Winston hit Fiji in 2016, causing extensive property and infrastructure damage and lost production, particularly in agriculture. Economic growth fell in 2016 to 0.4% from 3.8% in the previous year.

Fiji's susceptibility to such events is exacerbated by climate change, which is foreseen to have severe effects on the economy by undermining agriculture and tourism, causing extensive damage to infrastructure, and worsening poverty and hardship, particularly for the majority of the population who live in risk-prone coastal areas.

A major challenge therefore facing Fiji is to build urban infrastructure that can stand up to climate change while conserving the environment. Mainstreaming climate resilience in public investment decisions will increase costs and financing requirements. The government needs to carefully consider the fiscal risks associated with disasters, and to weigh the costs of financing before versus after a disaster strikes. While it has increased spending on resilient infrastructure, the government has simultaneously maintained fiscal policies that ensure macroeconomic stability. A cost-effective strategy of sovereign risk financing will need to be developed to achieve an optimal layering of disaster risk, including coverage for small and recurrent losses, contingent credit, and financial instruments such as reinsurance and catastrophe financing for the high costs imposed by disasters. Private sector financing may need to be actively promoted to supplement public sector efforts.

3.32.6 Remittances

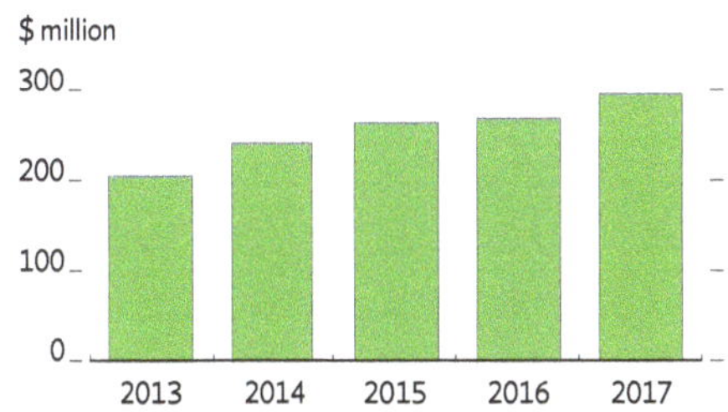

Sources: Reserve Bank of Fiji; ADB estimates.

Papua New Guinea

Growth remained soft in 2017 as foreign exchange shortages and fiscal difficulties continued to pose challenges. Asia-Pacific Economic Cooperation meetings will provide economic stimulus in 2018, but a recent earthquake will weigh on hydrocarbon exports. If fiscal balance could be achieved without reliance on volatile resource income, government finances would be secure when prices were low, and savings when prices were favorable could be channeled into a sovereign wealth fund.

Economic performance

Growth in 2017 is estimated at 2.2%, a slight increase from 2016 but below the 5.4% average realized over the past decade (Figure 3.33.1). Soft international commodity prices have caused large shortfalls in government revenues in recent years, ushering in a period of low growth and fiscal consolidation. Mining, which provides about 10% of GDP in Papua New Guinea (PNG), is estimated to have contributed more than half of GDP growth in 2017. Preliminary data indicate that the sector expanded by 13.6% during the year. The country's three largest mines, Lihir, Ok Tedi, and Porgera, which together provide more than three-quarters of mining revenue, all saw output expand. Ok Tedi returned to full-year production in 2017, and Lihir increased output by improving operational efficiency. There were also increased production and sales from Ramu NiCo, the country's fourth largest mine, so named for its nickel and cobalt. Gold remains the most important metal export by value, contributing over three-quarters of PNG metal revenue, followed by copper at 12%.

Oil and gas, the second-largest component of GDP at 16%, benefited from higher prices in 2017. However, oil production declined as oil fields aged, while gas production was steady.

The agriculture, forestry, and fisheries sector, which provides about 18% of GDP, grew by an estimated 2.6% in 2017, down from 3.4% in 2016. This sector, which employs some 85% of people living in rural areas, includes agriculture for domestic supply, commercial agriculture for export, and forest and marine production for export. The contribution to GDP from coffee, cocoa, and timber shrank in 2017, partly because of weaker prices, while the contribution from palm oil was higher on modest price and production increases.

3.33.1 Economic growth

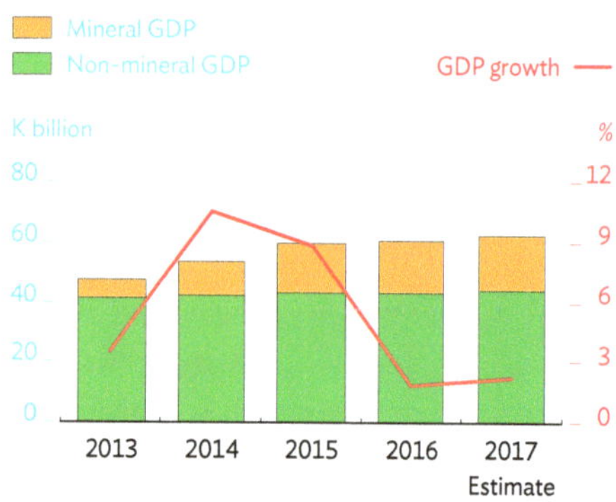

Sources: Papua New Guinea national budget documents, various years; ADB estimates.

3.33.2 Inflation

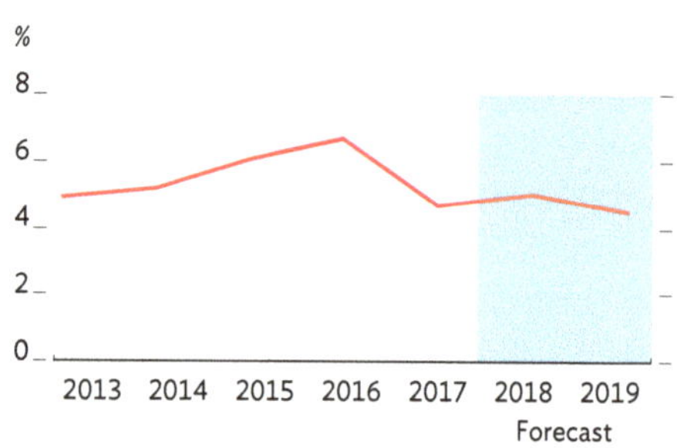

Source: Bank of Papua New Guinea Quarterly Statistical Tables.

This chapter was written by Edward Faber of the Papua New Guinea Resident Mission, ADB, Port Moresby.

On the demand side, private consumption remained constrained by difficulties in accessing foreign exchange and the resulting damage to business confidence, with wholesale and retail trade and the transport and storage industries both estimated to have expanded by only 2.0% in 2017. On the other hand, sustained public investment was largely responsible for water supply and waste management growth by 5.5%, and electricity and gas growth by 4.0%. In addition, boosts came from government spending related to elections in mid-2017 and preparations for the Asia-Pacific Economic Cooperation (APEC) meetings to be held in 2018.

Inflation eased to 4.7% in 2017 from 6.7% in 2016 as prices for some seasonal produce such as betel nut, fruit, and vegetables moderated after spiking because of the drought in 2016 (Figure 3.33.2). A stable exchange rate for the PNG kina against the US dollar during the year limited any pass-through of imported inflation. In 2017, inflation was once again highest, at 11.5%, for alcoholic beverages, tobacco, and betel nut, but this was down from 26.1% in 2016. Health-care costs came next, with inflation accelerating to 10.4% in 2017 from 8.0% in 2016.

The fiscal deficit was estimated to equal 2.5% of GDP in 2017, compared with a deficit of 4.6% in 2016 (Figure 3.33.3). This reflected a 5.3% reduction in expenditure over the year against an increase in revenue by 4.7%. The ratio of debt to GDP in 2017 stood at the equivalent of 32.1% of GDP, slightly lower than the 32.6% recorded in 2016 and within the revised 35.0% legislated limit.

The Bank of Papua New Guinea, the central bank, maintained its neutral monetary policy during 2017, leaving its main policy rate, called the kina facility rate, unchanged at 6.25% throughout the year. However, excess liquidity in the banking system renders monetary policy largely ineffective. Broad money supply declined by an estimated 0.9% in 2017 as credit to the private sector faltered.

The foreign exchange rate remained stable throughout 2017, at around K3.18 to the US dollar. The central bank tries to manage foreign exchange imbalances by selectively intervening in currency markets. A foreign exchange trading band determines the speed of PNG kina depreciation.

The current account recorded a large surplus in 2017 equal to 13.9% of GDP. However, the surplus did not translate into higher foreign exchange reserves as they were matched by a deficit in the financial account caused by debt repayment on a large liquefied natural gas project and the use of offshore foreign currency accounts by mining firms and oil and gas companies (Figure 3.33.4). Foreign exchange reserves were therefore static in 2017. As of October 2017, they stood at $1.7 billion, providing 6 months of import cover.

3.33.3 Fiscal performance

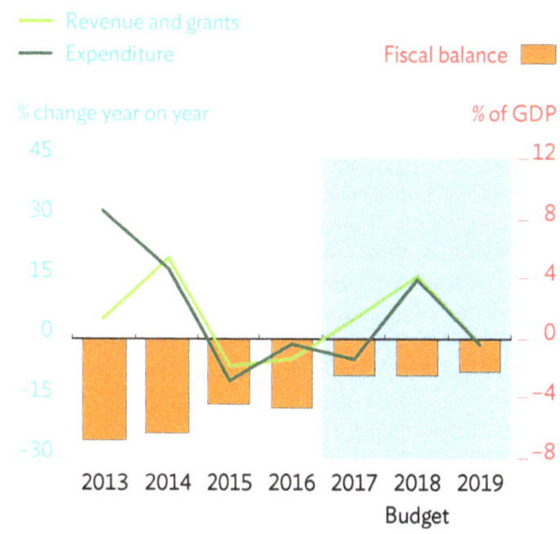

Sources: National budget documents, various years.

3.33.4 Liquefied natural gas exports and gross international reserves

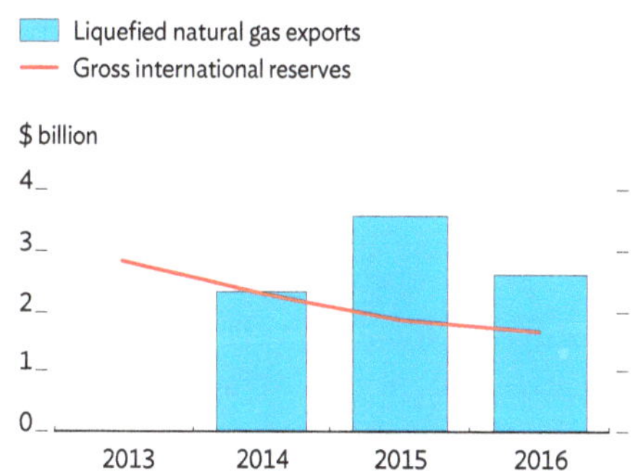

Sources: Bank of Papua New Guinea Quarterly Statistical Tables; International Monetary Fund. 2017. Article IV Consultation Staff Report. Washington, DC.

Economic prospects

Growth is projected to remain relatively modest in 2018 and 2019. Most sectors are expected to expand, with the APEC meetings providing an additional boost in 2018. However, a recent earthquake will hold back growth in oil and gas in 2018. Continued difficulty in accessing foreign currency and fiscal constraints will also limit growth.

Mining is expected to grow moderately during the forecast period, though growth may be tempered by recent earthquake damage to the Porgera mine. The country's largest mines are not expected to expand production significantly, but growth is expected at the Ramu NiCo mine and some smaller mining operations. Improved metal prices will translate into higher growth. Oil and gas are expected to contract in 2018 as oil production declines and the recent earthquake forces some oil and gas operations to suspend activity for an undetermined period. A rebound could follow as early as the latter part of 2018, however, with a return to full production.

3.33.1 Selected economic indicators (%)

	2018	2019
GDP growth	1.8	2.7
Inflation	5.0	4.5
Current account balance (share of GDP)	13.4	13.8

Source: ADB estimates.

The agriculture, forestry, and fishery sector is projected to grow by about 3% in 2018 and 2019 as output increases for all major crops. Coffee production is expected to rebound in 2018 with favorable growing conditions, cocoa production is seen to increase as the area under cultivation expands, copra and copra oil are expected to continue to benefit from heightened international demand in recent years, and palm oil production, which accounts for some 45% of agricultural exports, should grow modestly. Agricultural production for the domestic market will expand as well in line with a growing economy, an expanding population, and investment in the sector.

On the demand side, the APEC meetings in 2018 will boost consumption of goods and services. Several meetings will be held during the year, culminating in the main event in November. The PNG Treasury expects APEC-related growth at 6.5% in administration and support services, 6.2% in transport and storage, 5.3% in hotels and restaurants, and 5.2% in information and communication technology. Construction on government infrastructure projects, such as renovation of the Highlands Highway, will contribute to growth, as will earthquake relief and reconstruction.

Inflation is forecast to accelerate to 5.0% in 2018. Pass-through from higher oil prices will exert upward pressure, as will recent hikes in excise taxes on fuel and higher import tariffs under the 2018 budget. For example, diesel prices are expected to rise by 5.8% with new excise taxes. Demand related to the APEC meetings is expected to exert additional pressure on prices. Further, potential exists for currency depreciation and resulting imported inflation. In 2019, inflation is expected to ease to 4.5% as the APEC effect dissipates and growth remains relatively soft.

Under its fiscal consolidation strategy, the government is targeting deficits equal to 2.5% of GDP in 2018 and 2.2% in 2019. While budget expenditure is forecast to increase by 14.7% in 2018, partly to pay for APEC preparations, the government intends to counter it with a 16.0% increase in revenue. According to budget projections, over half of increased revenue is expected to be higher dividends from state-owned enterprises and one-off balance transfers from state authorities such as the National Fisheries Authority, which are reported to hold large idle cash balances. A further portion is expected to come from improved revenue collection, as well as higher tax collection resulting from APEC activity. Achieving the deficit target is likely to be a challenge, raising the prospect of midyear budget revisions, as have occurred in recent years. An additional weight on the budget will be government expenditure on relief and reconstruction following the recent earthquake.

To finance the deficit, the government is looking to external financing from multilateral organizations and international markets, and it is considering a sovereign bond issue. Development partner transactions in the pipeline worth about $600 million are likely to bring funds to PNG in the forecast period. However, additional foreign currency borrowing comes with elevated risk should the currency depreciate. Financing from domestic sources, which accounts for 72.8% of government debt, has become increasingly tight as some foreign banks operating in PNG have hit ceilings for such investment. The central bank has therefore ended up purchasing government securities on occasion that the market declined to take up. It has, however, succeeded in selling on almost half of its securities purchases under a new program that allows the general public to invest directly in government securities.

The current account is forecast to sustain a surplus equal to 13.4% of GDP in 2018 and 13.8% in 2019, largely from higher exports of liquefied natural gas. However, foreign exchange reserves will not improve commensurately as a significant portion of foreign exchange proceeds from mining and gas companies will not be remitted to PNG.

3.33.5 Resource revenue

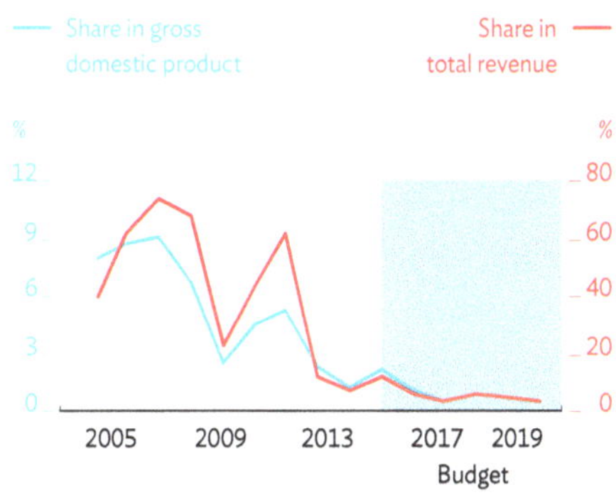

Sources: National budget documents, various years; national final budget outcome reports, various years; ADB estimates.

Policy challenge—fiscal consolidation

PNG ran a broadly balanced budget in the 10 years to 2012. During that time, the economy grew strongly and the ratio of debt to GDP declined from 71.0% to 16.3%, leaving PNG finances in a strong position. However, at the end of 2012, commodity prices began to fall, inflicting a significant shock to the PNG economy and undermining government revenue. Notably, resource revenue from mining and petroleum taxes and dividends were hit, falling from more than a quarter of total revenue during the boom years to under 5% in 2016 and 2017 (Figure 3.33.5). Increased revenue was matched by greater expenditure with large increases in wages, public office rentals, health-care and education subsidies, and debt-service costs. These trends brought fiscal deficits equal to 6.9% of GDP in 2013, 6.3% in 2014, 4.5% in 2015, and 4.6% in 2016. Financing these deficits became a challenge.

In mid-2017, PNG appeared to be on a path to another large deficit, initially expected to equal 3.8% of GDP. However, the outcome was better, estimated at 2.5%, because a new government that assumed office in August 2017 took tough action to reduce expenditure in the 2017 supplementary budget, mostly by cutting capital expenditure programs at the provincial and district level.

This was followed by the release in November 2017 of the new Medium Term Fiscal Strategy, 2018–2022, which aims to keep the deficit below 2.5% of GDP in 2018 and scale it back to 1.0% by 2022. The strategy incorporates medium-term revenue, expenditure, and debt strategies.

Under the Medium Term Revenue Strategy, the government has developed a plan to improve tax compliance, collection, and administration. This includes enhancing information technology systems in the Inland Revenue Commission, establishing a dedicated office to handle large taxpayers, and drafting a new law to simplify and modernize tax administration. The strategy proposes to broaden the tax base and review revenue collection from mines, which have traditionally benefited from concessions.

Under the expenditure strategy, the government will tackle the burgeoning public wage bill (Figure 3.33.6). Its aim is to limit wage bill growth to no more than 5% annually and reduce the wage bill from the current 49% of revenue (excluding resource and grant proceeds) to less than 40% by 2022. Finally, the debt strategy seeks to roll total government debt back below 30% of GDP by 2022 from the current 32% and to reduce the government's reliance on the domestic Treasury bill market by tapping external sources (Figure 3.33.7).

Committing to the Medium Term Fiscal Strategy and its path toward fiscal consolidation is essential. It will also be a challenge. If successful, however, it will help restore confidence in the economy and ease pressure from deficit financing.

Another challenge to address in the medium to long term is the economy's vulnerability to commodity price volatility. To this end, PNG should continue its efforts to set up a sovereign wealth fund and implement fiscal anchors that consider commodity price volatility and enable PNG to save when prices are favorable.

The Medium Term Fiscal Strategy has a plan to adopt a new fiscal anchor called a non-resource primary balance (NRPB), which is expressed as a percentage of GDP. The NRPB is the budget deficit or surplus from resource revenue excluding interest payments. The PNG NRPB was a deficit

3.33.6 Public wage bill

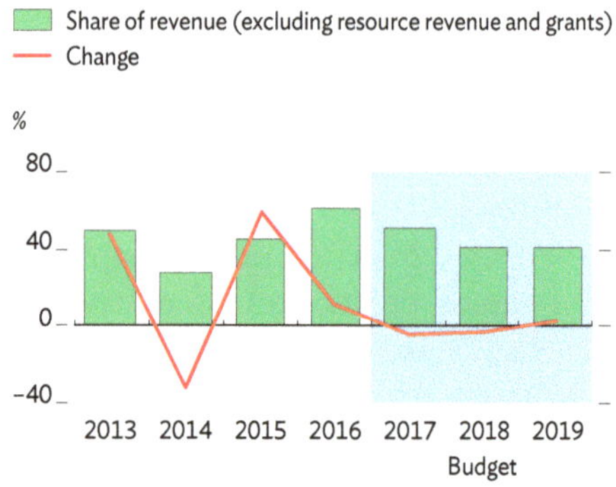

Sources: National budget documents, various years.

3.33.7 Public debt

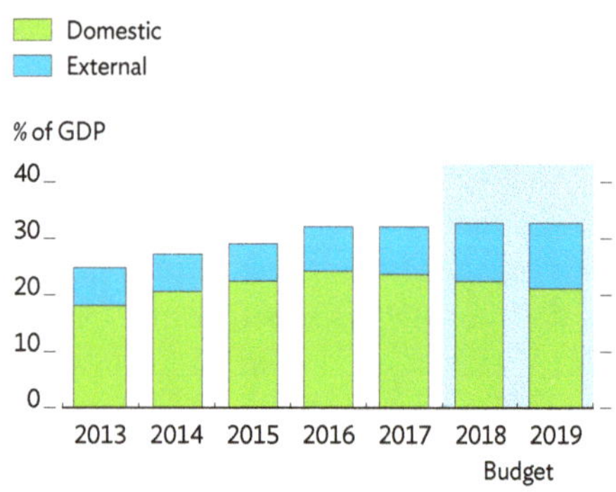

Sources: National budget documents, various years.

equal to 4.2% of GDP in 2016 and 1.2% in 2017. Over the medium term, the fiscal strategy targets an NRPB of zero, meaning a balanced budget before interest costs and without considering resource revenue. This would allow resource revenue to flow into savings, ideally into a sovereign wealth fund. If resource revenue picks up significantly, the ratio could be adjusted to, for example, a deficit equal to 1.0% of GDP. An NRPB would be useful because it would fix government budgeting to the relatively stable segment of the economy outside of the resource sector. However, the real test for PNG will be committing to these rules as production and prices pick up over the medium term.

Solomon Islands

Cash crops, fishing revenue, and construction remained strong in 2017, but economic growth nevertheless slowed as logging exports declined. Inflation decelerated on lower food prices, and the current account deficit almost halved. Slower growth is expected in 2018 and 2019 as new construction only partly offsets a likely further decline in logging output. Progress is being made in implementing a much-needed national transport plan, but challenges remain.

Economic performance

Economic growth slowed to 3.2% in 2017 (Figure 3.34.1). Log output decreased by almost 2% in 2017 to 2.65 million cubic meters from a high of 2.69 million cubic meters in 2016 (Figure 3.34.2). Meanwhile, the output of other major primary products increased, copra by 35% and fish by 15%. Mining and tourism also expanded significantly, albeit from low bases.

Industry grew strongly, driven by construction to upgrade Kukum Highway and the Mataniko Bridge. Manufacturing contributed to growth as well with fish processing in particular continuing to expand as in recent years.

The government maintained an expansionary budget in 2017 with a budget deficit estimated to equal 4.0% of GDP. Revenue collection rose but fell short of the government target. Meanwhile, government spending expanded by an estimated 4.8%, which included a significant increase for international scholarships for tertiary education. Government cash reserves, held at the Central Bank of Solomon Islands, have declined significantly to less than 1 month of recurrent spending, undermining their usefulness as a fiscal buffer. A weakened fiscal position prompted the government to delay payment to contractors and service providers, worsening domestic arrears.

Inflation decelerated in 2017 (Figure 3.34.3). Although fuel prices rose, prices were lower for imported and domestically produced food, which accounts for 42.9% of the consumer price index. The central bank maintained its accommodative monetary stance and left the cash reserve requirement on banks at 7.5%. Despite sufficient liquidity, growth in credit to the private sector has slowed in recent years.

The current account deficit almost halved in 2017 from the equivalent of 4.9% of GDP in 2016 to 2.5%, reflecting low international food prices, strong exports, and continued inflows

3.34.1 Supply-side contributions to growth

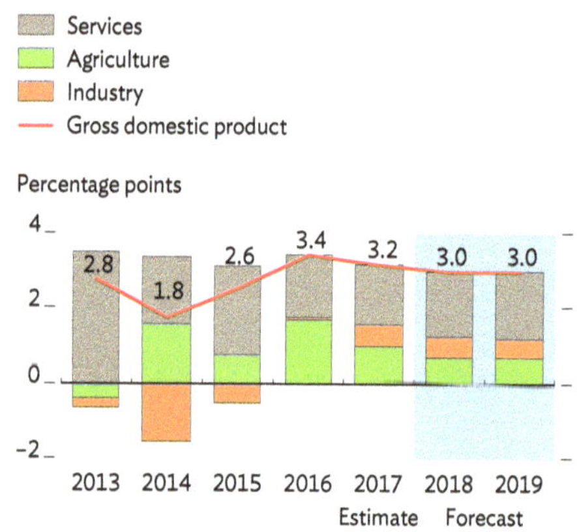

Sources: Ministry of Finance and Treasury; ADB estimates.

3.34.2 Logging output

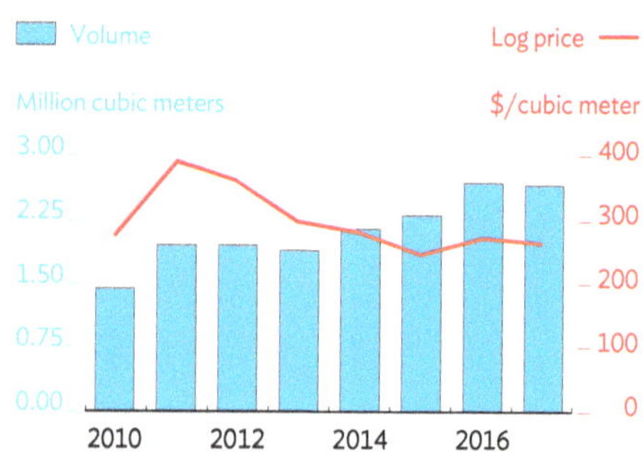

Sources: Central Bank of Solomon Islands; ADB estimates.

This chapter was written by Jacqueline Connell of the Pacific Liaison and Coordination Office, ADB, Sydney, and by Prince Cruz, consultant, Pacific Department, ADB, Manila.

of grants from development partners. Merchandise exports grew by an estimated 12.0% in 2017, up from fractional 0.6% growth in 2016. After several years of rising log output, the production reversal in 2017 and lower prices saw log exports drop by an estimated 5.5% in 2017 from 2016. Conversely, following several years of contraction, mineral exports rose with the resumption of production and exports from bauxite mines (Figure 3.34.4). Service exports grew by 19.1%, largely reflecting higher tourism as cruise ships arrived on a regular basis and air arrivals increased by more than 10.0% (Figure 3.34.5). The 75th anniversary in 2017 of the Guadalcanal landing in World War II attracted increased tourist visits from the US. Merchandise imports rose by an estimated 12.1% in 2017 owing to higher machinery and fuel imports.

3.34.3 Inflation

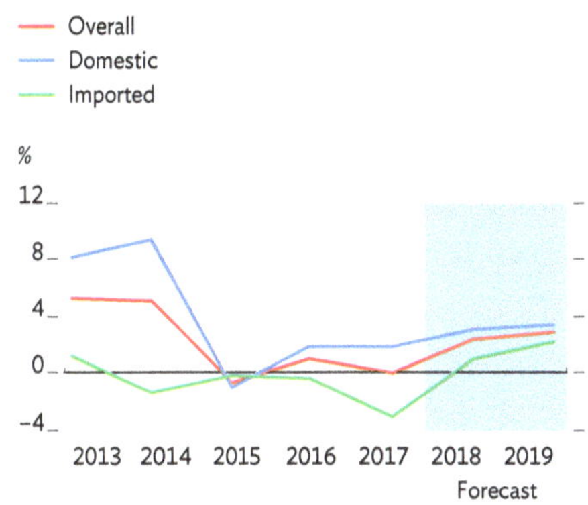

Sources: Central Bank of Solomon Islands; ADB estimates.

Economic prospects

Growth is projected to moderate in 2018 and 2019. A decline in log output is expected to be partly offset by greater output of nickel and bauxite and by construction associated with the planned rehabilitation of the Gold Ridge gold mine. Supported by development partners, the Tina River Hydropower Development Project and undersea cable project are expected to contribute to growth starting in 2019. A delay to their implementation would pose a risk to the outlook. Other risks would be delays to the planned upgrade of several airports, which could constrain tourism growth.

The government operated on a recurrent budget in the first quarter of 2018, following a change in administration in November 2017. There can be no new capital expenditure until the 2018 budget is passed, which is expected in April. The government is likely to face spending pressures in the approach to elections in early 2019. On top of these pressures, payment of domestic arrears accrued in 2017 will likely keep the fiscal deficit at about 4% of GDP in 2018 and 2019 (Figure 3.34.6).

Inflation is expected to pick up in 2018 and 2019 as international commodity prices rise. The current account deficit will likely narrow in 2018 before widening again in 2019 with rising imports to support large infrastructure projects (Figure 3.34.7). Rising prices for oil, which accounts for approximately 20% of imports, could similarly cause the current account deficit to widen in 2019.

Logs and timber, which declined as a share of exports from an estimated 72% in 2016 to 63% in 2017, will likely experience further gradual declines. In recent years, production has routinely surprised on the upside, but its eventual decline seems inevitable because output has long been far from sustainable. A risk to the outlook is an unexpectedly rapid collapse of the logging industry, which could be triggered by environmental or government pressures.

3.34.4 Mineral exports

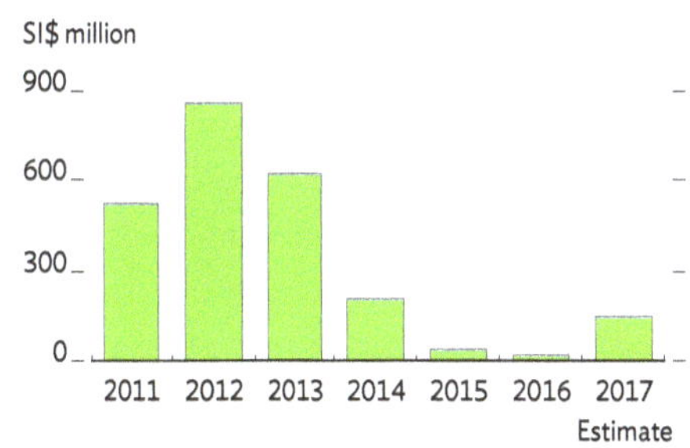

Sources: Central Bank of Solomon Islands; ADB estimates.

3.34.1 Selected economic indicators (%)

	2018	2019
GDP growth	3.0	3.0
Inflation	2.5	3.0
Current account balance (share of GDP)	-2.1	-2.5

Source: ADB estimates.

3.34.5 Visitor arrivals by mode of travel

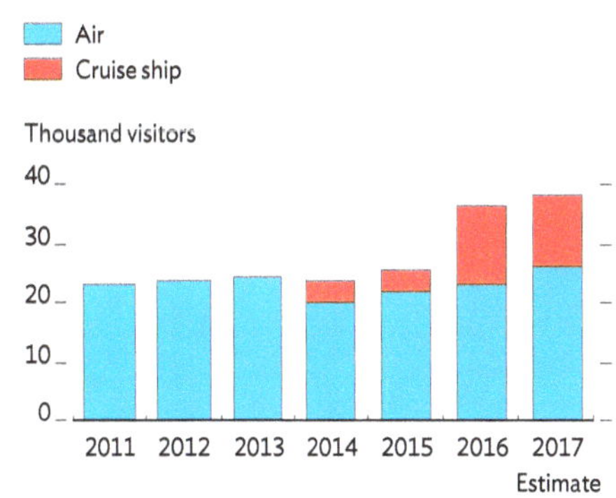

Sources: Central Bank of Solomon Islands; ADB estimates.

Another risk to the outlook is a significant slowdown in the People's Republic of China, which has become the key export market for commodities from the Solomon Islands. Meanwhile, relatively high foreign reserves, sufficient to cover 8 months of imports, and ongoing assistance from development partners help ensure that Solomon Islands continues to maintain a strong external position.

3.34.6 Fiscal balance

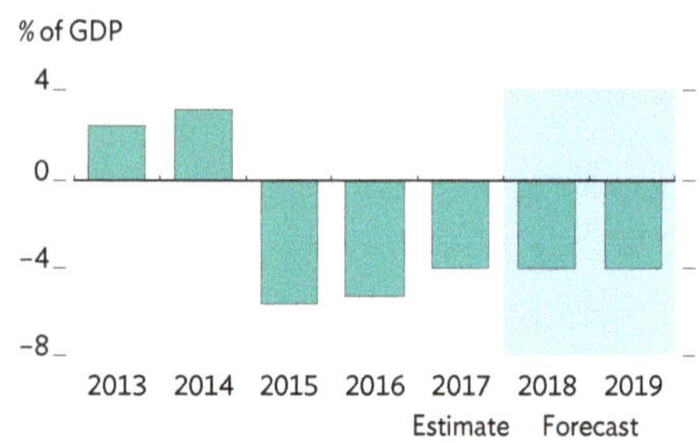

Source: Ministry of Finance and Treasury; ADB estimates.

Policy challenge—improving transport connectivity

Because the population of Solomon Islands is spread over many islands, disasters and climate change challenge its transport network. Some 60% of the population lives on islands other than the main island of Guadalcanal and relies on a limited network of sea and air transport links. Most wharves and domestic airfields on the outer islands need rehabilitation. These transport difficulties constrain tourism, limit access to basic services, and restrict economic growth.

A significant challenge for Solomon Islands is to improve its transport infrastructure in line with its limited resources. Providing recurrent budgets for maintenance is important as well because inadequate maintenance can accelerate wear and tear on transport assets, lengthen journey times, and cause accidents.

In 2016, the government updated its strategy with the National Transport Plan, 2017–2036 and affirmed the role of the National Transport Fund as the key mechanism for maintaining transport infrastructure with support from development partners. The plan identifies transport priorities, maps the number of potential beneficiaries for each project, and estimates project cost. As the total cost of priority projects is greater than the entire GDP for 2016, assistance from development partners is critical. The National Transport Plan provides a roadmap toward better coordination between government agencies, the public, and development partners.

Recognizing the country's dependence on maritime transport, the government has supported shipping operators directly and indirectly through grants offered to members of Parliament. While little evidence is available yet on the development impact of shipping grants made to members of Parliament, the practice raises broader questions on the social benefits and commercial viability of various transport options, especially in remote areas. The limited resources available to the government make it vital to align funding with transport priorities. Ensuring that accountability frameworks are in place is equally important to maximize the benefits of investments in Solomon Islands' transport infrastructure.

3.34.7 Current account balance

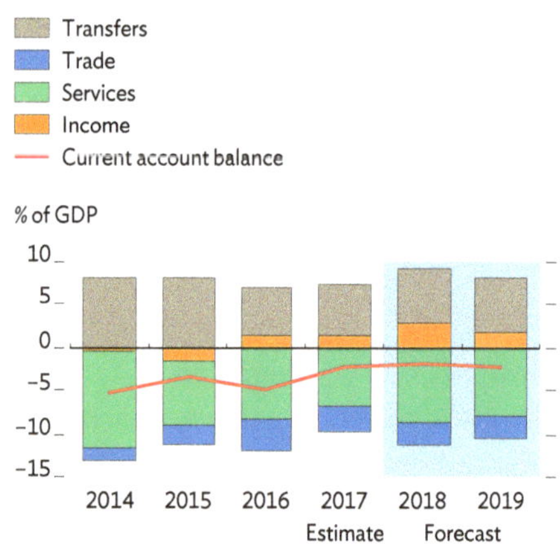

Sources: Central Bank of Solomon Islands; ADB estimates.

Timor-Leste

The economy contracted as political impasse held back public spending and private investment slowed. Prospects hinge on decisive results in this year's election and a restoration of public spending to complement large private projects in the near term. Recent developments in oil and gas boost the outlook over the longer term. Renewed emphasis on skills development and a more facilitating approach to labor migration would give young people better access to employment.

Economic performance

Sharply reduced public spending and a slowdown in private investment caused GDP excluding the large offshore petroleum sector (hereafter GDP) to contract by 2.0% in 2017 (Figure 3.35.1). Public expenditure excluding off-budget grants from development partners fell by 26.8%. Spending cuts were concentrated in capital investment, which plunged by 56.6%. Recurrent spending fell by 8.4% with reductions by 13.4% in purchases of goods and services and by 21.1% in transfer payments to the Special Administrative Region of Oe-Cusse Ambeno (Figure 3.35.2). Development partner grants fell by 36.0% to the equivalent of 8.8% of GDP.

Lower public spending in 2017 was linked to political events. Plans for government investment were scaled back in preparation for presidential elections in March and parliamentary elections in July. After no party won a majority in Parliament, protracted negotiations yielded a coalition government in September. However, the government's 5-year program and a proposal to increase the 2017 budget by 16.1% were rejected by Parliament.

The slowdown in public capital investment reduced demand for machinery and construction services. Agriculture, which generated 16.8% of GDP, also faced challenges in 2017. Production of paddy and maize, the two main staple crops, was hit by erratic rains. Cereal production was, at 130,000 tons, stable from 2016 but 20% below the 5-year average. Erratic weather also hit coffee, the main cash crop, pushing yield down by more than half and coffee export earnings down by 48.6%.

Many indicators reflected challenging conditions in 2017. Growth in household electricity consumption, for example, slowed from 35.5% in 2016 to 11.2%. Growth in electricity use by businesses also slowed, and motorbike registration fell by

3.35.1 Supply-side contributions to growth

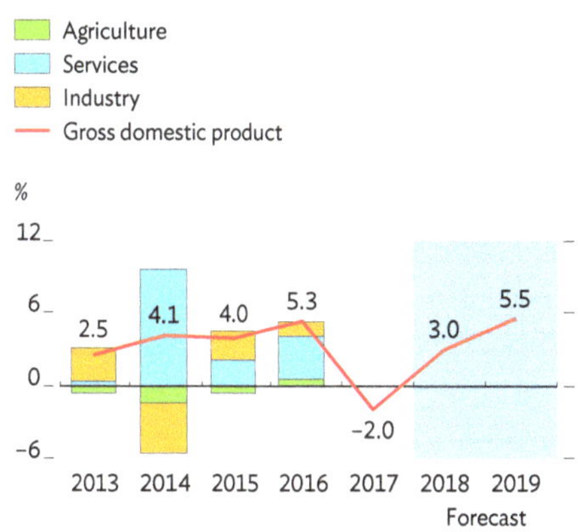

Sources: Statistics Timor-Leste; ADB estimates.

3.35.2 Public expenditure components

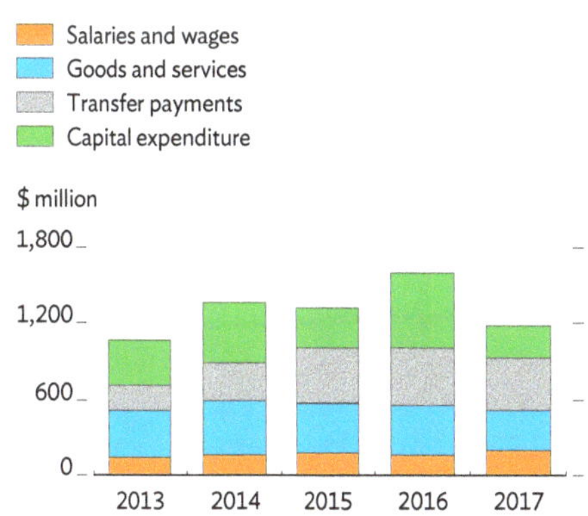

Source: Timor-Leste Budget Transparency Portal.

This chapter was written by David Freedman of the Timor-Leste Resident Mission, ADB, Dili.

4.6% after several years of double-digit growth. On the other hand, fiscal policy supported private consumption, with social assistance payments higher by 1.7% and government spending on salaries and wages up by 14.8%. International visitor arrivals were a bright spot, up by 12.0%.

A fifth bank commenced operations in Timor-Leste in 2017. Other developments in finance reflected trends in the wider economy. Slower public spending saw bank deposit growth halve from an annual average of 30.7% in 2015–2016 to 14.9% in 2017. Lending to the private sector expanded by 7.5% year on year in the first 3 quarters with large increases for construction. Bank deposits and net foreign asset holdings grew by 10.6% to $1.25 billion, equal to 75.0% of GDP.

Timor-Leste emerged from deflation in 2017 with the consumer price index up by 0.6%. However, inflation was lower than projected as economic activity faltered and reflected mainly higher food prices, especially in the capital. There were modest declines in communications and housing costs.

Government revenue exceeded expectations. Timor-Leste received $417.7 million in petroleum taxes and royalties in 2017, up from $223.9 million in 2016 as oil and gas prices rose and the government completed agreed repayments to field operators (Figure 3.35.3). However, production from the Bayu-Undan oil field continued to decline, falling by 18% in 2017. Domestic revenue was in line with budget forecasts. Petroleum Fund of Timor-Leste investments performed exceptionally well. Its bond and equity investments earned $301.0 million, equal to 17.9% of GDP, and generated a return on assets of 10.4%, the highest since the fund was established in 2005.

The fund ended the year with a balance of $16.8 billion, or $13,500 per capita (Figure 3.35.4). Strong performance in petroleum taxes and Petroleum Fund investments was reflected in the current account surplus, estimated to equal 0.8% of GDP, up from a deficit of 30.7% in 2016 despite higher merchandise imports. Also reflected in the surplus was a narrower service trade deficit as construction slowed.

Economic prospects

Growth is projected to accelerate to 3.0% in 2018 and 5.5% in 2019 on new government programs and renewed investor confidence. Inflation is also projected to accelerate as the economy picks up, to 2.0% in 2018 and 3.0% in 2019 on higher food and fuel prices (Figure 3.35.5).

Economic prospects are linked to the political outlook. Fresh parliamentary elections will be held in May 2018, and a new government is likely to be sworn in by July, but this could be delayed if election results fail again to be decisive. Election campaigns will begin in April and boost economic activity across the country. However, government expenditure

3.35.3 Petroleum taxes and royalties

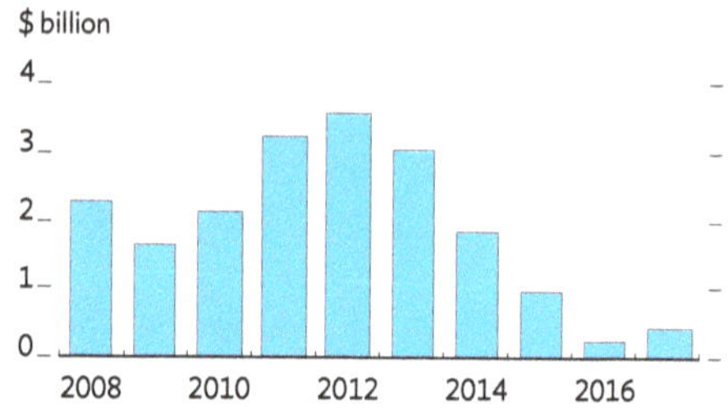

Sources: Timor-Leste Petroleum Fund reports, various years.

3.35.4 Petroleum Fund balance at year-end

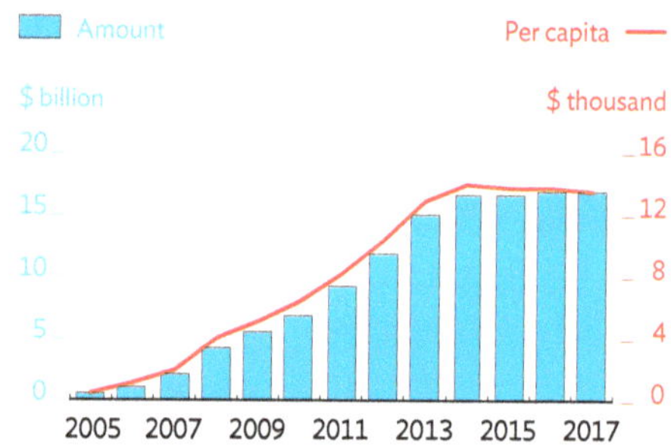

Sources: Timor-Leste Petroleum Fund reports, various years; Timor-Leste National Census 2015.

3.35.5 Inflation

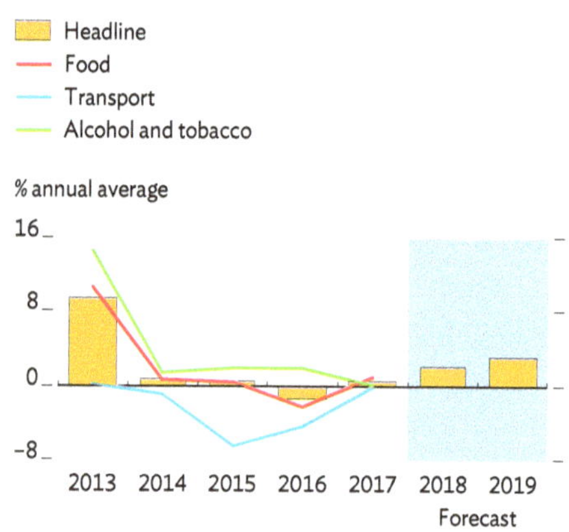

Sources: Statistics Timor-Leste; ADB estimates.

leading up to the elections is likely to be constrained for lack of an approved budget for 2018. In the meantime, the government is restricted to monthly appropriations of no more than a twelfth of the annual budget for 2017. This so-called duodecimal regime does not automatically enable the government to use the petroleum fund to cover expenditure, as the law stipulates that withdrawals from the fund can be made only with approval from Parliament. Government cash holdings were estimated at $369.6 million at the end of December 2017. With these reserves and domestic revenue, the government should be able to sustain operations until the elections, but expenditure in the first half of 2018 will likely be significantly lower than in recent years. The government may seek parliamentary approval for petroleum fund withdrawals to ensure that execution of the duodecimal budget is not constrained.

Lower public expenditure in the first half of 2018 is likely to be offset by accelerated spending after a new government is formed. It will immediately be tasked with formulating a budget for the remainder of 2018 and another for 2019 and may use this opportunity to scale up spending. The private sector should also provide a boost in 2018. The Tibar Bay port project secured its environmental license in February 2018, with construction expected to begin in the second half of the year. Total investment in the port is estimated at $278.3 million, equal to 16.7% of GDP.

Several other large private investment projects are poised to move ahead in 2018 and 2019. Investors are preparing to build a $100 million hotel and apartment complex on the outskirts of Dili beginning in the second half of 2018. Other resort developments are being considered, and plans for a $200 million cement factory near Baucau may go ahead before the end of 2019. However, as political stability and government support are essential for private investment, there are clear risks that project timelines may slip.

Agriculture is expected to pick up in 2018 with a large increase in coffee production and improved prospects for maize and paddy following good rains. Oil and gas exploration onshore, led by a state-owned enterprise, is set to continue in 2018 and 2019. New wells planned for the offshore Bayu-Undan oil field should help slow a decline in production—and in taxes and royalties received—extending the field's life by 2 years to 2022. As a consequence, the forecast for Bayu-Undan production from 2018 to 2022 has almost tripled, with discounted revenue to Timor-Leste in this period now projected at $1.3 billion, up from a previous estimate of $0.3 billion. This pushes the petroleum fund's estimated sustainable income—the amount that can be withdrawn from the fund each year without depleting it—up by 13.1% to $544.8 million.

3.35.1 Selected economic indicators (%)

	2018	2019
GDP growth	3.0	5.5
Inflation	2.0	3.0
Current account balance (share of GDP)	-15.2	-22.0

Source: ADB estimates.

3.35.6 Current account components

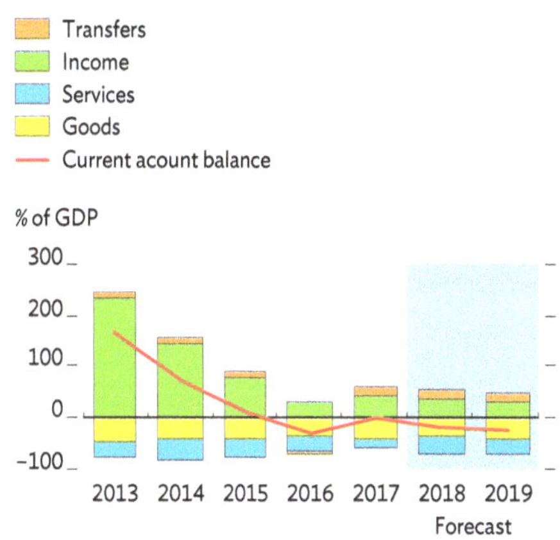

Sources: Central Bank of Timor-Leste; ADB estimates.

3.35.7 Growth in GDP and private employment

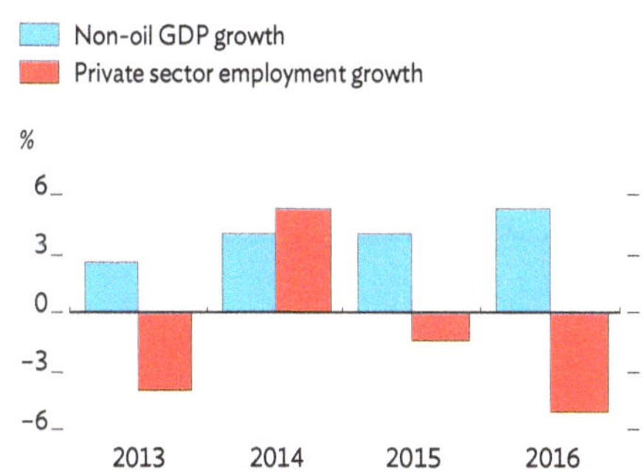

Sources: Timor-Leste Business Activity Survey 2016; Timor-Leste National Accounts 2016.

Longer-term prospects for oil and gas are promising. On 6 March 2018, the governments of Australia and Timor-Leste signed a treaty that establishes a permanent maritime boundary between them, defines the latter's exclusive economic zone, and paves the way for developing Greater Sunrise, a large oil and gas field in the Timor Sea. Under the treaty, Timor-Leste will receive 70% of production taxes and royalties on oil and gas from Greater Sunrise processed in Timor-Leste and 80% on production processed in Australia. The undiscounted value of Timor-Leste's share of these revenues is estimated at between $21 billion and $28 billion. Further, the treaty increases Timor-Leste's share of Bayu-Undan revenues from 90% to 100% and gives the country exclusive rights to any revenue from the development of the smaller Buffalo oil field.

The new treaty awaits ratification by both Australia and Timor-Leste. A number of conditions need to be met before Greater Sunrise can be developed, which may not happen until well into the 2020s. For now, the treaty will likely reassure policy makers about long-term fiscal sustainability and may accelerate infrastructure development on the south coast. Rising imports for public and private investments and a gradual decline in production from Bayu-Undan will mean continued current account deficits, projected to equal 15.2% of GDP in 2018 and 22.0% in 2019 (Figure 3.35.6).

3.35.8 Private employment by sector

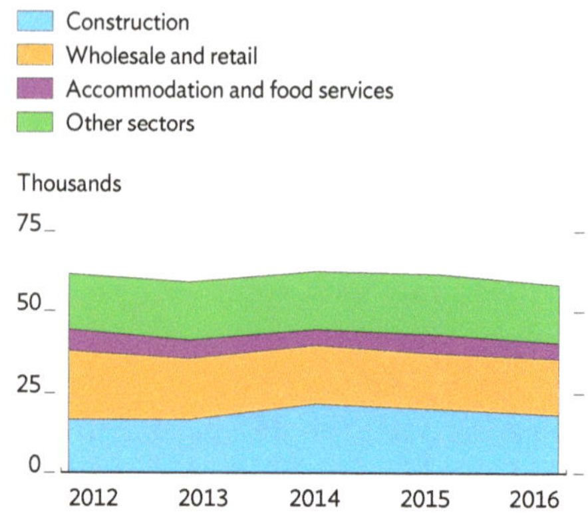

Source: Timor-Leste Business Activity Survey.

Policy challenge—providing opportunities for young workers

Timor-Leste struggles to employ a young and growing population. A recent survey found that, while GDP grew by 16.9% from 2012 to 2016, formal employment in the private sector fell by 5.4% in that period (Figure 3.35.7). Formal employment in 2016 stood at only 58,200 jobs, or 7.7% of the working-age population. Construction, which was the largest private employer, with 32% of the total, is highly dependent on public expenditure.

Declining employment from 2012 to 2016 reflected fewer jobs in retail, wholesale, restaurants, and accommodation, though the actual change may be less than surveyed as micro enterprises are not included (Figure 3.35.8). An annual enterprise skills survey with wider coverage found slightly higher employment in the private sector, up by 3.7% in the first 10 months of 2017. In any case, the current pace of job creation is clearly far too low, with only 4,000 new jobs each year (Figure 3.35.9).

Sustained job creation will depend on the development of tradable sectors such as tourism, agribusiness, and manufacturing. Supportive public policy can help to develop

3.35.9 Working-age population and employment

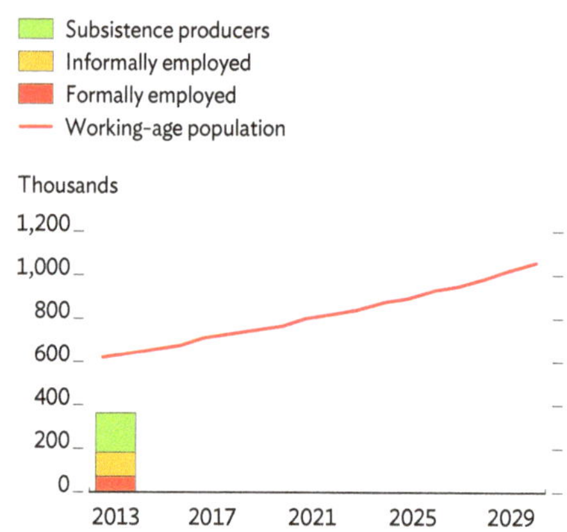

Sources: Timor-Leste Labour Force Survey. 2013; Timor-Leste Census 2010.

these industries by stimulating investment and new business formation. Improving basic education and developing more market-oriented technical and vocational training can narrow skills mismatches and enable young people entering the workforce to take advantage of new opportunities.

Labor mobility offers promise as part of an integrated employment strategy. Most Timorese are eligible for Portuguese citizenship, enabling them to work in the European Union, including 16,000–19,000 in the United Kingdom and smaller numbers in Portugal and other countries. Remittances from migrant workers, including more than $28 million from the United Kingdom in 2017, are increasingly important to Timorese households.

More government support for labor mobility can help to expand opportunities for Timorese workers. The government has long-established programs with Australia and the Republic of Korea to facilitate labor migration, with 750 Timorese currently participating. Such government-to-government programs could be expanded in the coming years with more partner governments and concerted efforts to identify suitable workers. The government should also consider options for supporting migration to the European Union. Gaps in public records leave some Timorese struggling to prove that they are entitled to Portuguese citizenship. Others struggle to meet the cost of migration to Europe or to prepare for the opportunities available there. A more proactive and facilitating approach to skills development and labor migration would help to address the job shortage in Timor-Leste and expand workers' access to opportunities in other countries.

Vanuatu

Economic recovery continued in 2017, propelled by elevated construction and strong agriculture and tourism. With several large infrastructure projects completed last year, growth is expected to moderate in 2018 and 2019. Vanuatu's ambitious infrastructure pipeline is supporting its current and future growth prospects, but the accompanying rise in public debt poses challenges for fiscal management.

Economic performance

GDP growth was steady in 2017, driven by construction and the continued recovery of agriculture and tourism from the impact of Cyclone Pam in 2015 (Figure 3.36.1). Tourism was buoyed by the 2017 Pacific Mini Games, which took place in Port Vila, and the return of codeshare flights operated by Qantas and Air Vanuatu. Air arrivals increased by an estimated 12% in 2017. In contrast, cruise ship arrivals fell by an estimated 11% from a record high in 2016 as several cruise ships cancelled trips to the newly upgraded Luganville wharf due to initial uncertainty about its operability (Figure 3.36.2).

Agriculture continued to recover from Cyclone Pam, with sector growth estimated at 5% in 2017. Production of major crops such as copra and kava exceeded pre-cyclone levels, but recovery in livestock production, mainly of cattle, has been slower.

Industry continued to expand with construction completed on international wharfs at Lapetasi and Luganville and tourist infrastructure in Port Vila. Private investment in hotels and other tourism projects also drove construction.

A fiscal deficit in 2017 equal to 2.0% of GDP reversed a 2.5% surplus in 2016. Despite capital expenditure remaining largely unchanged from 2016—and significantly lower than the budgeted fivefold increase—total government spending increased by an estimated 22% over the previous year. A large part of the increase covered overdue payments for civil servants, costs associated with the Pacific Mini Games, and tertiary scholarships.

Inflation accelerated to an estimated 3.2% in 2017. The largest increase was for domestic food, followed by higher transport costs because of higher global fuel prices in the second half of the year (Figure 3.36.3). Growth in domestic credit remained subdued.

3.36.1 Supply-side contributions to growth

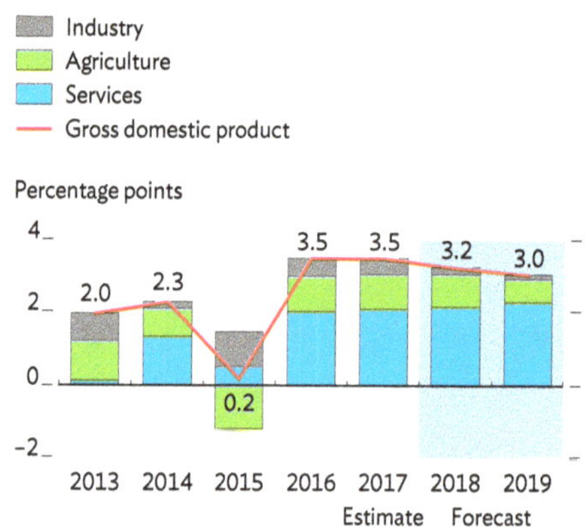

Sources: Vanuatu National Statistics Office; ADB estimates.

3.36.2 Visitor arrivals by mode of travel

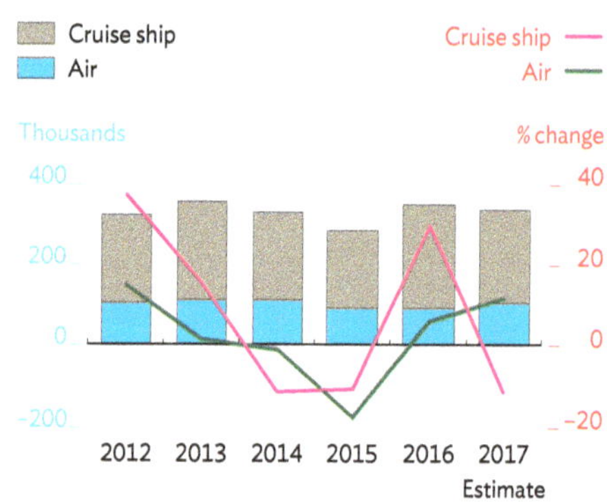

Sources: Vanuatu National Statistics Office; ADB estimates.

This chapter was written by Jacqueline Connell of the Pacific Liaison and Coordination Office, ADB, Sydney, and by Prince Cruz, consultant, Pacific Department, ADB, Manila.

The current account deficit halved to the equivalent of 2.1% of GDP in 2017 from 4.1% in 2016 with higher agricultural exports and increased tourism. Imports decreased with the completion of large projects. Official reserves were high, sufficient to cover 11.3 months of imports at the end of 2017.

Economic prospects

Economic growth is forecast to slow to 3.2% in 2018 and 3.0% in 2019. The services sector, which provides nearly two-thirds of GDP, is projected to continue to expand slightly on higher tourism and public administration. Growth in agriculture is expected to stabilize. Construction is set to remain strong in 2018 as some delayed reconstruction gets under way, but it is expected to wind down in 2019 and contribute less to growth that year. The government hopes it can raise its tax revenues with a value-added tax (VAT) rate rise from 12.5% to 15.0% effective in January 2018. It projects that higher VAT collections will supply the bulk of the 24.5% increase in budgeted domestic revenues (i.e., excluding grants) in 2018. The government also foresees its wages and salary bill to rise by 23.3% to implement the verdict of the Government Remuneration Tribunal, which ruled in favor of higher public service wages. In addition, as the grace period on some loans expires, interest payments are budgeted to increase from 4% of public revenues in 2017 to 5% in 2018. Fiscal deficits equal to about 1.8% of GDP are expected in 2018 and 2019.

Domestic inflation is projected to pick up to 4.8% in 2018, fueled by the VAT rate increase and higher public service remuneration, which may induce demands for similar wage hikes in the private sector. In 2019, inflation is expected to ease to 2.5%, which would be above the average of 1.5% over the past decade but below the 4.0% target set by the Reserve Bank of Vanuatu.

The current account deficit is expected to narrow in 2018, thanks to higher earnings from agriculture and tourism. With cruise ships already returning to the international wharf at Luganville, visitor arrivals are expected to increase in 2018. Airport upgrades in Port Vila, Luganville, and Tanna are expected to increase air arrivals, with new international routes possibly opening to Port Vila. Compared with arrivals on cruise ships, visitors by air contribute more to tourism earnings because they stay longer and consume more goods and services onshore. Meanwhile, the production of key agricultural products is expected to continue growing. The deficit is projected to increase slightly in 2019, however, because higher commodity prices will likely drive imports higher.

3.36.3 Inflation

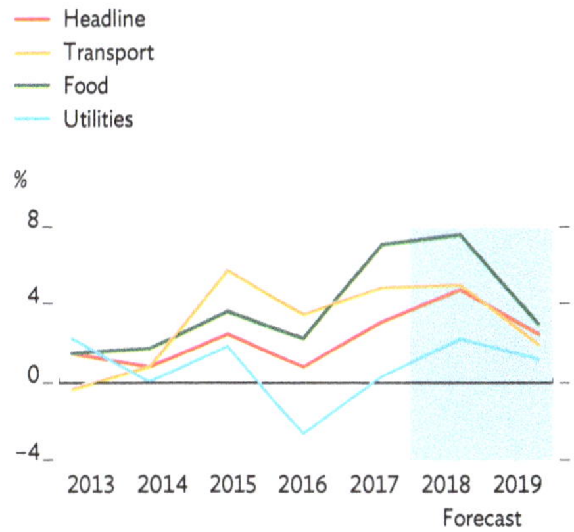

Sources: Vanuatu National Statistics Office; ADB estimates.

3.36.1 Selected economic indicators (%)

	2018	2019
GDP growth	3.2	3.0
Inflation	4.8	2.5
Current account balance (share of GDP)	-1.0	-1.1

Source: ADB estimates

3.36.4 Domestic revenues (excluding grants)

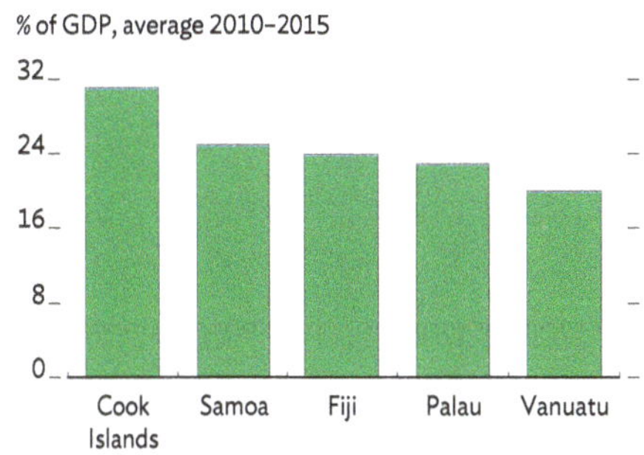

Source: *Asian Development Outlook* database.

A downside risk to the outlook is delay in implementing the large public infrastructure project pipeline. Implementation of development projects that outpaced expectations, on the other hand, would likely boost growth in 2018 and widen the current account deficit because of the need for higher capital imports.

Policy challenge—financing growth

The Government of Vanuatu is implementing a large infrastructure pipeline with a view to boosting productivity, particularly in the key tourism and agriculture sectors. While much of the infrastructure spending is expected to be sourced from concessional loans and development grants, public debt is increasing rapidly.

Recognizing the need to expand its revenue to maintain public investment and to service debt, the government has embarked on a revenue reform initiative. Vanuatu's domestic revenue has been low relative to comparable Pacific island economies (Figure 3.36.4).

Vanuatu raises most of its revenue through VAT and import tariffs, and from the sale of second citizenships to wealthy investors (Figure 3.36.5). The recent increase in the VAT rate will boost revenue, particularly from tourist spending. The government has resolved to introduce an income tax in the future, which would ease Vanuatu's reliance on more regressive taxes like the VAT.

The government needs to balance expansion of its revenue base with continued support for private sector growth. As it increases taxes on businesses, the government should ensure that other costs of doing business are minimized. While expanding its revenue base, the government needs to ensure as well that its tax administration is properly resourced to deal with tax policy changes. Updating the financial management information system, training staff to operate it, and enhancing human resource capacity in tax administration would help to support the government's revenue reform initiative.

3.36.5 Government revenue

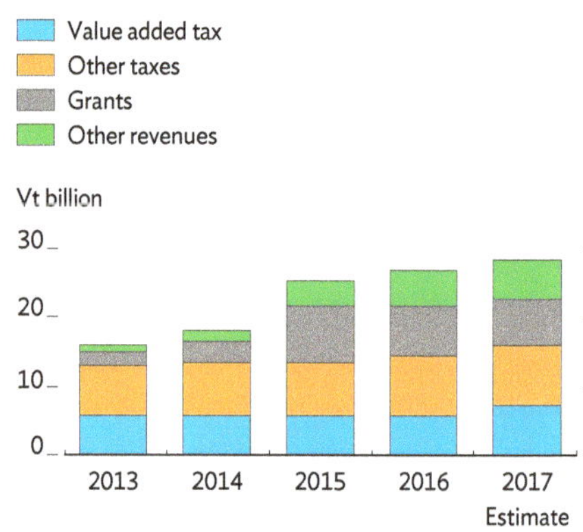

Sources: Reserve Bank of Vanuatu; ADB estimates.

North Pacific economies

Growth in 2017 followed recent trends, with infrastructure investment boosting economic activity in the Republic of the Marshall Islands and the Federated States of Micronesia, while a tourism downturn persisted in Palau. The outlook is similarly mixed and depends on the same growth drivers. Improving education can equip a young labor force with better skills to fill domestic employment gaps and raise potential growth over the long term.

Economic performance

The drivers of growth in three North Pacific economies in fiscal year 2017 (FY2017, ended 30 September 2017) have been the same as in recent years (Figure 3.37.1). Infrastructure investment fueled faster expansion in the Republic of the Marshall Islands (RMI) and the Federated States of Micronesia (FSM). In Palau, on the other hand, an ongoing tourism slump caused slight economic contraction.

In the RMI, growth more than doubled to 4.0% on stimulus from public investments funded by development partners, including infrastructure grants under the Compact of Free Association with the US. Among these were two saltwater reverse osmosis plants in Ebeye able to desalinate 1,600 cubic meters per day.

Similarly, the FSM recovered from slight contraction to 2.0% growth as public investments picked up moderately, despite a temporary suspension of US grants because of concern about project management. Under transitional arrangements, the FSM government will engage the US Army Corps of Engineers to help manage and implement projects. Previously approved projects—including a Kosrae State Hospital upgrade and the reconstruction of homes and public facilities damaged by Typhoon Maysak on Chuuk and Yap—were unaffected by the suspension and contributed to growth last year.

A tourism downturn in Palau worsened, pushing the economy into a contraction of 0.5% in FY2017. Meanwhile, revised official estimates show growth in FY2016 much weaker than previously estimated, highlighting the extent of the current economic slowdown. Tourist arrivals fell by 22.8% in FY2017, compounding a 13.1% decline in FY2016 (Figure 3.37.2).

This chapter was written by Norio Usui, Rommel Rabanal, and Cara Tinio of the Pacific Department, ADB, Manila.

3.37.1 GDP growth in the North Pacific economies

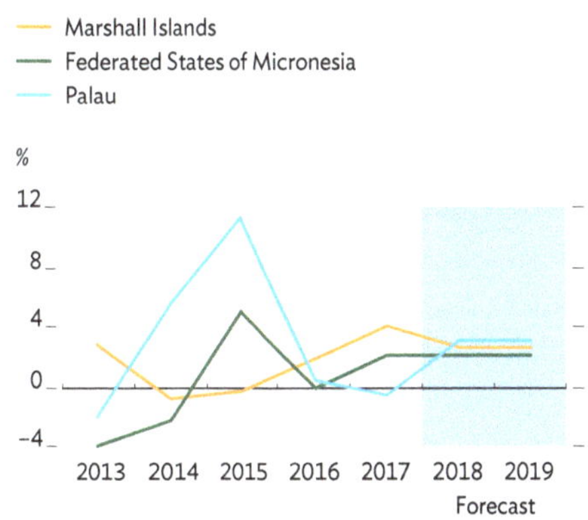

Note: Years are fiscal years ending on 30 September of the same calendar year.

Source: ADB estimates using data from the *Republic of the Marshall Islands, Federated States of Micronesia, and Republic of Palau FY2016 Economic Reviews*.

3.37.2 Visitor arrivals in Palau by source

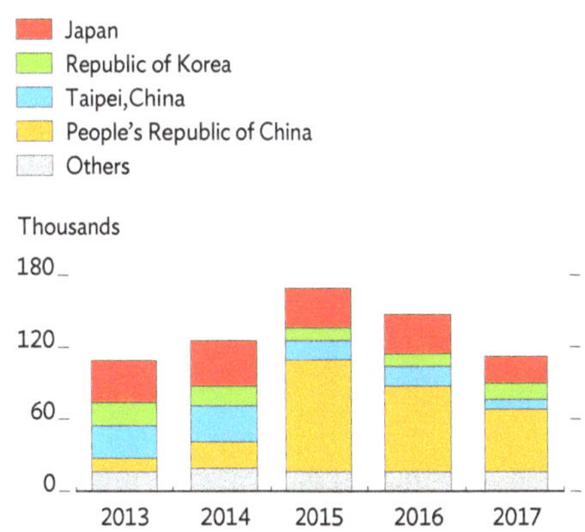

Note: Years are fiscal years ending on 30 September of the same calendar year.

Source: Palau Bureau of Labor and Immigration.

This reflected the closure of Jellyfish Lake, a major tourist attraction, but also appreciation of the US dollar, the local currency. A sharp fall in the number of tourists from the People's Republic of China, by 26.8%, accounted for much of the decline, but arrivals from traditional markets also fell, with Japan down 22.4% and Taipei,China down 43.2%. Slow implementation of projects funded by development partners worsened the downturn.

Inflationary pressures increased but remained modest in all three economies in FY2017, driven by higher fuel prices and their spillover effects on consumer goods such as clothing and processed food, most of which must be shipped from abroad. All three economies saw inflation return following price declines in the previous year.

Fiscal positions have weakened across the North Pacific. Preliminary estimates suggest that the Government of the RMI incurred a fiscal deficit equal to 2.0% of GDP in FY2017, reversing a surplus of 4.0% the previous year. Expenditures grew by 60.9%, far outpacing a 23.3% increase in revenues and grants partly because they included a transfer of $3 million to the Marshall Islands Social Security Authority as part of reform to the Social Security Fund.

Fiscal performance varied considerably within the FSM, with the national government running a large surplus and most states recording small deficits. State governments are responsible for major public services but have been constrained by declines in the real value of US compact grants, while the national government has benefited from higher revenue from fishing license fees (Figure 3.37.3). In FY2017, the national government recorded a fiscal surplus equal to 7.0% of GDP, down from 7.4% in the previous year because of significantly higher expenditures.

Palau's fiscal surplus similarly narrowed to the equivalent of 4.0% of GDP, from 4.7% in FY2016, as the falloff in tourism sharply dragged down revenues. This contrasted with the previous year, when tax revenues increased despite weak tourism because the downturn was concentrated in lower-spending market segments.

Current account balances likewise suffered in all three economies. In the RMI and the FSM, surpluses narrowed in FY2017 as imports of construction materials and fuel for public investments expanded. Fishing license revenues continued to increase in the RMI but appear to have reached a plateau in the FSM. Palau's current account is usually in deficit as large surpluses in secondary income such as remittances are insufficient to offset shortfalls in the trade and primary income balances. The deficit further widened in FY2017 with declining tourism receipts.

3.37.1 Selected economic indicators (%)

Federated States of Micronesia	2018	2019
GDP growth	2.0	2.0
Inflation	1.0	1.0
Current account balance (share of GDP)	2.0	2.0
Marshall Islands		
GDP growth	2.5	2.5
Inflation	1.0	1.0
Current account balance (share of GDP)	7.0	8.0
Palau		
GDP growth	3.0	3.0
Inflation	1.5	1.5
Current account balance (share of GDP)	-16.0	-16.0

Note: Years are fiscal years ending on 30 September of the same calendar year.

Source: ADB estimates.

3.37.3 Fishing license revenue in the Federated States of Micronesia

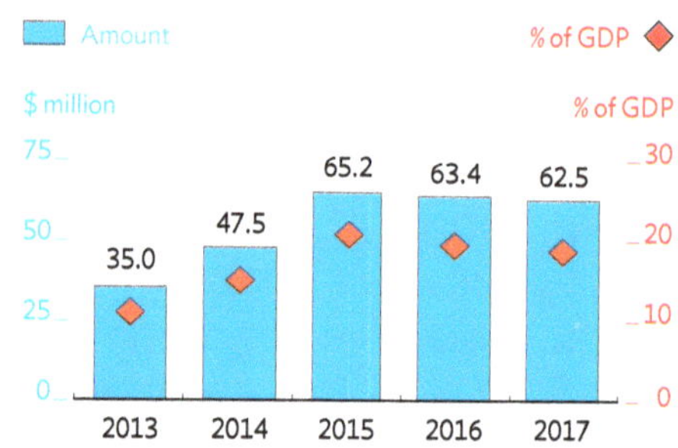

Note: Years are fiscal years ending on 30 September of the same calendar year.

Source: ADB estimates using data from the *Federated States of Micronesia FY2016 Economic Review.*

Economic prospects

The outlook for the North Pacific economies in the near term is mixed. In the RMI, growth is expected to slow in FY2018, albeit from a relatively high base, and remain at the same rate in FY2019 as local capacity constraints likely slow project implementation. The RMI has a large pool of funds from development partners to draw from, with over $200 million in potential project funding available from various multilateral and bilateral partners, including support for renewable energy projects. However, limited capacity to implement projects and a lack of alternative domestic opportunities hamper the economy.

GDP growth in the FSM is projected to remain stable. Although unspent compact infrastructure grants present an opportunity to reinvigorate the economy, public investments are projected to increase only gradually because of limited project implementation capacity.

The Infrastructure Development Plan, FY2016–FY2025 will continue to guide FSM capital spending priorities, especially investments to mitigate risks from disasters and climate change. Although the plan was expected to facilitate the implementation of projects funded through the US compact and by other development partners, recent project management issues have stalled progress. A sustainable solution to capacity issues would help harness more than $150 million in infrastructure grants that have been unspent since the start of the amended compact in 2004. This would both stimulate the economy in the near term and raise potential growth through longer-term productivity enhancements.

Palau is likely to return to steady, moderate growth in FY2018 and FY2019, supported by the commencement of private investment in new hotels and of public infrastructure projects funded by development partners. Gradual recovery in tourist arrivals is foreseen, but there is a risk that numbers could continue to fall because the People's Republic of China has imposed restrictions on advertisements for group tours to destinations not formally approved by the government.

Inflation is projected to rise slightly in all three economies in FY2018 before leveling off in FY2019, reflecting international food and fuel price trends (Figure 3.37.4). Rising commodity prices in the import bill are expected to further narrow the FSM current account surplus slightly. By contrast, the current account positions of the RMI and Palau are expected to improve despite larger commodity import bills. Project completion in the RMI will slow capital equipment imports, and in Palau the expected recovery in visitor arrivals should boost tourism receipts.

Fiscal sustainability remains a major concern. The fiscal deficit for the RMI is expected to widen gradually in FY2018 and FY2019 because of delayed reform to state-owned enterprises and the social security system. Subsidies and other

3.37.4 Inflation in the North Pacific economies and oil prices

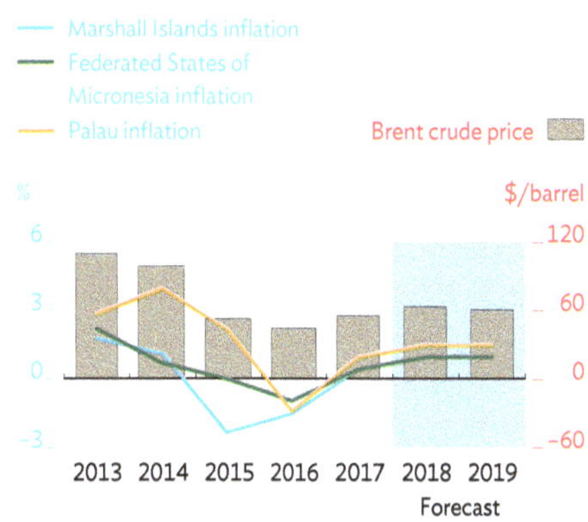

Note: Years are fiscal years ending on 30 September of the same calendar year.

Source: ADB estimates using data from the *Republic of the Marshall Islands, Federated States of Micronesia, and Republic of Palau FY2016 Economic Reviews.*

transfers have risen significantly in recent years, mirroring a structural increase in fishing license revenues since the full implementation of a vessel day scheme in 2012 (Figure 3.37.5).

To ensure that the proceeds of the RMI Compact Trust Fund are sufficient to replace grants that expire in 2023, the government would need to make annual deposits equal to 5% of GDP. Meanwhile, the combined savings in the FSM Compact Trust Fund and the FSM Trust Fund are not currently on track to generate sufficient investment income to replace expiring grants by 2023, according to a recent assessment by the International Monetary Fund. It recommends gradual fiscal adjustment to raise trust fund deposits by the equivalent of 4% of GDP to generate the investment income required and to ensure long-term sustainability.

3.37.5 Fishing license revenues and components of public spending in the Marshall Islands

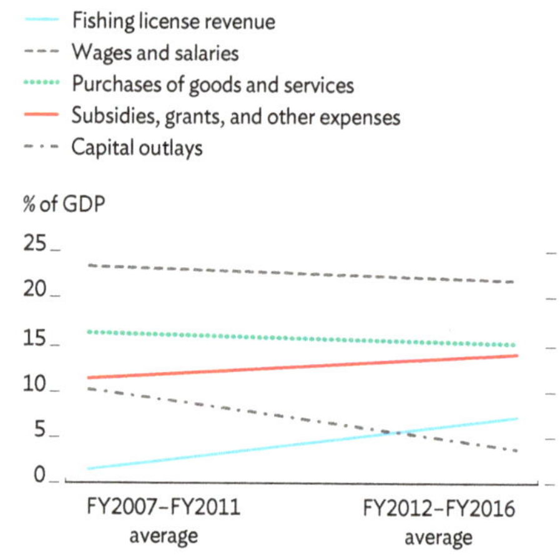

Source: ADB estimates using data from the *Republic of Marshall Islands FY2016 Economic Review*.

Policy challenge—raising the quality of basic education

Investment in education promises to increase lifetime earnings and improve health benefits, social equity, and cohesion—and ultimately reduce poverty. Following recent gains in expanding access to schooling, the North Pacific economies must now improve the quality of basic education. A 2013 review observed that students in the FSM and the RMI have difficulty achieving basic literacy standards in either the local language or English, as well as numeracy. Many fail to finish high school or else graduate without job skills.

Student performance is low. In the FSM, results from national standardized tests in 2012–2017 showed only 22.0% of sixth graders meeting minimum competency expectations in mathematics. In reading, the share was only 29.3% despite marked improvement in this subject from earlier test results (Figure 3.37.6). The corresponding figures in the RMI were 19.7% in mathematics and 18.5% in reading, with little if any progress over time.

Weak education outcomes stem from a combination of factors, most notably deficient teacher quality. The minimum qualification for teaching—a 2-year associate's degree—has not been completed by 17% of teachers in the FSM and 38% in the RMI. Professional learning opportunities are similarly deficient. In Palau, a practice certification test in 2013 found teachers scoring particularly low in math, with writing and reading results only slightly better. Even so, Palau outperformed all other participants, including the RMI and the FSM, in a Pacific literacy and numeracy assessment undertaken in 2015.

A project currently under way in the RMI and the FSM aims to improve the quality of basic education by strengthening teacher preservice and in-service programs. The project

3.37.6 Literacy and numeracy in the Federated States of Micronesia and the Marshall Islands

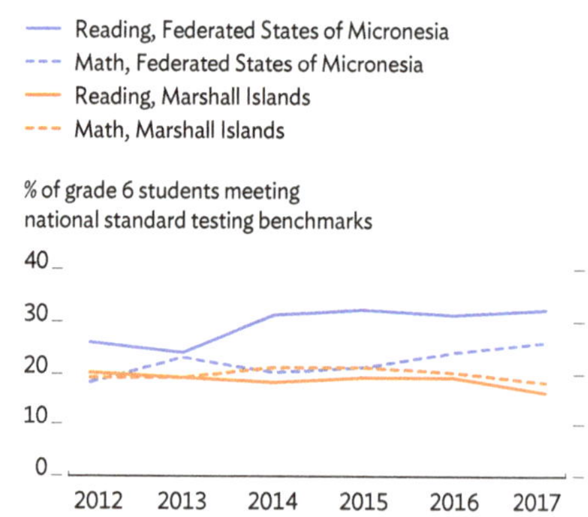

Note: Years are school years starting in August of the previous year and ending in May.

Sources: FSM National Minimum Competency Standard-Based Test Annual Final Report, various years; and Republic of the Marshall Islands Ministry of Education. 2013. Ministry of Education Strategic Plan for FY2013–2016. Majuro.

supports the implementation of a teacher-education program that includes experiential learning by doing, as well as the use of open education resources to facilitate curriculum improvement. Further, the project will train 400 teachers in the RMI and 800 in the FSM in the Quality Pedagogy Framework, an evidence-based approach to improved learning. Additional teaching and learning resources beyond textbooks—including readers in the vernacular language, hands-on manipulatives for numeracy skills, e-resources, open education resources, and low-cost mobile learning tools—will be made available to a range of learners, including in rural areas and on remote outer islands without internet access.

Addressing low student learning outcomes in primary education is vital to averting magnified learning issues at higher levels that are more expensive to resolve. A young population in the North Pacific offers a substantial labor force that can be harnessed to maximize potential growth (Figure 3.37.7). Quality basic education provides a stable foundation for developing employment skills through, for example, stronger technical and vocational education and training. This can facilitate skills matching to fill domestic employment gaps in key sectors such as tourism in Palau and agribusiness or fisheries in the RMI and the FSM. More broadly, sustained investment in human capital over the longer term will help ease current capacity constraints that limit the growth potential of these small and dispersed economies.

3.37.7 Youth employment rates, latest available year

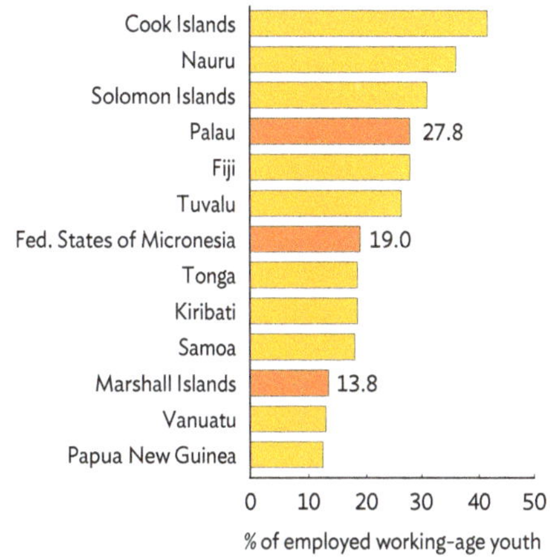

Source: *Secretariat of the Pacific Community National Minimum Development Indicators database.*

South Pacific economies

Tourism supported moderate growth in the Cook Islands, Samoa, and Tonga last year. Growth in Samoa also benefited from strong agriculture, commerce, and communications, and in Tonga from active electricity, construction, and mining and quarrying industries. Growth this year and next will likely moderate further with higher fuel costs and, in Tonga, damage from Cyclone Gita. These economies need to mitigate economic and climate shock risks to sustain economic growth.

Economic performance

Growth in the Cook Islands in fiscal year 2017 (FY2017, ended 30 June 2017 in all three South Pacific economies) was 3.5%, substantially slower than in the previous year, though only fishing failed to expand (Figure 3.38.1). Visitor arrivals to the Cook Islands rose by 14.9% from all leading markets, with the most additional visitors from New Zealand (Figure 3.38.2). The increase in tourism contributed to growth in retail, hotels and restaurants, and transport and communications. Utilities expanded by an estimated 24.2% with the implementation of water supply, sanitation, and renewable energy projects on outer islands.

Samoa also slowed considerably in FY2017, with declines in construction as large capital projects neared completion, communications, and fishing, which more than offset expansion in commerce and agriculture. Hotel and restaurant business grew modestly as visitor arrivals were maintained.

Tonga grew by an estimated 2.8% in FY2017, slower than in the previous year. Agriculture, construction, electricity, and mining and quarrying contributed to growth, but financial services declined. Growth has been supported by infrastructure rehabilitation, a $30 million upgrade of the Faua domestic wharf on the island of Nuku'alofa, improved tourism, and continued recovery in remittances.

In the Cook Islands, prices declined in FY2017 by 0.1%, as in FY2016 (Figure 3.38.3). Despite increases in import prices, lower costs for air transportation, mortgages and rents, and alcohol prolonged deflation. In Samoa, rising import prices, particularly for fuel, and increased taxes on tobacco and alcohol accelerated inflation to 1.4%. Average food prices were also higher. In general, prices for locally produced goods and services declined while prices for imports increased.

3.38.1 GDP growth in the South Pacific

Note: Years are fiscal years ending on 30 June of that year.
Sources: Cook Islands Statistics Office; Samoa Bureau of Statistics; Tonga Department of Statistics; ADB estimates.

3.38.2 Visitor arrivals to the South Pacific

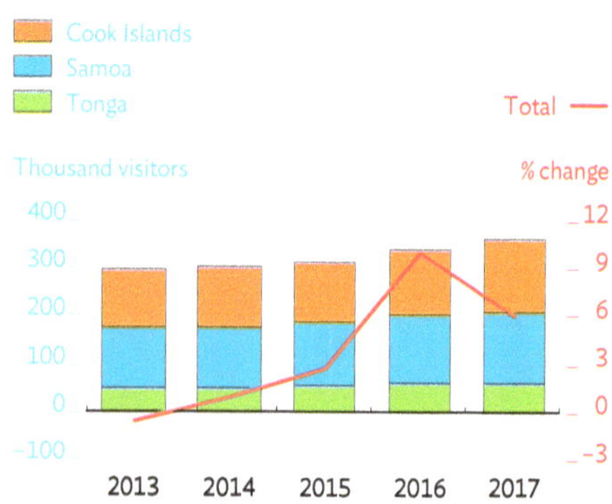

Note: Years are fiscal years ending on 30 June of that year.
Sources: Cook Islands Statistics Office; Samoa Bureau of Statistics; National Reserve Bank of Tonga.

This chapter was written by Shiu Raj Singh of the South Pacific Subregional Office, ADB, Suva; Cara Tinio and Laisiasa Tora of the Pacific Department, ADB, Manila; and Noel Del Castillo, consultant, Pacific Department, ADB, Manila.

High growth in agriculture strengthened supply to the food manufacturing industry and helped stabilize prices for domestically produced food. In Tonga, prices increased by 7.4% in FY2017, largely because of higher customs duties and excise taxes.

The Cook Islands regularly records current account surpluses because high income from tourism offsets deficits in merchandise trade and investment income. In FY2017, the current account surplus was estimated to equal 25.5% of GDP, little changed from FY2016 (Figure 3.38.4). In Samoa, the current account deficit narrowed significantly to 3.0% of GDP from 5.8% in the previous year on lower imports of goods and services, as well as increased service credits and remittances. In Tonga, the current account deficit equaled 12.2% of GDP in FY2017, which was slightly lower than in FY2016 as exports continued to grow. At the end of FY2017, Samoa's gross international reserves provided 3.6 months of import cover, and Tonga's reserves 7.6 months.

The Cook Islands ran a fiscal surplus equal to 7.3% of GDP in FY2017, up from 3.9% on higher collections of income and value-added taxes, and increased fisheries revenue and grants, as well as stable operating expenditures. Net public debt, all of it external, fell from the equivalent of 24.8% of GDP in FY2016 to 17.9% in FY2017, well below the government ceiling of 35.0%. The government maintained a debt-service reserve equal to 4.4% of GDP in FY2017.

In Samoa, the fiscal deficit widened in FY2017 to the equivalent of 1.1% of GDP from 0.4% in the previous year, but deficit expansion was contained by rigorous expenditure control in line with the government's emphasis on consolidation, as well as higher tax and nontax revenue. An operating surplus equal to 1.5% of GDP was achieved after 5 years of operating deficits since FY2012. At the end of the fiscal year, external debt equaled 47.7% of GDP, down from 50.7% at the end of FY2016.

Tonga's fiscal deficit remained unchanged at 0.4% of GDP in FY2017 as higher tax revenue balanced higher operating expenditure, including a steeper wage bill. Debt was estimated to equal 42.4% of GDP at the end of FY2017.

Economic prospects

Growth is set to moderate in all three South Pacific economies over the forecast period. Expansion in the Cook Islands is projected to continue at 3.5% in FY2018. Significant contributions will come from tourism, and large projects to improve water supply and sanitation, and internet connectivity. However, growth is projected to slow slightly in FY2019 as these infrastructure projects reach completion.

3.38.3 Inflation

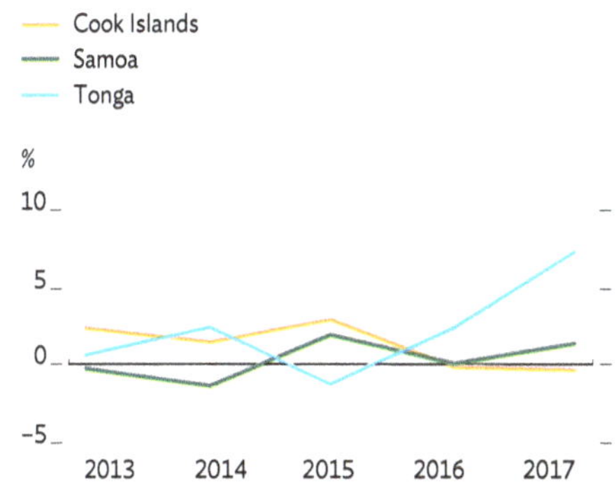

Note: Years are fiscal years ending on 30 June of that year.
Sources: Cook Islands Statistics Office; Samoa Bureau of Statistics; Tonga Department of Statistics; ADB estimates.

3.38.4 Current account balance

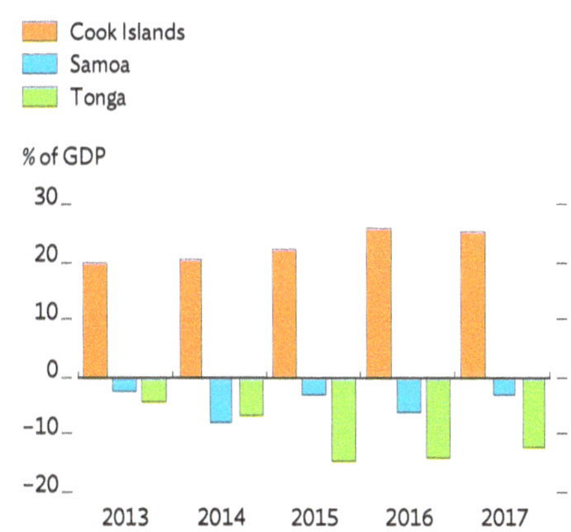

Note: Years are fiscal years ending on 30 June of that year.
Sources: Cook Islands Ministry of Finance and Economic Management; Central Bank of Samoa; Tonga Ministry of Finance and National Planning.

In Samoa, the forecast is for significantly slower growth in FY2018 with expected declines in manufacturing, because an operation assembling automotive wire harnesses closed, and transportation, because of higher fuel prices. Fishing is forecast to level off. Growth is seen to increase to 2.0% in FY2019, supported by tourism and stronger communications following the establishment of high-speed broadband links with Fiji. A service depot for submarine cables now being established is expected to boost employment and output.

Tropical Cyclone Gita struck Tonga in February 2018. It was among the most powerful cyclones in Tongan history and caused severe damage on the main island of Tongatapu and neighboring ‘Eua to government buildings, homes, and infrastructure for basic services, including water supply, sanitation and waste management, electricity, and communications. With agriculture, fishing, and tourism affected, the economy is now forecast to shrink by 0.3% in FY2018. However, as in other Pacific island economies following disasters, growth is expected to rebound on reconstruction and recovery in agriculture and tourism, in Tonga's case to 1.9% in FY2019. The government's immediate cyclone response plan envisages funding at $20 million, or the equivalent of 4% of GDP.

Inflation is expected to remain moderate in all three economies to the forecast horizon, in line with international price movements. Higher international oil prices will likely push inflation in the Cook Islands to 0.5% in FY2018 and 1.0% in FY2019 and in Samoa to 2.0% and then 3.0%. Supply disruption in Tonga will drive inflation to 3.8% in FY2018 before it subsides to 0.5% in FY2019.

The Cook Islands will likely return to fiscal deficits. A budgeted deficit equal to 8.7% of GDP in FY2018 stems largely from ambitious investments in water supply, renewable energy, and roads (Figure 3.38.5). In FY2019, the deficit is expected to shrink to 3.8%. Although a decline in capital expenditure will be largely paralleled by reduced grants from development partners, tax collection is expected to improve. Despite projected fiscal deficits, economic growth and cash balances on hand should keep public debt manageable. Debt is expected to be no more than the equivalent of 28.1% of GDP in FY2018 and 25.0% in FY2019.

Samoa's fiscal deficit is budgeted to equal 3.5% of GDP in both fiscal years. In the past 2 years, actual fiscal deficits have turned out lower than budgeted because of stringent expenditure control and diligent revenue collection. Higher deficits than in recent years are projected because the government will need to boost output through fiscal stimulus following contraction in fishing and nonfood manufacturing.

In Tonga, the fiscal deficit is forecast to remain near pre-cyclone levels as emergency response will be funded

3.38.5 Fiscal balance

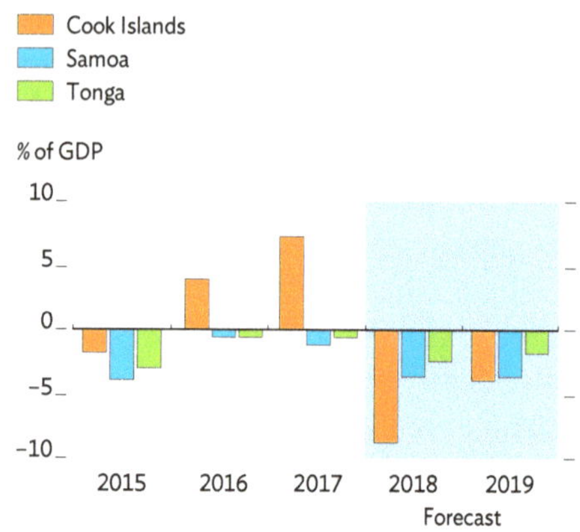

Note: Years are fiscal years ending on 30 June of that year.
Sources: Cook Islands Ministry of Finance and Economic Management; Samoa Ministry of Finance; Tonga Ministry of Finance and National Planning.

3.38.1 Selected economic indicators (%)

Cook Islands	2018	2019
GDP growth	3.5	3.0
Inflation	0.5	1.0
Current account balance (share of GDP)	23.6	21.7
Samoa		
GDP growth	0.5	2.0
Inflation	2.0	3.0
Current account balance (share of GDP)	-4.3	-3.2
Tonga		
GDP growth	-0.3	1.9
Inflation	3.8	0.5
Current account balance (share of GDP)	-14.8	-15.9

Note: Years are fiscal years ending on 30 June of that year.
Source: ADB estimates.

by grants. Primarily because the government has resolutely avoided any new borrowing that was not concessional, Tonga's external debt is expected to grow slowly, reaching the equivalent of 43.2% of GDP in FY2018 and 44.6% in FY2019.

Debt sustainability analyses in 2017, which included climate risk in their baseline assumptions, raised the risk of debt distress from moderate to high for both Samoa and Tonga. From 2018, both economies are eligible only for grants from multilateral development banks, not loans.

The Cook Islands is forecast to run current account surpluses in FY2018 and FY2019. Increased tourism earnings will likely offset higher imports of goods and services for public investment projects implemented in the next 2 years, but the surplus will narrow in FY2019 because of increased imports. Samoa's current account deficit is projected to widen again to the equivalent of 4.3% of GDP in FY2018 and 3.2% in FY2019 on higher merchandise trade deficits. In Tonga, the current account deficit is expected to jump to the equivalent of 14.8% of GDP in FY2018 and 15.9% in FY2019 on higher imports of food and reconstruction materials.

3.38.6 Tonga's public wage bill

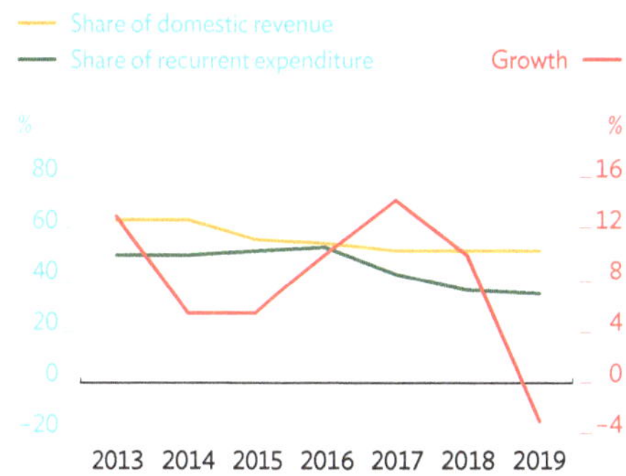

Note: Years are fiscal years ending on 30 June of that year.
Sources: Government of Tonga budget statements, various years; ADB estimates.

Policy challenge—ensuring economic resilience

The Cook Islands is set to become the first Pacific island nation to reach developed status based on income per capita. Any resulting decrease in grant inflows can be countered with improved mobilization of domestic revenue. With few feasible livelihood options, the country can only become more dependent on tourism. It has benefited from tourism for many years and taken steps to mitigate risks posed by disasters: developing contingent financing options, reducing debt when possible, and strengthening cash reserves. Ensuring the sustainability of tourism requires, however, policy and infrastructure development that is sensitive to the impact of tourism on the environment and local sociocultural frameworks. As in other tourism-dependent economies, the Cook Islands may wish to target the higher end of the market to rationalize capacity expansion without sacrificing potential income.

Samoa is highly vulnerable to disasters. This was demonstrated in September 2009, when a tsunami wiped out long stretches of the south and southeast coasts of the main island of Upolu, killing 143 people, injuring 310, and otherwise affecting over 12,000. Then in 2012, Tropical Cyclone Evan destroyed over 600 homes, killed 14 people, displaced more than 7,500, and caused economic damage and production losses estimated to exceed $210 million, or nearly a third of GDP. The government has responded with measures to make infrastructure assets and coastal communities climate resilient. However, Samoa has yet to integrate climate resilience and disaster risk management into its national development plans and policies. It will need to develop strategies to cope with disasters, ensure climate proofing, establish appropriate institutions, and maintain sufficient reserves to finance disaster response and recovery.

Tonga must restrain public wage expenditure. Government spending on salaries crowds out public investment and asset maintenance, undermines the implementation of national development priorities, and worsens exposure to shocks, including debt distress. Government spending on salaries rose by 14.3% in FY2017. Recognizing the serious implications for fiscal and debt sustainability, the government approved a new public service salary structure with a revised pay scale that provides remuneration based on updated performance assessments. The structure is expected to save costs by ending automatic salary progression. In addition, the FY2018 budget targets a public wage bill not to exceed 53% of domestic revenues or 45% of operating expenditure (Figure 3.38.6). The government must sustain reform to establish the fiscal discipline needed to insulate the country from shocks.

Small island economies

Prospects for three small island economies in the Pacific vary, with growth forecast to accelerate in Kiribati and Tuvalu but decelerate in Nauru. Public investments financed by development partners increased significantly in 2016 and 2017 and will continue to drive economic growth in 2018 and 2019. Further, public investments provide vital infrastructure that will allow these economies to reap the benefits of improved maritime links.

Economic performance

Kiribati is enjoying sustained economic growth that averaged 3.2% from 2012 to 2016. Growth accelerated to 2.5% in 2017 from 1.8% in 2016 on fishery revenue receipts that were 2.6% higher than in 2016 (Figure 3.39.1). Higher revenue financed higher public expenditure, particularly for wages, which increased by 14.5% in 2017, and transfers to the outer islands, up by 30.2%. In addition, growth continues to be driven by infrastructure investments supported by development partners, which equal in value 49.5% of GDP.

Nauru saw growth slow to an estimated 4.0% in fiscal year 2017 (FY2017, ended 30 June 2017) as phosphate exports weakened and activities connected with the Regional Processing Center (RPC), an Australian facility for asylum seekers, reached a plateau. The service sector, having replaced the phosphate industry as the main source of growth in 2013, provided an estimated 75% of GDP in FY2017.

In Tuvalu, the economy expanded by 3.2% in 2017, slightly up from 2016. Although fishing license revenues declined by 19% from the previous year, they continued to drive growth in tandem with projects supported by development partners whose total value equaled 35.6% of GDP in 2017 (Figure 3.39.2). Growth was well above its long-term average of 2.1%. Consumption spending increased on a 2.5% boost to public sector wages that came on top of a 10.0% increment in 2016.

All three economies use the Australian dollar as their currency, and this, along with subdued global food prices, has brought price stability in recent years. In Kiribati and Tuvalu, inflation accelerated in 2017 as economic activity picked up. In Nauru, inflation slowed to an estimated 5.0%, in line with moderating economic activity.

3.39.1 GDP growth

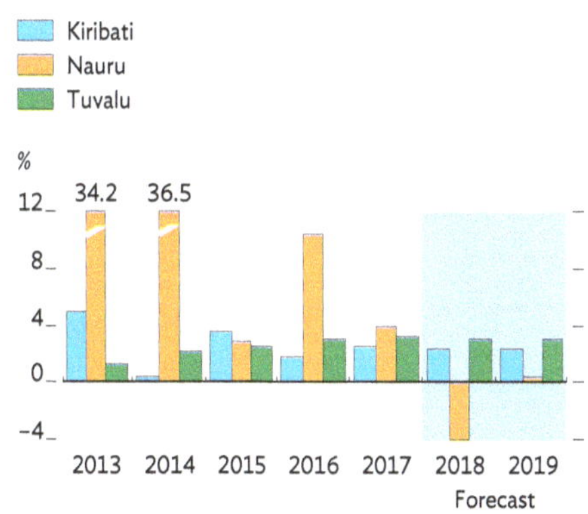

Note: Years are fiscal years ending on 30 June of that year for Nauru and coinciding with the calendar year for Kiribati and Tuvalu.

Sources: Kiribati National Statistics Office; Nauru budget documents; Tuvalu Central Statistics Division; ADB estimates.

3.39.2 Fishing license revenue

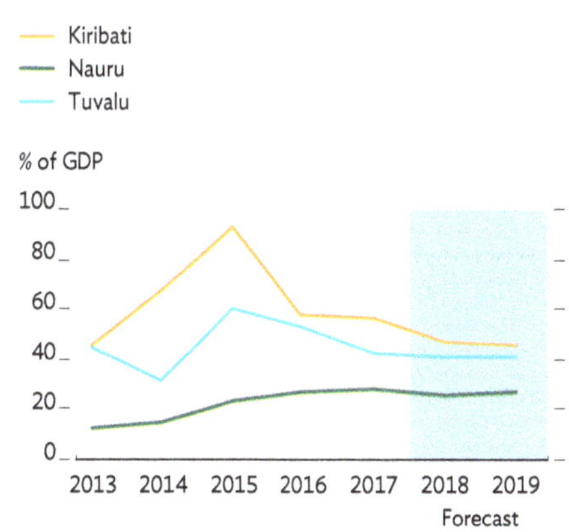

Note: Years are fiscal years ending on 30 June of that year for Nauru and coinciding with the calendar year for Kiribati and Tuvalu.

Sources: Kiribati National Statistics Office; Nauru budget documents; Tuvalu Central Statistics Division; ADB estimates.

This chapter was written by Jacqueline Connell of the Pacific Liaison and Coordination Office, ADB, Sydney; Laisiasa Tora of the Pacific Department, ADB, Manila; and Prince Cruz and Noel Del Castillo, consultants, Pacific Department, ADB, Manila.

Current account inflows come largely from fishing license fees, investment income from sovereign wealth funds, and grant-financed infrastructure investments (Figure 3.39.3). Higher imports of goods and services for construction projects, funded through loans from development partners, widened the current account deficit in Tuvalu and narrowed the surplus in Kiribati.

In Kiribati, increased outlays for copra subsidies and other spending more than offset strong revenue collection, causing a fiscal deficit equal to 9.2% of GDP that reversed a 4.0% surplus in the previous year. In Nauru, government spending including RPC expenses continued to increase, by 17.4% over FY2016, narrowing the fiscal surplus to the equivalent of 10.4% of GDP in FY2017—the surplus becoming a deficit equal to 1.1% of GDP when including contributions to the intergenerational trust fund. In Tuvalu, fiscal management in recent years has prudently focused on replenishing and maintaining fiscal buffers: the Consolidated Investment Fund and the Tuvalu Survival Fund, set up to finance future budgets and climate resilience. In 2017, a fiscal surplus equal to 10.9% of GDP largely reflected budget support grants and windfall fishing revenue that offset falling tax revenue.

3.39.3 Grants

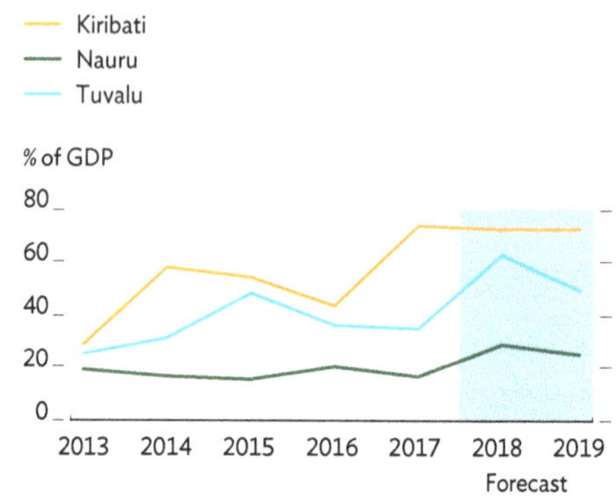

Note: Years are fiscal years ending on 30 June of that year for Nauru and coinciding with the calendar year for Kiribati and Tuvalu.

Sources: Kiribati National Statistics Office; Nauru budget documents; Tuvalu Central Statistics Division; ADB estimates.

Economic prospects

Growth is forecast to moderate in all three small island economies over the forecast period. In Kiribati, major projects will continue, but revenue from fishing licenses is projected to decline. In Nauru, the economy is expected to contract in FY2018 as some refugees are resettled in the US, and the RPC, which provides some 35% of GDP, scales down. While fishery revenue is likely to remain stable, phosphate exports are expected to shrink as deposits diminish. Secondary mining, below the surface, offers some promise but would require significant investment. Economic contraction in Nauru will be partly offset by the planned construction of a seaport starting in FY2019, though possible delays pose a downside risk to the outlook (an upside risk is a delay in scaling down the RPC). In Tuvalu, the economy is expected to grow moderately as construction on public projects continues.

Inflation is forecast to accelerate slightly in Kiribati in 2018 and 2019 as global commodity prices rise (Figure 3.39.4). In Nauru, on the other hand, inflation is projected to ease to 2% in both fiscal years as the economy slows and inflation stays stable in Australia, Nauru's main trade partner. In Tuvalu, inflation will likely ease in 2018 as demand slows, then rise again in 2019 on higher international food and fuel prices.

The fiscal deficit in Kiribati is projected to narrow to the equivalent of 7.3% of GDP in 2018 before widening again to 10.9% in 2019 as fishing revenue declines and as grants for

3.39.4 Inflation

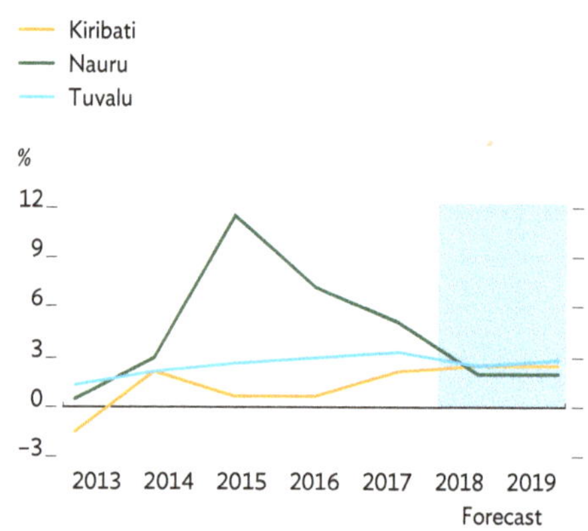

Note: Years are fiscal years ending on 30 June of that year for Nauru and coinciding with the calendar year for Kiribati and Tuvalu.

Sources: Kiribati National Statistics Office; Nauru budget documents; Tuvalu Central Statistics Division; ADB estimates.

outer island development and copra subsidies remain high, having almost doubled from 10.7% in 2015 to 20.8% in 2017. In Nauru, lower RPC revenue is expected to be partly offset in both fiscal years by development partner support for the budget and contributions to the intergenerational trust fund. With total revenue expected to decline in FY2019, fiscal discipline is needed to accommodate capital spending, and particularly the government's investment in construction of the new seaport. In Tuvalu, the fiscal deficit is expected to widen in 2018 and 2019 as revenues from fishing license fees and other taxes decline.

The current account surplus in Kiribati will narrow considerably as fishing revenue slows and imports of materials increase for infrastructure projects. In Tuvalu, the current account deficit is expected to widen to about 30% of GDP in 2018 and 2019 because the goods and services deficit continues to outpace inflows from fishing license fees and development grants. Current transfers to the government, mostly budget support grants from development partners, are expected to be higher in 2018 and then constant in 2019.

3.39.1 Selected economic indicators (%)

Kiribati	2018	2019
GDP growth	2.3	2.3
Inflation	2.5	2.5
Current account balance (share of GDP)	4.3	2.3
Nauru		
GDP growth	-4.0	0.5
Inflation	2.0	2.0
Current account balance (share of GDP)	...	...
Tuvalu		
GDP growth	3.0	3.0
Inflation	2.5	2.8
Current account balance (share of GDP)	-31.4	-29.1

... = data not available.

Note: Years are fiscal years ending on 30 June of that year for Nauru and coinciding with the calendar year for Kiribati and Tuvalu.

Source: ADB estimates.

Policy challenge—improved sea links to support development

Consisting of geographically remote and dispersed islands with poor transport links, the small island economies are challenged to move people and commodities (Figure 3.39.5).

In Kiribati, whose 33 islands are spread across 3.5 million square kilometers of ocean, high transport costs impede mobility and access to employment and social services. Shipping services provide vital links but infrequent service beyond the environs of Tarawa, the capital. In 2008, the government established Kiribati Shipping Services Limited to fill the transportation deficit, but its fleet has deteriorated under poor maintenance and management. The government recently acquired two new vessels and is reviewing technical assistance recommendations from development partners toward developing a long-term strategy to ensure corporate sustainability.

Nauru conducts more than 95% of its international trade by sea. A fringing reef requires most cargo to be ferried on small barges from offshore moorings to the dock. Turnaround that takes on average 21 days drives up shipping costs. Rough seas regularly render the port inoperable, typically closing it for 3 months of the year. The resulting interruption of food and fuel supplies increases prices. The construction of a new climate-resilient deepwater seaport will enable more efficient and reliable loading and unloading, which should ease Nauru's high cost of living and encourage trade and economic

3.39.5 Ratio of exclusive economic zone to land area

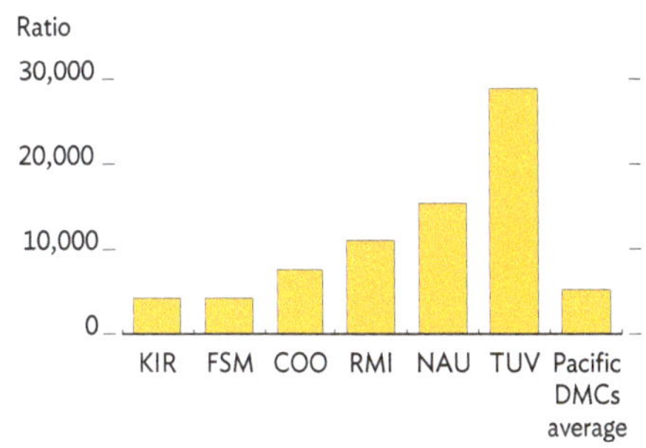

COO = Cook Islands, DMC = developing member country, FSM = Federated States of Micronesia, KIR = Kiribati, NAU = Nauru, RMI = Republic of Marshall Islands, TUV = Tuvalu.

Source: Asian Development Bank. 2016. *Pacific Economic Monitor July 2016.*

integration. With support from development partners, the government plans to establish a maintenance fund to be financed through budget allocations and port revenue.

Tuvalu, with nine atolls stretching over 900,000 square kilometers of the southwest Pacific, views transportation as a primary concern. Because many islands are too small for airfields, marine transport is the only option for transporting essential goods such as food and fuel or people seeking medical care or education. As inadequate docks preclude access by larger vessels, small vessels must be used to ferry goods and people. This is safe only in daylight and with smooth seas, making transport costly and inefficient. In 2015, the Government of Tuvalu adopted its National Strategy for Sustainable Development, 2016–2020, which includes strategies to provide efficient, high-quality infrastructure and support services. However, further project support may be needed to expedite the creation of transport infrastructure.

STATISTICAL APPENDIX

Statistical notes and tables

The statistical appendix presents selected economic indicators for the 45 developing member economies of the Asian Development Bank (ADB) in 18 tables. The economies are grouped into five subregions: Central Asia, East Asia, South Asia, Southeast Asia, and the Pacific. Most of the tables contain historical data from 2013 to 2017; some have forecasts for 2018 and 2019.

The data were standardized to the degree possible to allow comparability over time and across economies, but differences in statistical methodology, definitions, coverage, and practices make full comparability impossible. The national income accounts section is based on the United Nations System of National Accounts, while the data on balance of payments are based on International Monetary Fund (IMF) accounting standards. Historical data were obtained from official sources, statistical publications, and databases, as well as documents of ADB, the IMF, and the World Bank. For some economies, data for 2017 are estimated from the latest available information. Projections for 2018 and 2019 are generally ADB estimates made on the bases of available quarterly or monthly data, though some projections are from governments.

Most economies report by calendar year. The following record their government finance data by fiscal year: Brunei Darussalam; Fiji; Hong Kong, China; the Kyrgyz Republic; the Lao People's Democratic Republic (Lao PDR); Singapore; Tajikistan; Thailand; and Uzbekistan. South Asian countries (except for Maldives and Sri Lanka), the Cook Islands, the Federated States of Micronesia, the Republic of Marshall Islands, Nauru, Myanmar, Palau, Samoa, and Tonga report all variables by fiscal year.

Regional and subregional averages or totals are provided for seven tables (A1, A2, A6, A11, A12, A13, and A14). For tables A1, A2, A6, A11, A12 and A14, the averages are computed using weights derived from gross national income (GNI) in current US dollars following the World Bank Atlas method. The GNI data for 2013–2016 were obtained from the World Bank's World Development Indicators online. Weights for 2016 were carried over through 2019. The GNI data for the Cook Islands and Taipei,China were estimated using the Atlas conversion factor. For Table A13, the regional and subregional totals were computed based on a consistent sum, which means that if country data are missing for a given year, the sum excludes that country.

Tables A1, A2, A3, A4, and A5. These tables show data on output growth, production, and demand. Changes to the national income accounts series for some countries have been made to accommodate a change in source, methodology, and/or base year. The series for Afghanistan, Bhutan, India, Myanmar, and Pakistan reflect fiscal year data, rather than calendar year data, while those for Timor-Leste reflect GDP excluding the offshore petroleum sector.

Table A1: Growth rate of GDP (% per year). The table shows annual growth rates of GDP valued at constant market prices, factor costs, or basic prices. GDP at market prices is the aggregation of value added by all resident producers at producers' prices including taxes less subsidies on imports plus all nondeductible value-added or similar taxes. Constant factor cost measures differ from market price measures in that they exclude taxes on production and include subsidies. Basic price valuation is the factor cost plus some taxes on production, such as property and payroll taxes, and less some subsidies, such as for labor but not for products. Most economies use constant market price valuation. Pakistan and Nepal use constant factor costs, while Fiji and Maldives use basic prices.

Table A2: Growth rate of per capita GDP (% per year). The table provides the growth rates of real per capita GDP, which is defined as GDP at constant prices divided by the population. Data on per capita gross national income in US dollar terms (Atlas method) for 2016 are also shown, sourced from the World Bank's World Development Indicators online. The data for the Cook Islands and Taipei,China were estimated using the Atlas conversion factor.

Table A3: Growth rate of value added in agriculture (% per year). The table shows the growth rates of value added in agriculture at constant prices and agriculture's share of GDP in 2016 at current prices. The agriculture sector comprises plant crops, livestock, poultry, fisheries, and forestry.

Table A4: Growth rate of value added in industry (% per year). The table provides the growth rates of value added in industry at constant prices and industry's share of GDP in 2016 at current prices. This sector comprises manufacturing, mining and quarrying, construction, and utilities.

Table A5: Growth rate of value added in services (% per year). The table gives the growth rates of value added in services at constant prices and services' share of GDP in 2016 at current prices. Subsectors generally include trade, banking, finance, real estate, public administration, and other services. For Malaysia, electricity, gas, water supply, and waste management are included under services.

Table A6: Inflation (% per year). Data on inflation rates are period averages. The inflation rates presented are based on consumer price indexes. The consumer price indexes of the following economies are for a given city or group of consumers only: Cambodia is for Phnom Penh, the Marshall Islands is for Majuro, and Solomon Islands is for Honiara.

Table A7: Change in money supply (% per year). This table tracks the annual percentage change in the end-of-period supply of broad money as represented by M2 for most countries. M2 is defined as the sum of M1 and quasi-money, where M1 denotes currency in circulation plus demand deposits, and quasi-money consists of time and savings deposits including foreign currency deposits.

Tables A8, A9, and A10: Government finance. These tables give the revenue and expenditure transactions and the fiscal balance of the central government expressed as a percentage of GDP in nominal terms. For Cambodia, India, Kazakhstan, the Kyrgyz Republic, Mongolia, the People's Republic of China, and Tajikistan, transactions are those reported by the general government.

Table A8: Central government revenues (% of GDP). Central government revenues comprise all nonrepayable receipts, both current and capital, plus grants. These amounts are computed as a percentage of GDP at current prices. For the Republic of Korea, revenues exclude social security contributions. For Singapore, revenues include the contribution from net investment returns. For Kazakhstan, revenues include transfers from the national fund. Grants are excluded in Cambodia, the Lao PDR, Malaysia, Singapore, and Thailand; revenues from disinvestment are included for India; and only current revenues are included for Bangladesh.

Table A9: Central government expenditures (% of GDP). Central government expenditures comprise all nonrepayable payments to both current and capital expenses, plus net lending. These amounts are computed as a share of GDP at current prices. For Thailand, expenditures refer to budgetary expenditures excluding externally financed expenditures and borrowing. Those for Tajikistan include externally financed public investment programs. One-time expenditures are excluded for Pakistan.

Table A10: Fiscal balance of the central government (% of GDP). Fiscal balance is the difference between central government revenues and expenditures. The difference is computed as a share of GDP at current prices. Data variations may arise from statistical discrepancies when, for example, balancing items for both central and local governments, and from differences in the concept used in the individual computations of revenues and expenditures as compared with the calculation of the fiscal balance. For Fiji, the fiscal balance excludes loan repayments. For Thailand, the fiscal balance is the cash balance of the combined budgetary and nonbudgetary balances. For Uzbekistan, the augmented fiscal balance includes the Fund for Reconstruction and Development. Some off-budget accounts are included in the computation of the fiscal balance for Turkmenistan.

Tables A11, A12, A13, and A14: Balance of payments. These tables show selected international economic transactions of countries as recorded in the balance of payments. These items cover annual flows.

Tables A11 and A12: Growth rates of merchandise exports and imports (% per year). These tables show the annual growth rates of exports and imports of goods. Data are in million US dollars, primarily obtained from the balance-of-payments accounts of each economy. Exports are reported free on board. Import data are reported free on board, except for the following economies, which value them on the basis of cost, insurance, and freight: Afghanistan; Bhutan; Hong Kong, China; India; the Lao PDR; Myanmar; Singapore; and Thailand.

Table A13: Trade balance ($ million). The trade balance is the difference between merchandise exports and merchandise imports. Figures in this table are based on the export and import amounts used to generate tables A11 and A12.

Table A14: Current account balance (% of GDP). The current account balance is the sum of the balance of trade for merchandise, net trade in services and factor income, and net transfers. The values reported are divided by GDP at current prices in US dollars. In the case of Cambodia, the Lao PDR, and Viet Nam, official transfers are excluded from the current account balance.

Table A15: Exchange rates to the US dollar (annual average). Annual average exchange rates are quoted as the local currency per US dollar.

Table A16: Gross international reserves ($ million). Gross international reserves are defined as the US dollar value of holdings of foreign exchange, special drawing rights, reserve position in the IMF, and gold at the end of a given period. For Taipei,China, this heading refers to foreign exchange reserves only. In some economies, the rubric is foreign assets and reserves of national monetary authorities and national oil funds, e.g., net foreign reserves of the State Bank of Pakistan. The data for India are as of 2 March 2018.

Table A17: External debt outstanding ($ million). For most economies, external debt outstanding, public and private, includes medium- and long-term debt, short-term debt, and IMF credit. For Cambodia and the Lao PDR, only public external debt is reported. For the Kyrgyz Republic, Singapore, Sri Lanka, and Thailand, the figures for 2017 are as of the end of September.

Table A18: Debt service ratio (% of exports of goods and services). This table generally presents the total debt service payments of each economy, which comprise principal repayments (excluding on short-term debt) and interest payments on outstanding external debt, as a percentage of exports of goods and services. For Cambodia and the Lao PDR, debt service refers to external public debt only. For Viet Nam, exports of goods are used as the denominator in the calculation of the ratio; for the Philippines, exports of goods, services, and income are used as the denominator. For Bangladesh, the ratio represents debt service payments on medium- and long-term loans as a percentage of exports of goods, nonfactor services, and workers' remittances. For Azerbaijan, the ratio represents public and publicly guaranteed external debt service payments as a percentage of exports of goods and nonfactor services.

Table A1 Growth rate of GDP (% per year)

	2013	2014	2015	2016	2017	2018	2019
Central Asia	6.6	5.1	3.1	2.7	4.3	4.0	4.2
Armenia	3.3	3.6	3.2	0.2	7.5	4.0	4.2
Azerbaijan	5.8	2.8	1.1	-3.1	0.1	1.7	2.0
Georgia	3.4	4.6	2.9	2.8	5.0	4.5	4.7
Kazakhstan	6.0	4.2	1.2	1.1	4.0	3.2	3.5
Kyrgyz Republic	10.9	4.0	3.9	4.3	4.6	3.5	4.0
Tajikistan	7.4	6.7	6.0	6.9	7.1	6.0	6.5
Turkmenistan	10.2	10.3	6.5	6.2	6.5	6.5	6.7
Uzbekistan	8.0	8.0	7.9	7.8	5.3	5.5	5.6
East Asia	6.8	6.6	6.1	6.0	6.3	6.0	5.8
Hong Kong, China	3.1	2.8	2.4	2.1	3.8	3.2	3.0
Mongolia	11.6	7.9	2.4	1.2	5.1	3.8	4.3
People's Republic of China	7.8	7.3	6.9	6.7	6.9	6.6	6.4
Republic of Korea	2.9	3.3	2.8	2.9	3.1	3.0	2.9
Taipei,China	2.2	4.0	0.8	1.4	2.9	2.9	2.8
South Asia	6.0	6.9	7.4	6.7	6.4	7.0	7.2
Afghanistan	5.7	2.7	1.3	2.4	2.5	2.5	2.5
Bangladesh	6.0	6.1	6.6	7.1	7.3	7.0	7.2
Bhutan	3.6	4.0	6.2	7.3	7.5	7.1	7.4
India	6.4	7.4	8.2	7.1	6.6	7.3	7.6
Maldives	7.3	7.3	2.2	6.2	6.5	6.7	6.8
Nepal	3.8	5.7	3.0	0.0	6.9	4.9	5.5
Pakistan	3.7	4.1	4.1	4.5	5.3	5.6	5.1
Sri Lanka	3.4	5.0	5.0	4.5	3.1	4.2	4.8
Southeast Asia	5.2	4.7	4.6	4.7	5.2	5.2	5.2
Brunei Darussalam	-2.1	-2.5	-0.4	-2.5	0.8	1.5	2.0
Cambodia	7.4	7.1	7.0	7.0	7.0	7.0	7.0
Indonesia	5.6	5.0	4.9	5.0	5.1	5.3	5.3
Lao People's Dem. Rep.	8.0	7.6	7.3	7.0	6.8	6.8	7.0
Malaysia	4.7	6.0	5.0	4.2	5.9	5.3	5.0
Myanmar	8.4	8.0	7.0	5.9	6.8	6.8	7.2
Philippines	7.1	6.1	6.1	6.9	6.7	6.8	6.9
Singapore	5.1	3.9	2.2	2.4	3.6	3.1	2.9
Thailand	2.7	1.0	3.0	3.3	3.9	4.0	4.1
Viet Nam	5.4	6.0	6.7	6.2	6.8	7.1	6.8
The Pacific	3.5	9.6	8.1	2.4	2.2	2.2	3.0
Cook Islands	0.5	3.2	3.2	8.8	3.5	3.5	3.0
Federated States of Micronesia	-3.9	-2.2	4.9	-0.1	2.0	2.0	2.0
Fiji	4.7	5.6	3.8	0.4	3.9	3.6	3.3
Kiribati	5.0	0.4	3.5	1.8	2.5	2.3	2.3
Marshall Islands	2.9	-0.8	-0.4	1.9	4.0	2.5	2.5
Nauru	34.2	36.5	2.8	10.4	4.0	-4.0	0.5
Palau	-2.1	5.4	11.4	0.5	-0.5	3.0	3.0
Papua New Guinea	3.8	12.5	10.5	2.0	2.2	1.8	2.7
Samoa	-1.9	1.2	1.6	7.1	2.5	0.5	2.0
Solomon Islands	2.8	1.8	2.6	3.4	3.2	3.0	3.0
Timor-Leste	2.5	4.1	4.0	5.3	-2.0	3.0	5.5
Tonga	-3.1	2.1	3.7	3.1	2.8	-0.3	1.9
Tuvalu	1.3	2.2	2.6	3.0	3.2	3.0	3.0
Vanuatu	2.0	2.3	0.2	3.5	3.5	3.2	3.0
Developing Asia	6.4	6.3	6.0	5.9	6.1	6.0	5.9
Developing Asia excluding the NIEs	7.0	6.8	6.6	6.4	6.6	6.5	6.4

Note: The newly industrialized economies (NIEs) are Hong Kong, China; the Republic of Korea; Singapore; and Taipei,China.

Table A2 Growth rate of per capita GDP (% per year)

	2013	2014	2015	2016	2017	2018	2019	Per capita GNI, $, 2016
Central Asia	5.1	3.6	1.7	1.3	3.0	2.9	2.9	
Armenia	3.3	3.9	3.5	0.6	7.9	4.3	4.5	3,770
Azerbaijan	4.5	1.5	−0.1	−4.3	−1.0	0.6	0.7	4,760
Georgia	3.7	4.4	2.6	2.7	5.0	4.5	4.7	3,830
Kazakhstan	4.3	2.5	−0.3	−0.2	2.8	2.4	2.2	8,810
Kyrgyz Republic	8.7	2.0	1.8	2.2	2.5	1.9	2.3	1,100
Tajikistan	5.4	4.3	3.5	4.6	5.7	3.8	4.2	1,110
Turkmenistan	8.9	8.9	5.1	4.8	5.1	5.1	5.3	6,670
Uzbekistan	6.6	5.9	6.2	6.0	3.7	3.9	4.0	2,220
East Asia	6.3	6.1	5.6	5.4	5.7	5.5	5.3	
Hong Kong, China	2.7	2.0	1.5	1.5	3.0	2.4	2.3	43,240
Mongolia	9.4	5.6	0.2	−0.8	3.1	1.8	2.4	3,590
People's Republic of China	7.2	6.8	6.4	6.1	6.3	6.1	5.9	8,250
Republic of Korea	2.4	2.7	2.2	2.5	2.7	2.6	2.6	27,600
Taipei,China	1.8	3.8	0.5	1.2	2.7	2.9	2.7	23,015
South Asia	4.5	5.5	6.0	5.3	4.6	5.5	5.7	
Afghanistan	3.2	0.3	−1.0	−5.4	0.0	1.1	1.1	570
Bangladesh	4.6	4.6	5.1	5.7	6.0	5.7	5.8	1,330
Bhutan	1.8	2.3	4.5	5.7	6.0	5.7	6.1	2,510
India	5.0	6.1	6.8	5.8	5.3	6.0	6.3	1,670
Maldives	5.1	4.9	−1.6	2.4	2.1	2.4	2.4	10,630
Nepal	2.3	4.2	1.5	−1.4	5.5	3.5	4.1	730
Pakistan	1.6	2.0	2.0	2.5	−1.0	2.7	2.2	1,500
Sri Lanka	2.6	4.0	4.0	3.3	2.0	3.2	3.8	3,780
Southeast Asia	3.4	3.4	3.7	3.4	4.2	4.0	4.0	
Brunei Darussalam	−3.5	−4.0	−1.8	−3.9	−0.6	0.3	0.8	32,860
Cambodia	5.6	5.4	5.3	5.3	5.3	5.4	5.5	1,140
Indonesia	3.1	3.7	4.5	3.7	3.8	4.1	4.0	3,400
Lao People's Dem. Rep.	6.5	6.1	5.7	5.5	5.3	5.3	5.5	2,150
Malaysia	2.7	3.6	3.0	2.7	4.5	3.5	3.2	9,860
Myanmar	7.5	10.1	6.1	4.9	5.9	5.9	6.3	1,190
Philippines	5.2	4.4	4.9	4.6	5.0	5.1	5.2	3,580
Singapore	3.4	2.5	1.0	1.1	3.5	1.9	2.0	51,880
Thailand	2.2	0.5	2.1	3.0	3.4	3.5	3.6	5,640
Viet Nam	4.3	4.9	5.5	5.1	5.8	6.1	5.8	2,100
The Pacific	1.1	7.0	5.5	−0.4	−0.2	−0.2	0.5	
Cook Islands	5.3	3.2	2.6	4.3	3.6	3.6	3.1	16,398
Federated States of Micronesia	−3.9	−2.1	5.0	0.1	2.2	2.3	2.2	3,550
Fiji	4.1	5.0	3.3	−0.2	3.4	3.0	2.7	4,780
Kiribati	3.6	−0.9	2.1	0.6	1.3	1.1	1.1	2,270
Marshall Islands	2.5	−1.1	−0.7	1.5	1.7	2.1	−1.4	4,630
Nauru	30.4	34.8	−10.9	5.5	1.1	−0.8	0.5	10,750
Palau	−1.6	4.4	10.3	−0.5	−1.5	2.0	2.0	12,330
Papua New Guinea	0.7	9.1	7.2	−1.0	−0.9	−1.3	−0.4	2,680
Samoa	−2.8	0.4	0.8	6.3	1.6	−0.3	1.2	4,120
Solomon Islands	0.5	−0.5	1.0	−6.7	0.4	0.2	0.2	1,880
Timor-Leste	0.6	2.3	2.0	3.4	−3.7	1.1	3.6	2,060
Tonga	−3.3	1.6	3.5	2.9	2.5	−0.5	1.6	4,060
Tuvalu	0.0	−0.2	0.8	14.7	2.0	1.8	1.8	5,090
Vanuatu	−0.5	−0.1	−2.2	−0.9	1.0	0.7	0.5	3,395
Developing Asia	5.6	5.5	5.3	5.1	5.3	5.3	5.2	
Developing Asia excluding the NIEs	6.1	6.0	5.9	5.5	5.6	5.7	5.6	

GNI = gross national income.

Note: The newly industrialized economies (NIEs) are Hong Kong, China; the Republic of Korea; Singapore; and Taipei,China.

Table A3 Growth rate of value added in agriculture (% per year)

	2013	2014	2015	2016	2017	Sector share, 2016, %
Central Asia						
Armenia	7.6	6.1	13.2	-5.8	-4.0	17.4
Azerbaijan	4.9	-2.6	6.6	2.6	4.2	6.1
Georgia	11.3	1.6	1.6	0.3	-2.7	9.0
Kazakhstan	11.2	1.3	3.5	5.4	2.9	4.8
Kyrgyz Republic	2.6	-0.5	6.2	2.9	2.2	14.8
Tajikistan	7.6	4.5	3.2	5.2	6.8	23.3
Turkmenistan	10.0	4.2	7.9	12.0	5.0	13.4
Uzbekistan	6.8	6.9	6.8	6.6	2.0	17.6
East Asia						
Hong Kong, China	4.9	-6.0	-6.8	-2.0	-0.7	0.1
Mongolia	19.2	13.7	10.7	6.2	2.3	12.7
People's Republic of China	3.8	4.1	3.9	3.3	3.9	7.7
Republic of Korea	3.1	3.6	-0.4	-2.8	0.3	2.1
Taipei,China	1.3	0.5	-7.5	-10.1	6.0	1.8
South Asia						
Afghanistan	0.0	-0.1	-5.7	6.0	1.5	22.7
Bangladesh	2.5	4.4	3.3	2.8	3.0	14.8
Bhutan	2.3	2.4	3.7	4.3	3.5	17.4
India	5.6	-0.2	0.6	6.3	3.0	17.9
Maldives	6.9	-0.3	-0.5	1.4	3.3	6.8
Nepal	1.1	4.5	1.1	0.0	5.3	31.6
Pakistan	2.7	2.5	2.1	0.3	3.5	24.6
Sri Lanka	3.2	4.6	4.7	-3.8	-0.8	8.2
Southeast Asia						
Brunei Darussalam	-1.2	4.7	6.4	-3.6	-1.9	1.2
Cambodia	1.6	0.3	0.2	1.4	1.7	26.3
Indonesia	4.2	4.2	3.8	3.4	3.8	14.0
Lao People's Dem. Rep.	2.8	4.1	3.6	2.8	2.8	19.5
Malaysia	2.0	2.0	1.3	-5.1	7.2	8.8
Myanmar	3.6	2.8	3.4	-0.4	...	25.5
Philippines	1.1	1.7	0.1	-1.3	3.9	9.7
Singapore	4.5	7.3	-7.0	-1.5	-8.4	0.0
Thailand	0.7	-0.3	-6.3	-2.5	6.2	8.5
Viet Nam	2.6	3.4	2.4	1.4	2.9	17.3
The Pacific						
Cook Islands	-2.8	9.8	6.5	2.8	-4.3	8.5
Federated States of Micronesia	-6.4	6.0	10.7	-7.3	...	28.8
Fiji	6.7	1.9	6.3	-7.4	4.7	13.6
Kiribati	-0.7	5.9	-0.8	...	...	...
Marshall Islands	3.4	-1.5	0.5	-2.3	...	16.1
Nauru	5.3	9.5	5.2	...	...	...
Palau	-8.6	-5.1	-4.4	3.7	...	3.4
Papua New Guinea	4.7	3.3	2.2	3.4	2.6	18.5
Samoa	-2.4	9.6	-0.3	8.1	6.5	9.5
Solomon Islands	-1.3	5.8	2.5	5.8	3.0	27.3
Timor-Leste	-5.2	-3.1	-4.3	3.0	...	16.9
Tonga	3.7	3.1	...	...	...	...
Tuvalu	-11.5	2.2	2.6	3.0	3.2	22.3
Vanuatu	4.8	4.2	-15.8	5.1	5.0	22.2

... = data not available.

Table A4 Growth rate of value added in industry (% per year)

	2013	2014	2015	2016	2017	Sector share, 2016, %
Central Asia						
Armenia	0.5	-2.3	2.8	-0.9	8.0	26.9
Azerbaijan	4.9	0.5	-1.9	-5.9	-3.6	51.8
Georgia	2.4	4.6	4.1	6.0	5.6	24.9
Kazakhstan	3.1	1.5	-0.3	1.0	6.2	33.9
Kyrgyz Republic	30.5	5.7	2.9	7.1	9.3	30.6
Tajikistan	3.9	5.1	11.2	16.0	21.3	29.6
Turkmenistan	7.3	11.4	3.1	1.2	5.5	51.0
Uzbekistan	9.2	7.9	8.2	6.6	4.8	32.9
East Asia						
Hong Kong, China	1.7	7.8	2.5	3.0	2.7	7.7
Mongolia	14.6	12.7	9.9	-0.6	-1.0	36.7
People's Republic of China	8.0	7.4	6.2	6.3	6.1	46.8
Republic of Korea	3.3	3.1	2.4	3.3	4.6	38.7
Taipei,China	1.7	7.0	-0.2	2.7	3.9	36.6
South Asia						
Afghanistan	3.7	2.8	4.2	-0.8	2.0	21.9
Bangladesh	9.6	8.2	9.7	11.1	10.2	28.8
Bhutan	5.3	3.8	6.0	7.5	7.7	43.3
India	3.8	7.0	9.8	6.8	4.8	29.3
Maldives	-6.0	16.2	16.5	15.1	7.4	11.2
Nepal	2.7	7.1	1.4	-6.3	10.9	14.2
Pakistan	0.8	4.5	5.2	5.8	5.0	19.4
Sri Lanka	4.1	4.7	2.2	5.8	3.9	29.8
Southeast Asia						
Brunei Darussalam	-5.6	-4.4	0.0	-2.9	0.7	56.5
Cambodia	10.7	10.1	11.7	10.5	9.7	31.3
Indonesia	4.3	4.2	3.0	3.8	4.1	40.8
Lao People's Dem. Rep.	7.7	7.3	7.0	12.0	9.5	32.5
Malaysia	3.6	6.0	5.4	4.2	4.9	36.1
Myanmar	11.4	12.1	8.3	8.9	...	35.0
Philippines	9.2	7.8	6.4	8.4	7.2	30.8
Singapore	2.0	3.6	-2.7	3.2	5.7	25.2
Thailand	1.5	0.0	3.0	2.9	1.6	35.8
Viet Nam	5.1	6.4	9.6	7.6	8.0	39.1
The Pacific						
Cook Islands	-3.7	-6.8	-26.1	26.4	6.8	7.5
Federated States of Micronesia	-19.6	-28.3	-6.0	5.8	...	6.5
Fiji	4.4	1.2	3.5	0.9	3.5	17.5
Kiribati	25.9	5.6	13.7	...	...	...
Marshall Islands	7.1	-14.8	-1.9	17.4	...	14.3
Nauru	-28.5	-3.6	-17.1	...	...	...
Palau	-15.4	7.3	22.3	5.0	...	8.4
Papua New Guinea	2.0	36.7	31.2	4.5	2.8	37.2
Samoa	-3.2	3.8	-6.2	7.3	-1.8	23.6
Solomon Islands	-2.0	-13.0	-5.0	0.9	5.5	14.7
Timor-Leste	41.1	-10.9	22.2	7.6	...	18.6
Tonga	-14.3	1.3	...	...	...	...
Tuvalu	52.0	2.2	2.6	3.0	3.2	8.7
Vanuatu	9.8	3.2	35.4	4.3	4.0	11.1

... = data not available.

Table A5 Growth rate of value added in services (% per year)

	2013	2014	2015	2016	2017	Sector share, 2016, %
Central Asia						
Armenia	2.8	6.7	1.0	4.0	10.4	55.7
Azerbaijan	7.2	7.4	4.5	-0.7	3.5	42.1
Georgia	3.5	4.6	3.1	2.4	5.5	66.1
Kazakhstan	6.9	5.7	3.1	0.9	2.7	61.3
Kyrgyz Republic	4.7	4.6	3.7	3.4	2.6	54.7
Tajikistan	19.3	1.0	-7.1	-0.3	1.8	47.1
Turkmenistan	12.7	10.6	10.0	11.0	8.9	35.6
Uzbekistan	7.8	8.5	8.4	9.3	6.9	49.5
East Asia						
Hong Kong, China	2.7	2.5	1.7	2.3	3.5	92.2
Mongolia	7.8	7.8	0.6	1.5	8.5	50.5
People's Republic of China	8.3	7.8	8.2	7.7	8.0	45.5
Republic of Korea	2.9	3.3	2.8	2.5	2.1	59.2
Taipei,China	2.1	2.8	1.7	1.2	2.2	61.5
South Asia						
Afghanistan	5.3	4.4	1.9	2.2	3.3	55.4
Bangladesh	5.5	5.6	5.8	6.2	6.7	56.5
Bhutan	1.1	5.0	8.3	9.2	9.2	39.2
India	7.7	9.8	9.6	7.5	8.3	52.8
Maldives	8.8	7.0	1.4	5.2	6.7	82.0
Nepal	5.7	6.2	4.6	2.1	6.9	54.2
Pakistan	5.1	4.5	4.4	5.5	6.0	56.0
Sri Lanka	3.8	4.8	6.0	4.7	3.2	62.1
Southeast Asia						
Brunei Darussalam	4.7	0.6	-1.2	-1.6	1.0	42.4
Cambodia	8.7	8.7	7.1	6.8	7.1	42.4
Indonesia	6.4	6.0	5.5	5.7	5.7	45.3
Lao People's Dem. Rep.	9.7	8.1	8.0	4.7	6.2	48.0
Malaysia	5.9	6.6	5.1	5.6	6.2	55.1
Myanmar	10.3	9.1	8.7	8.0	...	39.5
Philippines	7.0	6.0	6.9	7.4	6.7	59.5
Singapore	7.1	4.3	3.6	1.6	2.9	74.8
Thailand	4.1	2.0	4.9	4.6	5.3	55.7
Viet Nam	6.7	6.2	6.3	7.0	7.4	43.6
The Pacific						
Cook Islands	0.0	4.0	6.3	7.4	5.1	84.0
Federated States of Micronesia	-0.7	-1.3	3.0	2.4	...	64.8
Fiji	4.5	7.4	3.6	1.4	3.9	68.9
Kiribati	2.6	-0.2	6.5	...	...	...
Marshall Islands	1.5	2.6	1.8	1.0	...	69.7
Nauru	60.7	41.9	11.6	...	...	...
Palau	-0.7	6.3	10.3	1.4	...	88.3
Papua New Guinea	3.9	-0.7	-0.2	0.2	1.8	44.3
Samoa	-1.1	-1.1	5.1	6.9	3.4	67.0
Solomon Islands	7.6	3.9	5.0	3.3	3.0	58.0
Timor-Leste	1.4	7.5	4.9	5.9	...	64.5
Tonga	-0.5	1.6	...	...	...	...
Tuvalu	1.3	2.2	2.6	3.0	3.2	69.0
Vanuatu	0.1	2.4	2.0	2.9	3.1	66.6

... = data not available.

Table A6 Inflation (% per year)

	2013	2014	2015	2016	2017	2018	2019
Central Asia	5.9	5.9	6.3	10.6	9.2	8.5	7.9
Armenia	5.8	3.0	3.7	–1.4	1.0	2.7	2.2
Azerbaijan	2.4	1.4	4.0	12.4	12.9	7.0	8.0
Georgia	–0.5	3.1	4.0	2.1	6.0	3.5	3.0
Kazakhstan	5.8	6.7	6.6	14.6	7.4	6.8	6.2
Kyrgyz Republic	6.6	7.5	6.5	0.4	3.2	4.0	4.5
Tajikistan	3.7	6.1	5.1	6.1	6.7	7.5	7.0
Turkmenistan	6.8	6.0	6.4	6.0	8.0	8.0	8.0
Uzbekistan	11.7	9.1	8.5	8.0	14.4	16.0	14.0
East Asia	2.4	1.9	1.3	1.9	1.6	2.3	2.2
Hong Kong, China	4.3	4.4	3.0	2.4	1.5	2.2	2.1
Mongolia	9.9	12.8	6.6	1.1	4.3	8.0	7.0
People's Republic of China	2.6	2.0	1.4	2.0	1.6	2.4	2.3
Republic of Korea	1.3	1.3	0.7	1.0	1.9	1.9	2.0
Taipei,China	0.8	1.2	–0.3	1.4	0.6	1.1	1.1
South Asia	8.9	6.3	4.9	4.5	4.0	4.7	5.1
Afghanistan	7.4	4.7	0.7	4.4	5.0	5.0	5.0
Bangladesh	6.8	7.3	6.4	5.9	5.4	6.1	6.3
Bhutan	8.8	9.6	6.6	3.3	4.3	4.6	5.4
India	9.4	6.0	4.9	4.5	3.7	4.6	5.0
Maldives	3.8	2.1	1.0	0.5	2.8	3.1	3.0
Nepal	9.9	9.1	7.2	9.9	4.5	5.5	6.0
Pakistan	7.3	8.6	4.5	2.9	4.2	4.5	4.8
Sri Lanka	6.9	3.3	3.8	4.0	7.7	5.2	5.0
Southeast Asia	4.2	4.1	2.8	2.1	2.8	3.0	3.0
Brunei Darussalam	0.4	–0.2	–0.4	–0.7	–0.2	0.1	0.1
Cambodia	3.0	3.9	1.2	3.0	2.9	3.2	3.5
Indonesia	6.4	6.4	6.4	3.5	3.8	3.8	4.0
Lao People's Dem. Rep.	6.4	4.1	1.3	1.6	0.8	2.0	2.5
Malaysia	2.1	3.1	2.1	2.1	3.8	2.6	1.8
Myanmar	5.7	5.1	10.0	6.8	5.3	6.2	6.0
Philippines	2.9	4.1	1.4	1.8	3.2	4.0	3.9
Singapore	2.4	1.0	–0.5	–0.5	0.6	0.9	1.4
Thailand	2.2	1.9	–0.9	0.2	0.7	1.2	1.3
Viet Nam	6.6	4.1	0.6	2.7	3.5	3.7	4.0
The Pacific	4.9	3.8	4.3	4.8	3.8	4.1	3.9
Cook Islands	2.6	1.6	3.0	–0.1	–0.1	0.5	1.0
Federated States of Micronesia	2.1	0.7	0.0	–1.0	0.5	1.0	1.0
Fiji	2.9	0.6	1.4	3.9	3.3	3.0	3.0
Kiribati	–1.5	2.1	0.6	0.7	2.2	2.5	2.5
Marshall Islands	1.9	1.1	–2.3	–1.5	0.5	1.0	1.0
Nauru	0.5	3.0	11.4	8.2	5.0	2.0	2.0
Palau	2.8	4.0	2.2	–1.3	1.0	1.5	1.5
Papua New Guinea	5.0	5.2	6.0	6.7	4.7	5.0	4.5
Samoa	–0.2	–1.2	1.9	0.1	1.4	2.0	3.0
Solomon Islands	5.4	5.2	–0.5	1.1	0.1	2.5	3.0
Timor-Leste	9.4	0.7	0.6	–1.3	0.6	2.0	3.0
Tonga	0.8	2.5	–1.0	2.6	7.4	3.8	0.5
Tuvalu	2.0	1.1	3.2	3.5	2.9	2.5	2.8
Vanuatu	1.4	1.0	2.5	0.9	3.2	4.8	2.5
Developing Asia	3.7	3.0	2.2	2.4	2.3	2.9	2.9
Developing Asia excluding the NIEs	4.1	3.2	2.4	2.7	2.4	3.0	3.0

Note: The newly industrialized economies (NIEs) are Hong Kong, China; the Republic of Korea; Singapore; and Taipei,China.

Table A7 Change in money supply (% per year)

	2013	2014	2015	2016	2017
Central Asia					
Armenia	14.8	8.3	10.8	17.5	18.5
Azerbaijan	15.0	11.8	-1.1	-2.0	9.0
Georgia	24.5	13.8	19.3	20.2	14.8
Kazakhstan	10.2	10.4	33.8	15.6	-1.7
Kyrgyz Republic	22.8	3.0	14.9	14.6	17.9
Tajikistan	19.7	7.1	18.7	37.1	21.8
Turkmenistan	31.2	11.4	16.1	9.4	9.3
Uzbekistan	22.4	18.0	20.7	27.0	40.2
East Asia					
Hong Kong, China	12.4	9.5	5.5	7.7	10.0
Mongolia	19.3	24.7	-1.3	10.5	24.2
People's Republic of China	13.6	11.0	13.3	11.3	8.2
Republic of Korea	4.6	8.1	8.2	7.1	5.1
Taipei,China	5.8	6.1	5.8	3.6	3.6
South Asia					
Afghanistan	9.4	8.6	3.1	9.7	4.1
Bangladesh	16.7	16.1	12.4	16.3	10.9
Bhutan	3.3	26.0	3.8	23.0	...
India	13.4	10.9	10.1	8.1	8.4
Maldives	18.4	14.9	12.1	-0.2	5.2
Nepal	16.4	19.1	19.9	19.5	15.5
Pakistan	15.9	12.5	13.2	13.7	13.7
Sri Lanka	16.7	13.4	17.8	18.4	16.7
Southeast Asia					
Brunei Darussalam	1.5	3.2	-1.8	1.5	-0.4
Cambodia	14.6	29.9	14.7	17.9	23.8
Indonesia	12.8	11.9	9.0	10.0	8.3
Lao People's Dem. Rep.	18.6	23.5	14.7	10.9	12.9
Malaysia	7.3	7.0	2.7	3.1	4.7
Myanmar	31.7	17.6	26.3	19.4	16.5
Philippines	31.8	11.2	9.4	12.8	11.9
Singapore	4.3	3.3	1.5	8.0	3.2
Thailand	7.3	4.7	4.4	4.2	5.1
Viet Nam	18.8	17.7	16.2	18.0	16.0
The Pacific					
Cook Islands	-25.6	3.0	9.6	-2.7	12.3
Federated States of Micronesia	-4.9	5.1	-5.1	-3.8	-1.8
Fiji	19.0	10.4	13.9	6.3	...
Kiribati	...	...	...	...	...
Marshall Islands	...	...	...	...	...
Nauru	...	...	...	...	...
Palau	4.5	24.7	2.6	...	...
Papua New Guinea	6.7	3.4	8.1	10.9	-0.9
Samoa	-0.8	18.7	0.6	7.1	7.8
Solomon Islands	12.5	5.5	15.0	13.4	-0.7
Timor-Leste	22.9	19.9	7.1	14.2	12.1
Tonga	7.0	7.9	2.4	12.6	...
Tuvalu	...	...	...	...	...
Vanuatu	-5.5	8.6	11.3	10.7	...

... = data not available.

Table A8 Central government revenues (% of GDP)

	2013	2014	2015	2016	2017
Central Asia					
Armenia	23.5	23.7	23.2	23.1	22.2
Azerbaijan	33.5	31.2	31.5	29.0	23.5
Georgia	27.7	27.9	28.2	28.4	28.7
Kazakhstan	17.7	18.5	18.7	19.8	22.4
Kyrgyz Republic	28.7	29.8	29.8	27.4	28.7
Tajikistan	26.9	28.4	30.1	32.1	31.0
Turkmenistan	17.1	17.9	16.5	12.8	12.2
Uzbekistan	36.2	35.4	35.4	35.0	33.0
East Asia					
Hong Kong, China	21.3	21.2	18.8	23.0	23.0
Mongolia	31.2	28.4	25.8	24.4	29.2
People's Republic of China	21.7	21.8	22.1	21.5	20.9
Republic of Korea	20.0	17.1	17.3	18.1	22.8
Taipei,China	11.4	10.7	11.3	11.1	10.6
South Asia					
Afghanistan	24.3	24.0	24.5	26.1	24.0
Bangladesh	10.7	10.4	9.6	10.0	10.2
Bhutan	30.2	33.6	28.8	29.9	30.3
India	19.7	19.2	17.9	20.0	19.9
Maldives	23.5	26.7	28.1	28.6	29.0
Nepal	19.5	20.6	20.8	23.2	24.6
Pakistan	14.6	15.8	15.3	16.6	16.7
Sri Lanka	12.0	11.6	13.3	14.2	14.4
Southeast Asia					
Brunei Darussalam	41.8	34.4	21.2	14.7	17.1
Cambodia	13.5	17.1	16.8	17.6	18.6
Indonesia	15.1	14.7	13.1	12.5	12.2
Lao People's Dem. Rep.	20.9	21.0	17.9	15.8	16.7
Malaysia	20.9	19.9	18.9	17.3	17.4
Myanmar	20.1	22.0	18.7	18.8	18.2
Philippines	14.9	15.1	15.8	15.2	15.7
Singapore	15.0	15.4	15.5	16.1	16.8
Thailand	16.8	15.7	16.1	16.6	15.2
Viet Nam	23.1	22.3	23.8	24.5	24.8
The Pacific					
Cook Islands	34.3	39.8	40.9	41.1	45.0
Federated States of Micronesia	62.0	64.8	66.0	68.7	...
Fiji	26.5	27.2	25.4	27.2	27.0
Kiribati	93.2	143.4	157.6	112.6	132.2
Marshall Islands	53.5	53.2	60.4	62.9	99.4
Nauru	58.9	76.8	81.2	115.2	110.3
Palau	40.4	43.3	38.6	43.1	...
Papua New Guinea	20.7	21.0	17.7	15.5	14.9
Samoa	29.7	32.5	29.9	34.1	31.5
Solomon Islands	43.3	43.4	45.8	37.3	38.6
Timor-Leste	305.1	175.7	104.0	54.4	62.1
Tonga	25.3	27.5	26.2	27.6	44.5
Tuvalu	109.8	129.8	159.1	158.6	136.2
Vanuatu	21.3	22.9	30.1	30.8	30.4

... = data not available.

Table A9 Central government expenditures (% of GDP)

	2013	2014	2015	2016	2017
Central Asia					
Armenia	25.1	25.6	27.9	28.5	27.0
Azerbaijan	32.8	31.7	32.7	29.4	25.1
Georgia	28.8	29.8	29.3	29.8	29.6
Kazakhstan	19.7	21.2	20.9	21.4	25.2
Kyrgyz Republic	29.3	30.3	31.3	31.8	31.8
Tajikistan	28.2	29.0	32.4	33.8	33.5
Turkmenistan	15.9	17.0	17.2	14.1	13.1
Uzbekistan	34.1	33.2	35.2	34.8	36.0
East Asia					
Hong Kong, China	20.3	18.0	18.2	18.6	17.8
Mongolia	32.2	32.1	30.8	39.7	33.1
People's Republic of China	23.6	23.6	25.5	25.2	24.6
Republic of Korea	16.5	19.1	19.7	19.5	24.7
Taipei,China	12.2	11.5	11.4	11.4	11.5
South Asia					
Afghanistan	25.0	25.7	25.9	26.0	23.9
Bangladesh	14.5	14.0	13.5	13.8	13.2
Bhutan	34.4	29.8	27.0	30.5	34.4
India	26.7	26.4	24.7	26.7	26.1
Maldives	27.0	29.1	34.8	39.0	31.0
Nepal	18.8	20.0	21.8	23.7	30.0
Pakistan	21.5	20.0	19.6	19.9	21.3
Sri Lanka	17.4	17.3	20.9	19.6	20.1
Southeast Asia					
Brunei Darussalam	34.1	35.4	35.7	35.7	30.2
Cambodia	20.7	20.9	19.4	20.5	19.5
Indonesia	17.3	16.8	15.7	15.0	14.7
Lao People's Dem. Rep.	25.2	23.8	22.4	20.5	21.7
Malaysia	24.7	23.3	22.1	20.4	20.3
Myanmar	21.4	22.9	23.2	21.3	21.7
Philippines	16.3	15.7	16.7	17.6	17.9
Singapore	13.6	14.4	16.1	16.6	16.5
Thailand	18.4	18.1	18.3	18.8	18.1
Viet Nam	28.8	26.4	28.2	28.7	28.2
The Pacific					
Cook Islands	34.0	39.9	42.5	37.2	37.7
Federated States of Micronesia	59.2	53.6	55.6	61.4	...
Fiji	23.8	28.4	26.2	29.7	26.6
Kiribati	83.8	118.8	114.6	108.6	141.1
Marshall Islands	53.7	50.0	57.5	58.9	99.4
Nauru	57.4	51.9	72.3	91.6	102.9
Palau	39.6	39.7	33.7	38.6	...
Papua New Guinea	27.6	27.3	22.2	20.0	17.4
Samoa	33.5	37.8	33.7	34.6	32.6
Solomon Islands	40.8	40.3	51.5	42.5	42.5
Timor-Leste	94.8	110.5	96.9	104.6	79.6
Tonga	26.5	25.7	29.1	28.1	44.9
Tuvalu	86.6	100.5	131.7	160.5	118.6
Vanuatu	22.3	22.1	24.1	28.3	32.5

... = data not available.

Table A10 Fiscal balance of the central government (% of GDP)

	2013	2014	2015	2016	2017
Central Asia					
Armenia	-1.6	-1.9	-4.8	-5.5	-4.8
Azerbaijan	0.7	-0.5	-1.2	-0.4	-1.6
Georgia	-1.1	-2.0	-1.1	-1.4	-0.9
Kazakhstan	-1.9	-2.7	-2.2	-1.6	-2.8
Kyrgyz Republic	-0.7	-0.5	-1.4	-4.4	-3.2
Tajikistan	-1.3	-0.6	-2.3	-1.7	-2.5
Turkmenistan	1.2	0.9	-0.7	-1.3	-0.9
Uzbekistan	2.7	2.1	0.2	0.2	-3.0
East Asia					
Hong Kong, China	1.0	3.2	0.6	4.5	5.2
Mongolia	-0.9	-3.7	-5.0	-15.3	-3.9
People's Republic of China	-1.8	-1.8	-3.4	-3.8	-3.7
Republic of Korea	3.5	-2.0	-2.4	-1.4	-2.0
Taipei,China	-0.9	-0.8	-0.1	-0.3	-0.9
South Asia					
Afghanistan	-0.6	-1.7	-1.4	0.1	0.1
Bangladesh	-3.8	-3.6	-3.9	-3.8	-3.1
Bhutan	-4.2	3.8	1.5	-1.1	-4.1
India	-6.9	-4.1	-3.9	-3.5	-3.5
Maldives	-3.5	-2.4	-6.7	-10.4	-2.0
Nepal	0.7	0.6	-1.0	-0.4	-5.4
Pakistan	-6.9	-4.2	-4.3	-3.3	-4.7
Sri Lanka	-5.4	-5.7	-7.6	-5.4	-5.8
Southeast Asia					
Brunei Darussalam	7.7	-1.0	-14.5	-21.0	-13.1
Cambodia	-7.2	-3.8	-2.6	-2.8	-0.9
Indonesia	-2.2	-2.1	-2.6	-2.5	-2.5
Lao People's Dem. Rep.	-4.3	-2.8	-4.5	-4.6	-4.8
Malaysia	-3.8	-3.4	-3.2	-3.1	-2.9
Myanmar	-1.3	-0.9	-4.4	-2.5	-3.5
Philippines	-1.4	-0.6	-0.9	-2.4	-2.2
Singapore	1.3	0.1	-1.0	1.4	2.1
Thailand	-1.6	-2.5	-2.5	-2.7	-2.7
Viet Nam	-5.7	-4.1	-4.4	-4.3	-3.5
The Pacific					
Cook Islands	0.2	-0.1	-1.6	3.9	7.3
Federated States of Micronesia	2.9	11.2	10.4	7.3	7.0
Fiji	-0.6	-4.3	-3.8	-5.5	-2.3
Kiribati	9.4	24.6	43.1	4.0	-8.9
Marshall Islands	-0.2	3.2	2.9	4.0	-2.0
Nauru	1.5	24.9	8.9	23.6	7.4
Palau	0.7	3.6	4.8	4.5	4.0
Papua New Guinea	-6.9	-6.3	-4.5	-4.6	-2.5
Samoa	-3.8	-5.3	-3.9	-0.4	-1.1
Solomon Islands	2.5	3.1	-5.7	-5.3	-4.0
Timor-Leste	210.3	65.1	7.2	-50.3	-17.5
Tonga	-1.3	1.7	-2.9	-0.4	-0.4
Tuvalu	23.1	29.3	27.4	-2.0	17.6
Vanuatu	-0.9	0.8	6.0	2.5	-2.0

... = data not available.

Table A11 Growth rate of merchandise exports (% per year)

	2013	2014	2015	2016	2017	2018	2019
Central Asia	0.8	-7.5	-34.6	-12.9	24.4	9.7	5.7
Armenia	7.9	3.8	-4.4	16.4	22.3	14.5	8.5
Azerbaijan	-2.6	-11.1	-44.8	-15.2	17.1	13.0	-3.5
Georgia	21.3	-4.1	-23.9	-5.4	18.8	5.0	11.6
Kazakhstan	-1.5	-6.2	-42.1	-19.9	32.2	9.0	5.0
Kyrgyz Republic	43.6	-12.4	-34.8	-0.7	14.4	8.0	14.0
Tajikistan	-14.4	-16.0	-8.9	0.8	9.4	15.0	20.0
Turkmenistan	-4.7	2.0	-38.5	-15.4	34.4	11.0	4.0
Uzbekistan	6.6	-14.8	-12.3	-3.7	11.0	8.0	10.0
East Asia	7.6	3.6	-5.5	-6.9	11.5	5.7	5.1
Hong Kong, China	8.0	1.6	-2.4	0.0	7.2	7.0	7.2
Mongolia	-0.3	44.3	-18.7	8.0	21.4	-0.7	1.7
People's Republic of China	8.9	4.4	-4.5	-7.2	11.4	5.0	4.5
Republic of Korea	2.4	-0.8	-11.4	-5.7	12.8	9.0	8.0
Taipei,China	-1.6	-0.8	-11.1	-8.0	12.9	10.2	9.2
South Asia	4.1	0.9	-12.8	3.6	9.2	8.2	9.5
Afghanistan	18.0	26.8	-9.8	6.8	16.7	20.0	25.0
Bangladesh	10.7	12.1	3.1	8.9	1.7	7.0	9.0
Bhutan	-11.5	-2.0	8.4	-14.7	12.2	3.0	5.0
India	3.9	-0.6	-15.9	5.2	11.0	8.0	9.0
Maldives	5.3	-9.1	-20.3	6.8	25.6	12.0	11.8
Nepal	-2.9	5.1	-3.9	-28.8	9.8	16.0	12.5
Pakistan	0.3	1.1	-3.9	-8.8	-0.2	10.5	13.0
Sri Lanka	6.3	7.1	-5.2	-2.2	10.2	5.0	6.0
Southeast Asia	-0.6	1.2	-11.3	-1.7	14.2	7.2	7.1
Brunei Darussalam	-8.1	-6.1	-44.9	-16.4	16.0	5.0	5.0
Cambodia	22.4	17.0	17.1	10.1	9.3	12.0	13.0
Indonesia	-2.8	-3.7	-14.9	-3.1	16.9	5.8	5.2
Lao People's Dem. Rep.	5.4	22.8	-12.9	17.0	16.1	4.3	10.2
Malaysia	-3.1	2.5	-15.9	-5.2	13.7	5.0	5.6
Myanmar	8.9	-7.8	-8.5	-0.3	15.0	11.0	12.0
Philippines	-4.0	11.9	-13.3	-1.1	12.8	6.8	6.3
Singapore	1.1	-1.7	-12.7	-5.5	9.3	5.8	6.5
Thailand	-0.1	-0.4	-5.6	0.1	9.7	9.0	10.0
Viet Nam	15.3	13.8	7.9	8.9	21.1	15.0	12.0
The Pacific	-10.5	32.9	-5.2	-2.5	0.2	1.8	5.5
Cook Islands	139.9	141.8	-17.0	-0.4	-16.4	-1.0	8.3
Federated States of Micronesia	-13.2	-23.9	4.4	24.7	...	...	...
Fiji	-4.8	5.1	-19.5	-4.9	9.7	3.0	4.0
Kiribati	-20.7	42.3	-16.0	5.7	-17.4	3.9	-0.9
Marshall Islands	-6.2	-15.0	-9.0	-26.0	...	...	...
Nauru	-14.1	-22.0	-55.2	20.2	-5.0	3.5	-4.1
Palau	-3.0	35.0	-15.3	22.6	...	...	...
Papua New Guinea	-6.0	47.2	-4.3	-6.5	0.6	-2.3	5.1
Samoa	-6.3	-9.5	11.6	33.2	-9.0	-2.9	6.5
Solomon Islands	-10.3	1.6	-7.5	0.6	12.0	7.8	4.1
Timor-Leste	-46.9	-9.5	12.5	11.1	-16.5	31.7	13.6
Tonga	-10.2	19.3	8.4	24.2	5.0	4.3	2.3
Tuvalu	-11.0	-5.2	-14.4	-0.9	4.0	10.1	-1.2
Vanuatu	-20.2	36.1	-16.6	-0.9	-5.2	5.3	5.2
Developing Asia	5.7	2.7	-7.9	-4.8	11.7	6.3	6.0
Developing Asia excluding the NIEs	6.3	3.2	-7.6	-4.7	11.7	6.0	5.7

... = data not available.

Note: The newly industrialized economies (NIEs) are Hong Kong, China; the Republic of Korea; Singapore; and Taipei,China.

Table A12 Growth rate of merchandise imports (% per year)

	2013	2014	2015	2016	2017	2018	2019
Central Asia	6.2	-7.0	-17.3	-10.2	7.8	5.7	7.3
Armenia	5.6	-2.0	-25.1	0.9	26.8	15.5	7.0
Azerbaijan	7.1	-16.3	4.7	-7.9	-2.5	-6.0	-6.0
Georgia	0.3	8.0	-10.8	-8.8	8.7	6.0	10.6
Kazakhstan	4.1	-13.3	-23.2	-17.1	13.1	9.1	11.1
Kyrgyz Republic	13.0	-5.8	-27.0	-3.0	11.4	12.0	11.0
Tajikistan	9.1	5.3	-20.8	-11.5	-8.5	5.0	10.0
Turkmenistan	11.7	1.8	-31.5	-6.2	-1.2	4.8	4.5
Uzbekistan	9.0	10.9	-11.0	-1.2	6.3	4.0	8.0
East Asia	5.9	0.6	-14.0	-4.9	16.0	8.6	6.7
Hong Kong, China	9.6	2.4	-4.0	-1.2	8.4	9.3	10.4
Mongolia	-6.2	-16.9	-27.1	-10.7	25.8	0.7	1.1
People's Republic of China	7.7	1.1	-13.4	-4.5	16.4	8.1	6.1
Republic of Korea	-3.4	-2.1	-19.8	-6.6	16.4	12.0	10.5
Taipei,China	-3.3	-2.7	-17.2	-9.3	12.3	9.1	9.2
South Asia	-5.8	0.4	-10.7	-0.4	19.4	11.5	10.0
Afghanistan	-9.3	-19.4	17.4	-19.6	14.7	1.1	6.1
Bangladesh	0.8	8.9	3.0	5.9	9.0	17.0	14.0
Bhutan	-8.8	0.5	8.8	4.9	-3.4	2.0	-1.0
India	-7.2	-1.0	-14.1	-1.0	21.0	11.0	10.0
Maldives	8.1	15.1	-3.4	10.6	11.9	11.2	10.8
Nepal	10.9	13.9	8.0	-7.1	29.4	18.0	15.0
Pakistan	-0.5	3.8	-0.7	-0.2	17.6	13.2	8.2
Sri Lanka	-6.2	7.9	-2.5	2.5	8.1	5.5	6.0
Southeast Asia	0.5	-1.8	-11.4	-0.4	15.2	9.7	9.2
Brunei Darussalam	19.3	-25.3	-12.3	-17.3	20.0	10.0	10.0
Cambodia	13.6	11.2	13.3	6.8	9.0	11.3	11.0
Indonesia	-1.3	-4.5	-19.7	-4.4	16.1	8.9	6.9
Lao People's Dem. Rep.	15.1	9.1	-5.8	-9.9	13.6	10.3	6.1
Malaysia	-0.3	0.6	-15.2	-3.8	14.0	5.8	6.2
Myanmar	14.5	-14.5	10.6	2.4	12.0	12.0	13.0
Philippines	-4.8	8.0	-1.0	17.7	14.2	7.0	7.3
Singapore	0.3	-4.5	-17.1	-5.7	12.4	7.2	7.8
Thailand	-0.1	-7.9	-10.6	-5.1	14.4	15.0	16.0
Viet Nam	16.5	12.0	12.0	7.0	22.3	17.0	15.0
The Pacific	-7.0	-21.0	-28.5	-7.0	7.4	1.2	3.7
Cook Islands	-2.8	7.9	-5.8	-4.9	9.3	5.5	6.8
Federated States of Micronesia	-2.3	-13.0	7.8	-4.6	...	...	...
Fiji	16.8	-3.2	-16.0	2.5	8.9	1.5	2.5
Kiribati	-5.6	2.8	9.6	-5.3	7.1	7.1	0.6
Marshall Islands	12.4	-8.3	-9.3	-6.3	...	...	...
Nauru	58.7	42.5	-18.6	0.0	8.7	0.9	-4.4
Palau	5.4	21.1	-11.5	1.7	...	...	...
Papua New Guinea	-16.1	-30.3	-41.2	-9.1	5.4	1.2	2.4
Samoa	-8.1	8.1	-4.0	-4.2	1.4	2.7	1.8
Solomon Islands	7.0	-1.0	-4.9	-6.2	12.1	3.7	6.7
Timor-Leste	3.7	-11.2	5.7	-14.4	21.8	-4.3	15.0
Tonga	-7.9	0.1	10.7	-2.4	15.9	9.9	8.8
Tuvalu	41.7	-15.6	-4.3	11.5	4.9	6.6	-1.6
Vanuatu	3.1	-5.6	17.2	7.3	-2.4	4.3	5.2
Developing Asia	3.4	0.0	-13.3	-3.7	16.3	9.1	7.5
Developing Asia excluding the NIEs	4.2	0.3	-12.7	-3.3	16.6	8.9	7.2

... = data not available.

Note: The newly industrialized economies (NIEs) are Hong Kong, China; the Republic of Korea; Singapore; and Taipei,China.

Table A13 Trade balance ($ million)

	2013	2014	2015	2016	2017	2018	2019
Central Asia	49,418	45,022	7,901	3,241	14,345	18,269	16,590
Armenia	-2,196	-2,055	-1,186	-944	-1,281	-1,503	-1,568
Azerbaijan	20,621	18,928	5,812	4,206	6,694	9,232	9,116
Georgia	-3,493	-4,280	-4,356	-3,869	-3,907	-4,180	-4,584
Kazakhstan	34,792	36,245	12,672	9,193	17,494	19,036	17,875
Kyrgyz Republic	-2,780	-2,808	-2,241	-2,137	-2,332	-2,685	-2,921
Tajikistan	-2,958	-3,361	-2,544	-2,132	-1,577	-1,536	-1,552
Turkmenistan	4,032	4,143	1,485	887	900	1,200	1,400
Uzbekistan	1,400	-1,790	-1,740	-1,964	-1,645	-1,295	-1,174
East Asia	465,798	551,904	749,251	668,216	654,494	617,873	591,139
Hong Kong, China	-27,913	-32,359	-22,871	-16,708	-24,000	-38,346	-61,051
Mongolia	-2,619	146	566	1,337	1,470	1,400	1,450
People's Republic of China	358,981	435,042	576,191	494,077	476,100	445,608	436,495
Republic of Korea	82,781	88,885	122,269	118,895	119,889	116,954	113,500
Taipei,China	54,567	60,191	73,095	70,615	81,035	92,257	100,745
South Asia	-193,044	-190,595	-178,560	-161,647	-227,020	-265,639	-295,853
Afghanistan	-8,450	-5,854	-7,086	-5,541	-6,342	-6,292	-6,481
Bangladesh	-7,009	-6,794	-6,965	-6,460	-9,472	-14,484	-18,332
Bhutan	-377	-393	-430	-565	-468	-472	-433
India	-147,609	-144,939	-130,079	-112,442	-164,069	-191,445	-213,948
Maldives	-1,372	-1,660	-1,655	-1,839	-2,023	-2,247	-2,486
Nepal	-5,263	-6,079	-6,689	-6,427	-8,458	-9,996	-11,518
Pakistan	-15,355	-16,590	-17,267	-19,283	-26,568	-30,667	-32,018
Sri Lanka	-7,609	-8,287	-8,389	-9,090	-9,620	-10,036	-10,638
Southeast Asia	100,789	137,221	134,318	129,504	124,914	105,773	82,909
Brunei Darussalam	6,924	7,443	2,910	2,461	2,745	2,723	2,684
Cambodia	-3,494	-3,483	-3,638	-3,575	-3,857	-4,212	-4,418
Indonesia	5,833	6,983	14,049	15,318	18,892	15,267	13,283
Lao People's Dem. Rep.	-3,299	-3,518	-3,624	-2,257	-2,454	-3,010	-2,979
Malaysia	30,642	34,626	27,967	24,439	27,463	27,688	28,294
Myanmar	-3,053	-1,859	-4,048	-4,394	-4,637	-5,303	-6,113
Philippines	-17,662	-17,330	-23,309	-35,549	-41,191	-44,209	-47,966
Singapore	76,145	85,032	89,817	85,479	84,701	85,245	86,332
Thailand	40	17,201	26,798	36,539	31,866	22,539	10,770
Viet Nam	8,713	12,126	7,396	11,042	11,385	9,044	3,023
The Pacific	-3,568	1,378	2,880	2,640	2,598	2,381	2,550
Cook Islands	-104	-102	-98	-92	-105	-111	-119
Federated States of Micronesia	-129	-117	-128	-110	...	...	...
Fiji	-1,159	-1,027	-906	-1,000	-1,081	-1,083	-1,094
Kiribati	-90	-90	-101	-95	-104	-111	-112
Marshall Islands	-61	-60	-55	-61	...	...	...
Nauru	5	-32	-43	-39	-45	-45	-43
Palau	-133	-160	-142	-141	...	...	...
Papua New Guinea	-517	4,248	5,735	5,428	5,342	5,128	5,460
Samoa	-281	-309	-293	-270	-278	-287	-291
Solomon Islands	-16	-5	-17	13	14	34	24
Timor-Leste	-679	-602	-635	-539	-664	-630	-725
Tonga	-172	-170	-188	-179	-210	-232	-254
Tuvalu	-13	-9	-10	-14	-14	-15	-14
Vanuatu	-217	-187	-239	-261	-256	-266	-280
Developing Asia	419,393	544,929	715,790	641,954	569,331	478,657	397,335
Developing Asia excluding the NIEs	233,812	343,180	453,479	383,673	307,705	222,547	157,810

... = data not available.

Note: The newly industrialized economies (NIEs) are Hong Kong, China; the Republic of Korea; Singapore; and Taipei,China.

Table A14 Current account balance (% of GDP)

	2013	2014	2015	2016	2017	2018	2019
Central Asia	1.8	2.3	-3.6	-6.5	-1.7	-2.1	-2.2
Armenia	-7.3	-7.6	-2.6	-2.3	-2.5	-3.2	-2.8
Azerbaijan	16.6	13.9	-0.4	-3.6	5.5	6.9	6.2
Georgia	-5.7	-10.6	-11.9	-12.8	-9.0	-9.5	-8.5
Kazakhstan	0.5	2.8	-2.8	-6.5	-3.0	-3.3	-3.4
Kyrgyz Republic	-14.1	-17.2	-16.2	-11.6	-4.8	-12.0	-10.0
Tajikistan	-7.7	-2.8	-6.2	-3.8	3.0	1.1	-3.0
Turkmenistan	-7.2	-6.4	-14.0	-21.0	-11.5	-9.0	-8.0
Uzbekistan	1.6	1.4	0.3	0.1	2.8	0.5	0.1
East Asia	2.4	3.0	3.7	2.8	2.4	2.1	1.9
Hong Kong, China	1.5	1.4	3.3	4.0	4.2	3.9	3.5
Mongolia	-37.6	-15.8	-8.1	-6.3	-10.2	-6.3	-7.0
People's Republic of China	1.5	2.3	2.7	1.8	1.4	1.3	1.2
Republic of Korea	6.2	6.0	7.7	7.0	5.1	4.9	4.8
Taipei,China	10.0	11.5	14.3	13.7	14.7	10.0	9.0
South Asia	-1.4	-1.1	-0.8	-0.8	-2.1	-2.5	-2.6
Afghanistan	8.7	5.8	7.5	7.1	4.5	3.3	2.6
Bangladesh	1.6	0.8	1.8	1.9	-0.6	-2.2	-1.9
Bhutan	-25.4	-26.4	-28.3	-31.2	-23.0	-22.2	-18.8
India	-1.7	-1.3	-1.1	-1.0	-2.0	-2.2	-2.4
Maldives	-3.9	-3.2	-7.6	-24.5	-21.7	-17.3	-17.1
Nepal	3.4	4.6	5.1	6.2	-0.4	-3.5	-5.8
Pakistan	-1.1	-1.3	-1.0	-1.7	-4.1	-4.9	-4.5
Sri Lanka	-3.5	-2.5	-2.3	-2.4	-3.0	-2.7	-2.5
Southeast Asia	1.6	3.1	3.2	3.6	3.5	2.7	2.5
Brunei Darussalam	20.9	30.7	16.7	15.5	19.0	14.0	14.0
Cambodia	-16.8	-13.6	-11.9	-11.2	-10.9	-11.1	-10.8
Indonesia	-3.2	-3.1	-2.0	-1.8	-1.7	-2.2	-2.2
Lao People's Dem. Rep.	-28.4	-20.0	-18.0	-14.1	-13.0	-14.9	-13.7
Malaysia	3.5	4.4	3.0	2.4	3.0	2.4	2.1
Myanmar	-4.9	-2.2	-5.1	-3.9	-5.0	-5.4	-5.5
Philippines	4.2	3.8	2.5	-0.4	-0.8	-1.0	-1.4
Singapore	16.5	18.7	18.6	19.0	18.8	19.0	19.0
Thailand	-1.2	3.7	8.0	11.7	10.8	8.0	7.5
Viet Nam	4.5	4.9	0.5	3.0	2.9	2.5	2.0
The Pacific	1.3	7.3	10.0	6.6	8.3	6.6	6.4
Cook Islands	20.2	20.2	22.5	25.8	25.5	23.6	21.7
Federated States of Micronesia	-10.4	1.3	3.0	3.9	2.8	2.0	2.0
Fiji	-9.7	-7.6	-3.1	-5.0	-5.2	-5.0	-4.8
Kiribati	19.6	53.0	47.4	18.9	13.8	4.3	2.3
Marshall Islands	-5.3	1.9	16.5	8.5	5.0	7.0	8.0
Nauru	18.8	-13.4	-9.4	1.7	0.5	...	...
Palau	-11.7	-15.1	-7.8	-10.9	-19.0	-16.0	-16.0
Papua New Guinea	-30.7	1.3	13.6	15.2	13.9	13.4	13.8
Samoa	-2.5	-8.1	-2.9	-5.8	-3.0	-4.3	-3.2
Solomon Islands	-4.4	-5.5	-3.4	-4.9	-2.5	-2.1	-2.5
Timor-Leste	168.9	75.2	14.9	-30.7	0.8	-15.2	-22.0
Tonga	-4.5	-6.8	-14.8	-13.9	-12.2	-14.8	-15.9
Tuvalu	1.5	12.8	9.9	-21.0	-26.8	-31.4	-29.1
Vanuatu	-3.3	-0.3	-8.9	-4.1	-2.1	-1.0	-1.1
Developing Asia	1.7	2.4	2.9	2.2	1.8	1.4	1.3
Developing Asia excluding the NIEs	0.7	1.5	1.8	1.1	0.8	0.5	0.4

... = data not available.

Note: The newly industrialized economies (NIEs) are Hong Kong, China; the Republic of Korea; Singapore; and Taipei,China.

Table A15 Exchange rates to the United States dollar (annual average)

	Currency	Symbol	2013	2014	2015	2016	2017
Central Asia							
Armenia	dram	AMD	409.6	415.9	477.9	480.5	482.7
Azerbaijan	Azerbaijan new manat	AZN	0.8	0.8	1.0	1.6	1.7
Georgia	lari	GEL	1.7	1.8	2.3	2.4	2.5
Kazakhstan	tenge	T	152.1	179.2	221.7	342.1	326.0
Kyrgyz Republic	som	Som	48.4	53.7	64.5	69.9	68.9
Tajikistan	somoni	TJS	4.8	5.0	6.2	7.9	8.6
Turkmenistan	Turkmen manat	TMM	2.9	2.9	3.5	3.5	3.5
Uzbekistan	sum	SUM	2,097.2	2,314.9	2,573.5	2,968.9	5,140.3
East Asia							
Hong Kong, China	Hong Kong dollar	HK$	7.8	7.8	7.8	7.8	7.8
Mongolia	togrog	MNT	1,523.9	1,817.9	1,970.3	2,145.5	2,439.8
People's Republic of China	yuan	CNY	6.2	6.1	6.2	6.7	6.7
Republic of Korea	won	W	1,095.4	1,052.2	1,133.1	1,163.3	1,122.3
Taipei,China	NT dollar	NT$	29.8	30.4	31.9	32.3	30.4
South Asia							
Afghanistan	afghani	AF	55.4	57.3	61.1	67.9	68.0
Bangladesh	taka	Tk	79.9	77.7	77.7	78.3	79.1
Bhutan	ngultrum	Nu	54.9	61.5	62.1	66.3	66.5
India	Indian rupee/s	₹	60.5	61.0	64.2	67.2	65.1
Maldives	rufiyaa	Rf	15.4	15.4	15.4	15.4	15.4
Nepal	Nepalese rupee/s	NRe/NRs	87.7	98.0	99.2	106.1	105.9
Pakistan	Pakistan rupee/s	PRe/PRs	96.7	102.9	101.5	104.4	104.7
Sri Lanka	Sri Lanka rupee/s	SLRe/SLRs	129.1	130.6	135.9	145.6	152.0
Southeast Asia							
Brunei Darussalam	Brunei dollar	B$	1.3	1.3	1.4	1.4	1.4
Cambodia	riel	KR	4,027.2	4,037.5	4,063.0	4,051.3	4,045.0
Indonesia	rupiah	Rp	10,461.2	11,865.2	13,389.4	13,308.7	13,380.8
Lao People's Dem. Rep.	kip	KN	7,821.0	8,049.0	8,113.0	8,130.0	8,235.0
Malaysia	ringgit	RM	3.2	3.3	3.9	4.1	4.3
Myanmar	kyat	MK	962.9	994.9	1,218.9	1,259.2	1,357.4
Philippines	peso	₱	42.4	44.4	45.5	47.5	50.4
Singapore	Singapore dollar	S$	1.3	1.3	1.4	1.4	1.4
Thailand	baht	B	30.7	32.5	34.3	35.3	33.9
Viet Nam	dong	D	20,934.6	21,148.8	21,675.6	21,931.0	22,370.3
The Pacific							
Cook Islands	New Zealand dollar	NZ$	1.2	1.2	1.3	1.5	1.4
Federated States of Micronesia	US dollar	US$	1.0	1.0	1.0	1.0	1.0
Fiji	Fiji dollar	F$	1.8	1.9	2.1	2.1	2.1
Kiribati	Australian dollar	A$	1.0	1.1	1.2	1.4	1.4
Marshall Islands	US dollar	US$	1.0	1.0	1.0	1.0	1.0
Nauru	Australian dollar	A$	1.0	1.1	1.2	1.4	1.4
Palau	US dollar	US$	1.0	1.0	1.0	1.0	1.0
Papua New Guinea	kina	K	2.2	2.4	2.8	3.1	3.2
Samoa	tala	ST	2.3	2.3	2.4	2.6	2.5
Solomon Islands	Sol. Islands dollar	SI$	7.3	7.4	7.9	8.1	7.9
Timor-Leste	US dollar	US$	1.0	1.0	1.0	1.0	1.0
Tonga	pa'anga	T$	1.7	1.8	1.9	2.2	2.2
Tuvalu	Australian dollar	A$	1.0	1.1	1.3	1.4	1.4
Vanuatu	vatu	Vt	96.9	102.4	116.3	110.8	109.0

Table A16 Gross international reserves ($ million)

	2013	2014	2015	2016	2017
Central Asia					
Armenia	2,252	1,489	1,775	2,204	2,314
Azerbaijan	14,153	13,758	5,017	3,974	5,335
Georgia	2,800	2,695	2,500	2,800	3,100
Kazakhstan	24,715	29,209	27,871	29,710	30,745
Kyrgyz Republic	2,238	1,958	1,778	1,969	2,177
Tajikistan	636	511	494	653	1,272
Turkmenistan	29,300	32,400	...	...	...
Uzbekistan	22,515	24,149	24,300	26,428	28,076
East Asia					
Hong Kong, China	311,209	328,516	358,823	386,241	431,370
Mongolia	2,248	1,650	1,323	1,296	3,008
People's Republic of China	3,880,383	3,899,285	3,406,112	3,097,845	3,235,895
Republic of Korea	346,460	363,593	367,962	371,102	389,267
Taipei,China	416,811	418,980	426,031	434,204	451,500
South Asia					
Afghanistan	6,873	7,311	6,808	7,582	8,159
Bangladesh	15,315	21,508	25,025	30,168	33,407
Bhutan	917	998	958	1,119	1,078
India	304,223	341,638	360,176	369,955	420,758
Maldives	368	615	564	467	586
Nepal	5,614	6,939	8,148	9,737	10,495
Pakistan	6,008	9,098	13,525	18,143	16,145
Sri Lanka	7,495	8,208	7,304	6,019	7,959
Southeast Asia					
Brunei Darussalam	3,575	3,648	3,367	3,489	3,289
Cambodia	3,642	4,391	5,093	6,731	8,758
Indonesia	99,387	111,862	105,931	116,362	130,196
Lao People's Dem. Rep.	662	816	987	815	979
Malaysia	134,911	115,937	95,290	94,525	102,446
Myanmar	4,444	5,125	4,764	5,134	5,370
Philippines	83,187	79,541	80,667	80,692	81,570
Singapore	273,065	256,860	247,747	246,575	269,018
Thailand	167,289	157,108	156,514	171,853	202,562
Viet Nam	25,955	34,330	28,298	41,000	54,489
The Pacific					
Cook Islands	...	...	...	...	...
Federated States of Micronesia	...	...	...	...	...
Fiji	966	905	926	1,921	2,138
Kiribati	...	...	...	...	...
Marshall Islands	...	...	...	...	...
Nauru	...	...	...	...	...
Palau	...	...	...	...	...
Papua New Guinea	2,826	2,305	1,865	1,681	1,696
Samoa	137	154	132	111	...
Solomon Islands	532	507	529	519	546
Timor-Leste	...	16,850	16,655	16,125	16,062
Tonga	148	159	143	166	170
Tuvalu	...	...	...	...	...
Vanuatu	180	185	256	302	...

... = data not available.

Table A17 External debt outstanding ($ million)

	2013	2014	2015	2016	2017
Central Asia					
Armenia	3,899	3,785	4,316	4,806	5,495
Azerbaijan	6,059	6,478	6,894	6,913	9,398
Georgia	10,542	10,718	11,983	13,246	14,183
Kazakhstan	150,033	157,562	153,422	163,632	167,485
Kyrgyz Republic	5,930	6,371	6,670	6,830	6,908
Tajikistan	2,152	2,098	2,183	2,276	2,833
Turkmenistan	8,653	8,043	8,354	...	...
Uzbekistan	7,500	8,399	11,800	13,100	15,000
East Asia					
Hong Kong, China	1,160,793	1,301,032	1,300,365	1,356,411	1,565,172
Mongolia	18,280	20,951	21,590	23,785	27,413
People's Republic of China	863,167	1,779,900	1,416,200	1,420,657	...
Republic of Korea	423,505	424,325	396,058	384,130	418,824
Taipei,China	170,134	177,945	158,954	172,238	181,938
South Asia					
Afghanistan	1,361	1,299	1,231	1,242	1,283
Bangladesh	22,381	24,388	23,901	26,306	28,566
Bhutan	1,607	1,759	1,855	2,316	2,505
India	446,178	474,675	485,052	471,824	495,686
Maldives	792	744	696	849	1,188
Nepal	3,510	3,617	3,391	3,642	4,025
Pakistan	60,900	65,269	65,169	73,870	83,092
Sri Lanka	39,905	42,914	44,797	46,586	...
Southeast Asia					
Brunei Darussalam	...	...	...	...	...
Cambodia	4,828	5,279	5,648	5,861	6,671
Indonesia	266,109	293,328	310,730	320,006	352,247
Lao People's Dem. Rep.	5,489	6,061	6,495	7,422	...
Malaysia	212,279	213,951	195,010	204,217	217,471
Myanmar	10,200	8,800	9,500	9,100	9,600
Philippines	78,489	77,674	77,474	74,763	73,098
Singapore	1,346,035	1,398,008	1,293,445	1,262,095	1,350,784
Thailand	141,933	141,715	131,078	132,194	148,995
Viet Nam	45,243	...	...	...	...
The Pacific					
Cook Islands	59	61	74	77	55
Federated States of Micronesia	88	90	81	80	...
Fiji	595	664	660	604	690
Kiribati	14	14	36	45	52
Marshall Islands	98	95	89	83	83
Nauru	52	44	39	35	36
Palau	65	71	64	75	...
Papua New Guinea	1,258	1,366	1,463	1,921	2,085
Samoa	414	415	442	399	401
Solomon Islands	102	89	83	78	89
Timor-Leste	6	22	46	77	87
Tonga	204	186	195	173	178
Tuvalu	20	22	18	17	16
Vanuatu	132	149	239	409	506

... = data not available.

Table A18 Debt service ratio (% of exports of goods and services)

	2013	2014	2015	2016	2017
Central Asia					
Armenia	27.3	6.8	4.4	4.7	5.7
Azerbaijan	...	...	...	...	...
Georgia	18.1	13.5	15.4	14.3	9.5
Kazakhstan	35.0	36.6	71.9	98.5	16.4
Kyrgyz Republic	20.3	26.9	42.4	38.2	...
Tajikistan	...	...	...	...	...
Turkmenistan	2.3	...	...	...	...
Uzbekistan	5.3	7.9	13.0	14.5	9.4
East Asia					
Hong Kong, China	49.0	60.0	65.8	73.4	80.5
Mongolia	50.6	39.8	41.6	88.6	21.1
People's Republic of China	1.6	2.6	5.0	6.0	...
Republic of Korea	7.2	7.9	8.9	9.0	10.0
Taipei,China	1.7	1.5	1.6	2.1	1.9
South Asia					
Afghanistan	...	...	...	...	...
Bangladesh	2.5	2.7	2.2	2.0	2.3
Bhutan	229.2	27.1	19.7	14.4	24.9
India	5.9	7.6	8.8	8.3	7.9
Maldives	2.1	2.3	2.3	2.6	2.6
Nepal	9.5	8.9	8.1	9.9	10.8
Pakistan	19.0	21.6	18.0	19.4	29.7
Sri Lanka	26.8	20.8	27.7	...	...
Southeast Asia					
Brunei Darussalam	...	...	...	...	...
Cambodia	1.1	1.2	1.1	1.4	1.4
Indonesia	18.4	24.0	30.6	35.4	25.2
Lao People's Dem. Rep.	5.1	5.7	6.5	8.1	...
Malaysia	10.7	11.4	15.7	16.0	13.9
Myanmar	4.9	5.0	4.7	4.7	4.1
Philippines	8.2	6.3	5.6	7.0	6.2
Singapore	...	...	...	...	...
Thailand	4.0	4.9	6.4	5.9	5.8
Viet Nam	...	...	...	...	...
The Pacific					
Cook Islands	7.2	6.2	6.2	5.8	5.9
Federated States of Micronesia	6.8	8.9	8.1	7.3	...
Fiji	1.6	1.7	1.9	...	...
Kiribati	11.1	33.4	2.7	4.5	3.2
Marshall Islands	7.1	7.1	11.4	12.8	...
Nauru	5.9	4.9	5.5	2.9	3.2
Palau	4.6	4.6	4.4	4.9	...
Papua New Guinea	1.4	1.1	0.9	1.4	1.6
Samoa	...	...	...	...	...
Solomon Islands	2.3	3.3	2.8	2.5	2.6
Timor-Leste	0.0	0.0	0.0	0.0	0.3
Tonga	7.5	9.2	9.8	9.4	8.8
Tuvalu	2.9	2.9	12.2	12.0	11.6
Vanuatu	1.0	1.0	1.9	2.2	2.0

... = data not available.

www.ingramcontent.com/pod-product-compliance
Lightning Source LLC
Chambersburg PA
CBHW041751220926
51847CB00014B/168
9789292611200